Sixth Edition

INTERNATIONAL
TRADE AND INVESTMENT

Franklin R. Root

The Wharton School
University of Pennsylvania

H62
PUBLISHED BY
SOUTH-WESTERN PUBLISHING CO.
CINCINNATI, OH   WEST CHICAGO, IL   DALLAS, TX   LIVERMORE, CA

Acquisitions Editor: James M. Keefe
Developmental Editor: Jeanne Busemeyer
Production Associate Editor: Diane Longworth Myers
Production House: WordCrafters Editorial Services Inc.
Cover and Interior Designer: Jim DeSollar
Marketing Manager: Scott Person

Library of Congress Cataloging-in-Publication Data

Root, Franklin R.
International trade and investment / Franklin R. Root. — 6th ed.
    p.   cm.
    ISBN 0-538-08620-3
    1. International trade.   2. International finance.
3. International economic relations.   4. International business
enterprises.   I. Title.
HF1411.R6345   1990
382—dc20   89-22032
                                                      CIP

1 2 3 4 5 6 7 8 D 6 5 4 3 2 1 0 9
Printed in the United States of America

Preface

International Trade and Investment offers the reader an integrated treatment of theory, policy, and enterprise in international trade and investment. A knowledge and understanding of these interdependent subjects is vital for all those who plan to enter an international business career or work for governments and international organizations in activities that relate to international economic relations. Apart from career interest, persons who want to improve their understanding of the world in which they live are seriously handicapped without an awareness, if not comprehension, of the economic dynamics and policy issues of trade and investment flows among nations.

Theory refers to the body of knowledge that seeks to explain the causal factors that determine the size, composition, and direction of international economic transactions. A grasp of theory enables us to analyze events occurring in the world economy and to evaluate the wisdom of national policies.

Policy encompasses the role of governments in their efforts to regulate, restrict, promote, or otherwise influence the conduct of international trade and investment. A study of national policies brings us to an intersection of international economics and international politics, an amalgam traditionally designated as political economy. This book carries the description and analysis of national policies to a greater depth than is customary in a basic text, with emphasis on contemporary problems and issues.

Enterprise designates the multinational enterprise, which undertakes production in many countries in pursuit of a global business strategy transcending national jurisdictions. Study of the multinational enterprise brings us face to face with the business firms that are responsible for much of the trade and most of the direct foreign investment in the world economy today.

International economists have traditionally maintained a *macroscopic* perspective on international economic relations by considering trade and investment only at the national level. This macroscopic approach is necessary but no longer sufficient to explain the behavior of the world economy. Possessing vast resources, multinational companies enjoy a market power that makes them independent actors in the international economic system, forcing changes in national economies and provoking policy responses by governments. Hence, to understand the contemporary world economy we must combine the traditional, macroscopic perspective with a *microscopic* perspective of the multinational enterprise. This text offers a systematic presentation of the multinational enterprise as the dominant institution in international trade and investment.

International Trade and Investment is a major revision of the previous edition, both in form and content. As for form, I have placed the treatment of *International Payments* after that of *International Trade*. As for content, I have revised every chapter and, in some instances, almost completely rewritten them to account for recent theoretical and policy developments. The treatment of international trade theory has been expanded from three to four chapters and that of trade policy from four to five chapters.

This revision was undertaken at a time of massive troubles afflicting the world economy. Indeed, the very existence of an open world economy remains threatened by trade wars and international financial collapse. I have tried in a period of rapid, often drastic, change to make this edition as up to date as possible without neglecting those conditions and forces that will shape our world a long time into the future.

In closing, let me express my thanks to readers and reviewers who cared enough about this text to make suggestions to improve it. I have worked hard to achieve a balance between theory, policy, and enterprise that I hope will please some of them without unduly annoying the rest.

Franklin R. Root
The Wharton School
University of Pennsylvania

Contents

PART THREE—INTERNATIONAL DEVELOPMENT

1
The International Economy and the National Interest

No nation inhabits an economic vacuum. Its industries, its commerce, its technology, its standard of living, and all the other facets of its economy are related to the economies of foreign nations by complex flows of goods, capital, technology, and enterprise. Every nation must come to terms with this interdependence, and every nation can enlarge the benefits and lessen the costs of interdependence through rational policies. But to do so, nations—individually and collectively— must base their policies on the objective analysis of international economic relations. It is the social function of international economists to develop the concepts and theories that make objective analysis possible.

From a broader perspective, every nation inhabits a global political and social environment as well as a global economic environment.[1] At the immediate, sensational level of perception, the international environment appears as a bewildering sequence of seemingly random events: A coup d'etat occurs in country A, prices rise in country B, the government of country C devalues its exchange rate, the government of country D expropriates a foreign-owned company, and so on. When each event is perceived as a unique, isolated phenomenon unrelated to other phenomena, then it is impossible to understand *why* the event has occurred. To comprehend the international environment, therefore, we must simplify by classifying individual events into groups or categories of events and by tracing out the relationships among these aggregates. In other words, we must construct a *system* characterized by defined elements (variables) and their interrelationships that together determine the behavior of the system. We are then able to interpret an event in terms of its place in the system. If the system

---

[1] Ecologists dramatically remind us that every nation also inhabits a global physical environment.

is a good approximation of the fundamental conditions and forces actually at work in the world, then we can also predict the consequences of an event with a reasonable degree of confidence. What we have done is to build a model that enables us to comprehend a reality that defies comprehension in the raw.

In our exploration of international economic relations, we shall make use of many concepts (such as the nation-state, gross national product, the balance of payments, and multinational enterprise) that bring together diverse phenomena and order them in ways that facilitate analysis. We shall also employ theories that seek to explain *why* the international economy behaves as it does, or how it *should* behave to maximize certain values. However, before proceeding with our study of the international economy, some preliminary remarks are in order about the *international political system*.

THE INTERNATIONAL POLITICAL SYSTEM

The human race is organized in a society of nation-states. The elemental constituents of a nation-state are a people, a territory, an economy, and a sovereign government. The necessary constituent of statehood is *national sovereignty*.

National Sovereignty

International law recognizes the national government as having exclusive jurisdiction over the territory of the state and as being the only legal representative of the state vis-à-vis other states. The state is not subordinate to any legal authority, and it has the right to abrogate any agreements with other states or with their citizens. Furthermore, national states have a legal monopoly on physical force both at home and abroad. Since states control the entire land surface of the earth, every individual and organization is a legal resident of a particular state and is subject to its authority.[2] Among its other consequences, the principle of national sovereignty raises many problems for international economic cooperation and for multinational enterprises that operate on the territory of more than one nation.

Although *legally* a state can do as it pleases, its actual conduct in international affairs is constrained by the power of other states. For a very weak state, national sovereignty may become a legal fiction even within its own territory.

---

[2] This system of sovereign territorial states was formally established by the Peace Treaty of Westphalia in 1648. At first limited to Europe, it has since spread to encompass the globe. See Joseph Frankel, *International Relations* (New York: Oxford University Press, 1964), p. 7.

External Relations of States

Each state seeks to have relations with other states that will sustain or promote its own national interests as they are conceived by government leaders. Foremost among these interests is the continuing survival of the state itself; economic growth and development are also prominent interests of contemporary states.

To carry out its foreign policies a state must be able to influence the behavior of other states. In this sense, *power* is the essence of international political relations. The elements of state power include the armed forces, economy, population, geography, government, morale, ideology, and other intangible factors. Because of the latter, precise measures of national power are illusory. Moreover, national power is a *relationship* between two or more states that depends, in part, on how each state perceives its own power compared with the power of others. History affords us many examples of misjudgments by states of their relative power positions.[3]

To say that international political relations are essentially power relations is not to say that they always involve conflict. National governments understand that the achievement of many, if not all, of their foreign policy goals depends on *cooperation* with other governments. States are willing, therefore, to take actions that benefit other states if those governments reciprocate in some measure. Cooperative arrangements among states are highly developed in economic and functional areas, such as trade, finance, communications, and transportation.

Antagonistic relations express a clash of interests between two or more states. When these interests are considered vital, they may limit or destroy cooperative arrangements. Because of the "cold war," for instance, trade between the United States and the Soviet Union has been restricted to very low levels.

Many international relations are *competitive* rather than cooperative or antagonistic. States exhibit various forms of rivalry that fall short of direct opposition to each other. They compete in economic performance, technological innovation, ideology, cultural achievements, and so on.

To conclude, the external relations of states are essentially power relations that are expressed in changing mixes of cooperation, competition, and antagonism. When account is taken of the existence of some 160 heterogeneous sovereign states, the pattern of international political relations becomes intricate indeed.

Nationalism

In the contemporary world, states are also nations. While the state is a political entity, the nation is an ethnic or social entity. When these two entities combine they form a *nation-state*.

---

[3] A recent example of such a misjudgment was the attempt by Argentina in 1982 to take over the Falkland Islands (a British crown colony) by military force.

The citizens of a nation experience a common identity stemming from a shared community, history, language, religion, race, or ideology. *Nationalism* is the emotional cement that binds a people together to make a nationality; it is marked by loyalty and devotion to a nation that exalt it above all other nations. At least since the French Revolution in the late eighteenth century, nationalism has been the driving force in the creation of new states. Born in Europe, nationalism was the primary force in the transformation of European colonies into independent states following World War II; it has now spread to all the world.

In the twentieth century it became a widely accepted principle that each national community merits its own government and political independence. Self-determination, however, has its practical limits. In recent years, several very small states have entered the United Nations, although their political and economic viability is highly questionable. At a time when sizable European states have begun a process of integration to overcome the liabilities of "smallness," the emergence of so many ministates in the past quarter century is a gross anomaly. The basic principle of self-determination also threatens the stability of older states that contain two or more ethnic groups, as witnessed by the separatist movements in Canada, Belgium, and Spain. Ironically, many new states in Africa that owe their birth to the principle of national self-determination may eventually founder on divisive tribal loyalties that take precedence over national loyalties. The tragic civil war in Nigeria has emphasized the formidable obstacles to nation building in a multiethnic state.

However, for the most part the states of the world command the loyalties of their peoples and may be accurately depicted as nation-states, namely, "a form of political organization under which a relatively homogeneous people inhabits a sovereign state."[4] Because the citizens of a modern state share a common national society and culture, national boundaries carry a sociocultural significance as well as a political one.

Nationalism injects an emotional energy into international relations, bedeviling cross-national communication and inciting governments to behavior that can undermine the achievement of their own political and economic goals. Encompassing a personal identification with, and a loyalty to, a particular state, nationalism often expresses negative attitudes toward other states. But nationalism is also a cultural phenomenon. Even before the emergence of nation-states, ethnic and tribal groups held attitudes toward other groups ranging from xenophobia (a hatred and fear of all foreigners) to, at times, cosmopolitanism (a sophisticated, open view of foreigners). Today, nationalistic attitudes toward economic relations with foreigners animate many government policies that restrict international trade and investment. When, for example, a business enterprise starts operations in a foreign country, its reception by the government and people

---

[4] *Webster's Ninth New Collegiate Dictionary*, s.v. "nation-state."

will depend in substantial measure on the blend of nationalism that predominates there.

International Organizations

Cooperation among nation-states has led to the creation of many international organizations to serve both political and economic purposes. Although these organizations seldom have any explicit supranational powers, they may gain an institutional strength over time that enables them to influence the behavior of individual states to a significant degree. Hence, they may assume an autonomous international role that makes them "actors" in the international political and economic systems along with the nation-states. For example, the policies of the International Monetary Fund (IMF) and the International Bank for Reconstruction and Development (IBRD) are more than a simple consensus of the national policies of their member states. Even more impressive in this regard is the European Community.

Summing up, the international political system comprises some 160 sovereign nation-states and their mutual power relations, which may be characterized as cooperative, competitive, or antagonistic. Nationalism, which generally carries an antiforeign bias, adds an emotional tone to the foreign policies of nation-states, making them less cooperative than would otherwise be the case. On the other hand, some international organizations have emerged as autonomous (or quasi-autonomous) actors in the international political system along with the nation-states.

THE INTERNATIONAL ECONOMIC SYSTEM

Every nation-state has an economy, and the mutual relations among national economies constitute the *international economic system.* Just as the distinguishing feature of the political relations among states is power, the distinguishing feature of their economic relations is *market transactions.* With the rather modest exception of unilateral transfers ("gifts"), international economic relations result from the exchange of assets having market value. The sum of a nation's economic transactions with the rest of the world over a period of time is recorded in its balance of payments. Transactions give rise to flows of merchandise, services, money, capital, technology, and enterprise, thereby creating patterns of interdependence among national economies. Shifts in the size and direction of these flows that are initiated in one national economy will affect, directly or indirectly, the behavior of other national economies. The economic theory that explains *why* these flows occur and *how* national economies as a whole interact with the world economy is one of the three themes that animate this book.

Contemporary nation-states, however, are not willing to allow their international economic relations to be determined *only* by market forces.

All national governments have foreign economic policies that are intended to regulate, restrict, promote, or otherwise influence international trade and investment. The description and evaluation of these policies is the second theme of this book.

The relative importance of noneconomic or political factors in the determination of foreign economic policies varies from one nation-state to another. However, we can loosely classify countries into two groups in that regard. International transactions of the *industrial countries* (mainly those in North America, Western Europe, and Japan) and of the *developing countries* (mainly nations in Africa, Asia, and Latin America) are predominantly undertaken by *private business firms*, most notably in the form of multinational enterprises. Because the motivation behind these transactions is economic gain, the trade and investment flows among these countries are mainly explicable in economic terms. Nonetheless, government policies in these countries both constrain and stimulate international economic transactions so as to bring about a divergence from the pattern of interdependence that would result purely from market forces.

The second group comprises the *centrally planned countries* (mainly countries of Eastern Europe, the Soviet Union, and China), which, in accordance with communist ideology, outlaw private enterprise. All foreign economic transactions are conducted by *state enterprises,* whose decisions are guided by national economic plans and foreign policy. Hence, the international economic relations of the communist countries are highly "politicized." Although state trading organizations may choose to maximize economic values (behaving like private firms), they can also choose to behave as purely political organizations, ignoring economic gain.[5]

It is fruitless to speculate in the abstract on whether international economic relations determine international political relations (as the Marxists contend) or whether international political relations determine international economic relations. International economic and political relations are interdependent; both the international economic system and the international political system are best regarded as subsystems of the same nation-state system. In some circumstances, political forces may dominate economic forces, while in other circumstances just the opposite occurs. One thing, however, is certain: Whenever a government considers the behavior of some or all of its country's international economic transactions as vital to national interests, the government will try to make that behavior conform to those interests.

---

[5] Several communist countries, notably China, have recently liberalized their economies by, for example, allowing their farmers to sell some of their crops on open markets and allowing state enterprises to form profit-oriented joint ventures with multinational enterprises of the industrial countries. Further progress in this direction will bring the communist countries to a fuller participation in the international economy. But at present, their economies remain predominantly under the control of government authorities.

THE MULTINATIONAL ENTERPRISE SYSTEM

International economists have traditionally maintained a *macroscopic perspective* on international economic relations. By considering trade and investment only on the national level, they have implicitly regarded national economies as the *agents* of international transactions. Although we shall rely on the macroscopic (or national) perspective in Parts One, Two, and Three, we must recognize that this perspective is necessary but no longer sufficient to explain the behavior of the international economy. Multinational enterprises have become responsible for a sizable (and increasing) share of world trade and for most international investment. As big, oligopolistic companies, multinational enterprises possess a market power that makes them independent actors in the international economic system. Unlike firms in purely competitive markets, multinational enterprises enjoy managerial discretion in their decisions; they do not simply respond to market conditions and public policies in a predetermined way. Indeed, their actions force changes in national economies and compel governments to respond to them. Thus, to understand the contemporary international economy we must supplement a macroscopic perspective with a *microscopic* perspective that considers the role of the multinational enterprise. This is the third theme of this book, which is taken up in Part Four. Here we make only a few additional comments on this subject.

A firm becomes a multinational enterprise when it extends its production and organization into foreign countries.[6] The *multinational enterprise system*, therefore, consists of a parent company; its producing and marketing affiliates in foreign countries; and the flows of products, services, capital, technology, management, and funds among them. These *intraenterprise transfers* (flows) cross national boundaries and therefore enter the balance of payments of nations in the same way as international transactions between independent buyers and sellers.

Although it has roots in the past, the multinational enterprise has become a dominant institution only in the last quarter century. Since the late 1950s, the political and economic systems of the industrial West have favored the spread of international production by corporations in search of market opportunity and lower costs. As a consequence, the traditional *international* economy of traders is giving way to a *world* economy of international producers. Our comprehension of this world economy is modest indeed. Part Four will be an exploration of new terrain in international economic relations.

---

[6] For a fuller definition, see Chapter 22.

DISTINCTIVE FEATURES OF INTERNATIONAL TRADE AND INVESTMENT

The distinctive features of international trade and investment are traceable to the environment in which they occur— the nation-state system and its political, sociocultural, and economic subsystems. In particular, national sovereignty is the ultimate source of most of the differences that distinguish international trade and investment from their domestic counterparts. Since we have already indicated some of the implications of these environmental systems for international trade and investment, this section is partly a recapitulation of our earlier discussion.

Different Languages and Customs

Most nations have a distinctive linguistic and cultural identity in addition to a basic political identity. This is not always true; we can all call to mind nations that have more than one official language and more than one cultural group in their populations. Moreover, several nations may share a common language and a common cultural heritage. Nevertheless, it is true that people tend to be like each other in more ways when they belong to the same nation than when they belong to different nations. Hence, international trade and investment, unlike most interregional trade and investment within nations, involve persons of different languages, customs, attitudes, values, and other cultural traits. Although such differences do not affect the basic economic similarity between interregional and international trade and investment, they do complicate relations between governments and introduce many new elements into the conduct of international business enterprise. As noted earlier, nationalism intensifies the sociocultural differences among the world's peoples.

Separate National Economic Policies

National economic policies may be compatible with the free flow of merchandise, services, and enterprise between nations, or they may be responsible for the regulation and suppression of that flow. As we shall discover, national economic policies that are apparently wholly domestic in nature may have profound effects on international trade and investment. To maintain an equilibrium in its international payments without resort to controls, a nation must keep its economy adjusted to the world economy. This means, for example, that it must pursue fiscal and monetary policies that keep its prices and costs competitive with those of other nations. It also means that there is sometimes a conflict between the aims of domestic policy and international adjustment. Because of political pressures, this conflict is often resolved in favor of the former, while international maladjustment is frozen by the imposition of controls over foreign trade and payments.

When certain nations adopt domestic policies that are detrimental to their external stability, all trading nations suffer the consequences. For the international economy to function in an atmosphere of freedom, there must be agreement among nations as to the criteria of sound domestic and international economic policies. It too often happens, however, that nations follow policies that are conceived in purely domestic terms, and the resulting welter of policies causes international maladjustments that are met by a rash of restrictive measures.[7] Unlike domestic trade and investment, therefore, international trade and investment is often subject to the influence of many separate national economic policies that are in disharmony with each other.

One consequence of separate national policies is jurisdictional overlap. For instance, a multinational enterprise may be taxed on the same income by two governments (double taxation). More generally, the enterprise may be subjected to the conflicting demands of both home and host governments in any number of policy areas.

National Monetary Systems

Unlike their domestic counterparts, international trade and investment take place between economies that have different monetary systems. This gives rise to the need to exchange one currency for another. The purchase and sale of foreign currency is conducted in the foreign exchange market, and the exchange ratio between currencies is known as the *exchange rate*. Dealings in foreign exchange often appear mysterious to the average person, and perhaps more than anything else, except nationalism, they have convinced the average person that international trade and investment are entirely distinct from the familiar domestic trade and investment. Even domestic producers have been daunted by the prospect of dealings in foreign exchange until relieved by the calm advice and aid of bankers.

Actually the presence of different monetary systems need not make the character of international trade and investment different from that of their domestic counterparts. When exchange rates are stable and currencies are freely convertible into each other, international payments are just as easily made as are domestic payments. In these circumstances the national monetary systems compose one international monetary system, and for all practical purposes they are one and the same. Before World War I such an international monetary system did in fact exist. National currencies were linked to gold and were freely transferable into each other; an international payment differed from a domestic payment only in that it involved residents of different countries.

Today the situation is far different, and international trade and in-

---

[7] A current example (discussed in Chapter 9) is the enormous U.S. trade deficit that has spawned growing demands for U.S. import protection.

vestment are sharply set off from domestic trade and investment by the restrictions imposed by many governments on transactions in foreign exchange and by variations in foreign exchange rates. Although the currencies of the industrial countries (mainly in North America, Western Europe, and Japan) are freely convertible at variable rates, the currencies of many nonindustrial countries and of all communist countries are inconvertible in one way or another. Currency inconvertibility can have profound effects on the conduct of international trade and investment. An importer may not be able to buy merchandise from a given country because of the impossibility of buying the necessary foreign exchange from his or her government. The importer may be compelled, therefore, to import inferior or higher priced goods from a country to which he or she is permitted to make payments. When currencies are freely convertible but only at variable rates (as today), foreign traders and investors may suffer exchange losses unless they can hedge against them. We should remember, however, that the exercise of national sovereignty to restrict international payments or follow policies that cause volatile exchange rates is a more significant feature of international trade and investment than the mere presence of national monetary systems.

Government Regulation of International Trade and Investment

Governments have interfered with international trade and investment ever since the beginnings of the nation-state system some five hundred years ago. Even during the last half of the nineteenth century, when the majority of governments followed a policy of laissez-faire with respect to domestic economic activities, the use of tariff protection was commonplace. Great Britain and the Netherlands were the only important trading nations that rid themselves of protective tariffs and adopted free trade in that period of liberal economic policies. Since World War I, all nations without exception have regulated their foreign trade and investment and have done so with many new control devices.

As noted previously, many contemporary governments restrict the convertibility of their currencies. This is known as *exchange control*. It allows a comprehensive regulation of the international movement not only of merchandise but of services and capital as well. Commodity trade is also regulated through quotas, licenses, tariffs, bilateral trading arrangements, commodity agreements, and other techniques. Restrictions are generally applied against imports, while exports may be stimulated by subsidies, exchange depreciation, bilateral agreements, and other methods. Mention should also be made of the fact that government regulation involves a great deal of red tape and bureaucratic delay, which are often potent deterrents to trade and to the entry of foreign firms.

The International Mobility of Factors of Production

In the nineteenth century, classical economists distinguished international trade from domestic trade by the criterion of factor mobility. It was assumed that the factors of production—capital, management, and labor—moved freely within a country but did not move between countries. For this reason international trade obeyed laws of economic behavior that differed from those of domestic trade.

As the nineteenth century progressed, these twin assumptions of perfect factor *mobility* within countries and perfect factor *immobility* between countries came more and more into conflict with the facts of economic life. Neoclassical economists observed that factors of production often did not move freely from one place to another inside the same country and, on the other hand, that a substantial migration of capital was proceeding from Europe to the other continents. Economists came to agree, therefore, that a sharp distinction between domestic interregional trade and international trade could not be drawn in terms of factor mobility. Rather, *both* kinds of trade were based on factor immobilities; that is, trade was a substitute for investment and other factor movements.

In the absence of political restrictions on the international movement of capital, enterprise, and persons, it is likely that factor mobility between countries would still be somewhat less than factor mobility within countries. International differences in customs and languages, distance, and the like would work in this direction. Under these circumstances no one would argue that factor movements between countries were essentially different from factor movements within countries. In actuality, as we all know, they *are* different, for nations throughout the world restrict immigration (and sometimes emigration) as well as the movement of capital and enterprise. Thus, the exercise of national sovereignty has greatly limited the international mobility of productive factors, and in so doing it has altered the scope and character of international trade and investment. At the same time, the multinational enterprise has remarkably accelerated the flow of factor services among countries since World War II.

To conclude, although the international mobility of factors tends to be less (and in the case of ordinary labor, much less) than their domestic mobility, the degree of factor mobility does not provide a *fundamental* distinction between domestic and international trade. It follows that international economic theory must encompass both trade flows and factor flows (mainly via the multinational enterprise) if it is to explain the behavior of the contemporary world economy.

THE NATIONAL INTEREST IN
INTERNATIONAL TRADE

What is the national interest in international trade? This question has colored many debates through the ages, and it will undoubtedly continue to do so in the future. In this introductory chapter we offer some preliminary remarks on the gains from trade at the levels of the nation, consumer, international business enterprise, and domestic import-competing enterprise.[8] We shall leave to Part Four a consideration of the national interest as it relates to international investment and to the multinational enterprise.

The National Gains from International Trade

Although conceivably a nation might have a sufficient variety of productive factors to produce every kind of good and service, it would not be able to produce each good and service with equal facility. The United States *could* produce handwoven rugs, but only at a high cost, since the production of such rugs requires great quantities of labor, which is expensive in this country. The production of handwoven rugs, however, would afford reasonable employment for the large supply of cheap labor in a country like India. It would be advantageous for the United States, therefore, to specialize in a commodity such as computers, whose production makes use of the abundant supply of technology in this country, and to export computers in exchange for handwoven rugs from India.

This example illustrates in a very simple way the gains that result from international specialization—each nation is able to utilize its productive factors in their most productive combinations. By raising the productivity of national economies, international specialization increases the output of goods and services. This is its economic justification and the principal justification of the international trade that makes possible such specialization.

The contribution of international trade is so immense that few countries could become self-sufficient even with the greatest effort. Contemporary economies have been shaped by the international trade and specialization of the past, and their continued viability is closely dependent on the world economy. For example, it is physically impossible for the United Kingdom or Japan to feed, clothe, and house their present populations at their current levels without imports from other countries. Economic self-sufficiency for these two nations would mean poverty standards of living unless emigration proved possible on a very large scale. The survival of these countries depends essentially on the export of manufactures that require

---

[8] The discussion of the basis and benefits of international trade in the following subsections is introductory to the detailed analysis of Chapters 2 through 6.

little space to produce in exchange for foodstuffs and raw materials that require great space to produce or are found in only certain areas of the earth.

The United Kingdom and Japan are examples of high dependence on international trade. But even countries that are able to supply their own peoples with the basic necessities of life out of domestic production would be faced with an unbearable decline in living standards if they were cut off from international trade.[9] New Zealand produces far more foodstuffs than are needed to nourish its sparse population, and it is able to trade this surplus for manufactures with industrial countries like the United Kingdom and Japan. Hence, for New Zealand, economic self-sufficiency would not mean starvation but rather the deprivation of manufactured goods that are necessary to sustain its current standard of living. Of course, New Zealand could produce some manufactures to take the place of imports, but its efforts in that direction would be limited by its scarce supplies of labor, capital, and industrial raw materials. The New Zealand economy is itself the product of international specialization and trade, and a far different and poorer economy would have evolved in the absence of world markets.

The United States, with its continental sweep and immense resources, could afford economic self-sufficiency with the least cost of any nation, with the possible exception of the Soviet Union. Perhaps this explains why Americans, more than people of other countries, are inclined to underestimate the importance of international trade.

But even for this country, the cost of self-sufficiency would be formidable. American consumers would experience an immediate pinch in their standards of living. An entire range of foodstuffs would no longer be available or would be available only at exorbitant prices. That American institution, the cup of coffee, would become a luxury to all but a few, and most of us would be forced to do without our daily stimulant or to use inferior substitutes. Even then, the sugar for our beverage would be an expensive item.

Of basic foodstuffs, we would, of course, have a plentiful supply. In fact, we would become embarrassed by growing stockpiles of agricultural products as farmers lost export outlets for over one half of their wheat crop, two fifths of their cotton crop, and large fractions of many other crops. Eventually many farmers would be ruined, and the agricultural sector of our economy would become less important.

Manufacturing industries would also face many difficulties. Without imports, many raw materials would no longer be available and inferior substitutes would replace them. Domestic supplies of other raw materials would no longer be supplemented by imports, and their prices would rise to increase costs of production all along the line. The loss of export markets would also cause severe dislocations in many manufacturing industries. But

---

[9] Much of the decline in living standards during a war is due to the cessation of international trade, as illustrated by the experience of neutral countries such as Sweden and Switzerland during World War II.

the most dramatic and profound consequence of economic self-sufficiency in the United States would be a drastic decline in the availability of energy in the form of petroleum. Now dependent on imports for over one third of its petroleum supply, a self-sufficient United States would become a country that could no longer sustain its contemporary energy-intensive economy and consumer lifestyle.

Thus, the outcome of economic self-sufficiency for the United States would be a fall in the American standard of living. Only those producers in direct competition with imports would benefit from self-sufficiency, but the improvement in their fortunes would be purchased at the cost of a general deterioration in the economic well-being of most Americans. Because of the rising dependence on imports of critical raw materials (particularly petroleum), the importance for the United States of foreign trade will grow in the future. More than at any time in the past, our economic prosperity in the years ahead rests upon an expanding world economy.

Domestic Specialization and Interregional Trade

The gains from specialization that are possible through international trade are fundamentally of the same nature as the gains from specialization achieved by interregional trade within a country. The distinctive features of international trade originate, for the most part, in the political fact of national sovereignty—not in economic conditions. Basically, trade within a country is identical with trade between countries. Both derive from the fact that individual regions and countries can gain through trade by specializing in the production of those goods and services that utilize the most productive combinations of their natural resources, labor, capital, management, and technology.

At the present time over half of the foreign trade of Western European countries is with each other. If these countries should one day federate and become one nation, this trade would become interregional rather than international, but its virtues would be neither greater nor less by reason of that change alone.[10] International trade and interregional trade are substitutes for each other. Thus, the explanation of the *relatively* small foreign trade of the United States is found in the vast interregional trade within its borders.

We readily comprehend the great advantages of regional specialization within the domestic economy. Nationalism may blind us to the benefits of international trade, but it does not stand in the way of our appreciation of domestic trade. It is true that local producers and merchants may seek to turn consumers away from products "imported" from other domestic regions,

---

[10] Undoubtedly trade between European countries would expand greatly if these nations merged into one political unit, since the restraints now imposed on this trade by individual governments would disappear. But this would not make interregional trade any "better" than international trade. See Chapter 10.

but these efforts are largely wasted since localities and regions do not have the authority to impose restrictions on interregional trade.[11] Moreover, almost all of us consider the national economy to be a single economy rather than an agglomeration of regional economies, and we oppose any interference with trade in the domestic market.

To illustrate, we would view as absurd a petition by New England textile producers requesting the federal government to impose restrictions on the sale of textiles produced in the South. We might sympathize with the plight of several New England communities as their chief industry shut its doors and headed south, but we would feel that such a situation is sure to occur now and then in a competitive economy and that in the long run everyone benefits by having goods and services produced in those places where costs are at a minimum. When, however, those same producers demand protection against imports of textiles from, say, Taiwan, their appeal sounds reasonable to many of us, despite the fact that the economic issue is the same, namely, whether domestic consumers are to have the right to purchase less expensive textiles made elsewhere.

To conclude, recognition of the basic similarity of interregional and international trade is essential to a proper understanding of the latter. That recognition will keep us from reaching the erroneous conclusion that, because of the many characteristics that distinguish international trade, it is a unique sort of trade and must be treated differently from domestic trade. Widespread awareness that the gains from international trade rest upon the same economic conditions as do the gains from domestic trade would eradicate much of the confusion and downright falsity that envelop public discussions of matters pertaining to our trade with other nations.

The Interest of Consumers

As consumers, all of us have an interest in international trade, although we are usually unaware of the influence of international trade on the prices, quality, and availability of goods. Goods are imported only because they are less expensive than domestic goods or are differentiated from them in one way or another. U.S. imports of watches from Hong Kong and cameras from Japan are examples of the first type of imports, while imports of perfumes from France, beer from Holland, and high-performance automobiles from West Germany are examples of the second type of imports. Without such imports the American consumer would pay a higher price for watches and cameras and would not have the opportunity to enjoy Chanel perfumes, Heineken beer, and Mercedes-Benz automobiles.

Imports of raw materials and other industrial goods likewise benefit

---

[11] Interstate trade barriers are forbidden by the United States Constitution. Despite this fact, individual states do restrain interstate trade in certain products (mostly agricultural) through a variety of devices ostensibly employed for other purposes, such as pest control and public safety. Arrangements between domestic producers to restrain interstate trade are forbidden by the antitrust laws.

the consumer by lowering domestic costs of production and in some instances enabling the production of goods that depend exclusively on foreign sources of supply. The consumer also has an interest in domestic exports, since they provide the means to pay for imports. Hence, as consumers, we all benefit from the greater abundance and variety of goods and the lower prices that international trade makes possible.

The contribution of international trade to the welfare of domestic consumers is the most basic of all. The end of economic activity is consumption; production is only a means to that end. A policy of production for the sake of production or of employment for the sake of employment ignores the fundamental reason for economic activity. Hence, economists have usually identified the national economic interest with the economic well-being of a nation's people. It follows that a sustainable policy or economic activity that adds to the supply of goods and services that people wish to consume is a policy or activity in the national interest. Conversely, a policy or economic activity that brings about a level of national consumption that is persistently below the level attainable by an alternative policy or activity is not in the national interest. This criterion of national interest may be modified to take into account illegal production, consumption harmful to health, the need to refrain from current domestic consumption to promote economic growth, and the like, but it differs from other criteria of national interest in its emphasis on consumer welfare. Of course, when a nation is at war, the aim of national survival takes precedence over consumer welfare or any other objective.

When we employ the criterion of consumer welfare to decide whether international trade is in the national interest, we find that increasing permanently the supply of goods and services available for domestic consumption benefits the nation. Moreover, all trading nations gain from international trade. This gain rests squarely on the specialization that arises from the opportunity to buy and sell in foreign markets.

The Interest of International Business Enterprises

The value of international trade to the manufacturers, extractive producers, intermediaries, transportation agencies, financial institutions, and other enterprises that engage in international trade is easily understood. Simply stated, international trade is a source of income and profits.

Domestic producers gain from international trade in many ways. They depend upon imports to meet their need for raw materials and productive equipment at a lower cost than if the same items were acquired from domestic sources of supply. Exports afford domestic producers a profit on sales, and they often make possible a larger scale of production with lower unit costs. Imports and exports, moreover, tend to moderate fluctuations in the supply, demand, and prices of individual goods. Sudden shifts in the availability of domestic raw materials may be offset by opposing shifts in raw material imports, and producers with substantial sales abroad are less sensitive to purely domestic economic conditions compared to producers in the same industries who dispose of their entire output at home.

A domestic concern may further find in export markets a means of additional growth that enables it to compete more effectively in the home market. Often the knowledge and experience gained from selling in foreign markets can be used to improve the efficiency and success of domestic marketing operations. In short, international trade allows domestic producers to escape the confines of the domestic market through imports that lower costs of production or improve the quality of the product and through exports that enhance sales and profits. For the multinational enterprise, international trade offers opportunities to link multicountry production bases with markets throughout the world.

International trade cannot be carried on by producers alone. Many specialized intermediaries and agencies are needed to conduct and facilitate its operations. This is particularly true of merchandise trade: The merchandise must be bought and sold; transportation services must be provided by railroads, ships, trucks, airplanes, and other agencies; international shipments must be insured, financed, and paid for; customs and other government requirements must be met; exports must be stimulated through advertising and other promotion devices; and so on. Specialized intermediaries and agencies are also needed in the field of international investment, in the tourist trade, and in other nonmerchandise transactions of an international character. All of the many business concerns involved in carrying out these functions have a direct stake in international trade. When international trade is booming, they experience expansion and profits. Conversely, when international trade enters a slump, these concerns are the first to suffer losses.

The Interest of Import-Competing Enterprises

The contribution of international trade to the many business enterprises involved cannot automatically be identified with the national interest, since other groups are also part of the national economy. Domestic producers who face close competition from imports may be injured by an expansion of international trade. Moreover, the labor used by such producers may suffer from unemployment or lower wages as a consequence of import competition. The adverse effects of import competition are particularly noticeable when import-competing industries are concentrated in specific localities. In measuring the national gain from international trade, therefore, the losses experienced by these groups must be set against the benefits received by other groups.

It must not be supposed, however, that the losses experienced by domestic producers and others hurt by import competition are permanent. In an expanding economy, labor, capital, and management are able to shift out of stagnant lines of production into more productive lines. Indeed, one of the virtues of a competitive economy lies in its flexibility in adjusting production to meet new technologies, new demands, and new competition—domestic or foreign.

Some Arguments Against International Trade

Despite the economic gain for the nation, many arguments have been voiced against international trade, including these:

1. A nation dependent on foreign sources of supply is in a particularly vulnerable position during a war.
2. International trade is a source of instability and interferes with economic planning.
3. International trade creates losses for those domestic industries whose products are displaced by imports.

International specialization brings to a nation a higher standard of living, but it also implies dependence on foreign markets as sources of supply and as outlets for domestic production. Some persons contemplate this dependence with marked distaste and argue that the national interest demands that it be lessened to one degree or another. The aversion toward international specialization is rationalized in many ways, and it often camouflages the interests of private groups that stand to gain from the removal of import competition. The most important ally of attacks against international specialization and trade is nationalism—the ideology that holds the nation-state to be the *only* source of political and economic security.

National Defense   It is argued that a nation dependent on foreign sources of supply is in a particularly vulnerable position during a war. The harrowing experience of the United Kingdom in both world wars is cited as proof of this assertion—twice the German submarine blockade almost brought the country to its knees by cutting off imports of food and raw materials. This is, of course, a political or military argument rather than an economic one, but it has many economic implications. Its proper evaluation requires not only a careful forecast of the probable nature of a future war but a searching study of the relationships between economic strength and military capacity as well. For example, if another world war promises destruction of everyone's productive facilities within a few hours, then it is the existing military strength that counts, and the military argument for economic self-sufficiency falls by the wayside.

In conclusion, there is no assurance that greater economic self-sufficiency will enhance a nation's military power, and by the same token there is no justification to deny out of hand the compatibility of international specialization and a nation's ability to defend itself against armed aggression.

Instability and Economic Planning   International trade is also condemned as a source of economic instability. This attitude gained prominence in the 1930s when depression spread from one country to another by disrupting the international flow of goods, services, and capital. In particular, foreign observers were wont to protest the folly of close dependence on such a volatile economy as that of the United States. In our own day this argument against international trade has been reinforced by government policies directed toward high employment and economic development. To many economic planners, foreign trade is a nuisance unless carefully controlled to fit the master economic plan. This is not the place to evaluate the bearing of international trade and investment on domestic stability, employment, and economic development, but it may be pointed out that most nations are unable to achieve the objectives of high employment and economic development except as members of a world trading system.

Protectionism   Traditionally the attacks against foreign trade have been leveled against imports. Several arguments in addition to those already mentioned have been used to justify the protection of domestic industry against foreign competition. These arguments are described and analyzed in Chapter 6, and we shall say nothing about them here except to indicate that insofar as protectionism lowers a nation's imports, it also eventually lowers a nation's exports (unless the protectionist country loans or gives away its exports), since other nations must finance their imports through exports.

The roll call of arguments against international specialization and trade is indeed a formidable one—national security, economic stability, full employment, economic development, economic planning, protectionism, and others of lesser note. All of these arguments pack a powerful emotional appeal to the person on the street. Nevertheless, international trade exhibits vitality and growth difficult to reconcile with its alleged disadvantages. It would appear that the supreme economic advantages of international specialization and trade, when weighed against the supreme economic costs of national self-sufficiency, cannot be denied by nationalistic fervor or the special pleading of private vested interests.

THE GOALS AND INSTRUMENTS OF FOREIGN ECONOMIC POLICY

We have observed that pervasive government regulation is a distinctive feature of international trade and investment. The regulations imposed by the government of one nation on its external economic relations with other nations constitute the instruments that the nation uses to carry out its foreign economic policy. Because much of this book deals with the foreign economic policies of the United States and other nations, it is fitting in this introductory chapter to offer some general observations on the nature of foreign economic policy, its possible goals, and the instruments that may be used to achieve those goals.

The rationale of government economic policies throughout the world is that national economies, if left alone, would fail to achieve goals that are deemed to be in the national interest, such as full employment, a "satisfactory" rate of growth, price stability, an equitable distribution of income, and a "strong" balance of payments. Basically, therefore, national economic policies may be viewed as a rejection in whole or in part of the social virtues of an atomistic, laissez-faire economy, in which levels of economic activity and resource allocation are determined by impersonal market forces with only a minimal government presence.

Although governments have sought to influence the internal and external behavior of national economies since the birth of the nation-state in the sixteenth century, the goals and instruments of their policies have frequently shifted over time. Up to the middle of the nineteenth century, the major countries for the most part followed mercantilistic policies that sought to advance power-political interests through a variety of controls on international trade and factor movements. The subsequent period, which ended with World War I, was marked by the ascendancy of a belief in the blessings of free, unfettered markets. Governments relied on monetary policy to smooth the operation of the international gold standard and generally relaxed or abandoned restrictions on external trade, while at home they accepted with equanimity the ups and downs of the business cycle. The global depression of the 1930s ended this laissez-faire posture, as governments everywhere undertook a variety of policy measures to stimulate economic recovery at home and to insulate the domestic economy from external influences. In the 1930s economic nationalism ran rampant, international cooperation almost disappeared, and international trade was throttled by tariffs, quotas, exchange controls, and other devices. In our own day, national governments are committed to a broad range of economic goals that they try to achieve in a world of growing economic interdependence.

Because there is no clear-cut distinction between a government's foreign and domestic policies, we may conceive foreign economic policy either broadly or narrowly, depending on our purposes. Broadly conceived, foreign economic policy embraces all of the varied activities of national governments that bear, directly or indirectly, upon the composition, direction, magnitude, and growth of international trade and factor flows. This conception of foreign economic policy covers not only such obvious examples as tariff policy but also domestic governmental measures, such as monetary and fiscal policy, that have an impact upon foreign trade and investment. Since economic activity is characterized by mutual interdependence, there are few, if any, economic policies of government that have only domestic effects.

Because of the signal importance of the American economy in the world, the economic policies of the U.S. government, whether ostensibly domestic or foreign, are of particular significance to the well-being of the world economy. Probably the greatest single contribution that the U.S. government can make toward the promotion and development of world trade and investment is the pursuit of policies at home that ensure the stable, noninflationary growth of the American economy. In this sense the fiscal and monetary policies of the government are more basic to U.S. foreign economic policy than, for example, its much touted actions in the field of tariff negotiation. Just as policies undertaken to achieve domestic goals (such as high employment) will have repercussions on a country's external economic relations, so will policies undertaken with respect to foreign trade, foreign aid, foreign investment, and the balance of payments have repercussions on the level, composition, and growth of national output and income; on employment; on prices; and on other aspects of the domestic economy.

In terms of *effects*, therefore, it is impossible to classify government policies as exclusively domestic or exclusively foreign. Instead, they may be regarded as occupying different positions along a continuum that stretches between an "internal effects" pole and an "external effects" pole. Policies that have only insignificant effects on foreign trade and investment (such as government subsidies for housing) are close to the "internal effects" pole, while policies that have insignificant domestic effects (such as lowering a revenue duty on an imported good with no domestic substitute) are close to the "external effects" pole. Most government policies, however, fall between these two poles, and growing international interdependence is pushing more and more policies toward the center.

The interdependence of domestic and foreign economic policy (however defined) is a fact that must be kept in mind throughout our study of international trade and investment. Unfortunately for the peace of mind of those people who like to have everything in watertight compartments, the political boundary of a nation cannot serve to demarcate domestic and foreign interests. For reasons of space and analytical convenience, in this text we are compelled to limit foreign economic policy to the activities of government that are *intended* to regulate, restrict, promote, or otherwise influence the conduct of international trade and investment. While employing this narrower definition in our subsequent description and analysis of foreign economic policy, we do not propose to neglect its close relationship with domestic economic policy.

Foreign Economic Policy and Private Interests

The foreign economic policy of governments is pervasive; it affects all of us in a number of ways—as consumers, as producers, and as citizens of a nation that itself is a member of the community of nations. Restrictive government policy forces us as consumers to pay a higher price for many imported goods and, at times, to do without them. On the other hand, liberal government policy enables us to reap the advantages of international specialization. As domestic producers we may be benefited or hurt by specific aspects of foreign economic policy, depending upon our place in the economy. As international traders and producers we may be thwarted in our efforts to sell and produce in foreign countries by policies that keep us out or limit our opportunities. As international lenders or borrowers we may be encouraged or constrained by government policies at home or abroad. Finally, the foreign economic policy of our government may earn us the goodwill and support of other nations, or it may provoke mistrust and retaliation.

Although we cannot escape the impact of the foreign economic policy of our government and others upon our lives and fortunes, we are usually ignorant of its source. The bearing of this policy on our interests as consumers is ordinarily indirect and can be traced only by careful economic analysis. Certainly, the average person on the street is unaware of the relationship between foreign economic policy and the availability and prices of the goods and services that compose our standard of living—particularly in the United States. Consequently, most of us care little about the foreign economic policy of our own government and few of us seek to change it.

The situation is far different for business enterprises that are directly engaged in international trade and investment or that face competition from imports. They know well that government actions in the world economy may spell the difference between profit and loss. Hence, they take steps to influence foreign economic policy in the direction that best accords with their interests. Because of the apathy of the general public, the individuals and groups that have an obvious financial stake in the foreign economic policy of their governments have been able to exert an extraordinary influence on policy formation. The effectiveness of protectionist lobbies in Washington and elsewhere is a good example.

The excessive weight given to private vested interests in the formulation and execution of foreign economic policy is not only undemocratic but also represents a yielding of the national interest to individual interests. Above our own individual welfare lies the welfare of the nation and the welfare of the community of nations, and, in the last analysis, they are inseparable. Enlightened self-interest demands, therefore, that we take full account of national and international interests in the formulation of foreign economic policy. To do so we must learn to evaluate foreign economic policy in light of these broad perspectives.

The Goals of Foreign Economic Policy

There are several ways to classify the goals that nations may strive to achieve in their foreign economic policy, and few classifications are apt to be exhaustive or mutually exclusive. We do not intend to catalog the many ends of foreign economic policy, but to illustrate their rich diversity we have chosen for discussion seven of the most fundamental goals. At this time we are not interested in an analysis of these goals; our purpose is simply one of identification.

Autarky   At one extreme is the objective of *autarky* or national self-suf-ficiency. A full autarkic policy aims to rid the nation of all dependence on international trade and investment because this dependence is feared for economic, political, or military reasons. Autarky is clearly inconsistent with the continuance of economic relations with other countries; the political counterpart of autarky is isolationism. Of course, most nations do not possess the domestic resources required to practice any significant degree of autarky. More common is a qualified autarkic policy that seeks self-sufficiency in only certain articles of trade, generally of a strategic military value.

Economic Welfare   At the opposite extreme to autarky lies the goal of *economic welfare* that springs from a conception of international trade and investment as an opportunity to reap the benefits of international special-ization. In Chapter 2 we present the cogent economic reasoning that un-derlies this conception of trade. Foreign economic policy in which the ob-jective of economic welfare plays a leading role seeks to expand international trade and investment by lowering or eliminating tariffs and other barriers to the free exchange of goods, services, and factors. As noted above, this liberal philosophy of trade was dominant in the period preceding World War I, when the United Kingdom, the paramount trading nation at that time, espoused a policy of free trade and most other nations used only the tariff in controlling trade. After World War II, economic welfare emerged once again as a prominent goal in the foreign economic policies of the industrial countries of the West, led by the United States.

Protectionism   Between the two extremes—autarky, which would regu-late foreign trade out of existence, and free trade, which would impose no restrictions whatsoever— there are many other goals that serve to motivate foreign economic policy. Chief among them is *protectionism*—the protection of domestic producers against the free competition of imports by regulating their volume through tariffs, quotas, and the like. Identification of a specific foreign economic policy as protectionist is sometimes difficult, since any policy that restricts imports has protectionist effects regardless of its objec-tive. Protectionism, therefore, has many guises and it shows a remarkable ability to adjust to new circumstances by employing arguments and strat-agems suited to the times. In the 1980s, protectionism became a stronger influence on the foreign economic policies of the industrial countries.

Stable Levels of Employment   Since the 1930s, *stability of the economy at high employment levels* has been among the most important objectives of national economic policy. Contemporary governments try to restrain infla-tion while at the same time sustaining employment, although they are commonly frustrated by conflicts between the policies needed to achieve these goals. When the aim of full-employment stability dominates the for-eign economic policy of a nation, international trade and capital movements are viewed as both a source of disturbances to the domestic economy and a means of compensating for disturbances originating within the economy.

Whether foreign trade and capital movements are restricted or encouraged depends mostly upon current levels of domestic economic activity.

Balance of Payments   Sooner or later, all nations are compelled to remedy deficits in their *balance of payments*, whether through market adjustments or controls. When a nation's reserves are low and its balance of payments is weak, the objective of payments equilibrium may come to dominate other objectives of its foreign economic policy and even of its domestic policy. In the decade following World War II, the elimination of the dollar shortage occupied first place among the foreign economic policy objectives of Western European countries. In the 1960s and again in the 1980s, the U.S. balance of payments problem overshadowed other foreign economic issues. As we shall observe, balance of payments policy may conflict with domestic policies of full employment and noninflationary growth.

Economic Development   Today the nonindustrial countries of Asia, Africa, and Latin America are striving to accelerate their economic growth and to raise the living standards of their peoples. The pressing concern of these nations with the mammoth problem of *economic development* has led their governments to regard international trade as an instrument to achieve such development to the exclusion of other ends. Thus, tariffs and other restrictive devices are employed to protect "infant industries" or to keep out "nonessential" consumer goods. On the other hand, capital goods and other "essential" imports are encouraged by subsidies or favorable exchange quotas. Exports may also be regulated in an attempt to promote economic development. Aside from these direct measures of control, economic development programs are likely to provoke disequilibrium in the balance of payments because of their inflationary impact on domestic income and price levels. Further controls may then be imposed to suppress the disequilibrium.

Economic Warfare   During periods of actual warfare the international economic policies of nations are directed toward the overriding objective of victory. Even in the absence of armed conflict, however, *economic warfare* is often among the goals of international economic policy. We live in a time of political tensions between great powers, and it is to be expected that these powers should use foreign economic policy to further their own political and military advantages and to limit the advantages of those opposed to their vital interests. Thus, the United States and its allies impose strategic controls on trade with the communist countries, and the latter follow a similar course of action against the United States. Foreign aid programs are also used to implement political objectives; indeed, the full range of foreign economic policy comes under the influence of this political contest among nations. The injection of political and military considerations into international economic policy is nothing new. After all, foreign economic policy is part of the foreign policy of the nation, and it is inevitably colored to some degree by national political aims. But the degree of coloring is important.

The Instruments of Foreign Economic Policy

Foreign economic policy involves instruments as well as goals. In accordance with our decision to use a narrower interpretation of the scope of foreign economic policy, we shall take policy instruments to signify the tools (market variables, such as exchange rates, and direct controls) that are employed by governments with the *intent* to influence the magnitude, composition, or direction of international trade and factor movements.

The instruments of foreign economic policy exhibit broad variety, and it will prove helpful to examine them in terms of four policy areas, three of which deal with different segments of the balance of payments and the other with the balance of payments as a whole.[12] Figure 1-1 lists these policy areas together with the principal policy instruments that are available to governments of countries with market economies.[13] The dots indicate the policy

---

[12] See Chapter 14 for a description of the balance of payments.

[13] The policy instruments available to governments in the centrally planned economies of Eastern Europe, the Soviet Union, and China take the form of official edicts, administrative decisions, and bilateral agreements, with only a very limited reliance on market instruments.

Figure 1-1   Areas and Instruments of Foreign Economic Policy

INSTRUMENTS \ AREAS	Trade Policy	Investment Policy	Foreign Aid Policy	Balance of Payments Policy
Tariffs	●			
Nontariff trade barriers	●			
Export promotion	●			
Foreign investment restrictions		●		
Foreign investment inducements		●		
Official grants and loans			●	
Fiscal				●
Monetary				●
Exchange-rate adjustment				●
Exchange control				●

instruments that are *primarily* associated with each policy area. However, it would be a mistake to identify a policy area with a particular set of policy instruments, for many of them may be used to achieve different policy goals depending on the circumstances. In particular, balance of payments policy may utilize *all* of the policy instruments shown in Figure 1-1. Actually these policy instruments are more accurately defined as "policy instrument types," since each consists of several specific policy tools. For instance, nontariff trade barriers include quotas, border taxes, customs procedures, antidumping regulations, domestic subsidies, and others.

Agreements and Treaties   Much of the foreign economic policy of a nation is effected through agreements and treaties with other nations. For the most part, the legal rights that individuals and business enterprises enjoy in a foreign country are those spelled out in treaties and agreements previously negotiated by their own governments. Thus, international treaties and agreements determine the treatment to be accorded foreigners and foreign interests. Generally speaking, this treatment is either *national* or *most-favored-nation treatment.* Under national treatment, foreigners possess the same rights as nationals. National treatment extends chiefly to the protection of life and property; no Mexican policeman, for instance, would ask for a birth certificate before coming to the rescue of a person in trouble. Most-favored-nation treatment is based on a different concept of equity; it means that a nation treats a second nation as favorably as it treats any third nation. The main purpose of most-favored-nation treatment is to eliminate national discrimination. Its greatest application is in the field of tariffs and other measures of commercial policy.[14]

Trade and Investment Policies   *Trade policy* refers to all government actions that seek to alter current account transactions, especially trade in merchandise.[15] Historically, the main instrument of trade policy has been the import tariff, but today nontariff barriers and export promotion are often of equal or greater importance.

Investment policy covers government actions both with respect to international long-term lending and borrowing (portfolio investment) and with respect to the international movement of business enterprise, which involves not only capital but management and technology as well (direct investment). Ordinarily the governments of investing nations restrict investment outflows only for balance of payments reasons; indeed, they may promote direct investment outflows via inducements of one sort or another. On the other hand, although the governments of borrowing or host nations seldom deter inflows of portfolio investment, they frequently do so with certain forms of direct investment while at the same time encouraging other forms. Because of the rapid development of multinational companies that

---

[14] See Chapter 7.

[15] Current account transactions are exports and imports of physical goods and services. See Chapter 14.

produce and sell throughout the world, foreign investment policy has assumed a critical importance for both home and host countries.[16]

Foreign Aid Policy   *Foreign aid policy* includes all of the activities involved in the field of governmental loans and grants that are intended to aid in the reconstruction, economic development, or military defense of recipient countries. Compared with the other policies, foreign aid policy is a newcomer; it was born out of the vicissitudes of the early postwar period, when Europe lay economically prostrate. Later, a recognition of the obligation to help in the development of the economically backward countries of the world provided another stimulus to foreign aid policy. Simultaneously, the threat of the cold war gave rise to large-scale U.S. programs of military and economic aid that sought to buttress the free world against internal and external communist aggression. Today, assistance for economic development is the most pervasive rationale for foreign aid. All of the industrial countries, many international organizations, and even the communist countries now have aid programs that transfer resources to the developing countries.[17]

Balance of Payments Policy   *Balance of payments policy* embraces all of the actions of governments to maintain or restore equilibrium in their external accounts. In the face of an enduring, fundamental disequilibrium, governments generally respond to a deficit (surplus) by (1) deflating (inflating) the domestic economy with monetary and fiscal instruments, (2) devaluing (revaluing) the exchange rate, or (3) imposing exchange controls over some or all international transactions.[18] These basic instruments of adjustment may be used singly or in combination, and at times they may be rejected by governments in favor of policy instruments, such as tariffs and quantitative import restrictions, that are normally associated with other policy areas.

The Diversity and Conflict of Goals

The goals of foreign economic policies are diverse on two counts: (1) each nation ordinarily pursues several goals simultaneously in its own foreign economic policy, and (2) the mix of goals pursued by one nation does not necessarily correspond to the goal mixes of other nations either over the short or long run.[19] If these diverse goals could be successfully attained by each and every nation, there would be no need for our analysis of foreign economic policy. As is true of all human affairs, however, no single nation or group of nations can fully achieve the many objectives of its foreign economic policy. This failure stems from inconsistencies and conflicts among

---

[16] See Chapter 24.

[17] See Chapter 21.

[18] Chapters 15 and 16 examine market adjustment to the balance of payments via changes in income, money, prices, and the exchange rate. Chapter 17 looks at exchange control.

[19] The mix of goals pursued by national governments changes over time. Hence, the diversity of goals is a continuing phenomenon.

goals at both national and international levels and from inadequacies in policy instruments. Let us turn first to the question of goal conflict.

Except possibly during a war, when the issue of national survival is paramount, no nation seeks to achieve a single objective in its foreign economic policy; rather, it has several objectives that reflect the complex needs and demands of the national society. A nation is made up of individuals and groups who occupy different positions in society, who do not equally benefit from the same economic events and government policies, and who have, therefore, diverse economic views and interests. It is to be expected that individuals and groups will try to direct government policies toward goals that they deem beneficial. This conflict of interests is not easily resolved, and often a government resolves it in a way that satisfies one or another vested interest while the national interest is sacrificed on the altar of political expediency.

Protectionism versus free trade is an age-old conflict in goals. Clearly a nation cannot pursue a policy of free trade and at the same time protect domestic industries against foreign competition. The justification of free trade is that it enables a nation to gain from international specialization, whereas protectionism precludes that possibility. And yet, nations are wont to subscribe to the principle of free trade and practice protectionism. Many other instances of an *internal* conflict of goals will be encountered in subsequent chapters, such as the conflict in many developing countries between autarky (economic nationalism) and economic development.

Some countries are extremely dependent upon international trade for their economic livelihood; other countries approach varying degrees of self-sufficiency. Some countries are industrialized and enjoy a high standard of living; other countries are in the early stages of economic development and many of their people live close to starvation. Some national economies are organized on a private enterprise basis; others have a feudalistic or socialistic basis of production. Some countries have strong balances of payments; others are hard pressed to meet their international obligations. These and the many other differences that distinguish one nation from another generate different and often conflicting attitudes and policies toward international trade and investment. One nation may seek to take advantage of the benefits of trade by lowering tariffs and other barriers while other nations are raising barriers to protect domestic industry or to meet a drain on international reserves. Such conflicts of national interest abound in the historical and contemporary economic policies of nations.

It is important to understand that the *external* conflict of economic goals does not arise out of diversity as such but rather out of the interdependence of national economies. If all nations were to adopt a policy of full autarky, there could be no external conflict of economic goals because there would be no flows of goods and factors linking their economies. By the same token, any increase in the degree of international economic interdependence (as is occurring today at a rapid pace) will heighten the probability of goal conflicts among economic policies that are determined at the national level.

Interdependence calls into question the effectiveness of economic policies determined solely on the national level as opposed to the international level.

A great deal of international economic policy consists of efforts to alleviate both the internal and external conflict of goals. Persuasion and compromise are the hallmarks of these efforts. Today it is clear that the external conflict of goals will not be lessened except through understanding and compromise among nations, buttressed by formal treaties and agreements. If one accepts the belief that some lessening of this conflict is better than no lessening at all, the spirit of compromise that is necessary to achieve it must also be accepted. As an ongoing process, cooperation can point the way toward international economic policies that will benefit all nations, not simply the few who are strong.

Contemporary Issues of Foreign Economic Policy

Following is a list of ten contemporary issues of foreign economic policy. We shall encounter all of these issues in our study of international trade and investment. These issues reflect the tensions between the forces of global interdependence, on the one hand, and the forces of national autonomy, on the other. Governments need somehow to reconcile the fact of global economic interdependence with responsibilities to their own peoples for jobs, stable prices, economic growth, an equitable distribution of real income, and security. The most promising approach—and perhaps the only workable approach—is to try to increase the coordination of economic policies among the world's nations.

1. U.S. competitiveness in a new global economy.
2. U.S. balance of payments deficit.
3. Japan's persistent export surplus with the United States and Western Europe.
4. The emergence of newly industrializing countries (NICs) as international competitors in manufactured products.
5. The conduct of trade between the market economies of the West and the centrally planned economies of the East.
6. The new protectionism.
7. The price and availability of petroleum.
8. The high volatility of foreign exchange rates.
9. The international debt burden of the developing countries.
10. Control of multinational enterprise.

SOME EMPIRICAL DIMENSIONS OF INTERNATIONAL TRADE

In closing this introductory chapter, four tables are offered that indicate some of the quantitative dimensions of world and U.S. trade.

The Ten Leading Exporting and Importing Countries

Table 1-1 lists the ten leading exporting and importing countries in 1987. These points may be drawn from an examination of the data.

1. Six of the major exporting countries and six of the major importing countries are located in Western Europe, showing the key role of that region in the world economy.
2. The order of countries is not always the same for both exports and imports. Most noteworthy in this regard is the United States, which ranks second in exports but first in imports (by an overwhelming margin). In the past, the United States has ranked first in both exports and imports; it is likely to regain first place in exports as it reduces its trade deficit.[20]
3. Although the precise ordering may change from one year to the next, the principal trading countries were the same in 1980, with the exception of Belgium-Luxembourg, which was replaced by Saudi Arabia on the export side after the quadrupling of oil prices in 1974 and their doubling in 1979–1980. The sharp decline in oil

_____

[20] See Chapter 19 for a discussion of the trade deficit in the U.S. balance of payments.

TABLE 1-1   The Ten Leading Exporting and Importing Countries in 1987 (Billions of Dollars)

Exports		Imports	
West Germany	239.8	United States	424.1
United States	252.9	West Germany	228.1
Japan	229.2	France	157.9
France	143.5	United Kingdom	154.4
United Kingdom	131.2	Japan	149.5
Italy	116.6	Italy	125.0
Soviet Union	97.3	Netherlands	91.3
Canada	94.4	Soviet Union	88.9
Netherlands	92.9	Canada	87.6
Belgium-Luxembourg	83.1	Belgium-Luxembourg	83.2
World[1]	2472.8	World	2568.9

[1]The value of world exports is somewhat less than the value of world imports due to the fact that most nations value exports f.o.b. (free on board) at the point of exportation and imports c.i.f. (cost, insurance, freight) at the point of importation. Thus, the value of world imports exceeds the value of world exports by an amount of transportation and other costs incurred in the physical movement of merchandise between countries.

Source: United Nations, _Monthly Bulletin of Statistics_ (July 1988), Table 50, pp. 102–23.

prices in the 1980s has knocked Saudi Arabia out of the ten top importers.

4. The total exports and imports of these ten countries were almost two-thirds of the respective world totals in 1987. Thus, the remaining 150 countries or so accounted for only one-third of world trade.

The Origin and Destination of World Exports

Table 1-2 depicts the origin and destination of world exports during the first half of 1987. The dominance of the industrial countries (the West) is clearly evident. In this period they generated seven-tenths of world exports (70.2 percent) and world imports (70.5 percent). Moreover, trade *between* the industrial countries accounted for 55.3 percent of total world trade. Thus, almost four-fifths of the industrial countries' exports went to other industrial countries.

U.S. exports (which are included in the figures of the industrial countries) were 9.5 percent of world exports in this period. About two-thirds of U.S. exports went to other industrial countries, with most of the remainder going to the developing countries.

The developing countries (the South) originated 20.1 percent and absorbed 20.0 percent of world exports. However, only 5.8 percent of world trade was *between* the developing countries, who trade far more with the industrial countries. Since 1973, the trade figures for the developing countries as a group have been misleading, because a small number of oil-exporting countries (which compose the OPEC export cartel) are responsible for a large (but highly variable) share of the exports of all developing countries. For this reason, OPEC trade is shown separately, although it is also included in the trade of the developing countries.

The centrally planned, communist countries (the East) originated only 9.7 percent of world exports in the first half of 1987. Over half of the international trade of the communist countries was with other communist countries.

Summing up, in the first half of 1987, 55.3 percent of world trade was among the industrial countries, 5.8 percent among the developing countries, and 5.5 percent among the centrally planned countries. Trade *between* the industrial and the developing countries (including OPEC) was 25.2 percent of world exports; trade between the industrial and communist countries, 4.9 percent; and trade between the developing and communist countries, 3.3 percent.

Composition of U.S. Trade

Tables 1-3 and 1-4 indicate the percentage composition of U.S. exports and imports respectively by principal end-use categories since 1946.

Since World War II, U.S. *exports* of manufactures have steadily ex-

TABLE 1-2   Origin and Destination of Exports as a Percentage of World Exports During the First Half of 1987

Exports from:	Industrial Countries[1]	United States	Developing Countries[2]	OPEC	Centrally Planned Countries	World
Industrial Countries[1]	55.3	10.6	12.5	2.5	2.4	70.2
United States	6.3		3.0	0.4	0.2	9.5
Developing Countries[2]	12.7	4.8	5.8	0.8	1.6	20.1
OPEC	3.1	0.7	2.1	0.1	0.2	5.4
Centrally Planned Countries[3]	2.5	0.2	1.7	0.2	5.5	9.7
World	70.5	15.6	20.0	3.5	9.5	100.0

[1]United States, Canada, Western Europe, Japan, Australia, New Zealand, and South Africa.
[2]Asia excluding Japan, Africa, the Middle East, and Latin America, Australia, New Zealand, South Africa, and the communist countries.
[3]Communist countries. The world and regional totals exclude the intertrade of the communist countries of Asia.

Source: Derived from United Nations, *Monthly Bulletin of Statistics* (December, 1987), Special Table E, pp. 270–73.

TABLE 1-3   Composition of U.S. Exports by Principal End-Use Categories, 1946–1987 (Percent)

End-Use Category	Average 1946–1958	Average 1966–1970	Average 1978–1980	Average 1985–1987
Manufactures	40.4	49.3	49.9	53.0
Capital goods[1]	25.1	33.0	33.4	35.4
Automotive[2]	7.4	9.4	9.4	11.0
Consumer goods[3]	7.9	6.9	7.1	6.6
Industrial supplies and materials	40.4	32.7	29.7	28.1
Food, feeds, beverages	16.5	15.0	17.2	10.4
All other[4]	2.7	3.0	3.2	8.5
Total exports[5]	100.0	100.0	100.0	100.0

[1]Excluding automotive products.
[2]Vehicles, parts, and engines.
[3]Excluding automotive and food products.
[4]Re-exports, low-value shipments, and miscellaneous special transactions.
[5]Excluding sales and transfers under military programs.

Source: Survey of Current Business, March 1971, June 1979, March 1981, and June 1988.

panded their share of total exports, whereas exports of industrial supplies and materials have experienced a diminishing share. Capital goods have dominated the growth in exports of manufactures, accounting for over one-third of the total in the period 1985–1987. The sharp jump in the share of automotive exports in the 1966–1970 period was entirely owing to the U.S.-Canadian Automotive Products Trade Act of 1965, which established free trade between the two countries in motor vehicles and original parts. Manufactured consumer goods (nonfood) have declined somewhat in relative importance. In sum, exports of manufactures now make up more than half of U.S. exports, and their share is almost certain to grow in the future.

Since World War II, the composition of U.S. *imports* has changed more drastically than the composition of U.S. exports. Imports of manufactures show an astounding increase in their share of total imports, rising from 10.7 percent in the 1946–1958 period to 61.0 percent in the 1985–1987 period. Capital goods, automotive products, and consumer goods each account for about one-third of the imports of manufactures. The dominance of manufactures in U.S. imports reflects the continuing industrialization of other countries and the closing of technology gaps between them and the United States. To what extent this dominance indicates the United States is suffering from deteriorating international competitiveness is a subject for Chapter 9.

TABLE 1-4   Composition of U.S. Imports by Principal End-Use Categories, 1946–1987 (Percent)

End-Use Category	Average 1946–1958	Average 1966–1970	Average 1978–1980	Average 1985–1987
Manufactures	10.7	38.4	39.2	61.0
Capital goods[1]	2.1	8.8	11.8	19.6
Automotive[2]	1.1	12.4	12.5	20.4
Consumer goods[3]	7.5	17.1	14.9	21.0
Industrial supplies and materials	58.9	41.7	50.8	29.7
Foods, feeds, beverages	27.8	15.9	8.2	6.4
All other[4]	2.6	4.0	1.8	2.9
Total imports[5]	100.0	100.0	100.0	100.0

[1]Excluding automotive products.
[2]Vehicles, parts, and engines.
[3]Excluding automotive and food products.
[4]Low-value shipments, U.S. goods returned, and miscellaneous special transactions.
[5]Excluding sales and transfers under military programs.

Source: Survey of Current Business, March 1971, June 1979, March 1981, and June 1988.

The falling share of industrial supplies and materials was reversed in the 1970s owing to the quadrupling of oil prices by OPEC and the growing dependence of the United States on oil imports. But the sharp decline of oil prices in the 1980s has brought about a resumption of the long-term decline in relative imports of industrial supplies and materials. Their future share in U.S. imports will depend mainly on the volume and price of petroleum imports.

U.S. High-Technology Exports and Imports

The most dynamic U.S. exports are the products of high-technology industries, which are defined as those industries that spend an above-average percentage of their net sales on research and development (R & D). High-technology products include communications equipment and electronic components; aircraft; scientific instruments; office, computing, and accounting machines; drugs and medicines; industrial inorganic chemicals; guided missiles and spacecraft; and plastics. Table 1-5 reveals that such products have contributed a growing share of U.S. exports of manufactures, reaching 42.2 percent in 1985. (In 1962—not shown in Table 1-5—they were only 29.5 percent.)

Clearly, the growth of high-technology exports has outstripped the growth of low-technology exports. It is evident that the United States has

TABLE 1-5   U.S. Exports of High-Technology Manufactures, 1978–1985 (Billions of Dollars)

	1978	1980	1985
High-technology exports	34.8	54.7	68.4
Other manufactured exports	66.6	101.1	93.5
Total exports	101.4	155.8	161.9
High-technology exports as a % of total exports	34.3%	35.1%	42.2%

Source: U.S. Department of Commerce, *United States Trade: Performance and Outlook,* Washington, D.C.: U.S. Government Printing Office, October 1986, Table 14, p. 131.

a competitive advantage (or a "comparative advantage," as described in Chapter 2) in the manufacture of new products that emerge from scientific research. But today the United States is only one of several countries offering high-technology products in world markets. As Table 1-6 shows, U.S. high-technology *imports* have experienced an even more explosive growth than U.S. high-technology exports, increasing their share of total U.S. imports of manufactures from 18.3 percent in 1978 to 24.1 percent in 1985. In sum, the United States is becoming more and more both an exporter and an importer of high-technology products.

The ever-increasing influence of technology on world trade has stimulated economists to develop technology theories of trade that are taken up

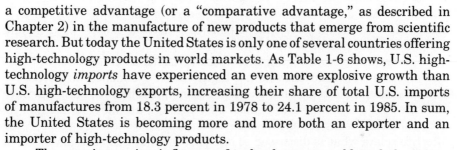

TABLE 1-6   U.S. Imports of High-Technology Manufactures, 1978–1985 (Billions of Dollars)

	1978	1980	1985
High-technology imports	20.3	28.0	64.8
Other manufactured imports	90.6	110.8	204.6
Total imports	110.9	138.8	269.4
High-technology imports as a % of total imports	18.3%	20.2%	24.1%

Source: U.S. Department of Commerce, *United States Trade: Performance and Outlook,* Washington, D.C.: U.S. Government Printing Office, October 1986, Table 14, p. 131.

in Chapter 5. For the present, it is enough to understand that the international competitiveness of the United States in the years ahead will depend more than ever before on its capacity to create new goods and services with advanced technologies.

WHAT LIES AHEAD

It is not possible to study all aspects of the international economy at the same time. We have chosen, therefore, to organize our study in four major parts based on the principal economic flows among nations: International flows of goods and services (Part One, "International Trade"), international flows of money and payments (Part Two, "International Payments"), international flows of development resources (Part Three, "International Development"), and international flows of direct investment and enterprise (Part Four, "International Investment and Multinational Enterprise"). Each part investigates both the theory and policy aspects of its subject in search of answers to the questions, What is the nature of the flows? Why do they occur? How do actual government policies constrain them? What should government policies be toward these flows?

The reader should regard these part divisions as dimensions of international economic relations that are highly interdependent. Our purpose is to understand the *whole* of international economic relations, but we believe that the whole can be comprehended only through an understanding of its constituent elements. It behooves the reader, therefore, to exert a continuing effort to relate what is discussed in one part to what has been discussed in other parts. We have tried to facilitate this effort by making frequent cross-references among the four parts.

SUMMARY

1. Every nation inhabits a global political and social environment as well as a global economic environment. To comprehend this international environment, we must simplify by classifying individual events into groups or categories of events and by tracing out the relationships among these aggregates. In other words, we must construct analytical systems.

2. The human race is organized in a society of nation-states. The elemental constituents of a nation-state are a people, a territory, an economy, and a sovereign government. The principle of national sovereignty gives each national government exclusive jurisdiction over the national territory and makes it the only legal representative of the nation vis-à-vis other nations. The *external political relations* of nation-

states are essentially power relations that are expressed in changing mixes of cooperation, competition, and antagonism. The *international political system* comprises some 160 sovereign nation-states and their mutual power relations. Nationalism makes nation-states less cooperative than would otherwise be the case.

3. Every nation-state has an economy, and the mutual relations among national economies constitute the *international economic system*. With the modest exception of gifts, international economic relations result from *transactions*, the exchange of assets having market value. The sum of a nation's economic transactions with the rest of the world over a period of time is recorded in its balance of payments.

4. It is fruitless to speculate in the abstract on whether international economic relations determine international political relations or vice versa. International economic and political relations are interdependent; both the international economic system and the international political system are best regarded as subsystems of the same nation-state system.

5. Although we shall rely on the macroscopic (or national) perspective in Parts One, Two, and Three, we must recognize that this perspective is necessary but no longer sufficient to explain the behavior of the international economy. Multinational enterprises have become responsible for a sizable (and increasing) share of world trade and for most international investment. The *multinational enterprise system* consists of a parent company; its producing and marketing affiliates in foreign countries; and the flows of products, services, capital, technology, management, and funds among them. Hence, *intraenterprise transfers* characterize this system.

6. The distinctive features of international trade and investment— different languages and customs, separate national economic policies, national monetary systems, government regulations, and the lower mobility of the factors of production—are traceable to the nation-state system and its subsystems.

7. The contribution of international trade is so immense that few countries could become self-sufficient even with the greatest effort. Even the United States would find the costs of self-sufficiency formidable. The benefits of international specialization are fundamentally of the same nature as the benefits of domestic interregional specialization. Thus, international trade and interregional trade are basically the same, and the distinctive features of international trade are largely owing to the political fact of national sovereignty.

8. The domestic consumers are benefited by international trade because it lowers the prices of goods and makes available goods that cannot be produced at home. If we agree that the proper end of economic activity is consumption, then we should agree that the interests of consumers in international trade are identical with the national interest. National

welfare is enhanced by international trade because such trade permits international specialization that leads to a more productive use of the natural resources, capital, and labor of nations.

9. It is easy to understand the contribution of international trade to the business enterprises that are engaged in the export and import of merchandise, services, and capital. They are interested in international trade as a source of income and profits. On the other hand, management, labor, and capital employed in domestic industries in close competition with imports from abroad may be injured by an expansion of international trade. It must be noted, however, that such injury is one of the costs of a competitive economic system.

10. There are several arguments against international specialization and trade—national security, economic stability, full employment, economic development, protection of domestic industries, and so on. Nevertheless, the advantages of international trade are so great that it exhibits vitality and growth.

11. For reasons of space and analytical convenience, we define foreign economic policy to include the activities of government that are *intended* to regulate, restrict, promote, or otherwise influence the conduct of international trade and investment. However, we do not propose to neglect the interdependence between foreign and domestic economic policies.

12. Enlightened self-interest demands that governments take full account of national and international interests as well as private interests in the formulation of foreign economic policy.

13. Seven fundamental goals that nations may pursue in their foreign economic policies are autarky, economic welfare, protectionism, full-employment stability, balance of payments equilibrium, economic development, and economic warfare.

14. It is helpful to examine the instruments of foreign economic policy in terms of four broad policy areas: trade policy, investment policy, foreign aid policy, and balance of payments policy.

15. The diversity of foreign economic policy goals engenders both internal and external conflicts. Interdependence among nations calls into question the effectiveness of economic policies determined solely on the national level as opposed to the international level. As an ongoing process, cooperation can point the way toward international economic policies that will benefit all nations, not simply the few who are strong.

16. The United States, West Germany, and Japan are the leaders in world trade. In the first half of 1987 about one-quarter of world trade was between the industrial countries and the developing countries (including OPEC) and more than half was among the industrial countries.

17. The composition of both U.S. exports and imports has shifted toward manufactured high-technology products and away from industrial supplies and materials.

QUESTIONS AND APPLICATIONS

1. What is a nation-state? What is the nation-state system? Compare the United States and four other nation-states of your own choosing in terms of territory, population, and gross national product.

2. Define the international political system. What is intended by the statement, "International political relations are essentially power relations"?

3. What is nationalism? Cite five cases of nationalism that have appeared in recent issues of *the New York Times* or other newspapers.

4. Define the international economic system. What is an economic transaction?

5. Why is a macroscopic or national perspective necessary but no longer sufficient to explain the behavior of the international economy? What is the multinational enterprise system?

6. What are the distinctive features of international trade and investment? Why are they distinctive?

7. What is the national interest in international trade? Why do we assert that the interest of consumers is identical with the national interest?

8. Which of the arguments against international trade presented in this chapter do you consider the most formidable? Why?

9. What is meant by the *instruments* of foreign economic policy?

10. Identify and discuss the goals of foreign economic policy.

11. Describe the four broad areas of foreign economic policy.

12. (a) Discuss the nature of the internal conflict of goals.
    (b) How does it differ from the external conflict of goals?

13. (a) Which are the principal trading countries?
    (b) How do you explain the rise of the United States to the position of first importer?

14. What have been the main shifts in the composition of U.S. exports and imports since World War II?

PART ONE

INTERNATIONAL TRADE

To grasp the significance of everyday events occurring in the vast field of activity that we call international trade, we must first gain an understanding of fundamental causal relationships, institutions, and unifying concepts. Accordingly, we begin Part One by considering in four chapters the theories and models that have been created by economists to explain international trade phenomena. By their very nature, theories and models are abstract, leaving out much of reality to focus on essential relationships. But they are indispensable prerequisites to an understanding of the trade policies that are treated in the remaining chapters of Part One.

2
Comparative Advantage and the Gains from Trade

Since the ending of the Middle Ages almost five centuries ago, two paradigms have dominated explanations of international trade: mercantilism (1500–1800) and comparative advantage (1800–   ). Both paradigms have had a profound effect on the trade policies of nations. The principle of comparative advantage remains today the single strongest intellectual influence on the trade policies of the United States and other industrial countries and is still accepted by the majority of economists. A natural starting point for an examination of international trade theory, therefore, is comparative advantage.

The principle of comparative advantage has an impressive lineage in economic thought. Its great progenitor was Adam Smith's *Wealth of Nations*, published in 1776.[1] Attacking the mercantilists, who argued for the regulation of trade to secure a "favorable balance of trade" (a surplus of exports over imports) that would bring in gold and silver in payment, Smith applied the doctrine of *laissez-faire* to international trade. All nations would benefit from unregulated, free trade that would allow individual countries to specialize in goods they were best suited to produce because of natural and acquired advantages. Smith's theory of trade has come to be known as the *theory of absolute advantage*.

The next and decisive step in the development of trade theory was the publication in 1817 of Ricardo's *On the Principles of Political Economy and Taxation*, which introduced the concept of *comparative advantage*.[2] Smith's

---

[1] Adam Smith, *An Inquiry into the Nature and Causes of the Wealth of Nations* (New York: Random House, 1937). For the classic exposition of mercantilist doctrine, see Thomas Mun, *England's Treasure by Forraign Trade* (Oxford: Basil Blackwell & Mott, 1949), first published in 1664.

[2] David Ricardo, *On the Principles of Political Economy and Taxation* (New York: E. P. Dutton, 1948).

theory of absolute advantage assumed that a country would always have a low-cost advantage in at least one product that it could export in exchange for other products. But suppose a country did not have an absolute cost advantage in *any* product? Ricardo answered that question with the theory of comparative advantage: Even if England were less efficient than Portugal in the production of both cloth and wine, it would still be of benefit for England to specialize in cloth production and Portugal in wine production if England were *comparatively* more efficient (or less inefficient) in cloth than in wine production.

In the century following Ricardo, many economists added refinements to the comparative advantage paradigm. As an example, John Stuart Mill (1806–1873) contributed the principle of reciprocal demand to explain the terms of trade. But the most significant new development came with the publication in 1933 of Ohlin's *Interregional and International Trade*.[3] Drawing on the pioneer work of Eli Heckscher, Ohlin further developed the proposition that a country exports those goods that use most intensively in their production the country's most abundant factors of production, and conversely. Ohlin replaced Ricardo's labor theory of value with a multiple-factor theory within a framework of mutually interdependent product and factor markets that determine trade. His theory is known as the Heckscher-Ohlin (H-O) model, and, together with subsequent refinements, it remains today the most widely accepted theory of international trade.

This chapter introduces the principle of comparative advantage by demonstrating how it answers three basic questions: (1) Why do countries export and import certain goods? (2) At which relative prices (terms of trade) do countries exchange goods? (3) What are the gains from international trade?

We start by developing the principle of comparative advantage through a series of arithmetical illustrations before turning to more sophisticated graphical illustrations later on in the chapter. Chapters 3 and 4 then examine particular theories that relate comparative advantage to certain attributes of trading countries, most notably, factor-of-production endowments, technology, economies of scale, product differentiation, and market structure.

ABSOLUTE INTERNATIONAL DIFFERENCES IN PRICES

Absolute differences between the prices of foreign goods and the prices of similar goods when produced at home are the *immediate* explanation of international trade. When these price differences are greater than the costs

---

[3] Bertil Ohlin, *Interregional and International Trade* (Cambridge: Harvard University Press, 1952).

of transferring the goods from one country to another, it becomes profitable for traders to import the goods from the lower-price country to the higher-price country. An extreme case arises when a country *must* obtain goods from abroad—or else go without them—because of the physical impossibility of producing them at home. Thus, a country totally lacking manganese has no choice but to import that commodity if it wants to produce specialized steels that include manganese as a vital element. In most instances, how- ever, a country is physically able to produce the goods that it imports but— and this is the important point—only at prices higher than it pays for imports. The United States *could* grow coffee and bananas but only at prices so high that few consumers would be able to afford them.

Absolute international differences in prices become evident only when there is an *exchange rate* that equates domestic and foreign currencies. For example, without an exchange rate between the dollar and the yen it would be impossible to compare the absolute prices of goods in the United States with the prices of similar goods in Japan. But when we know, say, that one dollar equals 200 yen ($1 = Y200), then direct price comparisons are possible and we can identify any differences in the prices of specific goods in the two countries.

Although absolute price differences measured by exchange rates are the immediate basis of international trade, they do not offer a *final* expla- nation. We want to know *why* such price differences exist and whether they are fortuitous or systematic.

DISSIMILAR RELATIVE-PRICE STRUCTURES IN TRADING COUNTRIES

What brings about absolute price differences among countries? The answer to this question is most unexpected: Absolute international price differences arise when the pretrade structures of *relative* prices within countries are dissimilar. This assertion underlies the principle of comparative advantage, and it may be demonstrated by a simple arithmetical example.

Let us assume a two-country, two-product world. In isolation the United States produces both beef and cameras, and Japan does the same. Let us also assume that the *relative* prices of beef and cameras are different between the two countries, as shown in Table 2-1.

In the United States the price ratio of a unit of beef to a camera is 1:2, whereas in Japan the ratio is 5:1. The ratios indicate that the United States has a *comparative advantage* in beef and a *comparative disadvantage* in cameras. The converse is true of Japan. Gainful trade will occur when the United States exports beef to Japan and imports cameras and Japan exports cameras and imports beef. We know this last statement to be true even though we have assumed no exchange rate that allows us to directly compare prices in the two countries.

TABLE 2-1   Different Price Ratios of Beef and Cameras in the United States and Japan

	United States (dollars)	Japan (yen)
Unit price of beef	10.00	5000.00
Unit price of cameras	20.00	1000.00

Because of its supply-and-demand conditions, the United States is able to produce 1 unit of beef or 0.5 cameras for the same price. Thus the *real* price of 1 unit of beef in the United States is 0.5 cameras (or, alternatively, the real price of 1 camera is 2 units of beef). However, Japan has dissimilar supply-and-demand conditions, and it is able to produce 1 unit of beef or 5 cameras for the same price. The real price of 1 unit of beef in Japan is 5 cameras (or, alternatively, the real price of 1 camera is 0.2 units of beef). Because the real prices of beef and cameras differ between the two countries, both can gain from trade with each other.

If, for example, the exchange rate is $1 = Y200, then the dollar prices of the two products in the United States and Japan before trade are shown in Table 2-2.

Clearly, the United States can gain from trade with Japan: For each unit of beef it exports it can obtain 2 cameras, whereas before trade it could obtain at home only 0.5 cameras for each unit of beef. At the same time, Japan can gain from trade with the United States: For each camera it exports it can obtain 0.5 units of beef, whereas before trade it could obtain at home only 0.2 units of beef. How can both countries gain from trade? We shall answer this question later in the chapter. Suffice it to say at this point that trade allows both countries to *specialize* in the production of that good in

TABLE 2-2   Dollar Prices of Beef and Cameras in the United States and Japan When 1 Dollar Equals 200 Yen

	United States (dollars)	Japan (dollars)
Unit price of beef	10.00	25.00
Unit price of cameras	20.00	5.00

which it has a comparative advantage, and as a result the combined output of the two countries is greater than before. The gains from trade come from this incremental output generated by a superior allocation of production.

We can now state the principle of comparative advantage: *Gainful trade will occur between countries when their pretrade relative price structures are different.* In general, let a_1 be the unit price of product a in country 1 and b_1 be the unit price of product b in country 1. Let a_2 be the unit price of product a and b_2 be the unit price of product b in country 2. Then trade is gainful when $a_1/b_1 \neq a_2/b_2$. If $a_1/b_1 > a_2/b_2$, then country 1 will import a and export b. If $a_1/b_1 < a_2/b_2$ (as in the example above), then country 1 will export a and import b, and conversely for country 2.

When price ratios are dissimilar between countries, there exists a range of exchange rates that allows for gainful trade. (Alternatively, at a given exchange rate, there exists a range of absolute price levels within the countries that allows for gainful trade.) One limit of this range is the exchange rate that makes the price of one product the same in both countries; the other limit is the exchange rate that makes the price of the second product the same in both countries. In our example, therefore, one limit is 1\$ = Y500 (making the dollar price of beef the same in the United States and Japan), and the other limit is 1\$ = Y50 (making the dollar price of a camera the same in the two countries). Trade is possible at either limit or at any exchange rate lying between them.

However, when trade occurs at one of the limits, then one country will neither gain nor lose from trade, because the rate of exchange between the export product and the import product will equal the pretrade *domestic* rate of exchange between the same goods in that country. To illustrate, when the exchange rate in our example is $1 = Y500, then Japan must export 5 cameras to obtain 1 unit of beef from the United States. But Japan could do just as well by producing the beef at home, where a unit is also exchanged for 5 cameras. At this rate of exchange, therefore, Japan neither loses nor gains from international trade; it will be indifferent to whether it trades or not. At this rate, the entire gain goes to the United States. At any exchange rate lying between these two limits, both countries gain, although not necessarily in the same degree. We have already shown how both countries gain from trade when the exchange rate is $1 = Y200.

Suppose the relative-price structures are similar in the United States and Japan? What then? In that case trade will not occur, because neither country can gain from trade. Table 2-3 illustrates this situation.

When price structures are similar, then the real price of a unit of beef (0.5 cameras) and the real price of a camera (2 units of beef) are the same in both countries. Any rate of exchange between the dollar and the yen will make the dollar (or yen) prices of a unit of beef and a camera either (1) the same in both countries, (2) higher in the United States than in Japan, or (3) lower in the United States than in Japan. The first situation—the identity of dollar (or yen) prices in both countries—clearly rules out international

TABLE 2-3   Identical Price Ratios of Beef and Cameras in the United States and Japan

	United States (dollars)	Japan (yen)
Unit price of beef	10.00	2000.00
Unit price of cameras	20.00	4000.00

trade. If the second or third situation exists, the United States will either import *both* products or export *both* products. But this is impossible, because exports must equal imports in the absence of loans or gifts (which is assumed in our two-country, two-product model). That is to say, exports must pay for imports in both countries.

THE GAINS FROM INTERNATIONAL TRADE

Through international trade a country is able to obtain more goods with which to satisfy the needs and desires of its people (the ultimate end of economic activity) than if it were to produce all goods at home. This is the true gain from international trade; it is the fruit of international specialization in accordance with the principle of comparative advantage.

In our two-country model, both countries can gain from trade when their relative price structures are dissimilar. But the division of gains depends on the *terms of trade* for the two traded goods. In turn, the terms of trade is determined by the demand of each country for the other's goods (reciprocal demand). A change in the terms of trade may occur through a change in the exchange rate between the currencies of the two countries or, alternatively, through a change in absolute price levels (inflation or deflation) within one or both countries.[4] In our presentation, we shall assume that a shift in the terms of trade is expressed through an alteration in the rate of exchange.

To illustrate the role of the terms of trade in the distribution of gains from trade, we return to our earlier example of dissimilar relative-price structures. As noted, there is a range of exchange rates that allow for gainful

---

[4] Whether a change in the terms of trade occurs through a movement of exchange rates or through a movement of price levels depends on the nature of the international monetary system. See Chapters 15 and 16.

trade (the range from $1 = Y500 to $1 = Y50). Over this range (including the two limits), the exchange rate is determined by the *reciprocal demand* of the United States and Japan. Because we are assuming the absence of any international lending that would finance a gap between exports and imports, the exchange rate must be such that the values of exports and imports of each country are equal. This is the *equilibrium rate of exchange*.

To show how reciprocal demand determines the equilibrium rate of exchange, let us assume an initial equilibrium rate of $1 = Y200. At this rate, the United States imports 1,000,000 cameras from Japan in exchange for 500,000 units of beef. The dollar prices of beef and cameras in both countries are as shown in Table 2-4. As observed earlier, for each unit of beef that the United States exports it can obtain 2 cameras, whereas before trade it could obtain at home only 0.5 cameras for each unit of beef. The United States, therefore, gains from trade 1.5 cameras (2 − 0.5 = 1.5) for each unit of beef it exports. Its total gain from trade is 750,000 (1.5 × 500,000) cameras.

At the same time, Japan obtains for each camera it exports 0.5 units of beef, whereas before trade it could obtain at home only 0.2 units of beef. Japan, therefore, gains 0.3 units of beef (0.5 − 0.2 = 0.3) for each camera it exports. Its total gain from trade is 300,000 (0.3 × 1,000,000) units of beef.

Now suppose that consumers in the United States demand 1,200,000 cameras from Japan instead of 1,000,000, but the demand for beef remains the same in Japan. At the exchange rate of $1 = Y200, therefore, U.S. imports would be $6,000,000 and U.S. exports would be $5,000,000. But, as noted earlier, this is not possible, for exports must pay for imports. Consequently, the higher U.S. demand for cameras will force up the dollar price of yen until a new equilibrium rate of exchange is achieved that brings about an equality between U.S. exports and imports. If 1,100,000 cameras are demanded by the United States and 600,000 units of beef are demanded by Japan, this new equilibrium rate might be $1 = Y183.33. The effect of this new exchange rate on the dollar prices of beef and cameras (the dollar

TABLE 2-4   Dollar Prices of Beef and Cameras in the United States and Japan When 1 Dollar Equals 200 Yen

	United States (dollars)	Japan (dollars)
Unit price of beef	10.00	25.00
Unit price of camera	20.00	5.00

prices in the United States and the yen prices in Japan remaining unchanged) is shown in Table 2-5.

At this new exchange rate the total value of imports equals exports in both countries ($6,000,000). The United States exports 600,000 units of beef for $6,000,000. With that amount of money, it can purchase 1,100,000 cameras.[5] But the *commodity terms of trade* have worsened for the United States. For each unit of beef it exports, it obtains only 1.83 cameras instead of the 2.0 cameras it obtained when the exchange rate was $1 = Y200. The United States must now pay more for its imports of cameras, whereas the dollar price of its beef exports has remained constant.[6] On the other hand, Japan's terms of trade have improved; it now obtains 0.55 units of beef for each camera it exports, as compared with 0.5 units at the earlier exchange rate.

The lesson we draw from this illustration is that the country with the more intense demand for the other country's goods will gain less from trade than the country with the less intense demand. More precisely, a country's gain from international trade will increase if its demand for imports falls relative to the foreign demand for its exports, and conversely. The division of gains between the trading countries is determined, therefore, by reciprocal demand.

Our analysis has provided us with an exact explanation of the gains from trade in terms of a two-country, two-product model. But we also need a broader interpretation of gains, because our model does not consider the

---

[5] The exchange rate and dollar price of cameras are rounded to two decimal places in the text. Using the more accurate exchange rate of 183.3333 and the dollar camera price of $5.4545464 gives 1,099,999.8 cameras, which when rounded becomes 1,100,000 cameras.

[6] The commodity terms of trade is the exchange ratio between a country's exports and imports, that is, between beef and cameras in this instance. In our illustration, the terms of trade was altered through a movement of the exchange rate (a *depreciation* of the dollar in terms of the yen) that was caused by a U.S. rise in the demand for cameras. If exchange rates were fixed, as under the international gold standard, then adjustment to a shift in demand would alter the terms of trade through changes in the domestic price levels of the two countries—a fall (deflation) of prices in the United States and a rise (inflation) of prices in Japan. See Chapters 15 and 16 for an analysis of adjustments to restore equilibrium in a country's international payments.

TABLE 2-5   Dollar Prices of Beef and Cameras in the United States and Japan When One Dollar Equals 183.3 Yen

	United States (dollars)	Japan (dollars)
Unit price of beef	10.00	27.27
Unit price of camera	20.00	5.45

enormous changes that international trade may bring to a country's economy over time. From this perspective, we can observe that the economies of most countries would be radically different if they had not developed as economies open to trade. For example, the Japanese economy is critically dependent on imports of petroleum and raw materials that are not available at home. To a somewhat lesser extent, the same is true of Western Europe. Even the continental economy of the United States would be seriously crippled without imports of petroleum and many raw materials. In short, the structure of national economies would be far different if countries were unable to use their comparative advantages in trade. Today's economies are largely a consequence of past international trade, and the gains from such trade are commensurate with the entire national economy.

In the foregoing presentation of the principle of comparative advantage, we started with absolute international price differences as the immediate (and familiar) basis of trade. We then demonstrated with arithmetical examples that absolute price differences arose when the relative price structures of countries differed. We now offer a more sophisticated graphical explanation of comparative advantage that is intended to reinforce and extend the reader's understanding of this fundamental principle.

GRAPHICAL PRESENTATION OF THE PRINCIPLE OF COMPARATIVE ADVANTAGE

We start our presentation with national production possibilities curves.

Production Possibilities: Constant Opportunity Costs

Assume there are only two countries in the world, the United States and France, and each produces only two commodities, beef and wine. Assume further that if each country uses *all* of its productive factors (land, labor, management, and capital) at a given level of technology, it can produce the alternative outputs of beef and wine shown in Table 2-6. Translating these

TABLE 2-6   Alternative Outputs

	Units of Beef	Units of Wine
United States	100	50
France	50	150

Figure 2-1   U.S. Production Possibilities: Constant Opportunity Costs

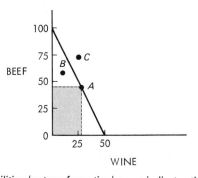

The U.S. production possibilities (or transformation) curve indicates the combination of beef and wine that U.S. factors of production can produce when they are fully employed and used efficiently at a given level of technology. Point A is one possible combination of beef and wine, but point B is a combination that is smaller than possible because of factor unemployment or inefficient factor use. Point C is a combination greater than the production capability of the United States at the given level of technology. In the absence of international trade, the United States can consume only beef-wine combinations that lie on or below its production possibilities curve.

output data into graphical form gives us the production possibilities (or transformation) curves shown in Figures 2-1 and 2-2.

The U.S. production possibilities curve (Figure 2-1) indicates the various combinations of beef and wine that the U.S. productive factors can produce when they are fully employed and used efficiently. For example, one possible output combination shown by point A on the curve represents 45 units of beef and 27.5 units of wine. Point B, on the other hand, represents a beef-wine combination that is smaller than possible production because of factor unemployment or inefficient use. Point C to the right of the curve denotes a beef-wine combination that is beyond the physical production capacity of the United States. Similar remarks can be made about the French production possibilities curve (Figure 2-2).

Both curves depict constant opportunity costs for beef and wine.[7] To increase the output of wine by 1 unit in the United States, factors must be taken away from the production of beef in such amount as to lower the output of beef by 2 units. Hence, the opportunity cost of 1 wine unit is 2 beef units, and this cost is not affected by the output levels of beef and wine. In France the opportunity cost of one wine unit is always one-third of a beef unit. These constant opportunity costs are shown by the constant slopes of

_____

[7] Constant opportunity costs imply that (1) the factors of production are perfect substitutes or are used in the same fixed proportions to produce both goods and (2) returns to scale are constant for both goods; that is to say, a doubling of all factor inputs will double output.

Figure 2-2   French Production Possibilities: Constant Opportunity Costs

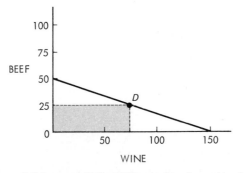

The French production possibilities curve indicates the combinations of beef and wine that factors of production in France can produce when they are fully employed and used efficiently at a given level of technology. One possible combination is denoted by D. In the absence of international trade, France can only consume wine-beef combinations that lie on or below its production possibilities curve.

the curves, -2 for the United States and $-\frac{1}{3}$ for France. The rate at which the output of one product must be reduced to increase the output of the other product is the *marginal rate of transformation (MRT)*.

In the case of the United States, the *MRT* of beef into wine is 2, which (disregarding sign) equals the slope of the production possibilities curve. When opportunity costs are constant, the *MRT* is also constant. Under conditions of pure competition, the *domestic terms of trade (DTT)* of beef for wine equal the *MRT* or slope of the production possibilities curve. In the United States 2 units of beef will exchange for 1 unit of wine while in France 1 unit of beef will exchange for 3 units of wine.

In the absence of trade, each country can elect to consume only a beef-wine combination that lies somewhere on its production possibilities curve, such as A in Figure 2-1 (45 beef units and 27.5 wine units) and D in Figure 2-2 (25 beef units and 75 wine units). The existence of different *MRTs*, however, offers both countries an opportunity to gain from mutual trade and to consume a beef-wine combination that lies beyond their production possibilities frontiers. This pleasant outcome will occur when beef and wine are traded at any *international terms of trade (ITT)* that fall between the two *DTTs*, which, in turn, are equal to the *MRTs*.

The gains from trade are depicted in Figures 2-3 and 2-4. Reciprocal demand determines an *ITT* (commodity terms of trade). This *ITT* is shown by the slope of the dashed lines, which is identical in both figures. At this *ITT* (1 beef unit = 1 wine unit), the United States will specialize completely in beef production, because it can obtain from France more wine for each

Figure 2-3   U.S. Gains from Trade: Constant Opportunity Costs

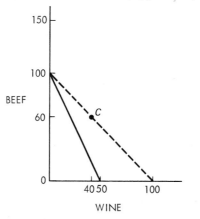

Reciprocal demand determines the international commodity terms of trade (*ITT*) depicted by the slope of the dashed line. At this *ITT*, the United States will specialize completely in beef production because it can obtain from France more wine for a unit of beef than at home. Here we assume that the United States decides to consume 40 units of wine, importing them from France in exchange for 40 units of beef. Hence the United States consumes a beef-wine combination denoted by *C*, a combination that is bigger than any combination the United States can produce (and consume) in the absence of trade.

unit of beef than it can at home. Conversely, France will specialize entirely in wine production, obtaining all its beef from the United States. If the United States chooses to consume 40 units of wine, it will import them from France in exchange for 40 units of beef.[8] The converse is true for France. As a result of trade, then, the United States is able to consume a beef-wine combination, indicated by point *C* on the international terms-of-trade line in Figure 2-3, that is superior to any combination the United States can produce in isolation. For France, point *D* in Figure 2-4 represents a beef-wine combination that is superior to any combination producible at home. Both countries gain from trade; because of specialization their combined output of beef and wine is higher than before, and the production increment is shared by consumers in both countries. (It might be helpful to look at the arithmetic recapitulation of the before- and after-trade situations presented in Table 2-7.)

   The *ITT* of 1 beef unit for 1 wine unit is an *equilibrium* rate because it clears the market; that is, exports equal imports. Any change in reciprocal demand, however, would establish a new equilibrium rate and thereby alter the division of gains. Gainful trade for both countries will occur at any *ITT*

---

[8] An explanation of consumption choices is offered in the next section.

Figure 2-4   French Gains from Trade: Constant Opportunity Costs

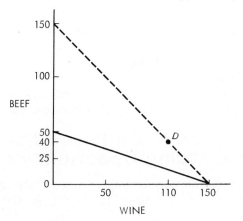

At the *ITT* established by reciprocal demand, France decides to consume a beef-wine combination denoted by *D*, which is superior to any combination that France can consume (or produce) in isolation. At this *ITT*, France will specialize completely in wine production.

TABLE 2-7   Comparison of Before- and After-Trade Combinations

	Before Trade					
	Production		Consumption		Gains from Trade	
	Beef	Wine	Beef	Wine	Beef	Wine
United States	45	27.5	45	27.5	0	0
France	25	75	25	75	0	0
Combined	70	102.5	70	102.5	0	0

	After Trade					
	Production		Consumption		Gains from Trade	
	Beef	Wine	Beef	Wine	Beef	Wine
United States	100	0	60	40	15	12.5
France	0	150	40	110	15	35
Combined	100	150	100	150	30	47.5

that falls between the two *DTTs*. At any rate beyond the range set by the two *DTTs*, only one country will gain, and trade will not occur because the other country will be better off without trade. When the *ITT* is the same as the *DTT* of one country, then that country will neither gain nor lose from trade and all the gain will go to the second country. This will happen when the trading economies differ so much in size that the bigger country cannot completely satisfy its demand for the product in which it has a comparative disadvantage through imports but must also rely on some domestic production. In that event, the bigger country will trade at its *DTT* and all the gain will go to the smaller country. Sometimes it pays to be small.

Production Possibilities: Increasing Opportunity Costs

The assumptions behind constant opportunity costs are highly unrealistic. In actuality, the factors of production are only partial substitutes for each other, and each good is produced with different factor combinations or intensities. With a given technology, good *A* will be generally more labor (and less capital) intensive in production than good *B*.[9] The existence of different factor intensities for two goods will make a country's production possibilities curve concave to the origin, indicating increasing opportunity costs.[10]

Such a curve is shown for the United States in Figure 2-5. Note that the *MRT* (the slope of curve *MN* at any point) is no longer constant. The meaning of increasing opportunity costs may be described as follows. Suppose the United States is producing only wine at *N*. Now it decides to produce 1 unit of beef. To do so, it must draw factors of production from wine, forcing a reduction in wine output. Note, however that this reduction is small (the slope of the production possibilities curve is steep near *N*), because the withdrawn factors of production are actually better suited to beef production than to wine production. But as the production of beef is progressively increased, greater and greater amounts of wine must be sacrificed to obtain 1 more unit of beef (the slope of the curve gets flatter and flatter). Why should the opportunity cost of beef increase? Because the factors of production drawn from wine production (such as land) are less and less suited to the production of beef. As the latter approaches *M*, very large quantities of wine must be given up to get 1 more unit of beef. Similarly, if the United States starts at *M* and then progressively transfers resources from beef to wine production, it will eventually encounter increasing opportunity costs.

What decides the *DTT* between beef and wine under conditions of

---

[9] However, good *A* may not have the same labor intensity at (1) different prices of labor relative to other factor prices, or (2) at different scales of output. It is even conceivable that good *A* will switch from a labor-intensive to a capital-intensive good at some factor price relationship or scale of output, a phenomenon known as *factor reversibility*.

[10] Even if factor intensities were the same, decreasing returns to scale (a doubling of all factor inputs causes less than a doubling of output) for one good would create increasing opportunity costs for both goods.

Figure 2-5   U.S. Production Possibilities: Increasing Opportunity Costs

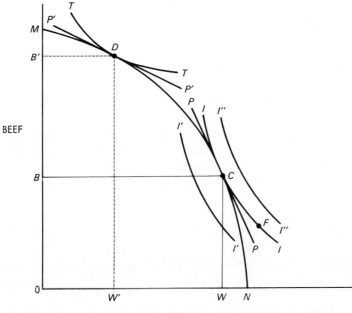

WINE

With increasing opportunity costs, the production possibilities curve becomes concave to the origin so that its slope is no longer constant but varies from point to point. The *domestic terms of trade (DTT)* between beef and wine is determined by the demand preferences of consumers. These preferences are depicted by indifference curves *I–I*, *I'–I'*, and *I"–I"*. The slope of an indifference curve at any point is the *marginal rate of substitution (MRS)* between, in this instance, beef and wine. The highest *attainable* level of consumer satisfaction in the absence of international trade occurs at the point of tangency (point *C*) between the production possibilities curve and an indifference curve. At that point (and no other), *MRT = MRS*, and the slope of this common tangent (indicated by the slope of *P–P*) is the *DTT*. Now suppose consumers experience a shift in preferences, preferring more beef and less wine. This shift generates a new indifference map indicated by *T–T*. Producers respond by moving out of wine into beef production until the *MRT* once again equals the *MRS* at point *D*, with a new *DTT* denoted by the slope of *P'–P'*. Hence, at point *D*, *MRT = MRS = DTT.*

increasing opportunity costs? The answer is the demand preferences or tastes of consumers—the combination of beef and wine that a nation's people want to consume. We can portray the demand preferences of U.S. consumers by an *indifference map* that consists of an infinite number of *indifference curves.* In Figure 2-5, *I*, *I'*, and *I"* represent indifference curves belonging to the same indifference map. *Each* indifference curve indicates all possible combinations of beef and wine that yield the same level of satisfaction; the nation's consumers are "indifferent" regarding the combinations lying on

Chapter 2 – Comparative Advantage and the Gains from Trade

an individual indifference curve. Thus, the combination of beef and wine indicated by point F on indifference curve I–I provides the same satisfaction to consumers as the combination at C. The slope of an indifference curve at any point is the *marginal rate of substitution in consumption (MRS)*, in this instance, the amount of beef consumers are willing to give up to obtain another unit of wine. The shape of each indifference curve is determined by consumer tastes; a change in tastes will generate a new family of indifference curves.[11]

It follows from the definition of an indifference curve that different indifference curves offer different levels of satisfaction. Graphically, the further an indifference curve is from the origin, the higher its level of satisfaction. Thus, in Figure 2-5, I''–I'' represents a higher level of satisfaction than I–I, which in turn represents a higher level of satisfaction than I'–I'. Consumers, therefore, will maximize their satisfaction by consuming a combination of beef and wine that lies on the *highest* indifference curve attainable with their income. This occurs at point C, where the U.S. production possibilities curve is tangent to I–I. At that point consumers obtain the combination of beef and wine that gives them the most satisfaction of any combination the nation is able to produce. Indifference curve I''–I'' is not attainable in the absence of international trade because it lies beyond the production possibilities curve. At point C the *MRT* equals the *MRS*—any movement away from this equality would lower welfare. The slope of their common tangent, indicated by P–P, is the *DTT* between beef and wine. Hence, at point C, $MRT = MRS = DTT$.

Suppose there occurs a change in taste that generates a new indifference map. What happens? T–T is the new indifference curve that is tangent to the production possibilities curve at point D. Compared to point C, consumers now want more beef and less wine. Their demand, therefore, will push up the price of beef relative to the price of wine (in barter terms, *decrease* the *MRS* of beef for wine). Producers will respond by shifting out of wine into beef production until the *MRT* once again equals the *MRS* at point D. Here their common tangent, P'–P', becomes the new *DTT*.

Let us now consider the gains from trade under increasing opportunity costs of production. Figures 2-6 and 2-7 depict the production possibilities and indifference curves for the United States and France. Before trade the United States produces at C on its production possibilities curve, producing

---

[11] Indifference curves were devised to analyze the preferences of the *individual* consumer, who presumably is able to determine the different combinations of two goods that would yield the same satisfaction. Can we add up the indifference curves of individuals to get a *community* indifference curve for the entire nation? Strictly speaking, the answer is no. Different consumers have dissimilar indifference maps that are literally incomparable. One person may want a lot of beef and only a little wine; another may want the converse. Although it is not possible to make interpersonal comparisons of welfare (satisfaction), the community indifference curve is most useful in demonstrating the influence of demand preferences on international trade. In so using it, however, we must bear in mind that its welfare implications are ambiguous. For a discussion of trade and welfare, see Chapter 6.

Figure 2-6   U.S. Gains from Trade: Increasing Opportunity Costs

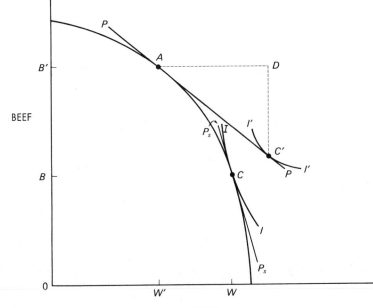

WINE

Before trade with France, the United States produces and consumes a beef-wine combination denoted by point *C*, where *MRT* = *MRS* = *DTT*. When trade opens up, reciprocal demand determines an *ITT* denoted by the slope of line *P–P*. In response to this *ITT*, which offers a higher price for beef than the *DTT*, the United States shifts production from *C* to *A*. At the same time, U.S. consumers respond to the *ITT* by choosing to consume a beef-wine combination located at point *C'* on line *P–P*. At this point, a new equilibrium is established where *MRT* = *MRS* = *ITT*. The United States clearly gains from trade with France because it now consumes a beef-wine combination that lies on a higher indifference curve (*I'–I'*) than before trade (*I–I*). The United States exports *D–C'* beef in exchange for imports of *A–D* wine.

(and consuming) 0–*B* beef and 0–*W* wine (Figure 2-6). The U.S. *DTT* line (P_s–P_s) is tangent to both the production possibilities curve and the indifference curve *I–I* at point *C*. Hence, *C* is an equilibrium position. Similarly, France produces and consumes at *K* (0–*G* beef and 0–*F* wine), where its *DTT* line (P_f–P_f) is tangent to its production possibilities curve and the indifference curve *T–T* (Figure 2-7). Since the slopes of the two *DTT* lines differ, there is a basis for gainful trade.

When trade opens up, reciprocal demand determines an *ITT* line (*P–P*) that is the same for both countries. Since the international barter price of beef is higher than its U.S. domestic price, U.S. producers will shift out of wine into beef until the *MRT* is equal to the new *MRS* at *A*. Here

Figure 2-7   French Gains from Trade: Increasing Opportunity Costs

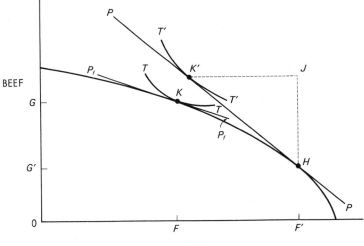

WINE

Before trade with the United States, France produces and consumes a beef-wine combination denoted by point *K*. When trade opens up, reciprocal demand establishes an *ITT* denoted by the slope of the line *P–P*. (Line *P–P*, of course, has the same slope as line *P–P* in Figure 2-6.) In response to this *ITT*, France shifts production from *K* to *H* and shifts consumption from *K* to *K'*. At point *K'*, *MRT = MRS = ITT*. France gains from trade because it now consumes a beef-wine combination that lies on a higher indifference curve (*T'–T'*) than before trade (*T–T*). France exports *K'–J* wine (equal to *A–D* wine in Figure 2-6) and imports *J–H* beef (equal to *D–C'* beef in Figure 2-6).

the United States specializes in beef (0–*B'*) but continues to produce some wine (0–*W'*). At the *ITT*, U.S. consumers choose to consume a beef-wine combination denoted by *C'*, the point of tangency between *P–P* and indifference curve *I'–I'*. The United States exports *D–C'* beef in exchange for *A–D* wine from France. After trade, U.S. beef consumption is domestic beef production (0–*B'*) *minus* beef exports (*D–C'*) and U.S. wine consumption is domestic production (0–*W'*) *plus* wine imports (*A–D*), a combination indicated by *C'*. The United States clearly gains from trade because it is able to reach a higher indifference curve. It has chosen to consume more beef (0–*C'* > 0–*B*) and more wine (0–*C'* > 0–*W*) than before trade.[12] Observe that international trade allows the United States to *separate* the production of beef and wine (point *A*) from the consumption of beef and wine (point *C'*).

In France, producers respond to *P–P* by shifting from beef to wine

---

[12] Instead of more of both goods, the gains from trade might be a combination that has more of one good and less of another than the pretrade combination, but the former would lie outside the production possibilities curve. The precise combination will depend on demand preferences.

production until, at *H, MRT* equals *MRS*. France exports K'–J wine in exchange for J–H beef, consuming a beef-wine combination denoted by K', where *P–P* is tangent to indifference curve T'–T'. This combination is superior to *K* because it lies on a higher indifference curve. France has chosen to consume more of both beef and wine than before trade.

Since U.S. exports of beef must equal French imports and vice versa, D–$C' = J$–H and A–$D = K'$–J. In after-trade equilibrium, the U.S. *MRT* is equal to the *ITT*, which in turn equals the *MRS*. Further, these rates are equal to the same marginal rates in France. Because of increasing opportunity costs, both countries continue to produce beef and wine.

Identical Production Possibilities
with Dissimilar Tastes

We have seen how dissimilar production possibilities curves of two countries afford a basis for gainful trade between them. But under conditions of increasing opportunity costs, dissimilar tastes in two countries can also provide a basis for gainful trade even when their production possibilities are the same.

Assume the United States and France have the same production possibilities curve *F–F* in Figure 2-8.[13] However, the Americans strongly prefer beef over wine, while French tastes run in the opposite direction, as shown by the indifference curves *I–I* and *T–T*, respectively. Consequently, before trade the United States chooses to produce and consume combination *C* of beef and wine with a domestic price line P_s–P_s. On the other hand, France chooses to produce and consume a great deal of wine and only a little beef, as shown by combination *K*, where its domestic price line P_f–P_f is tangent to its production possibilities curve and the indifference curve *T–T*. Since the *DTTs* are different at *C* and *K*, there is a basis for gainful trade.

With the opening of trade, reciprocal demand establishes an international price line *P–P*. U.S. producers adjust to *P–P* by moving from *C* to *G* (cutting down on beef production, increasing wine production), while French producers do the opposite, moving from *K* to *G*. U.S. consumers adjust to *P–P* by consuming combination C' of beef and wine, where *P–P* is tangent to the indifference curve I'–I'. Hence, the United States exports C'–B wine in exchange for B–G beef. French consumers choose combination K', where *P–P* is tangent to indifference curve T'–T'. France exports H–K' ($= B$–G) beef in exchange for G–H ($= C'$–B) wine. Both countries gain from trade because their consumption now lies on higher indifference curves. The United States now consumes more beef and the same amount of wine as before trade and France consumes more wine and slightly more beef. Where does this gain come from? Before trade the United States was highly specialized in beef production, using some factors of production that were much

---

[13] Only the *shape* of the two curves has to be identical, not the absolute size.

Figure 2-8   U.S. and French Gains from Trade: Dissimilar Tastes with Same Production Possibilities

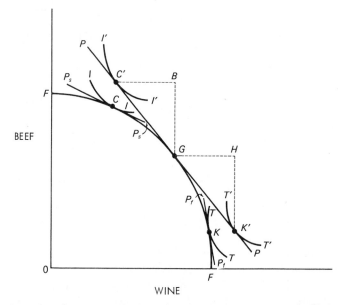

WINE

The United States and France have the same production possibilities curve (*F–F*). However, American consumers prefer a lot of beef and not much wine, while France consumers prefer the converse. Hence, before trade opens up, the United States produces and consumes at *C*, with a domestic price line P_s–P_s (whose slope equals the *DTT*). France produces and consumes at *K*, with a domestic price line P_f–P_f. Because the *DTT*s of the two countries differ, there is a basis for gainful trade. When trade opens up, reciprocal demand establishes an international price line whose slope equals the *ITT*. In response to this *ITT*, both countries shift production to *G* (where *MRT* = *ITT*); U.S. consumers move from *C* to *C'* (where *MRS* = *ITT*) and French consumers move from *K* to *K'* (where *MRS* = *ITT*). The United States exports *C'–B* (= *G–H*) wine and imports *B–G* (= *H–K'*) beef.

better suited to wine production. The converse was true for France. Trade permitted the United States to shift factors from beef to wine production and France to shift factors from wine to beef production. The gains from trade come from a lesser degree of specialization in production but a higher degree of specialization in consumption.

The assumption of similar production possibilities curves for two countries is, of course, unlikely to be matched in the real world. But can dissimilar tastes ever overwhelm dissimilar production possibilities so as to determine comparative advantage? Yes, theoretically. But the probability of such a situation may be regarded as very low. Actually, consumer tastes appear to be converging rather than diverging as "demonstration effects" penetrate all countries.[14] However, demand preferences must be taken into account in any full statement of the theory of comparative advantage, because they undoubtedly influence *DTTs* (price ratios).

Offer Curves: The Determination of the Terms of Trade

In the preceding analysis we have assumed an *ITT* between the United States and France by attributing it to reciprocal demand. We now utilize offer curves to demonstrate the precise determination of the terms of trade between two countries. In doing so, we shall make use of our example in the discussion of trade under constant opportunity costs on pages 49 through 54.

How is the dashed international price line (one beef equals one wine, or a ratio of 1:1) in Figures 2-3 and 2-5 determined? The answer is by the intersection of the U.S. and French offer curves. The U.S. offer curve indicates the amounts of beef (in which the United States has a comparative advantage) that the United States is willing to offer France for different amounts of wine (in which the United States has a comparative disadvantage). Similarly, the French offer curve indicates the amounts of wine that France is willing to offer the United States for different amounts of beef.

The U.S. offer curve is shown as 0–*A* in Figure 2-9.[15] The terms of trade for beef and wine at each point on the offer curve is the slope of the ray drawn from the origin through that point. Near the origin the U.S. offer curve has a terms of trade that matches the *DTT*, which is 2 units of beef for 1 unit of wine, as shown by the slope of the ray 0–*r* (2:1). At this terms of trade the United States is indifferent to trade with France but is willing to offer beef for small amounts of wine at its *DTT*. It should be obvious that the United States would not offer more than 2 units of beef for 1 unit of wine, because it could do better at home. For more and more wine imports, however, the United States is willing to offer only smaller and smaller amounts of beef for each additional unit of wine. The reason is that the marginal utility of wine decreases as the amount available to U.S. consumers increases relative to the amount of beef available to them. Hence, as the amount of wine increases, the U.S. offer curve bends further and further away from ray 0–*r*.[16]

At point *C* on the offer curve, the United States offers 0–b_1 beef for 0–w_1 wine at a terms of trade of 1:1, as shown by the slope of ray 0–*s*. At point *D* the United States is willing to export a larger amount of beef (0–b_2)

---

[14] Demonstration effects are transmitted via communication of all kinds (including travel) as well as via trade and investment. But see the discussion of income gaps in Chapter 4.

[15] The offer curve may be derived from a country's production possibilities curve and indifference map.

[16] Under conditions of increasing opportunity cost the offer curve bends away also because the marginal opportunity cost of beef increases in the United States as more and more beef is produced.

Figure 2-9   U.S. Offer Curve of Beef for Wine

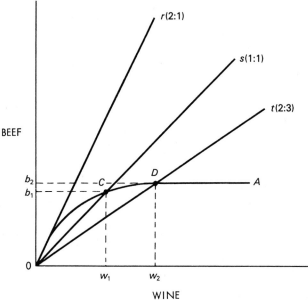

The U.S. offer curve (0–A) indicates the amounts of beef (in which the United States has a comparative advantage) that the United States is willing to offer France for different amounts of wine. The terms of trade between beef and wine at each point on the offer curve is the slope of the ray drawn from the origin through that point. Near the origin, the U.S. offer curve has terms of trade that match its *DTT*, as is shown by the slope of ray 0–r. But as the amount of wine increases, the marginal utility of wine falls, so that the U.S. offer curve bends further and further away from 0–r. At point *C*, the United States offers 0–b_1 beef for 0–w_1 wine at a terms of trade of 1:1. Beyond point *D*, the United States is unwilling to offer more beef for wine regardless of the terms of trade.

but only at terms of trade of 2:3, which would obtain 0–w_2 imports of wine. Beyond point *D* the United States is unwilling to offer more beef for wine regardless of how favorable the terms of trade become, as shown by the horizontal slope of *D–A*.

The French offer curve of wine for beef shows an unwillingness to export more wine for beef except at progressively more favorable terms of trade for that country.

The U.S. and French offer curves are brought together in Figure 2-10. Again 0–A is the U.S. offer curve, while 0–F is the French offer curve. Given these two offer curves, the equilibrium terms of trade are given by the slope of ray 0–t, which passes from the origin through the point of intersection of the curves at *E*. Why? Because only this terms of trade clears the market so that U.S. exports of beef equal U.S. imports of wine, and conversely for

Figure 2-10   U.S. and French Offer Curves: Determination of the Terms of Trade

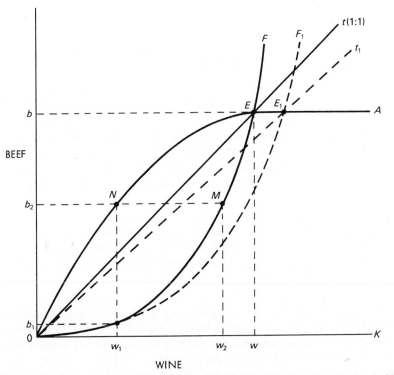

WINE

0–A is the U.S. offer curve and 0–F is the French offer curve. The equilibrium terms of trade (ITT) are determined by the intersection of the two offer curves at point E, where the ITT equals the slope of ray 0–t. Only this ITT (in this example, 1 unit of beef for 1 unit of wine) clears the market: At E, the amount of beef (0–b) that the United States offers for 0–w wine equals the amount of beef (0–b) that France is willing to take for 0–w wine. At any other point on either offer curve (such as K, N, or M), the ITT would fail to clear the market and would not last in a competitive market. If the French demand for beef increases while the U.S. demand for wine remains the same (as is shown by the shift of the French offer curve from 0–F to 0–f₁, then the terms of trade worsen for France and improve for the United States at the new equilibrium point E₁. To conclude, the ITT is determined by the intersection of the offer curves of the trading countries.

France. Only at E is the amount of beef (0–b) that the United States offers for 0–w wine equal to the amount of beef (0–b) that France offers to take for 0–w wine.[17]

At any other point on either offer curve the terms of trade would fail to clear the market and could not endure under pressure from competitive

---

[17] In our earlier example, at E the United States would export 40 units of beef and import 40 units of wine.

forces. Suppose, for example, that France offered to trade at point K on its offer curve by offering $0-w_1$ wine for $0-b_1$ beef. At the same time the United States would offer a large amount of beef ($0-b_2$) for $0-w_1$ wine, as shown by point N on its offer curve. But for $0-b_2$ beef, France would offer a larger amount of wine ($0-w_2$), as indicated by point M on its offer curve. The interaction of these offers would push the terms of trade to the point of intersection at E.

We can now make a precise statement of the principle of reciprocal demand. The terms of trade between two countries will be determined by the intersection of their respective offer curves.

We can also demonstrate the effects of a change in reciprocal demand with offer curves. Suppose that the French demand for beef increases while the U.S. demand for wine remains the same. This change in reciprocal demand is indicated by a shift to the right of the French offer curve from $0-F$ to $0-F_1$. Observe that this shift changes the intersection of the U.S. and French offer curves from E to E_1 and therefore results in new terms of trade, which is the slope of the ray $0-t_1$. The terms of trade are now worse for France than before the shift, and its gain from trade is also less. France now offers more wine for the same amount of beef (or takes less beef for the same amount of wine) than it did with its old offer curve $0-F$.

We have now completed our graphical presentation of the principle of comparative advantage. We have seen how dissimilar production possibilities curves, together with demand preferences as expressed by indifference curves (which may or may not be similar across countries), determine different $DTTs$ and thereby create a basis for gainful trade. When trade opens up, reciprocal demand (as demonstrated by offer curves) determines the ITT. In equilibrium, the $MRTs$ in both countries equal the ITT, which in turn equals the $MRSs$ in both countries. When money is introduced, dissimilar $DTTs$ become dissimilar price ratios (relative price structures), which, as stated in our earlier arithmetic presentation, make possible gainful international trade.

In the next three chapters, we investigate the principal explanations of comparative advantage: factor endowments, technology gaps, economies of scale, and product differentiation.

SUMMARY

1. The immediate basis of international trade lies in absolute international differences between the prices of foreign goods and the prices of similar goods produced at home.
2. Absolute international differences in prices between countries arise upon the establishment of an exchange rate when the price ratios (relative price structures) within each country are dissimilar, for then the opportunity costs of producing similar goods will differ between coun-

tries and each country will have a *comparative advantage* in producing some goods and a *comparative disadvantage* in producing other goods.

3. When price ratios are identical across countries, opportunity costs are also identical and there is no basis for gainful international trade.

4. When price ratios are dissimilar across countries, there is a range of exchange rates (or absolute price levels) that allow gainful international trade. The international commodity terms of trade associated with a given exchange rate determines the division of gains between the trading countries.

5. The slope of a country's production possibilities curve at any point is the *marginal rate of transformation (MRT)* at that point. The slope of a country's indifference curve at any point is the *marginal rate of substitution (MRS)* in consumption at that point. In the absence of international trade, equilibrium is achieved in both production and consumption at the point of tangency between the production possibilities curve and an indifference curve. This common tangency is the *domestic terms of trade (DTT)*. In equilibrium, therefore, *MRT* = *MRS* = *DTT*.

6. When the production possibilities curves of two countries have dissimilar shapes but their indifference curves have the same shape, then their pretrade *DTTs* will differ, providing a basis for gainful trade. Under conditions of increasing opportunity cost, posttrade equilibrium is achieved when the *MRT* and *MRS* of each country equal the *international terms of trade (ITT)*. This is the optimal welfare position.

7. Although dissimilar tastes (indifference curves) afford a separate basis for gainful trade, they are not likely to overwhelm the influence of dissimilar opportunity costs in production on the direction of trade.

8. The equilibrium terms of trade for two countries is determined by the intersection of their respective offer curves.

QUESTIONS AND APPLICATIONS

1. Assume that two countries (the United States and West Germany) produce and sell the same two commodities (steel and coal) at the following prices in their respective home markets before trade:

	United States (dollars)	West Germany (marks)
Unit price of steel	4.00	3.00
Unit price of coal	2.00	12.00

   (a) What are the opportunity costs of producing steel and coal in both countries?

   (b) Is gainful trade possible between the two countries? If so, what will be its nature?

   (c) Is there a range of exchange rates between the dollar and the mark that will permit gainful trade? If so, what is it?

2. Referring to question 1, what are the gains per unit of exports for each country when the exchange rate is $1 = DM2? When the exchange rate is $1 = DM6?

3. Does trade under constant opportunity costs necessarily lead to complete international specialization in production in the absence of any restrictions?

4. Why are the assumptions behind constant opportunity costs in production "highly unrealistic"?

5. In the absence of international trade, what determines the domestic barter rate of exchange between two goods under conditions of increasing opportunity cost?

6. After-trade equilibrium between two countries requires that $MRT = MRS = ITT$ across both countries. Why is that so?

7. Why is international specialization incomplete under conditions of increasing opportunity cost?

8. Draw production possibilities curves, for two countries, that have the *same* shapes under conditions of increasing opportunity cost.

   (a) Assuming similar tastes (indifference curves), demonstrate graphically that no gainful trade is possible.

   (b) Assuming dissimilar tastes, demonstrate graphically that gainful trade is possible.

9. Construct offer curves for two countries. Show how a decrease in demand for imports in one country will cause an improvement in its terms of trade.

SELECTED READINGS

See the list of readings given at the end of Chapter 3.

3

Comparative Advantage and Factor Endowments: The Heckscher-Ohlin Model

The Heckscher-Ohlin (H-O) model attributes comparative advantage to different proportions of national factor endowments of land, labor, and capital across countries.[1] In Chapter 2, we introduced the principle of comparative advantage with arithmetical examples and then followed with a more sophisticated graphical analysis. We do the same here to introduce the H-O model: first, an arithmetical example, and then a graphical derivation of a country's production possibilities curve from its factor endowments.

DISSIMILAR FACTOR ENDOWMENTS AND TRADE: AN ARITHMETICAL EXAMPLE

In Chapter 2, we learned that comparative advantage arises when relative price structures differ across countries. But why should they differ? The supply-side explanation is that dissimilar price ratios reflect dissimilar *cost* ratios. In a perfectly competitive market, the price of a good equals its marginal cost of production, which in turn reflects the prices of the marginal inputs of the factors of production—land, labor and capital—used to produce the good. Further, different goods are produced with different combinations of factor inputs. Hence if *factor-price ratios* (the ratios among rent, wages, and interest) differ across countries, then *goods-price ratios* will also differ. In one country wages may be low relative to rent, whereas in another country wages may be high relative to rent. Thus, the first country can produce

---

[1]For that reason, the H-O model is also called the *factor-proportions theory of international trade.*

TABLE 3-1   Unit Costs of Wheat and Textiles Deriving from Unit Prices of Land and Labor in the United States and Japan

	United States (dollars)	Japan (yen)
Unit price of land	1.00	800.0
Unit price of labor	2.00	200.0
Unit cost (price) of wheat	7.00	4200.0
Unit cost (price) of textiles	21.00	2800.0

goods that require a great deal of labor and not much land more cheaply than goods that require a great deal of land but not much labor. In the second country, the opposite is true.

To summarize, it is because factors of production are not perfect substitutes for each other and must be used in different combinations to produce different goods that dissimilar factor price ratios in two countries give rise to dissimilar commodity cost and price ratios that provide a basis for gainful trade.

The role of factor prices in the determination of cost (price) ratios may be clarified by a simple illustration. Assume that in the United States the price of a marginal unit of land is $1 and the price of a marginal unit of labor is $2 and that in Japan the price of a marginal unit of land is Y800 and the price of a marginal unit of labor is Y200. Thus, land is relatively cheap in the United States and relatively expensive in Japan, while the converse is true of labor. Assume further that to produce a unit of wheat in either country requires 5 units of land and 1 unit of labor and to produce a unit of textiles in either country requires 1 unit of land and 10 units of labor (see Table 3-1). These required inputs of land and labor are the *production functions* of wheat and textiles.[2]

The U.S. wheat-textile price ratio is 1:3 and the Japanese wheat-textile price ratio is 3:2. Clearly, the United States has a comparative advantage in the production of wheat and Japan has a comparative advantage in the production of textiles. This follows from the fact that wheat production is *land-intensive* and the United States can use its relatively cheap factor (land) to greatest advantage in that production. On the other hand, the United States has a comparative disadvantage in textile production, which is *labor-intensive* and requires comparatively large amounts of its relatively expensive factor (labor). The converse situation holds in Japan.

---

[2]The H-O model assumes that production functions are the *same* across countries. As we see in the next chapter, when production functions are *dissimilar* across countries, then technology gaps can be a source of comparative advantage.

But why should factor-price ratios differ across countries? The H-O model traces such differences to relative factor *endowments* (supplies) that are dissimilar across countries.[3] Countries differ greatly in their relative supplies of factors of production. A country like Canada has an abundant supply of natural resources (land) relative to its supplies of labor and capital. Therefore, rents in Canada are low relative to wages and interest. The Netherlands, on the other hand, has a relatively scarce supply of natural resources but relatively abundant supplies of labor and capital. In that country, rents are high relative to wages and interest. It is clear that such differences multiply when we consider that the individual factors of production are heterogeneous. Actually, there are several kinds of land factors and many varieties of labor and capital. For example, one country has a temperate climate, another has a tropical climate; one country has coal but lacks iron ore, another has iron ore but lacks coal; one country has large supplies of educated skilled workers, another has a predominantly illiterate, unskilled labor force; one country has steel plants, another has none; and so on. The number of specific factors is so large that any one country is certain to have factor-supply proportions that diverge in some respect from the proportions of other countries. Furthermore, as we shall see, national factor proportions change over time.

To conclude, the H-O model postulates that dissimilar commodity-price ratios (the immediate basis of gainful international trade) derive from dissimilar factor-price ratios and that these derive in turn from dissimilar factor proportions. A country has a comparative advantage in the production of goods that use relatively large amounts of its abundant factors of production and a comparative disadvantage in the production of goods that use relatively large amounts of its scarce factors of production. Indirectly, then, a country exports the services of its abundant factors of production and imports the services of its scarce factors of production.

DERIVATION OF A COUNTRY'S PRODUCTION POSSIBILITIES CURVE FROM ITS FACTOR ENDOWMENTS

In graphical language, the Heckscher-Ohlin model attributes the existence of dissimilar production possibilities curves among countries to dissimilar factor endowments. By using isoquant curves and the box diagram, we now

---

[3]Factor prices are determined by both factor supply and the demand for factor use in production. Hence, dissimilar factor price ratios across countries imply dissimilar factor supply or factor demand ratios across countries. By assuming that factor demand ratios are the same across countries (reflecting similar demand preferences) and that production functions are also the same across countries, the H-O model focuses on factor supply (endowment) as the sole explanation of factor price differences.

offer a formal derivation of a country's production possibilities curve from its factor endowments.

Production Functions: Isoquant Curves

A production function is the physical relationship between the output of a good and the necessary factor inputs. It indicates the *maximum* output attainable with a given combination of factor inputs as determined by the technical conditions of production. A production function may be expressed most simply as follows: $P_i = f(a, b, c, \ldots, n)$ where P is the output of good i and $a, b, c, \ldots, n$ are factor inputs. Such a function may be depicted by an isoquant (equal-product) curve.

Assume that the United States has only two factors—land and labor—to produce beef or wine. The isoquant curve b–b in Figure 3-1 shows the combinations of labor and land inputs needed to produce a specified output of beef, and curve w–w does the same for wine. An isoquant curve is convex to the origin because the removal of 1 unit of a factor from production requires the addition of increasingly large amounts of the second factor to maintain the same level of production. That is to say, labor and land are not perfect substitutes in production; they can only be substituted for one another at increasing opportunity costs.

We also assume that the production functions of beef and wine are homogeneous in the first degree so that they show constant returns to scale. Hence a doubling of labor and land inputs causes a doubling of output. Constant returns to scale are indicated in Figure 3-1 by b_1–b_1, which is twice the distance from 0 as b–b and therefore represents twice the output of b–b . For the same reason, w_1–w_1 represents twice the output of w–w.

The *least-cost combination* of factor inputs to produce a good is determined by the relative prices (or price ratio) and marginal physical products of the two factor inputs together with the budget constraint, that is, the amount of money the producer has to spend on factor inputs.[4] Two *iso-cost* curves are drawn in Figure 3-1, E_1–E_2 and E_1'–E_2'; each iso-cost curve indicates the combination of labor and land that the producer can obtain at the same cost. E_1'–E_2' represents twice the cost of E_1–E_2 because the former is twice the distance from the origin. The slope of an iso-cost curve is determined by the relative prices of labor and land. The producer can buy 0–E_1 of labor or 0–E_2 of land or any combination of labor and land that falls on that budget line. The least-cost combination of factor inputs is at the point of tangency between the given iso-cost curve and an isoquant. For the iso-cost curve E_1–E_2, the point of tangency for wine (isoquant w–w) is at g. Hence the producer will use 0–m of labor and 0–n of land to produce wine.

---

[4]The least cost rule expressed algebraically is $MPP_w/P_w = MPP_c/P_c = \ldots$. That is to say, the least-cost combination of factors occurs when the ratio of the marginal physical product and price of each factor (MPP_i/P_i) is equalized across all the factors used in the production of a good.

Figure 3-1   U.S. Production Functions for Wine and Beef: Determination of the Least-Cost Combination of Land and Labor

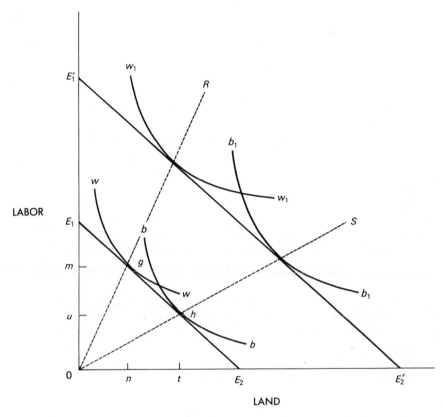

LABOR

LAND

The *b–b* curve is the *isoquant* for beef, indicating the combination of labor and land needed to produce a specified output of beef. Curve *w–w* is the isoquant for wine. We are assuming constant returns to scale: A doubling of labor and land inputs causes a doubling of output. Hence, the beef isoquant b_1–b_1 represents twice the output of *b–b* because it is twice the distance from 0 as *b–b*. For the same reason, w_1–w_1 represents twice the output of *w–w*. Two *iso-cost* curves, E_1–E_2 and E'_1–E'_2, indicate combinations of labor and land that a producer can obtain at the same cost. The *least-cost combination* of factor inputs is at the point of tangency between the given iso-cost curve and an isoquant curve, such as point *g* on isoquant *w–w*. Only at point *g* is the price ratio of labor and land inputs equal to the ratio of their marginal physical products. For beef, the least-cost combination is indicated by point *h*. Observe that the ratio of marginal physical products of labor and land is the same at points *g* and *h*. The 0–R and 0–S rays cross the low-cost points on *w–w* and *w'–w'* and *b–b* and *b'–b'*, respectively. Because 0–R has a steeper slope than 0–S, it is evident that the production of wine at *g* is more labor-intensive than the production of beef at *h*.

Only at point g is the price ratio of the labor and land inputs equal to the ratio of their marginal physical products. Putting the matter another way, w–w is the highest output of wine that can be obtained with the iso-cost curve E_1–E_2. For the same reason, h is the low-cost combination of factor inputs for beef.

Observe that the marginal rate of factor substitution in production is the same at points g and h because the slopes of the wine and beef isoquants are the same at those points. That is to say, the ratios of the marginal physical products of the two factors are the same in wine and beef production, and these ratios, in turn, equal the factor-price ratio. If this were not so, it would pay producers to shift factor inputs between wine and beef production until it became true.

If outlays are doubled by moving to iso-cost curve E_1'–E_2', the least-cost *proportions* of labor and land remain the same as long as the factor-price ratio does not change, which is true in this instance because the slopes of the two iso-cost curves are identical. We can show this by drawing ray 0–R from the origin to cross the least-cost points on w–w and w_1–w_1 and by drawing a second ray, 0–S, to cross the least-cost points on b–b and b_1–b_1. Since 0–R has a steeper slope than 0–S, it is evident that the production of wine at g is more labor-intensive than the production of beef at h (alternatively, beef is more land-intensive than wine). One of the assumptions of the H-O model is that wine will remain more labor-intensive and beef more land-intensive at all factor-price ratios, thereby ruling out factor reversibility. In Figure 3-1, this H-O assumption is preserved by making certain that the isoquants for wine and beef cross each other only once.

It is evident without a graphic exercise that a change in the factor-price ratio (a change in the slope of the iso-cost curve) will bring about a new least-cost combination of factor inputs. In sum, isoquant analysis demonstrates that the marginal rate of transformation of wine for beef as shown by a production possibilities curve (Figure 2-5) is based on factor-price ratios and given production functions. We are now prepared to show how a country's relative factor prices depend on its total factor endowments.

Factor Endowments: Box Diagram

Each vertical side of the box diagram in Figure 3-2 measures the *total* labor endowment of the United States and each horizontal side measures its *total* land endowment. Hence the total labor endowment is 0–D or, alternatively, $0'$–R, and the total land endowment is 0–R or, alternatively, $0'$–D. The diagonal 0–$0'$, drawn as a dashed line, indicates the overall factor intensity of the U.S. economy.

Assume that the United States is once again producing only wine and beef and that it has not yet entered international trade. Beef output is measured from the origin at 0 toward the right, and wine output is measured

Figure 3-2 U.S. Factor Endowments: Determination of Beef and Wine Outputs

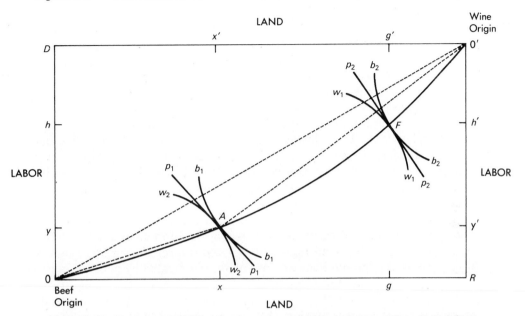

Each vertical side of the box diagram measures the *total labor endowment* of the United States and each horizontal side, its *total land endowment*. The diagonal 0–0′ (drawn as a dashed line) indicates the overall factor intensity of the U.S. economy. Assume that the United States produces both wine and beef and has not yet entered international trade. Any point inside the box represents a particular combination of wine and beef and also a particular combination of labor and land inputs at full employment. Although we can draw any number of isoquants indicating different output levels of wine and beef, we have drawn only two isoquants to avoid cluttering the diagram. The continuous line 0–0′ connects the points of tangency between *all* the beef and wine isoquants (such as points A and F). This line is called the *contract curve*; it represents all the *efficient* combinations of product outputs and factor inputs. Where the United States produces on its contract curve depends on the demand for wine and beef by U.S. consumers. Suppose consumers demand the combination denoted by point A. The ray 0–A (drawn as a dashed line) measures the factor intensity of beef output; the ray 0′–A does the same for wine. At point A, the United States uses 0–y labor and 0–x land to produce beef. How much labor and land is used to produce wine at point A? At that point, the factor-price line is p_1–p_1. An increase in demand for beef might cause production to move from point A to point F. How does the new factor-price line compare with the old one? The box diagram shows that with given isoquants (technology) the factor-price ratio is determined by the country's factor endowment and the relative demand for beef and wine.

from the origin at 0′ toward the left. Although we can draw any number of isoquants indicating different output levels for wine and beef, we have drawn only two isoquants for each product to avoid cluttering the diagram, namely, b_1–b_1 and b_2–b_2 for beef and w_1–w_1 and w_2–w_2 for wine.

Any point inside the box represents a particular combination of wine and beef and also a particular combination of labor and land inputs at full employment. If we draw a line that connects the points of tangency between all the beef and wine isoquants (such as points A and F), we obtain a curve 0–0', drawn as a continuous line, that represents all the *efficient* combinations of product outputs and factor inputs. This line is called the *contract curve*. At any point on the contract curve, the ratio between the marginal physical products of labor and land inputs are the same in the production of both wine and beef. Consequently, it is impossible to produce more wine without producing less beef, conversely. It follows that any point off the contract curve represents an *inefficient* combination of outputs and inputs that cannot endure under conditions of perfect competition.

Where will the United States produce on its contract curve? That depends on the demand for the two products by U.S. consumers. Suppose, for example, consumers demand the combination of wine and beef indicated by point A. By drawing ray 0–A (as a dashed line) we can measure the factor intensity of beef output, and we can do the same for wine output by drawing ray 0'–A. Thus to produce the amount of beef indicated by point A on the b_1–b_1 isoquant, the United States uses 0–x of land inputs and 0–y of labor inputs. The remaining land inputs (0'–x') and the remaining labor inputs (0'–y') are used to produce the amount of wine indicated by point A on the w_2–w_2 isoquant. Since the slope of ray 0–A is less than the slope of ray 0'–A, it is evident that the production of beef at point A is more land-intensive (or less labor-intensive) than the production of wine at point A.

From our earlier discussion of isoquants, we know that the labor/land price ratio must equal the slope of the isoquant curves at their point of tangency (A) because only then does the factor-price ratio equal the ratio of the marginal physical products of labor and land in beef and wine production. This is shown in Figure 3-2 by the factor-price line p_1–p_1.

Now suppose an increase in demand for beef causes production to move from A to F. We know that the price of beef would rise relative to the price of wine, but what would happen to the factor-price ratio? Because beef is land-intensive, an increase in beef production would require more land inputs than labor inputs. This more intense demand for land inputs would cause the price of land to rise relative to the price of labor. This is shown by the steeper slope of the new factor-price line (p_2–p_2) as compared with the old factor-price line (p_1–p_1). To increase beef output from point A to point F, producers have drawn x–g land inputs and y–h labor inputs from the production of wine. As the reader can discover by drawing rays, the production of both beef and wine is more labor-intensive at point F than at point A. Why is this so? Because the price of labor has fallen relative to the price of land, producers of both beef and wine will achieve the least-cost combination of inputs by substituting labor for capital. The box diagram shows, then, that with given isoquants (technology) the factor-price ratio is determined by the country's factor endowment and the relative demand for beef and wine.

Derivation of the Production-Possibilities Curve from the Box Diagram

The box diagram in Figure 3-2 contains all the information needed to construct the U.S. production possibilities curve. As we know, the slope of any point on the production possibilities curve is the marginal rate of transformation of beef for wine using the most efficient combination of factor inputs. Thus any point on the production possibilities curve corresponds uniquely with a point on the contract curve 0–0'. The production possibilities curve also indicates the quantities of beef and wine produced at each point on the curve. Similarly, each point on the contract curve indicates a particular quantity of beef and wine as measured by their isoquants, which are tangent at that point. All we need do, then, is to construct output scales for Figure 3-2 by measuring, say, beef along the bottom of the box (0–R) and wine along the left vertical side (0–D). The derivation of the production possibilities curve from the box diagram demonstrates that the *shape* of that curve is determined by the country's factor endowments at a given level of technology.

Dissimilar Factor Endowments as the Basis of Trade

We are now prepared to show how dissimilar factor endowments serve as a basis of trade between two countries.

Let us assume that France has a higher endowment of labor relative to land than does the United States. Then it follows that the French box diagram has a different shape than the U.S. box diagram. We show this in Figure 3-3 by superimposing the French box on the U.S. box. The diagonal in the French box (0–0") is steeper than the diagonal in the U.S. box (0–0'), indicating that the French economy is more labor-intensive than the U.S. economy. Accordingly, the French contract curve (shown as a solid line from 0 to 0") is steeper than the U.S. contract curve (shown as a solid line from 0 to 0'). Because French producers must combine more labor per unit of land than U.S. producers, the marginal physical product of labor is lower and the marginal physical product of land higher than in the United States. Therefore, the labor/land price ratio is lower in France than in the United States. (Keep in mind that the H-O model assumes isoquants are the same in both countries.) Hence, French producers will obtain their least-cost combinations of factor inputs in both wine and beef production by using more labor inputs relative to land inputs than U.S. producers.

Because the French and U.S. contract curves are dissimilar, we know that the French and U.S. production possibilities curves are dissimilar. *Hence, the different factor endowments of the two countries provide a basis for trade.* France has a comparative advantage in the labor-intensive good (wine) while the United States has a comparative advantage in the land-

Figure 3-3   United States and France: Dissimilar Contract Curves

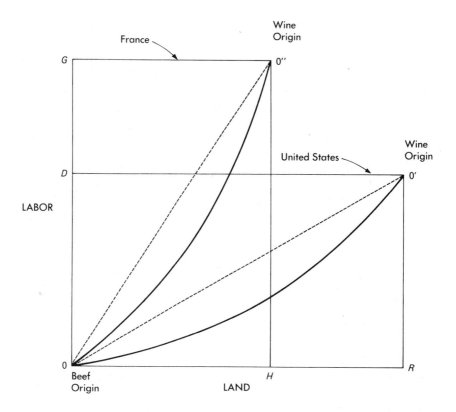

The diagonal (0–0″) in the French box diagram is steeper than the diagonal (0–0′) in the U.S. box diagram. The diagonals (shown as dashed lines) indicate that the French economy is more labor-intensive than the U.S. economy. Hence, the French contract curve (shown as a solid line from 0 to 0″) is steeper than the U.S. contract curve (shown as a solid line from 0 to 0′), as producers respond to a lower labor/land price ratio in France than in the United States. (Keep in mind that the H-O model assumes the same isoquants and demand preferences in both countries.) Because the French and U.S. contract curves are dissimilar, their production possibilities curves are also dissimilar. If wine is labor-intensive and beef is land-intensive, in which commodity does France have a comparative advantage? A comparative disadvantage?

intensive good (beef). To arrive at this conclusion, however, we have assumed that consumer preferences for wine and beef in France and the United States are not so different as to offset the influence of factor endowments on factor prices.

HETEROGENEITY AND CHANGE IN FACTOR ENDOWMENTS

The H-O theory of trade assumes that the individual factors of production are homogeneous and fixed in supply. Actually, there are many subvarieties of land, human factors, and capital. Furthermore, factor endowments (however defined) are continually changing over time through the effects of technical advance, population growth, and investment. This section considers the implications of factor heterogeneity and change (mostly growth) for international trade.

Land Factors

Land factors, or natural resources, comprise the many elements of the natural environment that contribute to the production of goods and services useful to society. Whether a natural element can and does contribute to production at any given time depends upon the society's capacity and willingness to utilize it.

Contrary to popular understanding, natural resources are dynamic rather than fixed in supply. Elements of the natural environment *become* natural resources as society develops the need and ability to use them in production. Over the centuries more and more of the natural environment has been transformed into natural resources. Early civilizations made only modest use of the natural environment, as do the Australian bush people even today. The availability of coal had no effect on the economy of the American Indians because they had no productive use for coal; consequently, it was not a natural resource for them. A generation ago much the same could be said of uranium for our own contemporary economy. The oceans will most likely become a much more important natural resource than they are at present. Fundamentally, therefore, what we call land factors, or natural resources, are dependent upon our technical knowledge and how we choose to use that knowledge. People must be aware of the existence of natural elements, must recognize their usefulness to them, and must want and know how to exploit them before they can become natural resources possessing an economic significance.

Natural resources are conventionally classified as agricultural land, forests, fisheries, and mineral deposits. Viewed broadly, natural resources also include topographical land features, solar radiation, water, winds, and any other natural elements that contribute directly or indirectly to economic activities. Each of these natural resource types has many variations. Agricultural lands differ in natural fertility, insolation, rainfall, latitude, height, and many other ways. Mineral deposits are even more diverse. Not only are there hundreds of different minerals, but deposits of one mineral will vary in size, accessibility, and quality. The many kinds of natural resources and the wide variations in their quality and other attributes preclude any precise measurement of the *totality* of national resource endowments or their comparison. Even international comparisons of one resource type, such as agricultural land, can be approximate only. Because of this complexity, sweeping statements about a country's resource endowment can be misleading. For example, although Switzerland is often described as "resource poor," its topographical features (especially the Alps) are a prime tourist attraction and also provide an abundant supply of waterpower for electricity generation.

It should be evident that national resource endowments are dynamic. Technological innovations develop new natural resources from materials that had no previous economic use, and they also improve the accessibility of existing resources. New discoveries (also aided by technological advances) add to the known supply of resources. Offsetting this expansion is the exhaustion of natural resources through use and misuse. Oil wells run dry, iron mines peter out, forests sometimes disappear, fertile grasslands can become dust bowls, water tables sink, and so on. Because of this exhaustion process (as well as higher usage), the United States must now import many minerals, such as iron ore and petroleum, that were formerly supplied entirely from domestic sources or even exported in large quantities.

Human Factors

International variations in human factor endowments are both quantitative and qualitative. Aside from variations in overall size that derive mainly, although not exclusively, from variations in population, the *composition* of labor and management often differs markedly among nations. In poor, underdeveloped economies the bulk of the labor force is unskilled and occupied in traditional forms of agriculture, only a small fraction is skilled in industrial pursuits, and an even smaller fraction has technical and management training. In contrast, the labor force in highly developed economies, such as the United States or Japan, is mainly composed of semiskilled and skilled workers in industry, white collar workers engaged in service occupations, and a significant proportion of technical and management people.

International differences in the *quality* of human factors are difficult to measure but nonetheless important. Again, they are most striking between poorly developed and highly developed economies. Qualitative variations arise because humans are shaped by an economic, political, social, and cultural milieu that is not everywhere the same nor is ever likely to be. Thus, there is a diversity among peoples in ways that influence economic performance, such as physical vigor, motivation, attitudes towards work, technical skills, organizational and management capacities, and many other attributes. In addition to disparities among individuals living in different cultures, there are also dissimilarities in social conditions that bear directly on economic performance. Some societies are rigid, offering little opportunity for lower class individuals; other societies are open, allowing individuals to move upward to higher social levels (or fall to lower levels). In a rigid society, movement from one labor group to another is a slow, painful process that limits the capacity of the economy to make positive adaptations to change.[5]

Qualitative disparities among the human factors of different countries are so pervasive that skilled workers (or any other subtype of labor) in one country are never quite the same as in another country and may, in fact, be very dissimilar. Such qualitative disparities influence comparative costs in the same way as quantitative disparities. If workers in one country are generally twice as productive as workers in a second country because of quality differences (as distinguished from differences arising from the use of complementary factors, especially capital), then the effect on comparative costs is equivalent to doubling the size of the first country's labor force.

The gist of this discussion is that *at any point of time* the human factor endowment of a nation will be heterogeneous and will differ both in composition and quality from the human factor endowments of other nations. This, as we know, is a basis for profitable international trade. But this is not all. Each nation's human factor endowment changes *through time,* injecting a dynamic element into its comparative cost structure.

Transformations in the level, composition, and quality of the labor force introduce continuing changes in the relative factor endowments of a nation and hence in its foreign trade. First, the overall supply of labor is strongly affected by the rate of growth and the age distribution of the population. Second, the many subtypes of labor—unskilled, semiskilled, technical, and so on—are subject to different rates of change. The radical expansion in the number of white collar workers and the simultaneous decline in the number of unskilled workers in the United States since the turn of the century are illustrative. Third, the quality of labor alters with changes in education, technology, and economic opportunity. An upgrading of labor has been particularly pronounced in this country—jobs once staffed by high school graduates are now staffed by college graduates. Because the formation of human skills requires saving and investment in education and training, economists regard human skills as *human capital.* As we shall see, the H-O model of trade has been extended to include the role of human skills in comparative advantage.

What we have said concerning labor is substantially true of another human agent of production—management. Changes in the size and the quality of the management force are largely determined by the freedom of economic opportunity, the rate of growth of the economy, and the rate of technological advance. When economic opportunity is impaired by a social caste system or by monopoly organization of the economy, when the economy is stagnant, or when the techniques of production are static, the manage-

---

[5]Even in the mobile societies of advanced economies, the subtypes of labor tend to form "noncompeting" groups, with little movement of people among them over the short run. The persistence of structural unemployment in the United States is a case in point. Many of the American unemployed are workers whose services are no longer in demand because of technological innovations that require more education and new skills.

Chapter 3 – Comparative Advantage and Factor Endowments: The Heckscher-Ohlin Model

ment factor will initiate few changes in its supply relative to the supplies of other factors of production.

In an economy like the United States, however, management is a most dynamic factor of production. In this country, management adapted to the operation of large-scale business has grown at a faster pace than other types of management; and the rapid rise of business schools suggests the qualitative changes that have occurred, and are occurring, in this factor.

Capital

Along with human skills, capital is the most dynamic factor of production, and it exhibits most strongly the influence of changing technology. An economy becomes more productive by increasing the supply of its capital relative to other factor supplies and by improving the quality of its capital. Today the American factory worker produces more in less time than did workers of previous generations, primarily because the worker today has more (and better) machines and more horsepower to help in the productive process.

Growth in the quantity and quality of capital is spurred by technological improvements. An advancing economy produces not only more factories, utilities, machines, and other varieties of capital, but also more productive factories, utilities, and so on, to take the place of the old. The growth of capital may markedly alter the relative factor endowment of a country within a generation. An outstanding contemporary example is Japan, which was transformed from a labor-intensive to a capital- and skills-intensive economy in the space of thirty years, and in the process became the world's second industrial power.

Drastic changes in a nation's capital supply cause substantial shifts in the nature of its foreign trade. The United States was once primarily an exporter of agricultural products and raw materials and an importer of manufactures. Now, with an abundant supply of capital, this country is a major exporter of manufactures and a heavy importer of raw materials.

Nations differ widely both in their stocks of capital goods and in their capacity to add to capital stocks through investment. Capital stocks constitute *real capital*, which includes many varieties of equipment, buildings, and other instruments of production, as well as *social capital*, such as transportation, communications, and educational facilities. Basically, however, real capital must be financed out of savings representing the surplus of current production over current consumption. Unlike real capital, investment funds *(financial capital)* may be viewed as a homogeneous factor of production commanding a single price, which is the long-term interest rate adjusted for variations in risk.

Consumption exhausts most of the production of poor economies unless austerity measures are undertaken by government authorities. Hence, the rates of investment of these poor economies tend to be low, perpetuating international differences in capital endowments. Because the supply of investment funds is low, long-term interest rates are high. Although investment funds flow from the more advanced economies, which have high rates of saving, to underdeveloped economies to earn higher returns, international investment can do no more than supplement domestic investment, which must carry the main responsibility of financing additions to a country's capital stock.[6] As a result of persisting disparities in existing capital stocks and the rate of new capital investment among nations, capital endowments will continue to be an important factor in the determination of international differences in comparative costs.

Effects on Trade: Factor Heterogeneity

The heterogeneity of factors of production raises the possibility that a given subfactor may be *unique* to a nation with no counterparts in other nations. We can visualize this possibility most easily in the case of a mineral exploitable in only one country, but it could also happen with a labor or capital subfactor, at least in the short run. The possibility of subfactor uniqueness is heightened for labor and management when we take into account the many qualitative differences arising out of dissimilar sociocultural environments.

Unlike comparative advantage arising from dissimilar proportions of the *same* factors, a country's possession of a unique factor gives it an *absolute* advantage in those goods requiring that factor in production. However, absolute advantage based on a unique factor is probably not too important: Few subfactors are unique (without any substitutes), and even so, they are not likely to remain unique indefinitely in a world of rapid technological change. In this regard we can call to mind how Chile lost its sodium nitrate monopoly during World War I when chemists discovered an economical process for making nitrates out of nitrogen drawn from the air. As we shall see later, however, a nation may gain an absolute advantage in trade through product innovations that are not matched (at least for a time) in the rest of the world.

More important, the existence of numerous subfactors indicates that national comparative cost structures are highly complex and that a broad similarity in the cost structures of two countries in terms of the three traditional factors most probably masks a rich diversity in their relative supplies of subfactors. For this reason, the possibility of identical comparative costs among nations is only theoretical. Nations can always find a basis to trade profitably with each other.

Effects on Trade: Factor Change

The effects of changes in a nation's factor endowments may be antitrade, neutral, or protrade. Figure 3-4 depicts these three possible outcomes.

Country X starts out with the production possibilities curve A–B. At

---

[6]Chapters 20 and 21 examine these and other aspects of underdeveloped economies.

Figure 3-4   Production Effects of Factor Growth with Constant Terms of Trade

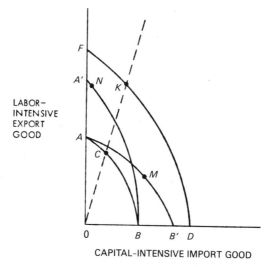

LABOR-
INTENSIVE
EXPORT
GOOD

CAPITAL-INTENSIVE IMPORT GOOD

Country X starts out with the production-possibilities curve A–B, producing combination C of both goods at a given terms of trade (which remains constant throughout this example). The country has a comparative advantage in the labor-intensive good which it exports in exchange for the capital-intensive good. Now suppose that country X's supplies of both labor and capital grow *in the same degree*, as depicted by the new production possibilities curve F–D. It now produces more of both goods but in the *same proportions* as at point C. Hence, the effect of these factor changes on trade is *neutral*: The shape of the production possibilities curve stays the same. But now suppose that the country's supply of capital grows while the supply of labor remains constant. This causes a shift from A–B to A–B', and the country now produces combination M, less of the labor-intensive (export) good and more of the capital-intensive (import) good. Because this unmatched growth in the country's relatively scarce factor lessens its comparative advantage, it is *antitrade*: There is less export of the labor-intensive good and less import of the capital-intensive good. When, however, the labor supply increases with no change in the capital supply, causing a shift from A–B to A'–B, then the effect is *protrade*: Combination N indicates more production of the labor-intensive commodity and less production of the capital-intensive good.

the given terms of trade, it produces combination C of both goods and has a comparative advantage in the labor-intensive good that it exports in exchange for imports of the capital-intensive good. Now suppose that its supplies of labor and capital grow in the same degree so that factor proportions remain the same.[7] As a result, the A–B curve shifts outward to make a new production possibilities curve, F–D. Since the terms of trade are constant, country X now produces combination K, which represents more of both goods

[7]That is to say, the country's box diagram for capital and labor factors keeps the same shape, although it is now larger.

but in the same proportion as combination C. (Both C and K lie on the same straight line drawn from the origin.) The effect of these factor changes on trade is *neutral* because they do not alter the comparative cost advantage (or disadvantage) of the country: The *shape* of the production possibilities curve stays the same.

What happens if only the supply of capital grows with no change in the labor supply? This is shown by a shift of A–B to A–B'. Assuming once again that the relative prices of the two goods are constant, then country X uses the new capital to produce more of the capital-intensive (import-competing) good, at the same time drawing some labor away from the production of the labor-intensive good. The resulting production mix at M has more of the import-competing good and less of the export good than the earlier mix at C. This increase in the country's relatively scarce factor (capital) is, therefore, *antitrade*; it has lessened the country's comparative advantage in the labor-intensive export good.[8]

Now take the converse situation: a growth in the labor endowment with no change in the capital endowment. A–B shifts to A'–B, with the country producing combination N, which has more of the labor-intensive, export good and less of the capital-intensive, import-competing good. Country X's comparative advantage in the labor-intensive good is now stronger than before and so, correspondingly, is its degree of specialization in that good. Hence, this increase in the country's relatively abundant factor is *protrade*.

Suppose both factors are growing but at different rates. In that event the output of both goods will increase, but the resulting production mix will differ from the pregrowth mix. The effect will be antitrade if the scarce factor grows more than the abundant factor and protrade if the abundant factor grows more than the scarce factor.

These *supply* effects of factor growth on trade may be intensified or weakened by the *consumption* effects of the higher real income (higher production) by country X. The consumption effect of a greater increase in the home demand for the import good than in the home demand for the export good is protrade, and vice versa. The *net* effects of factor growth on trade will depend, therefore, on both the production and consumption effects. A full analysis of factor growth effects on trade must also take into account any accompanying shifts in the terms of trade that were assumed to remain constant in the preceding analysis. Antitrade factor growth will tend to *improve* the terms of trade for country X because its import demand will fall relative to the foreign export demand from combined production and consumption effects. On the other hand, protrade factor growth will tend to *harm* country X's terms of trade. If the production effects of growth strongly increase the supply of the export good while its consumption (income) effects

---

[8]If this capital growth continues, at some point country X will develop a comparative advantage in the capital-intensive good and start exporting it in exchange for labor-intensive imports.

strongly increase the demand for the import good, then the terms of trade may become so adverse as to lower country X's *pregrowth* gains from trade, a situation designated as *immiserizing growth*.[9]

This short appraisal of factor endowments has shown that each of the factors of production is subjected to many influences that alter its supply within a nation over time. Factor changes are a continuing phenomenon within nations, causing shifts in factor proportions and in comparative cost structures. Hence, a nation's trade is not stereotyped or static but frequently changing in magnitude, composition, and direction at a rate that varies from time to time and from country to country.[10] It follows that nations must adjust continuously to shifts in comparative advantage because they cannot reasonably expect their future trade to be a mere repetition of their present trade. In this dynamic world, nations that quickly adapt their trade and economies to change (regardless of its origin) have an obvious advantage over nations with sluggish responses.

THE LEONTIEF PARADOX

No empirical study has cast more doubt on the conventional (Heckscher-Ohlin) theory of international trade than the *Leontief paradox*.

The central proposition of the H-O model of trade is that a country will export products that use intensively its relatively abundant factors of production and will import products that use intensively its relatively scarce factors of production. Using input-output tables covering 200 industries and 1947 trade figures, Wassily Leontief tested this proposition for the United States by comparing the capital/labor ratios in U.S. export industries and in U.S. industries producing import-type goods (import-competing industries). Much to his surprise, he found that the capital/labor ratio in the export industries was *lower* than the ratio in the import-competing industries. His principal findings, shown in Table 3-2, indicate that a million

---

[9]The question of immiserizing growth in the developing countries is raised in Chapter 21 when we look at the effect of international trade on growth rather than the effect of economic growth (factor change) on trade.

[10]In a study of Japan's trade, Peter Heller concluded that the shift in Japan's factor endowments from a relative labor abundance to a relative capital/human skills abundance over the period 1956–1969 strongly altered its comparative advantage in favor of capital- and skill-intensive exports. See Peter S. Heller, "Factor Endowment Change and Comparative Advantage: The Case of Japan, 1956–1969," *Review of Economics and Statistics*, August 1976, pp. 283–92. In another study, Bela Balassa analyzed the changing pattern of comparative advantage in 184 categories of manufactured goods for 36 countries. His results show that inter-country differences in the structure of exports are in large measure attributable to differences in physical and human capital endowments. These results can also be used to forecast the direction in which a country's comparative advantage is moving by projecting the future values of its physical and human capital endowments. See Bela Balassa, "The Changing Pattern of Comparative Advantage in Manufactured Goods," *Review of Economics and Statistics*, May 1979, pp. 259–66.

TABLE 3-2   Domestic Capital and Labor Requirements per Million Dollars of U.S. Exports and of Competitive Import Replacements of Average 1947 Composition

	Exports	Import Replacements
Capital (in 1947 dollars)	2,550,780	3,091,339
Labor (worker-years)	182	170
Capital per worker-year (dollars)	14,015	18,184

Source: Wassily Leontief, "Domestic Production and Foreign Trade; the American Capital Position Re-examined," in R. E. Caves and Harry C. Johnson (eds.), *Readings in International Economics* (Homewood, Ill.: Richard D. Irwin, 1968), pp. 503–27. This article was originally published in the *Proceedings of the American Philosophical Society* in September 1953.

dollars of import replacements requires more capital relative to labor to produce in the United States than a million dollars of U.S. exports.

Since the ratio of imports to exports in terms of capital per worker-year (18,184 ÷ 14,015) was 1.30, U.S. exports were *less* capital-intensive (or *more* labor-intensive) than U.S. import replacements, just the opposite of what would have been anticipated according to the H-O model for an "obviously" capital-abundant country such as the United States. Instead of capital-intensive exports and labor-intensive import replacements, Leontief showed that a representative bundle of U.S. import replacements required 30 percent more capital per worker-year to produce than a representative bundle of U.S. exports. This unexpected result came to be called the *Leontief paradox.*

Leontief confirmed this empirical finding in a second investigation that applied the same input-output matrix to U.S. trade in 1951. In this instance the import/export ratio was 1.06.[11] Baldwin applied 1958 input-output data to U.S. trade in 1962 and got the same paradoxical result, an import/export ratio of 1.27.[12] Other economists have made similar studies for Japan, West Germany, India, and Canada with paradoxical results.[13]

---

[11]Wassily W. Leontief, "Factor Proportions and the Structure of American Trade: Further Theoretical and Empirical Analysis," *Review of Economics and Statistics*, November 1956, pp. 386–407.

[12]Robert E. Baldwin, "Determinants of the Commodity Structure of U.S. Trade," *The American Economic Review*, March 1971, pp. 126–46.

[13]This was confirmed by Baldwin in a study of export/import capital intensities of some 30 countries. See Robert E. Baldwin, "Determinants of Trade and Foreign Investment: Further Evidence," *Review of Economics and Statistics*, February 1979, pp. 40–48. In opposition, Leamer argues that the paradox rests on a simple conceptual misunderstanding: When correct calculations are done, trade reveals the United States to be relatively abundant in capital compared with labor. See Edward E. Leamer, "The Leontief Paradox, Reconsidered," *Journal of*

The Leontief paradox has stimulated economists to search for explanations of the paradox and to test new trade hypotheses. The explanations fall into six major groups:

1. a *demand bias* in the United States in favor of capital-intensive goods
2. factor-intensity *reversal*
3. U.S. *import restrictions*
4. a scarcity of *natural resources* in the United States
5. the relative abundance of *skilled labor* in the United States
6. U.S. comparative advantage in *technology-intensive* industries

We shall briefly review the first four explanations in this section and then treat, at the end of this chapter and in Chapter 5, the skilled labor and technology explanations as new theories.

U.S. Demand Bias
for Capital-Intensive Goods

In Chapter 2 we demonstrated that dissimilar tastes could afford a basis for gainful trade between two countries. We also answered "yes, theoretically" to the question, Can dissimilar tastes ever overwhelm dissimilar production possibilities so that a nation exports the product in which it has a comparative cost disadvantage while importing the product in which it has a comparative cost advantage? It follows that a *possible* explanation of the Leontief paradox consistent with the H-O model is that a U.S. demand bias in favor of capital-intensive goods is so strong that it reverses the U.S. comparative cost advantage in such goods. However, we must reject this explanation on the facts. The evidence indicates that U.S. consumers allocate about the *same* share of their expenditures to capital goods as consumers in the other industrial countries.

Factor-Intensity Reversal

The H-O model assumes that the relative factor intensity of two or more goods remains the same (or at least does not change its order) at different factor prices; that is, the production of good A stays, say, capital-intensive as compared to the production of good B over any likely range of factor prices (wages, interest, rent). But suppose this assumption does not hold? Then at one set of factor prices, good A would be capital-intensive compared to good B, but at another set of factor prices it would become labor-intensive compared to good B. In this way factor reversibility would break the link between

Political Economy, June 1980, pp. 495–503. However, Brecher and Choudri point out that the correct calculations also imply that the United States has an abundance of labor, not compared with capital, but compared with the average of all resources. This U.S. export of labor services embodied in products contradicts the H-O model. See Richard A. Brecher and Ehsan U. Choudri, "The Leontief Paradox, Continued," *Journal of Political Economy*, August 1982, pp. 820–23.

factor endowments and comparative advantage. A labor-abundant country could conceivably have a comparative advantage in good A, exporting it to the capital-abundant country in exchange for good B.

A second possible explanation of the Leontief paradox, therefore, is that U.S. imports are produced abroad as labor-intensive and the same, or similar, goods are produced in the United States as capital-intensive. Is there evidence that factor reversibility actually occurs to a degree sufficient to support this explanation? Leontief himself has found little evidence of factor reversals.[14] Other investigations have come up with mixed results, but the weight of the evidence is against factor reversals on a significant scale. Although the agricultural sector is commonly cited as demonstrating factor reversal (e.g., capital-intensive rice production in the United States compared to labor-intensive production in Asia), it more likely demonstrates dissimilar production functions rather than different positions on the same production function.[15] To conclude, factor-intensity reversal attributable to different factor prices that reflect dissimilar factor endowments does not adequately explain the Leontief paradox.

U.S. Import Restrictions

In his original study, Leontief used the actual composition of U.S. imports in 1947 as the basis for the weights he assigned to the individual U.S. industries producing import-competing goods. But what if we suppose that U.S. tariffs and other restrictions were biased against the entry of labor-intensive imports to protect U.S. producers of similar products? In that event, Leontief's weights would result in a lower average labor intensity for U.S. import replacements than would occur in the absence of import restrictions. Under free trade the share of labor-intensive goods in U.S. imports would be higher than is actually the case.

In testing this explanation, Baldwin concluded that the capital/labor ratio of U.S. imports with no import restrictions would be about 5 percent lower than the ratio computed for actual imports.[16] This result offers a partial explanation of the Leontief paradox, but clearly it does not resolve the paradox.

Scarcity of Natural Resources

Leontief considered only capital and labor inputs, leaving out natural resource inputs. But if (1) the United States were heavily dependent on several natural resource imports, and (2) such imports required larger inputs of

---

[14]Wassily Leontief, "International Factor Costs and Factor Use," *The American Economic Review*, June 1964, pp. 335–45.

[15]See Chapter 5 for a discussion of dissimilar production functions caused by technology gaps. Footnote 1 in Chapter 5 points out the empirical difficulty of distinguishing the use of the same production function with different factor coefficients from the use of different production functions based on different technology.

[16]Baldwin, "Determinants of the Commodity Structure of U.S. Trade."

capital per worker-year to produce than imports that were not resource-intensive, then the link between natural resources and capital could explain the Leontief paradox. The United States would import domestically scarce imports of natural-resource products (in line with the H-O model) that were also capital-intensive.

This explanation has been proposed by Vanek.[17] It was apparently supported by Leontief in his second article, which showed that the paradox disappeared when natural-resource industries were excluded from the calculations. When Baldwin did the same, the import/export ratio of capital per worker-year fell from 1.27 to 1.04, not quite eliminating the paradox. He also found that the Leontief paradox did *not* appear in U.S. trade with Western Europe and Japan but did hold in U.S. trade with Canada, the developing countries, and all other countries.[18] These results are consistent with the Vanek hypothesis, because the latter three areas are all relatively abundant in natural resources.[19]

The evidence indicates that indeed there is a strong complementarity between certain raw materials, many of which are scarce in the United States, and capital. Hence, U.S. imports of natural-resource products make U.S. imports more capital-intensive than otherwise. At the same time, U.S. agricultural *exports*, which are capital-intensive, raise the average capital intensity of U.S. exports. The natural resource hypothesis, therefore, helps explain away the Leontief paradox on the import side, but it reinforces the paradox on the export side! As we have seen, the import effect more than offsets the export effect, so that the average import/export ratio becomes lower in the absence of natural-resource industries. In sum, natural resources offer a partial explanation of the Leontief paradox but not a resolution. Other factors are necessary for a more satisfactory explanation.

HUMAN-SKILLS THEORY OF TRADE

In our discussion of heterogeneity and change in factor endowments, we concluded that *at any point in time* the human factor endowment of a nation will be heterogeneous and will differ both in composition and quality from the human factor endowments of other nations. Although economists have long recognized these differences in human (labor) skills, the H-O theory of

---

[17]Jaroslav Vanek, "The Natural Resource Content of Foreign Trade, 1870–1955, and the Relative Abundance of Natural Resources in the United States," *Review of Economics and Statistics*, May 1959, pp. 146–53.

[18]Baldwin, "Determinants of the Commodity Structure of U.S. Trade."

[19]The results are consistent but not fully supportive, because U.S. imports from these three regions are *more* capital-intensive than U.S. exports to them, even when natural-resource industries are excluded from the calculations. On the other side, the disappearance of the paradox in U.S. trade with Western Europe and Japan cannot be taken as supportive of the H-O model, because the capital/labor variable did not appear as statistically significant in multiple regression analysis with respect to those two areas. See Baldwin.

trade has nonetheless treated labor as a single homogeneous factor of production.

Would a separation of the labor factor into two or more labor-skill factors explain the Leontief paradox in U.S. trade? In his original article, Leontief himself thought that the labor factor would explain the paradox. Suppose that 1 worker-year of American labor were equivalent to 3 worker-years of foreign labor. Then the total number of American workers should be multiplied by 3 in calculating the U.S. capital/labor ratio, which would make it smaller than in many other countries. Hence, the United States would be relatively rich in labor and poor in capital, and it would trade labor-intensive goods for capital-intensive goods. But what would make the productivity of American labor superior to that of foreign labor? Rejecting the H-O assumption of technological parity among nations, Leontief mentioned entrepreneurship, superior organization, and education as possible sources of higher productivity. His explanation of the paradox would appear, therefore, to belong with the technology theories taken up in Chapter 5.

The human-skills theory of trade explains the Leontief paradox in terms of a U.S. comparative abundance of professional skills and other high-level human skills. Instead of adjusting the U.S. capital/labor ratio by multiplying the denominator (labor) by three or some other multiple, as suggested by Leontief, the human-skills theorists increase the numerator (capital) by adding the value of labor skills. The Leontief approach would make the United States labor-abundant; the human-skills approach would make the United States capital-abundant by redefining capital to include human skills.

It is well known that U.S. export industries pay higher wages than U.S. import-competing industries.[20] Why should this be so? In answer, several empirical studies have shown that U.S. export industries employ higher proportions of highly skilled (and, therefore, highly paid) labor than do import-competing industries. As a consequence, the United States exports skill-intensive manufactures as compared with other countries.

Keesing applied U.S. skill coefficients involving eight categories of workers, based on the 1960 census of population, to the 1962 trade of the United States and 13 foreign countries, which were all industrial except for India and Hong Kong.[21] He found that U.S. exports of *manufactures* embody a higher proportion of skilled labor (the first seven categories of workers) than U.S. import-competing goods (55 percent as compared with 43 percent) and a correspondingly lower proportion of unskilled and semiskilled workers

---

[20]See the pioneer article by Irving B. Kravis, "Wages and Foreign Trade," *Review of Economic Statistics*, February 1956, pp. 14–30.

[21]Donald B. Keesing, "Labor Skills and Comparative Advantage," *The American Economic Review*, May 1966, pp. 249–58. Keesing's worker categories are (1) scientists and engineers; (2) technicians and draftspeople; (3) other professionals; (4) managers; (5) machinists, electricians, and tool and diemakers; (6) other skilled manual workers; (7) clerical and sales workers; and (8) unskilled and semiskilled workers.

(45 percent as compared with 57 percent). Also, of the 14 countries in the study, the United States had the most skill-intensive exports, which reflected the greatest relative abundance of professional and other hard-to-acquire skills. Thus, the United States enjoys a persistent comparative advantage in products that require high labor skills.

Baldwin made other comparisons of skill requirements of U.S. import replacements and U.S. exports in 1962.[22] Excluding natural-resource industries, he calculated that the average years of education of labor in import-replacement industries was 10.3 as compared with 10.7 in export industries (an import/export ratio of .96), and the proportion of scientists and engineers was .0228 compared with .0369 (an import/export ratio of .62). Baldwin also found a significant positive relationship between the percentage of scientists and engineers employed in an industry and the industry's net exports to Western Europe and Japan.

Like physical capital, the creation of labor skills requires saving and investment. Labor skills may, therefore, be regarded as *human capital*. Does the combination of physical and human capital explain the Leontief paradox? When Baldwin added the average costs of education of labor (but not the costs of on-the-job training) to physical capital and then divided the sum by worker-years, the import/export ratio for all U.S. industries remained above unity but fell to .97 when natural resource industries were excluded from the calculation. Using a different approach, Kenen valued labor skills indirectly by capitalizing the incremental income such skills earn for workers over the income of unskilled workers. When this extra income was capitalized at less than 12.7 percent, the combination of physical and human capital reversed the Leontief paradox.[23]

The evidence indicates that the relative abundance of professional and other highly skilled labor in the United States is a major source of its comparative advantage in manufactured products. The recognition of human skills as human capital also offers a partial explanation of the Leontief paradox. Rather than a separate theory, the human-skills approach may be regarded as a fruitful refinement of the conventional theory of trade. It adds a new factor of production (labor skills) to the H-O model and for that reason is sometimes called a "neofactor" theory. Against this view it can be argued that the human-skills theory is more properly regarded as a *technology* theory of trade because it rests on a country's possession of productive knowledge. When it is recalled that technological innovation undermines the critical assumptions of the H-O model (perfect competition, the sameness of production functions, and international factor immobility), the argument for treating human skills *directly* in a technology theory of trade appears most reasonable.[24] Efforts to rescue the H-O model by treating R & D as a

---

[22]Baldwin, "Determinants of the Commodity Structure of U.S. Trade."

[23]Peter B. Kenen, "Nature, Capital and Trade," *Journal of Political Economy*, October 1965, pp. 437–60.

[24]The argument for treating technology as a distinctive determinant of trade (neotechnology

form of capital (along with physical capital and human capital) are even more questionable.

In Chapters 4 and 5, we examine imperfect competition and technological innovation as possible sources of comparative advantage.

SUMMARY

1. Because factors of production are *not* perfect substitutes for each other and must be used in different combinations to produce different goods, dissimilar factor-price ratios give rise to dissimilar commodity cost and price ratios, which provide a basis for gainful trade.
2. The Heckscher-Ohlin (H-O) model traces dissimilar factor-price ratios across countries to dissimilar factor endowments of land, labor, and capital.
3. The least-cost combination of factor inputs to produce a good is at the point of tangency between a given iso-cost line and an isoquant.
4. A country's production possibilities curve may be derived from its box diagram. This demonstrates that the *shape* of the production possibilities curve is determined by a country's factor endowment at a given level of technology. Hence, dissimilar factor endowments among countries are the basis of their mutual trade. This is the fundamental proposition of the theory of comparative advantage.
5. Although the H-O theory assumes that the individual factors of production are homogeneous and fixed in supply, there are actually many subvarieties of land, human factors, and capital that are continually changing in supply over time through the effects of technical advance, population growth, and capital investment. The existence of numerous subfactors means that national comparative cost structures are highly complex, and the possibility of identical factor endowments among nations is only theoretical. The effects of changes in a nation's factor endowments may be antitrade, neutral, or protrade.
6. The central proposition of the H-O model of trade is that a country will export products that use intensively its relatively abundant factors of production and will import products that use intensively its relatively scarce factors of production. Much to his surprise, Leontief found in an empirical study that U.S. exports are labor-intensive and U.S. import replacements are capital-intensive, contrary to the H-O model.
7. The Leontief paradox has stimulated economists to find explanations for the paradox and to test new trade hypotheses. Explanations put forth

---

approach) instead of as a form—or forms— of capital within the H-O model (neofactor approach) is supported empirically by Hirsch. See Seev Hirsch, "Capital or Technology? Confronting the Neo-Factor Proportions and Neo-Technology Accounts of International Trade," *Weltwirtschaftliches Archiv Review of World Economics*, no. 4 (1974): 536–63.

to resolve the Leontief paradox include U.S. demand bias, factor-intensity reversal, U.S. import restrictions, and the scarcity of natural resources in the United States.

8. Two other approaches that help explain the Leontief paradox can be treated as new theories of trade: human skills and technology.

9. Supported by empirical evidence, the human-skills theory postulates that the United States has a relative abundance of professional and other highly skilled labor that is a major source of its comparative advantage in manufactured products.

QUESTIONS AND APPLICATIONS

1. (a) How does the H-O model explain dissimilar factor-price ratios across countries?
   (b) According to the H-O model, in which commodities will a country have a comparative advantage?

2. (a) Demonstrate graphically how a change in a country's factor-price ratio will bring about a new least-cost combination of factor inputs to produce a good.
   (b) At their least-cost combination of factor inputs, the marginal rates of factor substitution in production are the same for two goods. Why?

3. (a) Why is the contract curve in a country's box diagram composed of the loci of all the efficient combinations of product outputs and factor inputs?
   (b) Assuming two countries share the same technology, how can they have dissimilar contract curves?

4. Construct a country's box diagram. Derive that country's production possibilities curve from the box diagram.

5. Explain how dissimilar factor endowments afford a basis for gainful-trade.

6. What are the effects on international trade of factor heterogeneity? Of factor change?

7. What is the Leontief paradox? Evaluate the factor-intensity reversal and natural resource explanations of the Leontief paradox.

8. (a) What is the main proposition of the human-skills theory of trade?
   (b) What is the meaning of "human capital?"

SELECTED READINGS

Bhagwati, J. N. *International Trade: Selected Readings*. Cambridge: MIT Press, 1981. Part 1.

Caves, R. E., and H. G. Johnson, eds. *Readings in International Economics*. London: George Allen & Unwin, 1968. Parts 1, 2.

Corden, W. M. *Recent Developments in the Theory of International Trade*. Special Papers in International Economics, no. 7. Princeton, N.J.: Princeton University Press, 1965. Chapters 2–4.

Haberler, G. A. *Survey of International Trade Theory*. Special Papers in International Economics, no. 1. Princeton, N.J.: Princeton University Press, 1961. Chapters 2, 3.

Heller, H. Robert. *International Trade: Theory and Empirical Evidence*. 2d ed. Englewood Cliffs, N.J.: Prentice-Hall, 1973.

Hoover, E. M. *The Location of Economic Activity*. New York: McGraw-Hill, 1948.

Jones, R. M. *International Trade: Essays in Theory*. Studies in International Economics, vol. 4. New York: North-Holland, 1979.

Kindleberger, C. P. *Foreign Trade and the National Economy*. New Haven, Conn.: Yale University Press, 1962.

Ohlin, B. G. *Interregional and International Trade*. Cambridge: Harvard University Press, 1935. Part 2.

———. *Some Insufficiencies in the Theories of International Economic Relations*. Essays in International Finance, no. 134. Princeton, N.J.: Princeton University Press, 1979.

Ricardo, D. *Principles of Political Economy and Taxation*. New York: E. P. Dutton, 1912. Chapter 7.

4

Comparative Advantage: Transfer Costs, Imperfect Competition, and Intra-Industry Trade

Chapter 4 continues our search for explanations of comparative advantage and gainful international trade. We look first at the influence on international trade of transportation and other transfer costs that constrain the movement of goods among countries. We look next at a general source of comparative advantage that was assumed away by the H-O model: imperfect competition.

TRANSPORTATION AND OTHER TRANSFER COSTS

The movement of merchandise from one country to another involves a number of transfer costs. They may be classified as (1) costs of physical transfer and (2) costs associated with government regulation of international trade. Costs of physical transfer include the costs incurred in packing, transporting, and handling merchandise. Such costs are omnipresent, and they affect the movement of goods both within and between nations. Transfer costs also arise out of government regulation of foreign trade, such as import duties, quotas, and exchange restrictions.[1] These transfer costs differ from physical transfer costs in that they pertain only to international trade. Their nature and individual effects on trade are described in Chapter 7; for the present we shall restrict our discussion to the significance of physical transfer costs.

---

[1] Trade restrictions that prohibit trade either entirely or beyond specified amounts, such as import quotas, have the same economic effects as infinite transfer costs. It should be noted that international trade in services (banking, insurance, tourism, law, education, construction, and others) does not incur physical transfer costs but is subject to government regulation.

Physical transfer costs influence international trade in two ways. First, transfer costs increase the prices of imports and thereby restrict the opportunity for gainful trade. Second, transfer costs affect international trade by their bearing on the location of industry and the geographical pattern of production.

The Effects of Transportation Costs on International Trade

Transportation is the main source of physical transfer costs; handling and packing facilitate transportation and are subsidiary to it. To simplify matters, we shall confine our analysis to the effects of transportation costs on international trade. The effects of handling and packing costs are the same, but usually of lesser importance.

We can show the restrictive effects of transportation costs on the volume of international trade with partial equilibrium analysis that focuses on trade in a single good. The right side of Figure 4-1 indicates the demand and supply schedules for wool in England, and the left side indicates those schedules in Australia. (To get both countries in the same figure, it is necessary to invert the Australian schedules, which should be read from right to left because the amount of wool increases in that direction.) It is evident that the equilibrium price of wool in Australia before trade is much lower than its equilibrium price in England, as shown by the intersection of their schedules. When trade opens up, therefore, Australia will export wool to England.

In the absence of transportation costs, the trade in wool will reach equilibrium when the excess supply of wool in Australia equals the excess demand for wool in England. This occurs at price P, where Australia exports $A–B$ wool while England imports $C–D$ wool. In equilibrium, the price of wool is the same in both countries and the volume of exports equals the volume of imports. ($A–B$ equals $C–D$).

The introduction of transportation costs breaks the common international price into two prices: The English price is now higher than the Australian price by the transport cost per pound of wool. Equilibrium is achieved at an Australian price of P_a and an English price of P_e. At those prices, Australia exports $A'–B'$ wool while England imports $C'–D'$ ($= A'–B'$) wool. Transportation costs, therefore, have lowered the volume of wool traded from $A–B$ (or $C–D$) to $A'–B'$ (or $C'–D'$). Observe also that the decline in the volume of Australia's exports lowers the Australian price from P to P_a; hence, the rise in the English price from P to P_e is less than unit transportation costs. In this example, Australia continues to export wool to England, but if transportation costs exceeded the difference between the pretrade prices of wool in the two countries, then Australia would cease to export any wool to England.

Actually commodities vary greatly in their capacity to absorb transportation costs. Commodities that are heavy, bulky, and hard to handle

Figure 4-1   Effects of Transportation Costs on International Trade

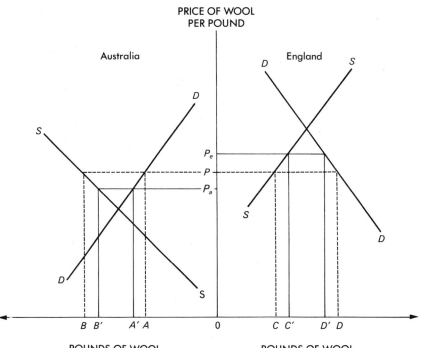

The right side of Figure 4-1 shows the supply and demand schedules for wool in England; the left side shows those schedules for Australia. (The Australian schedules should be read from right to left.) Before trade opens up, the price of wool in England is higher than its price in Australia, as indicated by the intersections of their respective supply and demand schedules. *In the absence of transportation costs,* trade between the two countries would occur at price P, where Australia exports A–B pounds of wool, which is the excess of its amount supplied (0–B) over its amount demanded (0–A). At the same time, England imports C–D (= A–B) pounds of wool, which is the excess of its amount demanded (0–D) over its amount supplied from domestic production (0–C). *When transportation costs are introduced,* the English price of wool will exceed the Australian price by the transportation cost per pound of wool. Equilibrium is achieved at an Australian price of P_a and an English price of P_e. Transportation costs equal $0–P_e$ minus $0–P_a$. Observe that transportation costs have lowered the volume of wool traded from A–B (or C–D) to A'–B' (or C'–D').

cannot absorb their transportation costs unless they command a high unit price. Bricks and sand are examples of this sort of commodity—to move them more than a short distance involves such high transportation costs that they cease to be competitive in price. On the other hand, commodities that take up little space or are easily handled may be economically transported over great distances even when their unit prices are low. The traditional staples of international trade, such as grains, wheat, cotton, and wool, are in the category of easy handling.

We may generalize this discussion of transportation costs in international trade by stating that the existence of transportation costs separates goods into two classes—*domestic* goods and *international* goods. Domestic goods do not enter international trade because transportation costs make it impossible to sell them at competitive prices in foreign markets.[2] International goods, however, are able to absorb transportation costs and still meet foreign competition.

The existence of transportation costs, like increasing costs of production (increasing opportunity costs), means that international specialization will not be complete. When transportation costs are taken into account, there will be a number of goods that can be acquired more cheaply from domestic industries despite the fact that foreign industries can produce the same goods at a lower cost. Low-cost housing construction in one country will not benefit home buyers in another country. There is, however, no sharp dividing line between domestic and international goods. A higher foreign demand may make it economically feasible to export a good that has not entered foreign trade in the past. An improvement in transportation that greatly lowers cost will convert many domestic goods into international goods.

This last observation suggests the tremendous effects upon international trade of the "transportation revolution" that occurred in the nineteenth century, particularly in its last quarter. Before this revolution, the vast hinterlands of North and South America and the productive resources of such countries as Australia and New Zealand were unable to supply the world market, centered in Europe, because of prohibitive costs of transportation. Argentine beef was left to rot in the sun because only skins and horns could be exported to Europe. Australia was able to export wool but not mutton. North American wheat could not compete in European markets. Hence, the railroad, the steamship, refrigeration, and many other improvements in transportation that came thick and fast after 1870 completely altered the character of world trade. A worldwide system of multilateral trade evolved to bring an ever-widening exchange of goods, illustrating in reverse the restrictive effects of transportation costs.

The Effects of Transportation Costs on the Location of Industry

Transportation costs also influence international trade by affecting the *location* of production. In seeking to minimize costs of production, business firms must take full account of the transportation costs incurred in acquiring

---

[2] Perishable goods are likely to be domestic goods unless techniques of preservation or very rapid means of transportation permit their sale at competitive prices in foreign markets. This is also true of the interregional trade, as is testified by the local character of milk and bread production.

raw materials and in marketing final products. The best location for a plant is the location that minimizes total costs of production, including all transportation costs. This location may be near raw materials (*resource-oriented*), near the market or markets of the final product (*market-oriented*), or somewhere in between (*footloose*), depending upon the character of production processes.

When the cost of transporting raw materials used by an industry is substantially higher than the cost of shipping its finished products to markets, then the industry will usually locate closer to its raw material sources than to its markets. This situation exists when the industrial processes characterizing an industry use large quantities of bulky, low-value raw materials and fuels that do not enter into the final product. Such processes are described as *weight losing* because the final product is so much less bulky or weighty than the materials and fuels necessary for its production. Steel, basic chemicals, aluminum, and lumber are among the products that utilize weight-losing industrial processes for their manufacture.

When the cost of transporting finished products is substantially higher than the cost of transporting the raw materials and fuels that are used in their manufacture, industries locate close to their markets. This relationship develops when industrial processes add bulk or weight in production; that is, they are *weight gaining*. Then industries try to postpone manufacture of the final product until it is physically close to its market. Although U.S. automobile companies have concentrated basic manufacture in the Detroit area, they have established regional assembly centers within the United States and assembly centers in many foreign countries because it is much cheaper to ship unassembled auto parts than the whole vehicle.[3] Many other manufactured goods are shipped as parts to assembly plants located near markets for the same reason. A prominent example of weight gaining occurs in the construction of buildings, where the final product is so much bulkier than its components. Thus, building construction is mainly an assembly job at the construction site. Beverage manufacture offers another example of how weight-gaining processes push final manufacture towards the market. Coca Cola and Pepsi Cola ship syrup concentrate to plants all over the world, which in turn add water to the concentrate and bottle the mixture. Even some Scotch whiskey comes to the United States in concentrated form. Finally, mention should be made of the extreme market orientation shown by service industries, such as wholesaling and retailing firms and transportation agencies.

When transportation costs are not an important factor on either the resource or market side, or when they tend to neutralize each other, and when location close to the market is not particularly advantageous, then

---

[3] Many countries also impose high duties on whole vehicles while imposing low or zero duties on vehicle parts to encourage assembly operations in their own territory.

industries are highly mobile or footloose, locating where the availability and cost of labor and other factors of production give them the lowest manufacturing cost. Companies producing electronic components, shoes, garments, containers, and small housewares offer examples of high locational mobility. U.S. electronics manufacturers ship their components to foreign countries, such as Taiwan and South Korea, for assembly by low-cost, semiskilled workers. The assemblies are then brought back to the United States where they are "packaged" for the domestic market.

The economics of location is extremely complex.[4] The fact that a firm may use several raw materials (including water, fuel, and power) drawn from different geographical areas and sell many products in several geographical markets can make it very difficult to determine the optimal location that minimizes transportation costs. This difficulty is compounded by the need to also consider the availability and cost of factors of production (land, labor, and capital) at different locations.[5] The availability of unskilled and semiskilled labor is often decisive in location decisions, especially in market-oriented and footloose industries.

In effect, the influence of transportation costs on the location of industry is a supply-side determinant of a nation's comparative advantage, along with factor endowments and technology gaps in production. The cost of overcoming geographical distance for a given product may vary from one place to another, both within and among nations, because of the location of raw materials or markets. In resource-oriented industries, transportation inputs may be a stronger influence on location and international specialization than relative supplies of productive factors. They will also be significant in determining international specialization in many market-oriented industries. Only in the case of footloose industries can we safely ignore the independent effects of transportation costs on location and international specialization.

In broader terms, the influence of transportation costs on location suggests that countries that are distant from world markets for finished goods and have no substantial domestic markets will tend to have a comparative disadvantage in market-oriented industries whereas countries close to world markets or with large domestic markets will attract market-oriented industries. Thus, the location of a country may give it an advantage in export markets even though its factor costs of producing some export goods are no lower (or are even higher) than the factor costs of producing similar goods in a country distant from those markets.

---

[4] Readers interested in location theory should look into Edgar M. Hoover, *The Location of Economic Activity* (New York: McGraw-Hill, 1948); and Walter Isard, *Location and Space-Economy* (New York: The Technology Press and John Wiley & Sons, 1956).

[5] Local taxes are also a factor in location. Many governments seek to attract industry to less-developed regions within their countries by offering preferential tax treatment to domestic and foreign investors.

IMPERFECT COMPETITION: MONOPOLY PROFITS, ECONOMIES OF SCALE, AND PRODUCT DIFFERENTIATION

The H-O model of trade rests on the assumptions of perfect competition, which are as follows: (1) Many independent firms produce a homogeneous product (hence, the individual firm cannot influence price); (2) there are no legal, financial, technical, or other obstacles to entry into the industry; (3) there are many independent *buyers*, none of whom can influence price; and (4) each firm has full knowledge of cost and demand data for both the present and the future (economic risk and uncertainty are nonexistent and pure profits are zero in equilibrium).

The first three assumptions are fairly representative of trade in basic foodstuffs and agricultural raw materials, although national farm programs and international commodity agreements have steadily introduced noncompetitive factors. However, international trade in minerals and manufactured goods departs in one way or another from the conditions of perfect competition. Although minerals are homogeneous commodities, their production and trade are usually dominated by a relatively small number of producers who can influence the market price and other conditions of sale. Much trade in manufactured goods also occurs under conditions of oligopoly (few sellers), and even when it does not, product differentiation is common. In brief, perfect competition is the exception rather than the rule in international trade.

The effects of this *imperfect* competition on international trade may be restrictive, neutral, or expansive, depending on the particular variety of imperfect competition in question and the policies of individual firms. In this section we sketch the principal types of imperfect competition and their most likely influence on the course of international trade. In particular, we wish to know whether international trade differs significantly from what it would be if all markets were perfectly competitive.

Imperfect competition in international trade may arise from monopoly, oligopoly, monopolistic competition, cartels, international commodity agreements, and state trading. Briefly, *monopoly* refers to a single seller; *oligopoly* to a small number of sellers who produce the same or a differentiated product; and *monopolistic competition* to a large number of sellers, each of whom produces a differentiated product with close substitutes. *Cartels* and *commodity agreements* involve restrictive arrangements among producers in various countries or among national governments.[6] *State trading* occurs when part or all of the foreign trade of a country is in the hands of its government. Today, the communist countries exhibit the most extreme form

---

[6] Restrictive business practices are treated in Chapter 24; cartels and international commodity agreements, in Chapter 21.

of state trading; communist government agencies are the sole buyers of all imports (monopsony) and the sole sellers of all exports (monopoly).

Monopoly and oligopoly may affect international trade via *monopoly profits, economies of scale,* or *technological innovation.* Monopolistic competition (and in some cases oligopoly) may also influence international trade via *nonprice competition,* which is its principal feature.

Monopoly Profits

Traditionally, economists have extolled perfect competition and deplored imperfect competition. This attitude is based on the theoretical finding that, unlike the case of perfect competition, the allocation of factors of production under imperfect competition does not maximize production and consumer satisfaction. Under perfect competition the price of a good tends to equal its lowest unit cost of production, and the cost of production includes only the profits necessary to attract and keep the management factor plus the other factor payments. Furthermore, the price of an individual factor in any employment is equal to the value of its marginal product in all employments. Thus, it is *not* possible to increase national output by reallocating factor supplies among different lines of production. As observed in Chapter 3, this means that national price and cost ratios are the same, and cost ratios reflect relative factor supplies and demands. Under the equilibrium conditions of perfect competition, therefore, comparative cost advantages and disadvantages are fully expressed in absolute international price differences.

Under monopoly and oligopoly, however, excess profits—profits not required to retain the management factor in production—may occur, although not necessarily. The existence of excess or *monopoly profits* makes the price of a good (or service) higher than its marginal cost of production and, for the nation as a whole, the price ratios between goods differ from their cost ratios. In this way, the international allocation of production (international specialization) is not fully adjusted to opportunity costs; in other words, the gains from trade are less.

Although the presence of excess profits distorts the price system and tends to restrict the volume of international trade, it does not follow that monopoly and oligopoly prices are necessarily higher than perfectly competitive prices or that the volume of trade is necessarily less under monopoly and oligopoly than under perfect competition. A monopolistic or oligopolistic industry may be able to achieve economies of scale and a rate of technological discovery and capital investment that would not be possible if the same industry were perfectly competitive. For example, perfect competition may require that an industry be made up of small firms unable to achieve economies of scale or engage in research on new products and processes.[7] When

---

[7] Until recently, this sort of situation has characterized the United States textile industry. Now bigger companies are being formed through mergers and acquisitions, and these companies are benefiting from economies of scale and more research. Many industries have started with

there are significant economies of scale, therefore, monopoly or oligopoly prices may be less than perfectly competitive prices, even though the former include excess profits and the latter do not. When this happens, the volume of international trade is greater under monopoly or oligopoly than under perfect competition. Of course, trade would be even greater if there were no excess profits. The effect of economies of scale on international trade deserves further attention.

Economies of Scale

The H-O model of trade denies any economies of scale by assuming that returns to scale are constant. Hence, a doubling of factor inputs can only double the output of a good, a tripling of inputs can only triple output, and so on.[8] Consequently, unit costs of production remain the same at different scales of output. But, in fact, firms in several industrial sectors, especially manufacturing, may experience economies of scale, in which case a doubling of inputs would more than double the output of a good and unit costs would *decrease* over the long run. The existence of economies of scale tends to create oligopolistic industries dominated by a small number of large firms.

Unlike increasing costs, decreasing costs enhance the opportunity for gainful trade. Unless their effects are blocked by tariffs or other restrictions, decreasing costs lead to complete international specialization. Thus, economies of scale provide a basis for international trade, along with differences in factor endowments and tastes.

Assume, for example, that two countries (A and B) have the same factor proportions, the same tastes, and the same level of technology. In terms of the H-O model discussed in Chapter 3, no gainful trade is possible under these conditions because cost and price ratios are identical. But now let us suppose that country A has a big domestic market that allows it to achieve economies of scale in producing a manufactured product (say, automobiles) whereas country B has only a small domestic market that limits it to high-cost, small-scale production of automobiles. This is shown in Figure 4-2. Although the long-run average cost (*LRAC*) curve is the same in both countries, the representative producer in country A is producing 0–G automobiles at a unit cost of 0–C whereas the representative producer in country B is producing 0–F automobiles on a smaller scale at a unit cost of 0–K. Thus, country A has a comparative advantage in automobiles based on economies of scale. When trade opens up, country A will export automobiles to country B and, in return, import a product from country B in which country A now has a comparative disadvantage because of the shift in opportunity cost ratios resulting from economies of scale. To eliminate country A's comparative advantage in automobiles, producers in country B

---

a large number of small firms, but subsequently economies of scale have transformed them into oligopolies. The histories of the U.S. automotive and steel industries offer instructive examples.

[8] In technical terms, production functions are assumed to be linearly homogeneous.

Figure 4-2   Long-Run Average Costs with Economies of Scale

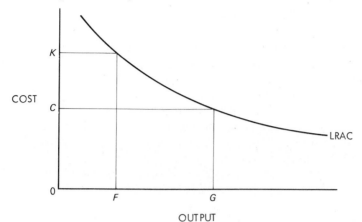

The declining long-run average cost (LRAC) curve reflects economies of scale in the manufacture of a product (say, an automobile). Assume that the LRAC curve for automobiles is the same in country A and in country B. However, the representative manufacturer in country A is producing 0–G automobiles at a cost of 0–C whereas the representative manufacturer in country B is producing 0–F automobiles at a cost of 0–K. Hence, manufacturers in country A produce at a lower cost than manufacturers in country B because of greater economies of scale. It follows that country A has a comparative advantage in automobiles and will export them to country B. This comparative advantage will endure as long as country B fails to match the economies of scale of country A.

would have to invest in new plant and equipment that would achieve the economies of scale enjoyed by producers in country A. But this would require both massive capital investment and time. And even if this investment were forthcoming, producers in country B would have to absorb losses until the new plants were actually in operation. Without government assistance, these obstacles might prove insurmountable, even over the long run.

The sources of internal economies of scale may be classified as specialization, technological innovation, and the experience curve.[9]

---

[9] For a review of the current state of theory and research on economies of scale, see Bela Gold, "Changing Perspectives on Size, Scale and Returns: An Interpretive Survey," *Journal of Economic Literature,* March 1981, pp. 5–33. Another source of decreasing unit costs may be found in *external* economies of scale that arise outside the firm or industry. The individual firm or industry functions within a broad economic environment, and its costs of production are dependent upon the efficiency of the economy as a whole. As an economy develops, transportation and communication facilities, raw materials, capital equipment, supplies and parts, skilled labor, financing, and so on, may become progressively more available and cheaper to the firm. The firm may also benefit from an expansion of its own industry. External economies—unlike internal economies—are compatible with perfect competition because they lower the costs curves of *all* firms.

Specialization can create economies of scale because a larger scale may enable a more productive use of specific factors of production. Giant machines, the assembly-line organization of production, high levels of labor and managerial specialization, extensive research and development, and mass marketing are economical only for firms that have reached a substantial size. Productivity increases at higher levels of output because indivisible factors of production can be more fully utilized, along with more specialized labor and management.

Specialization can also create internal economies of scale at the level of individual product runs when firms manufacture differentiated products. Assume, for instance, that two plants have the same size in countries A and B and both manufacture the same *type* of product. But the plant in country A produces a wider range of styles and sizes than the plant in country B. The second plant, therefore, is able to obtain greater economies of scale through longer production runs with resulting lower unit costs than the first plant.

Technological innovation in capital goods commonly enhances economies of scale over the long run. For example, twenty-five years ago an ammonia plant produced 150 tons a day; in 1970, 1,500 tons a day; and in 1980, 3,000 tons a day. Because increases in the scale of plants are so often associated with changes in technology, it is impossible to distinguish scale effects from technology effects in practice in any general way.[10] *Pure* scale effects occur only when the basic technology (production function) remains the same, as in automotive assembly plants or oil tankers, for instance. On the other hand, technological innovations can change production functions without creating scale economies, as is true of mini–steel mills.[11] The effects of technological innovation on trade (apart from any scale effects) are treated later in Chapter 5.

The *experience curve* traces a decrease in the average *total* costs of a product as a firm's *cumulative* volume of output grows over the long run. Substantial, if not conclusive, evidence regarding a wide range of products, including refrigerators, semiconductors, petrochemicals, paper, TV sets, beer, vacuum cleaners, primary aluminum, facial tissue, electric power,

---

[10] It may be done for very specific sectors. For example, differences between the basic oxygen and open hearth furnaces in steelmaking are attributable to technological differences and can be distinguished from scale differences within each category of furnace. See Gold, "Size, Scale, and Returns."

[11] Technological innovations are not always biased toward larger plants; they can also make smaller plants more economical. A case in point is the mini–steel mill, which is becoming more important in the United States. This mill depends solely on scrap metal, which is melted in electric furnaces and then poured into products. Further advances in technology are expected to enable the miniplant to manufacture certain products (such as sheet steel) that it cannot produce at present. See "The Rise of Mini–Steel Mills," *New York Times,* September 23, 1981, p. D1. More generally, factory automation can overcome the diseconomies of short production runs through "flexible" manufacturing systems. See "High Tech to the Rescue," *Business Week,* June 16, 1986, pp. 100–108.

motorcycles, and aircraft, supports the proposition that total product costs decline by a constant percentage (typically 25 to 30 percent) each time volume doubles. That is to say, unit costs decline in constant proportion to cumulative volume. For instance in less than two decades, Du Pont cut the cost of rayon fiber from 53 cents a pound to 17 cents.[12]

Why should total unit costs fall with cumulative output? The explanation covers the entire firm, not only economies in the single plant. As the firm gains experience with a product over time, it can cut costs through a combination of effects, such as spreading overhead over a bigger volume; improving the performance of workers and managers through greater specialization, more effective work design and layouts, and a growing familiarity with the product and related processes; and reducing inventory costs as production and marketing become better organized. In sum, unit costs drop as experience leads to a smoother coordination of tasks and their performance.

The experience curve is associated with the Boston Consulting Group, a management consulting firm, and it appears mainly in the management literature. Many economists remain skeptical of the proposition that performance improvements over time are necessarily caused by scale economies. But, as we have noted, there is now substantial empirical evidence that links total unit costs with cumulative output over the long run. Perhaps the major contribution of the experience curve concept lies in its focus on expanding production as a *process* within the firm that is improved with greater experience, a process ignored by the comparative statics approach of conventional economic theory. A second contribution is the extension of economies of scale to cover the firm's total costs, not only the costs of physical production at the plant level.

The implication of the experience curve is obvious: The firm that achieves the greatest market share in a product will gain a cost advantage over firms with smaller market shares. Cost reductions, of course, will not go on forever. At some point, incremental experience effects will become inconsequential or market demand will limit further growth.

Many American producers are able to compete effectively in the world market because their unit costs of production have been lowered through the economies of scale they have achieved in satisfying the vast domestic demand. On the other hand, countries with relatively abundant supplies of capital but only small domestic markets are seldom able to secure these

---

[12] William J. Abernathy and Kenneth Wayne, "Limits of the Learning Curve," *Harvard Business Review,* September–October 1974, p. 110. See also Samuel Hollander, *The Sources of Increased Efficiency: A Study of Du Pont's Rayon Plants* (Cambridge: MIT Press, 1965). For a more recent study of the experience curve, see Charles River Associates, *Innovation, Competition, and Government Policy in the Semi-Conductor Industry* (Lexington, Mass.: Lexington Books, 1980). The experience curve is also called the *learning curve,* although some writers view the experience curve as an extension of the learning curve to include other costs besides manufacturing costs.

economies of scale and therefore have a comparative disadvantage in goods that lend themselves to mass production.[13]

The Net Effect of Monopoly and Oligopoly on Trade

The *net* effect of monopoly and oligopoly on international trade may be detrimental or beneficial. Monopoly profits are always detrimental, but they may be more than offset by economies of scale and rapid technological advance. The net effect of *pure* monopoly on trade is probably detrimental in most cases. Lacking the spur of competition, a monopoly firm may become stagnant or actually retard technological improvements to sustain high profits. Nor is a monopoly firm necessarily a large-scale producer enjoying decreasing unit costs. For these reasons a monopoly, particularly an old monopoly, is apt to restrict the opportunity for international specialization and trade by holding prices far above costs and charging "what the traffic will bear." Fortunately pure monopoly is exceedingly rare in international trade. Its effects on trade, however, may be closely matched by cartels and state trading.

Oligopolies are very common in the mass-production industries, where a few firms can supply the entire market. In practice, oligopoly differs from monopoly in that there may be effective competition among oligopolists unless they organize a cartel or reach a less formal agreement not to compete, both of which are forbidden by American law but often permitted in foreign countries.[14] The possibility that the relatively small number of producers will "gang up" on buyers by agreeing to hold up prices, allocate markets, freeze technology, and the like is the greatest danger of oligopoly. When competition does exist in an oligopolistic industry, it will usually be *nonprice* competition in quality, style, or services rather than in prices. The heavy burden of fixed costs in the mass-production industries creates such a great risk of price wars that the firms within those industries tend to raise and lower prices together. We are all familiar with this sort of price behavior in cigarettes, automobiles, and gasoline—all products of oligopolistic industries.

When there is effective competition among oligopolistic firms, international trade will generally benefit from economies of scale and rapid improvements in technology. After all, the most dynamic industries are

---

[13] If international trade is free of official restrictions, then a small country may obtain the advantages of large-scale production by producing for the world market. But this is difficult and risky in the real world, where external markets may be suddenly closed off by foreign government action. One of the purposes of the European Community is to overcome this obstacle to large-scale production by creating free trade among its members. See Chapter 10.

[14] The Webb-Pomerene Act, however, does allow American producers to organize an *export* cartel.

likely to be industries in which oligopoly is the usual market arrangement.[15] The aggressive competition of oligopolies in this country and their willingness and ability to exploit foreign sources of supply and foreign market opportunities are mainly responsible for the expansion of U.S. trade in manufactured goods.[16]

Nonprice Competition: Product Differentiation

Most of the manufactured goods that enter international trade are sold in either oligopolistically or monopolistically competitive markets. In the latter variety of market, each good is produced by a large number of producers, but each producer has succeeded in differentiating the product from competitive products in some way. This differentiation is achieved by the technique of nonprice competition, which is the hallmark of monopolistic competition. Although price competition is close and competitors' prices can never be disregarded, it is nonprice competition in quality, style, and services that makes up the aggressive front of monopolistic competition.

American consumers encounter nonprice competition at every turn. Television, radio, and other advertising media daily assault our eyes and ears with clever appeals to buy this or that product. Price appeals are relatively rare, and they are usually drowned out by the host of selling points centered on nonprice factors. We are warned, cajoled, sweet-talked, entertained, and implored—all with the intent to make us rush out to buy brand X. American advertising has a pervasiveness and vigor that is seldom matched in other countries, but the use of advertising has risen sharply in all countries, much of it sponsored by international companies that market abroad.

Nonprice competition often employs appeals based on style factors. Not only is the style cycle of traditional style goods speeded up by this competition, but style is also created in goods that were formerly standardized. The evolution of the American automobile from the Model T to the contemporary stylized product is a case in point. Style introduces a rapid obsolescence of merchandise as each vogue has its day and then passes on; this raises problems of inventory, timing, and market information that are largely absent in the marketing of standardized merchandise. There is, however, another side of the coin—style obsolescence periodically renews demand by making buyers dissatisfied with their earlier acquisitions.

---

[15] In 1984, the fifty largest industrial companies in the world were all members of oligopolistic industries: petroleum, automotive, business machines, electrical, food products, communications equipment, chemical, steel, and aerospace. See "The World's Largest Industrial Corporations," *Fortune*, August 19, 1985, p. 179.

[16] The fifty largest industrial exporters in 1985 were large firms belonging to oligopolistic industries. The three "smallest" firms were two computer equipment companies with sales of $0.8 billion and $1.4 billion and a chemical company with sales of $1.6 billion. See "The 50 Leading Exporters," *Fortune*, August 18, 1986, p. 51. These fifty firms accounted for almost one-half of all U.S. exports of industrial products in 1985.

A great variety of services is also used to distinguish a product from its competitors—quick delivery, return guarantees, warranties, right of inspection before acceptance of merchandise, availability of repair parts, servicing of the product and instruction in its use, and so on. One reason for the establishment of overseas branches and subsidiaries by domestic concerns is to facilitate service competition.

The effect of nonprice competition on international trade is expansive. Nonprice competition stimulates demand by acquainting buyers with goods, by transforming latent demand into active demand, by introducing new products and new uses for old products, by heightening the availability of products, and in other ways. The dynamism of nonprice competition in creating new demand contrasts with the passivity of price competition—simply accepting demand and doing nothing to change it.

It is sometimes argued that nonprice competition restricts international trade because selling costs make prices higher than they would be under perfect competition. This accusation fails to note, however, that many goods do not sell themselves and that nonprice competition enlarges the sales of such goods beyond the levels attainable through perfect competition. Economies of scale may be possible only when production is bolstered through mass consumption that is induced by nonprice competition. The charge that nonprice competition is socially wasteful and costly is valid only when it does not enhance the demand for a product. This criticism is often leveled against cigarette advertising, which, it is alleged, does not raise the consumption of cigarettes but simply redistributes the existing demand among the individual producers.[17]

Over the long run, monopolistic competition forces an identity between costs and prices as products lose their differentiation through imitation by competitors. We may conclude, therefore, that nonprice competition brings a dynamic, expansive element to international trade without the distortion of chronic monopoly profits. This is not to deny the importance of price competition; nonprice competition does not take the place of price competition but rather supplements it. It does mean that the theory of comparative advantage must take into account nonprice competition as well as price competition if it is to explain international trade in manufactures.

Ignorance, Uncertainty, and Risk in International Trade

Ignorance and uncertainty are important sources of market imperfection in international trade that are assumed away in the H-O model. *Ignorance*

---

[17] Criticism of nonprice competition ultimately derives from welfare propositions, namely, that some things are better for society than others. The case for or against cigarette advertising is now complicated by the health issue. As for international advertising, a further point needs mention. International markets may differ greatly in the consumption levels and saturation percentages for the same product. Thus, the promotional elasticity of the same advertising

refers to a trader's incomplete knowledge about markets and costs in the present. This ignorance gap exists because information is not free; it is acquired only at a cost in time and money. For most business firms the acquisition of information about foreign markets is constrained by factors of distance, scarce or unreliable data, language and other cultural factors, and higher costs than for the acquisition of market information at home. Because of ignorance, traders do not fully utilize comparative advantage, and the gains from trade are correspondingly less. Thus, ignorance limits trade in much the same way as transfer costs. Conversely, improvements in market information widen the perceived opportunities for gainful trade among nations.

Uncertainty refers to a trader's incomplete knowledge about markets and costs in the future. Although the present is conceptually fully knowable (zero ignorance), only seers and astrologers claim to know the future with finality. For the rest of us (including the trader), the future offers an array of possible but uncertain events. In forecasting the future, therefore, the most that any trader can do is make probability judgments of possible future events and then relate those judgments to trading decisions. Although there are many forecasting techniques that may help the trader improve his or her judgments about the future, the trader must inevitably assume risks, because knowledge is never certain. Because of the greater number and variety of possible events in the world economy as compared to the domestic economy, firms tend to perceive risks in international trade (and investment) as higher than at home. Like ignorance, therefore, uncertainty also narrows the scope of international trade.

Another consequence of uncertainty is the appearance of windfall profits and losses and what may be called *entrepreneurial* profits and losses. *Windfall profits* accrue to the international trader when benefits from unexpected changes in the trading environment occur, such as an increase in market demand or a reduction in import duties. Windfall losses also come from unexpected events, such as the imposition of import barriers or the emergence of a strong competitor. *Entrepreneurial profits* are a reward for the *deliberate* assumption of risks by the trader. When, for example, a trader introduces a new product or enters a new market, risk is knowingly assumed in the expectation of a profit reward. Of course, the trader may be mistaken and end up with losses, but that is the meaning of risk. The presence of profits in international trade, therefore, is not necessarily a sign of monopoly; more commonly, profits arise from unexpected events and from the deliberate assumption of risk by the trader. Entrepreneurial profits play a key role in the dynamics of international trade. We shall have more to say about risk and uncertainty in Part Four.

---

may, and often does, vary widely among national markets. Finally, much criticism of nonprice competition either ignores product innovations or denies their usefulness.

INTRA-INDUSTRY TRADE: OVERLAPPING MARKET SEGMENTS, PRODUCT DIFFERENTIATION, AND ECONOMIES OF SCALE

According to the factor-endowments theory, international trade is based on dissimilar cost structures that mainly derive from differences in factor endowments: The greater the differences, the broader the opportunity for gainful trade. One would expect, therefore, that the greatest share of trade occurs between industrial (capital-abundant) countries on the one hand and nonindustrial (land- and labor-abundant) countries on the other and that this trade involves the exchange of manufactured goods for primary goods. However, the factual evidence points to a contrary state of affairs. Statistical data reveal that (1) the industrial countries generate about three-fourths of total world exports; (2) two-thirds of these exports go to the industrial countries themselves, and this trade is primarily (although not exclusively) an exchange of manufactures for manufactures; (3) in turn, much (certainly over half) of this manufactures-for-manufactures trade is *intra-industry* trade, that is, the simultaneous export and import of products belonging to the *same* industry; (4) furthermore, a great deal of this intra-industry trade is also *intrafirm* trade between multinational enterprises and their own foreign subsidiaries; (5) trade between the industrial and nonindustrial countries is only about one-third of world trade, mainly consisting of an exchange of manufactures for primary products; and (6) the economic structures of the industrial countries are becoming more, not less, similar. At the same time, income gaps are widening between the industrial group of countries and the nonindustrial group (with the exception of the newly industrializing countries).[18]

Overlapping Market Segments: The Linder Model

Dissatisfied with the glaring discrepancy between the trade patterns predicted by the conventional theory and actual trade patterns, Linder has advanced the most heterodox theory in international trade.[19] Linder asserts that differences in factor endowments explain trade in natural resource–intensive products but not in manufactures. His basic proposition is that the range of a country's manufactured exports is determined by *internal* demand. Thus, it is necessary (but not sufficient) that a product be consumed

---

[18] See Chapter 20.

[19] Staffan Burenstam Linder, *An Essay on Trade and Transformation* (New York: John Wiley & Sons, 1961). Discussion in the text is drawn from Chapters 2 and 3 of Linder's book.

or invested at home before it can become a potential export product. Comparative advantage in manufactures requires an earlier production for the domestic market. Linder supports this proposition by reference to the ignorance of entrepreneurs with regard to foreign markets as compared with domestic markets. He argues that an entrepreneur is not likely to think about satisfying a need that does not exist at home. Even if such a need were perceived, the entrepreneur might not conceive the product that would fill that need; and even if the right product were conceived and developed, it is still improbable that the product could be finally adapted to strange market conditions without prohibitive costs. Since internal demand also determines which products a country may import, the range of its potential exports is the same as, or included in, the range of its potential imports.

It follows that the more *similar* the demand preferences for manufactured goods in two countries, the more *intensive* is the potential trade in manufactures between them.[20] If two countries have the same demand structures, then their consumers and investors will demand the same goods with the same degrees of quality and sophistication. But what determines the structure of demand?

The most important influence, says Linder, is average or per capita income.[21] Countries with high per capita incomes will demand high-quality, "luxury" consumer goods and sophisticated capital goods, whereas low-per-capita-income countries will demand lower-quality, "necessity" consumer goods and less sophisticated capital goods. Consequently, differences in per capita incomes are a potential obstacle to trade: A rich country that has a comparative advantage in the production of high-quality, advanced manufactures will find its big export markets in other rich countries where people demand such products, not in poor countries, where the demand will always be small. By the same token, manufactured exports of the poor countries should find their best markets in other poor countries with similar demand structures. Linder does not rule out all trade in manufactures between rich and poor countries, because there will always be some overlapping of demand structures due to an unequal distribution of income: Some of the people in rich countries are poor and some of the people in poor countries are rich. But when the degree of overlap in demand structures is small, the potential trade in manufactures will also be small.

Figure 4-3 depicts the Linder model. Line 0–P shows the *average* relationship between per capita income and the quality/sophistication of each product demanded. Consumers in country A, with a per capita income of

---

[20] By "intensive" Linder does not mean the *absolute* size of trade between two countries, which is influenced by the absolute size of the trading economies, but rather the size of trade after adjustment for the size of the economies.

[21] The factor-endowments theory ignores the effects of per capita income differences on trade. It recognizes the influence of tastes (assumed to be marginal because of a similarity of tastes among countries), but tastes alone do not determine the structure of demand—they must be supported by purchasing power (income).

Figure 4-3   Overlapping Market Segments as a Determinant of Trade

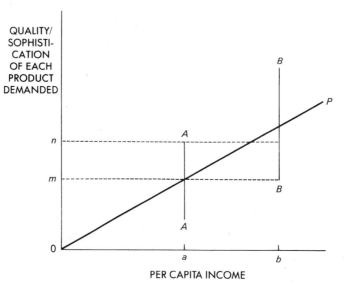

0–*P* shows the average relationship between per capita income and the quality/sophistication of each product demanded. Consumers in country A, with an *average* per capita income of 0–*a*, demand a *range* of product quality/sophistication, as indicated by *A–A*. Demand is for a range rather than a single level of quality/sophistication because consumers in country A fall into different income classes. It follows that consumers in country B, with a higher average per capita income (0–*b*), demand a higher range of (*B–B*) of product quality/sophistication. Because the two ranges overlap (*m–n*), there is a basis for trade between them.

0–*a*, demand a *range* of product quality/sophistication indicated by line *A–A*. Demand is for a range rather than a single level (which would be shown as a point on 0–*P*), because consumers in country A fall into different income classes. Country B has a higher per capita income than country A, and so its consumers demand a higher *average* product quality/sophistication—but they also demand a range because of different income classes. Since the two country ranges overlap (*m–n*), there is a basis for trade between them. Although Linder does not use the term, each country's range may be viewed as an aggregation of different *market segments*. Rephrasing Linder's proposition, then, we can say that countries will trade in manufactures when they have market segments in common.[22]

---

[22] Market segmentation is a key concept in modern marketing management. Marketing scholars have linked many factors in addition to income (such as age, occupation, and education) to market segments.

The situation is different for primary products. Because they are land-intensive, relative factor proportions are the main determinant of their prices. Linder arrives, therefore, at two explanations for trade, one for manufactures, the other for primary products. Trade in the former is caused by the same forces that cause domestic trade: economies of scale, product differentiation, and technology gaps. Linder concludes that the effect of per capita income levels on trade in manufactures may be constrained or distorted by entrepreneurial ignorance, cultural and political differences, transportation costs, and legislative obstacles such as tariffs.

Linder's model is consistent with the observed pattern of trade in manufactured products. Furthermore, it is in agreement with studies of international marketing at the enterprise level and with the product life cycle model. Only with rare exceptions do manufacturers enter into exports (or foreign investment) before establishing firm market positions at home. Once they do venture into exports, manufacturers usually find their most attractive markets in other industrial countries where incomes, tastes, and demand patterns most closely resemble those at home. In estimating sales potentials for their products in foreign markets, entrepreneurs give more weight to per capita income (and related phenomena) than they do to any other single economic factor.

Further observations about Linder's model can be made. Although Linder distinguishes between manufactures and primary products, a finer distinction exists between differentiated products and nondifferentiated commodities. As we observe later in our discussion of the product life cycle, when manufactured products become mature, they compete on the basis of price and cost. Unless economies of scale are significant, therefore, the factor endowments underlying costs are the principal explanation of trade in commodities, whether they are manufactures or primary products. Thus, poor countries have a comparative advantage in labor-intensive commodity manufactures such as basic textiles.

A second observation concerns the bearing of factor mobility, particularly management, on Linder's major proposition that countries only export manufactures that are first produced for the home market. Although this proposition appears to be generally true today, it will probably be less true in the future. International companies now establish manufacturing subsidiaries in poor countries as sources for products (mostly components rather than final products) that are exported to their operations in other countries. Because these arrangements are between a subsidiary and its parent, market separation is very low. Thus, the mobility of international companies may enable nonindustrial countries to export manufactured products that are not sold in their domestic markets.

A final observation is that the Linder model does not explain in a systematic fashion which *specific* manufactured goods a country will export and which it will import. More fundamentally, why should two countries that have the same factor endowments and that produce and consume the same types of products trade at all? The answer to this question must be found in a theory of intra-industry trade.

Toward a Theory of Intra-Industry Trade

Economists have not yet worked out a theory of intra-industry trade, but their efforts so far have enhanced the importance of theories relating to overlapping market segments, product differentiation, economies of scale, and direct foreign investment.

In a study of intra-industry trade, Grubel and Lloyd used the following index to measure it:

$$B = 1.0 - \frac{|X - M|}{X + M},$$

where B represents the degree of intra-industry trade and X and M represent exports and imports, respectively, of products that belong to the *same* industry.[23] B has a maximum value of 1.0 when exports equal imports for a given industry ($X - M = 0$) and a minimum value of zero when an industry has exports but no imports or no exports but imports. Using the three-digit Standard Industrial Trade Classification (SITC) to represent industries, Grubel and Lloyd calculated weighted averages of the index for ten industrial countries. The *combined* index for these countries in 1967 was 0.48, indicating that almost half the trade among the countries was in products belonging to the same industry. (For specific industries, the index ranged from 0.30 for mineral fuels, lubricants, and related industries to 0.66 for chemicals.) The combined index was 0.36 in 1959, 0.42 in 1964, and 0.48 in 1967. The index for countries in the European Economic Community was 0.67 in 1967.

Some intra-industry trade is in *homogeneous* or *nondifferentiated* products, such as raw materials and simple manufactures. The explanation of this trade is found in transfer costs, seasonal or other periodic variations in supply, and entrepôts. The production location of a homogeneous product (say, cement) in country A may be closer to a market area in country B than any production location in that country, and conversely. Hence, A exports cement to B while B exports cement to A. Again, countries in different climatic zones may trade in the same agricultural products, exporting them in one season and importing them in another, because storage costs exceed transportation costs. Entrepôt countries, such as Singapore, Hong Kong, and the Netherlands collect homogeneous goods through imports, sort and pack them, and then redistribute them through exports. Although intra-industry trade in homogeneous products should not be ignored, the available

---

[23] Herbert G. Grubel and P. J. Lloyd, *Intra-Industry Trade: The Theory and Measurement of International Trade in Differentiated Products* (New York: John Wiley & Sons, 1975), pp. 20 ff.

data indicate that most intra-industry trade is trade in *differentiated* products.

Linder's model of overlapping market segments offers a starting point to explain intra-industry trade in differentiated products. For example, manufacturers in the United States continually strive to develop and maintain differentiated products to obtain a competitive advantage in *specific* segments of the domestic market. When they are successful, differentiated products give manufacturers a degree of monopoly power, because demand curves are downward sloping rather than horizontal. The most prominent example of the pervasiveness of this strategy is the multitude of brands in the same consumer goods, but the strategy is also common for industrial products. A firm's products are distinguished from similar products of other firms in several ways, most commonly through style and design features, packaging, customer services, and promotion. Less commonly, a firm makes a technological breakthrough with a new type of product that, for a time, has no close substitutes.

When U.S. manufacturers look abroad for markets, they find them mainly in foreign countries that have market segments matching the segments they are currently exploiting in the U.S. market. According to the Linder model, these overlapping segments are found in foreign countries whose per capita incomes (level of economic development) are closest to that of the United States. Conversely, manufacturers in those countries export to the United States to exploit market segments similar to those at home.

Apart from marketing advantages, manufacturers may obtain *internal economies of scale* by specializing in differentiated products. In general, the fewer the number of differentiated products manufactured in a plant, the lower the unit costs; this is because of longer production runs and the experience curve. Thus a firm may gain a cost advantage over domestic and foreign competitors by specializing in a particular variant of a product while a firm in a second country gains a cost advantage by specializing in another variant of the same product. Economies of scale that are associated with product differentiation, therefore, also explain intra-industry trade.

It is evident that the explanation of intra-industry trade rests on factors that are *specific to the firm* (product differentiation and internal economies of scale) and on the existence of overlapping market segments. This firm-specific nature of intra-industry trade is highlighted when we recognize that about one-third of that trade occurs between multinational enterprises and their foreign subsidiaries.[24] Any theory of intra-industry trade, therefore, needs to be linked with a theory of foreign investment that explains the behavior of multinational enterprise.[25]

---

[24] In 1977, some 3500 U.S. parent companies exported $96.9 billion (80 percent of *total* U.S. exports), of which $31.8 billion or 32.8 percent was to their own foreign affiliates. For their exports of manufactures, intrafirm trade was 39.3 percent. See U.S. Department of Commerce, *U.S. Direct Investment Abroad, 1977* (Washington, D.C.: U.S. Government Printing Office, 1981), Table 3, T1, p. 395.

[25] See Chapter 23.

SUMMARY

1. Transfer costs may be divided into the costs of physical transfer and the costs associated with government regulation of foreign trade. The costs of physical transfer are mainly attributable to transportation. Transportation costs separate goods into two classes: domestic goods and international goods. Domestic goods do not enter international trade because transportation costs make it impossible to sell them at competitive prices in foreign markets. Hence, the existence of transportation costs narrows the opportunity for international trade.

2. Transportation costs also influence the location of industry and, thereby, the international specialization of production. In effect, transportation inputs must be viewed, along with the traditional factors of production, as a determinant of a nation's opportunity cost and comparative advantage.

3. International trade, especially in manufactured goods, departs in one way or another from the conditions of perfect competition. The monopoly profits of monopolies and oligopolies lower the gains from trade by introducing a discrepancy between national cost ratios and national price ratios. However, monopoly and oligopoly prices may be lower than perfectly competitive prices because of economies of scale and technological innovation.

4. Economies of scale may achieve decreasing unit costs over a broad range of output. Internal economies of scale are not compatible with perfect competition because they make possible the domination of markets by a small number of firms (oligopoly). But unlike increasing costs, economies of scale enhance the opportunities for gainful international trade and, along with differences in factor endowments and tastes, constitute a basis for trade. Hence, the net effects of oligopoly on trade may be detrimental (monopoly profits) or beneficial (economies of scale and technological innovation).

5. Nonprice competition deriving from product differentiation brings a dynamic, expansive element to international trade; in the case of monopolistic competition, it does so without the distortion of monopoly profits.

6. Ignorance and uncertainty are important sources of market imperfection in international trade that are assumed away in the Heckscher-Ohlin model. One consequence of uncertainty is the appearance of windfall and entrepreneurial profits and losses. Entrepreneurial profits are a reward for the deliberate assumption of risk, and they play a key role in the dynamics of international trade. Hence, the presence of profits in international trade is not necessarily a sign of monopoly power.

7. The Linder model asserts that the more *similar* the demand for manufactured products in two countries, the more intensive is the potential trade in manufactures between them. The principal determinant of similarity is per capita income. The Linder concept of overlapping market

segments, together with product differentiation and economies of scale, helps explain intra-industry trade.

QUESTIONS AND APPLICATIONS

1. How do transportation costs directly affect the volume of international trade?
2. What is meant by *weight-losing* and *weight-gaining* industrial processes? How do these processes influence location?
3. Why is the "economics of location" so complex?
4. What are the types of imperfect competition?
5. (a) What are the sources of economies of scale?
   (b) Why do decreasing costs lead inevitably to complete international specialization unless their effects are blocked by restrictions on trade?
6. Why may the *net* effect of monopoly and oligopoly on international trade be detrimental or beneficial?
7. (a) What is nonprice competition?
   (b) Why is its effect on international trade likely to be expansive?
8. (a) Do you consider ignorance and uncertainty to be greater in international trade than in domestic trade? Explain.
   (b) Do ignorance and uncertainty constrain international trade? Why or why not?
9. (a) How does the Linder model explain trade in manufactures among the industrial countries?
   (b) Does the trade in manufactures between the United States and Western Europe support this model?
   (c) What are the implications of the model for the developing countries?
10. (a) Why should overlapping market segments provide a basis for intra-industry trade in differentiated products?
    (b) Explain how economies of scale may promote intra-industry trade in differentiated products.

SELECTED READINGS

See the list of readings given at the end of Chapter 5.

5

Comparative Advantage: Technology, Factor Mobility, and Multinational Enterprise

We live in a world of continuing technological innovation. What are its implications for the comparative advantage of nations? This is the first subject addressed in this chapter. We also live in a world in which capital and advanced human skills move freely among nations. What are the implications of this international factor mobility for comparative advantage? Again, we live in a world of multinational enterprise. What are the features of multinational firms that need to be incorporated into a theory of international trade?

TECHNOLOGY THEORIES OF TRADE

The role that technology plays in shaping economic activities must be included in a theory of trade. In Chapter 3 we spoke of technological innovation as an agent of change in factor endowments. Here we take a closer look at the implications of technological innovation for a country's comparative advantage.

Technology is the accumulated knowledge, skills, and techniques that are applied to the production of goods and services. Inventions and discoveries are the source of technology, but they must be used in production to become innovations. Today, inventions and discoveries come mainly out of systematic research programs oriented toward technical innovations. The immense resources now devoted to research, along with the drive by management to apply its results to enterprise, have created an environment of explosive technological change, especially in advanced industrial economies. Technological innovations affect not only production and domestic and international trade but also the living styles of countless millions of people around the globe. One innovation alone—the automobile—has transformed societies throughout the world.

Technological innovations assume two basic forms: (1) new and more economical ways of producing existing products (new production functions) by innovations in producing specific products (such as a new way of making a chemical) or by general innovations affecting a broad range of production (such as automation), and (2) the production of wholly new products, both industrial and consumer (such as computers, televisions, plastics, and synthetic fibers to name only a few of the more prominent products introduced since the end of World War II), and improvements in existing products. These two forms are closely related; many new products, for example, are capital goods that make possible new production functions.

Because the influence of technological innovations on economic behavior is so pervasive, it has manifold effects on the volume, direction, and composition of international trade. Changing technology not only creates dissimilar production functions among countries at any given point of time but also transforms the trade of nations over time. We have already observed that technology determines what natural elements become land factors, making these factors dynamic rather than passive. Technology also vitally affects the training and education of labor, giving rise to qualitative differences among nations. Capital is directly influenced by technology because so much technology takes the form of capital equipment and, more basically, because technology contributes importantly to a nation's investment capacity by raising per capita productivity and real income.

The bearing of technology on international trade is not limited to the changes it provokes in the size and the quality of factor endowments. Technology also creates new production functions that raise the productivity of existing factors of production, and it profoundly affects the scope of international trade through innovations in transportation and communications. By fostering new products, technology has a direct impact on the composition and growth of international trade. The competitive strength of United States exports owes much to product innovations in capital and consumer goods— as older products, such as automobiles, are displaced by foreign competition, they are replaced by new products, such as computers, that for a time have no foreign counterparts. For this reason alone, a rapid rate of technological progress is a vital weapon in world markets.

The H-O model discussed in Chapter 3 made two implicit assumptions about technology: (1) the existence of a given state of technology, and (2) the same access to technology everywhere (that is, all countries use the same production functions). These assumptions do not hold in the real world. When we drop them, what happens to the factor proportions theory of trade?

Higher Factor Productivity via Innovation: Effects on Trade

When technological innovation takes the form of new ways to produce existing products, it pushes out a nation's production possibilities frontier. With new production functions the nation can now produce a greater output with the same endowment of productive factors. Indeed, technical advances in production are a major source of growth in contemporary economics. In effect, a new production function "saves" some or all the factors of production needed to produce a given level of output as compared with the old production function.

The effects of this saving may be neutral, protrade, or antitrade. Analytically, the situation is similar to the effects of factor growth on trade that were treated in Chapter 3. A technological innovation that causes a rise in the productivity of, say, labor has a production effect similar to an increase in the supply of labor. When an innovation saves all factors to the same degree, its effect on trade is neutral, as in the case when all factors grow to the same degree. However, when an innovation saves a country's relatively abundant factors but does not save its relatively scarce factors (or saves them to a lesser extent), then the effect will be protrade. The country will now have a greater comparative advantage than before in the production of goods that require relatively large amounts of its abundant factors. Conversely, when an innovation saves a country's relatively scarce factors more than it saves the relatively abundant factors, the effect will be antitrade, since production will shift toward goods that replace imports.

International Technology Gaps: Dissimilar Production Functions

Technical discoveries do not occur in all countries at the same pace. Neither do they spread instantaneously from one country to another, nor are they applied to production at the same rate in different countries. Advanced industrial countries generate most of the new technology, which then spreads to other countries after varying time lags. The most prominent example of this diffusion process is the Industrial Revolution (a combination of technical innovations involving the steam engine, new kinds of machinery, the factory system of organization, and other developments adding up to a transformation of the entire economy). The Industrial Revolution started in England in the eighteenth century, then spread to Western Europe and North America during the following century, to Japan and Russia early in this century, and is still spreading to many parts of South America, Africa, and Asia. Because this process is not instantaneous, we can distinguish between nations that are technological leaders and those that are technological followers.

At any given time, therefore, countries may be using different technologies to produce the same products; that is, *dissimilar* production functions exist. Since most technological innovations in production take the form of capital, a technological leader usually employs a capital-intensive method to produce a good that is traditionally labor- or land-intensive. Dissimilar production functions are strikingly evident in agriculture. Over the past generation, a technical revolution has transformed U.S. agriculture, encompassing a high level of mechanization, improved soil care, pest control, new varieties of seed, and so on, as well as large-scale organization of production characteristic of manufacturing more than traditional farming. U.S. agriculture has become capital-intensive (there are less than three million farmers and half of them produce almost all the commercial agricultural output), while in many countries it has remained labor-intensive. The employment of capital-intensive production functions (made possible by new technology) explains how the United States has retained, and probably increased, its comparative advantage in agriculture despite rising wage and land costs.

The point of this discussion is that a good cannot be uniquely defined as capital-intensive or labor-intensive (land-intensive), because it may be produced in *both* ways in countries using *different* production functions. Hence, the link between factor endowments and the *specific* kinds of products a country will export and import is now broken.[1] We can still say a nation will export those goods that use relatively large inputs of its abundant factors and import those goods that use relatively large inputs of its scarce factors, but we cannot say what those goods will be without knowing the production functions in question. In brief, by creating dissimilar production functions among nations, technological innovation can serve as a basis of international trade, along with dissimilar factor endowments, economies of scale, and product differentiation.

We can show this by means of a simple two-country (A and B), two-product (wheat and textiles), two-factor (labor and capital) model in which both countries have the same factor proportions (providing no basis for trade) but use different production functions to produce wheat. Specifically, both countries produce textiles with the same production function, which requires 3 units of labor and 2 units of capital to produce 1 unit of textiles. However, in producing 1 unit of wheat, country A uses 1 unit of labor and 4 units of capital (a capital-intensive process) whereas country B uses 5 units of labor and 1 unit of capital (the traditional labor-intensive process). Under these conditions, the two countries have different comparative costs: Country A

---

[1]This may also be true even when countries use the *same* production function for a specific product if there is a high degree of factor substitutability (that is, the technical coefficients of production can assume a broad range of values) such that at one set of factor prices the product is, say, capital-intensive whereas at another set of factor prices it becomes labor-intensive. Technically, this situation is called *factor reversal;* its frequency is a matter of dispute among economists. Part of the problem lies in the difficulty of distinguishing the use of the *same* production function with different coefficients of production on the one hand from the use of *different* production functions on the other in concrete situations where both differences may be operative.

TABLE 5-1   Effect of Dissimilar Production Functions on Comparative Advantage

	Country A (dollars)	Country B (pesos)
Unit price of labor	2	4
Unit price of capital	1	2
Unit cost of textiles	8	16
Unit cost of wheat	6	22

has a comparative advantage in wheat and country B a comparative advantage in textiles, and both will gain from trade (see Table 5-1).

International technology gaps in production functions have a dynamic impact on trade among nations as innovations open up new gaps and technological diffusion closes old gaps. There is ample evidence that both the opening and closing of technology gaps now occur much more rapidly than at any time in the past. Diffusion occurs in several ways. Technical and other news media transmit knowledge of new discoveries from one country to another, as does trade in new products. Companies in advanced countries like the United States license technical know-how and assistance to foreign companies in return for royalty payments and fees or set up their own operations abroad using new technology.[2] Diffusion is especially swift among the industrial countries because they have the capacity to use the new technical knowledge immediately. An outstanding example of this rapidity is the transistor. Developed by the United States, it was Japan that first used the transistor to make small radios, which then found a big market in the United States. Technological leadership is constantly threatened, therefore, by innovations elsewhere; nations must run hard to avoid falling behind. In the nineteenth century, comparative advantages changed slowly over a generation or more; in our own time, a country may enjoy a comparative advantage in a product for only a few years before technical diffusion and imitation or new technical discoveries wipe it out. The life cycle of new products offers the most dramatic evidence of this process.

International Technology Gaps: New Products

Commonly, technological innovations assume the form of new products or product improvements rather than new production functions for old prod-

---

[2]The role of international enterprise as a transfer agent for technology and technological innovation is examined in Chapter 22.

ucts. Such innovations may create entirely new industries. (In 1945, the television, jet travel, and digital computer industries were commercially nonexistent in the United States.) American manufacturers place thousands of new products on the home market every year, and sooner or later many of these products are exported to foreign markets. The technological leaders in American manufacturing are aerospace, electrical machinery (including communications), transportation equipment, chemicals (including pharmaceuticals), and nonelectrical machinery. It is hardly coincidental that these same industries are also the most aggressive competitors in world markets via direct exports and investment in foreign production.

New products do not always expand the volume of world trade; they may simply displace older *export* products or actually contract the volume of trade as substitutes for *import* products. Nylon has largely eliminated the raw silk trade, synthetic rubber casts a pall over the long-run future of natural rubber, and plastics have cut into the international trade of some traditional products. On balance, however, technological innovations in all their many forms have been, and continue to be, a positive force in world trade.

There is abundant evidence that the United States has a comparative advantage in research-intensive, high-technology products. One empirical study of nineteen U.S. industries found that the five industries with the strongest research effort (as measured both by total R & D expenditures as a percentage of sales and by the number of scientists and engineers in R & D as a percentage of total employment) accounted for 72.0 percent of U.S. exports of manufactures in 1962, although the same five industries were responsible for only 39.1 percent of U.S. total sales (domestic and export combined) of manufactured goods.[3]

These five high-technology industries—transportation, electrical machinery, instruments, chemicals, and nonelectrical machinery—also performed 89.4 percent of total U.S. R & D. They represent, therefore, both "the heart of U.S. export strength in manufactured products and the heart of its industrial research effort."[4]

This study also offered data on the characteristics of research-intensive industries. The data show that the industries with the largest research effort are also the industries with the strongest new-product orientation. Moreover, those industries make an intensive use of scientists and engineers in product and sales activities. The high-technology industries are also oligopolistic—dominated by a few large firms. On the other hand, two measures of capital intensity failed to show any systematic relationship with R & D

---

[3]William H. Gruber, Dileep Mehta, and Raymond Vernon. "The R & D Factor in International Trade and International Investment of United States Industries," *Journal of Political Economy*, February 1967, pp. 20–37. Other studies have confirmed the key role of technology as a determinant of U.S. exports. See, for example, Thomas C. Lowinger, "Human Capital and Technological Determinants of U.S. Industries' Revealed Comparative Advantage," *The Quarterly Review of Economics and Business*, Winter 1977, pp. 91–102.

[4]Gruber, Mehta, and Vernon, "The R & D Factor," p. 26.

intensity. The authors of the study concluded that these industries derive their large-scale economies and entry barriers to outsiders from successful product innovation and successful marketing rather than from capital intensity.

Technology theories postulate that certain countries have special advantages as innovators of new products. They also postulate that there is an "imitation lag" that prevents other countries from immediately duplicating in production the new products of the innovating country. These two conditions give rise to technology gaps in particular products that afford the innovating country an export monopoly during the period of imitation lag.

Posner has distinguished a *demand lag* and a *reaction lag* that together make up the imitation lag. The demand lag occurs because new foreign goods may not be regarded as perfect substitutes for old domestic goods. The reaction lag is the time between the production of a new product in the innovating country and the time when a potential producer in the local market views the new product as a competitive threat that should be met by local production.[5] The innovating country obtains an *export* advantage because the demand lag is ordinarily shorter than the reaction lag. The length of the reaction lag depends on economies of scale, tariffs, transportation costs, income elasticity of demand, and the income level and size of the foreign market.[6] Large economies of scale in production, low tariffs and transportation costs, a small income elasticity of demand, low income levels, and small market size act to favor a continuation of exports from the innovating country by delaying local production, and conversely. The innovating manufacturer enjoys an export monopoly advantage, but later imitators in other countries must depend on lower costs to justify local production.

Trade in electronic calculators illustrates the importance of technology gaps during the period 1962–1976, when the United States and Japan switched back and forth in technological leadership. It also illustrates that the demand lag facing the Japanese in the U.S. market (where the product was first developed) was nonexistent and that the reaction lags were very short. The transistorized electronic calculator was first developed in the United States in 1962, but the Japanese had imitated the product by 1964.[7] In subsequent years, the United States and Japan become the major producers of electronic calculators, and their relative positions in the U.S. market showed dramatic reversals over time. Starting in 1967 with 17

---

[5]Michael Posner, "International Trade and Technical Change," *Oxford Economic Papers,* Vol. 13 (October, 1961), pp. 323–41.

[6]Louis T. Wells, Jr., "International Trade: The Product Life Cycle Approach," in *The Product Life Cycle and International Trade,* ed. Louis T. Wells, Jr. (Boston: Harvard Business School, Division of Research, 1972), pp. 3–33.

[7]The following account is drawn from Badiul A. Majundar, "Innovations and International Trade: An Industry Study of Dynamic Competitive Advantage," *Kyklos,* no. 3 (1979): 559–69.

percent of the U.S. market, the Japanese gained a market share of 80 percent by 1971. After that year, their market share began to fall until 1974, when it reached 25 percent. In 1975, the Japanese once again started to gain market share, attaining 40 percent in 1976 (when this account ends).

These shifts in competitive advantage can be explained by shifts in technological leadership. In the period 1962–1966, the United States led, but in 1967 Sharp Corporation, a Japanese firm, introduced integrated circuits (ICs) and the metal oxide/large scale integration (MOS/LSI) that reduced the number of components in the calculator from 5000 to less than 1000. In 1969, the Japanese replaced ICs with only four MOS/LSI chips, cutting the number of components to 57. The next important step was taken by Bowmar Instrument, a U.S. company, when it developed the first single-chip calculator in 1971. With this innovation, the Americans regained technological leadership and, as we have noted, the Japanese suffered a loss in their share of the U.S. market. But this competitive advantage did not last very long. In 1973, the Sharp Corporation replaced the conventional circuit board with a soda-glass substrate that cut the number of components to fewer than forty. With this innovation, the Japanese began to recapture more and more of the U.S. market.

Technology gap theories as such do not explain why certain countries are technological leaders and other countries are technological followers. Nor do they satisfactorily explain imitation lags. The product life cycle model helps make these phenomena understandable.

The Product Life Cycle Model

Although the significance of product innovations has been largely ignored by economic theorists until recently, marketing scholars had earlier introduced the concept of the *product life cycle*. One version of this concept involves four successive stages: product introduction, product growth, product maturity, and product decline. Briefly, the life cycle starts when a company introduces a product that is entirely or partially differentiated from old products. (The introduction of the stainless steel razor blade by Wilkinson Sword in the early 1960s is a case in point.) In the first stage the product is a specialty and, for the time being, the manufacturer has a monopoly. However, most new products are soon imitated (or even improved upon) by competitors.[8] Hence, the original product loses its specialty status and instead becomes a growth product that is manufactured and sold by several companies. In this second stage, some product differentiation is maintained by individual manufacturers through promotion, packaging, and services (nonprice competition), but as more companies enter the market and the different brands become more and more alike to consumers, the product may

---

[8]Patent protection may inhibit imitation (as in the case of the Polaroid Land camera), but it is seldom complete. Furthermore, many new products are not patentable.

slip into the third stage as a mature product. Brand competition now gives way to price competition.

Vernon and others have used the concept of a product life cycle to explain the behavior of U.S. exports of manufactures.[9] A four-stage model is postulated: (1) The U.S. has an export monopoly in a new product, (2) foreign production begins, (3) foreign production becomes competitive in export markets, and (4) the U.S. imports the now-established product. Vernon asserts that U.S. producers are likely to be the first to exploit market opportunities for high-income and labor-saving new products, because such opportunities first appear in the affluent United States. Furthermore, they will first produce these new products in the United States, because close proximity to customers and suppliers is imperative for design and marketing flexibility. In this first stage, U.S. producers have a monopoly in export markets and they proceed to build up sales with no concern for local competition. However, during the second stage, producers in one or more industrial countries start to manufacture the product, whose design and production is now standardized.[10] Consequently, the overall rate of growth of U.S. exports declines and exports to the countries of foreign production become minimal. In the third stage, foreign producers displace U.S. exports in the remaining export markets. Finally, foreign producers achieve sufficient competitive strength (due to economies of scale and lower labor costs) to export to the United States itself. In short, the export effects of product innovation are undermined by technological diffusion and lower costs abroad.

Figures 5-1 and 5-2 depict the product cycle model of international trade for the innovating country and an imitating country, respectively. In Figure 5-1 the innovating country starts production of the new product at time 0, but it does not export that product until time A, when production exceeds domestic consumption. 0–A, therefore, is Posner's demand lag. At time B foreign production begins to compete against the innovating country's exports, which in turn begin to fall as a share of its production. 0–B is thus Posner's reaction lag. Exports, indicated by the vertically lined area, come to an end at time C, and the innovating country becomes an importer (shown by the diagonally lined area) of the once-new product.

In Figure 5-2, an imitating country starts to import the new product from the innovating country at time A'. If an imitating country is a high-income advanced country, then time A' most likely coincides with time A in Figure 5-1. But if it is a low-income, developing country, then time A' will come later; that is, the demand lag will be longer. Local production begins at time B', when the local market grows to sufficient size and cost conditions favor production against imports. Once again, if the imitating

---

[9]Raymond Vernon, "International Investment and International Trade in the Product Cycle," *The Quarterly Journal of Economics* (May, 1966), pp. 190–207. Louis T. Wells, Jr., "A Product Life Cycle for International Trade?" *Journal of Marketing* (July, 1968), pp. 1–6.

[10]Some of these foreign producers may be subsidiaries of American companies who anticipate later stages in the export life cycle. See Chapter 23.

Figure 5-1   Product Cycle Model of International Trade: Innovating Country

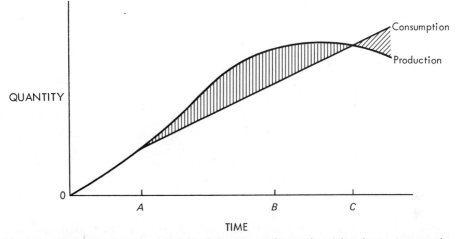

The innovating country starts production of the new product at time 0 but does not export the product until time *A*, when production exceeds *domestic* consumption. At time *B*, foreign production starts to compete against the innovating country's exports, which then begin to lose their share of the foreign market. Ultimately, exports come to an end at time *C* and the innovating country becomes an importer, as shown by the diagonally lined area.

country is an advanced country, then *B'* will coincide with *B* in Figure 5-1, whereas if it is a developing country, *B'* will come later after a longer reaction lag. With a lower price and stronger marketing effort resulting from local production, consumption rises more quickly. At time *C'*, when production begins to exceed consumption, the imitating country begins to export, at first to third countries and later to the innovating country. Thus, *C'* comes earlier in time than *C* in Figure 5-1.

An important feature of the product cycle model is the proposition that the factor proportions to produce a product will change in a systematic fashion as the product moves through its life cycle. The *new-product phase* (associated with the first production of the product in the innovating country and the early portion of the export monopoly stage) is characterized by unstable production functions, short production runs, and rapidly changing techniques that depend on scientists, engineers, and other highly skilled workers. Production, therefore, is skill-intensive rather than capital-intensive. In the *product-growth phase,* mass-production methods are introduced to exploit expanding markets, and consequently the factor inputs shift from skilled to semiskilled labor and from labor intensity to capital intensity overall. This growth phase is associated with the later portion of the export monopoly stage and the start of foreign production. The factor shifts continue

Figure 5-2   Product Cycle Model of International Trade: Imitating Country

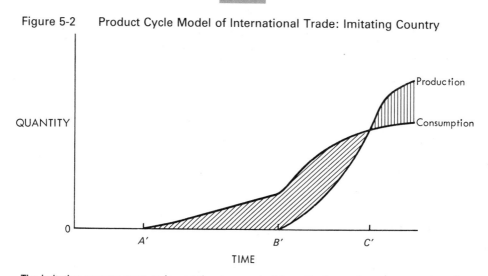

The imitating country starts to import the new product from the innovating country at time *A'*. Local production begins at time *B'*, when the local market grows to sufficient size and cost conditions favor local production against imports. At time *C'*, when production first exceeds consumption, the imitating country starts to export, at first to third countries and later to the innovating country.

in the *product-maturity phase,* which is characterized by long production runs with stable techniques; labor skills become relatively unimportant and production becomes more capital-intensive. This product phase is associated with the third stage of the product cycle model of international trade; the *product decline phase* is associated with the fourth stage.

These changes in factor requirements on the supply side are linked with systematic changes in market requirements on the demand side. In the new-product phase, the price elasticity of demand is low, since there are no close substitute products and most potential consumers remain ignorant of the new product. Also, the number of firms is small. In the product-growth phase, however, the individual firm experiences a rising price elasticity of demand as the product moves into mass consumption and the number of competitive firms becomes large. Finally, in the product-maturity phase, the product becomes fully standardized and there is intense price competition even though individual firms may maintain some differentiation through advertising and sales promotion.

Hirsch has used the product life cycle approach to determine the potential international competitiveness of industries in three groups of countries: (1) the most advanced industrial economies, led by the United States (Group *A*); (2) the smaller industrial economies, such as Holland, Switzerland, and Israel (Group *D*); and (3) the less-developed countries where some industrialization has started, such as India, Hong Kong, and Turkey (Group L).[11] Although Group A countries are capable of manufacturing new, growth, and mature products, Hirsch argues that they have a comparative advantage in *growth products* owing to their relative abundance of capital, management, and external economies and their large domestic markets. Group A countries also have a comparative advantage in *new products* whose manufacture is dependent on substantial capital and external economies, such as computers, aircraft, and atomic reactors. In turn, Group D countries have a comparative advantage in *new products* owing to their relative abundance of scientific and engineering know-how. But this advantage is limited to a certain range of new products, because Group D countries have a relative scarcity of external economies. This range is further reduced by the absence of large domestic markets and the high costs and risks incurred in the export of new products. Finally, Group L countries have a comparative advantage in *mature products* (such as steel, bulk chemicals, and other standardized manufactures) owing to their relative abundance of unskilled labor that more than compensates for their relative scarcity of capital (which, however, is less scarce than high-skill labor and external economies). Furthermore, mature products are easy to export to well-established markets.

Hirsch's analysis is an interesting attempt to synthesize a refined H-O model with the product life cycle model. The resulting model adds new factors of production (management, unskilled labor, scientific and engineering know-how, and external economies) to the conventional triad and links them to the phases of the product life cycle. Because time is an independent variable, this version of the factor endowments model (like the product life cycle model) is *dynamic,* with comparative advantage shifting from one group of countries to another as the product moves through its life cycle.

Several empirical investigations have been stimulated by the product life cycle model. For U.S. trade, Hirsch has studied the electronics industry; Stobaugh, the petrochemicals industry; and Wells, the consumer durables industries. For the trade of other countries, Tsurumi has studied Japan; Mousouris, Greece; and De La Torre, Mexico, Colombia, and Nicaragua.[12] These studies affirm the importance of technology in international trade and the usefulness of the product life cycle model to explain patterns of trade in manufactured goods.

In closing, however, we should point out that product life cycles may be determined by product differentiation as well as technological innovation.

---

[11]Seev Hirsch, *Location of Industry and International Competitiveness* (Oxford: Clarendon Press, 1967).

[12]The foregoing studies appear in Louis T. Wells, Jr., ed. *The Product Life Cycle and International Trade* (Boston: Harvard Business School, Division of Research, 1972), For a technology gap study, see Gary Hufbauer, *Synthetic Materials and the Theory of International Trade* (Cambridge: Harvard University Press, 1966). For a summary of empirical tests, see Rolando Polli and Victor Cook, "Validity of the Product Life Cycle," *The Journal of Business,* October 1969, pp. 385–400.

Indeed, it may be argued that new products are related more closely to product differentiation than to technological innovation. Only when a product becomes differentiated in the perceptions of foreign industrial or household consumers can it obtain an export monopoly advantage. Differentiation may derive from technological innovation (as is most likely true of any *radically* new product), but it may also derive from changes in style, design, packaging, promotion, and product-related services. Furthermore, not all technological innovations are embodied in products; process innovations may simply improve the manufacture of *existing* products. It follows that the life cycle model can be used to explain trade in differentiated products whether or not they are associated with technological innovations.[13]

FACTOR MOBILITY AND TRADE THEORY

The H-O theory of international trade presented in Chapter 3 assumed the absence of *any* factor movements among nations. Given this assumption, national factor endowments are determined only by *internal* conditions that perpetuate international dissimilarities in endowment structures and thereby afford a basis for gainful trade. The significance of this assumption for the H-O model of trade may be understood by tracing the implications of the contrary assumption, namely, perfect international factor mobility.

International Mobility of Factors

If labor, capital, and other factors moved freely among nations in response to opportunities for economic gain, they would move until the supply of each factor was everywhere fully adapted to demand and the price of each factor was the same in every country and in every use. Under the assumptions of the H-O theory, therefore, perfect international factor mobility would destroy the basis for gainful trade; given identical production functions, the shapes of all national production possibilities curves would be similar and the opportunity cost of any good would be the same in all countries. In the H-O model, factor mobility acts as a perfect substitute for goods mobility (trade).[14]

However useful they may be for economic analysis, the assumptions of perfect international factor mobility or immobility are fictions; neither

---

[13]Finger found that changes in the U.S. trade in manufactures were significantly associated with the rate of "product turnover." Product turnover (measured for a three-digit group of products as the number of seven-digit items that changed over a period relative to the total number of items in the group) is a proxy for product differentiation. See J. M. Finger, *Weltwirtschaftliches Archiv Review of World Economics,* no. 1 (1975): 79–99. For further observations on the product life cycle theory, see Chapter 23.

[14]When we drop the assumptions of the H-O model, this statement is no longer valid. Even with perfect factor mobility, opportunities for gainful trade would continue to be generated by economies of scale, product differentiation, and technology gaps.

is found to exist in the real world. Instead we find different degrees of factor mobility that vary among factors, among nations, and over time. Even within a country, noncompeting labor groups and other conditions constrain the free movement of factors and thereby provide an opportunity for interregional trade. Although factor mobility among countries is usually (but not always) lower than domestic mobility because of physical, social, and political obstacles, it is by no means small. Indeed, a key development in the world economy in recent years has been an extraordinary growth in international flows of management, capital, and technology, particularly among the advanced industrial countries. The principal agent in this factor transfer is the international enterprise (especially its most advanced form, the multinational corporation), which is the subject of Part Four. The emergence of customs unions and free trade areas, notably the European Community, has also encouraged the international movement of factors.

Resources *Natural resources* are completely immobile. It is not physically possible to move land area, climate, soil, forests, mines, land forms, and other "gifts of nature" from one place to another. Since the international distribution of natural resources is most haphazard, their immobility assures a permanent dissimilarity in the supplies of national land factors. This immobility is not a distinctive feature of international trade, however, because natural resources also cannot be moved among regions of the same country.

Labor *Ordinary workers* will not emigrate to a foreign country unless they are pressed by unhappy circumstances at home. Social inertia tends to keep people in their native countries. However, large masses of people have moved from one country to another, particularly during periods of widespread unrest brought on by natural disasters, revolution, or war at home.[15]

In our own day the absence of motivations to emigrate has been much less important than limited opportunities to emigrate in explaining the low international mobility of labor. All contemporary governments restrict immigration and some, such as the Soviet government, also restrict emigration. Actually the international mobility of ordinary labor is so low that international differences in relative labor supplies are probably growing wider due to disparate rates of population growth and capital accumulation.

The international mobility of *professional workers,* such as engineers and scientists, is much higher than that of ordinary workers. At times, the mobility of professional workers may be so high that national governments become concerned about "brain drains." The developing countries annually lose hundreds of their brightest professionals to North America and Europe,

---

[15]Many waves of migration to the United States have been associated with unrest in Europe and elsewhere. A recent example is the influx of Cubans and Vietnamese.

many of them recent graduates who decide not to return home. Undoubtedly, this mobility would be far higher if governments did not impose entry restrictions.

The international mobility of *managers* is probably higher today than at any time in the past. The multinational company with production and marketing affiliates in several countries has become a powerful vehicle for the transfer of managerial skills such as innovating, planning, directing, organizing, and controlling. A new type of international executive is now coming to the fore, an individual who is able to move quickly from a management post in one country to a new post in another country. Sophisticated, cosmopolitan, and highly educated, this new breed of international manager has the capacity to manage business operations effectively in a broad variety of national milieux. The movement of these managers has been enormously facilitated by jet travel.

Capital The international mobility of *capital goods* (construction, capital equipment, and inventories) varies with the nature of the goods. It is important to realize that a nation does not necessarily transfer capital to another nation by exporting capital goods to it. Instead, capital is transferred by international loans and investments (and occasionally by gifts) that provide the purchasing power needed to finance either the construction of capital goods in the borrowing country or the importation of capital goods from abroad. Therefore, the criterion of the international mobility of capital is the ease of foreign investment.

Viewed in this way, the international mobility of capital itself may be very high. During the nineteenth century and up to the 1930s, most international investment took the form of private lending via subscriptions to foreign bond issues. Although in the 1970s private lending of this sort and by banks once again became substantial, much private foreign investment today is undertaken by international companies that make direct equity investments in foreign affiliates. The rapid expansion of direct foreign investment by U.S., European, and Japanese companies is a dominant force in the evolution of the contemporary world economy.[16] Much capital also moves from rich to poor nations through international institutions, such as the World Bank, and through bilateral government aid programs.[17]

International Trade and Factor Movements as Substitutes

Both trade and factor movements act to bring about a superior allocation of production among nations. As we have seen, trade achieves this result, according to the H-O model through international specialization that allows nations to export products that require relatively abundant factors in their

---

[16]Chapter 23 explores the nature of private direct foreign investment.
[17]See Chapter 21 for a discussion of foreign aid.

production in exchange for products that require relatively scarce factors. More generally, trade enables a country to export products with low opportunity costs and import products with high opportunity costs.

Factor movements achieve a superior allocation of productive agents directly. Relatively abundant factors in country A (such as management and capital) move to country B, where the same factors are relatively scarce; they are then combined in production with country B's relatively abundant factors. In terms of price theory, factors move from country A, where their marginal productivities are low (because they are relatively abundant), to country B, where their marginal productivities are higher (because they are relatively scarce). Under conditions of perfect competition, the flow of factors continues until their marginal productivities (and prices) are the same in all countries. When this occurs, the international allocation of factors is perfect, because any further factor movement would lower production and consumer satisfaction for the world as a whole. Because of many obstacles and continuous economic change, this ideal allocation can never be achieved, even among regions of the same country; it can only be approached in varying degrees. Thus, the higher the mobility of factors among countries, the better the global allocation of factors and production. At the same time, factor mobility will tend to equalize factor prices among countries.

Does international trade also tend to equalize factor prices? To answer that question, let us assume that the United States has a comparative advantage in wheat production and a comparative disadvantage in textile production, while the converse holds in the United Kingdom. The production of wheat is land-intensive, and the United States has a relatively abundant supply of land, which thus commands a relatively low rent. The production of textiles is labor-intensive, and the United States has a relatively scarce supply of labor, which thus commands a relatively high wage. The opposite is true in the United Kingdom.

When trade begins, the demand facing United States wheat rises as foreign demand is added to domestic demand. With increasing unit costs, this higher demand leads to higher wheat prices and feeds back to create a higher demand and higher prices for the factors of production—especially land—used to produce wheat. At the same time, imports of textiles from the United Kingdom are displacing the United States' production of textiles. The falling demand for textiles initiates a falling demand and falling prices for the factor of production—especially labor—used to produce textiles. As a consequence, land rent rises relative to wages in the United States. Simultaneously, wages rise relative to land rent in the United Kingdom. Thus, the abundant factors (land in the United States, labor in the United Kingdom) become relatively more expensive while the scarce factors (labor in the United States, land in the United Kingdom) become relatively less expensive. It follows that the gap between the factor prices of the two countries becomes narrower.

Will international trade ever achieve a full equalization of factor prices between the trading countries? Only under these limiting assumptions could it ever happen: National factor endowments are not too unequal, there are no transfer costs, technology is the same in all countries, and there is only partial specialization (each country continues to produce some import-type goods).[18] But only the last assumption holds in the real world.

The foregoing analysis points to a *substitutive* relation between trade and factor movements. In the preceding example, a flow of labor from the United Kingdom to the United States would increase the opportunity cost of textiles in the first country and lower it in the second country, thereby narrowing the gainful opportunity for trade. The question whether there is a substitutive relation between foreign investment (capital outflow) and trade is a matter of controversy in the United States. Do restrictions on U.S. investment abroad raise or lower U.S. exports? What about U.S. imports? Labor unions assert that foreign investment causes a loss of jobs to American workers as U.S. companies transfer production to foreign locations. Some observations are made in the following section indicating that factor movements and trade may also be complementary.

International Trade and Factor Movements as Complements: Economic Integration

The conclusion that trade and factor movements are substitutes derives from the H-O factor endowments theory, which is concerned only with allocational efficiency under static conditions (perfect competition, fixed factor endowments, and no technology gaps). When these assumptions are dropped to allow for dynamic elements, it is no longer evident that international factor movements cause a general decrease in international trade. What the static analysis ignores are the effects of factor movements on economic growth and, particularly, economic integration.

As stated earlier, international factor flows are mainly initiated by multinational companies that transfer a mix of management, capital, and technology from one country to another. These factors are combined with local factors to manufacture products that, for the most part, are new to the host economy.[19] This process contributes both directly and indirectly to the growth of the economy.[20] By promoting economic growth, factor movements increase the capacity of nations to trade with one another; expansion occurs in both the size and diversity of production and markets. Although factor movements have displaced trade in some products, statistical data suggest

---

[18]The classic exposition of the factor-price equalization theorem is Paul A. Samuelson, "International Trade and the Equalization of Factor Prices," *Economic Journal*, June 1948, pp. 163–84.

[19]The term *host economy* refers to the country that receives the factor transfers.

[20]This is intended only as a general statement: Some factor transfers are more growth generating than others. For this and other qualifications, see Chapter 24.

that their growth effects on trade have been more powerful than their substitution effects. Trade and factor flows have expanded together for the world as a whole; in the European Community, factor transfers among the member countries have been accompanied by a growth in mutual trade that has exceeded the growth in trade with outside countries. At the enterprise level, it is also noteworthy that the principal exporters of manufactures from the United States are also the principal investors in production abroad.

Generally we are witnessing a process of economic integration on a global scale (particularly among the industrial countries) that is being carried forward by a complex mix of trade and factor flows. Economists generally agree that factor movements constitute a more powerful instrument for factor-price equalization than trade in products. Consequently, factor transfers can be expected to join national economies together to a higher degree than goods transfers alone. As local and regional markets earlier gave way to national markets, so national markets are now giving way to world markets. In the past, trade created an international economy; today, factor flows are creating a world economy.

MULTINATIONAL ENTERPRISE AND TRADE THEORY

Part Four is devoted to the theory and consequences of multinational enterprises that span the globe with their production, marketing, and financial operations. These firms are responsible for a large share of international trade and almost all direct foreign investment. Here we indicate only the principal features of multinational enterprises that need to be incorporated into a theory of trade in order to explain actual patterns of trade.

The multinational enterprise is the foremost agent in moving factors of production from one country to another. The intimate link between the trade and investment activities of multinational enterprises points to the need for a synthesis of trade and investment theories.

Multinational enterprises are large firms in oligopolistic industries. Furthermore, the manufacturing multinational enterprises are oligopolists producing and selling differentiated products. Strongly motivated by growth objectives and the maintenance of global market shares and sensitive to each other's behavior, multinational enterprises prefer to compete with new and differentiated products rather than with price. These firms are also characterized by economies of scale in production and organization that support their oligopolistic power.

Horizontally and vertically integrated across national boundaries, much of the international trade of multinational enterprises is among their national units. Indeed, one-third of U.S. exports of manufactures consist of transfers from U.S. parent companies to their foreign affiliates. The presence of intra-enterprise trade raises the question of how sensitive such trade is to costs, prices, and other economic forces. By assuming exchanges between independent sellers and buyers, trade theory has ignored the phenomenon of intrafirm trade.

Multinational enterprises are more technologically intensive than their domestic counterparts. It is no coincidence that the five most R & D-intensive and export-intensive U.S. industries identified by Gruber, Mehta, and Vernon are also the industries most dominated by multinational enterprises. Such companies have the global capability to transfer technology through export goods, directly through licensing, or through production in foreign countries. They have speeded up the international flow of technology, and they are mainly responsible for both the creation and destruction of international technology gaps.

With their international information networks, multinational enterprises have a greater capability than other firms to reduce the ignorance and uncertainty gaps that constrain international trade. Furthermore, their size and the geographical diversification of their operations enables multinational enterprises to assume risks that would turn away other firms. One consequence of this "scanning ability" may be to speed up the product trade cycle: Anticipating foreign imitation of a new product, the multinational enterprise may itself start production in foreign markets. Moreover, it may "short-circuit" the trade cycle by locating capital-intensive production in a capital-poor country, bringing in the capital and other scarce factors, such as technology.

By concentrating on trade only at the national level, economists until recently have left to marketing and management scholars the task of explaining the behavior of the international firm. As long as international trade was largely carried on by intermediaries and producers remained at home, this neglect was not serious. But today international firms have burst the confines of the individual nation-state to carry on their operations throughout the world. In the process, they bring to bear on international markets a mix of productive factors, technological innovation, and entrepreneurial drive. It is no longer possible to understand the trade of the industrial countries (notably the United States) unless full account is taken of the behavior of international firms. The theory of international trade must become part of a broader theory of international economic relations if we are to understand the forces now shaping the world economy.

CONCLUDING OBSERVATIONS ON COMPARATIVE ADVANTAGE

In this and in Chapters 3 and 4, we reviewed several theories that relate comparative advantage to certain attributes of trading countries: factor

TABLE 5-2   Principal Explanations of Comparative Advantage in International Trade

Explanations	Primary Goods		Manufactured Goods		
	Mineral	Agricul-tural	Early Phase	Middle Phase	Late Phase
Factor endowments	●	●			●
Technology gaps		●	●		
Economies of scale	●				●
Production differentiation				●	

proportions, technology, economies of scale, product differentiation, and preference similarity. Each of these theories concentrates on a particular determinant that explains international trade under certain circumstances. Collectively, therefore, the theories offer a comprehensive understanding of international trade. In general, they provide complementary rather than conflicting explanations.[21]

Table 5-2 indicates the *principal* explanations of comparative advantage depending on whether the product is (1) a primary or manufactured product, (2) a mineral or agricultural product (if a primary product), or (3) at an early, middle, or late stage of its life cycle (if a manufactured product).

Primary goods are nondifferentiated commodities whose prices are mainly set in commodity exchanges. Factor endowments are the main determinant of trade in such goods. However, a second-order distinction needs to be drawn between minerals and other (mostly agricultural) commodities. Big oligopolistic firms dominate the production and trade in minerals, such as petroleum, iron ore, bauxite, and copper ore. These firms exploit mineral deposits through large-scale, capital-intensive operations in mining, processing, transportation, and storage. Economies of scale, therefore, are an additional explanation of international trade in minerals. By and large, however, these firms share the same technology, and therefore technology gaps play only a modest role in minerals trade. In contrast, agricultural production is spread among many producers who have no marked economies of scale but who may be growing crops with dissimilar production functions,

---

[21]In a study of 24 countries, Hufbauer calculated significant correlations among the attributes that are featured in different trade theories. See Gary C. Hufbauer, "The Impact of National Characteristics and Technology on the Commodity Composition of Trade in Manufactured Goods," in *The Technology Factor in International Trade*, edited by Raymond Vernon (New York: Columbia University Press, 1970), p. 195.

as pointed out earlier. For that reason technology gaps, along with factor endowments, are a determinant of trade in agricultural goods.

The principal source of comparative advantage in manufactured goods depends on the phase of their life cycles. In the early phase, when the product is new, comparative advantage mainly derives from technology gaps. In the middle phase, when the innovating manufacturer's product has some imitators, product differentiation, sometimes accompanied by economies of scale, becomes the principal explanation of comparative advantage. In the late phase, when the product loses differentiation, factor endowments and economies of scale emerge as the dominant influences on comparative advantage.

Only trade in agricultural commodities and commodity-like manufactures in the late phase of their life cycles takes place in markets that approach the economist's model of perfect competition. In perfectly competitive markets, we can ignore the behavior of individual firms because they have no market power. In contrast, technology gaps, economies of scale, and product differentiation give to the individual firm some degree of monopoly power in its market. It follows, therefore, that an explanation of trade in new and differentiated manufactured products and in minerals must pay attention to the market behavior of individual firms, particularly of multinational corporations.

In the remaining chapters of Part One, we shall describe and evaluate the international trade policies of the United States and other countries. Apart from its purely intellectual appeal to economists, the principal justification of international economic theory is to give government policymakers a related set of concepts, models, and analytical tools that will help them (1) understand what is happening in the world economy, and (2) design policies that will best achieve national and international objectives and goals. Can contemporary trade theory make these contributions to policymakers?

We conclude that the several trade theories focus on different aspects of international trade phenomena and that collectively they offer a much better understanding of those phenomena than any single theory. Indeed, the policymaker today is a notable beneficiary of the renewed activity of international trade theorists. This is not to deny the desirability of a single theory that would incorporate systematically the insights of the several theories of trade and, at the same time, explain the behavior of multinational enterprises.

SUMMARY

1. Technological innovation influences trade through higher factor productivity, production functions, and new products. A new production

function "saves" some or all of the factors of production needed to produce a given level of output as compared with the old production function. The effects of this saving may be neutral, protrade, or antitrade.

2. At any given time, countries may be using different technologies to produce the same products; that is, they have dissimilar production functions (technology gap). Hence, there is no fixed relationship between factor endowments and the *specific* kinds of products a country will export and import. Technological innovation also creates technology gaps in new products, giving rise to international trade cycles.

3. There is also abundant evidence that the United States has a comparative advantage in research-intensive, high-technology products. Technology theories postulate that certain countries (notably the United States) have special advantages as innovators of new products and that there is an "imitation lag" that prevents other countries from immediately duplicating in production the new products of the innovating country. The consequence is a technology gap that affords the innovating country an export monopoly during the period of imitation lag.

4. One of the technology theories postulates a product life cycle model of international trade. In the four-stage model an innovating country (the United States) moves from being the sole exporter of a new product to being an importer of the same product at a future time when the product is no longer new. The factor requirements of a product, as well as its market, change in a systematic fashion during the product life cycle (i.e., new product, product growth, product maturity, and product decline).

5. No matter how useful they may be for economic analysis, the assumptions of perfect international factor mobility or immobility are fictions; neither is found to exist in the real world. Instead we find different degrees of factor mobility that vary among factors, among nations, and over time.

6. A key development in the world economy in recent years has been an extraordinary growth in international flows of management, capital, and technology under the aegis of the multinational enterprise. Both international trade and factor mobility tend to equalize factor prices among nations, pointing to a substitute relationship between the two. But factor movements may also generate trade by stimulating economic growth.

7. Today we are witnessing a process of global economic integration that is being carried forward by a complex mix of trade and factor flows.

8. It is no longer possible to understand the trade of the industrial countries unless full account is taken of the behavior of multinational firms.

9. The several trade theories are more complementary than conflicting, and together they can offer substantial help to government policymakers.

QUESTIONS AND APPLICATIONS

1. Although the terms are frequently used interchangeably, can you draw a meaningful distinction between *technology* as such and *technological innovation*? Illustrate your answer with examples.
2. **(a)** What is the meaning of *imitation lag*?
   (b) Why should the United States have "special advantages" as an innovator of new products?
3. **(a)** What are the four stages of the product life cycle model of international trade?
   (b) How do factor requirements and market conditions change during the four product phases of the product life cycle?
   (c) What are the implications of the product life cycle and Hirsch models for the international trade of the nonindustrial, developing countries?
4. Discuss the following statement: The human-skills and technology theories of trade are intimately related.
5. Explain how both trade and factor movements tend to equalize factor prices among nations. What conditions will prevent a full equalization of factor prices?
6. "The conclusion that trade and factor movements are substitutes derives from the factor endowments theory, which is concerned only with allocational efficiency under static conditions." Explain this statement.
7. Discuss four features of the multinational enterprise and their implications for international trade theory.
8. Do you agree that the different theories of trade are, for the most part, complementary rather than conflicting? Justify your answer.

SELECTED READINGS

Baldwin, Robert E., and J. David Richardson, eds. *International Trade and Finance: Readings.* Boston: Little, Brown, 1981. Part 1.

Bhagwati, Jagdish N., ed. *International Trade: Selected Readings.* Cambridge: MIT Press, 1981. Part 2.

Caves, Richard E., and Harry G. Johnson, eds. *Readings in International Economics.* Homewood, Ill.: Richard D. Irwin, 1968. Part 7.

Ethier, Wilfrid. "National and International Returns to Scale and the Modern Theory of Trade." *American Economic Review,* June 1982.

Giersch, Herbert, ed. *On the Economics of Intra-Industry Trade.* Tubingen: J. C. B. Mohr (Paul Siebeck), 1979.

Hirsch, Seev. *Location of Industry and International Competitiveness.* Oxford: Clarendon Press, 1967.

Leamer, Edward E. *Sources of Comparative Advantage: Theory and Evidence.* Cambridge: MIT Press, 1984.

Linder, S. Burenstam. *An Essay on Trade and Transformation.* New York: John Wiley & Sons, 1961.

Stern, Robert M. "Testing Trade Theories." In *International Trade and Finance,* edited by Peter B. Kenen. Cambridge: Cambridge University Press, 1975.

Vernon, Raymond, ed. *The Technology Factor in International Trade.* New York: Columbia University Press, 1970.

Wells, Louis T., Jr., ed. *The Product Life Cycle and International Trade.* Boston: Harvard Business School, Division of Research, 1972.

Whitman, Marina V. N. *International Trade and Investment: Two Perspectives.* Essays in International Finance, no. 143, Princeton, N.J.: Princeton University Press, 1981.

6

Free Trade and Arguments for Protection

International trade policy can be regarded as the result of the opposing forces of free trade and protection. Before examining the international trade policies of the United States and other countries, therefore, we need an understanding of the rationale for free trade and of the rival arguments for protection. As a policy, protection can use a broad variety of measures that restrict or otherwise distort flows of international trade. Our concern here is not with specific trade barriers, which are treated in the next chapter, but with why governments are inclined to use them in general.

The issue of *free trade* versus *protection* has been in dispute since the eighteenth century; the literature on this controversy is one of the most extensive in the annals of political economy. The arguments are often complex and subtle, although the controversy itself is obvious.

THE CASE FOR FREE TRADE

The principle of comparative advantage demonstrates that for the world as a whole free trade leads to a higher level of output and income than no trade (autarky). Free trade also enables each nation to obtain a higher level of production and consumption than can be obtained in isolation. Under perfect competition, free trade achieves a worldwide allocation of resources that meets the requirements of Pareto optimality: It is impossible to make anyone better off (through reallocation) without making someone else worse off. In the language of Chapter 2, free trade achieves an equality between each country's marginal rate of transformation in production (MRT) and its marginal rate of substitution in consumption (MRS) and the international terms of trade (ITT). In contrast, trade barriers *prevent* this equilibrium condition by creating divergences between the domestic and international prices of tradable goods. Hence, under protection, $MRT = MRS \neq ITT$. It follows, therefore, that trade barriers cause a suboptimal allocation of the world's factors of production and a lower world real income than would exist under free trade.

However, many contemporary economists (unlike their predecessors) are reluctant to support free trade without some reservations. Their qualifications of the free trade doctrine spring from two basic concerns: (1) the departure of actual markets from the conditions of perfect competition, and (2) the absence of any *necessary* correspondence between higher income and higher welfare at both national and international levels.

As we have discussed in earlier chapters, the most widely accepted theory of trade, the Heckscher-Ohlin (H-O) model, rests upon the assumptions of perfect competition: no monopoly or oligopoly; no product differentiation; no internal economies of scale; and no ignorance, uncertainty, or risk. Furthermore, the theory implicitly assumes that external economies and diseconomies do not cause a divergence between private and social benefits and costs, and that market prices truly indicate the full opportunity costs confronting a society.[1] Since these assumptions are only partially matched in actual markets, it follows that free trade will not achieve Pareto optimality and that more trade will not necessarily bring a higher allocative efficiency to national economies or to the world economy.

However, to say that the allocative efficiency of free trade may not be optimal is a poor argument for protection. Rather, it is an argument for direct measures to improve the functioning of competitive markets through antitrust policies that eliminate or restrain monopoly and oligopoly, through improvements in the flow of information to consumers and producers (to reduce ignorance and risk), through taxes and subsidies to remove any divergences between private and social benefits and costs, and through other measures that promote competition.

Actually protection is an ineffectual policy tool for overcoming the defects of imperfect competition as compared with more direct tools. Furthermore, there is little assurance that the trade restrictions actually imposed by a government will add to economic efficiency. When account is taken of protectionist politics, the probability is high that restrictions will *lower* economic efficiency—a policy of throwing out the baby with the bath water. The existence of market imperfections, therefore, has not turned economists into protectionists, although they may argue the desirability of selective restrictions in carefully defined circumstances (the "theory of the

---

[1] External economies exist when a firm (or industry) creates values for society that it cannot sell in a market (such as training workers who subsequently leave the firm for other employment). This situation makes the private value of the firm's output less than its social value. External diseconomies refer to social costs of production (such as pollution) that are not borne by the producer, making private costs less than social costs. In the case of external economies, the firm is producing too little to maximize social value; in the case of external diseconomies, too much.

second best" described later in this chapter). And, because of the possible existence of internal economies of scale as well as external economies, economists have also traditionally recognized (with qualifications) the legitimacy of the infant-industry argument for protection.

A second reason why most economists are reluctant to offer unqualified support of free trade is the question of economic welfare. Even if Pareto optimality were achieved in the allocation of national and world resources, it would not *necessarily* follow that free trade would also optimize national and world *welfare*. One problem is that competitive markets determine not only the prices of goods but also factor prices (incomes). By altering relative prices, free trade also alters income distribution among individuals and groups, both within and between nations. If the last (marginal) dollar of income earned by recipients in all countries provided the same satisfaction (welfare), then free trade under perfect competition would indeed maximize national and world welfare. Unfortunately, there is no objective way to make interpersonal comparisons of welfare. The presumption is strong, of course, that the marginal dollar received by a poor person contributes more welfare than the marginal dollar received by a rich person and, by extension, that poor countries benefit more than rich countries from the marginal income dollar. But in the final analysis this is an ethical judgment, not a scientific one.

The welfare question is hardly a general argument against free trade. A priori, there is no reason to believe that free trade worsens income distribution compared to no or restricted trade. In view of the motivations and political factors that actually determine protectionist policies, one can also be justifiably dubious that governments will select only those restrictions that improve national welfare, to say nothing of world welfare. Protection, therefore, is a singularly inappropriate policy to achieve higher levels of welfare for a group or nation.[2] Protection would sacrifice the gains from economic efficiency to an uncertain (and at times, perverse) welfare effect. More to the point, direct measures to redistribute income are available to all governments in the form of subsidies and taxation.[3]

To sum up, economic theory *cannot* demonstrate that under all circumstances free trade will improve efficiency or enhance economic welfare. In practice, however, most Western economists remain firmly on the side of

---

[2] What happens when governments seek to redistribute income by interfering with the market mechanism is clearly shown by agricultural programs that have promoted self-sufficiency at a cost of lower economic efficiency. A superior approach (granted the desirability of redistributing income to farmers) would be direct income subsidies financed out of general taxation, leaving markets free to allocate agricultural production both within and among nations.

[3] Mechanisms to redistribute income among countries are admittedly primitive compared to domestic mechanisms. There is no international authority to tax the rich and subsidize the poor. But attempts to achieve income redistribution between rich and poor countries via market restrictions (such as international commodity agreements) must reckon with the costs of lower economic efficiency. Direct income transfers avoid those costs.

freer, if not free, trade.[4] They remain skeptical of the capacity of governments to apply selective trade restrictions in such a way as to reach higher levels of economic efficiency or welfare. The history of protection is highly convincing on this score. At the same time, most economists would agree that free trade is not sufficient to achieve optimal world income and welfare but must be coupled with government policies that improve the efficiency of markets, achieve a better income distribution, and promote economic growth.

Strictly speaking, the argument for free trade (like all arguments for economic policies) is a conditional one. It states that *if* a nation wants to attain a higher level of economic efficiency, then it can do so by trading with other nations. But a nation can choose to reject economic efficiency for noneconomic values (such as the preservation of a social group or a way of life against foreign influences) and, in so doing, reject free trade in part or in whole.

Economists have long recognized the legitimacy of the national defense argument for trade protection. Commonly, however, nations have chosen trade protection in ignorance of its economic costs. Only the mythical economic person would argue that economic efficiency should be the exclusive goal of society, but only a fool would argue that economic efficiency does not matter at all.

One last comment is in order. No one, including the most ardent protectionist, opposes specialization and trade among the different regions of a country. And yet, the *economic* argument for free international trade is the same as the argument for unfettered interregional trade. The essential difference between external and internal trade is *political* only: One involves foreigners, the other does not. It is this difference that has nurtured protectionism through the ages; the principal ally of protectionism is economic nationalism.[5]

THE CASE FOR PROTECTION

Although in most circumstances the welfare of a country as a whole is reduced by import protection, the welfare of the specific factors of production associated with a protected industry will increase because of the income-redistribution effect.[6] In seeking protection, therefore, individual producers

---

[4] A survey of 100 economists in the United States on the proposition "Tariffs and import quotas reduce general economic welfare" obtained the following responses: *generally agree*—81, *agree with provisions*—16, *generally disagree*—3. See J. R. Kearl et al., "A Confusion of Economists?" *American Economic Review*, May 1979, p. 30.

[5] As we shall observe in Chapter 25, economic nationalism also nurtures resistance to foreign enterprise—another form of protectionism.

[6] See Figure 7-2. In the longer run, when there is time for factors to move into the protected industry, marginal factor returns in that industry will tend to equal marginal factor returns

and labor unions are trying to improve their own well-being. Hence, any attempt to lower or eliminate existing protection is stubbornly resisted, and continuing pressure is applied to national governments to initiate new protection. Frank recognition of the fact that certain groups would lose with a free trade policy is essential to any understanding of the political strength of protectionism. Indeed, the conflict between particular interests and the national interest is the dominant feature of the persistent controversy over free trade and protection.

In presenting their case to the public and government, protectionists would not get far if they argued in terms of their own private gain. Thus, all their arguments assert that protection benefits the national interest. In so many words, protectionists maintain that "what is good for my industry is also good for my country."[7] In defending this proposition they are usually supported by the nationalistic attitudes of their fellow citizens.

The arguments against free trade try to show that (1) its advantages are outweighed by its shortcomings; (2) the interdependence of nations implicit in free trade subjects national economies to uncertainties inherent in sudden changes in the policies of other nations that often cause serious dislocations, if not losses, far greater than the benefits to be derived from a free trade policy; and (3) the price system and perfect competition underlying the theory of free trade are, at best, only partially true in the real world, where prices and production are subjected to controls and rigidities that contribute to what has been referred to as a *disequilibrium system* (i.e., a system in which restrictions on consumers or producers are the tools of adjustment rather than price).

In the course of time many ingenious pleas have been advanced in direct support of protection. The pleas have been based on a variety of arguments, none of which possess unqualified economic validity. A few of these arguments rationalize short-term gains at the expense of long-term national benefits; others follow exactly the opposite approach; most of the remaining arguments have only partial economic validity or are completely fallacious, drawing their strength mainly from their engaging emotional mass appeal. The long series of arguments for protection may be classified into four categories: (1) fallacious arguments, (2) questionable arguments, (3) qualified arguments, and (4) sophisticated arguments.

FALLACIOUS ARGUMENTS FOR PROTECTION

Fallacious arguments for protection rely on plausibility or mass emotional appeal rather than economic logic.

---

in other (unprotected) industries. The ultimate beneficiary of protection is the factor (or factors) used intensively in the protected industry; other factors suffer a loss in welfare.

[7] For this reason, most protectionist arguments commit the *fallacy of composition:* What is true of the part is necessarily true of the whole.

Keep-Money-at-Home Argument

The proponents of this argument claim that when domestic residents buy imported goods, the country gets the goods and the foreigner gets the money. When, on the other hand, the residents buy domestic goods, it is argued that the country keeps both the goods and the money. Hence the country that prevents imports is richer for doing so.

The utter fallacy of this argument is rooted in the crudest form of mercantilistic theory, which maintained that money is wealth in itself. Money, as such, is a means of exchange. Money paid for imports must return sooner or later either in payment for exports or as investment, since it has no redemption value except in the country of its issue.

Home Market Argument

This argument claims that the domestic producer has a right to the domestic market and that by reducing or eliminating imports, more goods will be produced at home, more jobs will be created, and increased domestic activity will be the result. The fallacy of this argument stems from the fact that any shift from imports to domestic production is ultimately offset by a contraction of production for export. Unless a country is willing to give its goods away, it can only continue to export by continuing to import. Thus, the shift from foreign to domestic sources of supply does not in any way increase real purchasing power. In fact, the home market argument leads to a less efficient economy and a *decline* in real purchasing power.

Equalization-of-Costs Argument

Some protectionists have favored the so-called "scientific method of tariff making" that is intended to equalize the costs of production between foreign and domestic producers and to neutralize any advantage the foreigner may have over the domestic producer in lower taxes, cheaper labor, or other costs. This argument allegedly entails "fair competition," not the exclusion of imports. When, however, by reason of actual cost structure or artificial measures, costs of production become identical, the very basis of international trade disappears. The logical consequence of this pseudoscientific method is the elimination of trade between nations. Thus, the equalization-of-production-costs argument for protection is utterly fallacious and is one of the most deceitful ever advanced in support of protection.

A close examination of the equalization-of-costs argument reveals the presence of many problems. Producers in any country have different and constantly changing costs for the same products. Whose costs are to serve as a frame of reference?

If we aim for protection of *all* domestic producers against *all* foreign producers, we must equalize the lowest foreign costs with the highest costs of the least efficient domestic producers. To accomplish this, a very high duty is required to overcome the extreme cost differential. Domestic prices to the consumer must rise to the high level of the domestic marginal producer's cost. The efficient domestic producer will reap an extra monopoly profit, and the domestic consumer will be forced to subsidize the highest form of inefficiency.

In addition, the literal enforcement of such a policy entails considerable administrative difficulties in the collection of the necessary cost information for duty adjustments. This seems to be hardly worthwhile when the result can only be the prevention of imports, the ultimate elimination of trade, and the impairment of the country's standard of living—surely a misconception of the scientific approach, to say the least.

Despite these objections, a tariff provision to equalize the costs of production was actually incorporated in the United States Tariff Acts of 1922 and 1930. This provision, however, has been enforced only in a few instances.

In recent years, the equalization-of-cost argument has become the "fairness" argument. Its supporters allege that all they want is fair competition, that is, the equalization of wages and other factors affecting domestic and foreign costs. Then domestic firms would be able to compete against foreign firms on a "level playing field." Carried to an extreme, the fairness argument would block all international trade. It is nothing more than the old equalization-of-cost argument after a cosmetic face-lift.

Low Wage Argument

Some protectionists claim that a high-wage country cannot afford to trade with low-wage or "pauper labor" countries without risking a reduction in its own wages through competition with the low foreign wage level and thereby jeopardizing its standard of living. They assert further that to protect its workers from the competition of low-paid foreign workers, a high-wage country must impose a tariff duty on cheap goods that are imported from the low-wage countries.

More fundamentally, it is alleged that a country can only *lose* from trade with a low-wage country, since that country can undersell it. This argument has several weaknesses. First, we may ask how any trade is possible if the domestic country is undersold in *all* products for in that case it could not export anything nor, therefore, import anything. If only *some* products are in question, then the argument is absurd, since trade obviously requires that one country undersell the other country in some goods, and vice versa. Second, it must be pointed out that wages may be low and unit costs high when productivity is low. Thus, there is no necessary connection between low wages and low costs. Third, the low wage argument must bow to the logic of comparative advantage. As long as cost ratios are dissimilar, trade is profitable between countries regardless of absolute wage levels.

The proponents of the low wage argument are wrong when they suggest that high prices necessarily result from high wages and low prices from low wages. High wages in the United States are a consequence of the high productivity of American workers, who are aided in their tasks by the availability of raw materials, massive capital equipment, advanced technology, sophisticated management, and an elaborate infrastructure of communication, transportation, power, and other facilities. This high productivity explains both the high American standard of living and the ability of American exporters to compete effectively with foreign producers who pay far lower wages.[8] In light of the low-wage argument of U.S. protectionists, it is ironic that many producers in developing countries demand protection against U.S. products on the grounds that their (low-wage) industries cannot compete against the highly productive American industries!

It is true that domestic industries whose productivity is relatively low may find that high wages raise their costs above foreign costs. But such a situation is not a logical argument for protection. Rather, it is a signal for a reallocation of labor and capital to other lines of production that have a comparative advantage vis-à-vis foreign production. Such a reallocation occurs all the time as a result of domestic interregional competition, as witness, for example, the migration of the U.S. textile industry from New England to the South. It is the fear of a painful adjustment to import competition that really motivates the proponents of the low wage argument rather than the unlikely danger of a general deterioration of the country's standard of living. Import restrictions, however, are neither the most desirable nor the only solution to this problem. What is needed is government assistance that will facilitate an orderly redeployment of capital and workers so as to minimize adjustment costs while at the same time preserving the benefits of international trade.

Prevention-of-Injury Argument

The prevention-of-injury argument is designed to safeguard the vulnerability of an economy to increased imports subsequent to contemplated tariff concessions or to concessions already granted under trade agreements. The advocates of this argument proclaim their willingness to reduce and maintain low tariffs, provided that in so doing no domestic industry or producer is threatened by excessive imports resulting from such low rates of duties. Any contemplated concession must not reduce an existing rate to a preestimated low point, or *peril point,* that would jeopardize domestic producers. In addition, when previously reduced rates begin to threaten domestic producers, there should be an escape mechanism, or *escape clause,* to permit the restoration of higher rates or the tightening of quota controls.

On the surface, this argument sounds reasonable and implies an attitude of moderation. What this argument means in actual practice, how-

---

[8] Because of high worker productivity, the highest wages in the United States are generally found in the export industries, such as aerospace, electrical machinery, and chemicals. How, then, could anyone explain the existence of American exports if lower wages were the sole index of competitive advantage?

ever, is the elimination of international competition under comparative advantage when such competition threatens to divert a portion of the home market away from domestic producers, regardless of changed market conditions and technology at home and abroad.

The prevention-of-injury argument is closely related to the home market and equalization-of-production-costs arguments. It is an argument that is likely to encourage the perpetuation of static and regressive industries.

QUESTIONABLE ARGUMENTS FOR PROTECTION

Certain arguments for protection, although not entirely fallacious, represent an inferior policy or easily lend themselves to abuse.

Employment Argument

The basis for this argument is that the imposition of a tariff or other form of import restriction in periods of unemployment will reduce imports and generate home production. Increased domestic production in turn will increase employment and national income. Furthermore, since imports (like savings) cause a leakage in the domestic income stream, a reduction of imports will generate an even greater amount of domestic expenditure via the income multiplier.[9]

Another version of the employment argument asserts that widespread unemployment justifies any sort of production, regardless of comparative advantage, since it will make a net addition to a country's national income. Thus, a country will benefit by restricting imports and using idle factors to produce similar goods at home—the opportunity cost of imports is the exports that must be exchanged for them, whereas the opportunity cost of new domestic production is zero. Hence, international specialization and trade must give way to self-sufficiency when unemployment arises in the domestic economy.

This argument was especially persuasive during the Great Depression of the 1930s, but it rests upon several questionable assumptions: (1) full employment is the overriding national economic objective; (2) international trade must be sacrificed to attain full employment; and (3) the international consequences of a domestic full-employment policy can be safely ignored. We now turn to a brief evaluation of these assumptions.

First, employment for the sake of employment cannot be a sound national objective. Full employment is most productive when the factors of production are allocated in accordance with comparative advantage. In that way each factor is engaged in production in which its productivity is highest.

---

[9] See Chapter 15 for a discussion of the income multiplier.

Full employment is a means to the higher objective of national welfare, and this is maximized only when productivity cannot be raised by shifting factors of production from one economic activity to another. When imports are curtailed to afford opportunities for domestic employment, the losses occasioned by a lesser degree of international specialization must be set against any gains in national production.

Second, even if the gains in national production are greater than the losses brought about by the decline in international specialization, the policy of sacrificing international trade to increase domestic employment is not in the national interest, for there are other ways of stimulating employment that do not require the restriction of trade. An anticyclical employment policy should place main reliance on government fiscal and monetary policies that feed the inadequate stream of purchasing power. Not only will such policies alleviate unemployment in the domestic economy, but by sustaining or increasing imports they will also benefit foreign countries.

Third, the policy of curtailing imports to stimulate domestic employment is never in the interest of the community of nations. Actually that policy amounts to exporting unemployment to other nations, since the decline in imports will depress foreign economies. Moreover, foreign countries can retaliate by restricting their own imports. As a consequence, international relations become embittered, international trade spirals downward, and few countries are better off in terms of employment while many are much worse off in terms of economic welfare. This sequence took place to an unfortunate extent in the early thirties.

While condemning the policy of exporting one's unemployment, we must also recognize the fact that few nations are capable of overcoming massive unemployment by the use of fiscal and monetary policies alone unless international economic cooperation is forthcoming. Such policies tend to increase imports, yet at the same time exports may be falling because of recession abroad. Few nations have the reserves to finance the resulting gap between their exports and imports until recovery sets in abroad.[10] When, however, nations—particularly the major trading nations—cooperate with each other by extending credit and by harmonizing their domestic recovery measures, it may be possible for them to restore employment without seriously curtailing trade.

The foregoing remarks apply to *cyclical* unemployment that results from a deflationary gap in effective demand that cuts across all sectors of the economy. When protection is advocated as a remedy for *structural* unemployment, then the employment argument becomes even more questionable.

---

[10] In a floating-rate system, expansive monetary and fiscal policies to restore employment during a worldwide recession cause a depreciation of a country's currency unless other countries are following similar policies. The example of France in 1981–1982 is instructive in this regard. Deliberate *overdevaluation* of a currency to remedy unemployment is a beggar-my-neighbor policy of exporting unemployment, akin to import restrictions.

Structural unemployment occurs when the composition of a nation's output or the quality and supply of its factors of production fail to adapt to new patterns of demand and competition. That is to say, the *structure* of the economy is no longer suited to changing markets. Declining industries and regions make their appearance, and workers gradually lose their jobs while the rest of the economy is growing. The basic disturbance causing structural unemployment may originate at home, abroad (as specific export markets dry up or foreign competitors enter domestic markets [import competition]), or both at home and abroad.[11]

When import competition appears to be causing structural unemployment, workers and management in the affected industry are quick to demand that government curtail imports by higher tariffs, quotas, or other means. This protectionist solution attempts to preserve the status quo at the cost of losing the benefits of international specialization. If no other solution to the problem of structural unemployment were possible, protection would be justifiable as a way of utilizing labor and capital that would otherwise stand idle. But this is not the case. Basically, what is needed is a reallocation of productive factors, shifting the factors currently used in declining industries to expanding industries.

The capacity of an economy to adapt to change and thereby avoid or minimize structural imbalances is dependent primarily on the mobility of its factors of production and its overall rate of growth. When labor and capital move quickly out of declining industries into growing industries, then structural unemployment is transitional rather than prolonged. Mobility will be enhanced if the economy as a whole is growing, generating new opportunities for employment and capital investment. When, on the other hand, labor does not shift easily from one job to another or from one place to another, then structural unemployment may endure for a generation or more. Immobility is further intensified by a slowly growing economy.

All economies suffer from factor immobility, but it is most pervasive in underdeveloped countries, where economic, social, and cultural conditions favor stability over change. For such countries import protection may be necessary to give them time to transform their economies, but the ultimate solution is to develop a capacity to grow and adjust to change. For developed countries, however, protection is not a reasonable alternative to measures that are aimed directly at increasing labor and capital mobility. In the last analysis, the cause of structural unemployment lies in a failure to adapt to technological and other changes. As we have stressed earlier, the world economy is dynamic and nations can obtain the full advantages of inter-

---

[11] Structural unemployment in the United States mainly results from changes within the economy, such as the automation of industry, the mechanization of agriculture, the migration of industry among regions, and the pervasive shift in demand toward services and away from physical goods. In recent years, however, structural unemployment in several industries has been intensified by a failure to compete effectively with foreign industries. The automotive and steel industries are leading examples. See Chapter 9 for a discussion of international competition in the contemporary world economy.

national specialization only by responding quickly to new market opportunities and competitive challenges.

Antidumping Argument

The dumping of goods in an importing country at prices below those prevailing in the exporting country may be beneficial or harmful, depending upon circumstances. If dumping is persistent, buyers in the importing country reap a continuous benefit that results from lower prices for foreign goods. If the importing country had no domestic industry competing with the dumped product, there is, of course, no argument for protection. If, on the other hand, such an industry exists, domestic producers are in no different position than if the dumping price resulted from a normal cost advantage in the exporting country. The fact that there is some unfairness to domestic producers in the situation is not a valid reason for protection since the nation as a whole is benefited.

When dumping is sporadic and is intended to harass a competing domestic industry or put it out of business in order to raise prices afterwards, dumping becomes undesirable. To prevent such *predatory dumping,* action is necessary. High protection that precludes the possibility of predatory dumping, however, inflicts upon the domestic economy a permanently higher cost that is totally unjustified. By administrative action or by antidumping duties, predatory dumping can be prevented if and when it occurs by making its practice costly and ineffective. Unfortunately, this *limited* use of antidumping measures is violated in practice: Governments do not distinguish between persistent and predatory dumping, and they frequently utilize devices in the name of antidumping that amount to sheer protection.

Bargaining-and-Retaliation Argument

It has been argued that a country with a protective tariff is in a better position to bargain with other countries for concessions on its exports than is a country that has nothing to offer in return. It follows, therefore, that a free trade (or low-tariff) country should adopt some form of protection to be in a bargaining position.

The logic of this argument is strong and such a policy may work out in actual practice. It does not, however, necessarily follow that the argument has economic validity. A free trade country that resorts to protection for purposes of bargaining sacrifices the benefits of international specialization. Furthermore, once protection is introduced, domestic industries develop behind its shield and become entrenched, exerting pressures upon their government when the time comes to give up such protection. Experience proves that this kind of pressure is usually most successful in preventing the return to freer trade, and therefore the country will, in all probability, become permanently committed to protection. Similarly, a country adopting a tariff for retaliation purposes is, so to speak, adding insult to injury by depriving itself of the benefits from unhindered imports. More to the point, retaliation can easily breed counterretaliation and a general worsening of trade relations rather than an abandonment of the measure that provoked the retaliation. To conclude, the bargaining-and-retaliation argument involves a certain loss and an uncertain gain and presents ample opportunity for abuse.

Reciprocity Argument

Closely related to the bargaining-and-retaliation argument is the reciprocity argument, which has been advocated by some members of the U.S. Congress in recent years. Whereas the former would impose higher tariffs (or other forms of protection) to gain bargaining leverage with other countries in negotiating reductions of their import barriers, the latter would have the United States impose *new* restrictions on imports from individual foreign countries unless those countries lowered their import barriers so as to give access to their markets "comparable" to their access to the U.S. market. The bargaining-and-retaliation argument holds out a carrot (lower import barriers) to get import concessions from other countries; the reciprocity argument waves a stick (higher import barriers) to get import concessions from other countries.

The reciprocity argument is beguiling because it appears to support freer trade. Starting from the premise that the U.S. market is more open to imports than foreign markets, it is alleged that the purpose of reciprocity is to gain access to foreign markets comparable to that afforded by the U.S. market. Only if a foreign country refused to grant this "reasonable" request for "equal access" by lowering its barriers against U.S. goods would the United States retaliate with higher protection against that country's goods. When the argument is closely examined, however, it becomes evident that its application would almost certainly lead to higher U.S. protection and counterretaliation by other countries. Indeed, this argument is more questionable than the bargaining-and-retaliation argument because it involves discrimination among countries as well as higher protection.

We shall encounter the reciprocity argument again in Chapter 9 when we examine U.S. trade policy. Here we merely point out two questionable aspects. First, what does "comparable access" mean? How would it be measured? The traditional measures are the general level of tariffs and the portion of a nation's market covered by nontariff trade barriers. By such measures, the United States is *not* more open than Japan and the European Community: Access is about the same. What supporters of reciprocity appear to have in mind as *the* measure of comparable access is the size of any U.S. trade deficit with a foreign country, Japan being foremost in mind. But this measure is absurd, for a country experiences import trade balances with some countries at the same time as it experiences export balances with other countries. Does a U.S. export balance with EC countries indicate that the United States does not offer them equal access to the U.S. market?

Second, almost certainly some countries would not be able to make concessions to satisfy the requirements of equal opportunity. The consequent imposition of new U.S. import restrictions on those countries' goods would trigger counterretaliation that would close off market opportunities for U.S. exports—a result directly opposite to that intended by the supporters of reciprocity.

Third, the unilateral imposition of higher U.S. import restrictions would incur all the costs of higher protection.

QUALIFIED ARGUMENTS FOR PROTECTION

Some arguments for protection find their justification either in noneconomic considerations, such as national defense, or in the expectation of long-term economic benefits that will more than compensate for the immediate cost of protection.

National Security Argument

It is argued that a nation dependent on foreign sources of supply is in a particularly vulnerable position during a war. The harrowing experience of the United Kingdom in both World Wars is cited as proof of this assertion— twice the German submarine blockade almost brought that country to its knees by cutting off imports of food and raw materials. This is, of course, a political or military argument rather than an economic one, but it has many economic implications. Its proper evaluation requires not only a careful forecast of the probable nature of a future war but a searching study of the relationship between economic strength and military capacity as well. For example, if another world war promises destruction of everyone's productive facilities within a few hours, then it is existing military strength that counts and the military argument for economic self-sufficiency falls by the wayside.

Few would disagree with the need to maintain an "adequate" national defense. Even Adam Smith, the venerable father of free trade, wrote in 1776 that "defense is much more important than opulence."[12] The problem lies in defining the specific requirements of national defense and the proper way to meet those requirements. Otherwise the national security argument may be used to justify complete self-sufficiency or the protection of *any* industry. Since most producers consider their activities essential to the defense of their country, the national security argument is particularly subject to abuse. In the United States, manufacturers of peanuts, candles, thumbtacks, umbrella frames, gloves, and many other products of ordinary consumption have all asked for protection on grounds of national security.

Today military experts are inclined to view future wars in terms of

---

[12] Adam Smith, *The Wealth of Nations* (New York: Random House, 1937), p. 431.

"adequate strength in a constant state of readiness" rather than in terms of "potential production capacity." If this is the true situation, then the protection of "strategic" domestic industries can make no contribution to national security. Apart from this consideration, direct subsidies are better policy tools than import restrictions to maintain defense industries: They are more precise in their effects, more subject to review, and less costly to the nation.[13]

In conclusion, there is no assurance that greater economic self-sufficiency will enhance a nation's military power, and by the same token there is no justification for denying out of hand the compatibility of free trade and a nation's ability to defend itself against armed aggression.

Infant Industry Argument

In its traditional form, the infant industry argument asserts that a new industry which has a potential comparative advantage may not get started in a country unless it is given temporary protection against foreign competition. Most often, the argument stresses the necessity of protected domestic markets that will offer an opportunity for economies of scale in production. Regarding the example presented in Figure 4-2, it would be argued that protection would enable local manufacturers to produce at least 0–G automobiles at a unit cost of 0–C, thereby making them competitive with foreign manufacturers who already enjoy economies of scale. Aside from economies of scale, protection would also afford local producers the time to improve their skills in management, production, marketing, and the application of technology. Once competitive strength was built up, protection would be abandoned for free trade.

The infant industry argument is associated with Alexander Hamilton, the first Secretary of the Treasury of the United States, and Frederick List, a German economist who lived in this country as a political refugee. Alexander Hamilton published his famous *Report on Manufacturers* in 1791, urging the use of tariffs to foster the growth of manufacturing and to strengthen the American economy, which was then predominantly agricultural. He contended that the vast resources of the country could be advantageously developed to compete with foreign industries that held a vast lead due to a prior start; that even though time and ingenuity could ultimately bring about such a development, governmental aid and promotion would speed up the process; and that the provision of governmental assistance would constitute only a temporary departure from the free trade doctrine, since it would soon bring about a more secure and steady demand for the surplus produce of the soil.[14]

---

[13] Because subsidies do not raise the price of the product in question, they avoid the consumption loss of tariffs or import quotas; they do, however, involve a production loss. (See Chapter 7 for a discussion of consumption and production losses due to protection.) The United States subsidizes its merchant marine for reasons of national security.

[14] Isaac Asher, *International Trade, Tariff and Commercial Policies* (Homewood, Ill.: Richard D. Irwin, 1948), Chapter 4.

Frederick List's historical approach to the question of free trade versus protection led him to the general conclusion that free trade is a cosmopolitan concept that is not necessarily in the best interest of a country in an intermediate stage of economic development.[15] Such a developing country could not readily develop new industries without temporary protection.

Economists have long accepted the *theoretical* validity of the infant industry argument, recognizing that the theory of trade is a static analysis that abstracts from economies of scale. On the other hand, they have raised many questions with regard to its practical application.

First, it is not at all self-evident that an infant industry requires protection to get started. After all, many new enterprises are able to compete with well-entrenched older enterprises *within* a country under conditions of free trade. Some of these new ventures may even displace the less-dynamic older ones through better management, product innovation, quick response to market opportunities, and the like. Why should international competition be any different? If the long-run outlook of a true infant industry is so good, why should domestic entrepreneurs need protection? After all, they can capitalize early losses as part of their initial investment, and as long as the eventual return will cover this investment at a satisfactory profit, they should go ahead. If the response to this line of reasoning is that a country lacks the necessary local entrepreneurs, then the remedy is not protection as such but rather state enterprise (assuming the government has the necessary entrepreneurial talents) or the attraction of foreign entrepreneurs.[16]

Second, it is most difficult for a government to identify an industry that deserves infant industry protection. The search for an industry that has a potential comparative advantage requires, in the words of one writer, "the skill of the engineer, the brain of the economist, and the audacity of the entrepreneur."[17] In light of historical experience, the probability of a mistake would certainly be very high. One illustration is the U.S. woolen-worsted industry. Started in the early years of this country as an infant industry, it must still be protected against import competition and shows no signs of being able to overcome its comparative disadvantage.

This last example indicates that a mistake tends to become irreversible. Once a new industry is protected, the pressure of vested interests prevents the removal of protection even (or especially) when it becomes evident that the industry will not be competitive. *Temporary* protection usually turns into *permanent* protection. The result is a misallocation of resources that thwarts rather than promotes economic development.

Third, even if the proper choice of an infant industry is made by a government, it does not necessarily follow that import protection is the best

---

[15] Frederick List, *The National System of Political Economy* (London: Longmans, Green & Co., 1922).

[16] Protection may be used to attract foreign entrepreneurs. See Chapter 24.

[17] John P. Powelson, *Latin America: Today's Economic and Social Revolution* (New York: McGraw-Hill, 1964), p. 198.

way to promote that industry. In particular, direct subsidies have several advantages over tariffs. For one thing, subsidies are less likely to end up as permanent protection, because they are dependent on annual appropriations. Protectionists oppose subsidies for this very reason, but manufacturers who honestly seek only infant industry protection should have no objection to them.

Although internal economies of scale are most often cited as the rationale for infant industry protection, a stronger case rests on *external* economies. Suppose the industry in question would powerfully stimulate the growth of other industries (and the economy in general) through its research and development activities, its training of managers and workers whose skills are transferable to other industries, its assistance to suppliers, and in other ways. Such an industry that generates many backward and forward linkages with other industries would have a social value greater than its private value. But since entrepreneurs could not retain this extra social value, they might not start the industry without protection of some sort. In this situation, protection would eliminate the disparity between private and social values and thereby improve the allocation of the country's resources. However, the practical application of protection to "strategic" industries encounters all of the difficulties already mentioned plus the added difficulty of identifying and measuring external benefits. The mistakes made by several developing countries in granting infant industry protection to supposedly strategic industries such as steel, chemicals, and automobiles testify to the perils of policy in this area.

To conclude, the infant industry argument is theoretically sound, especially in regard to external economies. But the difficulties of practical application ensure that infant industry protection often becomes permanent protection, with all its attendant costs. It should also be evident that the infant industry argument does not apply to industrial countries such as the United States.

Diversification Argument

The diversification argument for protection is actually two arguments that commonly masquerade as one. One argument urges import protection as a means to bring about a diversification of *exports* so as to lessen instability in export income. The second argument proposes import protection as a means to achieve diversification in the *domestic economy* and thereby promote economic growth. Both arguments are put forth mainly by representatives of the nonindustrial, developing nations.

The *diversification-for-export-stability* argument proceeds from the dependence of many developing countries on one or two agricultural or mineral products for most of their export income. This "overspecialization" makes such countries highly sensitive to supply or demand shifts in a single export product. Furthermore, it is widely accepted that primary commodities experience wide cyclical fluctuations in price because of low price elasticities of supply and demand.[18] In this context, therefore, the export stability argument becomes an argument for the substitution of manufactured exports for primary exports via import protection that fosters the development of domestic industry.

Theoretically, the diversification-for-export-stability argument derives its validity from a possible divergence of private and social values in a world of change and uncertainty. When private costs do not fully reflect social costs, then the gains from higher economic efficiency may be more than offset by long-run losses due to economic disruptions caused by dependence on foreign markets. The policy application of this argument, however, is fraught with difficulties (mainly, there is the problem of choosing the proper diversification mix and the means to achieve it). These difficulties tend to make import protection an ineffective policy tool compared with export subsidies and other measures of direct export promotion. Indeed, protection has a qualified validity *only* when export diversification requires the prior development of new industries to produce goods that are presently being imported by the country in question. Thus, the diversification-for-export-stability argument for protection is really a version of the infant industry argument that emphasizes export stability rather than economies of scale.

The *diversification-for-domestic-growth* argument rests upon the doctrine of "balanced" economic growth, which asserts the necessity for a simultaneous or parallel development of all industries throughout the economy.[19] This argument, therefore, may be used to justify a policy of general import substitution that cuts across all categories of industrial products. Lacking the specific criteria of the traditional infant industry argument, the diversification-for-domestic-growth argument lends itself to easy abuse by protectionists. At its extreme, it closely resembles the argument for autarky in its real consequences.

Following World War II, many developing countries, especially in Latin America, adopted indiscriminate policies of import substitution under the banner of economic growth. Although these policies did achieve varying degrees of industrial diversification, they did so only in the form of many high-cost industries that will require indefinite protection to survive. Furthermore, these noncompetitive industries can make no contribution to the expansion of industrial exports. By discarding all considerations of comparative advantage in headlong pursuit of industrialization, these countries have gratuitously forsaken the gains from international specialization. In practice, therefore, the diversification-for-domestic-growth argument represents a highly questionable extension of the infant industry argument. Unless diversification is introduced with extreme care, the national loss in economic efficiency (to say nothing of the international loss) brought about

---

[18] The export problems of the developing countries are explored in Chapter 21.

[19] In opposition, the doctrine of "unbalanced" economic growth emphasizes the need to concentrate on key or strategic industries that will stimulate general economic development. This doctrine is consistent with the traditional infant industry argument.

Chapter 6 – Free Trade and Arguments for Protection

by the sacrifice of international specialization may turn out to be greater than the realized gains of economic growth.

SOPHISTICATED ARGUMENTS FOR PROTECTION

This section looks at two arguments that may justify import restrictions under certain conditions: the terms-of-trade argument (optimum tariff) and the theory of the second best. Strictly speaking, they are not arguments for protection. The first is an argument for the exploitation of a national monopsony (or monopoly) position; the second is an argument for the imposition of a tariff as a second-best policy when the first-best policy (free trade) is not possible. We call these arguments "sophisticated" because they appear in the formidable literature of economic theory rather than in the mouths of protectionists.

Terms-of-Trade Argument and the Optimum Tariff

The terms-of-trade argument rests upon the proposition that at least part of a duty is absorbed by foreign suppliers when the price elasticity of import supply is less than infinite and the price elasticity of import demand is greater than zero. Given these elasticity conditions, the imposition of a duty raises the domestic price of the import good by less than the amount of the duty as foreign suppliers lower their prices in an attempt to maintain sales in the tariff-levying country (see Figure 7-1).[20] Hence, that country experiences an improvement in its terms of trade: The price it pays foreigners for the import good falls while the price it charges foreigners for its export goods remains the same.

The national gain from an improvement in the terms of trade, however, must be set against the national loss resulting from the trade effect of the tariff. In terms of Figure 7-2, the *net* national gain is the sum of the revenue effect (d) and the income-redistribution effect (r) *minus* the loss in consumers' surplus due to the negative trade effect (l and c). This analysis leads to the concept of the *optimum tariff* that maximizes the net national gain.

At one extreme, when the *entire* duty is absorbed by foreign suppliers (perfectly inelastic supply), the *net* national gain equals the revenue effect, which is fully traceable to an improvement in the terms of trade. Since the duty does not affect the price paid by domestic consumers, there is no change in consumers' surplus and the trade effect is zero. In this situation the optimal tariff rate is infinite; the tariff-levying country is a pure *monopsonist*

---

[20] The reader may wish to read the section "Economic Effects of Tariffs" in Chapter 7 before going on with this treatment of the optimum tariff.

that can continually improve its terms of trade by raising the duty while importing the same volume of the commodity in question.

At the other extreme, when import supply is perfectly elastic, the optimum tariff rate is zero. In this situation a country cannot improve its terms of trade by imposing a duty because the entire duty is absorbed by domestic consumers who pay a postduty price that is higher than the preduty price by the full amount of the duty. The outcome is depicted in Figure 7-2. Between the two extremes, the optimum tariff rate will depend on the price elasticities of import demand and import supply. In general, the more elastic the import demand and the more inelastic the import supply, the higher the optimum duty rate. However, this rate will be less than the rate that maximizes an improvement in the terms of trade because of the negative trade effect.

The terms-of-trade argument is not really an argument for protection, nor has it been used by protectionists. We have seen that the optimal tariff is highest when there is no protection effect, hardly a comforting thought to domestic producers who are anxious to keep out imports. When applied to imports, the terms-of-trade argument is rather an argument for the exploitation of monopsonistic power. It can be applied equally well to exports to justify an export tariff that improves the terms of trade by exploiting *monopolistic* power. The optimal tariff provides a gain to the tariff-levying country by causing the rest of the world to suffer a loss; and insofar as the optimal tariff lowers trade, it causes a net loss to the world economy.

Although the theoretical argument for an optimal tariff is valid (given its assumptions), its application in policy raises serious administrative, economic, and political questions. For one thing, the determination of the optimal tariff requires a knowledge of the relevant elasticities, which are likely to change over time. Their accurate measurement and the quick adjustment of the optimum rate to elasticity changes run far beyond the capabilities of economic analysts and tariff administrators. For another, an optimal tariff policy would transfer income from the poor to the rich countries that have monopsonistic power because of their huge markets.[21] This consequence would undercut the foreign aid programs of those same rich countries. Finally, an optimal tariff policy would probably effect its own failure by inciting retaliation by countries faced with a deterioration in their terms of trade. After a series of retaliations and counterretaliations, all trading nations would end up on lower indifference curves.

The Theory of the Second Best

The theory of the second best may be traced to the proposition that free trade will *not* necessarily achieve Pareto optimality in the worldwide al-

---

[21] A poor country, or organized group of poor countries, might have *monopoly* power in the export of some primary products, such as coffee and petroleum. An exploitation of this power by export tariffs or other means would transfer income from the rich to the poor countries. In the 1970s, OPEC (Organization of Petroleum Exporting Countries) used monopoly power to force up the price of petroleum exports.

location of production and consumption when private monopoly, government policies, and externalities create divergences between private and social costs and benefits. If policymakers cannot eliminate these divergences so as to pursue a first-best policy (free trade), then a second-best policy may require the introduction of new distortions (such as tariffs) that will neutralize or offset the existing distortions.[22]

The theory of the second best is applicable to all economic policy, not only trade policy. It recognizes that at any given time policymakers may confront many constraints that run beyond the constraints assumed by the theory of trade (factor supplies, tastes, technology, and foreign supply or demand conditions). Given the existence of constraints such as subsidies and taxes, the optimum values of other variables in the economy will differ from their values in perfectly competitive markets. That is to say, there will be a second-best optimum. The theory of the second best is pertinent to policymaking whenever market prices that guide the actions of producers and consumers fail to indicate the real opportunity costs of the economy and thereby cause discrepancies between private and social values.

The theory of the second best may justify *selective* import protection when price distortions make the private costs of particular domestic producers higher than the social costs to the country as a whole. Consider, for example, the cost effects of a selective excise tax imposed on a domestic producer. The tax makes the private costs (which include the tax) exceed the social costs (which do not include the tax, because it is an internal transfer from producers to the government of the same country). Hence, domestic production of the taxed product is less and imports of that product are greater than they would be in the absence of the tax. Since the country is obtaining additional imports at a higher social cost than if it were to obtain additional domestic output, the imposition of a "compensatory" import duty that would restrict imports and permit the expansion of domestic production would add to the nation's welfare up to the point where the marginal social costs of imports and domestic production became equal. Further restriction of imports beyond that point would lower the nation's welfare.

Probably the single most important application of the theory of the second best is to customs unions and free trade areas, such as the European Community and the European Free Trade Area, which are examined in Chapter 10. To put the matter simply for the time being, it can be demonstrated that the elimination of import restrictions among members of a customs union or free trade area may cause a loss of welfare to the world as a whole. In other words, not every step toward free trade is necessarily a step toward greater economic efficiency and higher welfare.

---

[22] The theory of the second best first appeared in J. E. Meade, *Theory of International Economic Policy*, vol. 2, *Trade and Welfare* (New York: Oxford University Press, 1955).

It should be evident that the theory of second best is not a general argument for protection. Under certain conditions, a selective import restriction may improve welfare, but in other circumstances (for example, when private cost is *less* than social cost), the theory of the second best may entail the elimination or reduction of a specific import restriction. In a sense all arguments for protection (aside from the purely fallacious) may be regarded as calling for second-best policies, since they all argue that certain constraints justify protection. Correctly interpreted, the theory of the second best says that *any* policy that reduces divergences between marginal social costs and benefits will improve economic efficiency. This theory is not an argument for wholesale government intervention in the marketplace, especially when divergences are the result of previous intervention. The theory of the second best focuses attention first on the possible removal of distortion-causing constraints; only when their removal is deemed unfeasible does a second-best policy become appropriate. The first-best policy remains free trade.

PERSISTENCE OF PROTECTION

Our examination of arguments for protection has revealed their vulnerability to economic analysis. Aside from the purely fallacious arguments, we have found that arguments for protection have only a conditional validity when they are evaluated from the perspective of economic efficiency. In most instances, protection is an inferior policy instrument, because other policies can achieve the same result (or a better one) at a smaller cost. Even in those rare situations when protection brings a net gain to the protectionist country, it brings a net loss to the world economy. Because of their conditional validity, the arguments for protection are commonly abused in practice; the criterion of economic efficiency is overwhelmed by political factors. In light of historical experience, protection once established tends to become a permanent institution under the relentless pressure of the vested interests it benefits, even when it outgrows any original usefulness for the nation.

If so little can be said in its favor, why is protection so persistent? Why do all nations of the world continue to implement this restrictive policy to one degree or another? The answers to these perplexing questions are not to be found in the realm of logic or economics. The answers, deeply embedded in human behavior, are found in the same forces of narrow self-interest, fear, ignorance, and prejudice that afflict international relations in general. So long as groups who gain from protection are able to persuade policymakers that their private interests coincide with the national interest, protection will continue to stultify the flow of trade among nations who are otherwise committed to competitive market economies. By the same token, the struggle for free or freer trade is a never-ending chronology of victories and defeats with no final outcome.

SUMMARY

1. The theory of comparative advantage demonstrates that for the world as a whole free trade leads to a higher level of output and income than autarky. However, many contemporary economists are reluctant to support free trade unreservedly. Economic theory cannot demonstrate that *in all circumstances* free trade will improve economic efficiency or enhance economic welfare.

2. The essential difference between external and internal trade is political only; it is this difference that has nurtured protectionism through the ages. The long series of arguments for protection may be classified into four categories: (1) fallacious arguments, (2) questionable arguments, (3) qualified arguments, and (4) sophisticated arguments.

3. Fallacious arguments rely on plausibility or mass emotional appeal rather than economic logic. The keep-money-at-home, home market, equalization-of-production-costs, low wage, and prevention-of-injury arguments are traditional fallacious arguments.

4. Certain arguments for protection, although not entirely fallacious, represent an inferior policy or easily lend themselves to abuse. These include the employment, antidumping, bargaining-and-retaliation, and reciprocity arguments.

5. Other arguments for protection (the national security, infant industry, and diversification arguments) find their justification either in non-economic considerations or in expectation of long-term economic benefits that will more than compensate for the immediate costs of protection.

6. Two arguments may justify import restrictions under certain conditions: the terms-of-trade argument (optimum tariff) and the theory of the second best. We call these arguments "sophisticated" because they appear in the literature of economic theory and have not been adopted by protectionist groups.

QUESTIONS AND APPLICATIONS

1. "Contemporary Western economists are reluctant to support the doctrine of free trade unreservedly but remain firmly on the side of a policy of freer, if not free, trade." What is the explanation of this seemingly contradictory statement?

2. Which is the strongest argument for protection? Why?

3. "Governments spend a great deal of effort promoting exports while, at the same time, they impose all kinds of restrictions on imports." Discuss.

4. Define a truly infant industry. On the basis of your definition, are there any infant industries in the United States?

5. Why is fiscal policy preferable to import restrictions as a response to cyclical unemployment?

6. In presenting its case for protection (import quotas), the American Textile Manufacturers Institute has made the following statement: "With very few exceptions, foreign-made textiles do not sell in the United States because they are better, more stylish, or made more efficiently. The basic reason foreign textiles sell in such volumes in this country is that they are produced at wages far below the legal minimum here." Assuming this statement is true, does the situation justify protection?

7. A spokesman for the U.S. steel industry concluded a plea for import quotas as follows: "Does America want and need a strong steel industry? Does it want to maintain the maximum number of jobs at high wage standards? Does it believe in fair play in the competition for its own markets? Does our nation's security demand all the strength in steel we can possibly achieve? If so, something has to be done. I believe the proposed legislation represents a realistic solution of this problem—fair to all—and that it is worthy of your sympathetic support." What arguments for protection are implied in these questions? Justify your own response to each question.

SELECTED READINGS

See the list of readings given at the end of Chapter 9.

7

Tariffs and Nontariff Trade Barriers

This chapter begins our examination of international trade policies by describing the nature and economic effects of the policy instruments used by governments to influence the flows of goods and services in the world economy.

The traditional policy instrument is the import *tariff*. But governments also resort to a bewildering variety of measures to restrict imports or subsidize exports. These measures are collectively designated as *nontariff trade barriers*.

TARIFFS AND TARIFF SYSTEMS

Simply stated, a tariff (or customs duty) is a tax imposed by a government on physical goods as they move into or out of a country. The taxation of trade is probably as old as trade itself. The first reference to the use of a customs duty appeared after the Crusades, and such duties have been in more or less constant use ever since. The Mercantilists of the eighteenth century were probably the first to make tariffs more an instrument of national control of international trade than a source of revenue. Tariffs have been used extensively ever since as a protective measure against foreign competition.

A *customs area* is a geographical area within which goods may move freely without being subjected to customs duties. The boundaries of a customs area generally, but not necessarily, coincide with national boundaries. When a customs area encompasses more than one distinct national area, it is known as a *customs union*. The economic significance of a customs area lies essentially in the movement of goods within the area without payment of tariffs or duties.

Before analyzing the economic effects of tariffs, we offer a brief description of their different forms, both as individual customs duties and as collective tariff systems.

Ad Valorem, Specific, and Compound Duties

There are two basic kinds of customs duties: ad valorem and specific. An *ad valorem duty* is stated in terms of a percentage of the value of an imported article, such as 10 or 20 percent ad valorem. A *specific duty,* on the other hand, is expressed in terms of an amount of money per quantity of goods, such as 20 cents per pound or per gallon. A combination of an ad valorem and a specific duty is called a *compound duty*.

Ad valorem duties generally lend themselves more satisfactorily to manufactured products, while specific duties are more adaptable to standardized and staple products. Ad valorem duties on higher-priced manufactured goods are considered more effective than specific duties, because a single ad valorem rate can usually maintain a certain degree of protection, especially under conditions of rising prices. A specific rate, on the other hand, has the advantage of being more protective in a declining market or in a business recession when cheaper goods are favored. A specific rate will, moreover, discourage imports of the cheaper grade within a class of products as compared with the more expensive variety. For example, a specific rate of $2 a pair on shoes will discourage imports valued at $10 a pair to a greater extent than those valued at $25 a pair.

Compound duties frequently apply to manufactured goods containing raw materials that are on the dutiable list. In such cases the specific portion of the duty—known as a *compensatory duty*—is levied to offset the duty that grants protection to the raw materials industry, while the ad valorem portion of the duty affords protection to the finished goods industry. In the United States, for example, the wool tariff provides for compound duties on worsteds to compensate domestic worsted producers for protection afforded the raw wool industry as well as to provide protection for their own woolen industry.

In recent decades, specific duties have given way to ad valorem duties in response to worldwide inflation and the growing importance of international trade in manufactures.

Tariff Systems

There are countless articles of commerce that move in international trade, and their number is constantly growing as newly developed products are added every day. For manageable tariff administration, some kind of comprehensive classification or "customs nomenclature" is necessary.

As a rule most countries have two major lists in their tariffs: (1) a dutiable list for goods subject to customs duties, and (2) a free list for goods permitted to enter duty free. Classification in the dutiable list may be made according to (1) an alphabetical arrangement, (2) the height of the duty, or

(3) the attributes of the goods. Each of these methods has its advantages and its drawbacks. The alphabetical and the height-of-the-duty methods are simple in form, but they tend to make reference to any particular product or group of related products difficult. The attribute method of classification is more logical and more widely used in modern tariff systems. In this method, classification may be made on the basis of the physical substance from which products are derived, the end use of the products, or the degree of processing.[1]

Tariff schedules may have one, two, or three different duties for each dutiable article. A nation is said to have a *single-column*, a *double-column*, or a *triple-column* tariff system according to the number of different duties appearing on its schedules for each product. When customs duties are established by law, they are called *autonomous*, but when they are the result of treaty agreements with other countries, they are called *conventional*.

A *single-column* schedule is essentially autonomous and nondiscriminatory, since it provides only one duty for each product, whatever the country of origin.[2] It is best suited for a country that has established a tariff purely for revenue or purely for protection and has no intention of bargaining. Under present international commercial relations, the rigidity of a single-column tariff system is a handicap when nations deal with other nations to resolve mutual trade problems.

A *double-column* schedule has two levels of duties for each product. When both levels are established by law and are not subject to modification by international agreements, the tariff system is autonomous and said to be of a "maximum-minimum form." When only the higher level of duties is established by law and the lower level is a composite of all the reduced duties granted to other nations by negotiation, the system is partly autonomous and partly conventional and is said to be of a "general and conventional form."

A *triple-column* schedule is generally used by countries that have close political affiliations with other countries. It is an extension of the double-column schedule by the addition of a third, lower scale that is reserved for intragroup application. This is known as a "preferential system," and it is designed to encourage trade between the different members of the system.

Mitigation of Tariffs

To harmonize the conflict between import protection and export promotion, tariff systems commonly mitigate the effects of duties through drawbacks,

---

[1] The Brussels Tariff Nomenclature (BTN), which classifies products according to their physical substance, has been adopted by some 100 countries that account for over two-thirds of total world trade. Among the industrial countries, only the United States continues to use its own tariff classification.

[2] A single-column tariff schedule may, however, be discriminatory if the duties are purposely chosen to restrict imports from particular countries.

bonded warehouses, and free zones. A *drawback* is a refund of duties and internal taxes to an exporter who exports a product that was previously imported into the country. The United States refunds 99 percent of the original tariff duties as a drawback.

Dutiable imports may be brought into a customs territory and left in *bonded warehouses* free of duty. Under strict governmental supervision, imported goods may be stored, repacked, manipulated, or further processed in bonded warehouses according to the laws of the particular country. The goods may be later reexported free of duty or withdrawn for domestic consumption upon payment of customs duties. When such goods have been processed in a bonded warehouse with additional domestic materials and later entered for consumption, only the import portion of the finished product is subject to duty.

A *free zone* is an isolated, enclosed area with no resident population (generally adjacent to a port) that offers extensive facilities for handling, storing, mixing, and manufacturing imported and domestic goods and materials without customs intervention or immediate disbursement of customs duties. The purpose of a free zone is to enlarge the benefits of a bonded warehouse by the elimination of the restrictive aspects of customs supervision and by offering more suitable manufacturing facilities.

Sometimes a free zone is referred to as a *free port,* but a true free port is a whole city, or section of a city, isolated from the rest of the country for customs purposes. There are very few free ports left in the world where the population may enjoy the benefit of relatively free trade. Hong Kong is the most important of such ports. In medieval Europe, however, free ports abounded along the Mediterranean and northern seas. Venice, Genoa, Naples, Marseilles, Hamburg, and Bremen were prosperous free ports and leading centers of trade for a long period of time. In the United States, free zones are commonly known as "foreign-trade zones" and are governed by an act of Congress passed in 1934 that provides for their establishment and operation.

ECONOMIC EFFECTS OF TARIFFS

Tariffs may be designed to collect revenue for the government or to protect domestic industries against foreign competition.[3] To best perform their *revenue function,* tariff duties are applied to commodities of wide consumption and the rates of these duties are kept low enough to maximize customs

---

[3] Revenue and protection are the principal functions of tariffs. At times, however, a government may raise tariff rates in response to a balance of payments deficit. In 1964, Great Britain imposed a 15 percent surcharge on all imports (roughly doubling the existing tariff level), which was then abandoned the following year. In 1971 both the United States and Denmark levied a 10 percent surcharge on most dutiable imports. Unlike tariffs for revenue or protection, such surcharges have an emergency, short-lived character.

collections. The same objective may also be attained by the imposition of a uniform low rate of duty on all merchandise crossing the border either as exports, imports, or in transit. The revenue function of a duty is a relative concept. A duty is always characterized by an element of protection, however small or unimportant, except, of course, when the taxed product is not domestically produced and the tariff serves a purely revenue function.

The *protection function* of the tariff depends upon a partial or complete restriction of imports. When complete protection is desired, a given duty must be high enough to cover the difference in the marginal cost of production between domestic and *all* foreign producers, including transportation and incidental expenses of importing. If the tariff is to be only partially protective, however, the duty must remain below this difference. When partial protection is desired, goods will continue to be imported, but they will be imported in smaller quantities and the government will collect customs duties. Therefore, the protection function—like the revenue function—will usually afford both protection and revenue, although its purpose is primarily one of protection.

The seeming incompatibility of the two functions in the same duty does not necessarily disqualify its adoption, since most countries generally desire both protection and revenue. In national tariff schedules, however, a tendency does exist to provide a certain number of generally low rates of duties designed essentially for revenue and other higher duty rates for protection.

The immediate effects of tariffs are those reflected in price changes and consequent adjustments in production and consumption. Because of the fact that tariffs for revenue have effects similar to but smaller than those of protection tariffs, our discussion shall be confined to protective tariffs, leaving it to the reader to make the appropriate application to revenue tariffs.

Price Effects of an Import Duty

The price effects of an import duty depend primarily on the elasticity of the supply schedule of the import good facing the duty-levying country.[4] Here we distinguish three price effects: (1) a rise in domestic price of less than the amount of the duty, (2) no change in domestic price, and (3) a rise in domestic price equal to the duty.

Price Rise of Less Than the Amount of the Duty A large trading country, such as the United States, can influence world prices because its imports are a significant fraction of international markets. That is to say, it has some degree of *monopsonistic* power in international markets. Hence, the supply schedules of most foreign products entering the U.S. market are *price-inelastic* to some degree. In this situation, the imposition of an import

---

[4] Price effects depend secondarily on the elasticity of the import demand schedule, which in turn depends on the elasticity of the domestic demand schedule and the elasticity of the supply schedule of the domestic import-competing good.

Figure 7-1   Price Rise Less Than the Amount of the Duty

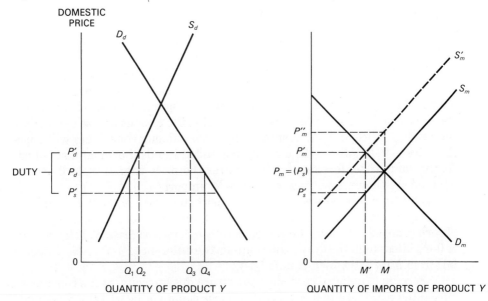

QUANTITY OF PRODUCT Y   QUANTITY OF IMPORTS OF PRODUCT Y

The diagram on the left shows the domestic demand schedule, D_d, and the domestic supply schedule, S_d, of product Y in country A. The diagram on the right shows country A's import demand schedule, D_m, and the import supply schedule, S_m, of product Y. The import demand schedule equals the excess of domestic demand over domestic supply at prices below the point of intersection of D_d and S_d. Before the imposition of an import duty, the domestic price of Y is 0–P_d. Now suppose country A imposes a duty. This causes the entire import supply schedule facing consumers in country A to shift upwards by the amount of the duty and a new supply schedule, S'_m, is established. Because foreign suppliers absorb some of the duty, the increase in the domestic price of Y from 0–P_d to 0–P'_d is less than the duty, which equals the difference P'_d–P'_s. Imports fall from M to M', which equals Q_2–Q_3.

duty on a product will cause foreign suppliers to lower the price, thereby absorbing some of the duty.[5] The postduty price for consumers in the tariff-levying country, therefore, will rise by less than the duty. Figure 7-1 demonstrates this price effect.

The diagram on the left shows the domestic demand schedule, D_d, and the domestic supply schedule, S_d, of product Y in country A. The diagram on the right shows the import demand schedule, D_m, and the import supply schedule, S_m, of product Y. The import demand schedule equals the excess of domestic demand over domestic supply at prices below the point of intersection of D_d and S_d. Before the imposition of an import duty, the domestic

---

[5] As we shall discuss later, absorption of the entire duty by foreign suppliers will occur only when the import supply schedule is *perfectly* inelastic.

price of Y is $0-P_d$. At that price, country A imports $0-M$ of product Y, an amount that equals the excess of domestic demand over domestic supply (Q_1-Q_4). Because there is no duty on imports of Y, the domestic consumer price $(0-P_d)$ equals the import supply price $(0-P_s)$, which in turn equals the import consumer price $(0-P_m)$.

Now suppose country A imposes a duty. This causes the entire import supply schedule facing consumers in country A to shift upwards by the amount of the duty and a new supply schedule, S'_m, is established. At each quantity of imports, the new supply price for consumers is higher than the old supply price by the amount of the duty. At quantity $0-M$, for instance, the duty equals $P_s-P''_m$.[6] The new supply schedule creates excess demand at the preduty price of $0-P_m$. Hence, competition among consumers will raise the price to $0-P'_m$, where the amount demanded equals the amount supplied. At the same time, foreign suppliers lower the price from $0-P_s$ to $0-P'_s$, for which price they are willing to offer $0-M'$ imports.

The difference between the new import consumer price $(0-P'_m)$ and the new import supply price $(0-P'_s)$ is the tariff duty. Because foreign suppliers absorb some of the duty, the increase in the domestic price of Y from $0-P_d$ to $0-P'_d$ is less than the duty, which equals the difference $P'_d-P'_s$. Also, imports fall from M to M', which equals Q_2-Q_3.

Foreign suppliers could shift the entire duty to country A's consumers only if the price rose to $0-P''_m$. But this price could not be sustained, because excess import supply would force it down to $0-P'_m$.

No Change in Price   When the duty-levying country is the sole buyer (monopsonist) of a good, then its import supply schedule is perfectly inelastic. Because foreign suppliers have no other market, they would lower price to absorb any import duty in order to maintain sales. Consequently, the price of the good for consumers in the duty-levying country would remain the same after imposition of the duty. This is shown in Figure 7-2.

The preduty domestic price of product Y $(0-P_d)$ equals the import supply price $(0-P_s)$, which in turn equals the import price for consumers of Y. Now suppose a duty is imposed equal to $P_s-P'_m$. If the duty is passed on fully to consumers of Y, then the import price rises to $0-P'_m$. But that price cannot endure, because there is an excess amount supplied: Competition among foreign suppliers forces down the price until the excess supply is wiped out at $0-P_m$. But to do this, suppliers need to absorb fully the duty by cutting their price by the amount of the duty from $0-P_s$ to $0-P'_s$. Consequently, the domestic price of Y remains $0-P_d$.

Foreign suppliers will continue to absorb the entire duty over the long run only if they can cover their costs at the supply price of $0-P'_s$. If the costs of marginal suppliers are *not* covered, then eventually they will eliminate or cut back production of Y. This cutback will appear as a loftward shift of

---

[6] Foreign suppliers view this postduty situation as a *downward* shift in the *demand* schedule facing their exports to country A: At each preduty price, they sell less than before.

Figure 7-2   No Effect of Import Duty on Price

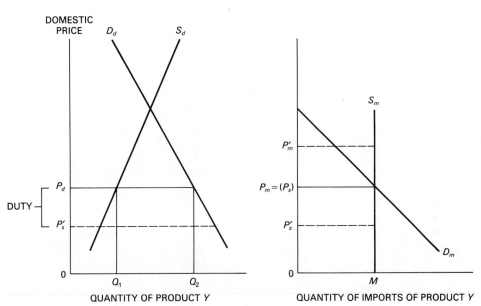

QUANTITY OF PRODUCT Y · QUANTITY OF IMPORTS OF PRODUCT Y

The preduty domestic price of product Y $(0-P_d)$ equals the import supply price $(0-P_s)$, which in turn equals the import price for consumers of Y. Now suppose a duty is imposed equal to $P_s-P'_m$. If the duty is passed on fully to consumers of Y, then the import price rises to $0-P'_m$. But that price cannot endure, because there is an excess amount supplied: Competition among foreign suppliers forces down the price until the excess supply is wiped out at $0-P_m$. Suppliers absorb fully the duty by cutting their price by the amount of the duty from $0-P_s$ to $0-P'_s$. Consequently, the domestic price of Y remains $0-P_d$. Foreign suppliers will continue to absorb the entire duty over the long run only if they can cover their costs at the supply price of $0-P'_s$.

the import supply schedule, bringing about a rise in the price of Y in country A. In sum, a perfectly inelastic import supply schedule is an extreme case that seldom exists in the real world, and even then the full absorption of an import duty will continue only if suppliers can cover all costs at their postduty price.

Price Rise Equal to the Amount of the Duty When a country is too small to influence the world price of a product by altering its import demand, then the import supply schedule is *perfectly elastic*. In this situation, an import duty raises the domestic price by the full amount of the duty. This is demonstrated in Figure 7-3.

Before the duty is imposed, country A imports $0-M$ of product Y at a price of $0-P_s$, which equals the domestic price of $0-P_d$. Now assume that

Figure 7-3   Price Rise Equal to Amount of Duty

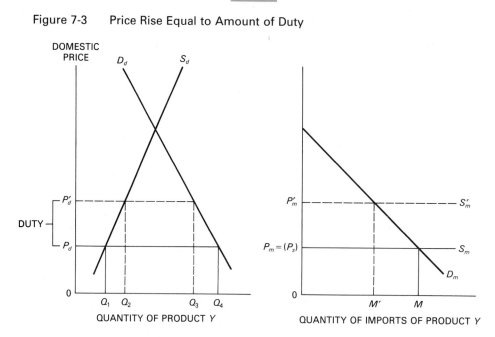

Before the duty is imposed, country A imports 0–M of product Y at a price of 0–P_s, which equals the domestic price of 0–P_d. Now assume that country A imposes an import duty. This shifts the import supply schedule facing country A's consumers upwards by the amount of the duty (which equals P_s–P'_m) and a new supply schedule, S'_m, is established. The new import price is 0–P'_m, as determined by the intersection of S'_m and D_m, and the new domestic price is 0–P'_d. The entire duty is borne by consumers as the price rises by the full amount of the duty.

country A imposes an import duty. This shifts the import supply schedule facing country A's consumers upwards by the amount of the duty (which equals P_s–P'_m), and a new supply schedule, S'_m, is established. The new equilibrium import price is 0–P'_m, as determined by the intersection of S'_m and D_m, and the new domestic price is 0–P'_d. Observe that the fall in imports from 0–M to 0–M' does *not* cause foreign suppliers to lower their price, because country A's imports are an inconsequential fraction of the world demand for product Y. Hence, the entire duty is borne by consumers in country A as the price rises by the full amount of the duty.[7]

---

[7] An import duty may raise the price to the consumer by *more* than the amount of the duty when the domestic channel of distribution is lengthy and the different middlemen add individual markups (calculated as a percentage of their selling prices) at each step of the marketing process.

Other Tariff Effects

Although an import duty may induce many changes in both the importing and exporting countries, its *direct* effects in the importing country may be classified as price, revenue, trade, protection, consumption, and income-redistribution effects. Figure 7-4 shows these effects under the simplifying assumption of a perfectly elastic foreign supply. At the prevailing price, $0-P_d$, the quantity demanded of a given product by country A is $0-Q$, determined by its domestic demand schedule, D_d, of which the portion $0-Q_1$ is domestically produced (determined by the intersection of the price, $0-P_d$, and the domestic supply schedule, S_d), and the remaining part, Q_1-Q, is imported.

Upon the introduction of a tariff by country A, a customs duty of, say, $P_d-P'_d$ is levied, raising the cost to domestic users from $0-P_d$ to $0-P'_d$. At this higher cost, the quantities demanded of the protected product are reduced from $0-Q$ to $0-Q_2$, of which $0-Q_3$ is domestically supplied and the remaining portion, Q_3-Q_2, is imported.

Figure 7-4   Effects of an Import Duty with a Perfectly Elastic Foreign Supply

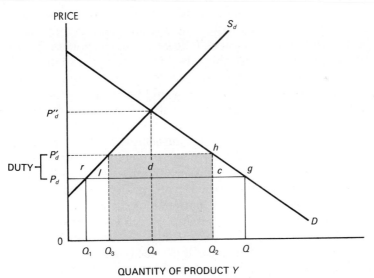

Before the duty, country A imports Q_1-Q at a price of $0-P_d$. Because the import supply schedule (not shown here) is perfectly elastic, the imposition of the duty raises the *price* by the full amount of the duty—from $0-P_d$ to $0-P'_d$. The *revenue* effect is the rectangle d, the *trade* effect is the drop in imports $(Q_1-Q_3 + Q_2-Q)$, the *protection* effect is Q_1-Q_3, and the *consumption* effect is Q_2-Q. The *income-redistribution* effect is the quadrangle r. The *net cost* (deadweight loss) of the tariff for country A is the sum of the triangles l and c.

The *price* effect is the increase in price to domestic consumers because of the duty. In this instance, consumers bear the full incidence of the duty (price rises by the full amount of the duty, $P_d–P'_d$, because the foreign supply price remains the same (foreign supply is perfectly elastic).

The *revenue* effect is the customs collections accruing to the government, represented by rectangle d. It is the product of the quantity of imports *times* the duty $P_d–P'_d$.

The *trade* effect is the decline in imports resulting from the duty. At the preduty price of $0–P_d$, imports were $Q_1–Q$; after the duty was imposed, they fell to $Q_3–Q_2$. The negative trade effect, therefore, is $Q_1–Q_3 + Q_2–Q$.

The *protection* effect is the increase in domestic production that is induced by the import duty, namely, $Q_1–Q_3$. This represents the substitution of domestic production for foreign production.

The *consumption* effect is the decrease in consumption resulting from the tariff. Because of a higher price, consumers cut their consumption of the product from $0–Q$ to $0–Q_2$. Hence, the consumption effect is $Q_2–Q$. (Note that the trade effect is the sum of the protection and consumption effects.)

The *income-redistribution* effect is the shift in income from domestic consumers to domestic producers. It is shown by quadrangle r, which measures the extra revenue, or pure rent, that is received by domestic producers above their supply price ($S–S$) as a result of the duty.

In a perfectly competitive economy, the *net cost* (deadweight loss) of the tariff to the domestic country is the sum of triangles l and c. The reasoning behind this conclusion is as follows. Some consumers enjoy an economic gain or surplus because they are willing to pay a higher price than the market price that they actually pay for some of the product. On the assumption that the prices consumers would be willing to pay for various quantities of the product measure the satisfactions they derive from the product, then the consumer surplus before the tariff is indicated by the area $d–g–P_d$ in Figure 7-4. The higher price caused by the tariff, however, reduces the consumer surplus to $d–h–P'_d$, resulting in a net loss of $P'_d–h–g–P_d$, which is equal to the sum of r, l, d, and c. Since the net loss in consumer surplus is partly offset by the national gain of r and d, the net national loss is the sum of l and c. Specifically, l is the national loss attributable to the substitution of higher-priced domestic production for lower-priced foreign production, and c is the national loss in consumption due to the higher postduty price, which causes the substitution of other goods providing less satisfaction than the foregone imports. When the tariff-levying country faces a perfectly elastic import supply, it always experiences a net national loss because domestic consumers bear the full incidence of the duty. When import supply is less than perfectly elastic, however, a country can improve its terms of trade by imposing a tariff and it may even enjoy a net national gain, a subject that was discussed in Chapter 6. If the duty is high enough to reach P''_d, there will be no imports—the entire quantity demanded, $0–Q_4$, will be supplied by the domestic producers at price $0–P''_d$.

With less-than-infinite foreign supply elasticity, the price effect would be less restrictive of imports and consumption, since the foreign price would drop, as established earlier in this chapter. This situation is likely if the importing country is a major consumer of the product.

Measurement of Tariff Systems

Several methods have been used to measure the trade and protection effects of national tariff systems.

Tariff Revenues   The most naive approach, favored by protectionists, is to divide a country's customs revenue by the total value of its imports. This method implicitly assumes that the protection effect of a tariff system is directly related to the duties collected on imports: The lower the ratio of customs revenue to imports, the lower the degree of protection. This assumption is demonstrably false. Suppose a country's duties are so high that no dutiable goods are imported—the trade effect is equal to the preduty import volume. In that event, no revenue would be collected—the ratio of revenue to imports would be zero! To conclude that the protection and trade effects are also zero would be patently absurd.

Height of Duties   Another approach is to add up all the duties in a tariff system and then calculate the unweighted average. A more sophisticated version of this method is to calculate an average of all duties weighted by the country's imports of each dutiable product. Thus, a product with imports of, say, $2 million is given twice the weight of a product with imports of $1 million.[8]

This approach assumes that trade and protection effects are proportional to the height of a duty and they are the same for all products and all countries. The unweighted average ignores the varying importance of different products in trade. On the other hand, an average that is weighted by the tariff-levying country's imports of each dutiable product has a downward bias: Prohibitory duties are not counted (since they keep out all imports) and the more restrictive a duty, the less its weight. Despite this drawback, both the United States and the European Community used such weighted averages to measure the heights of their own and the other's tariff

---

[8] In mathematical form, the simple unweighted average is

$$\sum_{t=1}^{t=n} = d_t/\mathrm{n},$$

where d represents the individual duty expressed as a percentage and n, the number of duties. The weighted average is

$$\sum_{t=1}^{t=n} = (d_t)i_t,$$

where i is the weight defined as the fractional share of dutiable imports associated with the individual duty. The sum of all the weights is one.

system during negotiations.[9] The downward bias would be moderated, if not overcome, by using as weights the value of *world* trade in each product.[10]

Effective versus Nominal Rates   As we have seen, an import duty raises the domestic price of a good (unless the elasticity of its foreign supply is zero) and thereby encourages consumers to shift from the foreign good to a domestic substitute. Thus, the nominal duty, together with the relevant elasticities, determines the *consumption* effect.

But for domestic producers the *protection* effect of a nominal duty on their final product is *enhanced* by the fact that their own production activity is responsible for only a part of the final product's value. At the same time, the protection effect of a nominal duty is *lowered* for domestic producers by any import duties on raw materials and other inputs that they use in manufacturing the final product. The tariff rate that is relevant to the protection effect, therefore, is the *effective* rate that takes into account both of these factors. The effective rate measures the degree of protection that is afforded the *value added* to the final product by domestic producers.

The formula for the calculation of the effective rate is

$$r = \frac{n - \Sigma pi}{1 - \Sigma p},$$

where r is the effective rate, n is the nominal rate, p is the proportion of the final product represented by imported or importable inputs in the absence of any import restrictions, and i is the nominal rate of duty on raw materials and other intermediate goods. The expression $1 - \Sigma_p$ is the value added to the final product by domestic producers as a proportion of the final value.

If no duties are imposed on imports of intermediate goods, then the formula becomes

$$r = \frac{n}{1 - \Sigma p}.$$

This gives the rate of protection against the value added by domestic producers (the final value of the product *minus* the value of importable inputs purchased from other producers, local or foreign).

Assume, for example, that a country places a 20 percent duty on imports of a final product but allows duty-free imports of intermediate goods that constitute one half of the final product's value. Then the effective rate is

---

[9] See Chapter 8.

[10] Due to lack of trade data, lack of comparability (different customs nomenclatures), and other statistical problems, weighting by world trade is generally considered impractical.

$$\frac{.20}{1 - \frac{1}{2}},$$

or 40 percent. Assuming a price rise equal to the duty, this 20 percent duty enables domestic producers of the final product to increase their value added by 40 percent more than in a free trade situation with no duties.

Continuing with this example, let us now assume that a 10 percent rate is applied to imports of intermediate goods. (If more than one input is involved, then the rate is a weighted average.) The effective rate becomes

$$\frac{.20 - \frac{1}{2}(.10)}{1 - \frac{1}{2}},$$

or 30 percent. Note that the tariff on intermediate goods has lowered the effective rate although it remains higher than the nominal rate. When the nominal rates applied to the final product and to intermediate goods are the same, then the effective rate is *equal* to the nominal rate for the final product. When the intermediate duty rate exceeds the final-product rate, then the effective rate becomes *less* than the nominal rate and may even be negative. Because national governments generally admit raw materials and other intermediate goods either duty-free or at a lower rate than finished goods to encourage local manufacture, effective tariff rates are usually higher than nominal rates.

Elasticities and Market Share Any method that pretends to measure the protection effect of a duty by its height (even when the effective rate is substituted for the nominal rate) implicitly ignores the foreign and domestic elasticities of supply and demand that vary from product to product and from country to country. A duty of any given height may or may not be restrictive, depending on the relevant elasticities. But elasticities are difficult to determine empirically, even for a single product. It is no wonder, then, that efforts to measure entire tariff systems comprising thousands of product classifications have relied on weighted averages of nominal or effective duties. Although such averages may be useful for intercountry and intertemporal comparisons, they should be interpreted only as crude indicators of the degree of tariff protection.

The elasticity of import demand is influenced by the *share* of imports in domestic consumption and domestic production as well as by domestic supply and demand elasticities.[11] Other things being equal, the smaller the import share, the greater the import elasticity. Given the domestic elasticities, therefore, a duty will restrict imports most when such imports are only marginal to domestic consumption and production, a situation that is probably more common in the United States than in most other countries.

---

[11] The formula is $e_m = e_d(C/M) + e_s(P/M)$, where e_m is the import demand elasticity, e_d and e_s are the domestic elasticities of demand and supply, respectively, C is domestic consumption, P is domestic production, and M is imports.

NONTARIFF TRADE BARRIERS: QUANTITATIVE RESTRICTIONS

As the industrial countries have progressively cut tariff rates under the auspices of the General Agreement on Tariffs and Trade, nontariff trade barriers have become more and more prominent.[12] The lowering of tariffs has been compared to the draining of a swamp: The lower water level has revealed all sorts of stumps and snags (nontariff barriers) that still make the swamp difficult to cross. We look first at quantitative trade restrictions, the most visible kind of nontariff barrier, and then offer a brief review of the many other kinds of nontariff barriers to international trade in goods and services.

Quantitative measures of restriction, like tariffs, are tools of national economic policy designed to regulate the international trade of a nation. Unlike tariffs, however, they impose absolute limitations upon foreign trade and inhibit market responses; this makes them extremely effective. Quantitative trade restrictions are used chiefly to afford protection to domestic producers or to bring about adjustment to a disturbed balance of payments. Quantitative restrictions ordinarily take the form of import quotas that are administered by the issuance of import licenses to individual traders.

Import Quotas

Three major types of import quotas are in use throughout the world: unilateral quotas, negotiated bilateral or multilateral quotas, and tariff quotas. All of them impose absolute limits in value or quantity on imports of a specific product or product group during a given period of time.

The *unilateral quota* is a fixed quota that is adopted without prior consultation or negotiation with other countries. It is imposed and administered solely by the importing country. Because of its unilateral aspect, this type of quota tends to create friction, antagonism, and retaliation abroad that undermines its ultimate success.

A unilateral quota may be *global* or *allocated,* depending upon whether or not the fixed volume of imports is specifically assigned by shares to different exporting countries or to individual domestic importers or foreign exporters. A *global quota* restricts the total volume without reference to countries of origin or to established importers and exporters engaged in the trade. In practice, the global quota becomes unwieldy because of the rush of both importers and exporters to secure as large a share as possible before the quota is exhausted. The result is frequently an excess of shipments over the quota, and charges of favoritism may be raised against traders fortunate enough to be the first to seize a lion's share of the business. To avoid the difficulties of a global quota system, a quota may be allocated by countries

---

[12] The General Agreement on Tariffs and Trade (GATT) is discussed in Chapter 8.

and by private traders on the basis of a prior representative period. This type of import quota is known as an *allocated quota.*

The administration of quotas is fraught with difficulties. Foreign traders feel encouraged to misrepresent their products to exempt them from quota classification; the traders may resort to methods ranging from simple persuasion to outright graft and corruption of government officials in charge of enforcement. To ease the administrative as well as political difficulties of unilateral quotas, many governments have turned to negotiated quotas.

Under the system of a *negotiated bilateral* or *multilateral quota,* the importing country negotiates with supplying countries, or with groups of exporters in those countries, before deciding the allotment of the quota by definite shares. Often the administration of licensing under a bilateral quota is left in the hands of the exporting countries.

A bilateral or multilateral quota tends to minimize pressure by domestic importers upon their own government and to increase cooperation by foreign exporters, thus enhancing the successful operation of the system. When licensing is entrusted to foreign private agencies, however, it often results in the bulk of trade falling into the hands of larger firms or of well-organized international cartels that are in a position to squeeze out most of the monopoly-like profit induced by the restriction of supply relative to demand in the quota country. Hence, domestic importers are deprived of this source of income and their government is deprived of the opportunity to tax such income.

In recent years the United States has restricted certain imports through negotiated quotas administered by the governments of supplying countries, the so-called *voluntary export quotas.* In 1981, for example, Japan agreed to impose "voluntary" quotas on exports of automobiles to the United States. Despite its name, a voluntary export quota is actually an import quota, since the initiative for its establishment comes from the importing country and the motivation is protection of domestic industry.

Under a *tariff quota* a specified quantity of a product is permitted to enter the country at a given rate of duty—or even duty-free. Any additional quantity that may be imported, however, must pay a higher duty. Thus, a tariff quota combines the features of both a tariff and a quota.

Export Quotas

Exports may also be subjected to quantitative restrictions by government action. Quantitative export controls are intended to accomplish one or more of the following objectives:

1. to prevent strategic goods from reaching the hands of unfriendly powers
2. to assure all or a significant proportion of certain products in short supply for the home market
3. to permit the control of surpluses on a national or an international basis to achieve production and price stability

These objectives can be attained more positively and with greater ease by quotas than by tariffs. Like import quotas, export quotas may be unilateral when they are established without prior agreement with other nations and bilateral or multilateral when they are the result of agreements. They are administered chiefly by licensing. Export controls have featured many schemes to improve the market and the price of raw materials. These controls are identified with export cartels and international commodity agreements discussed in Chapter 21.

The Economic Effects of Quotas

This section examines the nature of quota effects and offers a short comparison of quotas and tariffs.

The Nature of Quota Effects Figure 7-5 illustrates the effects of an import quota. Before the quota is imposed, country A imports $0–M$ of product Y at a price of $0–P'_s$, which equals the domestic price of $0–P_d$. Now suppose A imposes a quota that restricts imports to $0–M'$. The price that consumers are willing to pay for $0–M'$ of product Y rises to $0–P'_m$, and at the same time foreign suppliers would be willing to supply $0–M'$ of product Y at price $0–P'_s$ in a competitive market.

This price differential gives rise to a monopoly rent or *quota profits*, as indicated by the rectangles d and e. Who gets these profits? That depends on the institutional arrangements to administer the quota. Here we distinguish four possible arrangements and their consequences. (1) When the quota is a *global* quota that is not allocated to individual importers or exporters, then domestic importers and foreign exporters compete on a first-come, first-serve basis to fill the quota. In this situation, importers and exporters share the quota profits. (2) When the quota is allocated among foreign exporters, then they obtain all of the quota profits. (3) Similarly, when the quota is allocated among domestic importers, they obtain all of the quota profits. (4) Finally, when country A's government auctions quota allocations to the highest bidder in a competitive market, then it gets the quota profits.

A comparison of Figures 7-4 and 7-5 indicates that the price, trade, protection, and consumption effects of an import quota are the same as those of a tariff.[13] But the revenue effect of a quota is the same as that of a tariff only when the quota-levying government auctions quota allocations to the highest bidder in a competitive market. Otherwise, as we have noted, the revenue (quota profits) goes to domestic importers, foreign exporters, or both. When some or all quota profits go to foreign exporters, then the economic costs of the quota for the quota-levying country exceed the costs of a tariff duty that restricts trade in the same degree. Both the quota and the duty

---

[13] This statement assumes there is competition in the protected industry. Otherwise, a quota allows noncompeting domestic producers to raise the price to whatever the market will bear; a tariff would allow those same producers to raise the price at most by the amount of the duty.

Figure 7-5   Effects of an Import Quota

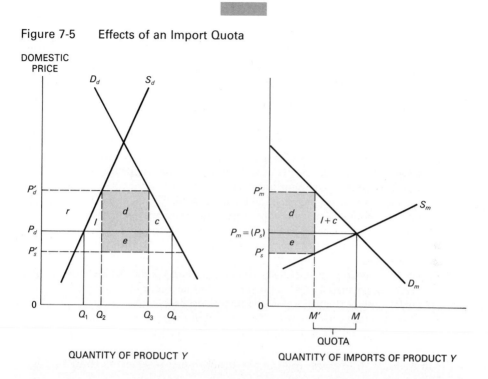

DOMESTIC PRICE

QUANTITY OF PRODUCT Y

QUANTITY OF IMPORTS OF PRODUCT Y

Before the quota is imposed, country A imports $0-M$ of product Y at a price of $0-P_s$, which equals the domestic price of $0-P_d$. Now country A imposes a quota that restricts imports to $0-M'$. The price that consumers are willing to pay for $0-M'$ of product Y rises to $0-P'_m$, and at the same time foreign suppliers would be willing to supply $0-M'$ of product Y at price $0-P'_s$ in a competitive market. This price differential gives rise to a monopoly rent or *quota profits*, as indicated by the rectangles d and e. Who gets these profits? That depends on the institutional arrangements for administering the quota. A comparison of Figures 7-4 and 7-5 indicates that the price, trade, protection, and consumption effects of an import quota are the same as those of a tariff.

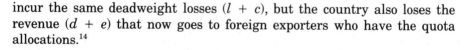

incur the same deadweight losses $(l + c)$, but the country also loses the revenue $(d + e)$ that now goes to foreign exporters who have the quota allocations.[14]

Quotas and Tariffs Compared   Quotas and tariffs are both tools of protection. Either may be used for discriminatory purposes in international trade.

Quotas, however, are absolute and inflexible, irrespective of prices and

---

[14] Rectangle e does not appear in Figure 7-4, which assumes a perfectly elastic import supply so that the import supply price remains the same after the duty. In contrast, Figure 7-5 assumes an inelastic import supply schedule; thus, if a tariff as restrictive as the quota were levied, then the import supply price would fall to $0-P'_s$.

elasticities. In contrast, the degree of protection afforded by tariffs is relative, since it is subject to market responses. Quotas separate markets pricewise and raise domestic prices above world prices by freezing import supply relative to domestic demand. On the other hand, the price effect of tariffs depends on market conditions of production and consumption. Quotas are not conducive to meting out equal treatment to different countries; tariffs, on the other hand, are more amenable to such treatment under the most-favored-nation concept.[15]

Several other differences between quotas and tariffs are noteworthy:

1. Quotas are better suited for quick emergency application by administrative action. Tariffs often require statutory legislation, which is too slow for immediate action.
2. Quotas are a direct source of monopoly profits. Tariffs do not necessarily induce monopolistic practices, and they are ordinarily less burdensome to consumers.
3. Quotas invariably stifle competition. Tariffs usually allow some competition.
4. Quotas are simpler and easier to manage than tariffs, but they deprive the government of the revenues that accrue from customs duties (unless the state auctions import licenses).
5. Because quotas are a more effective tool of restriction than tariffs, they are also a more potent weapon for retaliation and bargaining.

In general, therefore, quotas are much more restrictive than tariffs.

OTHER NONTARIFF TRADE BARRIERS

Other nontariff trade barriers form a heterogeneous collection of government policies and administrative practices that in one way or another either discriminate against imports or discriminate in favor of exports. Some nontariff measures are protectionist in both intent and effect, such as discriminatory taxes and customs valuations that do not reflect actual costs. But some nontariff measures may be protectionist in effect rather than in intent, for example, border tax adjustments and health regulations. Their immense variety, their concealment in otherwise legitimate practices, and their difficult-to-measure trade and protection effects combine to make international efforts to eliminate other nontariff trade barriers an exceedingly difficult enterprise as compared with tariffs and quantitative restrictions.[16] The fol-

---

[15] For a definition of the most-favored-nation concept (or principle), see Chapter 8, footnote 4.

[16] The inventory of nontariff barriers that is maintained by the General Agreement on Tariffs and Trade listed more than 600 official measures covering diverse manufactures in 1981. See "More Than 600 Hurdles to Trade in Industrial Products Cited," *Focus* (GATT Newsletter), February 1982, p. 2.

lowing sections simply identify the major kinds of nontariff trade barriers and their implications for international trade.

Customs Classification and Valuation

When a tariff is ad valorem, the duty imposed on a particular import good depends on how it is classified in the tariff schedule and how it is valued by the customs authorities. Complicated and obscure tariff nomenclatures coupled with ambiguous rules of classification give customs authorities plenty of opportunity for arbitrary classifications. The resulting uncertainty (and the higher duties in many instances) can act as a strong deterrent to trade.

Much more attention has been given to customs valuations that depart from the actual market value of the imported good. The "American Selling Price" (ASP) was a prime example of a customs valuation that restricts imports. The United States values most import goods at their "foreign export value," the market value at the foreign point of export. For benzenoid chemicals and a few other products, however, the customs valuation was the selling price within the United States (ordinarily much higher than the foreign export value) whenever it was determined that the import was "competitive" with or "like or similar" to a domestic product. Clearly both the intent and effect of the ASP was to afford the U.S. chemical industry higher protection than it would receive with the standard valuation. The United States agreed to eliminate the ASP (starting in 1980) pursuant to its agreement in the Tokyo Round of multilateral trade negotiations.[17]

Antidumping Regulations

The disparaging term *dumping* describes the practice of selling a product in one national market at a lower price than it is sold in another national market. Dumping, therefore, is price discrimination between national markets.

Economists distinguish between sporadic, predatory, and persistent dumping. *Sporadic dumping* occurs when producers dispose of unexpected surpluses abroad at lower prices than at home. *Predatory dumping* occurs when a producer uses low prices to weaken or drive out competitors in a foreign market. After competition is eliminated, the victorious producer is able to charge high, monopolistic prices. *Persistent dumping,* as its name indicates, refers to the continuing sale of a product at lower prices abroad than at home. Such dumping may reflect the existence of a foreign demand that is more price-elastic than domestic demand. Persistent dumping may also arise when a producer prices exports so as to cover only variable costs while absorbing the fixed costs in domestic sales.

Although persistent dumping benefits the importing country by im-

---

[17] See Chapter 8.

proving its terms of trade, governments consider all forms of dumping by foreign producers to be bad. Consequently, many governments have anti-dumping regulations that usually involve a remedial or punitive anti-dumping duty. This duty is intended to nullify the "harmful" effects of the lower dumping price on domestic producers. Article 6 of the General Agreement on Tariffs and Trade stipulates that two criteria must be met for the legitimate application of antidumping duties by member states: "sales at less than fair value" (sales abroad at prices lower than in the country of origin) and "material injury" to a domestic industry. It is widely recognized that antidumping regulations can easily be used for protection against foreign competition.

Subsidies

Many national governments, anxious to see a greater development of certain domestic industries, frequently pay *subsidies* to domestic producers or exporters to stimulate the expansion of such industries. Subsidies may be extended in the form of outright cash disbursements, tax exemptions, preferential exchange rates, governmental contracts with special privileges, or some other favorable treatment. The granting of subsidies results in a cost advantage to the recipient, and for all intents and purposes they are tantamount to an indirect form of protection.

Goods produced under a subsidy system that move in international trade tend to nullify the protective aspect of a tariff in the importing country. To reinstate the intended level of protection, the importing country may impose, in addition to the regular tariff duties, a special surtax or *countervailing duty,* which is generally equal to the amount of the foreign subsidy. In this manner, the landed cost to the domestic importer is raised by the amount of the subsidy granted to the foreign producer or exporter by the foreign government.

Direct export subsidies for manufactured goods are prohibited by the General Agreement for Tariffs and Trade.[18] However, most of the industrial countries provide special financing and insurance arrangements that enable exporters to extend easier credit terms to foreign buyers. Commonly exporters obtain credit at two or three percentage points below domestic market rates. This rate differential is a rough measure of the government subsidy. International efforts have been undertaken to harmonize national export credit policies, but many differences remain to distort the pattern of international trade.

Many domestic subsidies also influence imports, exports, or both. Agricultural support programs are notorious in this regard, as are subsidies for shipbuilding. Although the trade and protection effects of individual

---

[18] Member states are also committed to "seek to avoid" export subsidies on primary (mainly agricultural) exports and in no event to use subsidies to exceed their "equitable share" of export trade.

production and consumption subsidies may be difficult to trace, their existence is seldom in question when they are applied to products that enter international trade. Since domestic subsidies are justified as desirable internal policy measures, international negotiations to remove trade-distorting subsidies are sure to be slow and only partially successful.

Technical Standards and Health Regulations

Governments apply many regulations to imports with respect to safety, health, marking, labelling, packaging, and technical standards. Although generally desirable on social grounds, such regulations may discriminate against imports by imposing greater hardships on foreign than on domestic producers. At present, there is only a modest degree of international agreement on technical and health regulations. Products that may freely enter one country may be banned in another country, especially pharmaceuticals and foodstuffs. In illustration, American producers cannot export pickles to Norway, because that country forbids the entry of food products containing alum, an ingredient of American pickle preservatives. In turn, the United States forbids the import of live animals or fresh meat products from a country in which there are cases of hoof-and-mouth disease, even though the livestock in question may be grown in a region of the country that is free from that disease, a common situation in Argentina. In Canada, canned goods may be imported only in container sizes approved by the government. Despite some recent liberalization, the Japanese government still requires that some import goods be tested in Japan even when they have already been tested in the country of origin, a process that can take several years and result in substantial costs to foreign exporters.

Because of the increasing technical nature of products, rising living standards, and social pressures, we can expect a continuing proliferation of technical and health regulations. Foreign automobile producers, for instance, have complained that the unilateral U.S. safety regulations do not consider the special problems of the small car and hence discriminate against imports.

Government Procurement

The *procurement policies* of governments afford fertile soil for the discriminatory treatment of foreign products. The "Buy American" regulations of the U.S. government give domestic producers up to a 50 percent price spread advantage over foreign producers on Defense Department contracts and up to 12 percent on other government purchases. But the U.S. government procurement system relies mainly on competitive bidding open to all suppliers. This practice, coupled with the comparatively smaller role of the U.S. government in the economy, makes government procurement less discriminatory than in most other industrial countries. Generally, other countries practice procurement discrimination through administrative procedures (including closed bids) rather than through explicit laws or regulations. Discrimination, therefore, tends to be hidden and arbitrary. In Japan, for instance, the Nippon Telephone and Telegraph Public Corporation (NTT) procures its telecommunications products (spending over $3 billion per year in the early 1980s) mostly from four Japanese suppliers, shutting out foreign companies. After prolonged pressure by the U.S. government, NTT agreed in 1981 to accept for the first time open bids from foreign companies for some products.[19]

The very large numbers of goods and services directly purchased by national governments and the enormous influence they can exert over the procurement policies of both public-sector and private domestic firms have made preferential government procurement one of the most prominent trade issues in the 1980s, particularly in high-technology products and services.

Taxes

Besides the basic customs duties prescribed in tariff schedules, certain imports may be subjected to excise taxes and processing taxes. *Excise taxes* are collectible upon the entry of the goods through customs, whereas *processing taxes* are payable upon the first domestic processing in the case of certain raw material and semifinished commodities. The purpose of these special import taxes is generally to compensate for similar taxation of domestic goods. Very often, however, excise and processing taxes are levied exclusively on imports without corresponding levies on similar domestic products, or they may be levied when similar or competing products are not produced in the domestic market. When excise and processing taxes are assessed exclusively on imports, they become protective measures. They may be concealed behind a different rationale, but they are no less a part of a protective tariff system.

Some internal taxes obviously discriminate against imports from some or all foreign countries, such as *road taxes* that are based on the cylinder capacity or horsepower of a vehicle rather than its value. Another illustration is the French practice of placing a surtax on grain spirits when all domestic liquors are distilled from fruits. To make matters worse, all advertising of grain liquors is prohibited in France. Actually, all governments are guilty of discriminatory taxation of one kind or another.

Border tax adjustments have received much attention in recent years because of their widespread use by the European Community. Under GATT rules, a country that imposes a domestic *indirect* tax (a sales, turnover, excise, or value-added tax) on a good is permitted to give a tax rebate on exports of the same good and to levy an equivalent tax on imports of a similar good. In France, the border tax is about 20 percent of the duty-paid value of most industrial products. However, GATT prohibits any border adjustment for *direct* taxes, such as income, profits, payroll, social security,

---

[19] "Japan, The Doors of NTT Begin to Creak Open," *Business Week,* May 4, 1981, p. 67.

and property taxes. This system of border tax adjustment would be neutral in its effects on trade only if indirect taxes were fully shifted forward into prices while direct taxes were not shifted at all. Insofar as these conventional assumptions do not hold, border tax adjustments offer a trading advantage to countries relying primarily on indirect taxes for their revenue over other countries that depend mainly on direct taxes. The U.S. government (which depends mostly on direct taxes) has argued that the border taxes levied by the countries of the European Community in the process of harmonizing their tax systems do, in fact, discriminate against American goods.

Local Content and Foreign Investment Performance Requirements

Many governments, particularly in the developing countries, promote import substitution by imposing local-content regulations on certain industries. These regulations specify that a certain percentage of a good's value or certain inputs used in the manufacture of a good must be produced inside the country.

Local-content laws not only restrain imports but also are among the *performance requirements* commonly imposed on foreign investors by host governments in developing countries. Another common performance requirement is the obligation of a foreign-investing firm to export a certain proportion of its output from the host country. Such performance requirements distort international trade and investment and constitute an important source of nontariff barriers.

Nontariff Trade Barriers in Services

About one quarter of world trade is now in services: air and ocean transportation, banking, insurance, advertising, accounting, law, engineering, construction, franchising, tourism, education, health, business services, and others. Furthermore, service trade is growing more rapidly than merchandise trade. Despite its high growth rate, trade in services (commonly referred to as "invisible trade") is severely curtailed by nontariff trade barriers. The examples that follow indicate the nature of these barriers.

Many developing countries, having nationalized insurance companies, give their state insurance enterprises sole rights to domestic insurance business. Other countries refuse to license foreign-owned insurance companies. Norway, for instance, has not licensed a foreign insurance company in over 45 years.

National governments commonly discriminate against foreigners in their banking regulations. The United States is a major exception in this regard. For example, Canada limits foreign banks to a 25 percent interest in Canadian banks, and Japan makes it difficult for foreign banks to open branches and prohibits new foreign-owned banks from going into retail banking.

In shipping, many countries require that their own merchant fleets carry a certain fraction of their import and export cargoes. Generally, countries (including the United States) reserve intercoastal trade exclusively for domestic shipping companies.

Laws in many countries restrict the flow of data across their borders. For instance, Scandinavian governments require that most computer data be processed and stored within the country. West Germany prohibits the transmission of data outside the country unless some data processing is done within the country. Sweden does not permit the local offices of foreign companies to process payrolls abroad.

Many other restrictions on international trade in services distort the location of service activities and add to their costs. The U.S. government has compiled a list of 2,000 instances of barriers that stultify the flow of services among countries.

Concluding Remarks on Nontariff Trade Barriers

Our description of nontariff trade barriers is far from exhaustive. For example, governments may stipulate the minimum prices for certain imports, known as *trigger prices*. In the 1970s, the United States imposed trigger prices on imports of low-cost steel products. Mention should also be made of the cumbersome red tape in the administration of trade restrictions, which generates uncertainties and costs for international traders. Enough has been said, however, to demonstrate that nontariff trade barriers are bewildering in their variety, frequently hidden in administrative practices, and, in many instances, exceedingly difficult to eliminate through international negotiations. Furthermore, new nontariff barriers are continually created as governments respond to changing circumstances.

In the next chapter, we look at the progress that has been made in lessening tariff and nontariff trade barriers under the General Agreement on Tariffs and Trade.

SUMMARY

1. Despite the theoretical support for free trade, governments, more often than not, have interfered with the international movement of goods. These restrictive measures consist chiefly of (1) tariffs and (2) nontariff trade barriers.
2. Customs duties may be *ad valorem* or *specific*. Tariff schedules may have one, two, or three different duties for each dutiable article. Governments may mitigate the effects of their tariff rate systems through drawbacks, bonded warehouses, and free zones or ports.

3. Tariffs may be designed to serve a revenue function or a protection function. The revenue and protection functions are contradictory: A tariff maximizes revenue when it does not restrict imports; it maximizes protection when it eliminates imports.

4. Depending primarily on import supply elasticities, an import duty may raise the price of an import good (a) not at all, (b) less than the amount of the duty, or (c) equal to the amount of the duty.

5. In addition to price effects, an import duty has revenue, trade, protection, consumption, and income-redistribution effects.

6. Several methods have been used to measure the trade and protection effects of national tariff systems: (a) by tariff revenues, (b) by the height of duties (weighted or unweighted), (c) by effective rates rather than nominal rates, and (d) by elasticities and market share. Only the last method is fully justified by economic theory, but it is an enormous task to measure the elasticities of the thousands of products that make up a tariff system.

7. As the name implies, quantitative restrictions impose absolute limitations on foreign trade. Quantitative restrictions ordinarily take the form of import quotas administered by the issuance of import licenses to individual traders. Three major types of import quotas are in use throughout the world: unilateral quotas, negotiated quotas (bilateral or multilateral), and tariff quotas.

8. The economic effects of an import quota are similar to those of an import duty. Instead of generating government revenue, however, an import quota usually creates monopoly profits for the importers or exporters of the product in question.

9. Whereas quotas are absolute and inflexible regardless of prices and elasticities, the trade and protection effects of tariffs are dependent on the market conditions of production and consumption. In general, therefore, quotas are more restrictive than tariffs.

10. Besides quotas, nontariff barriers include a bewildering variety of government measures that in one way or another either discriminate against imports or discriminate in favor of exports. The major kinds of nontariff barriers include customs classification and valuation, antidumping regulations, subsidies, standards, government procurement, taxes, performance requirements, and restrictions on trade in services.

QUESTIONS AND APPLICATIONS

1. What is a tariff?
2. Distinguish between ad valorem, specific, and compound duties.
3. "Tariffs provide revenue for the government and protection for domestic industries. Therefore, the higher the rate of duties, the greater

the revenue and the greater the protection." Discuss the validity of this statement.

4. Utilizing supply-demand diagrams, indicate how the effects of an import duty change (a) when the import supply schedule becomes less elastic, (b) when the import demand schedule becomes more elastic, and (c) when the domestic supply schedule becomes more elastic.

5. If the duty on a final product import is 15 percent and the weighted average of duties on importable inputs that contribute one-fourth of the value of the final product is 10 percent, what is the *effective* rate of duty on the final product?

6. Distinguish between unilateral, negotiated, and tariff quotas.

7. Why and how do import quotas create monopoly profits?

8. Compare quotas with tariffs, identifying their similarities and differences.

9. "Quotas are positive regulations of international trade while the results of tariffs are uncertain. Since a country must know where it is heading, the use of quotas is therefore preferable to the use of tariffs." Evaluate this statement.

10. Discuss the meaning of the following statement: "The majority of non-tariff measures are protectionist in effect rather than in intent."

11. Why are direct export subsidies considered a nontariff trade barrier?

SELECTED READINGS

See the list of readings given at the end of Chapter 9.

8
Multilateral Trade Agreements Under GATT

As observed in Chapter 1, the rationale of government economic policies is that national economies, if left alone, would fail to achieve goals that are deemed to be in the national interest, such as full employment, price stability, a satisfactory rate of growth, an equitable distribution of income, and a strong balance of payments. Economic activity is characterized by a high degree of interdependence among the different nations of the world, and a policy in the best interests of a nation must take into account such interdependence, since it affects and, in turn, is affected by the policies of other nations. Consequently, a wise national economic policy must be conceived within a broad international frame of reference, especially when the nation involved holds a dominant position in world affairs and when its conduct is apt to have important repercussions abroad.

Unfortunately most nations, large and small, are inclined to disregard this dual aspect of their economic policies and to ignore the fact that by building roadblocks of interference on one side of the international highway of trade, they block the other side as well. The United States, like other nations, has been guilty of this shortsighted approach to economic policy at various periods of its history.

Although its earlier position of dominance has been eroded by the remarkable resurgence of Western Europe and Japan and the emergence of newly industrializing countries, such as South Korea and Taiwan, the United States continues to exert a pervasive influence on the world economy. With only 5 percent of the world's population, this country produces about one-quarter of the world's goods and services and accounts for about 12 percent of all international trade. Thus, the economic behavior of the United States can do much harm or good, depending upon the growth and stability of its economy as well as the direction of its foreign economic policy. A liberal U.S. trade policy enhances the gains from international specialization and helps promote world economic growth. Conversely, a protectionist trade policy runs the risk of widespread retaliation by other countries and a return to the "beggar-my-neighbor" policies of the 1930s.

Since World War II, the trade policies of the United States and other industrial nations have been conducted mainly within the framework laid down by the General Agreement on Tariffs and Trade, known as GATT. In this chapter we describe GATT and note its achievements, including the last completed negotiations under its auspices, known as the Tokyo Round. We then discuss the erosion of GATT as industrial countries have increasingly circumvented its provisions in recent years. We conclude with a preview of the key issues in the new round of multilateral trade negotiations now taking place—the Uruguay Round.

THE GENERAL AGREEMENT ON TARIFFS AND TRADE (GATT)

After World War II, several international measures were undertaken to liberalize trade and payments between nations. Plans for the creation of a liberal, multilateral system of world trade were started while the war was still in progress. Initiated for the most part by the United States, these plans envisaged the close economic cooperation of all nations in the fields of international trade, payments, and investment. At the time, it was widely believed that such cooperation, formalized by agreements and implemented by international organizations, would avoid the mistakes of the past and lay the cornerstones for a progressive world economy. The two notable achievements of this wartime planning were the International Monetary Fund and the International Bank for Reconstruction and Development. The first institution was to insure the free convertibility of currencies; the second was to supplement and stimulate the international flow of private capital.

Once the war had ended, it soon became apparent that the difficulties of postwar reconstruction in Europe and elsewhere had been greatly underestimated. Attention shifted from the now distant goal of a global system of multilateral trade to the immediate threat posed by Western Europe's economic distress and the spread of communism. The end of ambitious international planning was symbolized by the refusal of the United States Congress in 1950 to ratify the treaty establishing an International Trade Organization (ITO).[1]

---

[1] The ITO Charter was signed by representatives of 54 countries at Havana, Cuba, on March 24, 1948. The charter was an ambitious document, covering not only commercial policy but also such topics as employment, economic development, state trading, cartels, and intergovernmental commodity agreements. The charter has never been ratified by the signatory states. Late in 1950 the U.S. Department of State announced that it would no longer press for Congressional approval.

The effects of the failure of the ITO on international cooperation in commercial policy were considerably softened by the rise to prominence of the *General Agreement on Tariffs and Trade*. GATT was an almost casual offshoot of the international conference held at Geneva in 1947 to consider a draft charter for the ITO. There the United States initiated six months of continual negotiations with 22 other countries that led to commitments to bind or lower 45,000 tariff rates within the framework of principles and rules of procedure laid down by GATT.

GATT entered into force in 1948 with a membership of 23 industrial countries.[2] By the mid-1980s, its membership had risen to 90 countries that accounted for over four-fifths of world trade. In addition, over 30 other countries also apply GATT rules in their trade. All in all, therefore, about 120 countries subscribe to GATT's trading rules.[3]

Major Provisions of GATT

GATT contains numerous articles and annexes. The tariff schedules listing the thousands of concessions that have been negotiated by member countries are also part of the agreement. Despite its complexity, GATT comprises four basic elements:

1. the rule of nondiscrimination in trade relations between the participating countries
2. commitments to observe the negotiated tariff concessions
3. prohibitions against the use of quantitative restrictions (quotas) on exports and imports
4. special provisions to promote the trade of developing countries.

The remaining provisions of GATT are concerned with exceptions to these general principles, trade measures other than tariffs and quotas, and sundry procedural matters.

Tariffs GATT obligates each member to accord nondiscriminatory, *most-favored-nation* (MFN) treatment to all other members with respect to import and export duties (including allied charges), customs regulations, and internal taxes and regulations.[4] An exception to the rule of nondiscrimination is made in the case of well-known tariff preferences, such as those between the countries of the British Commonwealth. No new preferences may be

---

[2] A signatory of GATT is known as a *contracting party*, since, legally, GATT is not an organization. For convenience of exposition, however, we shall use the term "member" to refer to participation in GATT.

[3] China joined GATT in 1986 and shortly thereafter the Soviet Union asked to participate in GATT's new global trade talks (Uruguay Round). In the past, the Soviet Union has condemned GATT as an "instrument of Western imperialism."

[4] Under the most-favored-nation principle, any tariff concession granted by one country to any other country is automatically extended to all other countries. GATT members are obligated to apply the MFN principle only to other GATT members, but they are free to apply it to nonmember countries as well.

created, however, and existing preferences may not be increased. Frontier traffic, customs unions, free trade areas, and generalized systems of preferences extended by industrial countries to developing countries are exempted from the general rule of nondiscrimination.

GATT legalizes the schedules of tariff concessions negotiated by members and commits each member to their observance. An escape clause, however, allows any member to withdraw or modify a tariff concession (or other obligation) if, as a result of the tariff concession (or obligation), there is such an increase in imports as to cause, or threaten to cause, serious injury to domestic producers of like or directly competitive products. When a member uses the escape clause, it must consult with other members as to remedies; if agreement is not reached, those countries may withdraw equivalent concessions.[5]

Quantitative Restrictions   GATT sets forth a general rule prohibiting the use of quantitative import and export restrictions. There are, however, several exceptions to this rule. The four most important exceptions pertain to agriculture, the balance of payments, economic development, and national security.

The agreement sanctions the use of import restrictions on any agricultural or fishery product where restrictions are necessary for the enforcement of government programs in marketing, production control, or the removal of surpluses. This exception is important to the United States, which has placed import quotas on several agricultural products.

GATT also permits a member to apply import restrictions to safeguard its balance of payments when there is an imminent threat, or actual occurrence, of a serious decline in its monetary reserves or when its monetary reserves are very low. The member must consult with GATT with respect to the continuation or intensification of such restrictions. GATT must also consult with the International Monetary Fund when dealing with problems of monetary reserves, the balance of payments, and foreign exchange practices. Members of GATT are not to frustrate the intent of GATT by exchange action nor the intent of the Fund agreement by trade restrictions. A country that adheres to GATT but is not a member of the Fund must conclude a special exchange agreement with the contracting parties.

GATT recognizes the special position of the developing countries and allows such countries to use nondiscriminatory import quotas to encourage infant industries. Prior approval, however, must be obtained from the collective GATT membership.

A member of GATT may use trade controls for purposes of national security. The strategic controls on United States exports come under this exception.

---

[5] The *escape clause* is now referred to as the *safeguard provision,* a terminological shift that reflects a shift from "freer" trade to "managed trade." An example is the Multifiber Arrangement discussed in the section on trade disputes in Chapter 9.

In addition to these four major exceptions, there are many of lesser importance. For example, members may use trade restrictions to protect public morals, to implement sanitation regulations, to prevent deceptive trade practices, and to protect patents and copyrights. All quantitative restrictions permitted by GATT are to be applied in accordance with the most-favored-nation principle. Import licenses may not specify that goods be imported from a certain country.

Special Provisions to Promote the Trade of Developing Countries
In 1965 the contracting parties added a new Part IV—Trade and Development—to the general agreement in recognition of the need for a rapid and sustained expansion of the export earnings of the less-developed member countries. Under the terms of the three articles composing Part IV, the developed countries agree to undertake the following positive action "to the fullest extent possible": (1) give high priority to the reduction and elimination of barriers to products currently or potentially of particular export interest to less-developed contracting parties, (2) refrain from introducing or increasing customs duties or nontariff import barriers on such products, and (3) refrain from imposing new internal taxes that significantly hamper the consumption of primary products produced in the developing countries and accord high priority to the reduction or elimination of such taxes. In addition, the developed countries agree not to expect reciprocity for commitments made by them in trade negotiations to reduce or remove tariffs or other barriers to the trade of less-developed contracting parties. In return, the developing countries commit themselves to take "appropriate action" to implement the provisions of Part IV for the benefit of the trade of other less-developed contracting parties. A Committee on Trade and Development is charged with keeping under review the implementation of the provisions of Part IV.

Other Provisions Many other substantive matters are covered by the provisions of GATT: national treatment of internal taxation and regulation, motion picture films, antidumping and countervailing duties, customs valuation, customs formalities, marks of origin, subsidies, state trading, and the publication and administration of trade regulations. The intention of most of these provisions is to eliminate concealed protection or discrimination in international trade.

Several articles of GATT deal with procedural matters. In meetings, each member is entitled to one vote and, unless otherwise specified, decisions are to be taken by majority vote. A two-thirds majority vote is required to waive any obligation imposed on a member by the general agreement.[6] Articles also cover consultation procedures and the settlement of disputes between members.

---

[6] In practice, GATT decisions are generally arrived at by concensus rather than by vote.

Activities of GATT

The members of GATT meet in regular annual sessions and special tariff conferences. A Council of Representatives deals with matters between sessions and prepares the agenda for each session. In addition, intersessional working groups have been appointed at regular sessions to report on specific topics at subsequent sessions.

Adding further to the continuous influence of GATT has been the practice of member governments to consult with each other before the regular sessions. The membership has obtained a secretariat from the United Nations that, among other things, publishes an annual report. In these and other ways, GATT has behaved like an international organization and, as a matter of fact, has been more effective than some legitimate organizations.

The main activities of GATT fall into four categories: (1) tariff bargaining, (2) bargaining on nontariff trade barriers, (3) elimination of quantitative restrictions, and (4) settlement of disputes.

Tariff Bargaining   The parties to GATT have participated in eight tariff conferences to negotiate mutual tariff concessions, as indicated in Table 8-1. The initial conference at Geneva negotiated 45,000 different tariff rates, and today the schedules of GATT include products that make up more than half the world's trade. All of these rates have been either reduced or bound against any increase in the future.

The magnitude of this accomplishment is unprecedented in tariff history; it represents a new approach to the task of lowering tariff barriers.

TABLE 8-1   Multilateral Trade Negotiations under GATT

Date	Name	Outcome
1947	Geneva Round	45,000 tariff concessions representing half of world trade.
1949	Annecy Round	Modest tariff reductions.
1950–1951	Torquay Round	25 percent tariff reduction in relation to 1948 level.
1955–1956	Geneva Round	Modest tariff reductions.
1961–1962	Dillon Round	Modest tariff reductions.
1963–1967	Kennedy Round	Average tariff reduction of 35 percent for industrial products; only modest reductions for agricultural products. Antidumping code.
1973–1979	Tokyo Round	Average tariff reductions of 34 percent for industrial products. Nontariff trade barrier codes.
1986–	Uruguay Round	To be decided in forthcoming negotiations.

Source: Focus, GATT Newsletter, No. 44, March 1987, p. 5.

Before World War II the most successful attempt to reduce tariffs by reciprocal bargaining was the trade agreements program of the United States. That program was limited, however, by its bilateral nature. GATT has overcome this disability by applying multilaterally the underlying principles of the bilateral trade agreements of the 1930s.

The results of the round of tariff negotiations at each conference are not finalized until all of them are gathered into a single master agreement signed by the participating countries. The concessions in the master agreement then apply to trade between all members of GATT. In this way, each member receives the benefits of every tariff concession and becomes a party to every tariff agreement.

GATT has brilliantly overcome the difficulties of a purely bilateral trade agreements program: (1) the reluctance of nations to lower or bind tariff duties unless a large number of their trading partners are taking similar action, and (2) the time-consuming negotiation of individual trade agreements, each containing its own code of conduct and other provisions.[7] While it is negotiating, each member knows that other members are also negotiating and that the results of those negotiations will accrue to its benefit. Because the prospects of gain are greater, countries are apt to be more generous. Moreover, one set of rules applies to every tariff concession, and it is much more comprehensive in scope than would be possible in the case of individual bilateral agreements. GATT has also created an environment conducive to tariff bargaining, and it has often induced countries to bargain when they preferred to stand firm.

Bargaining on Nontariff Trade Barriers   The first six tariff conferences dealt only with tariffs, but it had become evident by the late 1960s that nontariff measures (apart from quantitative restrictions) were a more serious menace to international trade than were tariffs. Accordingly, the seventh conference (the Tokyo Round) undertook for the first time multilateral negotiations on several nontariff barriers. The outcome of this most recent conference is described later in this chapter.

Quantitative Restrictions   Until 1959 GATT made only slow progress toward the elimination of import restrictions (quotas). The majority of GATT members took advantage of the balance of payments exception to the general prohibition of import quotas. The restoration of currency convertibility by Western European countries at the end of 1958 broke this logjam. The major trading countries then abandoned quantitative import restrictions that were previously justified on grounds of a weak balance of payments or low mon-

---

[7] The superior effectiveness of the multilateral approach of GATT to the bilateral approach of the 1930s is clearly observable in the experience of the United States. During 1934–1945 this country negotiated trade agreements with 29 countries, but in a single GATT conference at Geneva in 1947 it completed negotiations with 22 other countries. The experience of the 1930s showed that the abandonment of protective import quotas through bilateral bargaining was virtually impossible.

etary reserves. However, the success of GATT in persuading industrial countries to eliminate import quotas on manufactured products in the 1960s is now being undermined by the reintroduction of such quotas through bilateral agreements known as voluntary export restrictions.

Settlement of Disputes   One of the most striking, but least publicized, of GATT's accomplishments is the settlement of trade disputes between members. Historically trade disputes have been matters strictly between the disputants; there was no third party to which they might appeal for a just solution. As a consequence, trade disputes often went unresolved for years, all the while embittering international relations. When disputes were settled in the past, it was usually a case of the weaker country giving way to the stronger. GATT has improved matters tremendously by adopting complaint procedures and by affording through its periodic meetings a world stage on which an aggrieved nation could voice its complaint.

A large number of disputes have been resolved by bilateral consultations without ever coming before the collective membership. The mere presence of GATT was probably helpful in these instances. Thus, the British government repealed a requirement forbidding the manufacture of cigarettes of pure Virginia tobacco when the United States protested the requirement as a violation of GATT.

When a dispute is not settled bilaterally, it may be taken by the complainant country to the collective membership at the next regular meeting on the basis that the treatment accorded to the commerce of the complainant country by the other disputant is impairing or nullifying benefits received under the agreement. A panel on complaints hears the disputants, deliberates, and drafts a report. The report is then acted upon by the membership. In this way GATT resolved an extremely bitter disagreement between Pakistan and India.

In the event that the GATT recommendation is not observed, the aggrieved party may be authorized to suspend the application of certain of its obligations to the trade of the other party. Thus, the Netherlands was allowed to place a limitation on wheat flour from the United States because of the damage caused its exports by U.S. dairy quotas.

In the 1980s, member countries have turned to GATT to help resolve an unprecedented number of serious trade disputes. For instance, the European Economic Community (EEC) has filed a complaint in GATT against Japanese trade practices, and the United States has filed petitions against European subsidies on agricultural exports. The United States has also started GATT proceedings against Canada on the performance requirements imposed on American investing companies (particularly the compulsory sourcing of Canadian products), which is the first time any country has asked GATT to deal with the trade aspects of foreign investment regulations. The number and importance of these disputes poses the greatest challenge ever faced by GATT's settlement machinery.

THE TOKYO ROUND OF MULTILATERAL TRADE NEGOTIATIONS (MTNs)

The Tokyo Round formally opened in Tokyo in September 1973, but bargaining did not start in earnest until January 1975, with the passage of the U.S. Trade Act of 1974. After five and a half years of acrimonious debates and tedious bargaining sessions, the Tokyo Round ended in April 1979 with the initialing of a comprehensive international trade pact.

What did the Tokyo Round accomplish? We offer the following summary descriptions of its major results.

Industrial Tariffs

Preceding the Tokyo Round, the sixth tariff conference (known as the Kennedy Round) had cut duties on industrial goods an average of 35 percent on some $40 billion of trade in 60,000 products. As a consequence of this reduction and reductions made in earlier conferences, the average tariff rates of the industrial countries were already very low by historical standards.

The Tokyo Round cut duties on industrial products an average of 30 percent on trade that amounted to more than $155 billion in 1977 dollars. The average tariff (weighted by actual trade flows) on manufactured products of the nine major industrial countries declined from 7.0 percent to 4.7 percent. The tariff cuts and resulting new tariffs on manufactures for the United States, the EC, and Japan are shown in Table 8-2. These tariff reductions were gradually applied over the seven-year period 1980–1987.

In addition to these MFN tariff reductions, several countries (including the United States) reached a *sectoral* agreement on trade in civil aircraft that eliminated all customs duties on civil aircraft, aircraft parts, and repairs on civil aircraft, effective January 1, 1980.

Agricultural Trade

The United States is vitally interested in reducing barriers to trade in agricultural products. As the world's most efficient agricultural producer, this country wants freer access to EC and Japanese markets. In opposition to this U.S. interest, the EC insists on the maintenance of its highly protectionist agricultural policy, which is viewed as an integral part of the Common Market.[8] At the same time, Japan strongly resists pressures to moderate protection of its high-cost farmers, who possess substantial political strength. Not surprisingly, then, the most contentious differences between the United States and these two parties in the Tokyo Round were in

---

[8] See Chapter 10.

TABLE 8-2   Average Tariff Rates on Manufactures for the United States, the European Economic Community, and Japan before and after Implementation of the Tokyo Round

Country/Country Group	Tariffs on Total Imports of Finished and Semifinished Manufactures		
	Pre-Tokyo	Post-Tokyo	Percentage Change
United States	7.0%	4.9%	30%
European Community	8.3	6.0	28
Japan	10.0	5.4	46

Note: These averages were calculated in two steps: First, a simple (unweighted) arithmetic average for each heading in the Brussels Tariff Nomenclature (BTN) was calculated; second, these averages were weighted according to the imports of the United States, the EC, and eight other industrial countries to get a total weighted average. This method is superior to an unweighted average or an average weighted by the imports of the country in question. See the discussion of effective versus nominal tariff rates in Chapter 7 for an explanation of tariff rate measurement.

Source: The World Bank, *World Development Report, 1987* (New York: Oxford University Press, 1987), Table 8.1, p. 136.

agricultural trade. At one point, for instance, the Japanese refusal to liberalize its import quotas on oranges threatened to halt negotiations.[9]

In the face of these deep-seated differences, the Tokyo Round made little progress toward cutting barriers on agricultural trade, as was also true of the earlier Kennedy Round.[10] Pervasive regulation, protection, and subsidies continue to distort international trade in temperate agricultural products.

Nontariff Trade Barriers

The distinctive hallmark of the Tokyo Round was a series of agreements on nontariff trade barriers. Earlier GATT conferences had paid little attention to such restrictions. In preparation for the Tokyo Round, the GATT secretariat compiled a list of more than 800 specific nontariff distortions of international trade. These were grouped into five broad categories: (1) government participation in trade (export subsidies, procurement, countervailing duties, etc.), (2) customs and administrative entry procedures (classification, valuation, customs formalities, etc.), (3) standards and packaging regulations, (4) specific limitations on trade (quotas, export restraints, li-

---

[9] "Japan's Tough Restrictions on Imported Oranges Endanger Settlement of U.S. Trade Agreements," *Wall Street Journal*, November 1, 1978, p. 48.

[10] Early in the conference, the industrial countries offered concessions on tropical agricultural products important to many developing countries.

censing, etc.), and (5) charges on imports (prior deposits, variable levies, etc.).

The Tokyo Round negotiated codes covering the first three categories, but it failed to reach agreement on the last two, with the exception of licensing. It also established standing committees to administer the individual codes that contain provisions for consultation and dispute settlement.

Subsidies and Countervailing Duty Code American firms frequently complain that foreign firms benefit from government assistance that allows them to sell their products in the United States at "unfairly" low prices and to displace American products in third-country markets. This code is intended to ensure that the subsidies used by member countries do not injure the interests of another member country. It prohibits outright *export* subsidies for manufactures and primary mineral products, but for agricultural products subsidies are prohibited only when they displace the exports of other members or undercut prices in a particular market. Criteria are to be set up to determine injury resulting from *domestic* subsidies, and upon a showing of injury, countries would be allowed to take countervailing duty action to offset subsidies.

Technical Barriers to Trade (Standards) Code This code seeks to ensure that product standards, product testing, and product certification systems that are adopted for reasons of safety, health, environmental protection, or other purposes do not create obstacles to trade. The code encourages the use of open procedures in the adoption of standards and the negotiation of international standards.

Government Procurement Code This code is designed to inhibit discrimination against foreign goods at all stages of government procurement so as to encourage more international competition. It prescribes specific rules on drafting the specifications of goods to be procured, advertising prospective purchases, the time allowed for the submission of bids, the qualifications of suppliers, the opening and evaluation of bids, the award of contracts, and the hearing and review of protests.

The code applies to individual government contracts to purchase physical goods worth more than SDR 150,000. Services are not covered by the code except those incidental to the purchase of physical goods. Also, the code does not apply to the purchase of goods involving national security or agricultural support programs.

Customs Valuation Code The method of valuation used by a country for imported goods can be as important as the rate of duty in determining the amount of duty. The code commits countries to base customs valuation on the actual price paid for a product, that is, its *invoice* value. Only when the invoice value of a product cannot be ascertained does the code allow countries to use other valuation bases in a manner stipulated by the code.

Import Licensing Code Complicated procedures and bureaucratic red tape in the administration of import licenses can thwart or delay imports. Under this code, countries are obligated to simplify their import-licensing systems and apply them in a nondiscriminatory manner. Importers have to go to only one administrative body to secure licenses, and a license may not be refused for minor errors in documentation or minor variations in the value, quantity, or weight of a product under license.

Revised Antidumping Code In addition to these five new codes, the Tokyo Round also revised the GATT Antidumping Code that had been in force for over 10 years. The revised code alters certain provisions to bring them into conformity with the code provisions on subsidies and countervailing duties. Both dumping (the action of a firm) and subsidies (the action of a government) can distort international competition in much the same way and may, in fact, occur together. The revised code redefines the determination of the cause and effects of dumping, clarifies the criterion of injury, and strengthens investigation procedures.

Safeguards Code An outstanding failure of the Tokyo Round was the inability of negotiators to agree on a safeguards code. *Safeguards* are temporary emergency actions, such as higher duties, quotas, and voluntary export restrictions, intended to protect industries suddenly threatened by a large increase in imports. Agreement on a safeguards code is vital to the maintenance of open international markets because governments are strongly inclined to pacify protectionist interest groups with safeguards unwarranted by objective circumstances and to make them a permanent form of protection. Intense protectionist pressures in the industrial countries hardened their negotiating positions in the Tokyo Round, preventing any agreement.

Concluding Observations on the Tokyo Round

The Tokyo Round was a holding action against growing forces of protection that threaten to undermine the international trading system. But it was not a victory over those forces. Indeed, trade disputes and protectionist measures have multiplied since the end of the Tokyo Round.

The major achievement of the Tokyo Round was the negotiation of codes on nontariff trade barriers that for the first time subjected them to international agreement. Its signal failures were the inability to agree on a safeguards code and to lower significantly the heavy restrictions on trade in agricultural products. Although positive, the reduction of duties on industrial products will have only a marginal effect on trade, because such duties were already low.

THE EROSION OF GATT

As members of GATT, the United States and other industrial countries are committed to observe the principle of nondiscrimination (unconditional MFN treatment) in their trade policies. This means that a member country's tariffs and nontariff trade barriers are to be applied equally to all other member countries. In sum, no member country is to give a special trading advantage to another member country. The industrial countries are also committed to abstain from quantitative restrictions on imports.

Under the present GATT safeguards or escape clause (Article XIX), a member country can withdraw or modify concessions previously granted to other members if it can demonstrate that imports of a certain product have increased to such an extent as to cause or threaten to cause serious injury to domestic producers. Furthermore, a country needs to apply safeguards in a nondiscriminatory fashion and to consult with the supplying countries. If those consultations do not lead to an agreement, then the supplying countries can withdraw "equivalent" concessions previously granted to the safeguards country.

Article XIX has not worked well in recent years. Starting in the 1970s, industrial countries have increasingly circumvented it by negotiating *bilateral* agreements with particular exporting countries to allocate market shares in specific sectors, such as textiles, steel, and semiconductors. Usually these agreements take the form of *voluntary export restrictions* (VERs) whereby the first party, an exporting country, agrees to limit quantitatively its exports of specific products to the second party, an importing country. VERs enable the importing country to discriminate among supplying countries with no offsetting concessions. A supplying country agrees to limit its exports because it faces the threat of more restrictive measures by the importing country. The United States and the EC have negotiated VERs with Japan, South Korea, Hong Kong, and other countries that cover TV sets, automobiles, footwear, ships, leather, steel, semiconductors, and other sectors.[11]

Bilateral agreements are *selective*, applying to a single exporting country (or country group in the case of the EC). They are, therefore, a clear violation of the principle of nondiscrimination. Because such agreements commonly use quotas (whether applied by the exporting or importing country), they also violate GATT's prohibition against quantitative restrictions. And, of course, they do not satisfy the safeguards criteria laid down in Article XIX.

Why have industrial countries applied import restrictions outside GATT? One reason that governments prefer bilateral agreements is that they appear less protectionist to consumers than import restrictions applied

---

[11] VERs and other bilateral restrictive agreements used by the United States are discussed in the section on the new protectionism in Chapter 9.

to *all* exporting countries. Also, the importing country can pretend that it supports free trade because the restrictions are imposed "voluntarily" by the exporting country. However, their main advantage is *selectivity*. By applying restrictions to imports of a product sector from a single country under a negotiated arrangement, bilateral agreements avoid giving other exporting countries the right to demand compensation or to retaliate under the dispute settlement provisions of GATT.

Clearly, a new safeguards agreement is needed to bring some order into a situation that is becoming anarchic. Without a new safeguards code, the industrial countries will continue to circumvent GATT with bilateral agreements that transform more and more of the international economy into *managed* trade, which is more responsive to political than to economic forces. A new code will have to allow selective restrictions. Otherwise, it will be ignored as Article XIX is today. The issues to be negotiated, therefore, are the rules, criteria, and surveillance arrangements that would govern selective safeguards. The failure to negotiate a new code in the Tokyo Round was a major setback for supporters of an open, multilateral trading system. In particular, it was a blow to the developing countries, whose exports of standard manufactured products, such as textiles, shoes, and steel, are frequently blocked by new import restrictions of the industrial countries.

THE URUGUAY ROUND OF NEW MULTILATERAL TRADE NEGOTIATIONS

A *declaration* adopted in September 1986 at Punta del Este, Uruguay, by GATT's member countries launched the Uruguay Round of trade negotiations.[12] The declaration was a victory for the United States, which had pressed hard for new trade talks that it hoped would stem the tide of protection both at home and abroad. Without a doubt, the Uruguay Round is the most ambitious and complex set of negotiations ever undertaken by GATT.

The *Trade Negotiations Committee* (TNC) oversees the conduct of the Uruguay Round. To carry out the negotiations, two groups were established: (1) the *Group on Negotiations on Goods* (GNG), whose purpose is to negotiate traditional trade issues and new issues relating to investment and intellectual property, and (2) the *Group on Negotiations on Services* (GNS), whose purpose is to negotiate trade in services. Negotiations now proceeding at the GATT headquarters in Geneva are due to end in 1990, but they could well last a decade.

Part I of the declaration covers trade in goods. It provides for a *standstill* and *rollback* of trade restrictions or other measures that distort trade (mem-

---

[12] GATT, "Launching of Uruguay Round," *Focus Newsletter,* October 1986, pp. 1 ff.

ber governments agree *not* to increase existing levels of protection and to phase out their existing violations of GATT). Part II covers negotiations on trade in services.

Trade in Goods

Fourteen *negotiation groups* have been set up under the GNG for the following subjects: tariffs, nontariff measures, tropical products, natural resource-based products, textiles and clothing, agriculture, GATT articles, safeguards, MFN agreements and arrangements, subsidies and countervailing measures, dispute settlement, industrial property rights, trade-related investment measures, and the functioning of the GATT system. We offer here comments on some of these subjects to indicate the complexity of negotiation issues.

In general, the level of tariff protection of the industrial countries is now so low as to have only minor significance. However, there remain two issues on which tariff negotiations might be fruitful: (1) Tariffs are higher for manufactures than for primary products, and (2) tariff protection in the developing countries remains very restrictive.

Tariff escalation occurs when duties increase as the degree of processing of a product increases (as a result, the finished product pays a higher duty than the previous semifinished product, which in turn pays a higher duty than the primary, commodity form of the product). The elimination of tariff escalation is of special importance to the developing countries as they try to convert their commodity exports into exports of manufactures. These countries will be the main beneficiaries of negotiations on tropical and natural resource-based products.

Tariffs are not only high in the developing countries but also much less *bound* than tariffs in the industrial countries. Consequently, the developing countries can raise tariffs at will without negotiating with other GATT members for grants of compensation under Article XXVIII. This special treatment is granted developing countries by Chapter IV of GATT. But what treatment should developing countries be given in tariff negotiations in the Uruguay Round? Should the advanced developing countries, such as Brazil and South Korea, be "graduated" to assume the same obligations in tariffs (and other trade measures) as the industrial countries?

Trade negotiations are also aimed at reducing or eliminating nontariff trade barriers. To advance that purpose, negotiators will try to improve, clarify, or expand agreements reached in the Tokyo Round. For instance, the United States believes that the subsidies and countervailing duty code badly needs strengthening in three areas. In particular, there needs to be (1) a definition of subsidies that are *potentially* injurious to the interests of trading countries, whether such subsidies are granted to exporters or to domestic firms; (2) an agreement on criteria to be used to determine the "material injury" that is required to justify remedial action (notably countervailing duties) by the injured country; and (3) the design of procedures and remedies that would redress injury but not overcompensate for it. Negotiations on subsidies are impeded by different attitudes toward them. Some countries believe that *all* subsidies distort international trade and deserve retaliation regardless of material injury, whereas other countries believe that retaliation is justified only when there is indisputable, substantial injury.[13]

Several *negotiating groups* are intended to strengthen the performance of GATT. The *Functioning of the GATT System Group* aims to enhance the surveillance by GATT of the trade policies and practices of member countries, improve decision-making, and strengthen GATT's relations with other international organizations, such as the IMF and the World Bank, so as to increase its contribution to global economic policymaking. The *GATT Articles Group* will review existing GATT articles, provisions, and rules ("disciplines") as requested by member countries. Two sets of negotiations of particular importance will be undertaken by the *Dispute Settlement Group* and the *Safeguards Group.*

It is widely agreed that prompt and effective settlement of trade disputes between member countries is essential to the GATT system. It is also widely agreed that dispute settlement needs to be improved by speeding up the settlement procedure and by strengthening the implementation of recommendations made by GATT panels. The United States is particularly unhappy with the present settlement provisions. For instance, in 1981 American pasta producers complained that European exporters of pasta were being subsidized by the EC in violation of GATT rules. It took two years to get a GATT panel ruling which found in favor of the United States. The EC then refused to adopt the panel ruling (as it was entitled to do under the current GATT dispute provision), and it negotiated on and off with the United States over the next four years before the dispute was settled on terms less favorable to the United States than the panel recommendation.

The failure to negotiate a safeguards code is the most important unfinished business of the Tokyo Round. We have already discussed the main safeguard issues. The declaration on the Uruguay Round states that the agreement on safeguards shall be based on the GATT principles and, among other features, shall contain the following: transparency (that is, safeguards are public knowledge), objective criteria for action (including the concept of serious injury), temporariness of safeguard restrictions, structural adjustment, compensation and retaliation, multilateral surveillance and dispute settlement, and application to all member countries.[14] The outcome of safeguard negotiations in the Uruguay Round will determine the ability of GATT to bring under its authority the trade restrictions (particularly, bi-

---

[13] For a detailed examination of this subject, see Gary C. Hufbauer, "Subsidy Issues after the Tokyo Round," in *Trade Policy in the 1980s,* edited by William R. Cline (Washington, D.C.: Institute for International Economics, 1983), pp. 327–61.

[14] GATT, "Launching of Uruguay Round," p. 4.

lateral market-sharing agreements) that have escaped its jurisdiction in recent years. Failure to negotiate an effective safeguards code will intensify the erosion of GATT, making it an agreement honored mainly in the breach.

Trade-related aspects of industrial property rights and trade-related investment measures are subjects that have never been negotiated in past GATT conferences. *Industrial property rights* refer to patents, trademarks, and copyrights that provide the owner with the right to exclusive use of the property in question (technology, products, printed materials). Industrial property rights are granted to individuals and business firms by national governments for designated periods of time. Their purpose is to encourage invention, discovery, and innovation. Negotiation issues include the adequacy of existing protection afforded industrial property rights; the enforcement of those rights by national governments, including action against counterfeit goods; and the abuse of industrial property rights to restrain legitimate trade.

Trade-related investment measures refer to restrictions imposed by host governments on the operations of subsidiaries owned by foreign firms when the restrictions have an impact on international trade. Such restrictions, which include local-content requirements and export requirements, are taken up in Chapter 24 in the discussion on host country policies toward multinational companies. The United States wants to bring trade-related investment measures under the same GATT regime that covers nontariff trade restrictions.

Trade in Services

With modest exceptions, the GATT articles cover only merchandise trade. And yet the most dynamic segment of international trade in recent years has been trade in services. Clearly, it is time to bring the international trade in services under the same GATT regime as trade in merchandise.

The declaration of the Uruguay Round states that the aim of negotiations on trade in services is to establish a multilateral framework of principles and rules to achieve the progressive liberalization and expansion of such trade. This will not be easy to accomplish.

An early task of the GNS will be to identify which activities are to be covered in negotiations. After all, what are international service transactions? Services include financial services (such as banking, insurance, and accounting), professional services (such as legal, educational, and medical), business services (such as advertising, consulting, and design), communications, transportation, construction, retail and wholesale trade, and tourism. Having decided on the services to be covered in the negotiations, the GNS will encounter severe problems in measuring the volume and direction of trade in those services because of a paucity of statistical data comparable across countries.

The GNS will then need to identify the specific barriers to trade in services, for example, government procurement of services that favors domestic suppliers, outright exclusion of foreign service companies, and discriminatory restraints on the activities of foreign-owned service establishments (such as limiting foreign insurance companies to the sale of certain policies or requiring foreign data-processing firms to process data locally).

The key challenge facing the GNS is to reach agreement on which government policies towards international trade in services are legitimate and which are illegitimate. There is no GATT experience to guide the group, and many policies on services are regarded by governments as domestic rather than international matters. The United States, the initiator of the service negotiations, believes that it has a comparative advantage in services that is all too often frustrated by barriers obstructing the sale of U.S. services in foreign countries. In contrast, several developing countries (notably Brazil and India) oppose the idea of service negotiations because they believe that restrictions are necessary to promote indigenous service firms.

It is evident that negotiations on services will sail into uncharted waters. Whether the negotiators can agree on a code (or codes) containing provisions for multilateral surveillance, complaint procedures, and dispute settlement remains to be seen. But at the very least, restrictions on the international trade in services are now recognized as a legitimate subject of GATT negotiations.

Concluding Observation

The Uruguay Round will determine whether the trend toward managed international trade or the principles of comparative advantage and free trade will prevail in the next century.

Successful negotiations could stimulate growth in the world economy by increasing market access, integrating the developing countries more closely with GATT, strengthening the Tokyo Round codes, and liberalizing trade in agriculture, textiles, and services. Successful negotiations could also remake GATT so that it could exert greater authority in the multilateral surveillance of trade practices, safeguards, and the settlement of disputes. The most vital issue is the safeguards question. If an effective safeguards code can be negotiated, then GATT will be able to resume its role as guardian of an open, multilateral trading system. If such a code cannot be negotiated, then GATT will continue to erode as the cartelization of trade replaces the liberalization of trade.

The key actor in the Uruguay Round is the United States. Although it can no longer dominate international trade talks, the United States remains the only country able to lead the world toward a more open economy through the power of its own trade policy. It is from this perspective that we turn in the next chapter to an examination of U.S. trade policy and the powerful forces that threaten to undermine it.

SUMMARY

1. Since World War II, the trade policies of the United States and other industrial nations have been conducted within the framework laid down by the General Agreement on Tariffs and Trade (GATT).

2. GATT comprises four basic elements: (1) the rule of nondiscrimination in trade relations between the participating countries, (2) commitments to observe negotiated tariff concessions, (3) prohibitions against the use of quantitative restrictions on exports and imports, and (4) special provisions to promote the trade of developing countries.

3. The principal activities of GATT are tariff bargaining, bargaining on nontariff trade barriers, and the settlement of disputes.

4. The distinctive hallmark of the Tokyo Round was a series of agreements on nontariff trade barriers: subsidies and countervailing duties, standards, government procurement, customs valuations, and import licensing. The Tokyo Round also revised the antidumping code but failed to agree on a safeguards code.

5. The influence of GATT has eroded since the 1970s as the industrial countries have negotiated bilateral agreements (notably voluntary export restrictions [VERs]) outside the framework of GATT's safeguards provision (Article XIX).

6. A declaration adopted in September 1986 at Punta del Este, Uruguay, by GATT's member countries launched the Uruguay Round of trade negotiations. To carry out negotiations, two groups were established: (1) the *Group on Negotiations on Goods* (GNG), whose purpose is to negotiate traditional trade issues and new issues relating to investment and intellectual property, and (2) the *Group on Negotiations on Services* (GNS), whose purpose is to negotiate trade in services.

7. Fourteen *negotiation groups* have been set up under GNG covering the following subjects: tariffs, nontariff measures, tropical products, natural resource–based products, textiles and clothing, agriculture, GATT articles, safeguards, most-favored-nation (MFN) agreements and arrangements, subsidies and countervailing measures, dispute settlement, industrial property rights, trade-related investment measures, and the functioning of the GATT system.

8. Two sets of negotiations of particular importance will be undertaken by the *Dispute Settlement Group* and the *Safeguards Group*. The outcome of safeguard negotiations will determine the ability of GATT to bring under its authority the trade restrictions (particularly, bilateral market-sharing agreements) that have escaped its jurisdiction in recent years. Failure to negotiate an effective safeguards code will intensify the erosion of GATT, making it an agreement honored mainly in the breach.

9. Trade-related aspects of industrial property rights and trade-related

investment measures are subjects that have never been negotiated in past GATT conferences.

10. The declaration of the Uruguay Round states that the aim of negotiations on trade in services is to establish a multilateral framework of principles and rules to achieve the progressive liberalization and expansion of such trade. This will not be easy to accomplish.

11. The Uruguay Round will determine whether the trend toward managed international trade or the principles of comparative advantage and free trade will prevail in the next century.

12. Although it can no longer dominate trade talks, the United States remains the only country able to lead the world toward a more open economy through the power of its own trade policy.

QUESTIONS AND APPLICATIONS

1. What are the major provisions of GATT? Describe the mechanism for tariff negotiations under GATT.

2. What is the most-favored-nation principle? What is its purpose in international trade policy?

3. (a) What were the aims of the Tokyo Round?
   (b) What did the United States hope to get in the Tokyo Round?
   (c) What were the key negotiating issues in the Tokyo Round?
   (d) What were the actual results of the Tokyo Round?

4. Why has Article XIX of GATT not worked well in recent years?

5. (a) What is a voluntary export restriction (VER)?
   (b) In what ways does a VER violate the basic principles of GATT?

6. Design an international safeguards code. Be prepared to defend the specific provisions in it.

7. On the basis of your own research, evaluate the role of GATT today.

8. (a) What is tariff escalation?
   (b) Why is tariff escalation important to developing countries?

9. "Some countries believe that *all* subsidies distort international trade and deserve retaliation regardless of material injury, whereas other countries believe that retaliation is justified only when there is indisputable, substantial injury." Discuss the merits of each position.

10. Why are negotiations on service trade in the Uruguay Round likely to be more difficult than negotiations on merchandise trade?

SELECTED READINGS

See the list of readings at the end of Chapter 9.

9

U.S. Trade Policy in an Era of Global Competition

Today, the United States faces formidable challenges in international trade and global competition. To cope with these challenges, this country needs to design a trade policy that will effectively promote its interests in an international economy that is undergoing deep-seated structural shifts.

Economic and technological forces are causing—and are almost certain to continue to cause—a migration of traditional industries, such as textiles and steel, from the industrial countries of the North to the developing countries of the South.[1] In particular, the closing of technology gaps, easier access to capital, and a supply of low-cost productive labor are transforming the economies of certain developing countries—the so-called newly industrializing countries (NICs)—as they actively compete in world markets with consumer electronics, light aircraft, automobiles, and other mature products. Undoubtedly, more NICs will appear in world markets in the next decade.[2] At the same time, economic and technological forces are causing a reallocation of resources in the North from capital-intensive traditional industries to knowledge-intensive or service-intensive emerging industries. In terms of trade theory, these changes represent systemic shifts in comparative advantage between the North and the South. In sum, economic and technological forces are fundamentally reshaping the world economy. In this new economy, the United States is no longer the dominant economic power it was in the three decades following World War II. Rather, it has

---

[1] The world's countries are commonly classified into three groups: South, East, and North. The *South* designates the nonindustrial countries of Asia, Africa, the Middle East, and Latin America. The *East* designates the Soviet Union, China, and other centrally planned (communist) countries. The *North* designates the industrial countries that belong to the Organization of Economic Cooperation and Development (OECD), mainly North American and Western European countries and Japan.

[2] Current NICs include Brazil, Hong Kong, India, Mexico, Taiwan, Singapore, and South Korea.

become a "first among equals," a country that can lead through example but not dominate other countries.

Apart from shifts in comparative advantage between the North and South, the dependence of the United States and other industrial countries on international trade has dramatically intensified over the past decade. Figure 9-1 shows that the import content of supplies of finished manufactures (import penetration ratio) has surged upwards for all industrial countries in the 1971–1985 period, rising from 15 percent in 1971 to 28 percent in 1985. For the United States, the proportion has increased from 9 percent in 1971 to 22 percent in 1985.

In this chapter, we first trace the historical evolution of U.S. trade policy to give us a perspective on present and prospective policy. We then examine the issue of declining U.S. competitiveness in world markets. The enormous U.S. trade deficit in the 1980s (which is commonly, but falsely, viewed as an indicator of declining competitiveness) has sparked a "new protectionism" in the United States, which is the next subject of this chapter. We then move on to a consideration of the special nature of trade with communist countries and of recent developments in U.S. trade policy. We close the chapter with some reflections on the open question, Whither U.S. trade policy?

THE EVOLUTION OF U.S. TRADE POLICY

Contemporary U.S. trade policy was born with the passage of the Reciprocal Trade Agreements Program in 1934. Since that time, the main thrust of U.S. trade policy has been the achievement and maintenance of an open world economy through cooperation with other nations to lessen barriers that stifle trade among them. After World War II, the United States became the leader in the movement toward freer trade, mainly through GATT, which was designed and promoted by this country.

Here we offer a description of the evolution of U.S. trade policy over the last half century and the contemporary expression of that policy.

Hawley-Smoot Act of 1930

Conceived at the beginning of an unprecedented world economic crisis, the Hawley-Smoot Act of 1930 was the crowning achievement of protectionism in this country. While the bill was still in the Senate, it brought protests from foreign nations and pleas from a group of American economists who opposed a policy fraught with disaster for the economy of this country and for the rest of the world. These economists pointed out that the contemplated action was unjustified either in principle or in practice and was sure to invite retaliation and threaten world peace. In spite of these warnings, the

Figure 9-1   Import Content of Supplies of Finished Manufactures in the Industrial
Countries, 1899–1985

%   0   10   20   30   40   50   60   70   80   90   100

United Kingdom

| 1899 |
| 1913 |
| 1950 |
| 1959 |
| 1963 |
| 1971 |
| **1985** |

France

| 1899 |
| 1913 |
| 1950 |
| 1959 |
| 1963 |
| 1971 |
| **1985** |

Germany

| 1899 |
| 1913 |
| 1950 |
| 1959 |
| 1963 |
| 1971 |
| **1985** |

Italy

| 1899 |
| 1913 |
| 1950 |
| 1959 |
| 1963 |
| 1971 |
| **1985** |

United States

| 1899 |
| 1913 |
| 1950 |
| 1959 |
| 1963 |
| 1971 |
| **1985** |

Japan

| 1899 |
| 1913 |
| 1950 |
| 1959 |
| 1963 |
| 1971 |
| **1985** |

Total for
6 Countries

| 1899 |
| 1913 |
| 1950 |
| 1959 |
| 1963 |
| 1971 |
| **1985** |

Total for 6
"Small" Industrial
Countries[1]

| 1899 |
| 1913 |
| 1950 |
| 1959 |
| 1963 |
| 1971 |
| **1985** |

Total for
All Industrial
Countries

| 1899 |
| 1913 |
| 1950 |
| 1959 |
| 1963 |
| 1971 |
| **1985** |

Source: The OECD Observer, No. 149, December 1987/January 1988, p. 16.
[1]Australia, Belgium-Luxembourg, Canada, Netherlands, Norway, and Sweden.

The extraordinary growth of international economic interdependence over the period 1971–1985 is demonstrated by the leap in imports of finished manufactures as a percentage of total supplies of manufactures in the industrial countries. With the exception of Japan, all the industrial countries are far more dependent on imports of manufactures today than at any other time in the period 1899–1985. And Japan is more dependent today than at any time since World War II.

act was passed by Congress and signed by President Hoover, unleashing a worldwide movement of retaliatory measures.[3]

> Few actions of the United States have been more detrimental to the foreign relations of this country than the Hawley-Smoot Tariff of 1930. Almost none of the rates could be justified in terms of the infant-industries argument or on grounds of national security. Many of the items on which tariffs were imposed or the rates raised were not in direct competition with any American product.[4]

Such inordinate action could not long endure without giving rise to countervailing forces for redress. After two years of the Hawley-Smoot tariff, the shrinkage of trade and the deterioration of the American economy were instrumental in convincing influential groups of the mutual relationship between imports and exports and of the effects of the American tariff policy upon the level of world trade. Their voices found more sympathetic ears in the new administration that took the reins of the government in 1932. Under the stewardship of President Roosevelt and his Secretary of State, Cordell Hull, brighter horizons were in sight.

The Reciprocal Trade Agreements Program, 1934–1962

In 1934, Congress passed the Reciprocal Trade Agreements (RTA) Act as an amendment to the Hawley-Smoot Tariff Act of 1930. The act ushered in an era of commercial liberalism in this country and paved the way for similar trends abroad that culminated after World War II in GATT.

The RTA Act of 1934 recognized the relationship between imports and exports and authorized the reduction of tariff rates up to 50 percent by means of bilateral trade agreements with foreign countries. Each agreement was to contain an *unconditional most-favored-nation* (MFN) clause so that all concessions made by either party to third countries would freely and automatically apply to the trade of the other party to an agreement. Thus, the United States would always receive MFN treatment of its exports from every agreement country. The United States would grant the concessions it gave to *all* countries, whether parties to the agreement or not.

During the war years, the extension of the RTA Act evoked little concern or opposition. After World War II, however, Congressional attitudes toward the program were mixed and, at times, uncertain. Periodic renewals

---

[3] According to the League of Nations Economic Survey of 1932–33, the Hawley-Smoot Tariff Act of 1930 was the signal for an outburst of tariff-making activity in other countries, partly, at least, by way of reprisal. Extensive increases in duties were made almost immediately by Canada, Cuba, Mexico, France, Italy, and Spain, followed by many other nations; and it was generally considered to be an unwarranted and unfriendly act of a creditor and powerful nation. See Asher Isaacs, *International Trade: Tariff and Commercial Policies* (Chicago: Richard D. Irwin, 1948), pp. 234–35.

[4] Raymond F. Mikesell, *United States Economic Policy and International Relations* (New York: McGraw-Hill, 1952), p. 62.

TABLE 9-1   Average Rates of Duty on Imports for Consumption under the U.S. Tariff Act of 1930, As Amended

Period	Dutiable Imports to Total Imports (Percent)	Duties Collected to Value of Dutiable Imports (Percent)
1931–1935	37.6	51.4
1936–1940	39.5	39.4
1941–1945	34.0	33.0
1946–1950	41.6	17.1
1951–1955	44.6	12.2
1956–1960	56.9	11.6
1961–1962	61.6	11.1

Source: Arranged from data in United States Department of Treasury, *Annual Reports of the Treasury on the State of the Finances* (Washington, D.C.: U.S. Government Printing Office, 1930–1964).

met with increased opposition. Although additional authority to reduce tariff rates was granted the president, other provisions were adopted to prevent actual or contemplated reductions from inflicting harm on domestic industries: (1) the *peril-point provision*, which required the Tariff Commission to set minimum rates for contemplated concessions below which domestic industries might be harmed by imports; (2) the *escape clause provision*, which permitted withdrawal of a tariff concession previously extended in an agreement; and (3) the *defense-essentiality amendment*, which called for the restriction of imports of a product whenever such imports threatened to impair the national security.[5]

The consequences of a general policy for an economy as complex as that of the United States defy any exact measurement. Hence, we cannot definitively measure the results of the RTA program. Nonetheless, the data on tariff rates do point out the long distance traveled from the highly protectionist Hawley-Smoot Act of 1930. As shown in Table 9-1, U.S. tariff rates fell from an average of 51.4 percent for dutiable imports in 1934 to 11.1 percent in 1962. Moreover, the percentage of dutiable imports to total imports rose from 37.6 percent to 61.6 percent over the same period.

Developments in the 1950s indicated a strong tendency in favor of moderation and even reversal of the country's liberal trade policy under the

---

[5] The Tariff Commission was a nonpolitical government agency whose function was the investigation, study, and submission of recommendations to the president on tariffs and other matters pertaining to the foreign trade of the United States. It was replaced in 1975 with the International Trade Commission.

RTA program, as evidenced by (1) the stiffening attacks upon this program in general, (2) the opposition to specific rate reductions already effected, and (3) the implications of escape-clause and peril-point legislation. Moreover, the item-by-item approach to bargaining under the RTA procedures, coupled with the principal-supplier concept as the basis for negotiation, resulted in a proliferation of tariff subclassifications for many products in order to confine the benefits of the lower duties to the negotiating parties. Otherwise these benefits would have accrued to third countries producing similar but not identical products without reciprocal concessions because of the *unconditional* MFN principle.[6] After thirty years of tariff reductions under the RTA program, over 400 U.S. industrial products remained unaffected by negotiations and subject to the high rates of the Hawley-Smoot Tariff of 1930—an inherent weakness of the item-by-item bargaining system.

In addition to domestic protectionist policies that weakened the original intent of the RTA Act, international developments (most notably, the abandonment by the European Community [EC] in 1960–1961 of the item-by-item approach to negotiations and the built-in preferential treatment within the EC and the European Free Trade Association [EFTA] were creating a new situation and putting the United States at a distinct disadvantage.

The Trade Expansion Act of 1962

The Trade Expansion Act of 1962 was a direct response to the progressive establishment of a customs union by EC.[7] The provisions of this act gave the president sweeping authority to reduce or eliminate U.S. import duties in return for similar concessions from the EC and third countries.

The key importance of EC markets to the United States and the threat that these markets would become limited by protectionist policies convinced the new Kennedy administration that the United States must make a strong effort to bargain down EC trade barriers and prevent, or mitigate, the trade diversion that menaced the export interests of countries outside the community. The persisting U.S. balance of payments deficit lent urgency to this decision.

During the five-year period from July 1, 1962, to June 30, 1967—the life of the new act— the president was authorized to do any of the following:

1. To reduce by as much as 50 percent the rates of duties existing as of July 1, 1962.

---

[6] Under the MFN policy any reduction in a nation's tariff is automatically extended to all nations, except, at times, to those considered politically or economically inimical. Item-by-item bargaining refers to tariff negotiations centered on specific products as opposed to across-the-board negotiations centered on linear percentage reductions in the entire tariff schedule for all products. In following the principal-supplier concept, the United States offered concessions in negotiations with another country only on products for which that country was the major supplier to the United States.

[7] See Chapter 10.

2. To reduce up to 100 percent the tariff rates on the products of industries where the United States and the EC combined represented 80 percent or more of the free-world trade.[8]
3. To reduce to zero tariff duties of 5 percent or less existing as of July 1962.
4. To eliminate tariffs on tropical products by agreement with the EC subject to its extending comparable treatment and without discrimination as to source of supply of these products, but only if such products were not produced in the United States in significant quantities.
5. To eliminate tariffs on certain farm products if in the opinion of the president such action would tend to assure the maintenance or expansion of U.S. exports of like articles.

Except for the tropical products authority, which might be applied when proclaimed, the act required that all other negotiable cuts be put into effect in at least five installments, a year apart (the first when concessions were proclaimed), to allow domestic producers time to adjust to foreign competition. Backed by the Trade Expansion Act, the United States called for a new GATT tariff conference, which became known as the Kennedy Round.

The Trade Act of 1974

Between the end of the Kennedy Round in 1967 and the end of 1974, protectionist forces in the United States prevented the passage of new liberal trade legislation. After pending in Congress for nearly two years, the Trade Act of 1974 became law on January 3, 1975. The act was a mixed bag of liberal and restrictive provisions that revised many elements of U.S. trade policy.

The Trade Act of 1974 gave the president the *negotiating authorities* that were necessary for U.S. participation in the Tokyo Round. The president could reduce by as much as 60 percent all tariff rates that were above 5 percent *ad valorem* and eliminate all tariff rates of 5 percent *ad valorem* or below. But any duty reductions had to be staged over ten years at a prescribed rate of decrease per year.

The president could also reduce, eliminate, or harmonize nontariff barriers under a "fast-track" procedure for Congressional approval. This procedure forbade amendments to an implementing bill and imposed time limits on its consideration by Congress.

The Trade Act of 1974 also made *adjustment assistance* for workers, firms, and communities injured by increased imports more accessible than they had been under the Trade Expansion Act of 1962.[9] The benefits could

---

[8] The 80 percent authority was rendered almost useless by the failure of Britain to enter the EEC.

[9] Under the Trade Expansion Act of 1962, the rules for trade adjustment assistance were so stringent that not a single firm or worker qualified for assistance in the 1960s. In 1975 the Labor Department made 18,000 Chrysler workers eligible for benefits under the new act.

take the form of unemployment compensation and assistance in job search, training, and relocation for workers; loans and technical assistance for firms; and, for the first time, loans and grants to firms who would locate in communities adversely affected by import competition. Adjustment assistance explicitly recognizes that a policy of freer trade also demands a policy to facilitate the adaptation of workers and others to the new conditions of import competition.

The Trade Act of 1974 made it much easier for a domestic industry to get safeguard protection against import competition. Under the previous escape-clause law, to get protection an industry had to demonstrate that higher imports were caused by an earlier tariff concession and that these higher imports were the "major" cause (greater than all other causes) of injury or threat of injury. The 1974 act eliminated the causal link between increased imports and concessions and required that imports be only a "substantial" cause (not less than any other cause) of injury or threat of injury.

Upon a determination of injury by the International Trade Commission (ITC), the president had to impose a higher duty or quota or negotiate an orderly marketing agreement with foreign suppliers unless any of these actions would hurt the U.S. economic interest. However, if the president took no action or an action different from the ITC recommendation, then Congress could overrule by a concurrent resolution. Import protection would be granted for a five-year period, with a single extension of three years. These restrictive provisions could be softened in practice by the right of the ITC to recommend adjustment assistance as an alternative to import protection.

The Trade Act of 1974 also gave the president more authority to retaliate against "unfair trade practices." The president could retaliate on a nondiscriminatory or a selective basis by withdrawing tariff concessions or by imposing import restrictions. The act tightened provisions of existing laws against dumping, export subsidies, and unfair practices.

The issue of Soviet emigration restrictions delayed passage for over a year, despite the fact that the central purpose of the act was to allow negotiations with the noncommunist industrial countries. The Trade Act authorized the president to extend nondiscriminatory MFN treatment to imports from non–market economy (communist) countries, but only if the president found that such countries were not denying their citizens freedom of emigration. The extension of U.S. government credits and investment guarantees to communist countries would also depend on the same finding. Furthermore, any granting of MFN treatment to imports from a communist country had to be done under a bilateral commercial agreement requiring approval by Congress.

Another provision authorized the president to extend preferential duty-free treatment to a broad range of manufactured products imported directly from developing countries for a period up to ten years. We shall examine the question of tariff preferences in Chapter 21.

The Trade Act of 1979

Although Congress had delegated tariff-cutting authority to the president in the Trade Act of 1974, Congressional approval was needed for the nontariff agreements negotiated in the Tokyo Round. Accordingly, President Carter submitted to Congress in June 1979 a text of the nontariff agreements, a draft of an implementing bill, and a statement of administrative action. The implementing bill became law as the Trade Act of 1979. It revised the law and rules governing antidumping, countervailing duties, customs valuation (including the abandonment of the American Selling Price), government procurement, and standards to make them conform with the new GATT codes. The act did not grant the president any new authority to lower trade barriers. Provisions of the 1974 trade act relating to adjustment assistance, safeguard protection, unfair trade practices, trade with communist countries, and preferential treatment of imports from developing countries continued to remain in force.

The Trade Act of 1974 and the Trade Act of 1979 provided the legislative framework for U.S. trade policy in the 1980s. Not until 1988 were these acts superseded by the Omnibus Trade and Competitiveness Act, which responded to concerns about the decline of U.S. competitiveness in world markets and to the influence of protectionist interests.

THE DECLINE OF U.S. COMPETITIVENESS IN WORLD MARKETS

National competitiveness is a country-level concept that cannot be expressed in income or balance sheet statements, as can the competitiveness of individual firms or industries. The President's Commission on Industrial Competitiveness adopted the following definition: *National competitiveness is the degree to which a nation can, under free and fair market conditions, produce goods and services that meet the test of international markets while simultaneously expanding the real incomes of its citizens.*[10] National competitiveness, therefore, means the ability to compete in free and open markets (1) without resort to protectionist restrictions and (2) while maintaining and improving real incomes (which rules out competing in ways that lower real incomes, such as a continuing depreciation of the country's currency in foreign exchange markets).[11] We shall use this definition in our treatment of international competitiveness.

It is common to view a growing external trade deficit as a symptom of declining national competitiveness. But the trade balance is a misleading

---

[10] *Global Competition: The New Reality*, Report of the President's Commission on Industrial Competitiveness, vol. 3 (Washington, D.C.: U.S. Government Printing Office, 1985).

[11] For an explanation of depreciation and its effects, see Chapter 16. *Real* income is nominal income adjusted for changes in the price level in order to measure its power to purchase goods and services, that is, to obtain a given standard of living.

measure of competitiveness because it is sensitive to temporary shifts in real exchange rates and to the business cycle. Changes in the share of a country's exports in international markets and changes in imports as a fraction of domestic production (import penetration ratio) are also defective measures of competitiveness, although less so when measured over a period of time long enough to eliminate transitory influences (say, five years). Much more reliable indicators of national competitiveness measure changes in the stock and use of a country's human and physical capital, such as the amount of capital per worker, the proportion of scientists and engineers in the work force, and productivity.

The trend in a country's productivity (usually expressed as output per man-hour) relative to those of other countries is the single most important indicator of changing competitiveness. If a country's productivity rises at a lower rate than the productivity of other countries, then its costs per unit of output will increase relative to foreign unit costs when measured at a constant rate of exchange. Consequently, the country cannot compete in world markets while expanding the real income of its people. Furthermore, a country can raise its real standard of living only when its productivity gains are greater than its population gains.

Is the United States losing its international competitiveness? Although this remains a controversial question in the national debate over U.S. economic policy, a comparison of U.S. and foreign productivity trends points to a persistent deterioration in the *relative* strength of the United States in the world economy. But before examining these trends, we will look first at the U.S. trade balance and the U.S. export share in manufactures.

The U.S. Trade Deficit

The astounding rise—without precedent—of the U.S. merchandise trade deficit in the 1980s is shown in Table 9-2. The popular press has pointed to this deficit as proof of a declining U.S. competitiveness, and spokespersons for industries facing import competition have used it as an argument for protection.

Table 9-2 reveals a volatile trade balance over the period 1970-1987. That balance was slightly positive in 1970, turned negative in 1971, and then became positive again in 1975. In 1976, the trade balance turned negative, but it showed improvement in the 1978–1980 period. Starting in 1981, however, the gap widened, exhibiting explosive growth after 1982. Why these shifts? As we shall learn in Part 2, (1) the trade balance (like the balance of payments as a whole) is determined mainly by changes in *macroeconomic* variables such as a country's real income, price level, interest rate, and rate of exchange; (2) over the long run, the trade balance plus the balance on trade in services (the net balance on current account) *must* net out to zero, because the rest of the world will not indefinitely finance a country's deficit on merchandise and service trade; and (3) a persistent current account deficit will be eventually eliminated through a decrease in

TABLE 9-2   U.S. Merchandise Trade Balance, 1970–1987 (Billions of Dollars)

Year	Exports	Imports	Balance
1970	43.2	42.4	0.8
1971	44.1	48.3	−4.2
1972	49.8	58.9	−9.1
1973	71.3	73.6	−2.3
1974	98.7	110.9	−12.2
1975	108.1	105.9	2.2
1976	115.4	132.5	−17.1
1977	121.3	160.4	−39.1
1978	143.8	186.0	−42.2
1979	182.0	222.2	−40.2
1980	220.8	257.0	−36.2
1981	233.6	273.4	−39.8
1982	212.3	254.9	−42.6
1983	200.5	269.9	−69.4
1984	224.0	346.4	−122.4
1985	218.8	352.5	−133.7
1986	226.8	383.0	−156.2
1987	252.9	424.1	−171.2

Source: U.S. Department of Commerce, *United States Trade, Performance and Outlook* (Washington, D.C.: U.S. Government Printing Office, October 1986), Table 1, p. 111; and *Federal Reserve Bulletin,* December 1987 and July 1988, Table 3.11, p. A54.

the deficit country's real income relative to that of its trading partners, usually brought about by a depreciation of its currency.

And so, it is simply wrong to argue that the U.S. trade deficit is an unequivocal sign that the United States is losing its international competitiveness.[12] Indeed, the shifts in the U.S. trade balance over the period 1970–1987 make a mockery of that argument. Does anyone believe that U.S. international competitiveness started out well in 1970, then worsened in 1971–1972, got better in 1973, then worsened again in 1974, and so on? Although the trade deficit is *not* an indicator of declining U.S. competitiveness, it has nonetheless greatly intensified the demand for protection by U.S. industries.

The U.S. Share in World Exports of Manufactures

Table 9-3 depicts the export shares of manufactured products over the period 1975–1986 for the top five exporting countries. In 1975, the U.S. share was

---

[12] The macroeconomic causes of the U.S. trade deficit are discussed in Chapter 19.

15.1 percent, but it fell steadily to reach 11.0 percent in 1986. Is this secular decline (which started in the 1960s) evidence of a decline in U.S. competitiveness? Not necessarily.

Export shares are a faulty measure of competitiveness for several reasons. Movements in exchange rates—unrelated to long-run competitiveness— can radically alter the real volume of trade flows over the short run. Exchange rate movements can also cause accounting distortions in trade patterns, because the exports of all countries must be translated into a common currency, usually the dollar (as in Table 9-3). Hence, a stronger dollar (an increase in its value relative to other currencies) lowers the dollar-denominated values of foreign-country exports, thereby pushing up the nominal U.S. share even though the *real* U.S. share (measured by quantity) may be constant or falling. A weaker U.S. dollar has the opposite effect. In the late 1970s, the U.S. dollar weakened, but in the first half of the 1980s, it became very strong.

As other countries industrialize, the U.S. share of manufactured exports is certain to fall, but, at the same time, the *absolute* value of U.S. manufactured exports may *increase* in a growing world economy. Export market shares are also sensitive to the business cycle. If, for example, the U.S. economy is growing more rapidly than the world economy, then exports of foreign manufactures to the United States will grow more rapidly than exports of U.S. manufactures to the rest of the world.

Enough has been said to explain why a shift in export market shares *alone* is an unreliable indicator of national competitiveness. However, if other leading industrial countries are maintaining their export shares while the United States is losing its share *over the long run* (a decade or more),

TABLE 9-3   Percentage Shares of Manufactured Exports of the United States, West Germany, Japan, France, and the United Kingdom, 1975–1986

Countries	1975	1980	1985	1986
United States	15.1	13.9	13.2	11.0
West Germany	16.9	16.0	14.7	16.1
Japan	11.3	12.0	15.5	15.0
France	8.4	8.1	6.7	6.8
United Kingdom	7.8	7.8	6.2	5.9
Total for 5 Countries	59.5	57.7	56.2	54.8
Rest of World	40.5	42.3	43.8	45.2
World	100.0	100.0	100.0	100.0

Note: Individual entries may not add to 100.0 percent because of rounding.

Source: Derived from United Nations, *Monthly Bulletin of Statistics,* March 1988, Special Table F, p. 273.

this shift points to a loss of U.S. competitiveness even though it does not prove it. Observe in Table 9-3 that West Germany held on to its share of 16 percent while Japan achieved a sharp jump in its share, moving from 11.3 percent to 15.0 percent over the period 1975–1986. These two countries now have larger shares of world exports of manufactures than the United States.

Import penetration ratios (imports as a share of domestic production) are also poor indicators of national competitiveness. Like export market shares, they are also sensitive to exchange rates and the business cycle. More fundamentally, import penetration ratios are bound to increase as the world economy becomes more integrated, as shown in Figure 9-1.

The Deterioration of U.S. Productivity

A country's economy can grow either through an increase in its factor inputs (land, labor, and capital) or through higher productivity (more efficient use of those inputs). The first way is called *extensive* growth; the second, *intensive* growth.

Productivity is usually expressed as *labor* productivity, namely, the output per hour of labor. Changes in a country's labor productivity come from (1) changes in the amounts of other factors of production used with labor, particularly changes in the capital/labor ratio (the land/labor ratio is comparatively stable); (2) changes in the mix of sectors with different labor productivities that make up the national output, notably a shift from the manufacturing sector (relatively high productivity) to the service and government sectors (relatively low productivity); and (3) changes in *total* factor productivity.[13]

We shall use *labor productivity in manufacturing* to compare productivity performance across countries because there are no reliable comparative data on total factor productivity and on productivity in the service and government sectors. Another reason is that a country's standard of living is closely tied to its labor productivity. By focusing on manufactures, we eliminate change in the sector mix as an explanatory variable. But the variables indicated in (1) and (3) remain as sources of changes in labor productivity. It is evident, therefore, that labor productivity reflects not only changes in the efficiency of labor but also changes in other factors, particularly capital, that are combined with labor in production.

A country can sustain its competitiveness in world markets only it its productivity performance keeps pace with that of other countries. As observed earlier, if a country's growth in productivity remains persistently

---

[13] *Total factor productivity* attempts to measure changes in the more efficient use of *all* factors of production. It is commonly derived as a residual after subtracting the contributions of additional amounts of land, labor, and capital to the growth of the gross domestic product. Because land grows slowly if at all, a good approximation of this residual is obtained by subtracting the additional contributions of labor and capital.

below that of other countries, then its unit costs of production will become *relatively* higher than those of its competitors in world markets. Symptoms of this relative productivity decline are likely to appear initially as falling export market shares in individual industries and in trade deficits. Subsequently, in adjusting to persistent balance of payments deficits, the country's currency will lose value and its standard of living will stagnate or even decline (a weaker currency means that the country will receive less for its exports and pay more for its imports). In sum, by competing with relatively low wages and profits, the country would *not* be competitive in a way that would help to increase the real incomes of its people. Thus the key to long-run competitiveness (accompanied by rises in real per capita income) is a country's ability to achieve productivity gains that match those of other countries.

Figure 9-2 demonstrates that productivity growth in the United States over the period 1960–1985 has lagged behind that of the other two leading industrial countries. As a result of this lag, Japan and West Germany now have productivity levels in manufacturing that match or even exceed the U.S. level. This is shown for Japan in Figure 9-3.

What explains the poor productivity performance of the United States over the last quarter century? Many variables can affect productivity, including changes in plant and capital equipment, technology, skill levels of workers and managers, organization of the workplace, labor-management relations, and the scale of operations. The relative importance of these variables varies across countries and in a single country over time. Economists would agree, however, that changes in plant and equipment and in technology are *always* major sources of productivity gains.[14] We need, therefore, to say something about those two factors.

Comparative Investment   Table 9-4 compares investment and saving in the United States, Japan, and West Germany for the 1975–1984 and 1985–1987 periods.

Several points deserve emphasis. First, gross private investment as a percentage of gross national product (GNP) was far less in the United States than in Japan in both periods. The U.S. percentage equalled the West German percentage in the first period but fell behind in the second period.

Second, gross private saving as a percentage of GNP was much less in

---

[14] Many empirical studies support this agreement. Mohr, for example, in comparing the slowdown in growth of output per hour in the United States in the period 1973–1978 with the period 1948–66, attributed 25–30 percent of the slowdown to lower capital formation and a decline in capital quality and 20–50 percent in residual productivity (mainly attributable to advances in knowledge). See Martin N. Baily and Alok K. Chakrabarti, *Innovation and the Productivity Crisis* (Washington, D.C.: Brookings Institution, 1988), Table 2-2, p. 32. For the results of other studies, see Committee for Economic Development, *Productivity Policy: Key to the Nation's Economic Future* (New York: Committee for Economic Development, 1983), Chapter 4.

Figure 9-2   Indexed Labor-Productivity Growth Rates for Manufacturing Industries of the United States, Japan, and West Germany, 1960–1985 (1960 = 100)

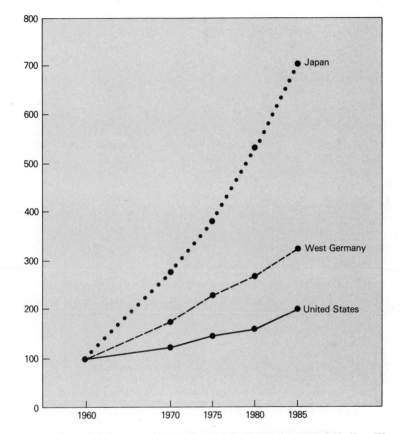

Source: Compiled from U.S. Department of Labor, *Monthly Labor Review,* May 1988, Table 47, p. 105.

Labor productivity in the manufacturing sector has grown much more rapidly in Japan and West
Germany—the other major industrial countries—than in the United States. This means that the
U.S. manufacturing sector as a whole has become less competitive in international markets. Also,
real income in the United States has grown less rapidly than in Japan and West Germany.

the United States than in Japan and West Germany, with the difference
widening between the two periods.

   Third, in the earlier period, a negative government saving/investment
balance (budget deficit) in the United States was slightly greater than the
positive private saving/investment balance. But this situation changed
abruptly in the 1985–1987 period: The private balance became negative and

Figure 9-3   Convergence of U.S. and Japanese Manufacturing Productivity Levels, 1960–1984

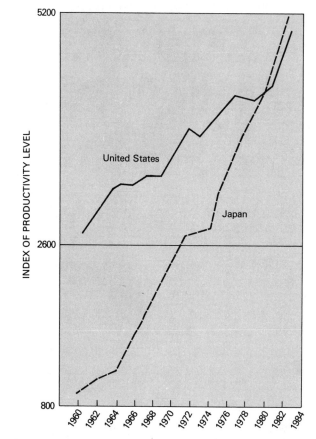

Source: Based on Committee for Economic Development, *Work and Change, Labor Adjustment Policies in a Competitive World* (New York: Committee for Economic Development, 1987), Figure 22, p. 25.

In 1960, U.S. labor productivity in manufacturing was about three times Japanese labor productivity. However, the much more rapid growth of Japanese productivity after that year brought about a convergence of U.S. and Japanese productivity levels by 1980. Japanese productivity in manufacturing has now moved ahead of U.S. productivity.

the negative government balance increased in size. Consequently, domestic investment exceeded domestic saving (the overall saving/investment balance) by an extraordinary amount equal to 3.4 percent of U.S. GNP. This could only happen because the United States borrowed that much from the rest of the world, as indicated by the negative balance on current account

	Average 1975–1984			Average 1985–1987		
	U.S.	Japan	West Germany	U.S.	Japan	West Germany
Gross private investment	16.3	24.8	16.4	16.3	26.7	17.2
Gross private saving	17.8	29.3	19.8	16.0	31.4	22.1
Private saving/investment balance	1.5	4.5	3.4	-0.3	4.7	4.9
Government saving/investment balance	-1.9	-3.8	-3.1	-3.1	-0.8	-1.3
Overall saving/investment balance	-0.4	0.7	0.3	-3.4	3.9	3.6

Note: The saving/investment balance is defined as gross saving minus gross investment. The overall saving/investment balance is the sum of the government and private saving/investment balances; it is by definition equal to the net balance on current account.

Source: Derived from The World Bank, *World Development Report, 1988* (New York: Oxford University Press, 1988), Table 1.2, p. 19.

of the U.S. balance of payments.[15] In other words, foreign countries financed over one-fifth (3.4 percent/16.3 percent) of gross private investment in the United States in the 1985–1987 period. In the absence of this financing, therefore, the U.S. investment performance would have been even worse in the later period: 12.9 percent compared with Japan's 26.7 percent and West Germany's 17.2 percent. The financing came mainly from the latter countries, which each had a *positive* overall saving/investment balance about equal to the U.S. negative balance. As explained in Chapter 19, this imbalance between saving and investment in the United States cannot continue in the long run, because foreign countries will not be willing to finance such a large U.S. current account deficit forever. This country, therefore, must adopt policies that will lead to an improvement in its saving and investment performance to match that of Japan and West Germany.

Technology Innovation The second major source of productivity gains is the application of new knowledge to the manufacture and innovation of products.[16] Table 9-5 indicates that Japan and West Germany have caught up with the United States in gross domestic expenditure on R & D expressed as a percentage of GNP.

But this comparison understates the impact on productivity of the relative decline in U.S. R & D expenditure, because a much larger fraction of U.S. R & D is allocated to defense and not intended to improve the manufacture and innovation of commercial products. As shown in Table 9-6, 33.6 percent of U.S. R & D expenditure in 1985 was spent for defense, compared with 0.7 percent for Japan and 4.5 percent for West Germany. Hence, R & D financed by industry and aimed at strengthening the competitiveness of business enterprise was only 48.4 percent of U.S. R & D,

---

[15] For the relationship between the national income accounts and the balance of payments, see Chapter 15.

[16] See Chapter 5 for a discussion of technology theories of trade.

TABLE 9-5   Gross Domestic Expenditure on R & D as a Percentage of Gross Domestic Product in the United States, Japan, and West Germany, 1970–1985

	1970	1975	1981	1985
United States	2.8	2.4	2.4	2.8
Japan	1.8	2.0	2.3	2.8
West Germany	2.1	2.2	2.4	2.7

Source: Derived from the Organization for Economic Cooperation and Development, *The OECD Observer,* January 1986; and *OECD Science and Technology Indicators, 1988.*

TABLE 9-6   Public and Private Financing of Gross Domestic Expenditure on
R & D in the United States, Japan, and West Germany in 1985
(Percent)

Source of Financing	United States	Japan	West Germany
Public	49.8	21.0	37.6
Defense R & D	33.6	0.7	4.5
Other R & D	16.2	20.3	33.1
Private	50.2	79.0	62.4
Industry	48.4	68.9	60.9
Other	1.8	10.1	1.5
All Sources	100.0	100.0	100.0

Source: Derived from the Organization for Economic Cooperation and Development, *The OECD Observer,* January 1986; and *OECD Science and Technology Indicators, 1988.*

compared with 68.9 percent for Japan and 60.9 percent for West Germany. It is necessary, therefore, to *lower* the U.S. percentages in Table 9-5 by about one-third to compare *commercially oriented* R & D that directly enhances productivity performance. Clearly, if the present trend in R & D continues, the United States will become progressively a technological follower rather than the technological leader it has been in the past.

Profile of U.S. Competitiveness

The President's Commission on Industrial Competitiveness drew up a profile of U.S. competitive advantages as of the beginning of 1985. This is depicted in Figure 9-4.

Major *disadvantages* were high capital costs (real interest rates), a strong dollar exchange rate, and high labor costs. Minor disadvantages were U.S. trade policy and international trade laws. The single current major *advantage* was product technology; process technology (new production functions) and labor quality were cited as minor advantages.

The commission made several recommendations to shift the disadvantages toward parity (except labor costs, which reflect the high living standard of American workers) and to transform minor advantages into major ones, including incentives for private-sector R & D, more investment in new manufacturing technologies, more protection of industrial property rights (patents, trademarks, and copyrights), a cut in the federal budget deficit to increase the supply of capital available to private investment at lower real interest rates, more worker training, and the establishment of a department of international trade to make trade a national priority.

So far the most evident improvement in competitive advantage has

Figure 9-4   Competitive Advantages of the United States in 1985

	Disadvantage		Parity	Advantage	
	Major	Minor		Minor	Major
Product Technology					●→○
Process Technology				●———————→○	
Capital Cost	●———————————→ ○				
Exchange Rate	●———→○				
Labor Cost	●				
Labor Quality				●————————→ ○	
U.S. Trade Policy		●———————→ ○			
International Trade Laws		●———————→ ○			

● 1985   ○ Potential
Source: President's Commission on Industrial Competitiveness, 1985.

In 1985, the United States suffered from the major competitive disadvantages of high capital costs, a strong dollar, and high labor costs. In contrast, product technology was its only major *advantage.* Since 1985, depreciation has eliminated the strong dollar as a competitive disadvantage, but the United States has not yet gained parity with other countries (notably Japan and West Germany) in capital costs. Nor has it made process technology and labor quality major competitive advantages.

come from the sharp depreciation of the dollar which started in 1985. But as we have stated earlier, depreciation will not by itself improve U.S. competitiveness when defined in terms of expanding real incomes for Americans. What, then, is the outlook for U.S. competitiveness? A study sponsored by the Federal Reserve Bank of New York points to improvements since 1985 in U.S. relative prices, reflecting both the dollar depreciation and low domestic inflation.[17] The latter has been aided by a substantial rise in U.S.

---

[17] S. Hickok, L. Bell, and J. Ceglowski, *U.S. Manufactured Goods Competitiveness: Recent Changes and Future Prospects*, Research Paper no. 8801 (New York: Federal Reserve Bank of New York, February 1988).

manufacturing productivity. The study also cites an improvement in the quality performance of several important U.S. products, such as automobiles. The study concludes that the United States has clearly gained in competitive strength since 1985, spurred by increased investment, R & D efforts, industrial restructuring, and work reorganization.

This optimism about U.S. national competitiveness needs to be tempered by two considerations. First, an improvement through dollar depreciation will constrain the ability of the United States to expand the real income of Americans. Second, the United States continues to depend heavily on foreign capital to sustain private investment because of its savings deficiency, which is mainly caused by the federal budget deficit. Our own conclusion, therefore, is that the achievement and maintenance of national competitiveness will remain a major challenge for the American people throughout the 1990s and beyond.

THE NEW PROTECTIONISM

The progressive liberalization of international trade initiated by the United States after World War II came to a halt in the mid-1970s, when a resurging protectionism in new forms swamped further efforts to lower trade barriers in the industrial world. As we observed in Chapter 8, the Tokyo Round of 1974–1979 was at best a holding action against protectionist forces, and it failed to reach agreement on a new safeguards code.

The proliferation of protection since the mid-1970s is a consequence of both short-run cyclical developments and long-run structural shifts, notably the sharp recessions precipitated by the two OPEC oil crises (1973–1974 and 1979–1980), which were accompanied by high levels of unemployment; the strong U.S. dollar of 1980–1985, coupled with enormous trade deficits; the decline in U.S. competitiveness; and the explosive rise in the economic interdependence of the industrial countries. Slower growth, unemployment, and intense import competition have created a political environment favorable to protectionist interests, particularly in the United States.

No new arguments have been advanced to justify the protectionist revival, but the old arguments examined in Chapter 6—the employment, low-wage, fairness, antidumping, bargaining-and-retaliation, reciprocity, and national security arguments—have been dressed in new clothing to suit the times. The advocates of a particular trade restriction usually claim to be against protectionism in general. The rhetoric of freer trade is still voiced: Each act of protection is viewed as an exception to the rule or as a means to open up export markets by pressuring foreign countries to eliminate import restrictions. Despite these pretentions, the resurgence of protectionism has inspired manifold trade disputes among the three giants of world trade: the United States, the EEC, and Japan.

The revival of protectionism since the mid-1970s is called the "new protectionism" because it relies heavily on new forms of nontariff trade barriers (NTBs), notably voluntary export restraints (VERs) and orderly marketing agreements (OMAs).[18] A detailed analysis of the extent of NTBs by the World Bank showed that 16 percent of industrial-country imports in 1986 were subject to "hard-core" NTBs compared with 13 percent in 1981. For the United States, the share of imports covered by hard-core NTBs in 1986 was 15 percent, compared with 9 percent in 1981.[19] The new protectionism sometimes takes ingenious forms, such as the action of the French government to restrict imports of videocassette recorders (VCRs) by requiring their customs clearance only at Poitiers.[20]

A second feature of the new protectionism is its focus on a comparatively small number of sectors: steel, automobiles, textiles and apparel, televisions, machine tools, footware, VCRs, semiconductors, and ships. From the end of World War II until 1974, the United States adopted only two special measures of protection for manufactured products, apart from the cotton textiles arrangement. One was for canned tuna in 1951 and the second was for carbon steel in 1969; together, these products accounted for only a minute share of total U.S. imports.[21] But since 1974, this country has established VERs and other hard-core NTBs for all of the sectors listed above except VCRs and ships.

A third feature of the new protectionism is its bilateral application, which violates GATT's principle of nondiscrimination (most-favored-nation policy). VERs, OMAs, and subsidies are initiated by the United States and other industrial countries outside Article XIX of GATT, the safeguards article. Hence, countries hurt by these restrictions seldom invoke Article XIX, which provides for compensatory or retaliatory actions when authorized by GATT. This, of course, is viewed as an advantage by the country imposing such restrictions.

A fourth feature of the new protectionism is its lack of "transparency." The new protectionist devices allow for a great deal of administrative discretion, which can be used to hide their effects from outsiders. Again, this

---

[18] For a definition of VERs, see "The Erosion of GATT" in Chapter 8. Unlike VERs, OMAs rely on restrictions imposed by the importing country. Both VERs and OMAs are negotiated bilaterally between the importing and exporting countries.

[19] The World Bank, *World Development Report 1987* (New York: Oxford University Press, 1987), Table 8.3, p. 142. Hard-core NTBs are those most likely to have significant restrictive effects: import prohibitions, quantitative restrictions, discretionary licensing, VERs, OMAs, and variable levies.

[20] In October 1981, the French government decreed that all imports of VCRs would have to pass through customs at Poitiers, a small inland town with a small customs office. At Poitiers, the officials opened each VCR container, painstakingly examined all documents, and disassembled several VCRs to establish if they were actually manufactured in their reputed country of origin. Before the use of Poitiers, more than 64,000 VCRs, mainly from Japan, entered France each month, but afterwards, less than 10,000 VCRs cleared customs each month. This restriction was lifted by the French government in 1982 after the European Community negotiated a VER with Japan that limited its VCR exports to the entire community.

[21] The World Bank, *World Development Report 1987,* pp. 139–40.

is an advantage to the restricting country, for it can then claim that a device is *not* protectionist.

Trade Disputes

We do not have the space to describe the many trade disputes that the United States has had with Japan, the EC, and other countries in recent years. For the most part, these disputes have revolved around U.S. allegations of unfair trade practices (dumping and government subsidies) and high nontariff barriers that keep out U.S. goods and services, especially in Japan. We offer below a short review of the issues involved in the more prominent disputes—steel, automobiles, textiles, and semiconductors. But first we list some representative headlines that appeared in the press during the period from October 1985 to July 1988. These headlines eloquently express the "flavor" of recent trade disputes:

"Three U.S. Firms File Trade Complaint against Japan Semiconductor Makers" (*Wall Street Journal*, October 1, 1985, p. 5)

"U.S.-South Korean Trade Tensions Rise, Koreans See Ally Turning against Them" (*Wall Street Journal*, January 8, 1986, p. 30)

"Japan Chips Found Dumped" (*New York Times*, January 23, 1986, p. D4)

"E.C. Retaliates for U.S. Unilateral Actions on Semi-finished Steel" (*European Community News,* January 28, 1986)

"U.S. Aides Say Japan Shuts Out Foreigners on Airport Contracts" (*Wall Street Journal*, March 3, 1986, p. 35)

"Canada Sets Tariff Retaliation, U.S. Surprised by Magnitude of Action"(*New York Times*, June 3, 1986, p. D1)

"Canada's Quick Retaliation for Shingles Tariff Prompts Some on the Hill to Rethink Protectionism" (*Wall Street Journal*, June 19, 1986, p. 64)

"U.S. and Europe Settle Pasta and Citrus Dispute" (*New York Times*, August 11, 1986, p. D1)

"E.C. and U.S. Withdraw Punitive Trade Measures, Settle Two Major Disputes" (*European Community News*, September 11, 1986)

"Japan Agrees to Eliminate Cigarette Tariffs" (*Wall Street Journal*, October 6, 1986, p. 35)

"U.S. Puts 15% Tariff on Lumber, Canada Found to Subsidize Its Producers" (*New York Times*, October 17, 1986, p. D1)

"Big Canada Duty Put on Corn, A Response to Charges of Unfair Subsidy" (*New York Times*, November 8, 1986, p. 37)

"Trade Pact Is Set with Europeans, Dispute Ended on Grain Sales to Spain" (*New York Times*, January 20, 1987, p. D1)

"Reagan Slaps 100% Tariffs on 4 Types of Japan Goods" (*Asian Wall Street Journal Weekly*, April 20, 1987, p. 26)

"Reagan Lifts Some of Japan Sanctions" (*New York Times*, November 5, 1987, p. D5)

"Reagan Imposes Punitive Tariffs against Brazil" (*New York Times*, November 14, 1987, p. 1)

"Brazil Exporters Move to Stop U.S. Sanctions" (*New York Times*, November 23, 1987, p. D1)

"Japan Dumping of Trucks Charged" (*New York Times*, March 31, 1988, p. D1)

"U.S.-Japan Talks on Beef, Citrus Quotas Collapse; New GATT Request Is Planned" (*Wall Street Journal*, May 4, 1988, p. 3)

"GATT to Act on Beef in U.S.-Japan Impasse" (*New York Times*, May 5, 1988, p. D1)

"U.S. and Japan Clear a Trade Hurdle, Tokyo's Lifting of Quotas on Beef and Oranges Has Symbolic Value" (*New York Times*, June 21, 1988, p. D6)

"U.S. Sets Brazil Curbs Over Patent 'Piracy'" (*New York Times*, July 23, 1988, p. 35)

Steel The U.S. steel industry has steadily declined in international competitiveness since World War II. The reasons for this decline are manifold, but two stand out: a failure to innovate in production processes and high wage costs. Starting in the 1950s, U.S. steel companies ignored new production technology (notably, the basic oxygen process) and the threat of import competition. By the 1970s, Japan had become the leader in steel technology, and today American steel firms obtain technical assistance from Japanese firms. In the 1970s, the output per worker-hour in Japanese steel plants was more than 50 percent higher than in U.S. plants. Low productivity was compounded by high wages paid to American steel workers, some 80 percent above the average wages in U.S. manufacturing and more than twice the wages paid in the Japanese steel industry. In the first half of the 1980s, the international competitive disadvantages of the U.S. steel were intensified by a strong U.S. dollar. By the mid-1980s, imports of steel from Japan and other countries had captured one-quarter of the U.S. market.

The American steel industry reacted to import competition primarily by getting import protection. In the late 1960s and early 1970s, imports from Japan and Europe were restricted through voluntary export quotas. Foreign producers responded by shifting their exports from basic steel products to specialty steel, which in turn caused problems for U.S. specialty steel producers. In 1978, import protection took a new form—the *trigger-pricing mechanism* (TPM). The TPM established reference prices pegged to the lowest-cost international producer, namely, Japan. Any steel imports below their reference prices were subject to antidumping duties imposed within 60 to 90 days. The U.S. steel industry had become disenchanted with the TPM by 1980, alleging that the trigger prices were too low and their enforcement by the U.S. Treasury Department too lax.

The U.S. government ended the TPM in January 1982, when the major U.S. steel producers filed petitions with the International Trade Commission (ITC) and the Department of Commerce for relief from injury caused by the sale of steel in the United States at below-fair-market prices by subsidized foreign producers, mainly located in Western Europe. These petitions then underwent a long legal process that ended in October 1982 when the International Trade Commission ruled that several European steel firms illegally dumped steel in the United States by selling at prices below "fair value." Rather than face higher duties (ranging up to 26 percent) European steel producers agreed to limit their shipments during 1983–1986 to 5.5 percent of the U.S. market, down from 6.4 percent.

In response to a petition filed by the United Steelworkers of America and the Bethlehem Steel Corporation under Section 201 (the "escape clause") of the Trade Act of 1974, the ITC ruled in 1984 that certain carbon and alloy steel products (amounting to 70 percent of *all* steel imports) were being imported into the United States in such quantities as to be a substantial cause or threat of serious injury to the domestic industry. The ITC recommended that the president impose a combination of tariffs and quotas on these imports. However, such action by the United States would have allowed foreign steel-exporting countries to demand compensation under the rules of GATT for lost exports to the United States (possibly amounting to several billion dollars). Compensation would take the form of lower restrictions on U.S. imports of other products. In the event compensation could not be agreed to, the injured countries could retaliate by eliminating an equal amount of imports from the United States—again under GATT rules. To avert this compensation-retaliation procedure, the president negotiated VERs with 29 countries limiting their steel exports to the United States. These agreements are intended to hold steel imports to about 20 percent of U.S. domestic consumption. The agreements, scheduled to expire in September 1989 originally, have been extended to March 1992.

In spite of twenty years of continuous protection, the international competitive position of the U.S. steel industry remains precarious. Market forces have caused a restructuring of the steel industry but to a lesser degree than would have occurred in the absence of protection. In the 1980s, 444 steel mills were closed, employment was cut by 200,000 workers, and billions of dollars were spent on labor-saving equipment. Between 1982 and 1987, the U.S. capacity to produce steel dropped from 154 million tons to 112 million tons, but productivity rose over 25 percent.[22] In the late 1980s, the U.S. began to export steel, particularly in specialty products used in aerospace, chemical equipment, and nuclear plant construction. It would appear that this revival of the American steel industry is mostly due to the sharp depreciation of the dollar that started in 1985. If so, international competitiveness as defined earlier in this chapter remains an elusive goal. In any

---

[22] "Is Steel's Revival for Real," *Fortune*, October 26, 1987, p. 97.

event, the steel industry does not intend to give up its protection.

Further protection is unlikely to benefit the U.S. steel industry beyond providing *temporary* relief from import competition. In the long run, the U.S. steel industry—as well as the European and even Japanese steel industries—will be forced out of bulk steel manufacture by new low-cost producers in developing countries; it will turn instead to technology-intensive specialty steel manufacture, in which it will continue to have a comparative advantage. By delaying this inevitable adjustment, import protection not only injures the national interest but the U.S. steel industry itself.

Automobiles By 1980, automobiles—imported mostly from Japan—had captured more than 25 percent of the U.S. market. The competitive advantage of Japanese manufacturers over their American counterparts was based on lower costs and higher quality. Several studies indicated that the Japanese, at the 1980 dollar/yen exchange rate, could build a car and ship it to the United States for $1,300 to $1,700 less than it cost the Americans to build a comparable vehicle. This cost advantage was traceable to both higher productivity and lower wages. On the average, Japanese companies could manufacture an automobile in 30.8 hours compared to the 59.9 hours it took U.S. companies. Toyota, for instance, built cars with about one-third the worker-hours needed in the United States and paid its workers about half the U.S. wages.

Unlike the steel producers, the U.S. automobile companies conceded that the decline in their competitiveness was largely of their own doing: sloppy management, poor quality control, a failure to anticipate the shift toward smaller cars, poor employee relations, and so on. Nonetheless, the Ford Motor Company asked the U.S. government in 1980 to restrict imports of Japanese vehicles. The government responded by getting the Japanese to agree in March 1981 to limit their exports of automobiles to the United States for two, possibly three, years.

The automobile, VER was intended to be a *temporary* crutch for the U.S. industry, which was facing international competition and a domestic recession. But despite record profits earned by the American auto companies in the mid-1980s, the VER remains in existence to this day. The U.S. government stopped asking Japan for export restraints in 1985. However, the Japanese government voluntarily decided to keep them because they feared that an abandonment would trigger new protectionist demands in the United States and also because the Japanese auto industry was a beneficiary of the VER. The quota was 1.68 million cars per year for 1981–1983 and 1.85 million for 1984; it was then set at 2.3 million by the Japanese government for 1985 and later years.

The Japanese auto industry has responded to the VER in several ways. First, because the quota is expressed in physical units, the Japanese exports moved from low-priced compact cars to high-priced luxury cars. Second, the Japanese auto companies invested in manufacturing facilities in the United States: Five of these companies now have assembly plants here that by 1990 could be producing 1.3 million cars a year. Third, by curtailing the supply of cars to the American market, the VER enabled the Japanese to charge high prices and make big monopoly profits.[23] In effect, the VER created a Japanese export cartel that rationed automobiles to the United States at monopoly prices— all with the approval of the U.S. government!

Has the VER enabled the U.S. auto industry to become competitive with the Japanese industry? Undoubtedly, American automobile companies have greatly improved their productivity and quality through a massive restructuring involving sharp cuts in employment and large-scale investments in automation. But in the late 1980s, they still ran behind their Japanese competitors. A study sponsored by MIT's International Motor Vehicle Program measured productivity and quality in thirty-eight auto plants around the world in 1987. It found that the average Japanese plant was 39 percent more productive than the average U.S. plant and that Japanese cars sold in the United States averaged 44 assembly defects per 100 cars while American cars averaged 87.[24] By 1990, Japanese plants in the United States will account for 11 percent of automobile manufacturing capacity in North America. These plants, plus continuing imports from Japan, Europe, South Korea, and other Third World countries, will almost certainly increase the share of foreign competitors in the U.S. market. By the mid-1990s, the Japanese alone may well control one-third of that market.[25] In sum, the VER has been an ineffective instrument to restore competitiveness in the U.S. auto industry. Indeed, it can be argued that the VER has slowed the adjustment of American auto firms while it has enhanced the adjustment of Japanese auto firms. By accelerating the establishment of U.S. plants and causing a shift to luxury cars, the VER has made the Japanese stronger competitors in the U.S. market and much more able to cope with a weak dollar.

Textiles   Unlike steel and automobiles, the textile trade dispute is between the industrial and developing countries. Largely because of pressure from the United States, the International Cotton Textiles Arrangement was entered into by some thirty countries in 1962 under the auspices of GATT. The arrangement allowed a country suffering from "disruptive imports" of cotton textiles to request the exporting country to restrict its exports to a specified level. If agreement was not reached, then the importing country could impose a quota related to past imports. But the importing country was committed to increase regularly permitted levels of imports and to enlarge existing quotas.

---

[23] A study by the Federal Trade Commission calculated that the VER transferred $750 million a year from American consumers to Japanese auto firms. (At the same time, American consumers subsidized the U.S. auto firms at an annual rate of $100 million.) For this reason, the Japanese government has been content to maintain the VER since 1985. See "A Victory for Car Buyers," *The Economist*, March 9, 1985, p. 69.

[24] See "Japan's Carmakers Take on the World," *Fortune*, June 20, 1988, p. 69.

[25] Ibid., p. 67.

The present regime is the Multifiber Arrangement (MFA), which covers textiles made from both natural and manufactured products. The most recent renegotiation of the MFA occurred in 1986. It provides a legal framework within which importing and exporting countries can negotiate bilateral pacts on levels of trade. The MFA allows the United States to restrict textile imports without violating its GATT obligations. This country is currently party to textile agreements with thirty-six countries.

In spite of MFA protection, U.S. textile manufacturers have repeatedly sought new trade legislation that would further restrict imports. In 1985, President Reagan vetoed a bill that would have rolled back textile imports from Hong Kong, Taiwan, and South Korea by 30 percent and would have frozen import quotas for nine other countries at 1984 levels. Again, in 1988, the president vetoed a bill that would have limited growth of textile imports to 1 percent a year.[26] (In recent years, U.S. textile imports have risen about 17 percent a year.) According to the *Economist*, that bill made the MFA, which it tried to supersede, look like a "free trade charter."[27] This demand for more protection occurred at a time when U.S. textile companies were running their plants at 95 percent capacity, and the profit rate of the textile industry was higher than the average for U.S. manufacturing as a whole. Profits of the industry were up 54 percent over the two previous years and textile imports were lower in 1988 than in 1987.

In sum, the MFA is a multilateral approach to voluntary export quotas that is sanctioned by an international accord. As such, it is an egregious departure from the liberal trade principles of GATT, amounting to a cartelization of world trade in textiles.

Semiconductors   By 1985, U.S. semiconductor manufacturers had lost a key sector of their industry—dynamic-random-access memory (DRAM) chips—to Japanese manufacturers. DRAM chips are standard memory chips that store data in all sorts of electronic products, such as computers and videocassette recorders. The Japanese were able to dominate the DRAM chip market by drastic cuts in prices and continual improvements in quality. By 1985, only three U.S. companies still sold DRAM chips on the commercial market.[28]

In 1984, the Semiconductor Industry Association filed an unfair trade complaint with the U.S. government against Japanese semiconductor producers under Section 301 of the Trade Act of 1974. This was followed in 1985 by petitions of American semiconductor manufacturers asking the government to impose antidumping duties on imports from Japan of 64K DRAM chips and other memory chips. At the end of that year, the U.S. government itself filed an antidumping case against Japanese semiconductor manufacturers of 256K DRAM chips and, significantly, of future gen-

---

[26] "President Vetoes Bill That Limits Imported Textiles," *New York Times*, September 29, 1988, p. 1.
[27] "Cloth-Eared Protectionists," *The Economist*, September 17, 1988, p. 31.
[28] "Pushing America out of Chips," *New York Times*, June 16, 1985, p. F1.

erations of chips. By then, only two U.S. companies still remained in the market for DRAM chips: Texas Instruments and Micro Technology. In 1986, the government ruled that Japanese producers were selling DRAM and other chips in the U.S. market for less than production costs and were subject to antidumping duties of up to 35 percent.

The U.S. Department of Commerce and the Semiconductor Industry Association wanted to stop alleged Japanese dumping (denied by the Japanese) without going through cumbersome antidumping procedures that could take two years between the time of petition and the time of ruling. Accordingly, the U.S. and Japanese governments reached a semiconductor agreement in July 1986 in which the United States agreed not to retaliate for the dumping of Japanese chips in the American market in return for Japan's commitment to establish a price monitoring system and to obtain greater access to the Japanese market for U.S. semiconductor producers. The Japanese agreed not to sell their chips below a "fair market value" (assigned by the U.S. Department of Commerce) to the United States and other countries.

In the following year, the United States contended that Japan failed to comply with the semiconductor agreement: it had not improved U.S. access to the Japanese market and it continued to dump semiconductors in third-country markets. In retaliation, in April 1987 the president imposed 100 percent duties on imports of Japanese computers, TV sets, and power tools worth $300 million. (These duties were removed some months later.)

Two years after its negotiation, it had become evident that the semiconductor agreement was falling short of its objectives. (1) Dumping had stopped, but only to be replaced by a shortage of DRAM chips that hurt the U.S. computer industry. (2) U.S. semiconductor companies failed to reenter the DRAM chip business because of the expense and risk. (3) The share of U.S. semiconductor producers in the Japanese market failed to increase, remaining at 10 percent. Furthermore, the agreement led the Japanese government to limit semiconductor production, thereby helping to form an export cartel that can charge high prices for its chips.[29]

The Costs of Protection

Several recent studies have estimated the costs of protection in the United States. Although these studies differ in estimation procedures and cover different time periods and industries, the results are consistent.

Tarr and Morkre estimated annual costs to the U.S. economy of $12.7 billion from all tariffs and quotas on automobiles, textiles, steel, and sugar. This is a *net* measure of costs: losses to consumers offset by gains to domestic producers and the U.S. government.[30] Hickok estimated that U.S trade re-

---

[29] "U.S. Chip Pact Falls Short of Goals," *New York Times*, August 8, 1988, p. D1.

[30] David G. Tarr and Morris E. Morkre, *Aggregate Costs to the United States of Tariffs and Quotas on Automobiles, Steel, Sugar, and Textiles* (Washington, D.C.: Federal Trade Commission, December 1984).

strictions on clothing, sugar, and automobiles caused increased consumer expenditures of $14 billion in 1984.[31]

Hufbauer looked at 31 cases in which the United States imposed trade restrictions on trade volumes exceeding $100 million.[32] In all but six cases, annual consumer losses were greater than $100 million; for all cases together, the costs to consumers exceeded $50 billion. The Hufbauer estimates for textiles and apparel, carbon steel, and automobiles are shown in Table 9-7.

In Phase I of protection for textiles and apparel, the cost to consumers was $9.4 billion (the extra amount paid due to the protection-induced rise in prices), gains to domestic producers totalled $8.7 billion (more sales at higher protection-induced prices), and tariff revenue was $1.2 billion. The *efficiency loss* was $1.1 billion.[33] Also, observe that the cost to save a single job in this industry through Phase I protection was $22,000. For all three industries, the highest cost to consumers was $27 billion for Phase III protection of textiles and apparel. The highest cost per job saved was an extraordinary $620,000 for Phase II protection of carbon steel.

These estimates of the costs of protection are almost certainly too low, because they ignore the *dynamic* effects of protection, in particular, inefficient management and slower innovation bred by lower competition. The biggest cost of protection to a country over the longer run is the prolonged maladjustment of domestic industries to a changing world economy.

RECENT DEVELOPMENTS IN U.S. TRADE POLICY

This closing section reviews East-West trade, the U.S.-Canada Free Trade Agreement, and the Omnibus Trade and Competitiveness Act of 1988.

East-West Trade

Since shortly after the end of World War II, the United States has viewed its economic relations with the Soviet Union and other communist countries as a *political* question. Consequently, U.S. policy on East-West trade has been separate from its commercial policy toward noncommunist countries.

During the 1950s and 1960s the United States placed strategic controls on its exports to communist countries. The basic restrictive legislation was

[31] Susan Hickok, "The Consumer Cost of U.S. Trade Restraints," *Quarterly Review* (Federal Reserve Bank of New York), Summer 1985, pp. 1–12.

[32] Gary Hufbauer et al., *Trade Protection in the United States: 31 Case Studies* (Washington, D.C.: Institute for International Economics, 1986).

[33] Efficiency loss is the *deadweight* loss to the national economy traceable to the replacement of imports with less efficiently produced domestic output and the replacement by consumers of imports with substitute goods that offer less satisfaction. It is the sum of the triangles *l* and *c* in Figure 7-4.

TABLE 9-7   Distribution of Costs and Gains of Protection for the U.S. Textile and Apparel, Steel, and Automobile Industries
(Millions of Dollars Except "Per Job Saved" in Thousands of Dollars)

| Industry | Cost to Consumers | | Gains to Producers | Tariff Revenue | Gains to Foreigners | Efficiency Loss |
	Total	Per Job Saved				
Textiles and Apparel						
Phase I	9,400	22	8,700	1,158	—	1,100
Phase II	20,000	37	18,000	2,143	350	3,100
Phase III	27,000	42	22,000	2,535	1,800	4,850
Carbon Steel						
Phase I	1,970	240	1,330	290	330	50
Phase II	4,350	620	2,770	556	930	120
Automobiles	5,800	105	2,600	790	2,200	200

Source: Gary Hufbauer, et al., *Trade Protection in the United States: 31 Case Studies* (Washington, D.C.: Institute for International Economics, 1986) in the Federal Reserve Bank of St. Louis, *Review*, January–February 1988, p. 18.

(and is) the Export Control Act of 1949, as amended in subsequent years. Export restrictions were embodied in a list of some 1,300 product categories (including their associated technology) that could not be exported without prior approval from the U.S. Department of Commerce in the form of validated licenses. In all but 200 categories, equivalent products and technology became freely available in the 1960s to communist buyers from the other industrial countries of the West. As a direct consequence of controls, therefore, U.S. companies failed to profit from East-West business, to the detriment of U.S. exports and the balance of payments.

Owing largely to the political frictions resulting from the Vietnam war, efforts to lessen the severity of U.S. export controls were fruitless during the 1960s. Only at the end of the decade did the passage of the Export Administration Act of 1969 signal a distinct turn toward liberalization. The Export Control Act of 1949, as amended, had required the denial of export licenses to items that contributed significantly to the military *or* economic potential of a communist bloc country. The 1969 act eliminated the criterion of "economic potential." Under this legislation the Department of Commerce removed some 2,000 individual items from the export control list, bringing it into closer agreement with the export control lists of Western European countries and Japan.[34] Furthermore, the Department was likely to approve for export any listed item that was freely available from other Western countries.

The liberalization of U.S. export controls proceeded rapidly in the early 1970s, including a lifting of the U.S. embargo on trade with the People's Republic of China. At the end of the decade, however, the United States reversed the direction of its East-West policy, with the notable exception of its trade relations with China. In response to the Soviet invasion of Afghanistan in 1979 and the imposition of martial law in Poland in 1981, the United States applied economic sanctions to those two countries. But Western European countries and Japan were reluctant to do the same. This difference between the United States and its Western allies on the direction of East-West trade policy was the source of the pipeline controversy.

The Yamal pipeline, which would bring gas from Siberia to Western Europe, had been under discussion for many years. The West German government approved it in July 1980 and agreed to make large loans to the Soviet Union to help finance the pipeline, whose total cost will be over $10 billion. Other European countries followed suit. At the end of 1981, the United States applied sanctions on U.S. shipments of pipeline equipment to the Soviet Union in retaliation for the imposition of martial law in Poland, but it failed to persuade European countries to abandon the project. In June 1982, without prior consultation with its allies, the United States extended its sanctions to cover not only U.S. companies but also their overseas sub-

---

[34] Export controls are determined multilaterally by the NATO countries and Japan through the Coordinating Committee (COCOM). The COCOM list has been much smaller than the U.S. list.

sidiaries and non-U.S. firms producing pipeline equipment under licenses with U.S. companies. The European governments vehemently protested this extraterritorial application of U.S. policy, instructing their companies to honor their pipeline contracts with the Soviet Union. When several European firms did so by shipping equipment to the Soviet Union, the United States retaliated by prohibiting them from doing any further business with the United States (later softened to a prohibition against doing business in oil and gas equipment).

It is evident that this country acted far too late in its efforts to stop the Soviet pipeline. Also, U.S. attempts to apply its controls extraterritorially angered its NATO allies, who accused the United States of a double-standard, as the United States continued to ship large quantities of grain to the Soviet Union. U.S. pipeline policy, therefore, was not only ineffective but also damaged relations with its closest allies.

Another controversy arose in May 1987 when it was discovered that a Japanese company (Toshiba) and a Norwegian company (Kongsberg Vapenfabrik) shipped to the Soviet Union four milling machines and associated numerical control systems that make advanced propeller blades. With this equipment, the Soviet Union can make blades that reduce the noise of its submarines, making them more difficult to detect by the United States and its NATO allies. The shipment was a direct violation of Coordinating Committee (COCOM) controls. In response to U.S. protests, the Japanese government agreed to establish strategic export controls similar to those used by this country. Also, new efforts were undertaken to strengthen COCOM controls over exports of high-technology goods to communist countries.

Apart from the political aspects of U.S. East-West trade, there are economic and business problems that arise from the fact that communist countries trade through state agencies in conformance with a national economic plan. Among several of the questions that bear on state trading, two deserve our attention here: (1) the potential imbalance in the relative bargaining power of private firms *versus* monopsonistic state-trading agencies, and (2) market access for outside suppliers.

As to the first question, there is no easy answer. As long as the United States adheres to a private enterprise system, individual firms will have to negotiate on their own with Soviet and other state-trading organizations. Suffice it to say that there is no firm evidence of a *systemic* bargaining advantage for state-trading agencies. The presence of powerful multinational enterprises suggests that the bargaining advantage will not always go to the state trader.

As to the second question, it is evident that the traditional approach to the liberalization of trade (mutual concessions on tariffs and the elimination of nontariff barriers) will not assure access to the markets of communist countries. Their imports are dictated by a national economic plan and administered by government agencies. Although they may use tariffs and quotas, the communist countries do not rely on them to regulate trade.

Any concessions they may give in tariffs or quotas are meaningless, or nearly so. New approaches are required to liberalize trade with centrally planned, state-trading countries, such as bilateral or multilateral trade agreements with market access provisions.

The prospects of more open East-West trade in the 1990s are good. Both China and the Soviet Union are now trying to invigorate their economies by replacing central controls with decentralized markets.

U.S.-Canada Free Trade Agreement

After nearly three years of negotiation, President Reagan and Prime Minister Mulroney signed the U.S.-Canada Free Trade Agreement (FTA) on January 2, 1988. The agreement will create the world's largest free trade area.[35] Each year the United States and Canada exchange more goods and services than any other two countries. In 1987, two-way trade amounted to $166 billion.

The FTA is designed to (1) eliminate all tariffs by 1998 and substantially reduce other barriers to trade in goods and services between the two countries; (2) promote fair competition; (3) liberalize trade in agriculture, autos, energy, financial services, government procurement, and other areas; (4) liberalize conditions for investment; (5) establish effective administrative procedures and resolve disputes; and (6) lay the foundation for further bilateral and multilateral cooperation.[36]

The Omnibus Trade and Competitiveness Act of 1988

The huge, persistent U.S. trade deficits, together with intense lobbying by protectionist interests, led to the passage of the Omnibus Trade and Competitiveness Act of 1988, which runs for one thousand pages and contains a variety of provisions. We note here only the most significant ones.

Unfair Trade Practices   The act raises the probability that the United States will retaliate in the future against what it regards as the unfair trade practices of foreign countries.[37] The act instructs the Administration to identify countries that have persistent trade surpluses and that also maintain pervasive trade practices that are "unjustifiable" or "unreasonable." If negotiations fail to remove these practices, then the United States could retaliate by restricting an offending country's access to U.S. markets. Hence,

---

[35] The largest free trade area currently in operation is the European Community, which is treated in the next chapter. The FTA is the second free trade agreement signed by the United States; its first agreement was signed with Israel in 1985.

[36] U.S. Department of State, *U.S.-Canada Free Trade Agreement* (Washington, D.C.: June 1988).

[37] The act defines unfair practices to include workers' rights and the violation of intellectual property rights as well as tariff and nontariff trade barriers.

the act stresses *reciprocity*: obtaining from other countries the kind of access to their markets that the United States offers them.

The act gives the president specific authority to deny foreign companies access to the U.S. telecommunications market to the degree that foreign countries deny American companies access to their own telecommunications markets. (The main targets of this provision are Japan and West Germany.) Also, the act prevents foreign companies from serving as primary dealers in U.S. government securities unless their own governments allow American firms to compete on an equal basis with local primary dealers. (Japan is the chief target here.)

Although the act transfers from the president to the U.S. Trade Representative the authority to initiate investigations of unfair trade practices and to order sanctions, the president ultimately retains control over the timing and method of any retaliatory measures. The president can choose to act or not to act under this provision as his or her own judgment dictates. For instance, the president can deny an industry import protection on grounds that such protection would hurt the poor, hurt national security, or hurt American companies that depend on the import in question. In sum, the new trade legislation opens the door to major changes in U.S. trade policy, but it does not force the president to walk through that door.

Trade Relief   Under the act, industries seriously injured by imports could receive some protection if they are willing to make a "positive adjustment" to foreign competition. Firms obtaining such relief would have to agree to a five-year plan to restore their competitiveness.

Worker Assistance   The act creates a $1 billion retraining program (financed by an import fee) to help workers displaced by imports. Also, as noted above, worker rights in foreign countries are one of the factors in determining unfair trade practices.

Intellectual Property   The act has measures to enhance the protection afforded by U.S. patents, copyrights, and other intellectual (industrial) property rights. It strengthens the ability of U.S. companies to block imports—without the need to prove damages—if patents are violated.

Use of the Metric System   Under the act, the government is required to use the metric system of measurement in its procurement, grants, and other business-related activities. The government and business firms are also required to use the metric system in the documentation of exports and imports as mandated by the International Convention on the Harmonized System, the classification of international goods that has been adopted by all major trading countries. However, private firms remain free to decide whether or not to convert to the metric system. The United States, Burma, and Brunei are the only countries in the world that have *not* gone metric. The lack of metric product designs and labeling constrains U.S. exports, amounting to a self-imposed nontariff trade barrier.

Negotiating Authority   The act grants to the president authority to continue negotiations under the Uruguay Round sponsored by GATT. As observed in Chapter 8, the United States intends to use these negotiations to open foreign markets for banking, insurance, and other services; to gain protection for patents, trademarks, copyrights, and other intellectual property rights; to liberalize rules pertaining to direct foreign investment; and to cut tariffs by up to 50 percent. Further, the act establishes a procedure—voting up or down without any amendments—to expedite the ratification by Congress of Uruguay Round agreements submitted by June 1, 1991.

Competitiveness   The act does little to improve U.S. competitiveness as we have defined it. It makes mention of education reforms to increase the language and technical skills of American workers and managers, but it provides only modest funding for that purpose. It calls on the National Bureau of Standards (renamed the National Institute of Standards and Technology) and other government agencies to allocate more resources to the transfer of government technology to private companies.

Closing Observations   Japan and the European Community have strongly criticized the Omnibus Trade and Competitiveness Act of 1988 as protectionist legislation that allows the U.S. government to act unilaterally in settling trade disputes.[38] In rebuttal, supporters of the act argue that it will open up markets rather than close them, because of the U.S. threat to retaliate against unfair trade barriers. (But suppose other countries deny they have unfair trade barriers and refuse to eliminate them, retaliating instead against the U.S. retaliation?)

Most observers would agree that the original language of the act was much more protectionist, with provisions that would have *compelled* the president to take restrictive or retaliatory actions. By giving the president discretionary authority, the act will have a major impact on trade policy only if the president aggressively tries to force other countries to open up their markets to U.S. products. Widespread acts of "retaliation" or "reciprocity" by the United States could well start a trade war. It is evident, then, that the direction of U.S. trade policy in the 1990s will depend critically on the president.

SUMMARY

1.   Today, the United States faces formidable challenges in international trade and global competition. To cope with these challenges, this country needs to design and carry out a trade policy that will effectively

---

[38] It is estimated that lobbyists for foreign governments spent more than $100 million in trying to stop the trade bill in Congress. See "Major Trade Bill Sent to President by Senate, 85-11," *New York Times*, August 4, 1988, p. 1.

promote its interests in an international economy undergoing deep-seated structural shifts.

2. Apart from shifts in comparative advantage between the North and South, the dependence of the United States and the other industrial countries on international trade has dramatically intensified over the past decade.

3. Modern U.S. trade policy was born with the passage of the Reciprocal Trade Agreements Act of 1934. After World War II, the United States became the leader in the movement toward freer trade. The Trade Act of 1974 and the Trade Act of 1979 provided the legislative framework for U.S. trade policy in the 1980s.

4. National competitiveness is the degree to which a nation can, under free and fair market conditions, produce goods and services that meet the test of international markets while simultaneously expanding the real incomes of its citizens.

5. The U.S. trade deficit in the 1980s experienced an astounding rise. However, this deficit is not a sign of declining U.S. competitiveness, because the trade balance is determined by macroeconomic variables such as real income, the price level, the interest rate, and the rate of exchange. Export shares and import penetration ratios of manufactures are also inadequate indicators of competitiveness.

6. A country can sustain its competitiveness in world markets only if its productivity performance keeps pace with that of other countries. Labor productivity in the manufacturing sector has grown much more rapidly in Japan and West Germany than in the United States. As a result, Japan and West Germany now have productivity levels in manufacturing that match or even exceed the U.S. level.

7. The achievement and maintenance of national competitiveness will remain a major challenge for the American people throughout the 1990s and beyond.

8. The revival of protectionism since the mid-1970s is called the "new protectionism" because it relies heavily on new forms of nontariff trade barriers, notably voluntary export restraints (VERs) and orderly marketing agreements (OMAs). Other features of the new protectionism are its focus on a comparatively small number of industries, its bilateral application (which violates GATT's principle of nondiscrimination), and its lack of transparency.

9. In recent years, the United States has experienced numerous trade disputes with the European Community, Japan, and other countries. For the most part, these disputes revolve around American allegations of unfair trade practices (dumping and government subsidies) relating to U.S. imports and allegations of high nontariff trade barriers that keep U.S. goods out of foreign markets.

10. A review of U.S. protection for steel, automobiles, textiles, and semiconductors indicates that import restrictions have offered only short-

term benefits to these industries at a very heavy cost to the American consumer.

11. Since shortly after the end of World War II, the United States has viewed its economic relations with the Soviet Union and other communist countries as a *political* question.

12. The U.S.-Canada Free Trade Agreement will create the world's largest free trade areas.

13. The direction of U.S. trade policy in the 1990s will depend critically on how the president uses his discretionary authority under the Omnibus Trade and Competitiveness Act of 1988.

QUESTIONS AND APPLICATIONS

1. Why is the Reciprocal Trade Agreements Program described as a "watershed" in U.S. trade policy?

2. Identify and be prepared to discuss the major provisions of the Trade Act of 1974 and the Trade Act of 1979.

3. Define *national competitiveness*.

4. "A growing external trade deficit is commonly viewed as a symptom of declining national competitiveness." Comment on this statement.

5. What is the single most important indicator of changes in national competitiveness? Why?

6. (a) Is the United States losing its international competitiveness? Be prepared to defend your position.

   (b) Prepare a report on the international competitiveness of a particular U.S. industry.

7. (a) What is the "new protectionism"?

   (b) Explain the resurgence of protectionism in the United States since the mid-1970s.

8. Undertake research to identify and describe the major protectionist interests in the United States.

9. Undertake research on new developments relating to international trade disputes in steel, autos, textiles, and semiconductors.

10. (a) What are the distinctive features of East-West trade?

    (b) What should U.S. policy be toward East-West trade? Why?

11. (a) What are the key provisions of the Omnibus Trade and Competitiveness Act of 1988?

    (b) What are the implications of these provisions for U.S. trade policy?

12. Be prepared to engage in a debate on "Protectionism versus Free Trade in the 1990s."

SELECTED READINGS

Baily, Martin N., and Alok K. Chakrabarti. *Innovation and the Productivity Crisis*. Washington, D.C.: Brookings Institution, 1988.

Cline, William R., ed. *Trade Policy in the 1980s*. Washington, D.C.: Institute for International Economics, 1983.

Finger, J. Michael, and Andrzej Olechowski, eds. *The Uruquay Round*. Washington, D.C.: The World Bank, 1987.

General Agreement on Tariffs and Trade. *Activities in (year)*. Geneva: General Agreement on Tariffs and Trade. Annual.

General Agreement on Tariffs and Trade. *Focus*. Monthly.

General Agreement on Tariffs and Trade. *What It Is, What It Does*. Geneva: General Agreement on Tariffs and Trade. Current edition.

Guile, Bruce R., and Harvey Brooks. *Technology and Global Industry*. Washington, D.C.: National Academy Press, 1987.

Hufbauer, Gary C., and Howard F. Rosen. *Trade Policy for Troubled Industries*. Washington, D.C.: Institute for International Economics, March 1986.

Krugman, Paul R., ed. *Strategic Trade Policy and the New International Economics*. Cambridge: MIT Press, 1986.

Lawrence, Robert Z. *Can America Compete?* Washington, D.C.: Brookings Institution, 1984.

Lawrence, Robert Z., and Robert E. Litan. *Saving Free Trade*. Washington, D.C.: Brookings Institution, 1986.

Macbean, A. I., and P. N. Snowden. *International Institutions in Trade and Finance*. London: George Allen & Unwin, 1981. Chapter 4.

Organization for Economic Cooperation and Development. *Costs and Benefits of Protection*. Paris: Organization for Economic Cooperation and Development, 1985

Pierre, Andrew, J., ed. *A High Technology Gap? Europe, America, and Japan*. New York: Council on Foreign Relations, 1987.

Schlossstein, Steven. *Trade War*. New York: Congdon & Weed, 1984.

Spence, A. Michael, and Heather A. Hazard, eds. *International Competitiveness*. Cambridge, Mass.: Ballinger Publishing, 1988.

Teece, David, ed. *The Competitive Challenge*. Cambridge, Mass.: Ballinger Publishing, 1987.

Tiffany, Paul A. *The Decline of American Steel*. New York: Oxford University Press, 1988.

U.S. International Trade Commission. *Annual Report*. Washingon, D.C.: U.S. Government Printing Office. Annual.

U.S. Trade Representative. *Annual Report of the President of the United States on the Trade Agreements Program*. Washington, D.C.: U.S. Government Printing Office. Annual.

10

The European Community and the Theory of Economic Integration

Postwar European economic cooperation began with the establishment of the Organization for European Economic Cooperation (OEEC) in 1948 to allocate Marshall Plan aid and accelerate the recovery of Western Europe. In the 1950s, quotas and payments restrictions on intra-OEEC trade were rapidly dismantled, and European countries grew accustomed to close cooperation on trade and other economic matters. However, many Europeans, as well as Americans, considered economic cooperation under the auspices of the OEEC inadequate to cope with Europe's problems. They argued that only economic integration transcending national boundaries would enable Europe to match the continental economies of the United States and the Soviet Union. Economic integration would create the large competitive markets that are the necessary counterparts of mass production and economies of scale, and it would stimulate a more efficient allocation of labor, materials, and capital.

Supported by the United States, the drive toward European economic unity gained strength in the 1950s despite widespread doubts as to its ultimate success. Its first notable success was the establishment of the European Coal and Steel Community (ECSC) in 1952 to create a common market in coal, steel, and iron ore that encompassed the six nations of France, West Germany, Italy, Belgium, the Netherlands, and Luxembourg. The second big step toward economic unity was the negotiation and approval by these same countries of a treaty establishing the European Economic Community (EEC) in 1957.[1] (It has now become standard practice to use

---

[1] The treaty was signed in Rome on March 25, 1957, and was then ratified by the six countries. A separate treaty setting up a European Atomic Energy Community (Euratom) was signed and ratified at the same time. Both the EC and Euratom treaties went into effect on January 1, 1958. Fusion of the three communities (EEC, ECSC, and Euratom) into a single European Community was substantively accomplished in 1967.

the designation *European Community* [EC] in place of *European Economic Community*.)

The failure of negotiations for an OEEC-wide free trade area led to the formation of the European Free Trade Association (EFTA) in 1960 by Great Britain, the three Scandinavian countries, Switzerland, Austria, and Portugal. During the 1960s Western Europe remained at "sixes and sevens," but the split between the EC and the EFTA is now minimal. Great Britain, Denmark, and Ireland entered the Community at the beginning of 1973 and the other EFTA countries made free trade arrangements with the Community short of full membership.[2]

The main feature of the European Community is the creation of a customs union for both industrial and agricultural goods, involving the abolition of all restrictions on trade among member countries and the erection of a common external tariff. But the EC goes much further than this. A second objective is the establishment of a *common market* with free movement of labor, capital, and other factors of production as well as products. A third objective is a full *economic union*, with free movement of products, persons, services, and capital, and the harmonization and unification of social, fiscal, and monetary policies. The ultimate objective is a *political union* of the member countries.

The formation of the EC introduced a new force to world trade and provoked a major attempt by the United States to negotiate with the EC to lower tariffs and other trade barriers. In this chapter we shall first describe the principal features of the EC and its progress toward the creation of a customs and economic union. Next, we shall consider some of the effects of European integration on international trade in light of economic theory. Finally, we shall examine the policies of EC toward the outside world, including the common external tariff, agricultural protection, the EFTA, the developing countries, and the United States. Before moving on to a consideration of the EC, it is instructive to outline the forms or stages of economic integration (Table 10-1).

A *free trade area* is established when a group of countries abolishes restrictions on mutual trade but each member country retains its own tariff and quota system on trade with third countries. An *industrial free trade area* covers only trade in industrial products whereas a *full free trade area* includes all products. As an industrial free trade area, EFTA represents only a modest form of economic integration.

A *customs union* is created when a group of countries removes all restrictions on mutual trade and also sets up a common system of tariffs and quotas with respect to third countries. A customs union becomes a *common market* with the removal of all restrictions on the movement of productive factors—labor, capital, and enterprise. The EC is now in this stage of evolution but is attempting to become an economic union.

---

[2] With the entry of Greece in 1981 and Spain and Portugal in 1986, the EC now has 12 members.

TABLE 10-1   Stages of International Economic Integration

Stage of Integration	Abolition of Tariffs and Quotas among Members	Common Tariff and Quota System	Abolition of Restrictions on Factor Movements	Harmonization and Unification of Economic Policies and Institutions
1. Industrial free trade area	Yes[1]	No	No	No
2. Full free trade area	Yes	No	No	No
3. Customs union	Yes	Yes	No	No
4. Common market	Yes	Yes	Yes	No
5. Economic union	Yes	Yes	Yes	Yes

[1]Industrial goods only.

The completion of the final stage of *economic union* involves a full integration of the member economies with supranational authorities responsible for economic policymaking. In particular, an economic union requires a single monetary system and central bank, a unified fiscal system, and a common foreign economic policy. The task of creating an economic union differs significantly from the steps necessary to establish the less ambitious forms of economic integration. A free trade area, a customs union, or a common market mainly result from the abolition of restrictions, whereas an economic union demands a positive agreement to transfer economic sovereignty to new supranational institutions.

THE CREATION OF A CUSTOMS UNION

The treaty establishing the EC is a lengthy document comprising over 200 articles. The treaty lays down a timetable for the progressive development of a customs union but goes far beyond this goal—it contains numerous provisions relating to the free movement of persons, services, and capital; transportation; rules governing competition; the harmonization of laws, economic policies, and social policies; and the organs of the EC.

Institutions of the European Community

The basic institutions, or organs, of the Community are five in number: European Commission, Council of Ministers, European Parliament, Court of Justice, and European Council. The *Commission* is the executive body of the EC and has two main functions. First, it administers the treaty and other EC policies. Second, it initiates new policies by making proposals to the Council. The Commission represents the Community rather than the member states, and it is the driving force in the EC.

All members of the *Council of Ministers* represent their own national governments. For the most part, the Council makes final policy decisions but can do so only on proposals by the Commission. At first, Council decisions required a unanimous vote, but they now require only a majority vote. It is through the Council that national governments influence and control the evolution of the EC by approving, amending, or rejecting Commission proposals.

The *European Parliament* draws its members from general elections in the member countries. However, the Parliament does not pass laws and is not a true legislature, since this function is performed jointly by the Commission and the Council. The Commission must report to the Parliament annually, and the Parliament must be consulted before certain specific decisions are made. But the only important power of the Parliament is the right to remove the Commission by a motion of censure voted by a two-thirds majority.

The *Court of Justice* has the sole power to decide on the constitutionality of acts performed by the Commission and the Council. The Court's judgments have the force of law throughout the Community and they are binding on all parties, whether individuals, business firms, national governments, or other Community institutions.

The *European Council* is composed of the 12 heads of state of the member countries and the EC Commission president. It holds summit meetings three times a year. The Council provides the main political guidance of the EC.

Free Trade in Industrial Products

The European Community became a full customs union in July 1968, when tariffs and quantitative restrictions were removed on all trade among its original member countries and a common tariff system was established vis-à-vis nonmember countries. Behind this signal achievement lay a decade of commitment that was tested by a series of hard-fought negotiations, especially in agricultural policy.

Although trade in industrial products within the EC is no longer obstructed by tariffs and quotas, it is not yet as free as trade within a single country. Many nontariff barriers continue to clog the arteries of commerce, such as differences in customs classification, varying taxation systems, border restrictions (for security, health, and technical reasons), and state monopolies. The Commission is working steadily on measures to harmonize customs legislation and eliminate licenses, visas, permits, and other export-import formalities so that the common market will have the same characteristics as a domestic market. However, certain barriers (for example, "tax frontiers" resulting from different tax systems) cannot be eliminated until the member countries agree to transfer more sovereignty to the EC.

Free Trade in Agricultural Products

Each of the original six countries came into the EC with its own domestic farm program involving price supports and import restrictions. This situation called for a different approach to free trade in agricultural products, namely, the establishment of a common agricultural policy that would not only free intra-EC trade but, at the same time, improve the economic position of EC farmers.

Negotiations for a Common Agricultural Policy The EC treaty does not spell out the details of a common agricultural policy; they have been worked out in a series of laborious negotiations that at times threatened the very existence of the organization. The EC took its first big step toward a common agricultural policy in January 1962, when the Council of Ministers (after a marathon session ending at 5 A.M.) agreed on the basic features of that policy and on regulations for grains, pork, eggs, poultry, fruit, vegetables, and wine. These regulations went into effect on July 30, 1962. The second big step was taken at the end of 1963 (the "Christmas eve" marathon) when the Council agreed on a common policy for rice, beef, veal, dairy products, vegetable oil, and oilseeds. By November 1964, when regulations covering these products went into effect, 85 percent of the agricultural output of the Community was under common organization.

These first two agreements did not extend to the common prices that would rule once a single agricultural market was fully established in the Community. This was the next order of business, and it proved exceptionally arduous. The key factor was the common price of grain. West Germany, the high-cost producer, tried to stall agreement on a common grain price while France, the low-cost producer, pressed hard for its early establishment. The issue was finally resolved in December 1964 (in another marathon conference, which ended at 5:15 A.M.), when the Council agreed on a common grain price—closer to the French than to the West German price—applicable to member countries no later than mid-1967.

The adoption of a common grain price broke a logjam; it was then possible to start negotiations on other common agricultural prices. The EC countries became full participants in a common agricultural policy when all remaining restrictions on their mutual trade in farm products were swept away at the end of June 1968.

Structure of the Common Agricultural Policy Although the farm problems in the EC and the United States have common features, their impact on international trade is very different. The EC is still the largest importer of farm products in the world, whereas the United States is the world's largest exporter. Hence, U.S. agricultural policy is aimed at opening up (and keeping open) foreign markets to American farm products, with import restrictions playing only a modest role except in the case of dairy products. In contrast, agricultural policy in the EC—a net importer of farm products— is based primarily on the restriction of imports. In this way the EC hopes to avoid production controls and surpluses by placing the burden of adjustment on third-country suppliers, notably the United States.

The structure of the common agricultural policy in the EC is illustrated by the common grain policy. First, there is a *target price*. This is the base price for grains and is to be established annually at the market of the region in the Community with the least adequate supplies. Farmers receive subsidies to sell their crops at prices as close as possible to the target price.

Second, there is an *intervention price*. This is the price (determined annually) at which the Community will buy from producers. It is the guaranteed minimum selling price.

Third, there is a *threshold price*. This is the price used to calculate the variable levy on imported grains. The threshold price is fixed at a level that will bring the selling price of imported grains up to the level of the target price in the region of the Community with the least adequate supplies.

Fourth, the *variable import levy* is a tariff imposed on grain imports from countries outside the group. It is determined daily and is equal to the difference between the world price for grain imports and the Community threshold price, taking any quality differences into account.

A hypothetical illustration involving common wheat may help to clarify the price structure of the common grain policy and the determination of the variable import levy:

		Per Metric Ton
1. Target price		$290
2. Intervention price		$200
3. Threshold price		
Target price	$290	
Less transportation and		
marketing costs	5	$285
4. Variable import levy		
Threshold price	$285	
Less adjusted world price	$125	$160

In conclusion, two points need stressing. First, there are no production controls: The EC must buy any quantity of a commodity offered at the intervention price. Second, variable import levies make third countries *residual* suppliers of farm products; imports are allowed only when EC producers fail to meet the EC's market demand. Consequently, the target prices are a key concern of the United States and other outside suppliers. High target prices encourage EC production and cut down on imports; low target prices greatly mitigate this effect.

Operation of the Common Agricultural Policy In the 1960s the EC countries introduced a common agricultural policy that eliminated restrictions on mutual trade and established single target and intervention prices for all the member nations. In the 1970s the common agricultural policy was plagued by food surpluses and a continuing deterioration of farm income relative to other sectors.

High support prices encouraged overproduction in butter, sugar, wine, beef, grains, and other products. The story of the beef surplus is illustrative. In the early 1970s the EC was importing large amounts of beef while piling up surpluses of grain and dairy products. The EC decided, therefore, to stimulate beef production by introducing a high intervention price in 1973. But then the recession in 1974 curtailed beef demand, forcing the EC to absorb vast amounts of unsold beef. Furthermore, sharp increases in fertilizer and petroleum prices led farmers in the fall of 1974 to slaughter their cattle en masse. With its beef policy in complete disarray, the EC embargoed all beef imports, much to the discomfort of its traditional suppliers, such as Australia and Argentina. The supplying countries in a formal protest charged that the EC embargo violated the GATT, forced down beef prices, and contradicted EC affirmations of a free trade policy.[3]

In the 1980s, the EC "solved" the problem of surpluses: It stepped up agricultural exports through massive subsidies made necessary by high domestic prices. It became the world's largest exporter of dairy products, sugar, barley, wheat flour, and poultry. It also became the second largest exporter of beef, although per capita beef consumption is comparatively low in the EC, held down by high prices. Only a few years before, the EC was a net importer of most of these products. Subsidized exports cut deeply into the agricultural exports of the United States and other countries to their traditional markets outside the EC.

In the early 1980s, then, the common agricultural policy was caught in a vicious spiral of ever-rising costs with no end in sight: Ever-higher support prices caused more surpluses, which in turn required ever-higher export subsidies to eliminate them. The cost of protecting agriculture was absorbing over two-thirds of the EC's budget. Moreover, protection had failed to halt the slippage of farm income.

Only in recent years has the EC begun to take corrective measures to reduce agricultural surpluses, including cutting the size of dairy herds to lower milk output, reducing cereal prices by changing intervention prices and by instituting a new mechanism that will automatically lower prices if cereal production rises above a certain level, and placing a ceiling on the annual increase in the common agricultural policy budget.[4] Although these efforts are in the right direction, EC target prices remain far above world prices, thereby stimulating excess production that is exported via subsidies to the rest of the world. Consequently, agricultural trade frictions between

---

[3] "Inflation Climbs the 'Beef Mountain,'" *European Community*, November 1974, pp. 6–7. In 1976 the EC cut its import of soybeans (mostly from the United States) to encourage the use of its "skimmed milk powder mountain" as cattle feed.

[4] *A Letter from Europe*, no. 5 (Washington, D.C.: Delegation of the European Community, June 14, 1988).

the EC and other countries (particularly the United States) are certain to continue. Because the common agricultural policy is viewed as a vital element of economic integration and because the farm lobbies in the EC are strong, any fundamental reform of the policy may prove to be impossible.

BUILDING A COMMON MARKET

To establish a common market that will match the freedom of national markets, the EC must go far beyond the traditional dimensions of a customs union. To enhance the gains from a superior allocation of resources, factors of production must be free to move among the member countries and thereby equalize factor returns for all the members. Furthermore, as noted earlier, many nontariff measures that restrict trade or confer artificial competitive advantages on the producers of only one of the member countries must be eliminated if the pattern of EC production and trade is to reflect fully the forces of competition, costs, and markets.

Free Movement of Labor Capital, and Enterprise

EC workers and their dependents can now move freely among the member countries in response to employment opportunities. Information on such opportunities is coordinated by an EC agency. When moving to a country, workers receive the same rights and social security benefits as nationals, and they also retain any rights and benefits they have earned through employment in another member country.

The EC has achieved unconditional freedom of movement for direct investment, personal capital transfers, and short- and medium-term commercial credits. However, some member countries still maintain discriminatory controls on new security issues and noncommercial loans and credits.

The EC has eliminated many restrictions on the right of member-country nationals to establish businesses and provide services throughout the member nations. Council measures have been applied to manufacturing, trading, agriculture, forestry, mining and prospecting, insurance, and other fields. However, many complexities have slowed progress toward the mutual recognition of diplomas and the right of professional people, such as lawyers and physicians, to practice freely anywhere in member countries. Furthermore, national differences in company laws and public buying preferences accorded national firms continue to obstruct the freedom of establishment for Community enterprise.

Rules Governing Competition

The Treaty of Rome gives to the Commission specific powers to prevent the formation of or to break up cartels and monopolies that lessen competition in the common market. The overriding purpose of this antitrust policy is to prevent private business agreements and industrial concentrations from nullifying Communitywide competition. Private restrictions are not to be allowed to replace the disappearing tariffs and other restrictions.

Although the EC antitrust provisions (Articles 85 and 86) have been influenced by United States antitrust legislation, there is a fundamental difference in philosophy between the two. Under U.S. law all "unreasonable" restraints on trade are illegal, and agreements to fix prices, allocate markets, and so on, are illegal per se regardless of their effects. In contrast, the EC distinguishes between "good" and "bad" cartels and monopolies. Business agreements and concentrations that help improve the production or distribution of goods or promote technical and economic progress are legal in the EC, provided that they do not eliminate competition in a "substantial" part of the market.

The administration of antitrust policy in the EC also differs from that in the United States. All cartels must register with the Commission, and to become legal they must be granted dispensation. Failure to register makes a private agreement null and void, and the Commission may impose retroactive penalties on the guilty parties. In the United States there is no prior registration because all cartels are illegal by their very nature; instead, each case is decided on its merits and the parties involved are presumed innocent until proven guilty.

How effective is EC antitrust policy? Certainly the Commission has ample authority to dismantle or regulate cartels and monopolies. The Commission has very sharp teeth: It may impose fines ranging up to $1 million or 10 percent of annual sales on companies that willfully violate or ignore its antitrust directives. The effectiveness of antitrust policy in the EC depends, therefore, mainly on how the Commission uses its powers.

In the 1960s the Commission focused its efforts on the elimination or modification of restrictive agreements among companies in sales, distribution, and patents under Article 85 of the EC treaty.[5] The first important antitrust decision came in 1964, when the Commission forbade the German electronics firm, Grundig, to operate under an agreement giving a French firm, Consten, exclusive rights to Grundig sales in France. Since then the Commission has imposed heavy fines on firms participating in cartels and has clarified its interpretation of unfair business practices in a body of case law.

In the 1970s the Commission turned to "abuses of dominant position" under Article 86. Its first case was brought against Continental Can, a U.S. multinational company, and its European subsidiary, Europemballage, which were accused of violating Article 86 by acquiring control of the leading

---

[5] Article 85 applies to anticompetitive agreements among companies; Article 86, to monopoly power of one or more companies. These two articles are comparable to Sections 1 and 2 of the Sherman Act in the United States. For a discussion of U.S. antitrust policy and the multinational enterprise, see Chapter 24.

Dutch metal container manufacturer. On appeal by Continental Can, the European Court of Justice in 1973 overturned the Commission's case on factual grounds; namely, the Commission had not proved that the merger eliminated competition in metal cans for fish and meat products in sufficient degree to justify its dissolution under Article 86. But the Commission also won a victory: The Court of Justice affirmed the right of the Commission to control mergers under Article 86. In a flurry of Article 86 cases, the Commission fined the Belgian subsidiary of General Motors over $120,000 for restraining automobile dealers and buyers from importing Opel cars (made by General Motors in West Germany) into Belgium outside that company's distribution system; the Swiss multinational drug company, Hoffman-La Roche, $360,000 for abusing its dominant position in the Community vitamins market; and the U.S. multinational food company, United Brands, $1.2 million for abuse of dominant position in the Community banana market. In 1984, the Commission settled an antitrust suit with IBM. The latter agreed to disclose sufficient information to enable competitors to connect hardware and software products to IBM's System/370.

Viewed broadly, the EC's antitrust policy represents a radical break with the past. Although this policy is limited to trade among the member countries and does not apply to purely domestic trade or to trade with nonmember countries, the Commission has already gone a long way toward establishing a common policy on competition in the EC, a policy of the kind that is indispensable for a common market.

Harmonization of Indirect Taxes

When indirect taxes on goods and services differ among countries, the consequence is a "tax frontier" that inhibits trade and distorts competition. Furthermore, since the traditional treatment of indirect taxes in international trade involves a reimbursement of taxes to exporters by the exporting country and the imposition of taxes on importers (equal to domestic indirect taxes), any uncertainty with regard to these taxes can lead to either excessive reimbursements or excessive border taxes.[6]

TOWARD AN ECONOMIC UNION

The EC is much more than a customs union; it seeks to integrate all facets of the national member economies. The result would be an economic union—a single economic system embracing the entire EC. It was recognized from the start that a truly successful customs union would not be possible if each member country were free to choose its own policies without regard to the others.

---

[6] The role of border tax adjustments as a nontariff barrier is identified in Chapter 7.

Harmonization is a key word in the evolution of the economic union. Harmonization calls for the gradual elimination of differences in national legislation and administrative practices and policies and their eventual integration to form a Community-wide policy carried out by common institutions. Since economic integration involves all aspects of the national economies, harmonization must proceed simultaneously on many fronts: antitrust policy, transportation and energy policy, trade policy, monetary and fiscal policy, wage and social policy, and so on. Actual progress toward economic union of the EC countries has been very uneven—substantial in those areas where the Treaty of Rome makes specific provision but only modest in those areas where economic integration has to be negotiated in the Council of Ministers.[7]

A Single European Market by 1992

The drive for a common market and economic union faltered badly in the 1970s and first half of the 1980s as two oil crises and a slowdown in economic growth accompanied by high unemployment caused member countries to turn inward and institute policies that prevented any further progress toward integration. The twenty-fifth anniversary of the EC was celebrated amidst a general pessimism about its future. By the mid-1980s, it had become evident that the Community would stagnate and possibly break up unless the remaining barriers on trade and factor movements among the member countries were abolished. It had also become evident that the EC was losing ground to the United States and Japan in the global competition of high-technology industries.

Faced with these gloomy prospects, the EC in 1987 made a dramatic effort to "relaunch" the drive toward economic union by adopting the Single European Act (SEA), which commits the Community to establish a *single market* by the end of 1992. The SEA defines a single market as an area without internal frontiers that insures the free movement of goods, persons, services, and capital. By sweeping away frontiers, the EC will create the largest single market in the world, with 320 million people. Moreover, the probability of success has been magnified by the adoption of a rule of majority voting instead of unanimous voting in the Council of Ministers for many of the decisions needed to complete the single market.

To achieve a single market by the target date, the EC will need to eliminate nontariff barriers (including different technical standards and government procurement preferences), liberalize services (such as banking, insurance, transportation, data processing, and telecommunications), harmonize taxation by reducing the differentials in coverage and rates among the current national systems, and liberalize capital movements. Significant progress has already been made. Perhaps the most notable step to date is an EC directive requiring all member countries to remove all remaining

---

[7] The Treaty of Rome does not specifically call for economic union.

restrictions on capital movements within the EC.[8] Instead of trying to harmonize all national policies, the EC has applied in some instances the principle of *mutual recognition*, which states that provisions in force in a member country must be recognized as equivalent to those applied by another member country. Under this principle, banks, for example, in one EC country would be able to operate in all EC countries *without* a prior harmonization of banking regulations. Probably the toughest challenge will be the elimination of differences in taxation; these differences, if allowed to continue in the single market, would not only distort trade but would justify the maintenance of border customs posts that the EC Commission wants to eliminate. A Europe truly without frontiers (comparable to the United States) can only come about, therefore, if and when the member countries are willing to give up much of their sovereignty over taxation.

What will be the economic gains for the EC from a single internal market? Table 10-2 shows the estimates of a study sponsored by the EC Commission. Over a period of five to six years, the microeconomic effects of the single market are expected to increase the EC's gross domestic product (GDP) by 4.25 to 6.50 percent. (The *macroeconomic* effects, not shown in Table 10-2, are expected to create as many as two million new jobs, to lower average consumer prices by 6 percent, and to improve the EC's current account in the balance of payments by 1 percent of its GDP.)

The European Monetary System

Following the collapse of the international monetary system in 1971, the EC countries agreed to maintain stable exchange rates among their currencies by preventing fluctuations of more than 2.25 percent. This arrangement was called the "European snake in the tunnel," because the Community currencies floated as a group against outside currencies such as the dollar. By 1978, the snake had turned into a worm, with only the West German deutsche mark, the Belgian franc, the Dutch guilder, and the Danish krone adhering to mutually stable exchange rates.[9] And so, a new effort to achieve monetary cooperation was launched in 1979 with the establishment of the European Monetary System (EMS).

The aim of the EMS is to foster "closer monetary cooperation leading to a zone of monetary stability in Europe."[10] EMS has three interrelated parts: (1) a commitment by its member countries to prevent movements greater than 2.25 percent around parity in bilateral exchange rates with other member countries[11]; (2) the European Monetary Cooperation Fund, which allocates European Currency Units (ECUs) to the members' central banks in exchange for 20 percent of the gold and dollar holdings of those

---

[8] *European Community News* (Washington, D.C.), no. 21/88, July 18, 1988.

[9] See Chapter 19 for a description of international monetary relations during this period.

[10] International Monetary Fund, *Annual Report 1979* (Washington, D.C.: International Monetary Fund, 1979), p. 40.

[11] The Italian lira is allowed to move 6 percent around parity before intervention.

TABLE 10-2　　Microeconomic Estimates of Potential Gains for the EC Resulting from Completion of the Internal Market

	Billions ECU*	% of GDP
1. Gains from removal of barriers affecting trade	8–9	0.2–0.3
2. Gains from removal of barriers affecting overall production	57–71	2.0–2.4
3. Gains from removing barriers (subtotal)	65–80	2.2–2.7
4. Gains from exploiting economies of scale more fully	61	2.1
5. Gains from intensified competition reducing business ineffectiveness and monopoly profits	46	1.6
6. Gains from market integration (subtotal)	62**–107	2.1**–3.7
7. Total Gains		
For 7 member states at 1985 prices	127–187	4.25–6.5
For 12 member states at 1988 prices	170–250	4.25–6.5

* 1 ECU = $1.25 on March 31, 1988.

** This alternative estimate for the sum of line 6 cannot be broken down between the two lines 4 and 5.

Note: All figures except in the last line are expressed at 1985 prices and relate to seven member states (Germany, France, Italy, Great Britain, Belgium, the Netherlands, and Luxembourg). The aggregate result is scaled up in terms of the twelve member states' 1988 GDP in the last line.

Source: E.C. Commission.

central banks[12] (ECUs are used in all intrasystem balance of payments settlements); and (3) the provision of credit facilities for compensatory financing of balance of payments deficits. All the EC countries are members of EMS except Great Britain (which refused to join) and the new entrant to the EC, Greece.

The EMS may be regarded as a qualified success. Despite several realignments, variations in exchange rates among its members have been much less than variations against other currencies. Furthermore, the realignments have become less frequent as the EC countries have achieved a greater convergence of economic policies. In particular, national disparities in interest rates and price inflation have narrowed greatly compared with the early 1980s. One continuing weakness, however, is the nonparticipation of the United Kingdom.

The SEA affirms the will to build a monetary union (relying mainly

---

[12] The ECU is an artificial currency (with no coins or banknotes) whose value is the weighted average of the national currencies of the member countries. Hence, the U.S. dollar value of the ECU varies with changes in the exchange rates between the dollar and EC national currencies.

on the EMS and ECU) as a key element in the formation of an economic union. The freedom of capital movements will make or break the EMS, because the member countries will have to maintain currency alignments without resort to controls over the sudden movements of money between them. Hence, if the EMS is to work, the EC countries will have to surrender monetary sovereignty to the EMS, which ultimately involves the creation of a European central bank and a single European currency. If this happens, the EC will be firmly on the road to political union.

Toward a Political Union?

From the beginning the ultimate objective of the EC has been political union—the establishment of a United States of Europe. Attempts in the early postwar years to move directly toward political union in Western Europe were frustrated by national jealousies and ambitions. It was then that individuals like Maurice Schuman and Jean Monnet turned toward economic integration as a means to achieve eventual political integration. The first concrete success in this direction was the creation of the European Coal and Steel Community in 1952, which pooled the coal and steel resources of the six countries. (Other countries, notably Great Britain, stayed out of the ECSC precisely because of its political implications.) In the early 1950s a new attempt to bring about political union by direct means was thwarted when in 1954 the French Assembly rejected the European Defense Community Treaty. Meanwhile, to the surprise of many, the ECSC got off to a strong start and progressively demonstrated that economic integration was not an illusion but a practical achievement. Its success led to the more ambitious EC treaty in 1957. The diplomats who drafted and negotiated the Treaty of Rome firmly believed that they were building a new Europe and that gradual economic integration over the transitional period would be crowned by a political federation of the member countries.

It can be argued that the Community is already a political union in specific areas of economic and social policy. Certainly the member countries have given up much of their sovereignty in international trade and agriculture. On the other hand, it is also true that the national governments still retain control: The Commission proposes but the Council of Ministers disposes. The Community institutions are supranational only to a limited degree; real power remains with the national governments. As long as this situation prevails, political union remains a distant goal.

In 1982, the EC celebrated its twenty-fifth anniversary. It could look back on many accomplishments: the creation of a free trade area, the substantial creation of a common market, the creation of a common agricultural policy, the creation of the European Monetary System, and the addition of Great Britain, Ireland, Denmark, and Greece as members. Nonetheless, the anniversary was marked, as noted earlier, by uncertainty and foreboding over the future of the EC as the forces of recession, nationalism, and protectionism strained the unity of the Community. But in the late 1980s, the mood of the EC became optimistic. The commitment to achieve a "Europe without frontiers" by the end of 1992 is a rededication of the EC to its original goal of political union.

In the previous edition of this book, the question was raised, Can the EC regain its earlier momentum toward economic and political unity? The answer to this question became in the late 1980s a resounding yes.

THE THEORY OF ECONOMIC INTEGRATION

Before reviewing the external economic relations of the Community, it will be instructive to delineate the theoretical benefits and costs of regional economic integration.

Static Effects of a Customs Union

The theory of customs unions, a relatively new branch of economics, represents an extension of tariff theory to multinational discriminatory systems.[13] This theory analyzes the static, one-for-all changes in trade and welfare induced by the formation of a customs union or a free trade area.

Trade Effects   Because a customs union involves both free trade among its member countries (liberalization) and, at the same time, restrictions on imports from nonmember or third countries (protection), it has both positive and negative effects on trade. A positive effect occurs when the elimination of internal tariffs and other barriers stimulates *new* trade among the member countries that does not displace third-country imports. That is to say, the customs union induces a shift from a high-cost producer inside the union to a lower-cost producer also inside the union. This positive effect is called *trade creation*. On the other hand, a negative trade effect occurs when member countries now buy from each other what they formerly bought from third countries. Known as *trade diversion*, this negative effect results from a shift from a low-cost producer outside the union to a higher-cost producer inside the union.

A simple model will clarify the meaning of trade creation and trade diversion. Let us assume three countries (A, B, and C) that are each capable of producing wheat and automobiles. Country A is the high-cost producer of both products, country B is the low-cost producer of automobiles, and country C is the low-cost producer of wheat. In the absence of restrictions, therefore, country A would import automobiles from country B and wheat from country C. Actually, however, country A keeps out automobile imports with a tariff and imports wheat despite a tariff. Now suppose country A and

---

[13] The pioneer work in this field is Viner's. See J. Viner, *The Customs Union Issue* (New York: Carnegie Endowment for International Peace, 1950). The theoretical effects of a tariff are discussed in Chapter 7.

TABLE 10-3   Positive Trade Effect of a Customs Union: Trade Creation
(Dollars)

	Country A	Country B	Country C
Unit cost (price) of automobile production	1,500	1,300	1,400
Cost plus country A's duty (20%)	1,500	1,560	1,680
Cost plus common duty (10%) after formation of customs union	1,500	1,300	1,540

country B form a customs union, leaving country C outside the union as a third country. The trade effects on automobiles and wheat are shown in Tables 10-3 and 10-4, respectively.

After the formation of the customs union, buyers in country A shift from high-cost domestic automobiles to country B's automobiles, which can now be purchased at country B's domestic cost because country A's 20 percent duty is abolished within the union. These imports represent trade creation because they do not displace automobile imports from country C, which are nonexistent. However, this is not true in the case of wheat. Buyers in country A shift from country C's wheat to country B's wheat, which they can obtain free of duty after the formation of the customs union. Although country C is the low-cost producer, it must pay a 20 percent duty to sell in country A, making its wheat noncompetitive with country B's.

Under what circumstances is a custom union likely to create trade rather than divert it? First, trade creation is enhanced when the economies

TABLE 10-4   Negative Trade Effect of a Customs Union: Trade Diversion
(Dollars)

	Country A	Country B	Country C
Unit cost (price) of wheat production	5.00	4.20	3.80
Cost plus country A's duty (25%)	5.00	5.25	4.75
Cost plus common duty (20%) after formation of customs union	5.00	4.20	4.56

of the member countries are very *competitive* and have overlapping patterns of production. Then there are plenty of opportunities for specialization and trade among them. Conversely, when the pre-union economies are complementary, then the opportunities for new trade are limited, because the economies are already specialized with respect to each other. Second, trade creation is positively related to the size of the customs union (as measured by its share of world trade and production), because the larger the size, the greater the probability the lowest-cost producers will be located inside the union. Conversely, a customs union of small economic size is more likely to induce trade diversion. Third, the higher the pre-union duties of the member countries, the greater the likelihood of trade creation in products that were formerly protected against imports. Finally, the smaller the distances among member countries, the greater the scope for trade creation (because of low physical transfer costs).

Welfare Effects   Customs union theory is concerned with the static effects of a customs union on *world* welfare rather than on the welfare of individual member or nonmember countries. From this perspective, the customs union "problem" is viewed as a special case of the theory of the second best.[14] Starting from the premise that universal free trade would achieve the most efficient allocation of the world's resources and consumption (Paretian optimum), it does not follow that free trade among a limited number of countries would *necessarily* raise world welfare. Rather, the *net* welfare effect of a customs union would depend on the net balance of the production and consumption effects associated with trade creation and trade diversion, together with any changes in income distribution.

As to the production effects, trade creation improves the world's economic efficiency (and thereby raises its potential welfare) by substituting lower-cost production for higher-cost production. Conversely, trade diversion lowers the world's potential welfare by substituting higher-cost production within the union for lower-cost production outside the union.

As we have seen, trade restrictions also have *consumption* effects because they introduce discrepancies between the relative prices at which goods can be purchased (the international terms of trade) and their relative costs of production (the marginal rate of transformation).[15] By reducing this discrepancy, trade liberalization allows consumers to move to a higher level of satisfaction (higher indifference curve). It follows that trade creation has a positive consumption effect on welfare, because it brings the production possibilities and the consumer preferences of the union into conformity. Conversely, trade diversion has a negative consumption effect, because it widens the gap between the preferences of consumers in the union on one hand and the world's production possibilities on the other.[16] Trade creation enhances consumer choice; trade diversion constricts it.

---

[14] See Chapter 6 for an explanation of the theory of the second best.
[15] For a review of these terms, see Chapter 2.
[16] This statement is true from the perspective of universal free trade, but it should be

To sum up, a customs union will improve world economic efficiency and potential welfare when trade creation outweighs trade diversion. However, *potential* welfare is not the same as *actual* welfare. Actual welfare depends not only on economic efficiency (the size of the pie) but also on income distribution (the sharing of the pie). In particular, income redistribution between the customs union and outsiders must be taken into account in any thorough evaluation of its welfare effects.

Dynamic Effects of a Customs Union

The static theory of customs union ignores the many dynamic effects of customs unions (and other forms of economic integration) on *economic growth*. A customs union can promote economic welfare not only by inducing higher allocative efficiency (a movement *along* the production possibilities frontier) but also by stimulating growth (an *outward* movement of the production possibilities frontier). Indeed, the impact of its dynamic effects on world welfare may well overwhelm any negative static effects. Here only brief mention will be made of the many ways a customs union may promote economic growth.

The most obvious consequence of a customs union is *market extension*: Producers (and consumers) enjoy free access to the national markets of all member countries, whereas formerly their access was hindered or blocked by import restrictions. Market extension sets in motion many forces. It makes possible *economies of scale* in many industries that could not be achieved in narrow national markets. A broader market also intensifies *competition*, forcing producers to cut costs, sell more aggressively, and look for new products. The combination of economies of scale and heightened competition is also apt to foster an increase in *enterprise size*, whether through internal growth, merger, or acquisition. Bigger firms, in turn, have more capacity to finance research and development and thereby complete more effectively in *product innovation*.

To take advantage of new market opportunities and withstand the pressures of new competition, firms are compelled to make *investments* in plant and equipment that directly create new employment and income. Furthermore, the quality of investment will improve because investment decisions are made in light of cost and market conditions throughout the union. By forcing the development of industrial centers that serve the enlarged market, a customs union also creates external economies; interactions among the many specialized firms in those centers bring costs down for all

---

recognized that consumers may *actually* gain in a trade-diverting member country when they are able to obtain the product in question at a lower price than before. Note in Table 10-4 that consumers in country A can obtain wheat at a unit price of $4.20 after formation of the customs union, whereas they paid $4.75 before its formation. Of course, the consumers' gain would be greater under universal free trade because they could then obtain wheat at a unit price of $3.80. If the pre-union price of wheat to consumers in country A were lower than the post-union price, then consumers would suffer an actual loss. This would happen if country A did not impose a pre-union duty on imports of wheat from country C.

of them. Moreover, a bigger market induces new investment in infrastructure (such as transportation, power, and communications), which in turn promotes general economic efficiency and growth. Mention should also be made of the reduction in risk and uncertainty for entrepreneurs. With assured access to the markets of the member countries, a customs union's internal trade more closely resembles domestic interregional trade than international trade. Faced with less uncertainty, therefore, entrepreneurs within the union are encouraged to make investments in plants and research to exploit the extended market over the long run.

It is to be expected that the greater the degree of economic integration, the greater the impact of these dynamic effects on growth. The liberalization of factor movements (common market) is especially noteworthy in this regard. It is not too much to say that the presence or absence of dynamic effects spell the success or failure of a customs union and more advanced forms of economic integration.

Static and Dynamic Effects of the EC

This section offers a few empirical observations about the probable welfare effects of the European Community. On general grounds, one would expect that trade creation resulting from the common market would outweigh any trade diversion; the member countries have competitive economies, the share of the EC in world trade and production is high, the pre-union tariffs of the member countries were restrictive, and the member countries are geographically contiguous. Data on trade support this expectation regarding manufactures but point to substantial trade diversion in the case of agricultural products.

One study calculated that the *trade creation* effects of the EC for industrial products totalled $2.3 billion in 1967, whereas the *trade diversion* effects totalled $0.9 million, of which the United States experienced $0.26 billion.[17] Several other studies of the trade effects of the EC in the 1960s agree that the trade creation in manufactured products exceeded trade diversion on the order of four times. Based on a study of the trade effects in the 1970s, MacBean and Snowden concluded that with the exception of agriculture, there was no evidence of increased trade diversion compared with the 1960s.[18]

A full analysis of the net welfare effect would need to establish what would have happened to the trade flows of the member countries if the EC had *not* been created and then compare this hypothetical result against actual trade flows. Given its hypothetical nature, as well as the difficulty in identifying and measuring dynamic effects, such an analysis could only reach "most probable" rather than definite conclusions.

---

[17] "The Trade Effects of EFTA and the EEC," *EFTA Bulletin,* June 1972, Tables 10 and 14, pp. 16–17.

[18] A. I. MacBean and P. N. Snowden, *International Institutions in Trade and Finance* (London: George Allen & Unwin, 1981), p. 157.

EXTERNAL ECONOMIC RELATIONS
OF THE COMMUNITY

The European Community and the United States are giants of world trade. Excluding trade among its members, the enlarged Community of twelve countries accounts for about 20 percent of world exports, and the United States for about 15 percent. Furthermore, the EC's gross domestic product is now comparable with that of the United States. Because of its economic size and dynamism, the external policies of the EC have a pervasive influence on the composition, direction, and volume of international trade and investment.

The basic policy of the EC toward third countries is expressed by the common external tariff and the variable import levies on agricultural products. The discrimination inherent in the common tariff and variable levies is a cause of concern to all third countries. This concern was behind the efforts to bargain down the EC tariffs in the Kennedy Round and again in the Tokyo Round. This closing section briefly describes the relations of the Community with the EFTA, with the countries that have been granted preferential status, and with the United States.

The Community and the EFTA

The EFTA is an industrial *free trade area* that was fully established at the end of 1966 with the abolition of all restrictions on trade in manufactured goods among its member countries.[19] Unlike the EC, each member country retains its own tariff and quota system and follows its own trade policies with respect to third countries.

The principal motivation behind the formation of the EFTA in 1960 was to set the stage for later negotiations with the EC to work toward a regional trading arrangement that would cover the whole of Western Europe. Because of the remarkable success of the EC, Great Britain opened negotiations in 1961 to enter the EC as a full member. By 1962 all EFTA members had expressed their willingness to join the EC or enter into an association with it. The United Kingdom, Denmark, and Ireland became full members of the Community at the beginning of 1973. The remaining EFTA members asked for arrangements short of full membership in the Community. In 1972, agreement was reached to establish a free trade area embracing these countries and the EC that covers industrial products but not farm products. Today the Community of twelve countries and the six countries of the EFTA share an industrial free trade area that encompasses over 350 million people and about one-third of world trade.

---

[19] The original seven member countries of the EFTA were Austria, Denmark, Norway, Sweden, Switzerland, Portugal, and Great Britain. Finland and Iceland subsequently joined the association.

The EC's drive for a single market at the end of 1992 threatens to upset the free trade arrangements with EFTA countries. EFTA representatives now talk of creating a "European economic space" (in parallel with progress toward the EC's internal market) that would demand a much higher degree of integration between EFTA countries and the EC.

Preferential Arrangements

The Community has entered into preferential arrangements of one kind or another with many countries that give them free access to the common market. *Association agreements* that envisage the creation of customs unions and eventual Community membership have been signed with Turkey, Malta, and Cyprus. *Preferential trade agreements* have been entered into with all the EFTA countries, as noted previously. Other preferential agreements have been reached with Morocco, Tunisia, Algeria, Egypt, Lebanon, and Israel in accordance with the EC's Mediterranean policy. Finally, the Community has entered a global agreement, known as the *Lome Convention*, with 65 countries of Africa, the Caribbean, and the Pacific region.[20]

The EC's preferential arrangements have been criticized by GATT, UNCTAD, and many third countries, notably the United States. They allege that the proliferation of these accords causes negative trade diversions (which particularly hurt tropical countries in Latin America and elsewhere that export the same products, such as coffee, cocoa, cotton, and bananas) and endangers the most-favored-nation principle (nondiscrimination). In reply, the Community points out that a preponderance of its trade is nondiscriminatory and that its preferential policy is limited to agreements with European countries that cannot become full members of the Community, countries of the Mediterranean basin, and Lome Convention countries.

The United States and the Community

The United States has consistently supported the EC in its efforts to build economic and political unity in Western Europe. At the same time, several issues have aggravated U.S.-EC trade relations, issues that first came to a head in the Kennedy Round of 1963–1967: the common agricultural policy (variable levies), tariff disparities, and nontariff trade barriers. As we saw in Chapter 8, these same issues reappeared in the Tokyo Round.

Although the EC remains the largest U.S. export market, this country has been irritated by the trade diversion effects of the common agricultural policy and EC preferential agreements in the Mediterranean. The entry of Great Britain, Ireland, and Denmark into the Community caused a sharp drop in U.S. agricultural exports to those countries, while preferential ar-

---

[20] The first Lome Convention ran from 1975 to 1980. The third Lome Convention runs from 1985 to 1990. It provides financial assistance to the developing countries and duty free access for their exports to the Community, with the exception of temperate food products protected by the common agricultural policy.

rangements in the Mediterranean have hurt U.S. citrus exports.[21] Conversely, the Community has frequently protested, and occasionally retaliated against, new U.S. import restrictions, and it is very sensitive to protectionism in the United States.

In the 1980s, trade relations between the United States and the Community dramatically worsened as protectionist forces gained strength on both sides of the Atlantic, raising the spectre of a trade war between the two giants. U.S.-EC disputes on agricultural trade have been chronic since the institution of the common agricultural policy in mid-1962. Both the United States and the Community heavily subsidize agriculture. The U.S. proposal to eliminate *all* forms of agricultural subsidies within ten years is vigorously opposed by the EC, which favors a gradual reduction in subsidies.

So far, the United States and the EC have avoided an all-out trade war, but specific disputes arise almost daily. These are some recent examples:

The EC has warned that if the United States adopts protectionist trade legislation, it will be forced to take similar measures.

The United States has challenged the subsidies received by Airbus Industries, a four-nation European consortium that manufactures commercial aircraft in direct competition with the American companies Boeing and McDonnell-Douglas. The EC argues that the U.S. government supports its aircraft industry with defense contracts and government-funded R & D.

The United States has asked a GATT panel to examine the legality of an EC directive that bans imports of meat containing growth hormones. In response, the EC has pointed out that the ban also applies within the Community.

The U.S. government has agreed to investigate a complaint filed by the American Soybean Association charging that EC subsidies discriminate against imports of U.S. soybeans and soybean meal. In response, the EC has noted that it regularly takes about one-half of all U.S. exports of soybeans and soybean meal.

The EC has asked the United States for consultations on a waiver granted by GATT in 1955 that allows the United States to limit imports of dairy products, sugar, cotton, and peanuts. The EC argues that the use of this waiver is not consistent with its original purpose—helping the United States solve its agriculture surplus problems.

Noting that some Europeans want to erect a "protective curtain" around their internal market, a U.S. official has warned the EC that the United States would find it "unacceptable" if the EC's 1992 integration restricts U.S. access to EC markets.[22]

---

[21] The share of the EC (excluding Greece) in U.S. agricultural exports to the world fell from 33.4 percent in 1958 to 21.6 percent in 1980. See U.S. Department of State, *U.S. Trade with the European Community,* Special Report no. 84 (June 28, 1981), Table IV, p. 5.

[22] "U.S. Warns Europe on Trade Plan," *New York Times,* August 5, 1988, p. D1.

Together the European Community and the United States account for over one-third of world trade and over 70 percent of the industrial world's gross domestic product, and they are major markets for each other. It is not too much to say that their mutual trade relations are crucial to the maintenance of an open international economy. It is imperative, therefore, that these two trading partners work out their trade differences in a spirit of understanding and cooperation, avoiding unilateral actions on issues of mutual concern. The EC's new drive toward a single market by the end of 1992 needs to be coupled with a new drive by both the EC and the United States toward strengthening an open world economy in the GATT negotiations now underway.

SUMMARY

1. The European Community started its official existence at the beginning of 1958. The main feature of the EC is the creation, in planned stages, of a *customs union* for both industrial and agricultural goods. A second objective is the establishment of a *common market,* with free movement of labor, capital, and other factors of production, as well as products. A third objective is a full *economic union,* with free movement of persons, services, and capital and progressive harmonization of social, fiscal, and monetary policies. The ultimate objective is *political union* of the member countries.
2. The basic institutions of the Community are five in number: European Commission, Council of Ministers, European Parliament, Court of Justice, and European Council.
3. The EC became a full customs union in 1968, when tariffs and quantitative restrictions were completely removed on all trade among its member countries and a common tariff system was fully established vis-à-vis nonmember countries. However, nontariff barriers (such as different national technical standards, government procurement preferences, and regulations covering banking, insurance, and other services) continue to restrain trade among the member countries.
4. Through a series of laborious negotiations the EC has developed a common agricultural policy involving target, intervention, and threshold prices and variable import levies. Two points need stressing: There are no production controls, and the variable import levies make third countries, such as the United States, residual suppliers of farm products.
5. The EC has also built a common market with free movements of productive factors among the member countries, namely, labor, capital, and enterprise. But the common market is not complete, since several national policies and regulations continue to curtail factor movements

within the Community. The EC has rules governing competition and a value-added tax system.

6. After earlier failures, the European Monetary System was created in 1979. It requires member countries to prevent movements greater than 2.25 percent around parity in bilateral exchange rates with other member countries.

7. The drive to complete the common market and move on to economic union faltered badly in the 1970s and first half of the 1980s. In 1987, the EC made a dramatic move to "relaunch" this drive by adopting the Single European Act, which commits the Community to the creation of a *single market* by the end of 1992. Such a market would resemble the U.S. market in its free movement of goods and factor services and in its economic size.

8. It can be argued that the Community is already a political union in specific areas of economic and social policy. But it is also true that the Community institutions are supranational only to a limited degree and that real power remains with the national governments. As long as this situation prevails, political union is a distant goal. The commitment to achieve a "Europe without frontiers" by the end of 1992 is a rededication of the EC to its original goal of political union.

9. The theory of customs unions analyzes the static, once-for-all changes in trade and welfare induced by the formation of a customs union or free trade area. The result of such changes culminates in either trade creation or trade diversion. A customs union will improve world economic efficiency and potential welfare when trade creation outweighs trade diversion. Aside from its static effects, a customs union may have many dynamic effects on economic growth and welfare: market extension, economies of scale, competition, enterprise size, and others. In the case of the EC, positive dynamic effects have been supplemented by trade creation in manufactures but partially offset by trade diversion in agriculture.

10. The basic policy of the EC toward third countries is expressed by the common external tariff and the variable import levies on agricultural products. But the EC has departed from the most-favored-nation principle by entering into preferential arrangements with EFTA, Lome Convention, and Mediterranean countries.

11. In the early 1970s, Western Europe remained split between the EC and EFTA. However, Great Britain, Ireland, and Denmark became full members of the EC in 1973, and agreements have established free trade in industrial products between the EC and the remaining EFTA countries.

12. Despite the achievements of the Tokyo Round, trade relations between the United States and the EC reached a crisis stage in the 1980s as protectionism grew on both sides of the Atlantic.

QUESTIONS AND APPLICATIONS

1. Distinguish between the following forms of economic integration: free trade area, customs union, common market, and economic union.
2. Identify the institutions of the EC and describe their functions.
3. What is the structure of the common agricultural policy? How does this structure affect EC imports of farm products?
4. Evaluate the performance of the EC in establishing a customs union and a common market.
5. What is a "tax frontier"? How is the EC seeking to eliminate it?
6. **(a)** What is the Single European Act?
   (b) What must the EC do to achieve a single market by the end of 1992?
7. Compare the advantages and disadvantages of the concepts of *harmonization* and *mutual recognition* with reference to the completion of the single market.
8. **(a)** Describe the major features of the European Monetary System.
   (b) Why is a convergence of economic policies necessary to the long-run success of the EMS?
9. Is economic union possible without political union? Explain your answer.
10. **(a)** Explain the meaning of *trade diversion* and *trade creation* in customs union theory.
    (b) Identify and explain the dynamic effects of a customs union.
11. **(a)** What is the EFTA?
    (b) What is the EFTA's relation to the EC?
12. Prepare an up-to-date report on trade relations between the United States and the EC.

SELECTED READINGS

Cohen, Benjamin J. *The European Monetary System.* Essays in International Finance, no. 142. Princeton, N.J.: Princeton University Press, June 1981.

De Vries, Tom. *On the Meaning and Future of the European Monetary System.* Essays in International Finance, no. 138, Princeton, N.J.: Princeton University Press, September 1980.

Commission of the European Communities. *Completing the Internal Market for Industrial Products.* Luxembourg: Office for Official Publications of the European Communities, 1986.

European Community. *Europe.* Bimonthly.

European Community. *General Report on the Activities of the Community.* Annual.

European Free Trade Association. *EFTA Bulletin*. Bimonthly.

European Free Trade Association. *EFTA: What It Is, What It Does*. Current Edition.

Lipsey, R. "The Theory of Customs Unions: A General Survey," *Economic Journal* 70 (1960): 496–513. Reprinted in *Readings in International Economics*, edited by R. E.Caves and H. G. Johnson. Homewood, Ill.: Richard D. Irwin, 1968.

MacBean, A. I., and P. N. Snowden. *International Institutions in Trade and Finance*. London: George Allen & Unwin, 1981. Chapter 8.

Robson, Peter. *The Economics of International Integration*. London: George Allen & Unwin, 1980. Chapters 2 and 3.

Swann, D. *The Economics of the Common Market*. 5th ed. Baltimore: Penguin Books, 1984.

PART TWO
INTERNATIONAL PAYMENTS

International trade and investment take place within an international monetary system composed of national monetary systems and their linkages through foreign exchange markets. Although the international monetary system is intended to facilitate flows of trade and investment, governments sometimes use (or abuse) it to restrict such flows. Part Two addresses the many theoretical and policy issues that arise from the money transactions that tie together the world's countries. Our analytical focus is the adjustment processes that bring national economies into equilibrium with economic forces outside their borders. Chapters on the theory of adjustment prepare us to understand the complexities of national payments policies in the context of the contemporary international monetary system.

11

The Mechanism of International Payments and Foreign Exchange Markets

How are international payments made? What is the role of commercial banks in international payments? What is foreign exchange? What is the structure of the foreign exchange market in the United States? Why can we speak of a *global* foreign exchange market? What is the role of international financial centers in international payments? These are the principal questions addressed in this opening chapter on international payments. Chapter 12 continues our study by examining the determination of exchange rates in foreign exchange markets, and Chapter 13 looks at speculation and hedging in foreign exchange markets.

THE MECHANISM OF INTERNATIONAL PAYMENTS

When an American resident buys something from, say, a Japanese resident, how can the American pay the Japanese? After all, the American wants to pay in dollars while the Japanese wants to receive payment in yen. Evidently, the American needs to find someone who is willing to sell to him the required amount of yen in exchange for dollars. Fortunately, it is not necessary for the American to search far and wide for that someone, because commercial banks in the United States and Japan offer facilities to transfer payments between the two countries.

Fundamentally, the mechanism of *international* payments is similar to the mechanism of *domestic* payments within the United States. Most payments in this country are made through checks drawn by persons and business firms on banks that cause shifts in the ownership of bank deposits from the payers to payees. Banknotes are used mostly for retail transactions, and even here their importance has fallen with the growth of credit cards.

Most international payments also involve shifts in the ownership of bank deposits. But these shifts are now between residents of different countries, and they are brought about by international bank transfers and bank drafts rather than by checks, because few individuals or nonbank institutions maintain deposits in *foreign* banks.[1] An international *bank transfer* is an order sent (usually through an electronic network) by a bank in one country to a bank in another country instructing the latter to debit the deposit account of the former and credit the account of a designated person or institution. Banks can also make international payments through a *bank draft*. Take, for example, the American who wants to send funds to a Japanese. To do so, he can purchase a draft from a U.S. bank that orders a Japanese bank to make payment of a specified amount in yen to a designated person or institution upon presentation of the draft. Bank transfers and bank drafts are possible because banks in one country maintain deposit balances with banks in other countries. Only a small fraction of international payments (mostly tourist purchases) are made with banknotes.

International payments are more risky than domestic payments for several reasons. First, the domestic-currency value of a prospective foreign-currency payment depends on the exchange rate between the two currencies. This *foreign exchange risk* is highest when exchange rates are free to respond to market forces, as is true of the major currencies today. A second risk of international payments is the *inconvertibility risk*: the inability of the holder of a country's currency to convert it into the currency of another country because of exchange restrictions imposed by the government. A third risk is the *default risk*, the risk that the debtor will fail to pay the creditor. Although default risk is also present in domestic payments (unlike foreign exchange and inconvertibility risks), it is higher in international payments because legal action against defaulting debtors in foreign countries is more costly, more time consuming, and less successful than legal action against domestic debtors.

We shall consider how firms can hedge against foreign exchange risks in Chapter 13. International traders try to minimize inconvertibility and default risks by adapting the method of international payment to the circumstances. To understand this point, we turn to a brief description of methods of payment in international trade.

Methods of Payment in International Trade

The principal methods of payment in international trade are cash in advance, commercial letters of credit, commercial drafts drawn on the buyer,

---

[1] The multinational corporation is an exception to this statement, maintaining bank deposits in several countries. It is able, therefore, to make international payments by writing corporate checks.

open account, and consignment. Generally, sellers (exporters) want to get paid quickly in their own currency while foreign buyers (importers) want to pay in their own currency only after delivery or resale of the goods. The method of payment agreed upon by a seller and a buyer depends, therefore, on their relative bargaining power. A strong seller can insist on cash in advance or an irrevocable letter of credit; a strong buyer can insist on open account or consignment. Payment through commercial drafts is more likely to accommodate the interests of both the exporter and importer than other methods of payment.

Exporters may try to minimize buyer default risk by insisting on cash in advance or an irrevocable letter of credit or by investigating the credit standing of importers before arranging more lenient methods of payment. The risk of currency inconvertibility, however, is country-specific, not buyer-specific. A Mexican importer, for example, may be quite willing to pay an American exporter, but the importer cannot obtain a license to buy dollars from the exchange control authorities. As discussed in Chapter 17, countries impose exchange controls in response to persistent deficits in their balance of payments. To minimize payment risks, therefore, exporters must consider not only the creditworthiness of individual importers but also the actual and prospective convertibility of the importer's currency.

Cash in Advance   This is a relatively uncommon method of international payment because of the burden that it places on the buyer. A seller may demand such terms when he judges the credit standing of the buyer is very poor or the risk of inconvertibility is very high. However, even in those circumstances, the seller may not demand cash in advance if he would thereby lose sales to competitors.

Confirmed, Irrevocable Letter of Credit   When an exporter is not receiving cash in advance but does not want to rely on an importer's promise to pay, he may request a confirmed, irrevocable letter of credit. A letter of credit is an instrument issued by the importer's bank that obligates that bank to honor drafts drawn against it by the exporter (beneficiary) in accordance with specified terms. These terms include the amount of the credit, tenor of the draft, general description of the merchandise, documents required, and expiration date.[2] The letter of credit becomes *confirmed* when a bank in the exporter's country also promises to honor drafts drawn under it. But the bank in the exporter's country will not confirm a letter of credit unless the foreign issuing bank makes it *irrevocable* so that it cannot be cancelled or altered except with the agreement of all the parties.

Under letter-of-credit export financing, the following basic steps occur: (1) The importer's bank issues an irrevocable letter of credit covering a specific shipment of merchandise, naming the exporter as beneficiary. (2) A

---

[2] The tenor of a draft determines its time of payment. A *sight* draft is payable at the time that it is presented to the drawee (the confirming bank under a confirmed letter of credit). A *time* draft is payable a certain number of days after sight or on a certain date.

bank in the exporter's country confirms the letter of credit, informing the exporter about it. (3) The exporter arranges for shipment of the merchandise to the importer, receiving from the shipping company a *bill of lading*.[3] (4) The exporter draws a draft on the confirming bank. (5) The exporter presents the draft (along with the bill of lading and other required documents) for payment or acceptance.[4]

In sum, payment under a confirmed commercial letter of credit is highly advantageous to the exporter, because it means payment at the time of shipment with hardly any risk of nonpayment as long as the exporter keeps to the conditions of the letter of credit. But this method is burdensome to the importer because he may need to make a substantial advance payment to his bank to arrange the letter of credit. Importers, therefore, tend to buy from exporters who offer more lenient terms. Consequently, to stay competitive, experienced exporters require letters of credit only when there are high default or inconvertibility risks.

Commercial Drafts   A commercial draft is a bill of exchange drawn by an exporter against an importer. A bill of exchange is an unconditional order in writing addressed by one party (the drawer) to a second party (the drawee), and it requires the latter to make payment of a specified sum in money at a fixed and determinable future time to a third party (the payee). A bill of exchange becomes a bill of *foreign* exchange when the drawer and drawee are residents of different countries. Bills of exchange are negotiable instruments that are transferable from one holder to another through endorsement. Such a bill is shown in Figure 11-1.

The sequence of steps in commercial draft payment is as follows: (1) The exporter draws a draft against the importer that orders payment on presentation (sight draft) or payment on a determinable date after presentation (time draft). The terms of the draft, therefore, are "documents against payment" (D/P) or "documents against acceptance" (D/A). (2) The exporter submits the draft and accompanying shipping documents (including the bill of lading) to the exporter's own bank for collection. (3) The bank forwards the draft and shipping documents to its correspondent bank in the importer's country, which in turn presents it to the importer. (4) If the draft is payable on sight, then the importer must make immediate payment to the exporter in order to obtain the bill of lading, which is needed to acquire physical possession of the export shipment. (5) If the draft is payable at a certain

---

[3] The ocean (or airway) bill of lading issued by the international carrier serves three functions: (1) It is a receipt for merchandise delivered to the carrier; (2) it is a contract for services to be provided by the carrier; and (3) when made out to the order of the exporter, it is a document of title that is needed to obtain the merchandise at the point of destination. As we shall note, it is this last function that makes the bill of lading important for international payments under commercial drafts. In addition to the bill of lading, several other documents may be required by a letter of credit, notably invoices and insurance certificates.

[4] A sight draft will be paid immediately by the bank; a time draft will be "accepted" by the bank, obligating it to make payment on the due date. A bank acceptance is readily sold for cash in the acceptance market.

Figure 11-1   A Commercial Bill of Exchange

$ 2,000.80	Philadelphia, May 20	19 __

Thirty days after sight of this First of Exchange (Second Unpaid) **PAY TO THE**

ORDER OF _The Bank of Philadelphia_

Two thousand and 80/100 — — — — — — — — — — — — — — — **DOLLARS**

VALUE RECEIVED AND CHARGE TO ACCOUNT OF

TO _LaFleur Importers_ } *Atlas Exporting Co.*

NO. _894_   _Paris, France_ } *R.J. Shaeffer, Treasurer*

time in the future, then the importer must "accept" the draft in order to obtain the bill of lading. This *trade acceptance* is held by the correspondent bank, and when it becomes due, it is presented to the importer for payment.

We have described what is called payment through *documentary* draft—a draft that is accompanied by documents that can be obtained by the importer only after payment or acceptance of the draft. The documentary draft is by far the most common method of financing international trade; it is also a very old method that can trace its beginnings back to the Italian city-states of the Middle Ages. The exporter's protection depends mainly on keeping title to the merchandise until the importer either pays or becomes obligated to pay.[5] But this method of payment is more risky than cash in advance or a letter of credit, for it depends on the importer (buyer) alone for payment. Even with a sight draft, the importer may refuse the shipment, leaving the exporter to incur the costs of disposing the merchandise elsewhere. With a time draft, the importer may default at maturity. Finally, documentary draft payment is subject to the risk of currency inconvertibility.

Open Account   This is a method of payment whereby the seller simply sends an invoice to the buyer, who is then expected to pay within a designated time. By far the most common method in domestic business, open account is usually restricted in international business to an exporter's own foreign sales affiliates and to intrafirm transactions of transnational corporations. It offers little protection against buyer default or currency in-

---

[5] This protection is forgone with a *clean* draft. In that case, the documents are sent directly to the importer, and the exporter submits only his or her draft to the bank for collection. Hence the importer can obtain the merchandise without paying or accepting the draft. Clean drafts should be used only when the exporter has full confidence in the importer.

convertibility. In the event of default, the exporter has no documentary evidence (draft acceptance) of the buyer's obligation to pay, and legal action to collect a debt is much more expensive and time consuming than at home. The lack of documentary evidence of the importer's obligation to pay may also make it more difficult for an importer to obtain foreign exchange when the currency is inconvertible.

Consignment   Under this method, the buyer is not obligated to pay until he has sold the merchandise. It is so disadvantageous to the seller that it is seldom used in international trade. As is true of the open account method, consignment sales are mostly limited to shipments to an exporter's own foreign affiliates. It suffers all the disabilities of the open account method and has the added disadvantage that the time of payment is uncertain.

International Payments as Cross-National Transfers in the Ownership of Bank Deposits

We can now bring together our discussion of bank transfers and methods of payment in international trade by demonstrating the mechanism of international payments with the T accounts of banks in the United States and Japan. T accounts are designed to show *changes* in assets and liabilities. To simplify our presentation, we assume that the banking system of each country is represented by a single bank.

To start, suppose an American importer wants to make a payment in yen to a Japanese exporter. The importer goes to the U.S. bank where he or she buys a draft that orders the Japanese bank to make payment of a certain sum in yen to the Japanese exporter. The American importer pays for the draft with a dollar check drawn on his or her own account with the U.S. bank, the amount being determined by the current dollar-yen rate of exchange. This transaction shows up in the T account of the U.S. bank as follows:

Assets	Liabilities
– Demand deposit in Japanese bank	– Demand deposit (American importer)

In effect, the importer purchases a yen deposit in the Japanese bank with a dollar deposit in the U.S. bank. The latter experiences a reduction in its yen-deposit assets that is offset by an equivalent reduction in its dollar-deposit liabilities as determined by the current dollar-yen exchange rate. Banks get compensated for arranging international payments by selling foreign currencies at a higher price than the price they pay for them.

The transaction appears in the T account of the Japanese bank as follows:

Assets	Liabilities
	− Demand deposit (U.S. bank)
	+ Demand deposit (Japanese importer)

The Japanese importer gets paid with a yen deposit in the Japanese bank. This increase in the deposit liability of the Japanese bank is offset by an equal decrease in the deposit liability owing the U.S. bank.

Let us now take the example of an American exporter who receives payment in yen from a Japanese importer. The importer sends a check drawn on his account with the Japanese bank to the American exporter, who deposits the check with the U.S. bank. This bank then forwards it to the Japanese bank for collection. Once collection is completed, the following changes appear in the U.S. bank's T account:

Assets	Liabilities
+ Demand deposit (Japanese bank)	+ Demand deposit (American exporter)

In effect, the exporter sells a yen deposit to the American bank exchange for a dollar deposit. The result of this transaction, therefore, is that the U.S. bank now has a yen deposit that it can sell to an American resident who needs yen.

The T account of the Japanese bank looks like this:

Assets	Liabilities
	− Demand deposit (Japanese importer)
	+ Demand deposit (U.S. bank)

The Japanese bank experiences an increase in a deposit liability owing the American bank that is offset by an equivalent decrease in the deposit liability owing the importer.

We can now see that international payments occur through shifts in the ownership of bank deposits, with banks acting as intermediaries. In our first example, a yen payment by the American importer to the Japanese exporter resulted in a shift in the ownership of a yen deposit from an American resident (the U.S. bank) to a Japanese resident (the exporter).[6] In the

---

[6] We are speaking here of a payment in *yen*. If the Japanese exporter had billed in dollars, then payment would occur through a shift in ownership of deposits in the U.S. bank: a decrease in the importer's deposit and an equivalent increase in the Japanese bank's deposit. If payment was made in a third currency, say, pounds sterling, then a deposit in a British bank would be transferred from American ownership (U.S. bank) to Japanese ownership (Japanese bank). Regardless of the currency of payment, therefore, payment occurs through transfers in the ownership of bank deposits.

second example, a yen payment by a Japanese importer to an American exporter resulted in a shift in the ownership of a yen deposit from a Japanese resident (the importer) to an American resident (the U.S. bank).

THE FOREIGN EXCHANGE MARKET

The core of the foreign exchange market in the United States is a network of some 120 commercial banks, located principally in New York, that buy and sell foreign-currency bank deposits known as foreign exchange. More generally, *foreign exchange* is a financial asset that represents a money claim held by a resident of one country against a resident of another country. Foreign exchange may be banknotes (currency), bank deposits, bills of exchange, or any other highly liquid claims. Because bank deposits are the principal medium of international payment, *foreign exchange* usually refers to foreign-currency bank deposits.

Structure of the Market

Figure 11-2 depicts the foreign exchange market in the United States.

Traditionally, the foreign exchange (FX) market has comprised two submarkets: the *FX retail market* and the *FX interbank (wholesale) market*. However, a third submarket, the *FX futures/options market*, came into existence in the 1970s with the inauguration of trading in foreign exchange futures and options by certain commodity and stock exchanges in this country. Together, these three submarkets form an integrated foreign exchange market.

Unlike the futures/options market, the FX retail and interbank markets do not have physical trading centers. They are over-the-counter markets. Customers transact business directly with local banks, and financial center banks transact business directly or through FX brokers with other financial center banks. Participants in the retail market are individuals, international firms, and nonbank financial institutions that buy foreign exchange from local commercial banks or sell foreign exchange to them. In turn, local banks obtain foreign exchange from and sell foreign exchange to large financial center banks mainly located in New York. Participants in the interbank market are the financial center banks. Most foreign exchange transactions are entered over the telephone between the specialist divisions of these banks, either directly or through brokers.

Foreign exchange transactions in the retail and interbank markets may be classified as spot and forward. *Spot* transactions are conducted at current exchange rates for immediate delivery of foreign exchange. Immediate delivery is over the counter in the retail market and within two business days in the interbank market. *Forward* transactions are conducted

Figure 11-2   Structure of the Foreign Exchange (FX) Market in the United States

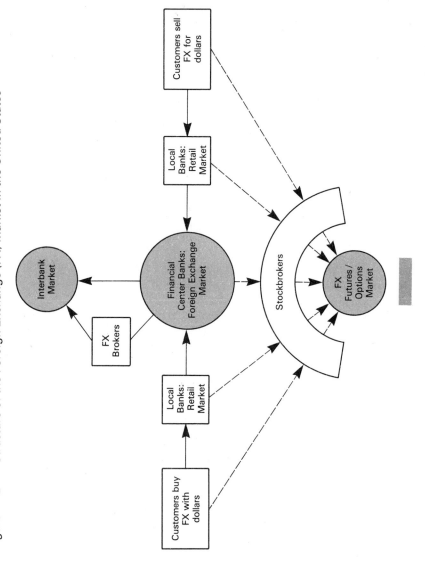

at forward exchange rates for the delivery of foreign exchange at a designated date more than two days in the future.

Nonbank customers, local banks, and financial center banks all participate through stockbrokers in exchanges that trade in FX futures and options. A FX futures contract is an agreement to purchase or sell a certain amount of designated foreign exchange at a specified price at a predetermined future time. FX contracts are of a standard size and settlement date. Before the settlement date, futures contracts may be resold at their market prices determined by trading on an organized exchange. The International Money Market (IMM) introduced trading in FX futures in 1972. IMM contracts appeal to individuals and small firms because they are convenient in size (for example, 25,000 pounds sterling, 125,000 Deutsche marks, and 100,000 Canadian dollars). Delivery dates for futures contracts are the third Wednesday of March, June, September, or December.

An FX option is the *right* to buy or sell foreign exchange within a specified future time at a specified price, known as the *strike* price. A *call* option is the right to buy at the strike price; a *put* option is the right to sell at the strike price. The Philadelphia Exchange was the the first to introduce FX options on spot currencies; later, the IMM offered options on FX futures contracts. We shall return to FX futures and options in Chapter 13 when we discuss hedging and speculation in foreign exchange.

Size of the Market

In 1986, for the first time, the central banks of the United States, Great Britain, and Japan—the three countries with the largest foreign exchange markets—undertook a coordinated survey of foreign exchange activities. The key findings of this survey are shown in Table 11-1.

The total volume of all three foreign exchange markets in New York, London, and Tokyo amounted to an astonishing average of *$188 billion each day* during March 1986. This figure does not include the activity of FX futures and options markets in those centers or the FX activity in other centers, such as Frankfurt, Zurich, Toronto, Singapore, and Hong Kong. It is certain, therefore, that in March 1986 the total volume of foreign exchange trading in the world averaged more than $200 billion a day. Foreign exchange markets now constitute the world's biggest financial market.[7]

The volume of foreign exchange trading has expanded at an unprecedented speed in recent years. In New York, volume has doubled since 1983, when the Federal Reserve Bank of New York reported an average of $23 billion per day for April of that year. In London, volume is almost twice the $50 billion figure cited for 1984. Volume in Tokyo has grown even faster: In April 1983, it was less than half the New York volume, but three years later it had gained parity.[8]

[7] A volume of $200 billion per day is twice the size of the U.S. government bond market and forty times the average daily volume of the New York stock exchange.

[8] "Recent Trends in the U.S. Foreign Exchange Market," *Quarterly Review* (Federal Reserve Bank of New York), Summer 1984, Tables 1 and 1, pp. 39, 41, and 46.

TABLE 11-1   Average Daily Trading of Foreign Exchange by Currency in New York, London, and Tokyo during March 1986

	Total (Billions of Dollars)	Percentage Distribution by Currency				
		Dollars	Marks	Yen	Pounds	Other*
New York	50	—	34	23	19	24
London	90	30	28	14	—	28
Tokyo	48	82	—	—	—	18**

* Mainly Swiss franc, French franc, Italian lira, Canadian dollar, and Dutch guilder.
** The percentages for marks and pounds are included.
Source: Federal Reserve Bank of New York, Bank of England, and Bank of Japan.

What explains this explosive growth? One cause is the high volatility in foreign exchange rates since the collapse of the Bretton Woods international monetary system in the early 1970s.[9] This volatility has encouraged widespread hedging and speculation by FX traders and international firms.

A second cause is the deregulation of capital markets, particularly in Western Europe and Japan. Deregulation enables holders of financial assets to move them more quickly from one country to another in search of higher yields and lower risks. In effect, a single global capital market is replacing separate national capital markets.[10]

A third cause is the technological innovation in electronic communications that has lowered the costs and increased the speed of international payments. Foreign exchange dealers are now connected worldwide by computer screens and telephone consoles. Electronic transfers have replaced checks as the principal means of payment. Each day billions of dollars of international currency transfers move in and out of New York via the Clearing House Interbank Payments System (CHIPS) operated by the New York Clearing House Association. Through CHIPS some 140 participating banks exchange irrevocable payment messages electronically throughout the day. At the end of the day, the banks settle their net positions by making or receiving a single payment to or from the CHIPS settlement account at the Federal Reserve System. In June 1986, the FX transfers of CHIPS averaged $23 billion each day, about half the total FX volume in New York. Over 80 percent of these transfers originate with foreign customers or the offshore offices of U.S. banks.[11]

Here is an example of how CHIPS works. (1) At 7 A.M. in Paris, a French vintner receives an order from a British importer for champagne to be bought with U.S. dollars. (2) At 9 A.M., the vintner orders its London warehouse to deliver the champagne to the importer. It does so. (3) At 12 noon, the importer instructs its London bank to pay the French vintner in U.S. dollars. (4) At 1 P.M., the London bank advises its New York office to pay. (5) At 3 P.M., payment is sent via CHIPS to the New York office of the vinter's French bank. (6) At 4 P.M., the French bank's New York office tells its Paris office that it has received payment. (7) At 6 P.M., the Paris bank pays the vintner.[12]

Only a small share of the world's FX trading (10 percent or so) involves the financing of international trade in goods and services. The bulk of trading now comes from international capital flows representing currency speculation and hedging or shifts in portfolio investments responding to interest

---

[9] See Chapter 18.

[10] Chapter 19 examines the formation of the global capital market.

[11] *Fedwire,* run by the Federal Reserve System, links almost 10,000 banks across the United States through a real-time electronics payments system. Most Fedwire transfers are in dollars. See "Large Dollar Payments Flows from New York," *Quarterly Review* (Federal Reserve Bank of New York), Winter 1987–1988, pp. 6–13.

[12] This example appears in "Risky Moments in the Money Markets," *U.S. News & World Report,* March 2, 1987, p. 45.

rate and risk differentials among countries. Furthermore, about 90 percent of FX turnover involves trading among the large financial center banks located mainly in New York, London, Tokyo; only a small share of trading is generated by outside firms and individuals. The banks profit from arbitrage but mostly from "positioning"—correctly anticipating daily movements in foreign exchange rates. *Positioning* is another name for speculation.

Table 11-1 reveals that the principal currencies traded in foreign exchange markets are the U.S. dollar, the West German mark, the Japanese yen, and the British pound sterling. The U.S. dollar is the leading international currency, used in more than half of all international payments in the world. The dominant (but declining) role of the U.S. dollar is examined in Chapter 19.

A GLOBAL FOREIGN EXCHANGE MARKET: EXCHANGE ARBITRAGE

Are currency prices (foreign exchange rates) the same across the several national foreign exchange markets? For example, is the dollar price of 1 pound sterling on any given day the same in New York, London, Tokyo, and other financial centers? Surprising as it may seem, the answer is yes. The explanation of this consistency is *exchange arbitrage*.

Fundamentally, exchange arbitrage is the sale of a given currency in one foreign exchange market and the simultaneous purchase of the same currency in another foreign exchange market. Arbitrage does not involve a speculative risk, because the arbitrage trader (arbitrager) fully offsets a sale in one market with a purchase in a second market. Opportunities for arbitrage profits are transitory, for the supply-demand effects of arbitrage quickly wipe out any discrepancies in the price of a currency across foreign exchange markets.

Suppose, for example, the pound sterling is trading at $1.32 in New York and at the same time is trading at $1.30 in London. This discrepancy provides an opportunity for arbitrage profits: Traders will buy pounds with dollars in London at $1.30 and simultaneously sell pounds for dollars in New York at $1.32. An arbitrager who bought and sold one million pounds would earn profits of $20,000 ($.02 multiplied by one million). But this rate discrepancy would quickly disappear: Higher demand for sterling in London would push up its dollar price while the increased supply of sterling in New York would push down its dollar price. Arbitrage would cease when the dollar price of sterling became the same in both markets, say, $1.31. This is an example of *bilateral* arbitrage involving two currencies.

Arbitrage also maintains consistency in *cross-rates* between two currencies through a third currency. Suppose that the West German mark is trading at $0.35 and the British pound sterling at $1.31 in New York. Then the mark-sterling cross-rate in New York is 3.74 marks per pound sterling. But let us further suppose that the price of sterling in Frankfurt is 3.70 marks. Because the *dollar* price of sterling at the mark-sterling cross-rate is cheaper in Frankfurt than in New York, arbitragers can profit by buying marks with dollars in New York, simultaneously selling the marks for sterling in Frankfurt, and simultaneously selling the sterling for dollars in New York. An arbitrager who undertook this set of transactions by starting with the purchase of 3.7 million marks in New York for $1.295 million would be able to sell the marks for 1 million pounds sterling in Frankfurt and then sell the sterling in New York for $1.310 million, for a profit of $.015 million (or $15,000). This is an example of *triangular* arbitrage involving three currencies.

Arbitrage creates a single integrated global market in foreign exchange. Actually, today almost all interbank transactions in foreign exchange both in the United States and abroad involve the purchase and sale of *dollars*. Thus even a British trader who wants to buy marks with sterling will first buy dollars with sterling and then sell the dollars for marks. This is done because the dollar is the principal currency for international trade and investment and the dollar market for each currency is consequently more active than the bilateral market between any pair of foreign currencies. Interbank trading directly through the dollar eliminates discrepancies between the dollar quotations of foreign currencies and their cross-rates.

Instant electronic communications have made arbitrage more effective than in the past. Arbitragers (mainly the financial center banks) rely on computer information systems and computer programs to identify and carry out arbitrage operations. Because of the time zones the major foreign exchange markets—New York, London and Tokyo—are located in, the global foreign exchange market is open for business 24 hours each day.

INTERNATIONAL FINANCIAL CENTERS

Domestic and foreign banks are able to act as dealers in foreign exchange because they are willing to hold balances in other countries. The mechanism of international payments, therefore, is based upon a pattern of interbank debt that covers the entire world. This pattern may be decentralized, centralized, or somewhere between these two extremes.

Decentralized and Centralized Systems of International Payment

When the banking system in one country is linked to the banking systems in all other countries by a series of bilateral debt arrangements (the number

Figure 11-3   Fully Decentralized System of International Payments: Six Countries

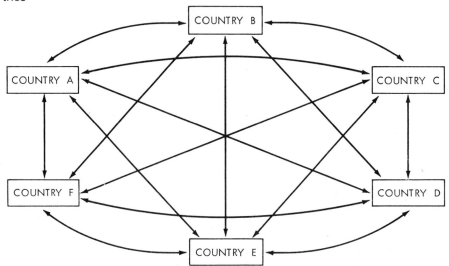

Arrows indicate reciprocal bank balances of foreign exchange dealers.

In a fully decentralized system of international payments, banks in one country maintain balances with banks in *all* other countries. Hence, international payments are made between two countries by shifts in the ownership of balances held in each other's banks.

of arrangements being equal to the number of other countries) and all international payments are cleared bilaterally, the system of international payment is fully decentralized. Figure 11-3 shows a fully decentralized payments system for a world of six countries.

When, on the other hand, banks in one country are linked to banks in other countries through balances maintained at *one* financial center and all international payments are cleared through this center, then the system of international payments is fully centralized. Figure 11-4 illustrates a fully centralized system of international payments for a world of six countries.

The London Financial Center before World War I

During the half century that preceded World War I, the system of international payments was highly centralized. The focus of this system was London. Banks throughout the world maintained sterling balances in London and transferred funds from one country to another by drawing sterling

Figure 11-4   Fully Centralized System of International Payments: Six Countries

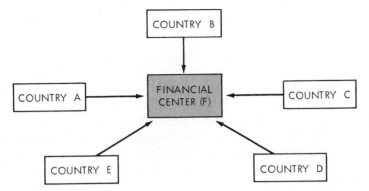

Direction of arrows indicates the location of foreign bank balances maintained by foreign exchange dealers.

In a fully centralized system of international payments, banks in different countries maintain balances with banks located in a single financial center. Hence, international payments are made via shifts in the national ownership of bank balances held in the financial center.

bills. A Brazilian exporting coffee to the United States would draw a sterling bill on the American importer, who, when the time came to buy, would remit a sterling draft. In this way international payments occurred through shifts in the ownership of sterling balances located in London. Although most countries were on the gold standard at this time, it was the pound sterling that made up most of the world's payments.

The prominence of London was due to many factors. First, Great Britain was the world's greatest importer, and its policy of free trade gave foreign suppliers easy access to its domestic market. Second, the London money market was unparalleled in its efficiency and resources—banks, acceptance houses, discount houses, dealers, and so on, made up a market in which sterling funds could be invested or borrowed on short term in any amount and at any time. Third, London was by far the paramount source of long-term investment capital; its highly evolved securities markets dealt in the securities of the entire world. First trader, first financier, and first investor of the world during a period when trade and finance were unrestricted by government policies, it was inevitable that most international payments should flow to, from, and through the London financial center.

The Rise of New York after World War I

During the 1920s New York and, to a lesser extent, Paris rose to challenge the financial supremacy of London. The blows that Great Britain had suffered during World War I and the simultaneous emergence of the United States as the leading international creditor were the main factors responsible for this development.

The resulting decentralization of the international payment system brought to the fore certain problems that had not existed in the earlier payments system centered in London. For one thing, there was less economy in the use of the world's supply of monetary gold. When there was only one dominant international financial center, there was little need for gold on the part of the peripheral countries, aside from domestic reserves, since foreign exchange could be easily borrowed from the center. When there were several financial centers, however, each center had to maintain individual gold reserves behind its international obligations, and the peripheral countries might also increase their gold holdings. In the 1920s the shortage of gold was also heightened by the large acquisitions of the United States during World War I.[13]

Another problem that arose in the 1920s was the movement of speculative capital between London and New York, stemming from the general uncertainty regarding the future course of exchange rates and from lack of faith in the ability of certain countries to maintain their newly restored gold standard. The movement of this capital was made easier by the decentralization of the international payment system; when there is only one financial center, there is less likelihood of a sudden flight of capital, since it can move only to a peripheral country. In the 1920s the volatility of short-term capital movements also heightened the gold shortage, since each financial center was compelled to maintain greater reserves behind its foreign obligations. Despite these drawbacks, the decentralized system of the 1920s, based on the London-New York axis, would probably have developed into a more workable arrangement in time. It was destroyed, however, by the onset of world depression in the early 1930s.

After World War II, the international monetary system came to rest on the dollar, and New York emerged as the dominant financial center. Foreign governments (central banks) maintained balances in New York that, together with gold, constituted their official international reserves. Private foreign banks also maintained sizable dollar balances to finance their FX transactions throughout the world.

The Emergence of Tokyo in the 1980s

In the 1980s, Japan became the world's leading exporter of capital and its greatest international creditor. At the same time, the United States became the world's leading *importer* of capital and its greatest international *debtor*. These twin developments have made Tokyo an international financial cen-

---

[13] U.S. gold reserves rose from $1.7 billion in December 1914 to $2.7 billion in December 1918. Reserves continued to rise until December 1924, when they reached $4.1 billion. Board of Governors of the Federal Reserve System, *Banking and Monetary Statistics* (Washington, D.C.: U.S. Government Printing Office, 1943), p. 544.

ter. Able to draw on a huge volume of domestic savings at comparatively low interest rates, Japan's banks and investment houses now wield formidable financial power in the international economy. Today, eight of the 10 largest banks in the world are Japanese.[14] In contrast, over the period 1984–1987 the share of the United States in international bank deposits fell from 76 to 38 percent and in international bond issues from 57 to 38 percent.[15] Also, the yen has assumed a more prominent role in the international monetary system as more countries hold yen as official monetary reserves and as more trade is financed in yen. Conversely, the decline in the value of the dollar has raised questions about the future role of the dollar.[16]

Tokyo's emergence as an international financial center has been held back by regulations that prevent its markets from becoming as liquid as New York's. Investors need access to a variety of financial instruments that can be easily bought or sold at any time. Deregulation is taking place, but it has not kept pace with the growth of Japan's financial power. In sum, if the yen remains strong and the dollar weak and if Tokyo's markets approach the liquidity of New York's, then Tokyo may well challenge New York in the 1990s as the premier international financial center.

SUMMARY

1. Most international payments involve shifts between domestic and foreign residents in the ownership of bank deposits. These shifts are brought about by international electronic bank transfers and bank drafts rather than by checks.

2. International payments are more risky than domestic payments because of the foreign exchange risk, the inconvertibility risk, and the default risk.

3. The principal methods of payment in international trade are cash in advance, commercial letters of credit, commercial drafts drawn on the buyer, open account, and consignment.

4. We can demonstrate the mechanism of international payments with the T accounts of U.S. and foreign banks: Payments occur through shifts in the domestic and foreign ownership of bank deposits, with banks acting as intermediaries.

5. The core of the foreign exchange market in the United States is a network of some 120 commercial banks, located principally in New York, that buy and sell foreign-currency deposits known as foreign exchange. Traditionally, the foreign exchange (FX) market has comprised two submarkets: FX retail market and the FX interbank market.

---

[14] See Chapter 20.
[15] "Will the Yen Push Aside the Dollar?" *Fortune*, December 5, 1988, p. 160.
[16] See Chapter 19.

However, a third submarket, the FX futures/options market, came into existence in the 1970s.

6. Apart from the distinction between retail and interbank transactions, foreign exchange transactions may be classified as spot and forward. Only a small number of currencies—commonly referred to as international currencies—are used to effect international payments. The leading international currency is the U.S. dollar.

7. The total volume on the three principal FX markets—New York, London and Tokyo—averaged $188 billion each day during March 1986. The explosive growth of FX markets is propelled by high volatility in exchange rates, deregulation, and electronic communication systems such as CHIPS.

8. The principal currencies traded in FX markets are the U.S. dollar, the West German mark, the Japanese yen, and the British pound sterling.

9. Exchange (or currency) arbitrage is the sale of a given currency in one foreign exchange market and the simultaneous purchase of the same currency in another foreign exchange market. Bilateral arbitrage maintains the same price for a given currency across foreign exchange markets; triangular arbitrage maintains consistency in cross-rates between two currencies through a third currency. The effect of currency arbitrage is to create a single integrated global market in foreign exchange.

10. London was the dominant international financial center before World War I, and New York became the dominant center after World War II. In the 1980s, Tokyo has emerged as a new international financial center to challenge the supremacy of New York.

QUESTIONS AND APPLICATIONS

1. Why are international payments more risky than domestic payments?
2. (a) What is a confirmed, irrevocable letter of credit?
   (b) What are the advantages and disadvantages of letter-of-credit payment for the exporter? For the importer?
3. (a) What is a commercial draft?
   (b) How is the bill of lading used in documentary draft payment to protect the interests of the exporter?
4. Demonstrate with the T accounts of U.S. and foreign banks what happens when (a) a U.S. resident makes a payment to a foreign resident in the latter's currency, (b) a U.S. resident receives a dollar payment from a foreign resident, and (c) a U.S. resident makes a payment to a foreign resident in a third-country currency.
5. (a) Identify the three submarkets composing the FX market.
   (b) What are the distinctive functions of each submarket?

6. **(a)** What is CHIPS?

   (b) How does CHIPS work?

7. **(a)** How does bilateral currency arbitrage make the dollar price of a foreign currency the same in different foreign exchange markets?

   (b) How does triangular currency arbitrage keep cross-rates consistent?

   (c) Suppose the dollar price of the French franc is $0.16 in New York while at the same time it is $0.17 in Paris. What would arbitragers do?

8. Explain what a decentralized system of international payments is. Explain what a centralized system is.

9. Be prepared to debate this proposition: "Tokyo will become the dominant international financial center in the 1990s, surpassing New York."

SELECTED READINGS

Chrystal, K. Alec. "A Guide to Foreign Exchange Markets." *Review* (The Federal Reserve Bank of St. Louis), March 1984, pp. 5–18.

Federal Reserve Bank of New York. "Recent Trends in the U.S. Foreign Exchange Market." *Quarterly Review* (Federal Reserve Bank of New York), Summer 1984, pp. 38–47.

_____. "Large Dollar Payment Flows from New York." *Quarterly Review* (Federal Reserve Bank of New York), Winter 1987–1988, pp. 6–13.

Kubarych, Roger M. *Foreign Exchange Markets in the United States*. New York: Federal Reserve Bank of New York, 1983.

Gendreau, Brian. "New Markets in Foreign Currency Options." *Business Review* (Federal Reserve Bank of Philadelphia), July-August 1984, pp. 3–12.

12

Foreign Exchange Rates and Their Determination

Foreign exchange rates are of key significance in directing the flow of merchandise, services, and capital between nations. In Chapter 11, we showed how arbitrage equates foreign exchange rates across the several national foreign exchange markets. This chapter explores the different kinds of exchange rate behavior.

THE RATE OF EXCHANGE

Foreign exchange is bought and sold in the foreign exchange market at a price that is called the *rate of exchange*. More specifically, the exchange rate is the *domestic* money price of foreign money, establishing an equivalence between dollars and British pounds sterling, dollars and French francs, dollars and Argentine pesos, and so on.[1] The daily quotations of foreign exchange are based on the price of bank (or electronic) transfers, which are the quickest means of international payment. Table 12-1 indicates the selling rates for bank transfers in New York on February 10 and February 13, 1989.

For most currencies only a "spot" rate is quoted. *Spot exchange* is foreign exchange for immediate delivery (ordinarily within one or two days).

---

[1] If there are n national currencies, then there are $n-1$ rates of exchange relating foreign currencies to the domestic currency. Foreign exchange rates may be quoted either as the *domestic* currency price for a unit of a given foreign currency or, alternatively, as the *foreign* currency price for a unit of domestic currency. Both terms are equivalent; one is simply the reciprocal of the other. European foreign exchange markets use the second term; until recently, the U.S. foreign exchange market used only the first term, but now quotes rates in both terms, as shown in Table 12-1. To explain the determination of foreign exchange rates, we shall use the first term, specifically, the dollar price of sterling.

TABLE 12-1 Selling Rates for Foreign Exchange (Bank Transfers) in New York on February 10 and February 13, 1989

Monday, February 13, 1989

The New York foreign exchange selling rates below apply to trading among banks in amounts of $1 million and more, as quoted at 3 p.m. Eastern time by Bankers Trust Co. Retail transactions provide fewer units of foreign currency per dollar.

Country	U.S. $ equiv. Mon.	U.S. $ equiv. Fri.	Currency per U.S. $ Mon.	Currency per U.S. $ Fri.
Argentina (Austral)	.38314	.043066	26.10	23.22
Australia (Dollar)	.8875	.8865	1.1267	1.1280
Austria (Schilling)	.07602	.07599	13.15	13.15
Bahrain (Dinar)	2.6525	2.6521	.37700	.37705
Belgium (Franc)				
Commercial rate	.02551	.02567	39.18	38.95
Financial rate	.02539	.02554	39.37	39.15
Brazil (Cruzado)	1.0101	1.0101	.99000	.99000
Britain (Pound)	1.7505	1.7482	.5712	.5720
30-Day Forward	1.7459	1.7435	.5727	.5735
90-Day Forward	1.7369	1.7343	.5757	.5766
180-Day Forward	1.7267	1.7243	.5791	.5799
Canada (Dollar)	.8428	.8435	1.1865	1.1855
30-Day Forward	.8418	.8423	1.1879	1.1871
90-Day Forward	.8390	.8395	1.1918	1.1911
180-Day Forward	.8352	.8355	1.1973	1.1968
Chile (Official rate)	.0040734	.0040816	245.49	245.00
China (Yuan)	.268672	.268672	3.7220	3.7220
Colombia (Peso)	.002865	.002857	349.00	350.00
Denmark (Krone)	.1374	.1373	7.2750	7.2820
Ecuador (Sucre)				
Floating rate	.001865	.001901	536.00	526.00
Finland (Markka)	.2319	.2316	4.3110	4.3165
France (Franc)	.1571	.1585	6.3635	6.3070
30-Day Forward	.1572	.1586	6.3610	6.3042
90-Day Forward	.1573	.1587	6.3547	6.2976
180-Day Forward	.1576	.1591	6.3450	6.2867
Greece (Drachma)	.006418	.006514	155.80	153.50
Hong Kong (Dollar)	.128254	.128205	7.7970	7.8000
India (Rupee)	.0656598	.0657030	15.23	15.22
Indonesia (Rupiah)	.0005780	.0005780	1730.00	1730.00
Ireland (Punt)	1.4262	1.4160	.7011	.7062
Israel (Shekel)	.5503	.5503	1.8170	1.8170
Italy (Lira)	.0007342	.0007330	1362.00	1364.25
Japan (Yen)	.0077942	.007771	128.30	128.67
30-Day Forward	.0078259	.007803	127.78	128.15
90-Day Forward	.0078932	.007869	126.69	127.07
180-Day Forward	.0079961	.007970	125.06	125.47
Kuwait (Dinar)	3.4714	3.4634	.2887	.2887
Malaysia (Ringgit)	.36603	.36616	2.7320	2.7310
Mexico (Peso)				
Floating rate	.00042918	.0004310	2330.00	2320.00
Netherland (Guilder)	.473596	.4792	2.1115	2.0867
New Zealand (Dollar)	.6185	.6180	1.6181	1.6181
Norway (Krone)	.1483	.1480	6.7450	6.7530
Pakistan (Rupee)	.05208	.05235	19.20	19.10
Peru (Inti)	.0006911	.0006153	1447.00	1625.00
Philippines (Peso)	.048309	.048309	20.70	20.70
Portugal (Escudo)	.006540	.006493	152.90	154.00
Saudi Arabia (Riyal)	.2666	.2667	3.7505	3.7495
Singapore (Dollar)	.5184	.5182	1.9290	1.9295
South Africa (Rand)				
Commercial rate	.4077	.4108	2.4525	2.4340
Financial rate	.2519	.2525	3.9700	3.9600
South Korea (Won)	.00147145	.0014690	679.60	680.70
Spain (Peseta)	.0086058	.0086090	116.20	116.15
Sweden (Krona)	.1576	.1575	6.3460	6.3485
Switzerland (Franc)	.6289	.6295	1.5900	1.5885
30-Day Forward	.6308	.6313	1.5853	1.5838
90-Day Forward	.6350	.6356	1.5749	1.5733
180-Day Forward	.6420	.6418	1.5576	1.5579
Taiwan (Dollar)	.03623	.03620	27.60	27.62
Thailand (Baht)	.03937	.039416	25.40	25.37
Turkey (Lira)	.0005316	.0005330	1881.00	1876.00
United Arab (Dirham)	.2722	.2722	3.6725	3.6725
Uruguay (New Peso)				
Financial	.002114	.002127	473.00	470.00
Venezuela (Bolivar)				
Floating rate	.02685	.02702	37.25	37.00
W. Germany (Mark)	.5348	.5347	1.8700	1.8700
30-Day Forward	.5361	.5361	1.8653	1.8653
90-Day Forward	.5404	.5390	1.8505	1.8552
180-Day Forward	.5432	.5433	1.8407	1.8403

Source: The Wall Street Journal, February 14, 1989.

For international currencies, however, the New York market also quotes "forward" rates for foreign exchange promised for delivery at a time in the future—30, 90, or 180 days. Unless otherwise noted, our analysis of exchange rate behavior relates to the spot rate.

Actually, there are several spot rates of exchange for a given currency. The price of bank transfers is the *base* rate of exchange, and other means of international payment—sight and time bills—usually sell at a discounted price below this base rate. The discounts reflect varying delays or risks of payment compared to the bank transfer. Even payment by a bank draft sent airmail requires two or three days between New York and London, and during that time the foreign exchange dealer has the use of both the domestic money paid for the draft and the foreign balance against which the draft is drawn. Time drafts postpone payment for a much longer period. The discount on a given kind of foreign exchange, say a 30-day bill, will depend upon the current rate of interest since, in effect, the buyer of the bill is lending money to the seller of the bill until its maturity date. Discounts from the base rate of exchange stem also from differences in the risk of payment. For that reason trade bills are quoted below bank bills of similar maturity.

The rates of different kinds of foreign exchange are thus linked to the base rate of exchange by discounts that take into account liquidity and risk factors. Although these discounts will vary with the two aforementioned factors, the resulting pattern of exchange rates will rise and fall with the base rate. In our analysis of the determination of foreign exchange rates, therefore, we shall consider the pattern of spot rates as one rate, namely, the base rate of exchange for bank transfers.

The behavior of exchange rates will depend upon the nature of the foreign exchange market. When there are no restrictions on private trading in the market and official agencies do not stand ready to stabilize the rate of exchange, the exchange rate will fluctuate from day to day in response to changes in the supply and demand of foreign exchange. When, however, government authorities follow a policy of stabilization but do not interfere with private market transactions in foreign exchange, the exchange rate will move only within narrow limits, although these limits may be substantially altered from time to time by official action. Finally, the government may restrict private transactions by becoming the sole buyer and seller of foreign exchange; the rate of exchange is then no longer determined by supply and demand but instead is the end product of bureaucratic decisions. We now examine more closely the determination of these three types of exchange rate behavior—freely fluctuating rates, stable rates, and controlled rates.

FREELY FLUCTUATING EXCHANGE RATES

When the rate of exchange is not stabilized or controlled by government authorities, the foreign exchange market very closely approaches the theoretical model of perfect competition. Except for the liquidity and risk differentials that discounts allow for, the foreign exchange of any given country is one homogeneous product. Moreover, the number of buyers and sellers of foreign exchange is so large that a single buyer or seller cannot measurably influence the rate of exchange but must accept it as given. In a free, unstabilized market, therefore, the rate of exchange is determined by the many individual acts of buying and selling, none of which individually is able to affect it but all of which interact to set its level.

The Demand for Foreign Exchange

In a free market the rate of exchange, like any other price, is determined by the interplay of supply and demand. The foreign exchange that is demanded at any time will depend upon the volume of international transfers that require payments to foreign residents. These transfers may be purchases of goods and services (*real* transfers) or purchases of financial assets (*financial* transfers).[2]

The amount of foreign exchange in demand varies inversely with its price—the amount demanded at a high rate is less than the amount demanded at a low rate, provided other conditions (such as prices, interest rates, and real incomes) remain the same. A high exchange rate makes foreign goods and services and financial assets more expensive to domestic buyers, who respond by reducing the volume of their purchases from foreigners. This, in turn, lessens the amount of foreign exchange demanded by domestic residents. Conversely, a low rate of exchange increases the amount of foreign exchange demanded.

The demand relationship of foreign exchange (here represented by the British pound sterling) is indicated in Figure 12-1 by the familiar downsloping demand schedule *D–D*. The schedule shows the quantity of sterling exchange demanded at each rate of exchange in the New York market; thus, it is an aggregate of all the individual demand schedules of those who wish to transfer funds abroad.

In analyzing the determination of the exchange rate, it is important to distinguish between a movement along a given demand schedule (change in the amount demanded) and a shift in the entire schedule (change in demand). We have noted that a movement along the demand schedule is downward from left to right because the exchange rate determines the domestic price of imports of goods, services, or capital and thereby affects their volume and the amount of foreign exchange demanded to pay for them. Changes in income, costs, prices, interest rates, tastes, and other factors may, however, cause shifts in imports independent of the exchange rate. When this happens, the entire demand schedule shifts either left or right, depending on whether there has been a decrease or an increase in the volume

---

[2] The demand for foreign exchange originates in the *debit* items composing the current and capital accounts of a country's balance of payments (see Chapter 14).

Figure 12-1   Demand for Sterling Exchange in New York

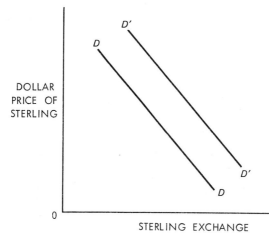

DOLLAR
PRICE OF
STERLING

0

STERLING EXCHANGE

The demand schedule for sterling exchange (representing foreign exchange in general) slopes downward from left to right because the *amount* of sterling demanded at a high rate is less than the *amount* demanded at a lower rate. A high rate of exchange makes foreign goods, services, and financial assets expensive to domestic buyers, and conversely. An *increase* in the demand for sterling would be indicated by a shift in the entire schedule to the right (from *D–D* to *D'–D'*); a *decrease* in demand would be indicated by a shift to the left.

of imports. For example, a rise in the national income of the United States will cause a rise in imports of merchandise and services, and this will shift the demand schedule for foreign exchange to the right as more foreign exchange is demanded at each rate of exchange. Such a development is shown in Figure 12-1 by *D'–D'*. Or the shift to *D'–D'* may be caused by a rise in real interest rates abroad, which would encourage U.S. residents to buy foreign securities.

The Supply of Foreign Exchange

The supply of foreign exchange in the foreign exchange market derives from international transfers that require money receipts from foreign residents, that is, from *credit* items in the balance of payments. Unlike the amount demanded, the amount of foreign exchange supplied to the market varies directly with the rate of exchange. When the rate of exchange is high, domestic prices appear low to foreigners, since they are able to acquire a unit of domestic money with a small expenditure of their own money. This cheapness stimulates domestic exports of real and financial assets and thereby brings a larger supply of foreign exchange into the market. Conversely, a low exchange rate restricts exports and lowers the amount of foreign exchange offered to the market.

Figure 12-2 shows the supply relationship of foreign exchange by a schedule that slopes upward from left to right. A shift of the entire supply schedule either to the left or right occurs with a change in economic variables that affect receipts of foreign exchange (other than the exchange rate).

For example, a shift to the left would occur if deflation abroad caused a decrease in American exports. This would decrease the amount of foreign exchange supplied to the market at each exchange rate. A decrease in the supply of sterling exchange in the New York market is shown in Figure 12-2 by S'–S'.

Determination of the Rate of Exchange

The rate of exchange is determined by the intersection of the demand and the supply schedules. At this rate of exchange, and at no other rate, the market is cleared; the rate will remain stable until a shift occurs in either one or both schedules. It is unlikely that this equilibrium rate of exchange will last very long or even be attained in a free, unstabilized foreign ex-

Figure 12-2   Supply of Sterling Exchange in New York

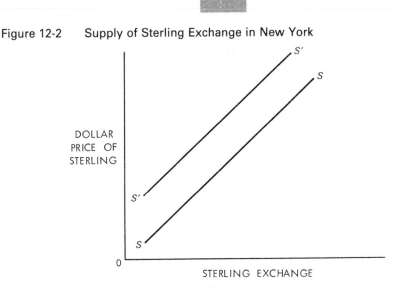

The supply schedule for sterling exchange slopes upward from left to right: When the exchange rate moves higher, domestic prices of goods, services, and financial assets appear lower to foreign buyers. This stimulates more domestic exports and brings in a larger *amount* of foreign exchange to the market. Conversely, lower rates reduce domestic exports, bringing in a lower *amount* of foreign exchange. A *decrease* in supply would be indicated by a shift of the entire schedule to the left (from S–S to S'–S'); an *increase* in supply would be indicated by a shift to the right.

change market, since continuing shifts in demand and supply will force continuing adjustments toward new equilibrium positions. Thus, the exchange rate will fluctuate continuously, just as the prices of securities traded in the security market continuously fluctuate. To simplify our analysis, however, we shall assume that there is time for the exchange rate to adjust fully to a change in demand or supply.

In Figure 12-3 the equilibrium rate of exchange is 0–R. At this rate the amount supplied is equal to the amount demanded, and both suppliers and buyers of foreign exchange are satisfied. Suppose now that the demand for sterling increases from D–D to D'–D', as in Figure 12-4. In response to this increase, the equilibrium rate rises from 0–R to 0–R', where once again the amounts of sterling exchange supplied and demanded are equal. This higher rate calls forth an increase in the amount supplied of E'–E', since it stimulates more American exports. Similarly, a shift of the demand schedule to the left (fall in demand) will bring about a decline in the rate of exchange. On the other hand, a shift in the *supply schedule* to the left (fall in supply) will raise the exchange rate and a shift to the right (rise in supply) will lower it.

Because foreign exchange is a store of value as well as an instrument of current payment, demand and supply schedules shift quickly in response to changes in *expectations* about the future behavior of economic variables,

Figure 12-3   Determination of Equilibrium Sterling Exchange Rate in New York

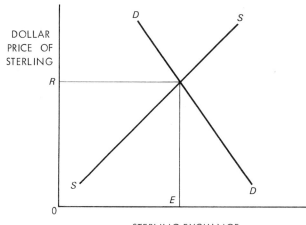

The equilibrium rate of exchange (0–R) is determined by the intersection of the demand and supply schedules. Only at 0–R does the amount demanded equal the amount supplied. Consequently, the market clears and both buyers and suppliers of sterling exchange are satisfied.

Figure 12-4   Determination of a New Equilibrium Sterling Exchange Rate in New York

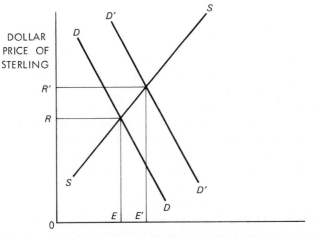

When the demand for sterling exchange *increases,* as shown by the shift from *D–D* to *D'–D'*, then the price of sterling rises to a new equilibrium level, 0–*R'*. At the new rate, the amount of sterling in demand and supply is 0–*E'*. The increase in the amount supplied (from 0–*E* to 0–*E'*) is induced by the higher rate of exchange, which encourages domestic exports.

notably expectations about future interest and inflation rates. Suppose, for example, traders alter their expectations about future rates of inflation, and now believe that the inflation rate will become much higher in the United States than in Britain. Consequently, they regard the pound sterling as a better store of value than the dollar, moving out of dollars into sterling. This new *speculative* demand for sterling is shown as a shift in the demand schedule to *D'–D'* in Figure 12-4, a rise in demand that causes a rise in the price of sterling.

In summary, the exchange rate in a free, unstabilized market is determined by the supply of and the demand for foreign exchange, which derive from exports and imports of merchandise, services, and securities (financial assets). The exchange rate itself also influences the volume of exports and imports, and this influence is shown by the shape of the demand and supply schedules of foreign exchange.[3]

---

[3] The influence of the exchange rate on the balance of payments is an important means of adjustment to disequilibrium and is taken up in Chapter 16.

STABLE EXCHANGE RATES

In this section several arguments for stable rates are presented, after which specific techniques of stabilization are discussed.

Arguments for Stable Rates

The contemporary system of fluctuating or floating exchange rates is a historical anomaly. Exchange rates have seldom been left free to vary with supply and demand. Even before World War I, when there was general agreement on the benefits of flexible market prices in merchandise, services, and securities, fluctuating exchange rates were viewed with marked distaste. At this time all of the leading trading nations were firm adherents of the gold standard, which provided fixed rates of exchange. Fluctuating exchange rates, therefore, were considered the mark of a failure to remain on the gold standard. Apart from the gold standard, however, there are strong arguments for stable exchange rates.

It is forcibly argued that the exchange rate is unlike the price of an ordinary commodity and that it is illogical to view the two in the same light. When the exchange rate varies, the prices of *all* exports are changed for foreign buyers and, simultaneously, the prices of *all* imports are changed for domestic buyers. These widespread price effects unloose a series of repercussions that extend throughout the domestic and foreign economies. This critical nature of the exchange rate, the argument runs, rules out the unlicensed freedom of the unstabilized foreign exchange market. It is also contended that fluctuating rates invite foreign exchange speculation that may intensify balance of payments difficulties. Less fundamental arguments for stable rates spring from considerations of trade and finance. Fluctuating rates provoke uncertainty in foreign payments and investments. The exporter is unable to make a sound calculation of the profit margin, since the domestic value of foreign exchange receipts depends upon an unstable rate of exchange. Lenders and borrowers are also subject to this exchange risk.[4]

Techniques of Stabilization

Unlike the controlled exchange market, the stabilized market imposes no restraints on private transactions in foreign exchange; the factors of supply and demand are fully operative. How, then, is it possible to prevent fluctuations in the rate of exchange? The answer lies in the open-market operations of government authorities that compensate for movements in the ordinary demand and supply of foreign exchange. Successful stabilization of the rate of exchange requires that the stabilization agency be able to offset movements in market supply and demand to any desired degree. To

---

[4] The case for fluctuating rates (also referred to as flexible or floating rates) is presented in Chapter 16.

do so, the agency must possess adequate supplies of domestic and foreign exchange.[5] Under the gold standard, stabilization is assured by the willingness of the monetary authorities to buy or sell gold without limit at a fixed price. This *passive* stabilization contrasts with *active* stabilization practices whereby government agencies buy and sell foreign exchange in the market to offset any undesired movements in exchange rates.

Passive Stabilization: The Gold Standard A country is on the *gold standard* when its basic monetary unit (dollar, pound sterling, franc, and so on) is defined in terms of a specified weight of gold and when its monetary authorities stand ready at all times to buy and sell gold in unlimited quantities at the rate fixed by the legal gold content of the monetary unit. As long as this second condition of unrestricted convertibility is observed, the gold value of the monetary unit cannot vary and the price of gold remains constant.

The minimum conditions for a true *international* gold standard are two: (1) two or more countries must adopt monetary units with a designated gold content, and (2) the monetary authorities of each country must permit the free, unlimited export and import of gold at a rate fixed by the gold content of the monetary unit. Since the gold standard creates fixed exchange rates only between countries on the gold standard, however, it makes its greatest contribution to exchange rate stability when several currencies, particularly key currencies such as the dollar and the pound sterling, are tied to gold.

Gold standard currencies hold a fixed relationship to each other because they all hold a fixed relationship to gold. Before World War I and during the last half of the 1920s, the British pound sterling was defined as 113 grains of gold and the United States dollar as 23.22 grains. The gold content of the pound, therefore, was 4.8665 times greater than the gold content of the dollar. This latter relationship was the *mint parity* of the pound and the dollar at the time—one pound sterling was equivalent to $4.8665. Any holder of 113 grains of gold could obtain one pound sterling from the British monetary authorities or, alternately, $4.8665 from the American authorities.

Under the gold standard, the mint parity and the exchange rate between two currencies need not be identical. Because of the costs of shipping gold from one country to another (freight, insurance, handling, and interest), the exchange rate is free to vary within narrow limits known as *gold points*. The higher the costs of shipping gold, the greater the spread between mint parity and the gold points. The costs of shipment, when added to mint parity, establish the *gold export point;* the costs of shipment, when subtracted from mint parity, establish the *gold import point*. When the exchange rate rises to the gold export point, gold begins to flow out of the country; on the other

---

[5] This may be illustrated by the price stabilization of wheat. To keep the price of wheat from falling below a minimum level, the stabilization authority must have enough dollars to buy all the wheat offered at that level; to keep the price of wheat from rising above a maximum level, the authority must have enough wheat to satisfy demand at that level.

hand, when the exchange rate falls to the gold import point, gold begins to flow into the country. These flows of gold provide the compensatory changes in the supply of and the demand for foreign exchange that are necessary to keep the foreign exchange rate from moving beyond the gold points.

This stabilizing function of gold flows under the international gold standard may be illustrated by an example. Let us assume that the mint parity of the pound sterling is $4.8665 and that shipping costs make the gold export point in New York $4.8865 and the gold import point, $4.8465. Now suppose that the rate of exchange in New York rises to the gold export point of $4.8865. The rate will not rise further because foreign exchange dealers can acquire all the pounds sterling they desire at a rate of $4.8865 by purchasing gold for dollars from the American monetary authorities, shipping the gold to London, and then selling the gold for pounds to the British monetary authorities. Thus, the supply of foreign exchange becomes perfectly elastic at the gold export point, and the rate of exchange cannot rise beyond it.[6]

Similarly, the gold import point sets a floor below which the rate of exchange cannot fall: Exchange dealers will not sell pounds at a rate below $4.8465 because they can obtain that many dollars for each pound sterling by converting pounds into gold in London, shipping the gold to New York, and then converting the gold into dollars. In other words, the demand for foreign exchange becomes perfectly elastic at the gold import point.[7]

When the rate of exchange is between the gold points, there is no longer an option on the part of dealers to acquire foreign exchange by gold exports or to dispose of foreign exchange by gold imports, since to do so would involve losses. If, in our example, the sterling exchange rate is $4.8665 (the mint parity), then to acquire or dispose of sterling by gold shipments would mean a loss of two American cents per pound sterling for each transaction (the costs of shipment). Between the gold points, therefore, the rate of exchange is determined as in a free, unstabilized market. The spread between the gold points, however, is so narrow that we may regard exchange rates under the gold standard as fixed.

It will be noted that this stabilization is achieved without any intervention in the foreign exchange market on the part of the monetary authorities, who behave simply as residual buyers and sellers of gold. Gold moves "automatically" from one country to another in response to the supply of and demand for foreign exchange.

Active Stabilization by Monetary Authorities. A true international gold standard has not functioned since the first half of the 1930s, and since that time exchange rates, unless controlled outright or left free to float, have been stabilized by official compensatory transactions in the foreign exchange market.[8] The policy objectives of active stabilization, however, differ con-

---

[6] All the foreign exchange that is demanded at the gold export point will be supplied.

[7] All the foreign exchange that is supplied at the gold import point will be demanded.

[8] The first stabilization agency was the British Exchange Equalization Account, which was

siderably from the policy objectives of passive stabilization under the gold standard. Under the old gold standard, the fundamental aim of international monetary policy was to remain on the gold standard and to avoid any change in the gold content of the monetary unit. The almost incidental result of this policy was a fixed exchange rate. As a matter of fact, the exchange rates of the major trading countries were fixed at the same level for several decades preceding World War I. In contrast, active stabilization seeks to achieve stability in the exchange rate but allows for occasional adjustments in the rate to correct disequilibrium in the balance of payments. This policy of "stable, yet flexible" rates attempts to secure the advantages of stability and, at the same time, to use the exchange rate as an instrument of international adjustment.

We have already briefly described the basic mechanism of exchange rate stabilization; we now look more closely into its actual operation. To stabilize the dollar price of sterling between, say $1.73 and $1.77, the United States monetary authorities (Treasury and Federal Reserve System) would require two assets: (1) dollars and (2) sterling exchange, other foreign exchange freely convertible into sterling, or gold. The dollars would be needed so that the authorities could buy all the sterling that might be offered in New York at $1.73, that is, so that they could make the demand for sterling perfectly elastic at that rate. Foreign exchange or gold would be needed so that the authorities could satisfy any demand for sterling at $1.77 thereby providing the ability to make the supply of sterling perfectly elastic at that rate.

As part of the government, the monetary authorities would have no difficulty in obtaining sufficient dollars for their operations, but the supply of foreign exchange and gold would be limited, since the government cannot create foreign exchange and domestic gold production is small. There is another reason why American monetary authorities would not be concerned over their holdings of dollars. As we have noted, domestic currency would be necessary to put a floor under the dollar price of sterling, that is, to avert a depreciation of sterling and a simultaneous appreciation of the dollar. Ordinarily, however, domestic authorities would not support the exchange value of a foreign currency; they would be interested only in one-sided stabilization, the avoidance of depreciation of the domestic currency. In practice, therefore, the U.S. authorities would impose a ceiling over the dollar price of sterling, while at the same time the British authorities would place a floor below the dollar price of sterling.[9] This division of labor would

---

established in 1932 after the United Kingdom abandoned the gold standard. Upon the devaluation of the dollar in 1934, the United States also established a stabilization agency, and by the end of 1930s, most countries had adopted a policy of exchange stabilization, whether implemented by special agencies, central banks, or treasuries.

[9] In other words, the British authorities would impose a ceiling over the pound price of dollars in London. In a stable-rate system, *depreciation* is commonly called *devaluation* (because it is a government action) and *appreciation* is called *revaluation*. We prefer to use *depreciation* and *appreciation* as the basic terms to indicate the direction of a movement in the exchange

Figure 12-5   Stabilization of the Dollar-Sterling Exchange Rate

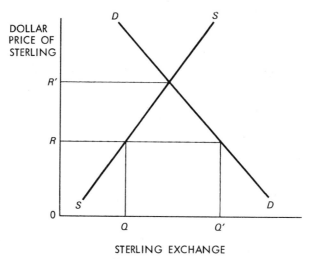

DOLLAR
PRICE OF
STERLING

STERLING EXCHANGE

In the absence of intervention by the monetary authorities, the equilibrium rate of exchange would be 0–R′. To fix the rate at 0–R, the authorities need to supply the market with Q–Q′ of sterling exchange taken from their international reserves.

also occur under gold standard stabilization: Gold would flow out of a country to maintain an upper price limit (gold export point) on foreign exchange and would flow into a country to maintain a lower price limit (gold import point).

A diagrammatic illustration of the mechanism of exchange rate stabilization is shown in Figure 12-5. Without the intervention of monetary authorities, the exchange rate would be 0–R′. But suppose the authorities want to hold the rate to 0–R. At that rate, the amount of foreign exchange supplied the market is Q–Q′ less than the amount demanded, which is the reason why 0–R is *not* the equilibrium rate. To maintain the rate at 0–R, therefore, the authorities must supply the market with Q–Q′ of foreign exchange, which will close the gap between the amounts supplied and demanded.[10] In other words, they must provide *compensatory financing* of the supply deficit.

rate. Hence we shall use them for that purpose in describing both variable and stable-rate systems. With respect to the latter, we shall also use devaluation and revaluation. In the contemporary "managed-float" system, it is not always clear when a depreciation (appreciation) is a devaluation (revaluation) because of the hidden role of governments in influencing exchange rates (see Chapter 19).

[10] Hence, Q–Q′ is the *deficit* in the official reserves transactions balance of the country's balance of payments (see Chapter 14).

CONTROLLED EXCHANGE RATES

Neither the fluctuating rate market nor the stabilized market imposes restrictions on private transactions in foreign exchange. A wide gulf separates these two markets from the controlled foreign exchange market, which prohibits private transactions not authorized by the control authority. The controlled exchange rate does not directly respond to shifts in supply and demand; government rationing supersedes the allocating function of the exchange rate and the currency becomes *inconvertible*. When exchange controls are relaxed, the job of maintaining stable exchange rates is passed on to stabilization agencies or their counterparts.

We shall examine the nature and the effects of exchange control in Chapter 17. At present we are interested only in the essential mechanism of exchange control—how it works in the foreign exchange market. To simplify our analysis, we assume a completely controlled market in which the control authority is the *exclusive* buyer from domestic residents and the *exclusive* seller of foreign exchange to domestic residents. All foreign exchange must be sold to the authority at its stipulated rate, and all foreign exchange must be bought from the authority at its stipulated rate. We further assume that there is only one rate of exchange, although in practice the control agency may charge a much higher rate than it pays for foreign exchange to earn a monopoly profit, or it may adopt several discriminatory rates.

The supply of foreign exchange is derived from the credit items of the balance of payments, and the control authorities have only a limited influence over it. To raise the supply of foreign exchange, steps must be taken to expand exports, encourage foreign loans, and the like. Many of these steps lie beyond the jurisdiction of the control agency. The agency, therefore, considers the supply of foreign exchange as relatively fixed with respect to its own powers, and its main task is the allocation of this fixed supply among those who demand it. This is usually done by an exchange or trade-licensing system—unless a domestic resident can obtain a license, foreign exchange cannot be secured. This rationing brings about a "suppressed disequilibrium" between supply and demand by forcibly choking off all excess demand.

The determination of the controlled rate of exchange is shown in Figure 12-6. If the market were free, the equilibrium rate of exchange would be ten pesos for one dollar where the supply and demand schedules intersect. At this equilibrium rate both the amount demanded and the amount supplied would be 0–E dollars. At the controlled rate of five pesos, however, the amount demanded (0–F) exceeds the amount supplied (0–G) by an amount of dollars (G–F); that is to say, the market is not cleared at the controlled rate. It follows that the control authority must suppress the excess demand (G–F) by issuing licenses only for the purchase of 0–G dollars; otherwise the authority will be unable to maintain the controlled rate.

Figure 12-6   The Controlled Rate of Exchange: Peso Country

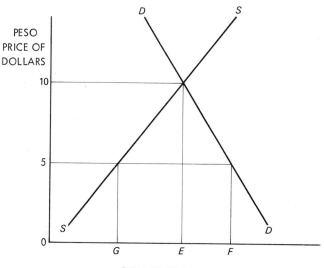

If the peso were freely convertible, the exchange rate would be 10 pesos. This is the *equilibrium* rate that clears the market. To control the rate at 5 pesos, the control authority (central bank) must suppress the excess demand (*G–F*) by issuing licenses to purchase only the amount of dollars supplied at the rate of 5 pesos (*0–G*). Exchange control substitutes a bureaucratic allocation of foreign exchange to buyers for an allocation determined by the free play of market forces.

We can draw the following conclusions from our analysis of the controlled rate of exchange: (1) The controlled rate is less than the equilibrium rate—the controlled rate overvalues the peso in terms of dollars; (2) the amount of dollars supplied to the market at the controlled rate is less than the amount supplied at the equilibrium rate (*0–G* compared with *0–E*)— the controlled rate discourages exports by making them more expensive to foreign buyers; (3) the market is not truly cleared—the excess demand (*G–F*) is not satisfied; and (4) the purchase of dollars at the controlled rate is smaller than the purchase at the equilibrium rate (*0–G* compared with *0–E*)— controlled market cuts imports below the level permitted by the free market.

EXCHANGE SPECULATION AND CAPITAL FLIGHT

In the previous pages we have covered many of the factors that determine exchange rates: the ordinary supply of and demand for foreign exchange, gold movements, the compensatory transactions of monetary authorities, and exchange controls. We now turn to a brief description and analysis of exchange speculation and capital flight, which may provoke violent disturbances in the rate of exchange.

Speculation Proper

Speculators purposely assume an open position in the foreign exchange market with the intent of making windfall profits from fluctuations in the rate of exchange. When speculators expect the exchange rate of a specific currency to rise in the near future, they go *long* on that currency by buying it. Conversely, when they expect the exchange rate of a currency to fall in the near future, they go *short,* either by selling the currency in the *forward* market for future delivery or by borrowing the currency on short term and then exchanging it for a currency they consider stable. When the expectations of speculators are not borne out, they suffer windfall losses. Curiously enough, however, if speculation in a currency is strong and one-sided, it may itself force the exchange rate to move in the anticipated direction.

By going long on a currency, speculators sustain its exchange rate—they increase demand and thus help ward off depreciation or even bring about appreciation. For this reason, monetary authorities, anxious to avert depreciation but not concerned about appreciation, tend to view long speculators with less distaste than short speculators.

Speculation may be *stabilizing* or *destabilizing*. Stabilizing speculation goes *against* the market. When the demand for a currency if falling (or its supply increasing), speculation helps to stabilize the exchange rate by going long and buying the currency. Conversely, when the exchange rate is rising, stabilizing speculation will retard the rise by going short and selling the currency. Stabilizing speculation was common under the gold standard before World War I, when everyone felt certain that the gold points would limit any movements in the exchange rate. Today, however, there is no such assurance, and speculation, by going *with* the market, may be destabilizing.

At times in the past, destabilizing speculation, coupled with capital flight, has swamped the ordinary transactions of the foreign exchange market and has plunged the exchange rate into a dizzy spiral of depreciation. When general confidence in the exchange rate of a currency is shaky, destabilizing speculation may become cumulative: Speculation provokes depreciation, and this in turn provokes further speculation. As was true of the German mark in the early 1920s and the Chinese yuan after World War II, this interaction may attain a truly fantastic velocity and bring about a rate of exchange that is below the true value of the currency even though domestic inflation may be running rampant.

Speculators believe that they can "outguess" the market; that is, they believe they can forecast exchange rates more accurately than market indicators such as forward exchange rates. Whether, in fact, speculators can do so is a question taken up in Chapter 13. Suffice it to say here that speculators commonly guess wrong, particularly in a floating-rate system. Since the onset of floating rates in 1973, banks in several countries have suffered massive foreign exchange losses, including the Franklin National Bank of New York (which was declared insolvent), the Herstatt Bank of West Germany (which was forced to close), the union Bank of Switzerland, and the Lloyds Bank of London.[11] Individual speculators have also been hurt badly by guessing wrong on the future behavior of foreign exchange rates.[12]

Capital Flight

Unlike speculation proper, *capital flight* is initiated not by the hope of gain but the fear of loss. When a country faces the prospect of exchange depreciation, the imposition of exchange controls, political instability, or war, domestic and foreign residents who own assets in that country seek safety by transferring funds to a country that is considered stable. The consequence may be a mass flight of capital that seriously weakens the currencies of some countries and brings unneeded foreign exchange and gold to other countries.

Speculative and flight capital movements inevitably occur when there is fear of exchange devaluation, exchange restrictions, or political instability. During the 1960s flows of speculative capital repeatedly threatened the stability of the pound sterling and the dollar. A massive flow of speculative capital out of the dollar in 1971 finally led to the abandonment of the gold convertibility of the dollar and a wholesale realignment of exchange rates, a subject which is taken up in Chapter 18.

SOME ADDITIONAL REMARKS ON THE DETERMINATION OF EXCHANGE RATES

In this chapter we have used a *balance of payments approach* to the determination of exchange rates: Exchange rates move to equilibrate the supply and demand of foreign exchange. As explained above, the supply of foreign exchange involves all credit transactions that appear in a country's balance of payments, and the demand for foreign exchange involves all debit transactions. But the different kinds of credit and debit transactions (current account, long-term capital account, short-term capital account, and official

---

[11] Franklin National's foreign exchange loss was nearly $50 million. See "What Really Went Wrong at Franklin National," *Fortune,* October 1974, pp. 118–227.

[12] A Mr. X lost $900,000 of his own money and was left owing another $1.8 million to five brokerage houses when the value of the Mexican peso dropped 40 percent within a few days in September 1976. Not too wisely, Mr. X was long on pesos: He had purchased forward pesos at predevaluation rates. See "No Mariachi Music, Please; Mr. X Isn't in a Fiesta Mood," *Wall Street Journal,* January 6, 1977, p. 1.

reserves account) do not all respond with the same speed to new economic (and political) circumstances. For that reason, we can draw a distinction between short- and long-run equilibrium in the foreign exchange market.

Flows of financial assets (including monies) that make up the short-term capital account and the official reserves account (when the monetary authorities seek to influence the exchange rate) respond quickly to international differences in interest rates and to shifting expectations of future exchange rates. Over the short run (say, up to six months), therefore, the supply and demand of foreign exchange are dominated by transfers of financial assets between the domestic and foreign countries. To explain the transfer mechanism, we must understand the forward exchange market, which is the subject of the next chapter.

In contrast to short-term financial assets, flows of goods, services, and investment capital respond more slowly to fundamental or real economic forces, such as changes in factor supply, economic growth (real income), technological innovation, productivity, and demand preferences. But these flows become the dominant influence on the long-run supply and demand of foreign exchange and, therefore, the long-run equilibrium rate of exchange.

The balance of payments approach to the determination of exchange rates is accepted by all economists. But economists may differ on the causal factors that lie behind the supply and demand of foreign exchange. Commonly, these differences relate to different emphases on short- and long-run equilibria in the foreign exchange market, but sometimes they also reflect basic theoretical disagreements. In Chapter 16 we shall take up alternative explanations of exchange rates. Our present task, however, is to complete our understanding of the balance of payments approach by looking at the flows of financial assets that determine short-run equilibrium in the foreign exchange market.

SUMMARY

1. The exchange rate is the domestic money price of foreign money. The domestic price of bank transfers is the base rate of exchange, and all other means of international payments usually sell at a discount from the base rate. Unless otherwise specified, we assume the exchange rate to be one rate, namely, the base rate. The behavior of the exchange rate will depend upon the nature of the foreign exchange market. We can distinguish three sorts of behavior: freely fluctuating rates, stable rates, and controlled rates.

2. Freely fluctuating rates result when the rate of exchange is free to respond to the movements of supply and demand. The rate of exchange is then determined by the intersection of the supply and demand sched-

ules, which in turn are determined by the credit and debit items of the balance of payments, respectively. The rate of exchange, however, also affects the balance of payments, and there is thus a mutual interdependence between them.

3. There are several arguments in favor of stable exchange rates. Under the gold standard, international gold movements prevent any variation in the exchange rate outside the narrow limits of the gold points. Exchange rates may also be stabilized by compensatory purchases and sales of foreign exchange on the part of government agencies.

4. Controlled rates result from the monopoly purchase and sale of foreign exchange by a government agency. The available foreign exchange is distributed by a rationing system, and because the controlled rate is maintained below the equilibrium rate, there is an excess demand that is not satisfied. The exchange rate is determined by bureaucratic decision rather than supply and demand.

5. Because foreign exchange is a store of value as well as an instrument of current payment, demand and supply schedules shift quickly in response to changes in expectations about the future behavior of economic variables.

6. Exchange speculation and capital flight also influence exchange rates. Because these short-term capital movements usually undermine the exchange rate and weaken the balance of payments, monetary authorities view them with marked distaste.

QUESTIONS AND APPLICATIONS

1. What is the base rate of exchange?
2. What are the three kinds of exchange rate behavior?
3. (a) How is the exchange rate determined when it is freely fluctuating?
   (b) Why, in Figure 12-1, does the demand schedule for foreign exchange slope downward form left to right?
   (c) Why, in Figure 12-2, does the supply schedule for foreign exchange slope upward from left to right?
4. Using graphs like those in this chapter, show the effects on the exchange rate of the following:
   (a) An increase in exports of merchandise.
   (b) An increase in domestic demand for foreign securities.
   (c) An increase in sale of domestic securities to foreigners.
   (d) A decrease in imports of services.
5. (a) What are the minimum conditions of an international gold standard?
   (b) Explain how the international gold standard prevents fluctuations of the exchange rate beyond the gold points.

6. What is the function of a stabilization agency? How does it perform this function?
7. Using a graph, show how exchange control determines the rate of exchange. Why is the market not cleared under exchange control?
8. (a) Distinguish between stabilizing and destabilizing speculation.
   (b) What is capital flight?

SELECTED READINGS

See the list of readings given at the end of Chapter 13.

13

Forward Exchange Speculation and Hedging Against Exchange Risks

This chapter continues our study of the foreign exchange market by analyzing the determination of forward exchange rates and the use of the forward market to protect against exchange risks. As we shall observe, transactions in the forward market also influence spot rates of foreign exchange.

THE FORWARD RATE OF EXCHANGE

The markets that we have previously analyzed deal in foreign exchange bought and sold for immediate delivery. Closely allied to these *spot* exchange markets are the *forward* exchange markets that deal not in foreign exchange but in promises to buy or sell foreign exchange at a specified rate and at a specified time in the future, with payment to be made upon delivery. These promises are known as *forward exchange,* and the price at which they are traded is the *forward rate of exchange.*[1]

The forward exchange market resembles the futures markets found in organized commodity exchanges, such as those for wheat and coffee. The primary function of any futures or forward market is to afford protection against the risk of price fluctuations. Forward exchange markets, therefore, are most useful when the rate of exchange is freely fluctuating and when there are significant exchange risks for those who are committed to make or receive international payments. When the rate of exchange is stabilized, forward exchange is most useful when there is a strong possibility that the exchange rate will be allowed to depreciate in the near future. Since the

---

[1] The forward rates for major international currencies on February 10 and February 13, 1989 are shown in Table 12-1.

forward exchange market must be free, it cannot function under exchange control.

Foreign exchange dealers commonly seek to balance their sales and purchases of forward exchange in a given currency to avoid the exchange risk, and they may refuse to enter forward contracts of long maturity because they cannot find an offsetting contract of equal maturity. At times, dealers may offset an open position in forward exchange with an opposing open position in spot exchange, a practice known as "swapping." At other times, dealers may function as professional risk bearers by deliberately assuming an open forward position in the expectation of making a speculative gain. Because of their own role as speculators, foreign exchange dealers are usually reluctant to enter forward contracts with individuals who want to speculate rather than protect themselves against an exchange risk.[2]

Two theories have been put forth to explain the determination of forward exchange rates: the traditional interest parity theory and the modern theory.

INTEREST PARITY THEORY

When short-term interest rates are higher in one national money market (say, London) than in another (say, New York), investors will be motivated to shift funds from New York to London. To do so, they must convert dollars into sterling for investment in London. But then they become exposed to an exchange risk: If the pound subsequently depreciates vis-à-vis the dollar, then when the investors convert from sterling back into dollars at the end of the investment period (maturity), they will experience an *exchange loss* that will offset, or more than offset, the gain in interest income. To avoid this possible exchange loss, therefore, dollar investors will *cover* against the exchange risk by selling sterling *forward* in an amount that fully equals their purchase of *spot* sterling plus the interest that will be earned in London. This practice is known as *interest arbitrage*. As we shall see, interest arbitrage establishes a link between the interest-rate differential of two national money markets and the forward rates of the respective currencies. This link is the basis of the interest parity theory.

---

[2] Although the traditional foreign exchange dealers (banks) continue to handle the bulk of forward exchange transactions, speculators have ample opportunities to trade in currency futures and options markets that have opened since the arrival of floating exchange rates in 1971, as described in Chapter 11. These markets appeal to the small investor who wants to speculate or to the small trader who wants to hedge against exchange risks. In contrast, the bank forward market deals primarily with the large transactions of banks, multinational companies, and big exporters and importers.

Algebraic Formulation of Interest Parity Theory

The interest parity theory is most easily explained algebraically. Let us assume that a U.S. investor has A dollars to invest in 90-day Treasury bills, either in New York or in London. If A dollars are invested in New York, the return (principal plus interest) at the end of 90 days will be

$$(1)\ A(1 + i_{US}/4),$$

where i_{US} is the annual interest rate on Treasury bills in New York. It is necessary to divide i by 4 because the maturity of the bills is 90 days, or one-fourth of a year.

Alternatively, if our investor buys A dollars worth of bills in London and covers against the exchange risk, the return at maturity will be

$$(2)\ (A/S)(1 + i_{UK}/4)F,$$

where S is the *spot* dollar-sterling rate of exchange (the dollar price of one pound sterling); i_{UK}, the interest rate in London; and F, the dollar-sterling forward rate of exchange (the dollar price of one pound sterling for delivery 90 days hence). The expression A/S is the amount of spot sterling that can be purchased with A dollars; the expression $(A/S)(1 + i_{UK}/4)$ is the amount of sterling the investor will receive at the end of 90 days; and the entire expression is the amount of dollars the investor will receive when the sterling amount is converted into dollars at the 90-days forward rate of exchange.

It is evident that if $A(1 + i_{US}) > (A/S)(1 + i_{UK})F$, then our investor will invest funds in New York, as will short-term investors in London. Hence, funds will move from London to New York. Conversely, if $A(1 + i_{US}) < (A/S)(1 + i_{UK})F$, then funds will move from New York to London. To illustrate, suppose that on a given day i_{US} is 6 percent, i_{UK} is 10 percent, the dollar-sterling exchange rate is $1.70, the rate on 90-day sterling is $1.65, and A is $100,000. In which market will our investor earn the highest return on Treasury bills, assuming that our investor covers the exchange risk in the forward market? Entering the appropriate values in equation (1), we have

$$\$100,000(1 + .06/4) = \$101,500.$$

Entering the appropriate values in equation (2), we have

$$(\$100,000/\$1.70)(1 + .10/4)\$1.65 = \$99,485.$$

Despite the higher interest rate in London, it is evident that our investor will place the funds in New York. If invested in London, the net interest gain (.04/4 or .01) would be more than offset by the loss on forward sterling. Under these conditions funds will move from London to New York.

The interest parity theory asserts the *interest arbitrage* will cause the forward rate to adjust to the interest rate differential until it reaches an equilibrium value at which it is no longer profitable to shift funds between the two money centers. In equilibrium, therefore,

$$(3) \ A(1 + i_{US}/4) = (A/S)(1 + i_{UK}/4)F^*,$$

where F^* is the equilibrium ("no-profit") forward exchange rate.

Solving equation (3) for F^*, we get

$$(4) \ F^* = \frac{S(1 + i_{US}/4)}{(1 + i_{UK}/4)}.$$

If we assume that i is adjusted for the length of the forward exchange contract, then equation (4) becomes

$$(5) \ F^* = \frac{S(1 + i_{US})}{(1 + i_{UK})}.$$

Transposing and subtracting 1 from both sides of equation (5), we get

$$(6) \ \frac{i_{US} - i_{UK}}{1 + i_{UK}} = \frac{F^* - S}{S}.$$

If i_{UK} is a small fraction (as it ordinarily is), then equation (6) can be approximated as

$$(7) \ i_{US} - i_{UK} = \frac{F^* - S}{S}.$$

This equation states that at interest parity, the interest rate differential between New York and London (the New York rate *minus* the London rate) is equal to the forward-spot rate differential (the forward rate *minus* the spot rate) as a percentage of the spot rate.[3] Solving equation (7) for F^*, we have

$$(8) \ F^* = S + S(i_{US} - i_{UK}).$$

Returning to our earlier example and assuming that the interest rates

---

[3] This equation is commonly used by arbitragers in practice.

and the spot rate are autonomous (do not change) with respect to interest arbitrage, what is the equilibrium forward rate of exchange? Entering the values into equation (8), we have

$$F^* = \$1.70 + \$1.70(.06/4 - .10/4) = \$1.683.$$

At this forward rate, the investor's rate of return in New York would equal the return in London *with* forward cover. This is true because the higher net interest rate in London for 90 days (1 percent) is exactly offset by the percentage discount on 90-day forward sterling (1 percent). The discount on forward sterling (\$1.683 - \$1.700, or -\$.017) may be expressed as an *implicit* interest rate, as shown on the right side of equation (7):

$$\frac{F^* - S}{S} = \frac{\$1.683 - \$1.70}{\$1.70} = -.01 = 1 \text{ percent discount.}$$

This is the implicit interest rate for 90-day forward sterling; hence, the annual rate is 4 percent, which equals the annual interest rate advantage of London over New York. In other words, the forward rate is at *interest parity*. As we showed above, our investor would end up with \$101,500 if the funds were invested in New York. If instead the funds were invested in London and covered against the exchange risk, the investor would receive at the end of 90 days the following *dollar* sum: (\$100,000/\$1.70)(1.025) × 1.6834 = \$101,500—exactly the same sum that would be received in New York.[4] Clearly, when the forward rate is at interest parity, investors in New York have no incentive to invest in London and investors in London have no incentive to invest in New York.

Graphic Demonstration of Interest Parity Theory

The interest parity theory is demonstrated graphically in Figure 13-1. The vertical axis measures the interest rate differential between New York and London. Above the origin the interest rate is higher in New York than in London; below the origin the interest rate is higher in London than in New York. The horizontal axis measures the implicit interest rate on forward sterling. To the right of the origin forward sterling sells at a premium over spot sterling; to the left of the origin it sells at a discount under spot sterling

---

[4] To obtain full arithmetic accuracy, we have calculated the equilibrium forward rate by using the mathematically correct equation derived from equation (6):

$$F^* = S + \frac{S(i_{US} - i_{UK})}{1 + i_{UK}},$$

which gives \$1.6834, as compared with \$1.683, which was derived from the approximate equation (8).

Figure 13-1   Interest Parity Theory: The Determination of the Forward Exchange Rate through Interest Arbitrage

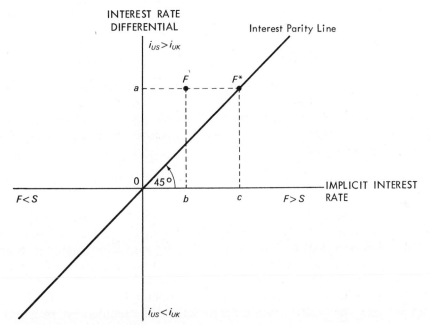

At every point on the interest parity line, the implicit interest rate on forward sterling ($F–S$) equals the interest rate differential ($i_{US} - i_{UK}$) between New York and London. According to the interest parity theory, the dollar-sterling forward rate will move to a point on the interest parity line. The forward rate F is in disequilibrium because the implicit premium interest rate on forward sterling (0–b) is less than the interest advantage of New York over London (0–a). Hence, funds will move from London to New York until a new equilibrium forward rate F^* makes the implicit premium interest rate on forward sterling (0–c) equal to New York's interest rate advantage (0–a).

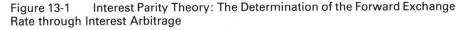

(as in our previous example). The interest parity line is drawn at a 45-degree angle to the origin (slope of 1) so that any point on it is equidistant from the two axes. According to the interest parity theory, the dollar-sterling forward rate will move to a point on the interest parity line at which the implicit interest rate equals the interest rate differential.

The forward rate F is in disequilibrium because 0–b (the implicit premium interest rate on forward sterling) is less than 0–a (the net interest advantage of New York over London). Hence, funds will move from London to New York as investors make an interest gain of 0–a and are able to cover the exchange risk by *buying* sterling forward (the same as *selling* dollars forward) at a premium over the spot rate that is less than their interest gain. Assuming that the interest differential is autonomous (constant), the purchase of forward sterling by interest arbitragers will raise its premium until the implicit interest reaches F^* on the interest parity line, where $0–c$ equals $0–a$. At any forward rate lying above the interest parity line, funds will move from London to New York; at any forward rate lying below the line, funds will move from New York to London.

Other Effects of Interest Arbitrage

Up to this point in our exposition of the interest parity theory, we have assumed that interest arbitrage brings about an adjustment of the forward rate to autonomous spot and interest rates. Actually, interest arbitrage will also affect those other variables. When, for example, funds move from New York to London because

$$(i_{US} - i_{UK}) < \frac{(F - S)}{S}$$

then: (1) the demand for spot sterling will push up the spot rate of exchange (S), (2) interest rates in New York (i_{US}) will rise as the supply of funds decreases, (3) interest rates in London (i_{UK}) will fall as the supply of funds increases, and (4) sales of forward sterling will lower the forward rate (F). All of these adjustments are equilibrating, helping to remove any discrepancy between the interest rate differential and the implicit interest rate.[5]

The Limitation of Interest Parity Theory

Does interest arbitrage *in practice* eliminate any discrepancy between interest rate differentials and implicit interest rates of forward exchange? The answer is no. The interest parity theory fails to explain fully the behavior of forward exchange rates because it ignores *speculation* in forward exchange. This omission is rectified by the modern theory of forward exchange that takes into account the actions of speculators and traders as well as arbitragers.

THE MODERN THEORY OF
FORWARD EXCHANGE

The modern theory of forward exchange postulates that the forward exchange rate is determined by the supply and demand schedules of arbitragers, traders, and speculators. To simplify our presentation we shall assume

---

[5] In terms of Figure 13-1, $0–a$ will decrease and thus the adjustment of F to F^* will be less than $b–c$.

that New York and London are the two money centers, the exchange rate is expressed as the dollar price of one pound sterling, and the interest rate differential and spot exchange rate are given (autonomous).

The Arbitragers' Schedule

Figure 13-2 depicts the arbitragers' schedule. The horizontal axis measures the quantity of forward sterling: sales to the left of the origin, purchases to the right of the origin. The vertical axis indicates the spot and forward rates of exchange.

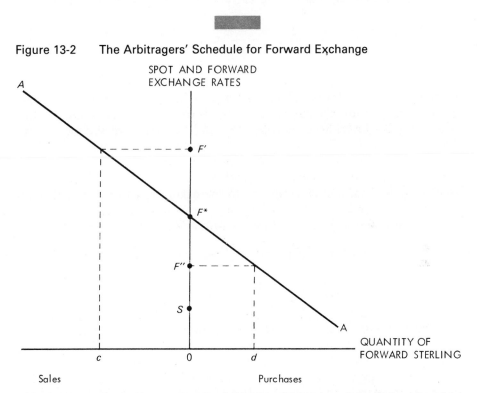

Figure 13-2   The Arbitragers' Schedule for Forward Exchange

The arbitragers' schedule indicates the sales (left of the origin) and purchases (right of the origin) of forward sterling that are undertaken by arbitragers at different spot and forward exchange rates. When the forward rate is at interest parity, then arbitragers neither buy nor sell forward sterling. This occurs at F^*, where the schedule crosses the vertical axis. Because this interest parity forward rate is above the spot rate (S), the interest rate differential favors New York. When the forward rate is at F' (above F^*), the percentage premium on forward sterling exceeds New York's interest advantage. Hence, arbitragers shift funds from New York to London, selling $0-c$ forward sterling to cover against the exchange risk. Conversely, at the forward rate of F'', arbitragers move funds from London to New York, buying $0-d$ forward sterling to cover against the exchange risk.

If the forward rate is at interest parity, then arbitragers will neither buy nor sell forward sterling. This is the point (F^*) where the schedule crosses the vertical axis. The fact that F^* lies above the spot rate (S) tells us that the interest rate differential favors New York. At the forward rate F' (above F^*), arbitragers will shift funds from New York to London, selling $0-c$ forward sterling. Recall equation (7):

$$i_{US} - i_{UK} = \frac{F^* - S}{S}.$$

With a given interest differential and spot rate, if $F' > F^* > S$, then

$$\frac{F' - S}{S} > \frac{F^* - S}{S} = i_{US} - i_{UK}.$$

Thus, at F' the percentage premium on forward sterling (implicit interest rate) exceeds the interest advantage of New York over London, providing arbitragers with an incentive to move funds from New York to London and cover with forward sales of sterling. At rate F'', arbitragers will move funds from London to New York, buying $0-d$ forward sterling to cover against the exchange risk. At that rate the premium on forward sterling is less than the interest rate advantage of New York over London. As the $A-A$ schedule shows, forward *sales* of sterling are an increasing function of the *absolute* difference $F-F^*$ when $F > F^*$. Conversely, forward *purchases* of sterling are an increasing function of the absolute difference $F-F^*$ when $F < F^*$.

The Traders' Schedule

A second actor in the forward market is the trader (exporter or importer of goods and services) who wants to hedge against an open position in foreign exchange. For example, a U.S. importer who must pay a certain amount of sterling in 90 days for imported goods is exposed to an exchange risk: If sterling appreciates in 90 days, more dollars must be paid for the goods than otherwise. Conversely, a U.S. exporter who will receive payment for goods in sterling 90 days hence is exposed to an exchange loss if sterling depreciates in that period. In the next section we shall look at the hedging options open to the trader to eliminate the exchange risk.[6] We shall also find that the traders' schedule takes the same form as the arbitragers' schedule. Therefore, we simply add the traders' schedule $(T-T)$ to the arbitragers' schedule $(A-A)$ to obtain a combined schedule $(AT-AT)$.

---

[6] If traders fail to hedge against the foreign exchange risk, then they become speculators in the spot market but do not influence the forward rate.

The Speculators' Schedule

The speculator deliberately assumes a foreign exchange risk in the expectation that future changes in the exchange rate will bring a profit. Speculation may be made in the spot or the forward market. However, deliberate speculation in the spot market requires either the purchase of a foreign currency with an immediate cash outlay (to go long) or the borrowing of a foreign currency with interest costs (to go short). In contrast, speculation in the forward market involves no cash outlay or interest cost beyond a small margin of 10 percent or less. Consequently, professional speculators choose to speculate in forward markets rather than in spot markets. Speculation in spot markets is mainly done by traders (including multinational enterprises) who fail to cover an existing foreign exchange exposure.

In our exposition of the speculators' schedule, we shall continue to use dollars and sterling. Then the speculator will *sell* sterling forward if the spot rate of sterling is expected to fall below the forward rate over the forward contract period. At the end of the contract period (say, 90 days) the speculator will buy sterling at the spot rate and sell it at the higher forward rate. Algebraically, the speculator will sell forward sterling if $E(S^t) < F$, where $E(S^t)$ is the speculator's expected spot rate at a future time t (which we take to be 90 days) and F is the price of forward sterling *now* for delivery at time t. If the speculator's expectation is realized by the market, then at time t the speculator's profit will be $A(F - S^t)$, where A is the amount of forward sterling the speculator originally sold. Assume, for example, that the current spot rate is \$1.75, $E(S^t)$ is \$1.65, and F for period t ($= 90$ days) is \$1.70. The speculator expects the spot sterling rate to fall below the forward rate in 90 days. Thus, the speculator decides to sell forward \$50,000 of sterling, which gives the speculator a commitment to sell £29,412 in 90 days at a rate of \$1.70. Ninety days pass and the spot rate indeed falls to \$1.65. Then the speculator buys £29,412 at the spot rate for \$48,530 (£29,412 $\times$ \$1.65) and sells those pounds for \$50,000 under the terms of the forward contract, making a profit of \$1,470. Of course, if the spot rate had remained above the forward rate, the speculator would have suffered a loss.

Conversely, if the speculator expects the spot rate to be above the forward rate at time t ($E(S^t) > F$), then A amount of forward sterling will be *bought*. If the expectation is realized, the profit will be $A(S^t - F)$ when the speculator buys sterling at the forward contract rate and sells it at the higher spot rate. On the other hand, if $S^t < F$, then $A(S^t - F)$ will be lost.

The speculators' schedule is depicted in Figure 13-3. If speculators expect that the spot rate of sterling at time t will equal the forward rate for period t, then they will neither sell nor buy forward sterling. This equality is at the point where the S–S schedule crosses the vertical axis. If, however, the forward rate is $F' > E(S^t)$, then speculators will sell 0–c pounds forward. The greater the positive gap $F' - E(S^t)$, the greater the sales of forward sterling by speculators. Conversely, if the forward rate is F'', speculators

Figure 13-3 The Speculators' Schedule for Forward Exchange

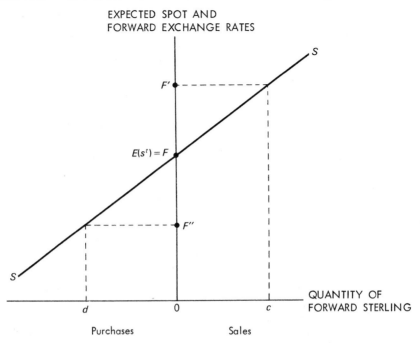

The speculators' schedule shows the amounts of forward sterling purchased and sold at various differences between the expected spot and forward exchange rates. At the intersection of *S–S* and the vertical axis, the spot rate expected to prevail at the end of the forward contract period is equal to the forward rate [$E(s^t) = F$]. Hence, speculators neither buy nor sell forward sterling. Speculators *buy* forward sterling when the forward rate is less than the expected spot rate [$F < E(S^t)$]. The greater this difference, the greater the purchases of forward sterling, as indicated by the positive slope of the schedule to the *left* of the point of intersection. Speculators *sell* forward sterling when the forward rate is higher than the expected spot rate [$F > E(S^t)$]. The greater this difference, the greater the sale of forward sterling. Accordingly, the schedule slopes upward to the *right* of the point of intersection.

will buy 0–*d* pounds forward. The greater the negative gap $F'' - E(S^t)$, the greater the purchases of forward sterling by speculators.[7]

The Determination of the Equilibrium Rate

The equilibrium rate of forward exchange is determined by the intersection of the *AT–AT* and *S–S* schedules, as shown in Figure 13-4. Since $F^* < S$,

---

[7] How much speculators are willing to risk depends not only on the size of the gap but also on their *confidence* in their expectations. The higher their confidence, the more speculators are willing to risk at a given gap (the more elastic is the *S–S* schedule), and conversely.

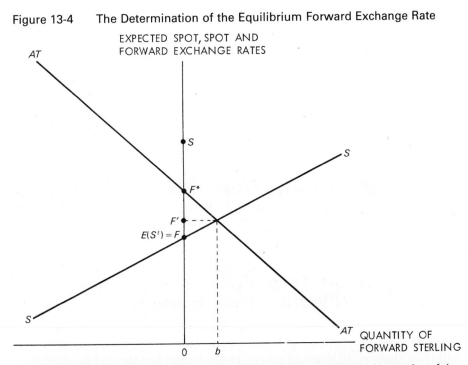

Figure 13-4   The Determination of the Equilibrium Forward Exchange Rate

The equilibrium rate of sterling forward exchange (F') is determined by the intersection of the arbitrager-trader schedule (AT–AT) and the speculator schedule (S–S). At F', arbitragers and traders want to *buy* 0–B of forward sterling while speculators want to *sell* 0–B of forward sterling. Hence, the market clears at F'. Because speculators expect a depreciation of the spot rate [from S to E(S')], the equilibrium rate F' lies below the interest parity rate F*, at which arbitragers and traders neither sell nor buy forward sterling. A shift in either schedule causes movement to a new equilibrium rate.

it follows that interest rates in London are higher than in New York. $E(S')$ lies below S, which indicates that speculators expect a sterling depreciation. The two schedules intersect to determine the equilibrium rate F'. At that rate arbitragers and traders will *buy* 0–b forward sterling while speculators will *sell* the same amount of forward sterling. Observe that the equilibrium rate (F') is below the interest parity rate (F^*) because of speculators' sales.

A shift in either schedule will bring about a new equilibrium rate. The AT–AT schedule will shift with changes in the spot rate and interest differential, because F^* would then change. The S–S schedule will shift with a change in speculators' expectations. For instance, if speculators become less bearish on the pound, then $E(S')$ will move closer to S; that is, the S–S schedule will shift upward to intersect AT–AT at a higher forward rate, since speculators will sell less forward sterling and thereby raise its price.

Finally, if $E(S^t) = F^*$, then there is no speculation and the forward rate is at interest parity.

FORECASTING EXCHANGE RATES

Although governments continue to influence exchange rates with compensatory financing, they no longer seek to maintain them at prescribed levels (par values). Hence, exchange rates are allowed to respond to market forces much more freely than in the past. The term "dirty float" is commonly used to describe this system.

The flexibility of exchange rates today has stimulated a strong interest in forecasting exchange rates and in hedging against exchange risks. International traders, lenders, speculators, multinational companies, and governments must all make decisions that are based in some measure on their expectations of future exchange rates.

Short-Term Forecasting in a Floating-Rate System

When exchange rates are free to respond immediately to market forces, they are subject to expectations and speculation. Rates are formed in anticipation of *future* supply and demand rather than present supply and demand.

Are *forward* rates of exchange good forecasters of floating *spot* rates of exchange? The answer is no. Forward rates commonly diverge from future spot rates.

Can speculators do consistently better than the forward market in forecasting exchange rates? Most economists would say no, because they believe the foreign exchange market is an *efficient market.*

A market is strongly efficient if (1) prices immediately reflect all information, and (2) all information is public (that is, there are no traders with private "inside" information). In such a market, prices respond to the random arrival of new information, and therefore they are unpredictable. A forecaster who is trying to outsmart the market is confronted with a fatal obstacle to any systematic analysis: There is no *time lag* between the appearance of disequilibrating economic forces (such as interest rates, prices, money supply, and strikes) and adjustments in the exchange rate. A competitive, informed market immediately reflects all relevant information in the behavior of the exchange rate. Paradoxically, a forecaster who was consistently successful would be copied by others, who would then make the forecasted rate the actual market rate, thereby preventing the initial forecaster from any longer outguessing the market! In brief, the purely floating exchange rate describes a "random walk" in the same way as stock market prices. In such a market the forecaster is not likely to do any better consistently than the forward market and may do worse. Only *systematic* government intervention in the market can make short-term forecasting a successful enterprise.[8]

Although the market efficiency hypothesis has not been conclusively demonstrated, no one has found a reliable approach to forecasting exchange rates over the short run. It is for this reason that international firms are inclined to hedge against exchange risks, an activity described in the next section.

Long-Term Forecasting: The Purchasing-Power Parity Doctrine

Although forecasting exchange rates in the short term is a dubious enterprise, it is possible to forecast *long-term* changes in exchange rates with more confidence. Over a period of three to five years, the external value of a currency *tends* to reflect changes in its purchasing power relative to the purchasing power of other currencies, a relationship known as *purchasing-power parity*.

The purchasing-power parity doctrine is most easily explained with a few equations. Let us assume we are talking about the United States and Argentina. According to the doctrine, a relative change in the price levels of the two countries caused by different rates of inflation will bring about the same relative change in the external values of the U.S. dollar and Argentine peso as expressed by the exchange rate linking the two currencies:

$$(9) \quad \frac{P_{t,us}/P_{t,arg}}{P_{0,us}/P_{0,arg}} = \frac{S_t}{S_0},$$

where P is the price level in the United States (subscript us) and in Argentina (subscript arg) at time t or at a previous time 0, and S is the U.S. dollar price of the Argentine peso at time t or at time 0.

Using indexes to express price levels, suppose $P_{t,us} = 125$, $P_{t,arg} = 200$, both $P_{0,us}$ and $P_{0,arg} = 100$, and $S_0 = \$.10$.[9] What, then, is S_t? Using equation (9), we find that $S_t = \$.0625$.

---

[8] See Laurent L. Jacque, "Management of Foreign Exchange Risk: A Review Article," *Journal of International Business Studies*, Spring-Summer 1981, p. 87. When governments adhere to an agreed set of rules in managing exchange rates, such as devaluation in the face of a persistent deficit, forecasting exchange rates is comparatively straightforward and likely to be successful. Generally this was the situation with the industrial countries under the Bretton Woods international monetary system, which collapsed in 1971. Moreover, the downside risk of actions taken on the basis of forecasts was limited: Either the exchange rate decreased as expected or the government held it stable.

[9] National price levels are a composite of many individual prices:

$$P_{US} = \sum_{i=1}^{i=n} P_i Q_i,$$

The purchasing-power parity doctrine can also be formulated in terms of inflation rates. Let $r_{t,us}$ be the rate of inflation in the United States over the period t, and $r_{t,arg}$ the rate of inflation in Argentina over the same period. Then, $P_{t,us} = P_{0,us}(1 + r_{t,us})$ and $P_{t,arg} = P_{0,arg}(1 + r_{t,arg})$. Substituting these expressions in equation (1), we obtain

$$(10) \quad \frac{1 + r_{t,us}}{1 + r_{t,arg}} = \frac{S_t}{S_0}.$$

Suppose $r_{t,us} = 25$ percent, $r_{t,arg} = 100$ percent, and $S_0 = $ U.S. \$.10. Then using equation (10), we find that $S_t = \$.0625$. This is the answer we got with equation (9) when using the same data expressed in terms of price levels.

Economists have raised several objections against the purchasing-power parity doctrine on both theoretical and empirical grounds. The principal theoretical objection to the doctrine lies in its inadequate coverage of the transactions that determine the rate of exchange. Only the price levels of goods are used to determine purchasing-power parities, whereas exchange rates are determined by capital transactions as well as goods transactions. On empirical grounds, the most serious objection is the question of the appropriate price indexes. To use the price indexes of export and import goods is almost a tautology: The relative price parities of homogeneous traded goods *should* be close to the actual exchange rate. Some economists also reject the use of wholesale price indexes because they may be heavily weighted with traded goods. The ideal index would be one based on the same assortment of goods in both countries, but governments do not compile such indexes. Pragmatically, the cost-of-living index would appear to be the most appropriate one to use in applying the purchasing-power parity doctrine. Other objections point to conditions that would create disparities between the purchasing-power parity exchange rate and the actual exchange rate over the short run, such as restrictions, the lagged response of officials in adjusting to payment disequilibria, the influence of exchange rate variations on the price level, and speculation.

Most critics of the purchasing-power parity doctrine do not reject it outright. It is widely accepted that in periods of rapid inflation the single most important determinant of change in exchange rates is the relative shift in the purchasing power of national currencies. Empirical studies have confirmed the usefulness of the doctrine to explain longer-term changes in exchange rates during periods of inflation. Table 13-1 shows the application of the doctrine to the dollar-cruzeiro exchange rate during a period when

---

where P_i is the price of an individual good and Q_i is the quantity purchased expressed as a fraction of the total quantity purchased of all goods. This weighted price average is converted into an index number to measure changes over time.

TABLE 13-1   Comparison of the Purchasing-Power Parity Dollar-Cruzeiro Exchange Rate with the Actual Exchange Rate over the Period 1970–1975

	1970	1971	1972	1973	1974	1975
U.S. cost-of-living index	100	104.3	107.7	114.4	127.0	138.5
Brazilian cost-of-living index	100	120	140	158	210	260
Purchasing-power parity exchange rate (dollars)	.202	.176	.155	.146	.122	.108
Actual exchange rate (dollars)	.202	.177	.161	.161	.134	.110

Source: International Monetary Fund, *International Financial Statistics* (Washington, D.C.: various monthly issues).

Brazil experienced a high rate of inflation and made frequent devaluations of its currency.

Over the period as a whole, the U.S. price level rose 38.5 percent, while the Brazilian price level rose 160 percent. According to the purchasing-power parity doctrine, the exchange rate should fall from $.202 in 1970 to $.108 in 1975. The actual exchange rate in 1975 was $.110. This is a very close fit; the discrepancy as a percentage of the actual rate is less than 2 percent. Even on an annual basis the fit is close: The greatest discrepancy (1973) is 9.3 percent.

To conclude, the purchasing-power parity doctrine is a good method to forecast exchange rates when changes in price levels are of a substantial magnitude. (Keep in mind, however, that the analyst must be able to forecast successfully the rates of inflation in the two countries.) Forecasts of long-term trends in a nation's exchange rate may be critical for international business decisions with long-time horizons, such as the country location of industrial plants. But parities cannot help businessmen forecast the exchange rate of a currency three or six months from now (the time horizon of most international payments) or one year from now (the time horizon for budgetary planning in the transnational corporation). In the short run, exchange rates may diverge considerably from purchasing-power parities because they are dominated by short-term interest rates and price expectations. Also, it takes time for the demand and supply of foreign exchange to adjust to inflation. Indeed, it is this lag that makes purchasing-power parities useful for forecasting: Inflation rates become "leading indicators" of future exchange rates.

HEDGING AGAINST FOREIGN EXCHANGE RISKS

Hedging is the procedure of balancing sales and purchases of an asset so there is no net open position on the market. If the hedge is perfect, the trader is protected against the risk of adverse changes in the price of the asset. In this section we examine the hedging of traders against foreign exchange risks originating in international *transactions* and the hedging of multinational companies against exchange risks originating in the *translation* of foreign currency balance sheets into dollar balance sheets. As we have demonstrated, the hedging transactions of international traders, along with the transactions of arbitragers, interact with speculators' transactions to determine the forward rate of exchange.

Hedging against Transaction Risks

Sales contracts between international traders ordinarily call for payment at a specified future time (for example, 60 days after sight) in either the exporter's or the importer's currency. It follows that the party to whom the currency of payment is foreign is exposed to an exchange risk; that is, the amount of payment or receipt in domestic currency is subject to variations in the exchange rate between the domestic and foreign currencies. This is a *transaction* risk that arises from the international sale and purchase of goods and services.

Unless traders are willing to speculate in foreign exchange (usually they are not when, as at present, exchange rates are floating), they will eliminate the exchange risk by hedging. They may hedge in the forward exchange market or in the related foreign exchange futures and options markets. Or they may hedge through the spot exchange and money markets (borrower arbitrage). Here we examine hedging in the forward market and through borrower arbitrage.

Hedging in the Forward Market Suppose a U.S. exporter sells merchandise to a British importer for £10,000 payable in 60 days. The exporter is exposed to a transaction exchange risk: If the pound depreciates over the next 60 days, the exporter will receive fewer dollars. To hedge against this risk, the exporter proceeds as follows. Assuming the exporter wants a *dollar* payment of $17,500 for the merchandise, the exporter calculates the *sterling* value of that amount at the 60-day rate on forward sterling, which we take to be $1.75 ($17,500/$1.75 = £10,000). When the sales contract with the British importer is signed, the exporter *immediately sells* £10,000 forward for 60 days at $1.75. If at the end of 60 days the spot sterling rate has fallen below $1.75, the exporter is fully protected because the exporter can sell the £10,000 received from the importer for $17,500 under the forward contract, which is the dollar amount wanted by the exporter for the merchandise.

Similarly, an American importer who must pay a certain amount of sterling in 60 days to a British exporter will *immediately buy* 60-day forward sterling for that same amount. At the end of 60 days the importer will pay for the goods with sterling purchased at the forward rate under the forward contract. By using the forward market to hedge, both the exporter and the importer have transformed an *uncertain* dollar amount into a *certain* dollar amount.

Hedging through the Spot Exchange and Money Markets: Borrower Arbitrage   A second hedging option for the U.S. exporter would be to borrow the present value of £10,000 in London for 60 days, immediately convert the sterling into dollars at the spot exchange rate, and then lend the funds in New York.[10] At the end of 60 days the exporter would repay the sterling loan (including interest) with the sterling received from the British importer and keep the following dollar amount:

$$\left(\frac{A}{1 + i_{UK}}\right) S(1 + i_{US}),$$

where A is the sterling amount due the exporter in 60 days (£10,000 in our example),

$$\frac{A}{1 + i_{UK}}$$

is the amount of sterling borrowed in London (the present value of A), S is the dollar-sterling spot exchange rate, and i_{UK} and i_{US} are respectively the London and New York interest rates adjusted to the 60-day period. If $S = \$1.80$, the annual $i_{UK} = .12$, and the annual $i_{US} = .09$, the exporter would end up with the following dollar amount at the end of 60 days:

$$\left(\frac{£10,000}{1 + .12/6}\right) \$1.80(1 + .09/6) = \$17,911.77.$$

In this example, the exporter would choose to hedge through the spot and money markets because only $17,500 would be received if the hedging had taken place in the forward market.

   More generally, the exporter would be indifferent as to the hedging option chosen if

$$(11)\ FA = \left(\frac{A}{1 + i_{UK}}\right) S(1 + i_{US}),$$

_____
   [10] The dollar funds could be kept in the exporter's business rather than lending them. We assume the cost of those funds kept is the interest foregone by not lending them.

where the left side of the equation indicates the dollar receipts from forward hedging (the forward rate *times* the amount of sterling sold forward) and the right side represents the dollar receipts from hedging through the spot and money markets.

Solving equation (11) for F, we get

$$(12)\ F = \frac{S(1 + i_{US})}{1 + i_{UK}}.$$

This equation is the same as equation (5), which defined the interest parity forward exchange rate. We can say, therefore, that when the exporter hedges through the spot and money markets, the exporter is behaving as an interest *arbitrager*.[11] If

$$FA > \frac{A}{1 + i_{UK}}\ S(1 + i_{US}),$$

then the exporter will hedge in the forward market and conversely.

Equation (11) also applies to the importer who is hedging against a sterling payment due in, say, 60 days. Instead of using the forward market, the importer can hedge as an arbitrager by borrowing in New York an amount of dollars that when converted into sterling at the spot rate and invested for 60 days in London would give the importer an amount equal to the sterling debt. But in the case of the importer we are talking of *payments* rather than *receipts*, as was true of the exporter. Thus, if

$$FA > \frac{A}{1 + i_{UK}}S(1 + i_{US}),$$

the importer will hedge as an arbitrager. Table 13-2 summarizes the hedging options of the exporter and importer.

Hedging against Translation Risks

In addition to the transactions risk they encounter as international traders, multinational enterprises with foreign subsidiaries are exposed to a foreign exchange *translation* risk because they are required to consolidate in a prescribed way the local-currency income and balance sheets of their subsidiaries with their own corporate statements.[12] Hence, they must "trans-

---

[11] More precisely, the exporter is a *borrower* arbitrager (who borrows funds in one money market to transfer to another money market) rather than an *owner* arbitrager (who invests personal funds, as in our discussion of the arbitragers' schedule). Because equations (12) and (5) are the same, we added the arbitragers' and traders' schedules to get a combined schedule in our earlier presentation of the modern theory of forward exchange. The hedging actions of traders will push the forward rate toward interest parity.

[12] See Chapter 22 for a description of multinational enterprises.

TABLE 13-2   Hedging Options of Exporters and Importers

	$FA > \dfrac{A}{1 + i_{UK}} S(1 + i_{US})$	$FA < \dfrac{A}{1 + i_{UK}} S(1 + i_{US})$
Exporter	Sells forward	Borrows in London Lends in New York
Importer	Borrows in New York Lends in London	Buys forward

late" financial statements expressed in a foreign currency into statements expressed in their home currency. Multinational corporations headquartered in different countries must conform to the accounting standards of each home country: French multinationals to French accounting rules, British multinationals to British accounting rules, and so on. In this section we shall discuss only the translation risk facing U.S. multinationals who keep their corporate accounts in dollars.

U.S. accounting rules (which became effective December 15, 1982) require U.S. companies to translate the local-currency balance sheets of their foreign subsidiaries at the exchange rate prevailing on the closing date and to translate local-currency income statements at the average rate for the period.[13] To simplify our presentation, we shall look only at the consolidation of balance sheets.

To illustrate the effects of these translation rules, Table 13-3 depicts the simplified balance sheet of the subsidiary in country X of a U.S. multinational company. To focus only on translation risk, we assume that the subsidiary has no assets or liabilities payable in foreign (nonlocal) currencies. Hence, it has no exposure to transaction risk, and the *local-currency* balance sheet will remain unaffected by variations in the exchange rate. Now suppose that the dollar price of country X's currency (francs) has depreciated 20 percent during the current quarter: On the last day of the preceding quarter, it was $.10; on the last day of the current quarter, it is $.08.

The first column of Table 13-3 shows the local-currency balance sheet of the subsidiary; the second column, the balance sheet translated into dollars at the *old* exchange rate according to U.S. accounting rules; and the

---

[13] This *current-rate* rule of the U.S. Financial Accounting Standards Board is entitled FASB 52. It replaces FASB 8, which required U.S. companies to translate the *monetary* assets and liabilities of their foreign subsidiaries at the current rates and the other items in the balance sheet (inventory and fixed assets) at historic rates in effect when the item was first added to the balance sheet.

TABLE 13-3   Effect of Local-Currency Depreciation on Dollar Translation of the Balance Sheet of a U.S. Company's Foreign Subsidiary in Country X

Balance Sheet Items	In Francs	In Dollars at Old Exchange Rate (1 franc = $.10)	In Dollars at New Exchange Rate (1 franc = $.08)
Assets			
Cash	100	10	8
Accounts receivable	200	20	16
Inventory	150	15	12
Fixed assets	500	50	40
Total assets	950	95	76
Liabilities and equity			
Accounts payable	50	5	4
Long-term liabilities	100	10	8
Owner's equity*	800	80	64
Total liabilities and equity	950	95	76
Translation gain or loss			− 16

*Residual item.

third column, the balance sheet translated into dollars at the *new* end-of-period exchange rate, as required by the rules. Observe that the U.S. company has incurred a translation *loss* of $16 that has reduced its equity from $80 to $64. Keep in mind that it is an *accounting* loss, not a *cash* loss.

Because of the accounting rules, the net exposure of a U.S. company to translation risk is $E = A - L$, where E is net exposure, A is assets, and L is liabilities. If local-currency $A > L$, then the U.S. parent company will experience a translation *loss* when the subsidiary's currency depreciates vis-à-vis the dollar, and conversely. In Table 13-3 the net exposure is $A - L = F950 - F150 = F800$. With this net exposure, the U.S. company incurred a translation loss when the franc depreciated $-.20(F800)($.10) = $16.

Translation gains and losses can be substantial. Thus, multinational managers sometimes have a strong incentive to eliminate or limit translation risk. Multinational companies can eliminate or limit translation risk by adjusting the balance sheets of foreign subsidiaries, by hedging in the forward market, and in other ways.[14]

---

[14] Readers interested in the hedging practices of multinational companies are referred to a basic text in international finance, such as David K. Eiteman and Arthur I. Stonehill, *Multinational Business Finance*, 4th ed. (Reading, Mass.: Addison-Wesley, 1988).

Adjusting the Foreign Subsidiary's Balance Sheet A multinational enterprise can lower its *exposure* to translation risk by adjusting the asset/liability ratio of a foreign subsidiary. Under present accounting rules (FASB 52), a U.S. company can reduce its translation exposure by decreasing local-currency assets or increasing local-currency liabilities so as to reduce owner's equity. The subsidiary depicted in Table 13-3 has a net exposure of F800 (F950 − F150). By decreasing its assets to, say, F700, the U.S. parent company could reduce net translation exposure to F550. However, apart from the direct costs of adjustment (higher interest costs for local borrowing, for instance), altering the asset/liability ratio to a substantial degree may cripple the operations of the subsidiary. Balance sheet adjustment, therefore, can reduce, but not eliminate entirely, the net translation exposure.

The multinational company may try to adjust a foreign subsidiary's balance sheet not to reduce translation exposure but rather to maximize translation gains and minimize translation losses. This is speculation, not hedging. The general approach is shown in Table 13-4. The successful application of this approach depends on correct forecasts of the *direction* of movements in the foreign exchange rate.

Hedging in the Forward Exchange Market To take care of any remaining translation risk after balance sheet adjustments, the multinational company can hedge in the forward market. Suppose, for example, a U.S. company has a translation exposure of £1 million $(A - L)$ in its British subsidiary and wants to protect itself against an expected sterling depreciation over the next quarter. We assume that the current spot rate of exchange (S) is $2.00, the 90-day forward rate is $1.90, and the company expects the spot rate in 90 days $[E(S^{90})]$ to be $1.80. Then the company sells forward £1 million for $1,900,000. If at the end of the quarter the spot rate has indeed fallen to $1.80 as expected, the company will suffer a translation loss of $200,000. But it will make $100,000 in the forward market by buying

TABLE 13-4   General Approach to Increase Translation Gains and Minimize Translation Losses through Balance Sheet Adjustments of Foreign Subsidiaries

	Assets of Foreign Subsidiary	Liabilities of Foreign Subsidiary
Strong local currency*	Increase	Decrease
Weak local currency*	Decrease	Increase

*Relative to the dollar.

£1 million in the spot market for $1,800,000 and selling it for $1,900,000 under the forward contract. Hence it has suffered a net loss of $100,000.

This example demonstrates that even when the multinational company correctly forecasts an exchange rate, it can have a net translation loss if it hedges only an amount equal to the translation exposure. In this instance the company would have to sell £2 million forward to fully offset its translation loss. A second point is that the company is behaving like a speculator: It can only make a forward profit if the spot rate at the end of the quarter is less than the forward rate ($S^{90} < F$). Otherwise it will make no profit or will even incur a loss.

More generally, a company's translation gain or loss is $E(S^0 - S^t)$, where E is the net translation exposure, S^0 is the spot exchange rate at the beginning of the quarter, and S^t is the spot exchange rate at the end of the quarter. A company's speculative gain or loss on the forward market is $A(F - S^t)$, where A is the amount hedged and F is the appropriate forward rate. Consequently, a hedge against translation risk will be perfect only when

$$(13)\ A\,(F\ -\ S^t)\ =\ E(S^0\ -\ S^t).$$

To make a perfect hedge, therefore, a company must correctly forecast the end-of-period exchange rate. If its forecast is incorrect, it will make a speculative gain or loss or break even on its forward contract. In other words, to make a perfect hedge against translation risk, a company must become a speculator successful in outguessing the market.

The substantial cash losses some multinational companies have experienced in attempting perfect hedges against expected translation losses have persuaded multinational managers to use a "loss minimizing" hedge that limits translation loss but does not eliminate it. Loss minimization requires that the amount hedged in the forward market *equals* the net translation exposure. Using equation (13), we can obtain the net hedging loss (H):

$$(14)\ H\ =\ E(S^0\ -\ S^t)\ -\ A\,(F\ -\ S^t).$$

By hedging on the forward market an amount equal to the translation exposure ($A\ =\ E$), equation (14) becomes

$$(15)\ H^*\ =\ E(S^0\ -\ S^t)\ -\ E(F\ -\ S^t)$$
$$=\ E(S^0\ -\ F),$$

where H^* is the loss-minimizing net hedging loss. Observe that H^* does not depend on the future exchange rate but on the difference between the current spot and forward rates, both of which are known to managers. The percentage cost of this hedge is

$$\frac{S^0 - F}{S^0},$$

which is the percentage discount on forward sterling for the period in question.

Returning to our earlier example, the company limited its translation loss to $100,000 by hedging an amount in the forward market equal to its translation exposure. The percentage cost of this protection is

$$\frac{\$2.00 - \$1.90}{\$2.00},$$

or 5 percent for 90 days. The company has replaced an uncertain translation loss with a certain loss of $100,000.

The cost of a risk-minimizing hedge has persuaded multinational managers to follow a *selective* hedging policy based on their expectations of future exchange rates. At times, therefore, they will remain deliberately exposed to a translation risk. The success of a selective policy is dependent on success in forecasting exchange rates.[15]

SUMMARY

1. Promises to buy or sell foreign exchange at a specified rate and at a specified time in the future with payment to be made upon delivery are known as forward exchange. The domestic currency price of forward exchange is the forward exchange rate.

2. Two theories have been put forth to explain the determination of forward exchange rates: the traditional interest parity theory and the modern theory. The former asserts that interest arbitrage will cause the forward rate of exchange to adjust to the interest rate differential until it reaches an equilibrium value at which it is no longer profitable to shift funds between the two money centers. In equilibrium, $F^* = S + S(i_{US} - i_{UK})$.

3. In addition to acting directly on the forward rate, interest arbitrage will also bring about adjustments in spot and interest rates that will help remove any discrepancy between the interest rate differential and the implicit interest rate.

4. The neglect by the interest parity theory of the influence of speculators

---

[15] We cannot take up here the question of whether translation risks *should* guide management decisions respecting foreign subsidiaries. Suffice it to say that a local-currency depreciation (or appreciation) will affect the cash flows and true economic value of a subsidiary in ways that have nothing to do with translation risk. See Chapter 16 for an analysis of the effects of exchange rate variations on a country's exports and imports.

on the forward rate is rectified by the modern theory of forward exchange, which takes into account the behavior of speculators (and traders) as well as arbitragers. The equilibrium rate of forward exchange is determined by the intersection of the *AT–AT* and *S–S* schedules. When there is speculative buying or selling, the equilibrium forward rate will diverge from the interest parity rate.

5. Although the market efficiency hypothesis has not been conclusively demonstrated for the foreign exchange market, no one has found a reliable approach to forecasting exchange rates over the short term. However, over the long term (three to five years), the external value of a currency tends to reflect changes in its purchasing power relative to the purchasing power of other currencies, a relationship known as purchasing-power parity.

6. Hedging is the balancing of sales and purchases of an asset so there is no net open position on the market. International traders hedge against transaction foreign exchange risk. Multinational companies with foreign subsidiaries hedge against translation foreign exchange risk.

7. International traders may hedge in (1) the forward exchange market and the related futures and options markets, or (2) through borrower arbitrage. When the forward exchange rate is at interest parity, traders are indifferent between (1) and (2). Thus, the trader who hedges is behaving as an interest arbitrager.

8. Multinational companies are exposed to a translation risk because they must "translate" the financial statements of their foreign subsidiaries expressed in local currencies into corporate statements expressed in dollars. They may limit translation risk (1) by adjusting subsidiaries' balance sheet items or (2) by hedging in the forward exchange market. To avoid speculative losses in the forward market, multinational managers may use a "loss-minimizing" hedge that limits but does not try to eliminate the translation risk.

QUESTIONS AND APPLICATIONS

1. **(a)** How does forward exchange differ from spot exchange?
   (b) What is the primary function of the forward market?
2. **(a)** Define interest arbitrage.
   (b) If $A(1 + i_{US}) > A/S(1 + i_{UK})F$, will the investor place funds in New York or in London? Why?
3. **(a)** What is the interest parity theory?
   (b) Explain the meaning of the following equation:

$$i_{US} - i_{UK} = \frac{F^* - S}{S}.$$

(c) Suppose $i_{US} = .10$ (annually), $i_{UK} = .14$ (annually), and $S = \$1.75$. What is the interest parity rate for 90-day forward sterling? Is it at a discount or a premium?

4. (a) Why is the forward rate at point F in Figure 13-1 in disequilibrium?

(b) Why is a forward rate lying below the horizontal axis to the left of the interest parity line in Figure 13-1 in disequilibrium?

5. Why may interest arbitrage fail to achieve interest parity in the forward rate?

6. (a) How does the modern theory explain the determination of forward exchange rates?

(b) In Figure 13-2, F^* lies above S. What does this tell us about the interest rate differential? Why?

7. (a) How does the speculator differ from the interest arbitrager?

(b) If $E(S^t) < F$, what will the speculator do? Why?

(c) Under which conditions will the speculator make a profit? A loss?

8. Reproduce Figure 13-4. Show what happens to the equilibrium forward exchange rate when the S–S schedule shifts downward. What would cause such a shift?

9. If the foreign exchange market is "efficient," why is successful short-run forecasting of the exchange rate impossible?

10. If 1900 Brazilian cruzeiros exchange for one dollar today, and the U.S. annual inflation rate is 5 percent while the Brazilian annual inflation rate is 80 percent, then what will be the purchasing-power parity rate of exchange a year from now?

11. (a) What are the hedging options of the international trader against a transaction foreign exchange risk?

(b) If

$$FA < \frac{A}{1 + i_{UK}} S(1 + i_{US}),$$

which hedging option will an importer choose? Why?

12. (a) What is the net exposure of a U.S. company to translation risk?

(b) How may a multinational company hedge its translation risk?

(c) What is the requirement for a "loss-minimizing" hedge? Why?

SELECTED READINGS

Grabbe, J. Orlin, *International Financial Markets*. New York: Elsevier, 1986. Chapters 3, 7, and 8.

Hardouvelis, Gikas A. "Economic News, Exchange Rates, and Interest Rates." *Journal of International Money and Finance* (1988): 23–35.

Isard, Peter. "Lessons from Empirical Models of Exchange Rates." *Staff Papers* (International Monetary Fund), March 1987, pp. 1–28.

Jacque, Laurent L. "Management of Foreign Exchange Risk." *Journal of International Business Studies,* Spring-Summer 1981, pp. 81–101.

Koedijk, Kees G., and Mack Ott. "Risk Aversion, Efficient Markets and the Forward Exchange Rate." *Review* (Federal Reserve Bank of St. Louis), December 1987, pp. 5–13.

Levich, Richard M. "Are Forward Exchange Rates Unbiased Predictors of Future Spot Rates?" *Columbia Journal of International Business,* Winter 1979, pp. 49–61.

McKinnon, Ronald I. *Money in International Exchange.* New York: Oxford University Press, 1979. Chapter 6.

Officer, Lawrence H. "The Purchasing-Power Parity Theory of Exchange Rates: A Review Article." *International Monetary Fund Staff Papers* 23 (March 1976): 1–60.

Stokes, Houston H., and Hugh Neuburger. "Interest Arbitrage, Forward Speculation, and the Determination of the Forward Exchange Rate." *Columbia Journal of International Business,* Winter 1979, pp. 86–98.

Westerfield, Janice M. "How U.S. Multinationals Manage Currency Risk." *Business Review* (Federal Reserve Bank of Philadelphia), March-April 1980, pp. 19–27.

Wilson, Peter. *International Economics, Theory, Evidence and Practice.* Lincoln, Nebr.: University of Nebraska Press, 1986. Chapter 14.

14

The Balance of International Payments

During the course of a year the residents of one country engage in a vast number and variety of transactions with residents of other countries—exports and imports of merchandise and services, cash payments and receipts, gold flows, gifts, loans and investments, and other transactions. These transactions are interrelated in many ways, and together they comprise the international trade and payments of the national economy. Before we can analyze and evaluate a nation's international transactions, however, they must be classified and aggregated to make a balance of payments.

As a statistical classification and summary of all economic transactions between domestic and foreign residents over a stipulated period (ordinarily one year), the *balance of payments* of a nation affords an overall view of its international economic position. For this reason, the balance of payments is particularly helpful to government authorities—treasuries, central banks, and stabilization agencies—who are directly charged with the responsibility of maintaining external economic stability. Moreover, international trade is so important to many countries that the balance of payments must be carefully considered in the formulation of domestic economic policies, such as employment, wage, and investment policies.

The balance of payments of a country may also influence the decisions of business people. The experienced international trader or investor does not overlook the intimate bearing of the balance of payments upon the foreign exchange market and the course of government policy. A domestic exporter may hesitate to deal with an importer if it is suspected that the authorities of the importer's country will shortly impose or tighten exchange controls in the face of an adverse balance of payments. Dealers in foreign exchange also pay close attention to the balance of payments of countries whose currencies they handle in daily transactions. Failure to realize the close dependence of international business upon the balance of payments of the domestic and foreign countries has often led to losses or even outright business failures.

THE COMPILATION OF THE BALANCE OF PAYMENTS

Three principles underlying the compilation of the balance of payments of a nation are worth special emphasis. First, only economic transactions between domestic and foreign *residents* are entered in the balance of payments. Second, a distinction is made between *debit* and *credit* transfers. Third, the balance of payments is a *double-entry* accounting statement.

The Concept of Residence

The balance of payments summarizes all economic transactions between domestic and foreign residents. Residence should not be confused with the legal notions of citizenship or nationality.

Individuals who represent their government in foreign countries, including members of the armed forces, are always considered residents of their own country. Thus, when a member of the American armed forces buys a glass of wine in France, an international transaction occurs that enters the balance of payments of both the United States and France.

Individuals who do not represent a government are considered to be residents of the country in which they have a permanent residence or in which they find their "center of interest." In some instances an individual's center of interest may be in doubt, but ordinarily such criteria as customary place of work, residence of employer, or principal source of income are sufficient to determine it. In the event of conflict, the permanent place of habitation takes precedence over center of interest. For example, an individual working at the United Nations in New York who does not represent a foreign government and who resides in New York permanently is treated as a resident of the United States despite the individual's foreign center of interest.

In preparing a balance of payments, the question of individual residence is much less important than the question of business residence. A corporation is a resident of the country in which it is incorporated, but its foreign branches and subsidiaries are viewed as foreign residents. Hence, shipments between an American concern and its overseas branch are international transactions and, as such, are entered in the U.S. balance of payments. At times the residence of a business may be difficult to decide. For example, a company may be incorporated in the domestic country, owned by residents of a second country, and conduct all of its business in a third country. In most instances, however, the residence of a business enterprise is readily apparent.

Government residence is the clearest of all: All government agencies are residents of their own country regardless of location.

Debit and Credit Entries in a Double-Entry System

With the exception of gifts, all international transactions represent a two-way exchange of assets between domestic and foreign residents.

Assets may be classified as *real* (goods and services) or *financial* (short- and long-term monetary claims, including money, which is the shortest-term claim). We can distinguish, therefore, three kinds of international transaction:

1. The exchange of goods or services for other goods or services.This is a *barter* transaction; both sides of the transaction are real.
2. The exchange of goods and services for money or other financial claims. These transactions are much more common than barter transactions. One side of the transaction is real and the other side is financial.
3. The exchange of financial claims, such as bonds or stock, for other financial claims, such as money. Both sides of this transaction are financial.

An international transaction, therefore, involves two opposing *transfers* of assets. Because the balance of payments is a double-entry accounting system, a transaction is entered twice: one transfer as a debit, the other transfer as a credit. *Hence, total debits and credits are always equal in a balance of payments.* This is an accounting equality that has no economic significance.

When is a transfer a debit entry? A credit entry? The accounting rules are depicted in Table 14-1.

A *debit* entry is made in a country's balance of payments for a transfer that either (1) *increases* the country's assets (something of value *owned*) or

TABLE 14-1   Accounting Rules for Entering Debits and Credits in the Balance of Payments

Direction of Change	International Assets	International Liabilities
Increase	Debit	Credit
Decrease	Credit	Debit

(2) *decreases* the country's liabilities (something of value *owed*). Conversely, a *credit* entry is made for a transfer that either (1) *decreases* the country's assets or (2) *increases* its liabilities.

A second way of distinguishing debit and credit transfers is as follows: A transfer that gives rise to money payments to foreign residents is a *debit* entry in the balance of payments; a transfer that gives rise to money receipts from foreign residents is a *credit* entry. This distinction, however, is less precise than the accounting distinction, and for that reason we shall use the latter in constructing the balance of payments.

Gifts are a special kind of international transaction and do not involve an exchange of assets. They are *unilateral transfers* of goods or services (gifts in kind) or of financial assets (money gifts). Despite this one-sidedness, gifts are entered twice in the balance of payments to preserve the double-entry accounting system. One entry records the actual unilateral transfer, and a second entry is made in a unilateral transfers account to record the missing side of the gift transaction.

Constructing the Balance of Payments

Table 14-2 depicts the conventional presentation of the balance of payments used by the International Monetary Fund (IMF). International transfers are grouped into three major accounts: the current account, the capital account, and the official reserves account. Entries in these accounts are recorded as *debits* or *credits*. The balance of payments is usually drawn up in the currency of the domestic country. Regardless of the currency in which they are made, international payments and receipts may be expressed in the domestic currency by the use of exchange rates for conversion from foreign to domestic currencies.

Current Account All international transfers of *goods and services* are placed in the current account. Goods are physical products commonly referred to as merchandise. Services are intangible products, such as transportation, travel, capital services (as measured by interest and dividend income), construction, technical assistance, industrial property rights (as measured by income from patents, trademarks, and copyrights), and business services.

The current account also includes a *unilateral transfers* subaccount that records offsetting entries for real or financial unilateral transfers that appear elsewhere in the balance of payments. Unilateral transfers include institutional gifts for missionary and charitable purposes; personal gifts; and government transfers, such as grants to foreign countries to assist their economic development.

Table 14-2 shows three net balance entries in the current account: the net balance on trade (merchandise), the net balance on goods and services, and the net balance on current account.

Capital Account The capital account includes all *financial* transfers be-

TABLE 14-2 Conventional Presentation of a Balance of Payments (Dollars)

	Debits	Credits	Net Debit (−) or Credit (+)
A. Current Account			
1. Goods	600	500	
		25	
Net Balance on Trade			−75
2. Services			
(a) Transportation	100	50	
(b) Travel	75	60	
(c) Investment	50	100	
(d) Other	25	50	
Net Balance on Goods and Services			−65
3. Unilateral Transfers	75	25	
Net Balance on Current Account			−115
B. Capital Account			
1. Long-term Capital			
(a) Direct Investment	100	50	
(b) Portfolio Investment	25	50	
2. Short-term Capital	500	600	
	260	250	
	25	50	
	50	100	
	50	25	
		100	
			+215
Net Balance on Capital Account			
C. Official Reserves Account			
1. Monetary Gold (net)	5		
2. Other Reserve Assets (net)	100		
3. Liabilities to Foreign Central Banks (net)		15	
Net Balance on Official Reserves Account			−90
Net Errors and Omissions	10		−10
Total Debits and Credits	2050	2050	

tween a country and the rest of the world, except for *official reserve transfers,* which are placed in a third major account.

One subaccount is *long-term capital*—financial claims and liabilities with an original maturity of more than one year. Long-term capital is further classified into direct investment and portfolio investment. *Direct investment* is defined as investment in enterprises located in one country but "effectively controlled" by residents in another country. Direct investment is a distinctive feature of international business because it usually involves the ownership of branches and subsidiaries abroad by domestic parent companies.[1]

Portfolio investment designates all long-term capital flows that do *not* give investors effective control over their investments.

Short-term capital—financial claims and liabilities, including money, with an original maturity of one year or less—includes international transfers of bank deposits and short-term securities, bank loans, and commercial claims and liabilities arising from the financing of current-account transfers.

Official Reserves Account The official reserves account records the international financial transfers of the country's monetary authorities (the Treasury Department and the Federal Reserve System in the United States and central banks in other countries). The national monetary authorities hold the country's international reserves of gold and foreign exchange, which are used to provide residual financing of balance of payment transactions (known as "compensatory compensation") in a stable-rate system or to influence the exchange rate in a floating-rate system. These same authorities also issue currency and create the domestic reserves for commercial banks. Their responsibility for monetary policy (the cost and availability of credit) gives them a powerful role in external payment adjustment in addition to compensatory financing.

Official reserve transfers are classified as monetary gold, other reserve assets (mostly foreign exchange), and liabilities owing foreign central banks. The terminology used for monetary gold flows is identical with that used for merchandise. A monetary gold export is a credit; a monetary gold import, a debit. Since monetary gold is an international financial asset (a claim on foreigners), a gold export is equivalent to a capital inflow, while a gold import is a capital outflow. Ordinarily, however, gold movements are designated as such rather than as capital flows.

Errors and Omissions Although the balance of payments is a double-entry account, governments do not draw up the balance of payments by recording each transaction twice. Governments simply do not have the necessary information on all of the many international transactions that take place over a year. Instead, they make single entries in the different accounts, depending on several sources of information that are not always consistent across accounts and vary in coverage and reliability. Consequently, *recorded* debits and credits are never equal in a country's balance of payments. To get that equality and thereby preserve the double-entry accounting system, an entry is made for "errors and omissions." In the balance of payments of the United States and other industrial countries, this entry is mainly at-

---

[1] The U.S. Department of Commerce defines a direct investment as an investment that gives the investor at least 10 percent ownership of a foreign entity. However, this percentage is a judgmental statistical criterion, for there is no single ownership percentage that separates foreign investments that carry managerial control from those that do not (see Chapter 23).

tributable to inadequate coverage of service and short-term capital transfers. But in some developing countries, the major source of errors and omissions is the illegal smuggling of goods, such as the narcotics exports of Colombia.

ENTERING TRANSACTIONS IN THE BALANCE OF PAYMENTS

We can now demonstrate how transactions are entered in the balance of payments shown in Table 14-2. To facilitate our discussion, let us assume that this is the balance of payments of the United States, although the entries are illustrative only.

To make the proper entries, we need to answer five questions: (1) Is the transfer a *real* or *financial transfer*? (2) If it is a real transfer, is it a *goods* or *services* transfer? (3) If it is a financial transfer, is it an *official reserve* transfer or a *nonreserve* transfer? (4) If it is a nonreserve financial transfer, is it a transfer of *short-term* or *long-term* capital? (5) Is the transfer a *debit* or *credit* entry?

Entering Current-Account Transactions

We start with a U.S. merchandise export valued at $500.[2] This export is a *real* transfer that goes into the current account (item A1). It is a *credit* entry because the export of merchandise *decreases* U.S. merchandise assets. (Alternatively, it is a credit entry because it gives rise to money receipts for U.S. residents.) The payment received from the foreign resident who bought the merchandise may take the form of dollars or of another country's currency. Both forms of payment are short-term *financial* transfers that are entered under item B2 of the capital account. The payment is a *debit* entry because it either decreases U.S. dollar liabilities owing foreigners (payment in dollars) or increases U.S. foreign-currency claims owed by foreigners (payment in a foreign currency).

A U.S. merchandise import of $600 is recorded as a *debit* in the current account. Payment for this import by a U.S. resident is recorded as a *credit* in the short-term capital account. These entries are the converse of those for a merchandise export.

The purchase by U.S. residents of transportation services from foreign shipping firms ($100), travel services abroad ($75), the capital services of foreign-owned investment in the United States as measured by interest and dividends paid to foreigners ($50), and other services from foreigners ($25) are entered as *debits* in the current account. These are real transfers that

---

[2] A country's balance of payments is drawn up in its own currency. Hence, any transfers expressed in a foreign currency must be converted into the domestic currency at the current exchange rate.

increase the assets of U.S. residents. Payment for these service imports (amounting altogether to $250) is entered in Table 14-2 as a single *credit* in the short-term capital account.

Conversely, the sale of services by U.S. residents to foreign residents is entered as a *credit* in the current account. Payments received by U.S. residents for these service exports (amounting to $260) are entered in Table 14-2 as a single *debit* in the short-term capital account.

Unilateral transfers to foreigners over the past year, amounting to $75, are entered as *debits* in the unilateral transfers account (A3). Keep in mind that this account is an accounting offset to the actual unilateral transfers, which take the form of goods and services or of money. Assuming that $25 of unilateral transfers are in merchandise (for example, shipments of U.S. agricultural products under a U.S. government aid program) and $50 in money, then $25 is entered as a *credit* in the goods account and $50 as a *credit* in the short-term capital account.

In the same year, unilateral transfers received by U.S. residents ($25) are entered as a *credit* in the unilateral transfers account. Because we are assuming that the actual transfers consisted entirely of money, they are recorded in Table 14-2 as a single *debit* entry in the short-term capital account.

We can now draw up the *net balances* in the current account. The net balance on trade is a *debit* of $75.[3] The net balance on goods and services is a *debit* of $65. The net balance on current account is a *debit* of $115.

Entering Capital Account Transactions

In addition to engaging in current-account transactions, U.S. residents during the year were lending to and borrowing from foreign residents. U.S. firms made *direct investments* totalling $100, as indicated by the *debit* entry in item B1(a). Direct investments abroad by U.S. firms are recorded as debits because U.S. residents *increased* their ownership claims, which constitute long-term capital assets. The firms financed their direct foreign investments in money (the most common form of payment), in goods and services, or a mix of both. We are assuming here that all payments to foreign residents for ownership claims were in money, and they are therefore recorded as *credits* in the short-term capital account.

Conversely, direct investment by foreign companies in the United States ($50) is recorded as a *credit* in item B1(a) of Table 14-2. The money received by U.S. residents from the sale of ownership rights to those foreign companies is recorded as a *debit* in the short-term capital account.

Over the year, U.S. residents also bought bonds and other long-term securities from foreign residents in the amount of $25. This *portfolio* investment is recorded as a *debit* in item B1(b) of Table 14-2 because it in-

---

[3] A debit trade balance is commonly designated an *import balance* or a *trade deficit*. On the other hand, a *credit* trade balance is designated an *export balance* or a *trade surplus*.

creases U.S. long-term claims on foreigners. Payment to foreign residents for these claims is recorded as a *credit* in the short-term capital account.

Conversely, foreign residents bought $50 of long-term securities from U.S. residents over the year. This inflow of portfolio investment is entered as a *credit* in item B1(b) because it increases U.S. long-term liabilities owing foreigners. Money receipts by U.S. residents from the sale of securities to foreigners are recorded as a $50 debit in the short-term capital account, representing an increase in U.S. short-term financial claims against foreigners.

So far all entries in the short-term capital account record payments or receipts for transfers entered in the current and long-term capital accounts. But short-term capital transfers also occur independently of those accounts. Banks, multinational enterprises, and persons located in the United States and abroad shift funds into and out of the United States to take advantage of interest-rate differentials among national money markets and to hedge against or speculate on movements in the exchange rate. Funds may also move out of countries judged to be high political risks into countries judged to be low political risks, a phenomenon called *capital flight*. Over the year, the United States received a *net inflow* of short-term capital, amounting to $100, due to these factors. This net inflow is entered as a *credit* in item B2 in Table 14-2 because it represents either a decrease in U.S. short-term claims on foreigners (as U.S.residents shift funds from abroad to the United States) or an increase in U.S. short-term liabilities owing foreigners (as foreign residents shift funds to the United States).

We can now calculate the net balance on capital account. Total debits add up to $1010; total credits, to $1225. The net balance, therefore, is a credit of $215.

Entering Official Reserves Transactions

Entries in the official reserves account are made on a net basis. Over the year, U.S. monetary authorities bought $5 of monetary gold from foreign central banks. This is regarded as a financial transfer because monetary gold is treated as a financial asset. Because an import of gold increases U.S. monetary gold assets, it is a *debit* entry. If the monetary authorities paid for this gold by crediting the accounts of the foreign central banks that sold it, then a *credit* entry is made in item C3 to record an increase in liabilities to foreign central banks.

The U.S. authorities also increased their holdings of other reserve assets (mostly foreign currencies) by a net of $100, as indicated by the *debit* entry in C2.[4] This increase in reserve assets was mostly offset by the net short-term capital inflow (credit entry) recorded in item B2. Lastly, U.S.

---

[4] In addition to foreign currencies (foreign exchange), other reserve assets include the U.S. reserve position with the IMF and special drawing rights (SDRs) issued by the IMF (see Chapters 18 and 19).

liabilities owing foreign central banks increased a net of $15, as shown by the *credit* entry in C3.

Entering Net Errors and Omissions

If we now add all the debit and credit entries in our balance of payments, we find that total credits exceed total debits by $10. Evidently, we have not recorded all transfers. Because the overall balance of payments *must* balance, we take care of this discrepancy by making a *debit* entry of $10 in the errors and omissions account. As noted earlier, the equality of total debits and credits has no economic significance.

Much of the errors and omissions entry derives from the comparatively poor record of private short-term capital movements. A radical shift in the size or sign of this entry from one payment period to the next is usually interpreted as a symptom of speculative or flight capital. Short-term capital may enter or leave a country outside the normal payment mechanism, especially when there is an intent to evade exchange controls and other official restrictions. In any event, short-term capital movements may either lead or lag behind the transactions they finance and thus show up in another payment period. For example, payment for a merchandise export shipped in December may not be recorded by a bank until January of the following year, or even later if the importer has received credit. Cash prepayment may cause the opposite situation.[5]

BALANCE OF PAYMENTS ANALYSIS: EQUILIBRIUM AND DISEQUILIBRIUM

A balance of payments is always in accounting balance, but it is not always in *equilibrium*. The essential meaning of equilibrium is a sustainable relationship between two or more economic variables, such as the supply, demand, and price of an individual good. A balance of payments is in equilibrium when the nation's economy is in "fundamental adjustment" to the world economy. Conversely, when the balance of payments is in disequilibrium, the national economy must undergo changes in its price level, income, exchange rate, or other economic variables to restore a sustainable relationship with the rest of the world. The concept of balance of payments equilibrium is a market adjustment concept. Thus, official measures to con-

---

[5] Statistical discrepancies also appear in the balance of payments for the world as a whole. It is evident that the total of *all* countries' current-account balances should add up to zero because countries can only trade with each other. And yet there was a discrepancy of $45 billion in aggregate current-account balances in 1987. Portfolio investment income credits were $45 billion less than debits, and the gap between merchandise exports and imports was $36 billion. See "In a Maze of Numbers," *The Economist*, August 20, 1988, pp. 61–62.

trol international transactions do not eliminate a deficit but merely suppress it.

Three balances are most useful when analyzing a balance of payments: the balance on *current account*, the balance on *basic transactions*, and the balance on *official reserve transactions*. These balances are calculated by "drawing a line" at certain places in the balance of payments and then by adding up all of the entries above the line. (The net balance on official reserves account equals the net balance on current and capital accounts but carries an opposite sign.) This is done in Table 14-3, which uses the same entries as appear in Table 14-2. To detect trends in these balances, it is necessary to analyze a country's balance of payments over several periods, say, each year for three to five years. However, we shall confine our analysis to a single year.

Long-run Equilibrium

Under what conditions are a nation's external economic relations sustainable over a period of time? If we take a very long time period measured in decades, the answer is plain. In the very long run, a nation *must* pay for

TABLE 14-3   Analytical Balances of the Balance of Payments (Dollars)

	Debits	Credits	Net Balance
A. Current Account			
1. Goods	600	525	
2. Services	250	260	
3. Unilateral Transfers	75	25	
Balance on Current Account			−115
B. Capital Account			
1. Long-term Capital			
(a) Direct Investment	100	50	
(b) Portfolio Investment	25	50	
Basic Balance			−140
2. Short-term Capital	910	1150	
3. Net Errors and Omissions	10		
Balance on Current and Capital Accounts			+90
C. Official Reserves Account			
1. Monetary Gold	5		
2. Other Reserve Assets	100		
3. Liabilities to Foreign Central Banks		15	
Balance on Official Reserves Account			−90

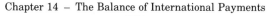

its imports of goods and services through its exports of goods and services. That is to say, in the very long run a nation cannot depend on international credit (whether short- or long-term) to finance a net import balance on current account. Nor can it hope to sustain a net export balance. Long-run equilibrium demands, therefore, that the net balance on goods and services become zero over the secular time period.

Long-run disequilibrium is measured by the net balance on *current account*. A net current-account *deficit* (debit balance) indicates that a country is spending more than it is earning in transactions with other countries. Conversely, a current-account *surplus* (credit balance) indicates that a country is earning more than it is spending in its international transactions. Because a current-account deficit or surplus needs to be financed, the net balance on current account also measures the *net* international lending or borrowing of a country over the year. A deficit is financed by net borrowing from foreign residents; a surplus is financed by net lending to foreign residents. In Table 14-3, the net balance on current account is a deficit of $115, indicating that the United States is spending more than it is earning internationally and, therefore, is a net borrower in the same amount from the rest of the world.

Intermediate-run Equilibrium

Ordinarily our time frame of reference in balance of payments analysis is much shorter than decades; it seldom exceeds three to five years, or about long enough to encompass short-run cyclical variations in national income. What are the conditions of balance of payments equilibrium over this time period? It is no longer necessary for the nation to balance imports against exports: It can sustain an import balance if *long-term* credits are available to finance it. Similarly, the nation can sustain an export balance on current account if it is willing to lend (or give) an equal amount on long term to the rest of the world. In such circumstances, there are no pressures for immediate adjustment of the balance of payments. Eventually, of course, a long-term borrower must repay the lender, but this is a future contingency that can be met or prepared for over a lengthy period of time.[6]

Intermediate-term disequilibrium in the balance of payments is measured by the net *basic* balance. The basic balance is the sum of the current account balance and the net movement of long-term capital. This balance is intended to measure the long-term or *structural* stability of a country's balance of payments. The transfers making up this balance are assumed to be insensitive to short-run changes in exchange rates and interest rates and to respond only to long-run changes in factors of production, productivity, technology, consumer preferences, competition, and other real (nonmone-

---

[6] A family that finances a home on a twenty-five-year mortgage offers a crude analogy. As long as the family is able to service the mortgage, it is not forced to make adjustments in income, expenditures, or savings. The situation is sustainable.

tary) economic variables. A basic deficit (debit balance) or a basic surplus (credit balance) extending over several years are both indicators of an intermediate-run disequilibrium, because external payments cannot be sustained without adjustments in the economic relationship between a country and the rest of the world. Table 14-3 shows that the U.S. balance of payments is in fundamental disequilibrium with a basic deficit of $140.

Short-run Equilibrium

In the short run (ranging from a moment to, say, a single year), equilibrium in the balance of payments exists when the monetary authorities make zero net use of international reserves: The amounts of foreign exchange in supply and demand are equal so there is no need for official intervention to maintain a fixed exchange rate. Further, short-run equilibrium implies the absence of any government measures to adjust international payments through direct controls.

Short-run disequilibrium is measured by the net balance on *official reserves* account. As noted earlier, a country's monetary authorities use international reserves of gold and foreign exchange to maintain or influence the exchange rate. Therefore, the direction and size of the reserve transactions balance is an indicator of pressures on the exchange rate. A *credit* balance indicates that the authorities used their reserves to prevent or limit a *depreciation* of the country's currency. A *debit* balance reveals that the authorities added to reserves to prevent or limit an *appreciation* of the country's currency.

In Table 14-3, the basic deficit (a debit of $140) was more than offset by a net short-term capital inflow (including net errors and omissions) amounting to a $230 credit. The net balance on current and capital accounts, therefore, was a surplus (a credit of $90). This surplus was financed by a net *increase* of the same amount in the country's international reserves: Holdings of reserve assets (monetary gold and foreign exchange) received from foreign residents during the year rose by $105 while liabilities owing foreign central banks rose by only $15, making a *debit* net balance on official reserves account of $90.

Sources of Disequilibrium

To add further to our understanding of equilibrium and disequilibrium in the balance of payments, we offer brief descriptions of the sources of disequilibrium as classified in the following broad categories:

1. seasonal and random disequilibrium
2. cyclical disequilibrium
3. structural disequilibrium
4. destabilizing speculation and capital flight
5. other sources of disequilibrium

We shall discuss these categories as sources of *deficit* disequilibrium, but since a deficit disequilibrium in one country implies a surplus disequilibrium in one or more other countries, it should be clear that they are also sources of *surplus* disequilibrium.

Seasonal and Random Disequilibrium   A nation's exports and imports vary seasonally due to seasonal changes in production and consumption, but usually this seasonal variation is not the same for both. The result is seasonal disequilibrium in the balance of payments. Seasonal disequilibrium is ordinarily of little consequence, since it is short-lived and self-reversible—a deficit in one season offsets a surplus in another.

Irregular, nonsystematic, short-lived disturbances may also cause disequilibrium in the balance of payments. The traditional example of this kind of disequilibrium is a crop failure that curtails exports or forces a nation to import foodstuffs. Labor strikes that tie up transportation or immobilize industries can also affect exports or imports and thus the balance of payments. Other sources of random disequilibrium include natural disasters such as floods and earthquakes. The foregoing random disturbances have a once-for-all impact on the balance of payments; they cause only a short-run disequilibrium. When disturbances are of such a magnitude as to have pervasive and lasting effects on the economy and trade of a nation (war, revolution, civil strife, and so on), then they are not random in the sense that we are using the term.

Cyclical Disequilibrium   Variations in the national incomes of trading countries, whether involving changes in price levels, changes in the levels of production and employment, or both, may lead to cyclical disequilibrium in the balance of payments. In the early 1930s massive deflations in real income and production (accompanied by widespread unemployment) occurred in the industrial countries of North America and Western Europe. In the nonindustrial countries, where the agricultural sector accounted for the bulk of national income, deflation mainly took the form of a catastrophic fall in prices, wages, and terms of trade rather than in production and employment. This global deflation caused enormous payment disequilibria, wrecked the international monetary system, and forced nations into competitive depreciations and the wholesale use of trade and payment restrictions.

Since the end of World War II the industrial countries have avoided profound deflation of the 1930s variety, but they have been far less successful in avoiding inflation generated by an effective demand running ahead of production. The situation in many developing countries has been far worse: "Runaway" inflation of 50 percent or more in a single year is not uncommon. Brazil and Argentina may be cited as examples. We can fairly say that inflation has been the single most important source of payment disequilibrium in the postwar years.

Cyclical disequilibrium may be a misnomer to denote payment disequilibrium caused by deflationary and inflationary movements in national income and price levels, because at most it is only roughly periodic. Usually, such movements are a source of intermediate-run disequilibrium lasting longer than a year.

Structural Disequilibrium   Shifts in the demand for *specific* export goods, whether brought about by changing tastes, a new distribution of income in export markets, or by changes in the availability or prices of competitive products offered by foreign suppliers, are common events in foreign trade. Shifts in the demand for import goods also occur for similar reasons. When a national economy is slow to adapt to these shifts, persistent structural disequilibrium appears in its balance of payments.

What is needed to remedy structural disequilibrium is a reallocation of production to conform to new patterns of demand and supply. Persistent structural disequilibrium may be viewed as a failure of the price system, which is supposed to guide and encourage reallocation in a market economy. Reallocation is sluggish when prices respond only slowly, if at all, to shift market conditions because of monopoly, administrative pricing, price agreements, import protection, or other arrangements that limit price competition.

Adjustments in production usually demand a reallocation in the use of factors of production. In the export sector, for example, labor and other factors must move out of lines of production no longer in demand in foreign markets and into lines that enjoy a comparative advantage. When wages and the prices of other factors employed in declining export industries are hard to lower (sticky downwards), the reallocating function of factor prices is crippled and must depend on the attraction of higher factor rewards in growing industries in the export sector or elsewhere in the economy. A more serious deterrent to a prompt reallocation of factors is low factor mobility, especially labor. This creates the problem of structural unemployment.

A structural disequilibrium unprecedented in scope and severity struck the world economy when the OPEC countries quadrupled oil prices in the early months of 1974. The enormity of the payment burden suddenly imposed on the oil-importing countries was substantially responsible for the economic crisis of the mid-1970s. The further doubling of already high oil prices in 1979 undoubtedly contributed to the worldwide recession in the early 1980s. The magnitude and pervasiveness of the balance of payments adjustments to the high cost of OPEC oil places this structural disequilibrium in a class by itself.[7]

To conclude, a wide variety of forces operating at home and abroad, such as technological and product innovations, new competition, changes in tastes, improvements in productivity, growing populations, and export cartels may cause shifts in the supply and demand of individual exports and imports that result in a structural disequilibrium in the balance of payments. Because it demands a reallocation of a country's productive capa-

---

[7] We shall have more to say about the OPEC cartel in Chapter 21.

bilities, adjustment to structural disequilibrium is certain to be painful to displaced workers and industries, and therefore the restoration of international competitiveness usually takes several years.

Destabilizing Speculation and Capital Flight Destabilizing speculation and capital flight (described in Chapter 12) constitute another source of payment disequilibrium. Although conceptually distinct, these short-term capital movements tend to occur together. Both intensify an existing disequilibrium, and capital flight may actually create one, since it is motivated by fears of safety that sometimes originate in conditions unrelated to the balance of payments, notably the prospect of war or revolution. In recent years the primary stimulus of destabilizing speculation and capital flight has been the expectation of depreciation in a major currency.

Other Sources of Disequilibrium The preceding four categories cover the main sources of disequilibrium, but they are not exhaustive. As we shall discover in Chapter 18, the U.S. payments deficit of the 1960s did not fit neatly into any one of these categories. And in the 1980s, an enormous current-account deficit in the U.S. balance of payments has been financed by massive capital inflows induced by persistently high interest rates.[8]

Disequilibrium may also originate in an unrealistic exchange rate, not uncommon when there is exchange control. Some economists also speak of *secular* disequilibrium, which arises from technological and other changes that occur slowly as an economy moves from one stage of growth to another over a period of decades.

Algebraic Summary of Equilibrium Conditions

In closing this section, we offer an algebraic summary of balance of payments equilibrium over the long run, the intermediate run, and the short run.

Over the long run, the equilibrium condition is $B_c = 0$, where B_c is the net balance on current account.

Over the intermediate run, the equilibrium condition is $B_c = B_{k,l}$, where $B_{k,l}$ is the net balance on *long-term* capital account.

Over the short run, the equilibrium condition is $B_r = 0$, where B_r is the net balance on official reserves account.

THE NEED FOR BALANCE OF PAYMENTS ADJUSTMENT

A country's balance of payments cannot remain indefinitely in disequilibrium. But adjustment may take several forms. Over the short run, a country may adjust to an official reserves *deficit* by attracting inflows of short-term

---

[8] See Chapter 19.

capital. But if the deficit persists, then a country must adjust in one of three ways: (1) through an internal deflation of prices and incomes relative to foreign prices and incomes, (2) through a depreciation of its rate of exchange, or (3) through an imposition of exchange and trade controls. Chapters 15, 16, and 17 investigate these three forms of adjustment to an international payments disequilibrium.

Market versus Nonmarket Adjustment

The first two methods of adjustment work through market processes involving changes in income, prices, exchange rates, money supplies, interest rates, and other economic phenomena. Market adjustment, however, does not imply the absence of governmental action. Indeed, successful market adjustment to an external deficit depends upon government fiscal and monetary policies directed toward reinforcing equilibrating market forces. Otherwise government monetary and fiscal policies, while not controlling or supplanting market adjustment, may counteract its equilibrating effects on the balance of payments by introducing disequilibrating changes in income, prices, and the like.

Nonmarket adjustment stands in sharp contrast to market adjustment. Government controls and regulatory devices replace the market to suppress an external deficit. Controlled adjustment is not true adjustment. Although the symptoms of disequilibrium (net official reserves balance in the balance of payments or depreciation of the exchange rate) are removed by direct controls, the causes of disequilibrium (cyclical, structural, and so on) are left untouched. The result is *suppressed disequilibrium*. Suppressed disequilibrium generally results from the widespread use of import quotas and exchange restrictions. But restrictive measures and direct controls may take any number of particular forms: tied loans and grants, ceilings on direct investment outflows, generalized tariff surcharges, domestic buying preferences, and restrictions on the purchase of foreign bonds and on bank loans to foreigners, to name only a few.

Varieties of Market Adjustment

Market adjustment to persistent disequilibrium takes two different paths depending upon whether exchange rates are stable or free to vary. When exchange rates are held stable, either through adherence to the gold standard or through official stabilization agencies, adjustment occurs in the balance of payments. When, on the other hand, the exchange rate is free to respond to fluctuations in supply and demand, disequilibrium shows up as a one-way movement of the exchange rate. Adjustment occurs within the foreign exchange market (with repercussions on domestic and foreign income and prices), and the exchange rate moves until an equality is established between the amounts of foreign exchange supplied and demanded for current-account and long-term capital transfers.

When monetary authorities try to influence exchange rates but not to peg them at a particular level (a policy known as "dirty float" in contrast to a "pure float"), then adjustment occurs in both the balance of payments and the foreign exchange market. This is the situation today for the world's major currencies.[9]

SUMMARY

1. The balance of payments is a statistical classification and summary of all economic transactions between residents of one country and residents of other countries over a stipulated period of time, ordinarily one year. Residence is primarily determined by permanent location and secondarily by "center of interest."
2. International transfers are grouped into three major balance of payments accounts: the current account, the capital account, and the official reserves account. Entries in these accounts are recorded as debits and credits.
3. Because the balance of payments is a double-entry accounting statement, total debits always equal total credits. This accounting equality has no economic significance.
4. An international transfer that increases a country's assets or decreases its liabilities is a debit entry in the balance of payments. Conversely, an international transfer that decreases a country's assets or increases its liabilities is a credit entry.
5. With the exception of gifts, all international transactions are two-way exchanges of assets between domestic and foreign residents. Each side of a transaction is a transfer of real or financial assets.
6. All international transfers of goods and services (real transfers) are placed in the current account. Except for official reserve transfers, all financial transfers between a country and the rest of the world are placed in the capital account. Finally, the international reserve transfers of a country's monetary authorities are placed in the official reserves account.
7. The three balances most useful in the analysis of the balance of payments are the balance on current account, the balance on basic transactions, and the balance on official reserve transactions.
8. *Long-run* equilibrium demands a zero net balance on current account ($B_c = 0$); *intermediate-term* equilibrium requires a zero net basic balance ($B_c + B_{k,l} = 0$); *short-term* equilibrium occurs when there is a zero net balance on official reserves account ($B_r = 0$). Short-term equilibrium also means equilibrium in the foreign exchange market.
9. Sources of disequilibrium in the balance of payments may be seasonal and random, cyclical, structural, speculation and capital flight, and other.

---

[9] See Chapter 19.

10. When a country experiences a persistent deficit in its balance of payments, it cannot rely indefinitely on net short-term capital inflows and international reserves to finance that deficit. The need for adjustment policies that will eliminate the deficit becomes critical when a country's international reserves fall to a minimal level.

11. A government may use three different modes of adjustment to remove a persistent disequilibrium in its balance of payments, either singly or in some combination: adjustment through deflation, adjustment through devaluation, and adjustment through controls.

QUESTIONS AND APPLICATIONS

1. What is the balance of international payments?
2. What determines whether a transfer is entered as a debit or a credit in the balance of payments?
3. What is the distinction between current transactions, capital transactions, and official reserve transactions?
4. Using the double-entry system, record the following international transactions in a hypothetical U.S. balance of payments: (a) an export of U.S. merchandise, valued at $500, for payment in dollars by a foreign resident; (b) the purchase of hotel services, valued at $100, by an American tourist in France; (c) the sale by the U.S. monetary authorities of gold (worth $1000) to the Bank of England; (d) the purchase of $200 of bonds by an American resident from a foreign resident; and (e) the acquisition by a U.S. multinational corporation of a firm in a foreign country in exchange for 1,000 dollars.
5. Why is the balance of payments always in an accounting balance?
6. What is the essential meaning of balance of payments equilibrium? Of disequilibrium?
7. Describe the major sources of disequilibrium.
8. What is the economic significance of the net balance on current account? The net balance on basic transactions? The net balance on official reserve transactions?
9. (a) Why is a country compelled to take adjustment measures to eliminate a persistent deficit in its balance of payments?
   (b) Which modes of adjustment may a country use to eliminate a persistent deficit?
10. Explain the difference between market and nonmarket adjustments.

SELECTED READINGS

International Monetary Fund. *Balance of Payments Manual.* Washington, D.C.: International Monetary Fund. Latest edition.

International Monetary Fund. *Balance of Payments Yearbook*. Washington, D.C.: International Monetary Fund. Annual.

Kuwayama, Patricia H. "Measuring the United States Balance of Payments." *Monthly Review* (Federal Reserve Bank of New York), August 1975, pp. 183–94.

Stern, Robert M., et al. *The Presentation of the U.S. Balance of Payments: A Symposium*. Essays in International Finance, no. 123. Princeton, N.J.: Princeton University Press, 1977.

United States Department of Commerce, Office of Business Economics. *Survey of Current Business*. Washington, D.C.: U.S. Government Printing Office. March, June, September, and December issues, annual.

15

International Payments Adjustment in a Fixed-Rate System

How do countries adjust to disequilibria in their balance of payments in an international monetary system that commits national governments to maintain fixed exchange rates? This is the question addressed in this chapter.

DETERMINANTS OF THE CURRENT AND CAPITAL ACCOUNTS

Current-account transfers and capital-account transfers in the balance of payments are influenced by different sets of economic variables.

The balance on current account depends on domestic real income, foreign real income, and the relative prices of domestically produced and foreign-produced goods and services. Expressed algebraically,

$$B_c = f(Y_d, Y_f, P/SP^*)$$

where B_c is the net balance on current account; Y_d, domestic real income; Y_f, foreign real income; P, the domestic price level; P^*, the foreign price level; and S, the spot foreign exchange rate.

The balance on capital account is dependent on the domestic interest rate relative to the foreign interest rate, the domestic profit rate relative to the foreign profit rate, and the expected exchange rate. Expressed algebraically,

$$B_k = f(i/i^*, r/r^*, E(S)),$$

where i is the domestic interest rate; i^*, the foreign interest rate; r, the domestic profit rate; r^*, the foreign profit rate; and $E(S)$, the expected exchange rate.

The combined net balance on current and capital accounts can deviate from zero only when it is financed by an opposing and equal balance on official reserves account (B_r). Compensatory financing is provided by the monetary authorities when they intervene in the foreign exchange market to maintain a fixed exchange rate. Hence, the net balance on official reserves account is *induced* by the combined net balance of the other two accounts. Expressed algebraically,

$$B_r = -(B_c + B_k).$$

To deal with the several independent variables that can play a role in the international adjustment process, we first analyze adjustment when capital is immobile among countries and then when capital is perfectly mobile among countries. In both cases, the exchange rate does not influence adjustment, because it is fixed. After this explanation of current-account and capital-account adjustment processes, we investigate the conditions of general equilibrium in an open economy.

Our first task is to examine the relationship between national income and the balance of payments.

NATIONAL INCOME, FOREIGN TRADE, AND DOMESTIC ABSORPTION

This section examines the relationships between national income and foreign trade and the conception of a balance of payments deficit (surplus) as an excess (deficiency) of domestic absorption.

The Gross National Product and Income Equations

The *gross national product* (GNP) of a nation is the market value of all final goods and services produced by the national economy over a period of time, which is usually a year. In practice, the GNP is estimated by aggregating the total expenditures on goods and services of individuals, business, government, and foreigners in the markets of the nation over the year. Since these are final expenditures, no single good or service is ever counted more than once.

In a *closed* economy with no foreign trade, all expenditures are domestic and GNP may be expressed as follows:

$$GNP = C + I + G,$$

where C represents expenditures by individuals for consumption; I, expenditures by business for gross investment (capital equipment, construction, and net additions to inventories); and G, expenditures by government for both consumption and investment.

In an *open* economy, however, GNP is affected by the exports and imports of goods and services that make up the current account of the nation's balance of payments. Exports measure the expenditures by foreigners in domestic markets and therefore are part of GNP. Imports, on the other hand, measure expenditures by domestic individuals, business, and government for goods and services produced by other nations and must be deducted from total expenditures to get the domestic gross national product. Hence, in an open economy GNP assumes this form:

$$(1)\ GNP = C + I + G + X - M,$$

where X represents expenditures on exports and M represents expenditures on imports. The expression $X - M$ links GNP to the balance of payments, because this expression is the net balance on goods and services, which is also the net foreign investment of the nation.[1] To show this, we can rewrite equation (1) as follows:

$$(2)\ GNP = C + I_d + G + (X - M),$$

where I_d represents *domestic* gross investment and $(X - M)$ represents net foreign investment.

The production of the goods and services making up the GNP generates an equal flow of income to the factors that contribute their productive services. Some of this income is spent by individuals on consumption and some is saved by them, some is saved by business as depreciation and "retained corporate profits," and the rest is taxed away by government. Thus, we can define *gross national income* (GNI) as follows:

$$(3)\ GNI = C + S_p + S_b + T,$$

where C represents income spent on consumption; S_p and S_b, personal and business saving, respectively; and T, income taxed away by government.

Since GNP is equal to GNI, we now have this identity:

$$(4)\ C + I_d + G + (X - M) = C + S_p + S_b + T.$$

Simplifying and transposing we get

---

[1] To simplify our exposition, in this chapter we shall assume the absence of unilateral transfers and therefore consider the balance on current account as synonymous with the balance on goods and services.

TABLE 15-1 Gross National Product and Income of the United States in 1988 (Billions of Dollars)

Symbol	GNP	Symbol	GNI
C	3226.0	C	3226.0
I_d	765.5	S_p	147.0
G	963.6	S_b	583.9
X	518.7	T	904.9
M	-611.9		
GNP	4861.8	GNI	4861.8

Source: Adapted from *Federal Reserve Bulletin* (Washington, D.C.: U.S. Government Printing Office, March 1989), pp. A53–A54.

$$(5)\ I_d + G + (X - M) = S_p + S_b + T.$$

$$(6)\ S_p + S_b + (T - G) - I_d = X - M.$$

Since $(T - G)$ is the excess of tax revenue over government expenditure, or *government saving*, $S_p + S_b + (T - G) = S$, where S represents *total* domestic saving. Thus,

$$(7)\ S - I_d = X - M.$$

This is a basic equation relating GNI (or GNP) to foreign trade. It states that any excess of exports over imports (current account surplus) is matched by an excess of domestic saving over domestic investment. Conversely, an excess of imports over exports (current account deficit) is matched by an excess of domestic investment over domestic saving. If domestic saving equals domestic investment, then exports also equal imports.

This discussion of GNI and GNP may take on more meaning for readers if we end it with a presentation of those two accounts for the United States in 1988. This presentation is given in Table 15-1. Readers may find it instructive to insert these figures into GNP and GNI equations.

Determination of National Income

How do *changes* in GNI (GNP) affect the balance of payments? How do changes in foreign trade affect GNI? To answer these questions, we must understand how national income is determined.[2]

---

[2] We can offer here only a very condensed version of the theory of income determination. For a fuller treatment see any introductory text on economics.

Figure 15-1   The Determination of Actual Gross National Product (Income) by Aggregate Demand

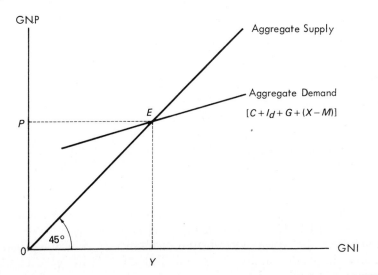

A country's GNP (national income) is determined by the intersection of the aggregate supply and demand schedules. The aggregate supply schedule shows the country's real output of goods and services. It is drawn at a 45° slope because at each point on the schedule GNP equals GNI. The aggregate demand schedule shows the *planned* expenditures of domestic consumers (C), investors (I_d), and government (G) plus the *net* planned expenditures of foreigners on domestic goods and services (X–M). Only at E is the level of national output (supply) equal to the level of planned expenditures, with GNP at 0–P (=0–Y). At any income level below 0–Y, aggregate demand exceeds aggregate supply. This excess demand stimulates more production of goods and services until that excess demand is eliminated at E. Conversely, at any income level above 0–Y, aggregate demand is less than aggregate supply, forcing a contraction of national output back to 0–Y (=0–P).

Although the *potential* size of the real GNP (the production possibilities frontier) depends on the supply and productivity of the nation's factors of production, its *actual* size is determined by the level of aggregate demand— the planned expenditures of domestic consumers, investors, and government agencies *plus* the net planned expenditures of foreigners [C + I_d + G + (X − M)]. In Figure 15-1, GNP is determined by the intersection of the aggregate demand schedule with the aggregate (real) supply schedule at E. The equilibrium level of GNP is 0–P, which generates an equal level of GNI; that is to say, 0–P = 0–Y.[3] Only at E is the level of national output

---

[3] Since the aggregate supply line is drawn at 45° to the origin, GNP = GNI at every point on the line. As noted above, GNP and GNI are always equal.

equal to the level of planned expenditures. At any income level below 0–Y, aggregate demand exceeds real output. This excess demand will stimulate producers to expand their output until the excess demand is eliminated at D. On the other hand, at any income level higher than 0–Y, aggregate demand falls short of aggregate supply. In this instance producers will respond by contracting output until the demand deficiency is eliminated at E. Hence, the only stable level of GNI is 0–Y, as determined by E.

In equilibrium, therefore,

$$(8)\ GNP = C + I_d + G + (X - M)$$
$$= GNI = C + S_p + S_b + T.$$

Although this equation appears to be the same as equation (4), it is not. The expenditures on the left side are planned or *ex ante* expenditures, whereas in equation (4) the expenditures are *ex post* expenditures that may or may not have been planned.

Any increase in planned expenditures will cause an increase in GNP and GNI, subject to the constraint of the production possibilities frontier. In Figure 15-2, the initial equilibrium position is E, where aggregate demand and aggregate supply are equal. But now an increase in planned domestic investment pushes up the aggregate demand schedule, creating excess demand at the existing level of GNI. Producers respond to this excess demand by expanding output to E', where planned expenditure once again equals aggregate supply. At this new equilibrium GNP is 0–P' and GNI is 0–Y'. In similar fashion, a *decrease* in the planned expenditure causes a contraction in GNP and GNI.

Equation (8) can be rewritten as follows:

$$(9)\ \underbrace{C + I_d + G + X}_{\substack{\text{Income} \\ \text{Injections}}} = \underbrace{C + S_p + S_b + T + M.}_{\substack{\text{Income} \\ \text{Leakages}}}$$

Simply put, all increases (decreases) in expenditures on domestic goods and services will increase (decrease) national income. The different expenditures, however, do not play the same role in initiating changes in national income. Basically, changes in domestic investment and government and export expenditures are *autonomous* with respect to national income. That is to say, they are not dependent on any prior change in income but rather cause changes in income. On the other hand, changes in consumption expenditures are *induced* by prior changes in national income and do not *initiate* changes in it. In other words, consumption expenditures do not determine national income but instead are determined by it. Henceforth, we shall refer to autonomous expenditures (domestic investment, government expenditures, and exports) as *income injections*.

Figure 15-2 The Determination of a New Equilibrium Level of Gross National Product (Income) by an Upward Shift in Aggregate Demand

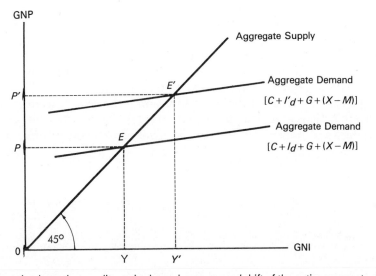

An increase in planned expenditures is shown by an *upward* shift of the entire aggregate demand schedule. The increase shown above is caused by a rise in domestic investment from I_d to I'_d that creates excess demand at 0–Y. In response, producers increase output from E to E', where planned expenditures once again equal aggregate supply at 0–P' (= 0–Y'). Conversely, a decrease in planned expenditures causes a *downward* shift in the entire aggregate demand schedule, thereby bringing about a contraction of GNP (= GNI).

In contrast to expenditures, domestic saving, taxes, and imports act to *depress* national income. Saving is a decision not to spend, taxes lower spendable income in the hands of individuals and business, and imports divert expenditures away from domestic goods and services to foreign output. For this reason we shall call them *income leakages*.

National income is in equilibrium when the expenditures that business, government, and foreigners *intend* to make in domestic markets equal saving, taxation, and imports, that is, when

$$(10)\ G + I_d + X = S_p + S_b + T + M.$$

To simplify matters we can view $(T - G)$ as part of domestic saving (S), along with S_p and S_b, reducing equation (10) to

$$(11)\ I_d + X = S + M.$$

This equation resembles equation (7) but is not the same, because in our present discussion we are speaking of *intended* expenditures, saving, and imports. Equation (7) always holds, but equation (11) holds only when national income is in equilibrium. If, for example, businesses end up the year with unwanted or unintended additions to their inventories, then they will take steps to reduce them and thus lower income in the following year. Only when intended income injections equal income leakages is national income "determined," that is, stable. We can draw here an analogy with the balance of payments. As we have seen, the balance of payments is always in accounting balance, but it is not always in equilibrium.

Figure 15-3 indicates the determination of national income in terms of income injections and leakages [equation (11)]. The $S + M$ schedule shows how savings and imports vary with the level of national income; it is the

Figure 15-3   The Determination of Gross National Income: Injection-Leakage Approach

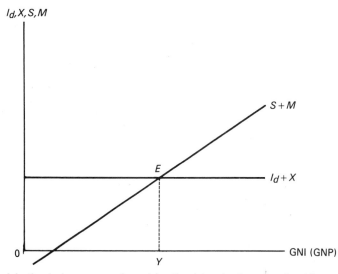

The income *injection-leakage* approach explains the determination of national income by the intersection of the combined savings and import (leakage) schedules ($S + M$) and the combined domestic investment and export (injection) schedules ($I_d + M$). Equilibrium income is 0–Y because at E the sum of leakages equals the sum of injections. The $S + M$ schedule slopes upward from left to right because leakages are a positive function of national income: The higher the income, the higher the leakages. The $I_d + X$ schedule has a zero slope because injections are autonomous (independent) with respect to national income. An upward shift in the $I_d + X$ schedule (autonomous *increase* in income injection) causes an expansion in national income to a new equilibrium level; a downward shift causes a contraction. The injection-leakage approach gives the same result as the *total expenditures* approach shown in Figure 15-1.

sum of the savings schedule (S) and the import schedule (M), which are not shown separately. The $I_d + X$ schedule is the sum of the domestic investment schedule (I_d) and the export schedule (X). Since both the domestic investment schedule and the export schedule are autonomous with respect to national income, the composite $I_d + X$ schedule is drawn parallel to the abscissa. The equilibrium level of income (0–Y) is determined by the intersection of the two composite schedules at E. An autonomous upward shift in the $I_d + X$ schedule will bring about a higher equilibrium level of national income, whereas a downward shift will bring about a lower level. This injection-leakage approach to national income determination gives the same result as the total-expenditures approach used in Figure 15-1.

Functional Relationship of Expenditures, Saving, and Imports to Real Domestic Income

In discussing the relationships between changes in expenditures, saving, and imports, on one hand, and changes in national income, on the other, we shall be talking of *real* income changes, that is, changes that are *not* accompanied by price changes. The assumptions underlying this condition are indicated later in the chapter.

As discussed in the previous section, changes in domestic investment and exports are independent of changes in domestic national income. Investment expenditure depends on the expected return on capital (marginal efficiency of capital) interacting with the cost of capital (interest rate). Changes in exports depend upon changes in tastes and real income in foreign countries. Consumption, saving, and imports, however, are all dependent on income.

The relation between consumption and income is known as the *marginal propensity to consume* (MPC), which is expressed as dC/dY, where dY is a change in national income and dC is the change in consumption induced by the change in income. If, for example, the MPC is 0.8, then a $100 change (increase or decrease) in national income will induce an $80 change in consumption. In brief, the marginal propensity to consume is the fraction or percentage of new income that is spent on consumption.

Some of the consumption expenditure goes to buy imports. Thus, the marginal propensity to consume *includes the marginal propensity to import* (MPM), which is expressed as dM/dY. The marginal propensity to import, then, is the percentage of new income that is spent on imports. If the MPM is 0.2, then a $100 change in national income will induce a $20 change in imports.

The expression dS/dY is the *marginal propensity to save* (MPS), which relates a change in national income to the change in saving induced by the former. Since income is either spent or saved, the MPC and MPS together always add up to 1. If the MPC is 0.8, then the MPS must be 0.2.

The marginal propensities are not necessarily the same at different levels of national income. For example, as family incomes rise beyond a subsistence level, the marginal propensity to consume may decline or, to say the same thing, the marginal propensity to save may increase. For the sake of simplicity, however, we shall assume in this and later discussions that the marginal propensities are constant.

Domestic and Foreign Trade Income Multipliers

Reverting to equation (11), an autonomous shift in domestic investment or in exports will cause a change in national income in the same direction. Increases in these expenditures will raise national income; decreases will lower it. Furthermore, the resulting change in national income will be a *multiple* of the autonomous change in investment or exports. This is because the income first generated by the autonomous expenditure will be respent by its recipients, which in turn will generate another change in income, and so on. This process of income change (expansion or contraction) will come to a stop when the income leakages induced by the income change become equal to the autonomous income injection. As we have noted, this is when $I_d + X = S + M$.

This relationship between an autonomous change in domestic investment and the subsequent change in national income that it induces is called the *domestic income multiplier,* or dY/dI_d. If the domestic multiplier is 2, then a \$100 increase (decrease) in domestic investment will cause a \$200 increase (decrease) in national income. We may derive the domestic income multiplier as follows:

$$(12)\ I_d + X = S + M.$$

Now introduce a change in domestic investment (dI) that will induce a change in domestic saving (dS) and imports (dM) via an induced change in national income. Since exports are not affected, we can rewrite equation (12):

$$(13)\ dI_d = dS + dM.$$

Dividing both sides of equation (13) into the induced change in national income (dY), we have

$$(14)\ dY/dI_d = \frac{dY}{dS + dM},\ \text{or}$$

$$(15)\ dY/dI_d = \frac{1}{dS/dY + dM/dY}$$

$$= \frac{1}{MPS + MPM}.$$

This last equation tells us that the domestic income multiplier (dY/dI_d) equals the *reciprocal of the sum of the marginal propensities to save and import*. If MPS is 0.1 and MPM is 0.1, then the multiplier is 1/0.2, or 5. Thus, an autonomous change in domestic investment of, say, $50 would cause a change of $250 in national income. In mathematical terms,

$$(16)\ dY = (dY/dI_d)\ dI_d,$$

which says that the change in income equals the multiplier dY/dI_d *times* the autonomous change in domestic investment (dI_d).

The relationship between an autonomous change in exports (dX) and the induced change in national income (dY) is known as the *foreign trade multiplier*. We can derive the foreign trade multiplier in exactly the same way we derived the domestic multiplier, and it assumes the same form:

$$\frac{dY}{dX} = \frac{1}{MPS + MPM}.$$

The induced change in national income will be the autonomous change in exports *times* the multiplier $[dX(dY/dX)]$.

We may summarize this exposition by saying that changes in national income are induced by autonomous changes in domestic investment or exports. The resulting change in national income will be the product of the autonomous change in investment or exports times the income multiplier. Both the domestic and foreign trade multipliers may be expressed as the reciprocal of the sum of the marginal propensities to save and import, or the reciprocal of the sum of the *income leakages*. National income will reach a new equilibrium position (and cease to change) when intended expenditures (income injections) equal the income leakages, that is, $I_d + X = S + M$.

ADJUSTMENT WITH NO INTERNATIONAL CAPITAL MOBILITY

In our exposition of international payments adjustment in this and the next two chapters, we shall use the net balance on official reserves account to measure disequilibrium in the balance of payments. A positive or negative balance on this account indicates that the monetary authorities are using international reserves to finance an opposing net balance on the combined current and capital accounts. When the net balance on official reserves account is zero, then the balance of payments is in *equilibrium*: $B_r = 0 = B_c + B_k$.[4]

How does a country adjust to a balance of payments disequilibrium when there is no net movement of capital between it and the rest of the world? In that case, $B_k = 0$ and therefore disequilibrium appears only in the current account: $B_r = -B_c \neq 0$. The elimination of the surplus or deficit on current account to restore equilibrium occurs through changes in domestic real income (GNP) and the relative prices of domestic and foreign goods and services.

International Adjustment and Domestic Absorption

Let us rewrite equation (2) as follows:

$$(17) \; X - M = GNP - (C + I_d + G).$$

This tells us that when exports are greater than imports, GNP (GNI) is greater than *domestic* expenditure on goods and services $(C + I_d + G)$ by the same amount. Conversely, when imports are greater than exports, GNP is less than domestic expenditure by the same amount.

We can rewrite equation (17):

$$(18) \; B_c = Y - A,$$

where B_c is the net current-account balance $(X - M)$, Y is the gross national product, and A is the domestic *absorption* of goods and services $(C + I_d + G)$. If $X < M$, then $B_c < 0$ and $Y < A$. Hence, to correct a current-account deficit, a country must either (1) *increase* its physical output of goods and services (Y) or (2) *decrease* its real absorption of goods and services (A).

The period of time allowed for adjustment to a persistent payments deficit is limited by the availability of compensatory financing, and for most countries it is probably not more than two or three years. When an economy is fully employed, further growth in GNP must depend mainly upon an improvement in productivity, which seldom goes beyond 5 percent a year and is often less. Under full-employment conditions, therefore, it is usually not possible to raise Y to any significant degree during the period allowed for payments adjustment. Thus, adjustment under full-employment conditions calls for *a reduction in domestic absorption (expenditure) in real terms* and thus a smaller allocation of goods and services to domestic use.

When the economy is at less than full employment, it may be possible to increase output (Y). But to improve the balance of payments, output must be increased without adding to the level of domestic absorption (A). This

---

[4] Whether or not this equilibrium is a short-run or intermediate-run equilibrium depends on the net balance on short-term capital flows, as discussed in the previous chapter.

requires that any new expenditure be switched from domestic absorption to expenditures by foreigners on exports and to expenditures on domestic goods that replace imports. To bring about such expenditure switching, either *prices* in the deficit country must be lowered relative to prices in the rest of the world (through internal deflation or exchange devaluation) or the reallocation must be accomplished by restrictions and controls. In the absence of switching, any increase in output will simply increase domestic absorption with no benefit to the balance of payments. If we assume that prices are fixed, then adjustment, even under less-than-full-employment conditions, must rely on *expenditure reduction* that cuts down on domestic absorption.

Equilibrating Changes in Domestic Absorption through Real Income Effects

We are now prepared to see how the foreign trade multiplier helps to bring about adjustment to a persistent deficit or surplus in the current account.

Operation of the Foreign Trade Multiplier To focus our analysis in this and the next section on equilibrating changes in real expenditure, we shall assume that goods and factor prices are *fixed*. We shall further assume that the economy of the country in payments disequilibrium is at less than full employment and has excess capacity to produce real output.

How does the foreign trade multiplier function to bring about an adjustment to persistent deficit disequilibrium in the balance of payments? We can indicate income adjustment most simply with a diagram. In Figure 15-4 the initial equilibrium income level is 0–Y, as determined by the intersection of the $X + I_d$ schedule (income injection) and the $M + S$ schedule (income leakage). The M and X schedules also intersect at 0–Y income: Imports equal exports, and hence the balance of payments is in equilibrium. The country is enjoying external balance but not internal balance.[5] Now, however, an autonomous drop in exports from X to X' creates a balance of payments deficit (dX) and also causes an equal drop in autonomous expenditure from $X + I_d$ to $X' + I_d$. This lower injection of spending forces a contraction of output that reduces national income to a new equilibrium level of 0–Y'. At 0–Y' no further changes occur in the level of income, because income injection ($X' + I_d$) once again equals income leakage ($M + S$).

Note that the decrease in income (dY) is greater than the autonomous decrease in exports (dX) as a result of the foreign trade multiplier. The multiplier is greater than one because the combined marginal propensity to import and save (the slope of the $M + S$ schedule) is less than 1. Income

---

[5] We are assuming in Figure 15-4 that full employment occurs only at a GNP higher than 0–Y. Internal balance means that 0–Y is accompanied by full employment. The problem of achieving internal and external balance at the same time is explored later. Observe that at 0–Y' there is neither internal nor external balance.

Figure 15-4   Income Adjustment to an Autonomous Decrease in Exports

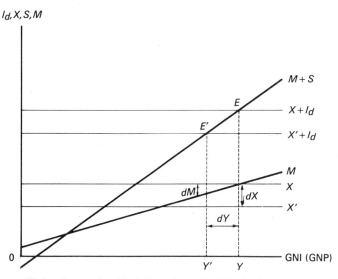

Initially, the equilibrium income level is 0–Y, as determined by the intersection at E of the $X + I_d$ schedule (injection) and the $M + S$ schedule (leakage). It so happens that the M and X schedules intersect at income level 0–Y. Hence, the balance of payments is also in equilibrium. Then, an autonomous decrease in the export schedule from X to X' causes a balance of payments deficit (dX) and also an equal decrease in the injection schedule from $X + I_d$ to $X' + I_d$, which forces a contraction of GNP from 0–Y to 0–Y', where income injection once again equals income leakage at point E'. The decrease in income (dY) exceeds the decrease in exports (dX) due to the foreign trade multiplier. Income adjustment to the balance of payments occurs through a decrease in imports (dM) induced by the decrease in income (dY). At the new equilibrium income (0–Y), adjustment to the balance of payments deficit remains incomplete (dM < dX) due to a positive savings leakage.

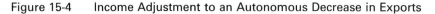

adjustment to the balance of payments deficit occurs through a fall in imports (dM) that is induced by the contraction in national income (dY) via the marginal propensity to import (the slope of the M schedule). In this instance, income adjustment is not sufficient to wipe out the entire deficit (dM < dX). As we shall observe shortly, adjustment through the foreign trade multiplier can be completed only when there is no savings leakage (MPS = 0). Figure 15-4 shows only the *final* effect of the foreign trade multiplier on national income and the balance of payments (imports). To gain an insight into the *process* of income adjustment, we now turn to arithmetic examples.

The Income Adjustment Process: No Savings Leakage   Let us suppose that exports of the domestic country fall $100 because of lower foreign demand and that this fall is permanent. Assuming a prior equilibrium, the balance of payments now has a persistent deficit, and long-run adjustment is necessary. We further assume the following marginal propensities in the deficit country: MPC = 1, MPM = 0.4, and MPS = 0. Thus, all new income is spent on consumption—0.4 on imports and 0.6 on domestic output. In the same way, a drop in income induces an equal decrease in consumption spread over imports and domestic output. There is no domestic savings leakage.

We now trace the equilibrating income effects of this permanent fall in exports as they occur over income periods. An income period is the time necessary to spend the income earned in the preceding income period and to earn the income that will be spent in the next income period. (It has been estimated that an income period in the United States economy has a duration of about three months.) Turning now to Table 15-2, we observe that there is no change in the level of exports in income period 0, and consequently there are no induced changes in imports, domestic consumption, or domestic income. In income period 1, however, exports drop $100 to a new level that is sustained throughout our example. This causes a decline of $100 in the income received by those domestic residents who produce and sell the merchandise and services comprising the $100 drop in exports.

In income period 2, these residents cut their spending on imports by $40 (0.4 *times* $100) and their spending on domestic output by $60 (0.6 *times* $100). As a result, a second group of residents who produce and sell domestic goods going to the first group of residents now suffer an income loss of $60. (What is spending to the buyer is income to the seller.) The $40 drop in imports reduces foreign income but not domestic income. Thus, in income period 2 domestic income falls by $160—an induced decline in domestic consumption ($60) plus the continuing negative export injection ($100). This

TABLE 15-2   Income Adjustment to a Payments Deficit with No Savings Leakage

Income Period	Period Export Income Injection	Period Import Income Leakage	Period Decrease in Domestic Consumption	Period Decrease in Consumption of Domestic Output
0	$ 0	$ 0	$ 0	$ 0
1	−100	0	0	−100
2	−100	−40	−60	−160
3	−100	−64	−96	−196
n	−100	−100	−150	−250

process of income deflation continues into income period 3, and domestic income falls $196 below its level in period 0.

As we know, the overall contraction in domestic income is determined by the foreign trade multiplier. In this case the multiplier is the reciprocal of the marginal propensity to import, because the marginal propensity to save is zero. Thus, the multiplier is 2.5 and domestic income will fall by 2.5 *times* $100, or $250, in income period n after all the multiplier effects have taken place. This decline in domestic income induces a $100 fall in imports that exactly matches the autonomous fall in exports, thereby restoring equilibrium in the balance of payments. The process of income contraction comes to a halt in income period n because the autonomous fall in export expenditure is fully offset by an induced decline in the import leakage, that is, $dM = dX$.

The Income Adjustment Process: Savings Leakage   When spending on imports is the only income leakage, then adjustment to a balance of payments deficit (surplus) in the current account is complete—imports fall (rise) until they exactly offset the autonomous decrease (increase) in exports. Income, however, is rarely spent entirely on consumption; part of it is generally saved, and this saving, as we have observed, constitutes a second income leakage. Because of the savings leakage, the foreign trade multiplier is too small to effect a full adjustment in the balance of payments—the induced change in imports is less than the autonomous change in exports. Table 15-3 demonstrates this incomplete adjustment by assuming MPC = 0.9, MPM = 0.4, and MPS = 0.1.

Because the combined marginal leakage propensity (marginal import propensity plus marginal savings propensity) is 0.5, the multiplier is only 2 (1/0.5), and domestic income does not contract sufficiently to induce a fall in imports equal to the autonomous fall in exports. Actually, imports fall

TABLE 15-3   Income Adjustment to a Payments Deficit with Savings Leakage

Income Period	Period Export Income Injection	Period Import Income Leakage	Period Savings Leakage	Period Decrease in Domestic Consumption	Period Decrease in Consumption of Domestic Output
0	$ 0	$ 0	$ 0	$ 0	$ 0
1	− 100	0	0	0	− 100
2	− 100	− 40	− 10	− 50	− 150
3	− 100	− 60	− 15	− 75	− 175
n	− 100	− 80	− 20	− 100	− 200

only $80, and thus there remains a $20 deficit (equal to the savings leakage) in the balance of payments. It is apparent, then, that the foreign trade multiplier will not effect full adjustment to disequilibrium when there is a domestic savings leakage.

The Foreign Repercussion Effect   The conclusion reached in the last paragraph is true but incomplete. To get a complete picture of income adjustment to payments disequilibrium, we must take note not only of domestic income changes induced by the balance of payments but also of income changes induced in foreign countries.

The autonomous fall in domestic exports appears to the rest of the world as a $100 fall in its imports that creates a *surplus* disequilibrium in its balance of payments. Now the foreign trade multiplier functions as soon as there is disequilibrium in the current account regardless of whether the disequilibrium results from a change in exports or a change in imports. Thus, the surplus disequilibrium in the rest of the world starts a cumulative expansive movement in foreign incomes, which in turn induces an increase in imports from the deficit country via the foreign marginal propensity to import. This complicated interaction between the foreign trade multipliers of different countries restrains the decline in income in the deficit country and the rise in income in the surplus country.

The foreign repercussion effect depends on foreign propensities to import and save. Returning to our previous example, let us now assume that the foreign propensity to import is 0.3 and the foreign propensity to save is 0.1. Then the foreign trade multiplier for the domestic country would be 1.25 rather than 2 and the domestic income would fall only $125.[6] Because in this instance we are assuming that the domestic and foreign propensities to save are both 0.1, foreign income would rise $125. Thus, the rest of the world would increase its imports from the domestic country by $37.5 (0.3 times $125) or, to say the same thing, the domestic country's exports would increase by $37.5. At the same time, the domestic country would reduce its imports by $50 (0.4 times $125). The end result of these income adjustments would be to decrease the domestic country's deficit from $100 to $12.5 because of a foreign repercussion effect of $37.5 and an induced import leakage of $50. Note that the deficit would be less than in our previous example ($12.5 compared to $20) but that adjustment would remain incomplete. This will always be the case unless the domestic savings leakage is offset by a change in domestic investment expenditure *induced* by monetary effects.

---

[6] The foreign trade multiplier that takes account of this interaction, or foreign repercussion effect, is

$$\frac{1}{MPS_d + MPM_d + MPM_f(MPS_d/MPS_f)},$$

where MPS_d and MPM_d are the marginal propensities to save and import, respectively, of the domestic country, and MPS_f and MPM_f are the marginal propensities to save and import, respectively, of the rest of the world.

The foreign repercussion effect will be insignificant for a country whose exports and imports are only a small part of world trade. However, for major trading countries like the United States, the foreign repercussion effect must be taken into account in estimating the foreign trade multiplier.

The Domestic Income Multiplier   We have now examined adjustment via the foreign trade multiplier, noting how income changes originating in the current account work toward the establishment of a new equilibrium. But all changes in income do not proceed from disequilibrium in the balance of payments. New income may also be created (or old income extinguished) by independent shifts in domestic investment (construction, capital equipment, inventories) or domestic government expenditures. These shifts in domestic expenditure cause a multiple expansion (or contraction) of domestic income via the *domestic* income multiplier. The change in domestic income then affects the level of imports through the marginal propensity to import, and the result, assuming a prior equilibrium, is a cyclical disequilibrium in the balance of payments.

Because of the domestic income multiplier, government fiscal and monetary policies become key instruments of balance of payments adjustment. By the same token, however, these policies may delay international adjustment by bringing about changes in domestic income that counteract the equilibrating income changes of the foreign trade multiplier. This situation often occurs since nations usually place the objectives of domestic full employment and rapid economic development above that of balance of payments equilibrium.

Equilibrating Changes in Domestic Absorption through Monetary Effects

We have seen that the foreign trade multiplier will fail to bring about full adjustment to a balance of payments disequilibrium when there is a domestic savings leakage. Since such a leakage is almost certain to exist, how then will full adjustment be achieved when all prices are fixed and unemployment prevails in the economy? The answer to this question lies in the *monetary effects* of a balance of payments disequilibrium on real expenditure (real income).

A current account surplus or deficit is financed by an opposing and equal net balance on official reserves account when, as we are presently assuming, there is zero net international movement of capital. A current account surplus *increases* the international reserves and monetary base of the domestic country; a current account deficit *decreases* the international reserves and monetary base of the domestic country. In turn, a rise in the monetary base increases the domestic country's money supply (stock) whereas a fall in the monetary base decreases its money supply. To understand this last statement, a few words are necessary on how a country's central bank creates the money stock.

Each country's central bank (the Federal Reserve System in the United States) creates money when it buys securities (bonds) or foreign exchange from others and it destroys money when it sells securities or foreign exchange to others.[7] When it buys securities or foreign exchange, the central bank pays for them with a check drawn against itself. The seller of bonds or foreign exchange to the central bank deposits this check with its commercial bank, which credits the seller's checking account. (The central bank then credits the account that the commercial bank maintains with it.) Hence, the *purchase* of bonds or foreign exchange by the central bank immediately creates an equal amount of money (the demand deposit of the seller). Conversely, the *sale* of bonds or foreign exchange by the central bank decreases the money stock: The buyer pays with a check drawn against its commercial bank, which debits the buyer's checking account. (The central bank then debits the commercial bank's account.)

The money creation (destruction) process does not stop with the initial creation (destruction) of the seller's (buyer's) demand deposit with its commercial bank. In the instance of a purchase of bonds or foreign exchange by the central bank, the new deposit that the commercial bank now holds in the central bank constitutes *reserves*. Because a commercial bank is required to hold reserves in the central bank that equal only a fraction of its demand deposits, an increase in reserves enables it to increase demand deposits through loans up to a multiple of the increase in reserves. If, for example, the required reserve ratio is 10 percent, then a $100 increase in the bank reserves can support a $1000 increase in the money stock. Conversely, a decrease in bank reserves causes a multiple decrease in the money stock. In sum, the supply of money (M^s) equals the money multiplier (m) times the monetary base (B):

$$(19)\ M^s = mB$$

The *monetary base* is composed of two elements: a *domestic* element (D) consisting of domestic credit created by the central bank (which is represented by commercial bank reserves and currency held by the nonbank public), and an *international* element (R) consisting of the domestic-currency value of the official international reserves held by the monetary authorities. In equation form,

$$(20)\ B = D + R.$$

The monetary base is sometimes called "high-powered money" because commercial banks can create demand deposits to a multiple (m) of their reserves. This money multiplier is assumed to be independent of changes in the monetary base.

---

[7] Money is a financial asset that can be used directly as a means of payment. The money stock of a country consists mostly of currency (banknotes and coins) in the hands of the public and the demand deposits of commercial banks.

To finance a surplus in the current account, the central bank buys foreign exchange, thereby increasing R and B. Conversely, to finance a deficit in the current account, the central bank sells foreign exchange, thereby decreasing R and B. The change in R over a period equals the net balance on official reserves account which, in turn, equals the net balance on current account (ignoring sign). That is to say, $dR = B_r = -B_c$.

How can these monetary effects change real domestic absorption and thus contribute to balance of payments adjustment? Let us first take up the case of a balance of payments surplus.

A current-account surplus that raises expenditure via the foreign trade multiplier adds to the cash balances of domestic residents. At first, these higher cash balances are needed to support the higher level of real expenditure in the economy caused by the foreign trade multiplier. But after the multiplier effect on expenditure (income) has come to an end, any remaining surplus will continue to increase cash balances relative to money expenditures. Eventually the cash balances held by domestic residents will exceed their transactions demand for money, and then they will invest excess cash in securities to obtain income.[8] This purchase of securities will drive up their prices and thus lower the rate of interest. The lower interest rate, in turn, will induce businesses to increase the planned level of their investments, thus injecting new real expenditure into the economy. The resulting new income will increase imports through the marginal propensity to import (MPM). Income generated by monetary effects will continue to rise until the balance of payments surplus is completely eliminated. Only then will the supply of money stop rising and the monetary effects come to an end.

In similar fashion, the net monetary effects that continue after incomplete adjustment via the foreign trade multiplier to a current account deficit will lower cash balances below the level that domestic residents want to maintain relative to their money expenditures. To restore that level, they will sell securities, thereby lowering security prices and pushing up the interest rate. In turn, the higher interest rate will induce businesses to reduce their planned investment expenditures. The resulting drop in income will lower imports through the marginal propensity to import until the balance of payments deficit is completely eliminated. Only then will the net monetary effects become zero.

How will the burden of adjustment be shared by the foreign trade multiplier and monetary effects? To eliminate a disequilibrium caused by an autonomous change in exports, the induced change in imports must equal that autonomous change.[9] Thus, the change in real expenditure (income) required for full adjustment is the change that makes $dM = dX$. Since the

---

[8] Because we are assuming zero international capital mobility, excess cash is invested only in *domestic* securities. Also, we continue to assume that consumption depends only on real income.

[9] For simplicity, we are assuming the absence of any foreign repercussion effect.

change in imports is $MPM(dY)$, we have the following equation for the change in income required for full adjustment:

$$(21)\ dY = dM(1/MPM) = dX(1/MPM).$$

Now we know that the change in income (dY') that will result from the foreign trade multiplier is

$$(22)\ dY' = dX \left(\frac{1}{MPM + MPS} \right).$$

Thus, the change in income via monetary effects that is necessary to achieve full adjustment is $dY - dY' = dY''$. Algebraically,

$$(23)\ dY'' = dX \left(\frac{1}{MPM} \right) - dX \left(\frac{1}{MPM + MPS} \right).$$

This reduces to

$$(24)\ dY'' = dX \left(\frac{MPS/MPM}{MPM + MPS} \right).$$

Thus, the necessary change in income via monetary effects is the autonomous change in exports multiplied by the ratio of the marginal propensity to save to the marginal propensity to import divided by the sum of the two propensities.

If $MPM > MPS$, then the foreign trade multiplier will assume the larger share of the adjustment burden, and conversely.[10] If $MPM = MPS$, then the foreign trade multiplier and the monetary effects will each account for one half the adjustment. To illustrate the adjustment, let us assume that $MPM = 0.2$ and $MPS = 0.2$. Then the multiplier is 2.5. If there is an autonomous drop in exports of $100, the foreign trade multiplier will decrease income by $250. Hence, imports will fall by $50 [.2 ($250)], leaving a continuing deficit in the balance of payments of $50. Full adjustment will require a further decrease in income of $250 via the monetary effects that are defined by equation (24).[11]

----

[10] If $MPM > MPS$, then

$$\left(\frac{1}{MPM + MPS} \right) > \frac{MPS}{MPM} \left(\frac{1}{MPM + MPS} \right).$$

[11] $dY'' = dX \left(\dfrac{MPS/MPM}{MPM + MPS} \right)$

$\qquad = \$100 \left(\dfrac{0.2/0.2}{0.2 + 0.2} \right) = \$250.$

Equilibrating Changes in Domestic Absorption through Price Effects

Until now we have assumed fixed prices to concentrate our attention on payments adjustment through *changes in real expenditure (income)* via the foreign trade multiplier and monetary effects. We now relax this assumption to allow for some price flexibility.

In the extreme case, when prices are fully flexible (perfectly competitive markets for goods and factors), the economy is at full employment, and exchange rates are stable, a country would adjust to a balance of payments disequilibrium *solely* through price changes, with no accompanying changes in real expenditure.

It is unlikely that the fixed prices of the income theory of adjustment or the flexible prices of the classical theory of adjustment would ever exist in the actual world.[12] The relative importance of income (through both the multiplier and monetary effects) and price adjustments in a particular instance, therefore, will depend on the degree of flexibility in prices and the degree of unemployment and excess capacity in deficit and surplus countries. In periods of massive unemployment, the income-adjustment model provides a more satisfactory explanation of the actual adjustment process; in periods of full employment and inflation, the classical model gains in relevance. In both situations, however, income and price changes interact to bring about adjustment to payments disequilibrium.

Switching Real Expenditure: Tradables and Nontradables Price effects help to eliminate a balance of payments *deficit* on current account by switching real domestic expenditure away from tradable goods and services to nontradable goods and services so as to reduce domestic absorption. Conversely, adjustment to a *surplus* involves switching real domestic expenditure away from nontradables to tradables, thereby increasing domestic absorption.

Tradable goods and services consist of exportables and importables. *Exportables* are goods and services actually exported by a country plus their close substitutes produced and consumed at home. *Importables* are goods and services actually imported by a country plus their close substitutes (import-competing goods and services) produced and consumed at home. *Nontradables* are goods and services both produced and consumed at home. Nontradables are *not* close substitutes for tradables and, in fact, consist mostly of services.

The *domestic* supply of exportables (S_x) equals the sum of the *domestic* demand for exportables (D_x) and actual exports (X), or

$$(25) \; S_x = D_x + X.$$

---

[12] The classical theory of adjustment is described in the following section.

Hence, exports equal the *excess domestic supply* of exportables, or

$$(26)\ X = S_x - D_x.$$

The *domestic* demand for importables (D_m) equals the sum of the domestic supply of import-competing goods and services (S_m) and actual imports (M), or

$$(27)\ D_m = S_m + M.$$

Hence actual imports equal the *excess domestic demand* for importables, or

$$(28)\ M = D_m - S_m.$$

Finally, the *domestic* demand for nontradables (D_n) equals their domestic supply (S_n), or

$$(29)\ D_n = S_n.$$

We can now derive the following equation for the net balance on current account:

$$(30)\ X - M = (S_x - D_x) - (D_m - S_m).$$

When exports equal imports, then the excess supply of exportables is equal to the excess demand for importables. When $S_x - D_x > D_m - S_m$, then the current account is in surplus, and conversely. We can restate equation (30) as follows:

$$(31)\ X - M = (S_x + S_m) - (D_x + D_m).$$

It follows that a deficit on current account can be reduced by increasing the domestic supply of tradables and, at the same time, decreasing the domestic demand for tradables. Assuming that real GNP is constant for the period in question, an increase in the supply of tradables can only occur through a transfer of resources from the production of nontradables. These supply and demand switches reduce domestic absorption, which, as we know, is necessary to reduce a deficit on current account.[13]

Let us now trace through the price adjustments that will accompany, in small or large degree, real-income adjustment to a current-account deficit.

---

[13] The total output (Y) of the economy is the sum of the domestic production of tradables and nontradables, or $S_x + S_m + S_n$. Substituting and transposing equation (18), we get the following statement for domestic absorption: $A = S_n + D_x + D_m$. To reduce absorption, therefore, the domestic supply of nontradables and the domestic demand for tradables must decrease, as stated in the text.

The deficit will induce a decline in money income and spending in the deficit country, which will in turn cause a general decline in prices (although the decline may be spotty and somewhat retarded because of market imperfections). The effect of this general price deflation is to encourage exports and discourage imports: With fixed exchange rates, domestic goods and services become cheaper to foreign buyers, while foreign goods and services become more expensive to domestic buyers.

In addition to the general decline in prices, a current-account deficit will also cause the prices of tradables to rise relative to the prices of nontradables. The prices of exportables are held up by export demand; the prices of importables are determined in the world market; but the prices of nontradables are subject entirely to the deficit-induced decline in domestic spending. These relative price changes switch domestic demand away from tradables to nontradables and switch domestic supply away from nontradables to tradables.

These general and relative price changes will continue until the deficit is eliminated. At that point, there are no further effects on domestic expenditure, and the demand-supply shifts between tradables and nontradables come to an end.

Simultaneously, surplus countries will experience an expansion of money income and spending. This will cause a general rise in the price level (unless there is widespread unemployment and excess capacity) and shifts in relative prices that will encourage imports and discourage exports.

In effect, general price adjustment works through a shift in the *terms of trade* of both the surplus and deficit countries.[14] The surplus country enjoys an improvement in its terms of trade as its import prices fall and its export prices rise, while the deficit country suffers a deterioration in its terms of trade as its import prices rise and its export prices fall.

Price Elasticities   The degree to which the terms of trade must shift in favor of the surplus country to remove disequilibrium in the balance of payments will depend upon the price elasticities of supply and demand of both exports and imports.[15] When elasticities are high, a relatively small

---

[14] For a definition of *commodity terms of trade*, see Chapter 2.

[15] The price elasticity of demand is this ratio: percentage change in amount of demanded/percentage change in price. (Algebraically speaking, this ratio carries a minus sign, since the amount demanded and price are inversely related. However, following common practice, we shall ignore the sign.) When demand elasticity is one, then the percentage changes in amount demanded and price are the same, and the amount spent on the product in question stays the same after a price change. When elasticity is greater than one, total expenditure increases (decreases) with a fall (rise) in price. When elasticity lies between one and zero, then total expenditure decreases with a fall in price. When elasticity is zero, then total expenditure decreases the same percentage as the fall in price. Similarly, the quantity supplied changes the same percentage, a greater percentage, or a lesser percentage than the percentage change in price, depending on whether the elasticity of supply is one, greater than one, or less than one. It should be noted that the amount supplied and price are positively related: They change in the same direction. The use of percentages to define elasticities is a crude simplification and an approximation only. Mathematically, elasticity is $(dQ/dP)(P/Q)$, where dQ/dP is the rate of change (derivative) of Q with respect to P.

change in prices calls forth a relatively large response in the quantity of exports and imports, and the terms of trade need change little to effect adjustment. With low elasticities, however, relatively large price changes will stimulate only relatively small changes in the quantity of exports and imports, and there must be a wide swing in the terms of trade to effect adjustment.

The price elasticities of export and import supply will depend upon the mobility of productive factors within both the surplus and deficit countries. When labor and other resources are induced by only slight variations in relative wages and other factor prices to move from one industry to another, the supply of goods is *elastic*—the amount supplied can be adjusted to changing demand with relatively small changes in the supply price. When, however, productive resources are relatively immobile, supply elasticities are low and any adjustment to balance of payments disequilibrium is impeded. In a many-nation world, the price elasticity of import supply for a specific country will also depend on whether foreign suppliers have alternative markets. When the domestic demand for import goods is small compared to the world demand, it will have little or no influence over import prices, and import supply will appear highly elastic to the domestic country.

The price elasticities of export and import demand will depend on the nature of the export and import goods and the availability of domestic substitutes. Thus, the demand for luxury imports is more elastic than the demand for essential imports and, other things being equal, the demand for imports with close domestic substitutes is more elastic than the demand for imports with only distant or no domestic substitutes. In a many-nation world, substitutes for imports from a given country may also be found in imports from other countries. Hence, the demand facing the exports of a country is apt to be less elastic than otherwise when that country supplies most of the world market—that is, when foreign customers have little opportunity to obtain similar goods elsewhere. Conversely, export demand is likely to be more elastic than otherwise when the exporting country supplies only a small portion of the world market.

Obstacles to Price Adjustment Fundamentally, international adjustment requires shifts in the level and composition of both supply and demand in the surplus and deficit countries. Equilibrating changes in prices are effective in bringing about such shifts when the price elasticities of supply and demand are high. Anything that lowers price elasticities, therefore, hinders price adjustment to balance of payments disequilibrium.

Price adjustment is undoubtedly less effective today than before World War I. As observed in Chapter 4, few contemporary markets are close to pure competition. Markets for agricultural staples, such as wheat, cotton, and coffee, are usually subject to price stabilization by government agencies, whereas the majority of markets for manufactured goods have monopolistic elements that allow the seller (or, in the case of monopsony, the buyer) some control over price. Administered pricing by large-scale oligopolistic industries and the enforcement of wage floors by powerful labor unions are common examples of price inflexibility in today's economies. Of special importance is the international cartel that outlaws price competition and fixes the pattern of foreign trade in its products. The widespread abandonment of price competition in favor of nonprice competition in quality, style, and services; government schemes to control production and marketing; and the innumerable devices used by governments to insulate the domestic economy from foreign economic influences have all diminished the importance of price adjustment.

Despite these developments, however, equilibrating changes in prices remain a significant instrument of international adjustment. The prices of many raw materials and foodstuffs in international trade remain uncontrolled and respond quickly to changes in supply and demand. Moreover, all international goods show plenty of price flexibility upward, as inflation has demonstrated time and again. We can conclude that price adjustment, when permitted, is an effective ally of income adjustment and that both are required in a fixed exchange rate system if exchange depreciation or suppressed disequilibrium is to be avoided.

The Classical Theory of Adjustment

The first coherent theory of international payments adjustment was devised by David Hume (1711–1776), British philosopher and economist extraordinary.[16] In opposition to the dominant mercantilist thought of the age, Hume asserted the impossibility of maintaining a chronic "favorable balance of trade" to acquire gold and silver (specie) from foreign countries.

The Price-Specie Flow Mechanism Hume's theory of adjustment has come down as the *price-specie flow mechanism*. It asserts that an inflow of specie resulting from an excess of exports over imports increases the nation's money supply and that the increased money supply, in turn, increases domestic prices. These higher prices then curtail exports. At the same time there occurs a fall in the money supply and prices in the foreign countries experiencing an outflow of specie. This decline in prices stimulates the exports of those countries, including exports to the country receiving specie. In this way international specie movements eliminate any disequilibrium in the balance of payments—higher prices in the surplus country cause its exports to fall and its imports to rise, while lower prices in the deficit country or countries cause exports to rise and imports to fall. International specie movements are, therefore, symptoms of payments disequilibrium, and they will continue until the money supplies and price levels of the trading nations achieve an equality between the exports and imports of each country.

Critique of the Price-Specie Flow Mechanism Succeeding generations of classical and neoclassical economists (Ricardo, Mill, Marshall, Taussig,

---

[16] This theory appeared in Hume's *Political Discourses*, published in Edinburgh in 1752.

and others) added refinements to Hume's price-specie flow mechanism but made no basic changes in it. The theory was modified to take account of service or "invisible" items in the balance of payments; short-term capital movements; the fractional reserve system of banking; and the differential price behavior of export goods, import-competing goods, and nontraded goods. However, the underlying assumptions of the theory—the quantity theory of money and the effect of price changes on exports and imports— were not effectively challenged until the Keynesian revolution in economic thinking of the late 1930s.

The price-specie flow mechanism is open to all criticisms that have been leveled against the quantity theory of money. This theory assumes that a change in the quantity of money will bring about a proportionate change in the price level. A change in the quantity of money will, however, affect prices only if it affects spending, and the change in spending induced by a given change in the money supply may be relatively large or small depending on its velocity of turnover. Moreover, the influence of a given change in spending on prices will vary according to the general level of employment and output and the degree of price flexibility in the economy. Hence, there is no direct or certain price response to a change in the money supply, and under conditions of excess productive capacity and unemployment or of imperfect competition, there may be little or no response.

The main criticism of the price-specie flow mechanism, however, is its emphasis upon price adjustment to the neglect of real income adjustment. Classical and neoclassical economists understood that a deficit country underwent a decline in its purchasing power relative to a surplus country and that this decline, along with the adverse shift in its terms of trade, brought about adjustment by raising its exports and lowering its imports. But this purchasing-power or nominal income effect was viewed as the incidental accompaniment of price changes, which were the main instruments of international adjustment. There was no conception of an *autonomous* change in income unrelated to a change in prices. In the classical world of full employment and purely competitive markets, this oversight was inevitable, for under such conditions a change in spending will cause a change in prices and there are no real income effects.

Writing in 1928, Taussig, the foremost neoclassical economist in America, felt that something was missing in the price-specie flow explanation of international payments adjustment, although he was unable to lay his finger on it. In speaking of adjustment to a movement of long-term investment capital, he wrote as follows:

> What is puzzling is the rapidity, almost simultaneity, of the commodity movements. The presumable intermediate state of gold flow and price changes is hard to discern, and certainly extremely short.[17]

---

[17] Frank W. Taussig, *International Trade* (New York: Macmillan, 1928), p. 260.

At another point he remarked,

> It must be confessed that here we have phenomena not fully understood. In part our information is insufficient; in part our understanding of other connected topics is also inadequate.[18]

Income and cash-balance adjustment are the keys to this puzzle.

ADJUSTMENT WITH INTERNATIONAL CAPITAL MOBILITY

In our treatment of current-account adjustment through changes in income and the price level, we have assumed until now that capital does not move between the domestic country and the rest of the world. But if in fact capital does so move, then a net balance on current account may be financed by an opposing net balance on capital account. When $B_c = -B_k$, then $B_c + B_k = 0$ and $B_r = 0$. Capital flows, therefore, can restore *temporary* equilibrium in the balance of payments.

International Differentials in Short-term Interest Rates

How is the adjustment process affected by international capital mobility? Let us trace adjustment to a current-account deficit. We continue to assume fixed exchange rates and, to simplify the presentation, we also assume fixed price levels. Under these assumptions, a decrease in the money stock induced by the current-account deficit is also a decrease in the *real* money stock of the deficit country.[19] This decrease will cause a *rise* in the short-term interest rate as residents of the deficit country try to restore their cash balances by selling financial assets (securities), thereby lowering the price of those assets. The higher interest rate in the deficit country creates a real interest-rate differential between it and the rest of the world that attracts an inflow of capital, thereby creating a surplus on capital account in the balance of payments. (Earlier, when we assumed *no* international capital mobility, a change in the interest rate in the deficit country could only induce a change in domestic investment.)

Not all forms of international capital transfer are sensitive to interest-rate differentials. Short-term capital (securities with a maturity of one year or less) moves quickly in response to differentials, as indicated in our presentation of interest arbitrage in Chapter 13. At the extreme of *perfect* international capital mobility, even a very small change in the rate of in-

---

[18] *Ibid.*, p. 239.

[19] The real money stock is the *nominal* money stock adjusted for the rate of inflation. In our example, the rate of inflation is zero because the price level is fixed. Hence, the real money stock equals the nominal money stock.

terest would cause massive short-term capital flows. In contrast, flows of direct foreign investment capital are *insensitive* to interest-rate differentials, responding instead to profit-rate differentials and other factors.[20] Flows of other long-term investment capital (evidenced by debt securities with distant maturities) respond to long-term interest rates that reflect the marginal productivity of real capital used to create wealth. Hence, under conditions of fixed exchange rates and price levels, international flows of direct foreign investment and other long-term capital are *autonomous*, remaining unaffected by changes in short-term interest rates.

Because only short-term capital flows are sensitive to the *liquidity effect* of changes in the money stock, the adjustment process in the capital account achieves only *temporary* equilibrium, which eliminates the need for net official reserve transfers but does not eliminate the source of *persistent* disequilibrium in the current account. The inflow of short-term capital comes to a halt when a rising interest rate equilibrates the demand and supply of money. This money market equilibrium will be coupled with equilibrium in the short-term capital market that (assuming perfect international mobility) occurs when there is no longer a differential in real interest rates between the deficit country and the rest of the world. Expressed algebraically,

$$(32)\ i - i^* = 0,$$

where i is the domestic interest rate and i^* is the foreign interest rate. (Keep in mind we are still assuming fixed exchange rates and price levels.)

If the current account deficit continues after equilibrium is established in the money and short-term capital markets, then the money stock will decrease further, causing a new round of adjustment in the capital account. Only when the combined net balance on the current account and the *autonomous* capital account (direct foreign investment and other long-term capital) equals zero will the balance of payments reach stable, intermediate-run equilibrium.

The International Portfolio Effect

The riskiness of a combination or portfolio of securities (as measured by the variability of returns) is less than the riskiness of the individual securities making up the portfolio when the riskiness of each security is in some degree independent of the riskiness of the others. Through diversification of their security holdings, therefore, investors can achieve lower risk at any given rate of return. The theory of *international* diversification predicts that capital will flow among countries even when interest rates are identical if the riskiness of financial assets is *not* perfectly correlated across countries. By diversifying internationally, investors seek to maximize their risk-adjusted

---

[20] For a review of the theory of direct foreign investment, see Chapter 23.

returns. It follows that a higher interest rate in a deficit country will immediately cause an inflow of short-term capital as investors throughout the world rearrange their holdings of securities so as to achieve new optimal portfolios. Once these optimal portfolios are established, capital movements will cease.

If financial assets denominated in different currencies also differ in riskiness, then investors will demand a *risk premium* for a higher risk. Hence, the equilibrium condition of equation (32) becomes

$$(33)\ i - i^* = v,$$

where v represents a risk premium expressed at an annual rate.

The short-term capital market is in equilibrium only when any remaining interest-rate differential is fully matched by a risk premium. When investors judge short-term financial assets in the deficit country to have the *same* degree of riskiness as in the rest of the world, then $v = 0$ and equation (33) reduces to equation (32). The international portfolio effect remains positive, however, even when the riskiness (variability of returns over time) of financial assets denominated in different currencies is the same—as long as that riskiness is not perfectly correlated over time.

The International Expectations Effect

As discussed above, an increase (decrease) in a country's money stock causes a decrease (increase) in real short-term interest rates through the *liquidity effect*. But if we drop our assumption of fixed price levels, then a change in the money stock can alter expectations about future price levels. This *expectations effect* opposes the liquidity effect. When investors expect inflation, they demand an *inflation premium* in the form of a higher interest rate, and conversely. Suppose that an increase in the money stock of a *surplus* country triggers expectations of a higher price level over the next year. Then, the liquidity effect, which acts to *lower* the interest rate, would be offset in some degree by the expectations effect, which acts to *rise* the interest rate. The latter might overwhelm the former so that the interest rate would rise in the surplus country rather than fall! The expectations effect, therefore, weakens the adjustment process: Movement toward equilibrium in the short-term capital market will require larger changes in the money stock and interest rate than would otherwise be the case.

When the price level is free to move, the equilibrium condition expressed by Equation (33) becomes

$$(34)\ i - i^* = v + \frac{E(P/P^*) - P/P^*}{P/P^*},$$

where $E(P/P^*)$ is the expected ratio between the domestic price level (P) and the foreign price level (P^*) over next year. Any remaining interest-rate differential equals the sum of the risk premium and the inflation premium (which is the expected annual change in the domestic price level relative to the foreign price level). The inflation premium is positive when the domestic country is expected to experience more inflation than the rest of the world. As we know from the purchasing-power parity doctrine, an international inflation differential eventually leads to an equal adjustment in the exchange rate. Hence,

$$\frac{E(P/P^*) - P/P^*}{P/P^*}$$

is equivalent to $[E(S) - S]/S$, which in turn is equivalent to $(F^* - S)/S$. Hence, equation (34) is equivalent over the longer run to the interest-parity equation (7) in Chapter 13, except for the risk premium, which is ignored in that equation.[21]

BALANCE OF PAYMENTS POLICY: INTERNAL AND EXTERNAL BALANCE

In Chapter 1 we spoke about the diversity and conflict of goals in foreign economic policy. Both internal and external goal conflicts make it impossible for a nation to fully achieve a particular goal without sacrificing in some degree the achievement of other goals. In no area of foreign economic policy is goal conflict more apparent than in balance of payments policy in a fixed system. It comes about when the goal of *internal balance* (full employment with price stability) is perceived by policymakers as incompatible with the goal of *external balance* (balance of payments equilibrium), or conversely. Here we call attention to this potential conflict, whose impact on the international monetary system is described in Chapters 18 and 19.

Inflation and recession are the two internal imbalances and deficits and surpluses are the two external imbalances. Conflict arises when the two goals become inconsistent so that an effort to achieve one goal renders more difficult or impossible the achievement of the other. Figure 15-5 depicts in summary fashion the incidence of conflict.

The three conditions relating to internal balance (inflation, recession, and balance) combine with the three conditions relating to external balance (deficit, surplus, and balance) to make a nine-cell matrix whose entries indicate when the policy requirements for internal and external balance (contraction, expansion or none) are consistent or in conflict. With generally inflationary situations in many countries, a common policy conflict is located in cell 1.2—inflation at home combined with a persistent balance of payments surplus. In the late 1950s, early 1960s, and again in the 1970s, the

---

[21] Equation (7): $i_{US} - i_{UK} = (F^* - S)/S$.

Figure 15-5   The Internal Conflict of Goals: Internal and External Balance

	BALANCE OF PAYMENTS →	Deficit	Surplus	Balance
DOMESTIC ECONOMY ↓	POLICY REQUIREMENT →	Contraction	Expansion	None
Inflation	Contraction	No conflict 1.1	Conflict 1.2	Conflict 1.3
Recession	Expansion	Conflict 2.1	No conflict 2.2	Conflict 2.3
Balance	None	Conflict 3.1	Conflict 3.2	No conflict 3.3

United States faced the policy conflict located in cell 2.1—unemployment at home with a persistent balance of payments deficit. This second policy dilemma is felt more keenly by governments than the first one, because both unemployment and a balance of payments deficit are widely viewed as more serious than inflation or a balance of payments surplus (which is often viewed as highly desirable).

When governments fail to resolve the conflict between internal and external balance in a stable-rate system with monetary and fiscal policies, they resort to other policy instruments, most notably an alteration in the exchange rate or the suppression of balance of payments disequilibrium with exchange controls. Flexible exchange rates and exchange control are the subjects of the next two chapters.

THE MONETARY APPROACH TO THE BALANCE OF PAYMENTS

In the 1970s, a period marked by high rates of inflation in the world economy, some economists advanced a new approach to the balance of payments. Although new, the monetary approach can trace its lineage back to Hume's price-specie flow mechanism, which explained payments adjustment in terms of changes in the money supply. But unlike Hume, today's monetarists do not rely on price effects to achieve equilibrium.

According to the monetary approach, the balance of payments is a monetary phenomenon determined by the demand and supply of money stocks. Whereas the conventional approach explains current-account adjustment by changes and switches in real expenditure, the monetary approach explains adjustment of the entire balance of payments by changes in the demand and supply of money.

In conventional balance of payments analysis, transfers in the current and long-term capital accounts are regarded as *autonomous* and transfers in the short-term capital and official reserves accounts are regarded as *compensatory*, passively financing the net balance on autonomous transactions. The monetary approach takes the opposite view: The official reserve transfers are *active* (or autonomous), responding to changes in the demand and supply of money, whereas all other transfers in the balance of payments are *passive*, adjusting to the official reserves balance. In sum, the conventional approach looks at the balance of payments from the "top down" and the monetary approach looks at the balance of payments from the "bottom up."

Money Demand and Supply

The monetary approach postulates that the cause of an international payments imbalance (defined as a nonzero balance on the official reserves account) is an excess demand or excess supply of money. An excess demand causes a payments surplus; an excess supply, a payments deficit. Balance of payments equilibrium is achieved only when the demand and supply of money are equal.

For monetarists, the demand for money (currency and demand deposits held by the public) is a stable function of a few macroeconomic variables:

$$(35)\ M^d = L(P,\ Y,\ i),$$

which states that the demand for nominal money balances (M^d) is a function (L) of the price level (P), real income (Y), and the interest rate (i).[22] An increase in P or Y causes an increase in M^d, because individuals and business firms need to finance a larger value of transactions—the so-called *transactions* demand for money. However, an increase in i causes a decrease in the demand for money, because it raises the opportunity cost of holding money—the so-called *hoarding* (or precautionary/speculative) demand for money.

The supply of money (M^s) equals the money multiplier (m) times the monetary base (B):

$$(36)\ M^s = mB = m(D + R).[23]$$

---

[22] This and the following equations are taken from Mordechai E. Kreinin and Lawrence H. Officer, *The Monetary Approach to the Balance of Payments*, Princeton Studies in International Finance, no. 43 (Princeton, N.J.: Princeton University Press, 1978), pp. 5 ff.

[23] See Equations (19) and (20).

Adjustment to Balance of Payments Disequilibrium

Equilibrium in the money market is an equality between the stock demand and stock supply of money:

$$(37)\ M^d = m(D + R).$$

Assuming a constant money multiplier, monetarists consider changes in the demand for money (ΔM^d) and in the domestic element of the monetary base (ΔD) as the initiating forces causing disequilibrium in the money market. Under fixed exchange rates, equilibrium is restored by changes in the international element of the reserve base (ΔR) that are expressed in the balance of payments as a net balance on official reserves account. We have, therefore,

$$(38)\ m\Delta R = \Delta M^d - m\Delta D,$$

which, in turn, equals the net balance on official reserves account.

The monetary approach explains payments adjustment in a fixed-rate system in the following way. Changes in the demand for money can occur quickly with changes in the price level, real income, or the interest rate. Also, changes in the domestic supply of money ($m\Delta D$) can occur quickly through the open-market operations of the central bank. Such changes create either an excess stock demand for money ($\Delta M^d > m\Delta D$) or an excess stock supply of money ($\Delta M^d < m\Delta D$). (Keep in mind that ΔM^d and ΔD are *not* flows over time but rather one-time changes in stocks.)

Any divergence between the demand and supply of money (disequilibrium in the money market) is eliminated by a one-time change in the international element of the monetary base (ΔR). Suppose $\Delta M^d > m\Delta D$, then the excess demand for money by individuals and business firms will cause them to build up their money stocks by cutting their purchases of foreign goods and services, by liquidating their foreign investments, or by borrowing from foreigners. These actions will draw foreign funds into the country and thereby create a balance of payments surplus. Monetarists are not concerned with where the official reserves account is offset in the remainder of the balance of payments. The important point is that the surplus will disappear as soon as the stock supply of money satisfies the stock demand for money balances.

Conversely, when $\Delta M^d < m\Delta D$, then individuals and firms act to reduce their money stocks by increasing their purchases of foreign goods and services, investing abroad, or lending to foreigners, thereby creating a balance of payments deficit. The deficit, therefore, is regarded as a spillover of the excess supply of money, and it will cease to exist when stock equilibrium is restored in the money market.

To monetarists, a *continuing* disequilibrium in the balance of payments is possible only when the monetary authorities offset ("sterilize") a change in international reserves with an opposing change in domestic credit created (or destroyed) by the central bank. The self-correcting mechanism takes time to work, but the monetarists have said little about the dynamic adjustment process of the economy necessary to reestablish equilibrium (or the time required). The monetary approach, therefore, deals only with the final, equilibrium position of the balance of payments and money market.

Some Closing Remarks about the Monetary Approach

The monetary approach to the balance of payments is posed as a direct challenge to the conventional approach. In sum, the monetarists argue that the demand for money balances relative to supply determines the level of real expenditure on goods and services, rejecting the conventional view that real expenditure decisions are the initiating forces and money is only a passive agent to finance expenditures.

The monetary approach has made an undeniable contribution to the theory of balance of payments adjustment by emphasizing the role of money, which has often been ignored in the real-expenditure approach. In so doing, it has made the theory more relevant to the inflationary conditions of recent years. For example, the monetary approach demonstrates a direct connection between excessive domestic credit creation and a balance of payments deficit.

But the monetarists would appear to have gone too far in singling out monetary variables as the *only* explanation of balance of payments disequilibria and in claiming that their approach is a *complete* substitute for the conventional approach. After all, *real* factors, such as economic growth, technological innovation, and shifts in international competitiveness (comparative advantage) can generate structural payments imbalances, and these real factors are not related to money variables in any systematic way.

By ignoring the *composition* of the balance of payments, the monetarists have also gone too far. For example, a current-account deficit has very different implications for the domestic economy (and calls for different policy responses) than a deficit on long- or short-term capital accounts. Also, the monetarists fail to distinguish between financing a current-account deficit through inflows of long-term capital and through inflows of short-term capital. As discussed in Chapter 14, short-term capital flows can provide only short-run adjustment.

Are the two approaches irreconcilable? Almost certainly, no. Economists have always recognized that there are two sides to transactions in goods, services, and securities, and in a monetary system (in contrast to a barter system), one of those sides is money. Hence, when the conventional approach looks at the real side of transactions and the monetary approach looks at the money side of transactions, they are looking at the same phenomenon. It remains true, therefore, that an imbalance on current account can be eliminated only by changing domestic absorption or (less likely) by changing physical output. We can justifiably view the monetary approach, therefore, as an additional explanation of the absorption process of adjustment.

GENERAL EQUILIBRIUM IN AN OPEN ECONOMY

Equilibrium in the balance of payments requires simultaneous equilibrium in a country's goods and money markets. We offer here in summary form a graphical depiction of general equilibrium in these three markets.

The IS Schedule

The IS schedule shown in Figure 15-6 indicates equilibrium in the goods market: It contains all combinations of interest rates and levels of national

Figure 15-6   The IS Schedule

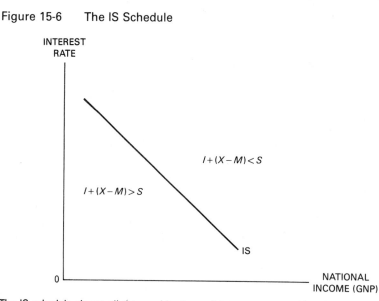

The IS schedule shows all the combinations of interest rates and levels of national income that equate aggregate demand and supply. The schedule slopes downward from left to right because equilibrium at higher levels of national income requires lower interest rates to induce higher domestic investment.

income that equate aggregate demand and supply.[24] Alternatively, it contains all combinations of interest rates and national income that equate income injections and leakages: $I + X = S + M$. This equilibrium condition may be rewritten as follows: $I + (X - M) = S$.

The IS curve slopes downward from left to right because equilibrium at higher levels of national income requires lower interest rates to induce higher domestic investment. At any point below and to the left of the IS schedule, $I + (X - M) > S$; at any point above and to the right of the IS schedule, $I + (X - M) < S$.

The IS schedule assumes that government spending (G) and X and M are fixed. Autonomous changes in any of these variables will cause a shift to the left or right of the entire IS schedule.

The LM Schedule

The LM schedule shown in Figure 15-7 depicts equilibrium in the money market. At each point on the schedule, the quantity of money demanded

---

[24] The IS schedule is derived from Figure 15-2.

Figure 15-7   The LM Schedule

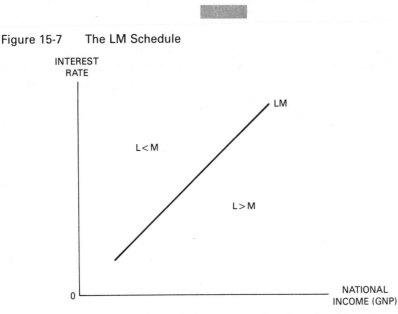

The LM schedule depicts equilibrium in the money market: At each point on the schedule, the quantity of money demanded (L) equals the money stock (M). The schedule slopes upward from left to right because the quantity of money demanded rises with a rise in national income and a new equilibrium can be achieved with a fixed stock of money only through a rise in the interest rate, which increases the opportunity cost of holding money.

(L) equals the money stock (M). The LM schedule slopes upward from left to right because as national income rises more money is demanded to support the greater volume of transactions in goods and services. With the money stock fixed, individuals try to obtain additional cash balances by selling securities, which lowers their price and thus pushes up the interest rate. Higher interest rates reduce the amount of money demanded by raising the opportunity cost of holding money, namely, the interest that could otherwise be earned from securities. Interest rates will raise until the money demanded once again equals the money stock. Hence, national income and interest rates must move in the same direction to maintain equilibrium in the money market.

Above and to the left of the LM schedule, the amount of money demanded is less than the money stock ($L < M$); below and to the right of the schedule, the amount of money demanded is greater than the money stock ($L > M$). Because the LM schedule assumes a fixed money stock, any increase in the money stock shifts the entire schedule to the right, and conversely.

The BOP Schedule

The BOP schedule presented in Figure 15-8 is the locus of all combinations of interest rates and national income levels at which the balance of payments is in equilibrium: $B_c + B_k = 0$. The foreign exchange market is also in equilibrium (with a zero net flow of foreign exchange into or out of the domestic country), because $B_r = 0$. The BOP curve slopes upward from left to right because at a fixed exchange rate higher levels of national income induce more imports (via the marginal propensity to import), which worsens the current account balance, and higher interest rates induce inflows of short-term capital, which improves the capital account balance.

At the lower end of the BOP schedule, low income levels create a surplus in the current account that is fully offset by a deficit on capital account induced by low interest rates: $B_c = -B_k$. At the higher end of the schedule, high income levels cause a deficit in the current account that is fully offset by a surplus on capital account resulting from capital inflows induced by high interest rates: $-B_c = B_k$. It follows that above and to the left of the BOP schedule the balance of payments is in *surplus disequilibrium* (BOP > 0), whereas below and to the right of the schedule the balance of payments is in *deficit disequilibrium* (BOP < 0).

The BOP schedule assumes fixed values for foreign income (Y_f), the relation between foreign and domestic prices as determined by both local-currency price levels and the foreign exchange rate (P/SP^*), the relation between domestic foreign profit rates (r/r^*), and the expected exchange rate [$E(S)$]. Changes in any of these variables will cause the entire schedule to shift to the left or right.

Figure 15-8   The BOP Schedule

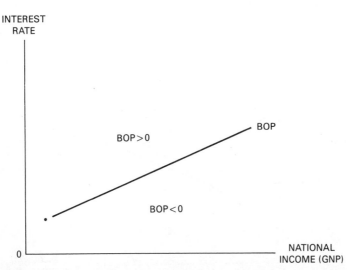

The BOP schedule shows all combinations of interest rates and national income levels at which the balance of payments is in equilibrium, with a zero net balance on official reserves account. (At the same time, the foreign exchange market is in equilibrium.) The schedule slopes upward from left to right because at a fixed exchange rate a rise in national income worsens the *current-account* balance, putting the balance of payments in deficit disequilibrium. A new equilibrium can be achieved only through a rise in the interest rate, which improves the *capital-account* balance.

Determination of General Equilibrium

General equilibrium in an open economy is determined graphically at the point of intersection of the IS, LM, and BOP schedules, indicating simultaneous equilibrium in the goods market, the money market, and the balance of payments (foreign exchange) market. In Figure 15-9, general equilibrium is determined at the rate of interest i and the national income level Y.

To conclude, the general equilibrium model demonstrates that balance of payments equilibrium requires simultaneous equilibrium in the goods and money markets. If one or both of these markets is in disequilibrium, then continuing changes in the interest rate and the level of national income will prevent the balance of payments from reaching equilibrium. But it is important to keep in mind that this model concerns only general equilibrium over the short run. As pointed out earlier, *intermediate* and *long-run* equilibrium in the balance of payments cannot be sustained with net flows of short-term capital.

Figure 15-9   General Equilibrium in an Open Economy: The Intersection of the IS, LM and BOP Schedules

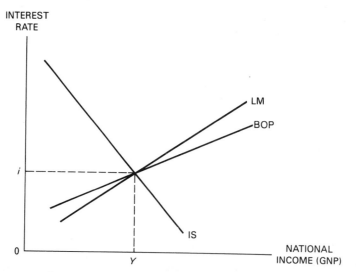

General equilibrium in an open economy is determined at the point of intersection of the IS, LM, and BOP schedules. Simultaneous equilibrium in the goods, money, and balance of payments (foreign exchange) markets occurs only at that point. General equilibrium occurs at an interest rate *i* and a national income level *Y*.

SUMMARY

1. The balance on current account depends on domestic real income, foreign real income, and the relative prices of domestic and foreign goods and services as determined by local-currency price levels and the rate of foreign exchange. The balance on capital account is dependent on the domestic interest rate relative to the foreign interest rate, the domestic profit rate relative to the foreign profit rate, and the expected exchange rate.

2. The gross national product (GNP) is the market value of all final goods and services produced by the national economy over the year; it is equal to the gross national income (GNI). $S - I_d = X - M$ is a basic equation relating GNI (or GNP) to foreign trade.

3. National income is in equilibrium when intended expenditures equal income leakages, that is, $I_d + X = S + M$. The foreign trade multiplier equals the reciprocal of the marginal propensities to save and import, or

$$\frac{dY}{dX} = \frac{1}{MPS + MPM}.$$

4. For our exposition of international payments adjustment in this and the next two chapters, we define balance of payments equilibrium as a zero net balance on official reserves account.

5. When the exchange rate is fixed and there is zero international mobility of capital, disequilibrium in the balance of payments appears as a surplus or deficit in the current account. Algebraically, $B_c = Y - A$. Adjustment to a *persistent deficit* in the current account requires the elimination of excess domestic absorption (reduction in real expenditure).

6. When prices are fixed, equilibrating changes in domestic absorption occur through changes in real income via the foreign trade multiplier and monetary effects.

7. When there is a savings leakage, adjustment to a payments disequilibrium via the foreign trade multiplier is incomplete, even after allowance is made for the foreign repercussion effect.

8. When prices are fixed and there is a savings leakage that causes incomplete adjustment via the foreign trade multiplier, the remaining adjustment depends on the monetary effects on real income.

9. When prices are flexible, adjustment to a balance of payments disequilibrium also occurs through changes in prices that *switch* expenditures among exportables, importables, and nontradables. Price elasticities determine the effectiveness of price adjustment.

10. The classical theory of adjustment in a fixed exchange rate system (the gold standard) is the price-specie flow mechanism, which stresses the equilibrating role of price changes but ignores changes in real income and cash balances.

11. When capital is internationally mobile, then adjustment can occur in the capital account, because interest-rate differentials stimulate short-term capital flows between deficit and surplus countries. In addition to current interest-rate differentials, portfolio and expectations effects influence the international movement of capital.

12. Balance of payments policy in a fixed-rate system is often constrained by a conflict between internal and external balance.

13. The monetary approach explains a balance of payments deficit as an excess supply of money stocks and a surplus as an excess demand for money stocks.

14. Equilibrium in the balance of payments requires simultaneous equilibrium in a country's goods and money markets.

QUESTIONS AND APPLICATIONS

1. Explain the following equation: $B_r = -(B_c + B_k)$.
2. (a) What are the components of gross national product and gross national income?
   (b) Why is GNP equal to GNI?
   (c) Derive the equation $I_d + X = S + M$ from the GNP and GNI equations.
3. (a) What are the equilibrium conditions of national income?
   (b) Derive both the domestic and foreign trade multipliers from the equation $I_d + X = S + M$.
4. Explain the following equation: $B_c = Y - A$.
5. (a) How does the foreign trade multiplier explain income adjustment to a current-account disequilibrium in the balance of payments?
   (b) When is income adjustment complete? Incomplete?
6. Explain the following equations: (1) $M = mB$ and (2) $B = D + R$.
7. (a) How do the monetary effects of a current-account deficit bring about equilibrating changes in domestic absorption?
   (b) Assuming fixed prices, what change in income via monetary effects is *necessary* to restore equilibrium after an autonomous change in exports?
8. (a) What determines the effectiveness of a shift in the terms of trade in bringing about adjustment in the balance of payments?
   (b) What are the obstacles to price adjustment?
9. Under what conditions is income adjustment likely to dominate adjustment to a net balance on current account when exchange rates are fixed? Under what conditions is price adjustment likely to dominate?
10. (a) Describe the classical theory of adjustment.
    (b) What is the main criticism of this theory?
11. (a) How does adjustment to a current-account surplus occur when there is international capital mobility?
    (b) Why does the adjustment process in the capital account restore only *temporary* equilibrium in the balance of payments?
12. Explain the following equation:

$$i - i^* = v + \frac{E(P/P^*) - P/P^*}{P/P^*}.$$

13. Explain why there is a policy conflict in cell 3.1 of Figure 15-5. Why is there no conflict in cell 2.2 of Figure 15-5?
14. (a) According to the monetary approach, what is the process of adjustment to a balance of payments *deficit*?
    (b) How does this explanation differ from the conventional explanation?

15. Using the monetary approach, trace the effect on the balance of payments of an increase in the interest rate.

16. (a) Define the IS, LM, and BOP schedules.
    (b) Why is equilibrium in an open economy determined by the intersection of these three schedules?

SELECTED READINGS

See the list of readings at the end of Chapter 16.

16

International Payments Adjustment in a Variable-Rate System

In a variable-rate system, adjustment to a payments disequilibrium occurs through an alteration in the rate of exchange. There are many possible kinds of variable-rate systems. At one extreme is the system of *flexible rates* (or purely floating), in which the rate of exchange is determined solely by supply and demand in the foreign exchange market with no attempt by government authorities to limit or moderate fluctuations.[1] At the other extreme is the *adjustable-peg* system, in which rates are fixed by government authorities in the short run and then adjusted once-for-all to a new stabilized level.[2] In between these two extremes there are any number of variant systems that have more rate variability than the adjustable-peg system but less variability than the flexible-rate system. We shall call these middle variants *managed floating-rate* systems, because the rate of exchange may vary beyond the limits imposed on fixed rates but is constrained within wider limits decided by monetary authorities. These limits may or may not change in line with market trends. In all of these systems, however, the rate of exchange continuously or occasionally varies and, in so doing, influences the balance of payments. This variability distinguishes them from a fixed-rate system.

After some introductory remarks, we shall take up, in turn, three different explanations of how exchange rates effect adjustment in the balance of payments: the elasticities approach, the absorption approach, and the monetary approach. In the final section, we shall look at general equilibrium in an open economy with flexible exchange rates.

---

[1] The determination of flexible (freely fluctuating) rates was examined in Chapter 12.

[2] Since the adjustable-peg system involves both stable and variable exchange rates, it may be considered a variant of either the stable-rate or variable-rate system. In Chapter 12, we described briefly the adjustable-peg system in our treatment of active stabilization. In this chapter our interest lies in the variable-rate element of the adjustable-peg system.

VARIABLE RATES: INTRODUCTION

It is important to distinguish between the continuous exchange rate adjustments in a flexible-rate system and occasional exchange rate adjustments in an adjustable-peg system. In both instances, exchange rates are used as an instrument for international payments adjustment, but the circumstances and theoretical arguments are different.

Adjustment Through Flexible Rates

Flexible exchange rates bring about an instantaneous adjustment of the amounts of foreign exchange demanded and supplied in the market. Over time, movements in the exchange rate achieve a succession of short-run equilibria that clear the market. Short-run disequilibrium does not appear in the balance of payments because there are no official reserve transfers to finance a deficit or surplus on the combined current and capital accounts. Algebraically, $B_r = 0$, and consequently $B_c + B_k = 0$. The equilibrium exchange rate is shown as $0-E'$ in Figure 16-1.

Figure 16-1   Exchange Depreciation with High Demand and Supply Elasticities

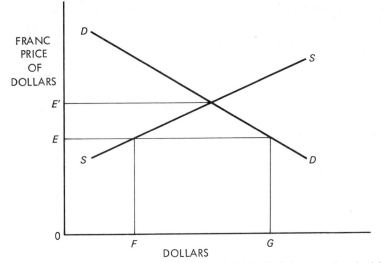

Before devaluation, the exchange rate is $0-E$ and the deficit is $F-G$. Because the elasticities of demand and supply are high, only a small devaluation from $0-E$ to $0-E'$ is needed to eliminate the deficit.

Adjustment Through Occasional Devaluation or Revaluation

What we have just said applies to a system in which exchange rates are *always* free to respond to changes in supply and demand. It does not apply to a payments system in which exchange rates are *occasionally* varied from one stable level to another stable level. In this system, short-run adjustment occurs as under a fixed-rate system, while a planned and limited variation in the exchange rate effects a longer-run adjustment. Under these conditions a variation in the exchange rate will have income and price effects, since it is closing a gap in the balance of payments—a gap that could not exist in a flexible-rate system due to the lack of any compensatory financing. In this adjustable-peg system, adjustment to persistent disequilibrium takes the form of *exchange devaluation* or *exchange revaluation*—a limited increase or limited decrease in the domestic price of foreign money.

Deciding on the Equilibrium Rate   In a freely fluctuating-rate system, the equilibrium rate is determined by the impersonal tug and pull of supply and demand. When, however, a nation that normally stabilizes its exchange rate decides to devalue to correct a deficit disequilibrium, the equilibrium rate of exchange is not known in advance, even though successful devaluation requires depreciation to the equilibrium rate. The exchange rate will, otherwise, continue to be too low, with domestic currency overvalued, or too high, with domestic currency undervalued.

One solution to this difficulty is to free the exchange rate to find its equilibrium rate in the market and then, when equilibrium is restored, to stabilize the rate at the new level. When exchange controls are in existence, either the illegal black market rate or the official "free" rate is sometimes taken to be the equilibrium rate of exchange.[3] Although these rates will usually reveal whether the domestic currency is overvalued or not, they are apt to be unreliable indicators of the equilibrium rate, since the forces of supply and demand acting to determine them often diverge widely from the forces that would exist in a freely fluctuating-rate market.

To estimate the equilibrium rate of exchange, the monetary authorities may apply the *purchasing-power parity doctrine*, a subject treated in Chapter 13. Or they can evaluate the many factors that determine the rate of exchange, including the likely responses of those same factors to a variation in the exchange rate itself.

We learned in Chapter 12 that there is a mutual interdependence between the exchange rate and the balance of payments. When changes in the balance of payments place it in deficit disequilibrium, exchange devaluation is successful only if it reverses those changes or induces new compensating changes. An intelligent policy of devaluation, therefore, depends

---

[3] See Chapter 17 for a description of the official " free" market with fluctuating exchange rates in multiple-rate systems of exchange control.

upon a careful appraisal of the sources of disequilibrium in the balance of payments and of the conditions (supply and demand elasticities, income, price, and monetary effects, and so on) that will determine the efficacy of a given devaluation in overcoming a specific disequilibrium. Even then, the dynamic nature of economic phenomena makes impossible any certain discovery of the equilibrium rate of exchange and any firm guarantee of successful devaluation. Deciding upon the equilibrium rate of exchange, then, is partly economic analysis and partly hunch.

Competitive Depreciation and Overvaluation Depreciation stimulates exports and simultaneously deters imports. During the 1930s many countries took advantage of this fact by depreciating their currencies beyond the equilibrium rate of exchange. Their purpose was to create a surplus in the balance of payments and thereby foster greater income and employment in the domestic economy. Since this policy required a deficit disequilibrium in the balance of payments of other countries that also faced depression, it amounted to exporting unemployment. For this reason, the attempt to depreciate more than other countries—*competitive depreciation*—has received the uncomplimentary designation of "beggar-my-neighbor policy." Competitive depreciation is not likely to be effective in the long run, since other countries will also depreciate in retaliation. The result for a country is usually a disruption of its foreign trade rather than any improvement in the domestic economy.

Competitive depreciation developed out of the rigors of international depression. In our own day, widespread inflation has led to *overvaluation* of the exchange rate through exchange control, especially in developing countries. Depreciation is feared for its inflationary impact on the domestic economy, and it is avoided even when overvaluation of the currency perpetuates a deficit in the balance of payments.

Arguments for Variable Exchange Rates

In Chapter 12 we noted some of the arguments for fixed exchange rates. We now turn the tables and present the argument for flexible exchange rates.

There is a strong theoretical case for flexible exchange rates. In highly simplified terms, it assumes this form. In a fixed-rate system, adjustment to a deficit is carried out by deflationary movements in domestic income and prices that contract real expenditure. All goes well if wages and prices are flexible downward, for then employment and output are sustained at their previous levels. But if wages and prices are *inflexible* downward, then a contraction in real expenditure involves a fall in employment and output. There is abundant evidence indicating that the second course of events is the more likely to happen in contemporary national economies. Unions set floors under wages that are supplemented by official minimum wage policies. Oligopolistic industries set administered prices that do not respond to a decline in effective demand. The decline is met instead by a cutback in production. Under these conditions, current-account adjustment in a fixed-rate system will cause a downward spiral in employment and output. On the other hand, governments are pledged to the maintenance of a high-employment economy. Hence, they will act to frustrate any deflation induced by a deficit in the balance of payments by making use of expansionary fiscal and monetary policies that sustain the level of real expenditure necessary for full employment.

Given contemporary government policies with respect to employment and economic stability, then, current-account adjustment in a fixed-rate system is not likely to be effective. There are two ways out of this impasse: (1) impose controls on trade and payments, or (2) devalue the rate of exchange. Controls, however, are incompatible with a market economy, and they provoke hostility and retaliation in foreign countries. We are left, then, with depreciation or, more comprehensively, variable exchange rates as the only mode of payments adjustment that is compatible both with domestic high-employment policies and the principle of free competition in world markets. Free exchange rates respond to disequilibrating forces and achieve a continuous adjustment in the balance of payments. This gives governments the freedom to follow domestic policies of high employment and growth without worrying about payments deficits.

The theoretical argument for an adjustable-peg system is less strong, because adjustment in the exchange rate is apt to be delayed and the degree of rate variation is determined by a government under circumstances that make the choice of the correct equilibrium rate a very difficult one. Delay in devaluating the exchange rate to correct a deficit is likely to occur in an adjustable-peg system for several reasons. The government often demonstrates a "fixed-rate complex" and makes the mistake of identifying its prestige with the maintenance of the existing rate. Or the government may repeatedly postpone rate adjustment in the renewed expectation that the disequilibrium will prove to be "temporary" after all. Or, having decided in principle on devaluation, the government may take a long time to reach a political consensus on the appropriate amount of devaluation. All this adds up to the fact that there is a strong probability that a government will put off devaluation until it is forced to act because its official reserves are running out and its international credit is exhausted. By that time it is clear to everyone that devaluation (or controls) is imminent, and this will stimulate massive capital flight and destabilizing speculation that will intensify the drain on reserves. In these circumstances a government may feel compelled to undertake a very large devaluation to put a stop to speculative activity. In the end the government devalues the exchange rate and blames the speculators for its troubles.

To sum up, in an adjustable-peg system, devaluation to eliminate a deficit is likely to come too late and be too big. Moreover, the deficit country must do most of the adjusting because there is little or no incentive for surplus countries to revalue their exchange rates. These drawbacks do not appear in a flexible-rate system shared by several countries: The exchange rates of all countries respond quickly to disturbances, and these prompt adjustments sustain a continuing equilibrium in international payments.

Despite the strong theoretical case for flexible exchange rates, governments and central bankers have been traditionally hostile to a flexible-rate system. Unfortunately the reputation of flexible rates has suffered from bad company in the past. Until the 1970s, flexible rates involving several major currencies had appeared two times during this century, but only by default: in the period following World War I before European countries returned to the gold standard in the middle 1920s, and in the 1930s, when global depression forced the wholesale abandonment of the international gold standard. Grave instability in international trade and payments characterized both periods. Not surprisingly, speculation and capital flight were rife; exchange rates behaved erratically, making sharp and sudden movements. Thus, flexible exchange rates came to be associated with instability, speculation, and generally bad times.

This presumed association rests on a confusion of symptom and cause. When underlying conditions are very unstable, then exchange rates will mirror this instability. The same conditions will provoke capital flight and unwanted shifts in domestic income and prices in a fixed-rate system. When underlying conditions are only moderately unstable, then fluctuations in exchange rates will also be moderate.

There is also a widespread belief that fluctuating rates introduce exchange risks that hinder international trade and investment. The rebuttal is that forward exchange markets quickly develop in a flexible-rate system, making possible the hedging of foreign exchange risks. Moreover, there are trading risks of another kind in a fixed-rate system caused by income and price adjustments, to say nothing of trade restrictions stemming from a failure, or rather frustration, of the market adjustment process.

Despite the traditional hostility to flexible rates, the collapse of the Bretton Woods (adjustable-peg) international monetary system at the end of 1971 has been followed by the contemporary floating-rate system, which is characterized by a far higher degree of exchange rate flexibility. When we examine the operation of the contemporary system in Chapter 19, we shall encounter once again the debate on fixed versus flexible exchange rates.

ELASTICITIES APPROACH TO EXCHANGE RATE ADJUSTMENT

The primary effect of an alteration in the exchange rate on the balance of payments depends on the sensitivity of the demand and supply of foreign exchange to the new price of foreign exchange. When demand and supply are very sensitive, or highly elastic, then a small movement in the exchange rate can be very effective in removing a disequilibrium. But when elasticities are low, a large movement in the exchange rate is necessary to restore or maintain equilibrium. Let us examine the role of elasticities for a depreciation (devaluation) of the exchange rate.

This effect of exchange depreciation is shown in Figures 16-1 and 16-2. We take as our example a depreciation of the French franc as viewed in the French foreign exchange market, where the foreign exchange rate is the franc price of dollars. Suppose the French government decides to devalue the franc to remove a deficit in the balance of payments. If, as in Figure 16-1, the elasticities of the demand and supply of foreign exchange (dollars) are high, then the devaluation will be very effective and will not need to be great. In Figure 16-1, the exchange rate before depreciation is 0–*E* and the deficit is *F–G*. This deficit is closed by a relatively slight devaluation from 0–*E* to 0–*E'*. On the other hand, when elasticities are low, a considerable devaluation is needed to bring about adjustment. In Figure 16-2, the exchange rate before devaluation is 0–*P* and the deficit is *M–N*. To wipe out

Figure 16-2   Exchange Depreciation with Low Demand and Supply Elasticities

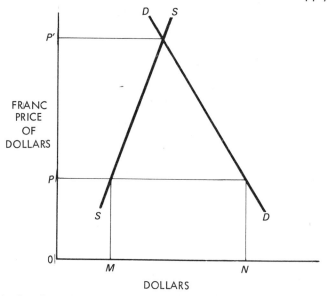

Before devaluation, the exchange rate is 0–*P* and the deficit is *M–N* (equal to *F–G* in Figure 16-1). Because the elasticities of demand and supply are low, a much larger devaluation from 0–*P* to 0–*P'* is needed to wipe out the deficit than was needed in Figure 16-1.

this deficit, the franc must be devalued from 0–P to 0–P'. Note that despite the fact that the deficit in Figure 16-2 is equal to the deficit in Figure 16-1, the exchange depreciation is much larger in the former case.

The Elasticity of Foreign Exchange Supply

The elasticity of the supply of foreign exchange is mainly dependent on the elasticity of foreign demand for domestic exports. Upon devaluation, the foreign exchange price of exports falls. When foreign demand is elastic, this decline in export prices will stimulate an expansion in the quantity exported that will be sufficient to enlarge total receipts of foreign exchange despite the lower prices in terms of foreign exchange. On the other hand, when the elasticity of foreign demand is low, total receipts of foreign exchange may even be smaller after devaluation. In this unlikely event, devaluation will widen the deficit insofar as the supply of foreign exchange is concerned.

We can distinguish three cases that demonstrate the influence of the elasticity of export demand on the elasticity of foreign exchange supply. (When *domestic* export prices do not change after devaluation because export *supply* is perfectly elastic, then the export demand elasticity *fully* determines the supply elasticity of foreign exchange.)

1. When the elasticity of export demand has a value of *one* (unit elastic), then a 10 percent devaluation causes a 10 percent increase in the quantity of exports.[4] Hence, the receipts of foreign exchange are the same before and after devaluation. The elasticity of *foreign exchange supply*, therefore, is zero—foreign exchange receipts do not respond to a variation in the exchange rate—and the effect of devaluation on the supply of foreign exchange is neutral.

2. When the elasticity of export demand is greater than one, then a 10 percent devaluation causes an increase of more than 10 percent in the quantity of exports. Receipts of foreign exchange, therefore, increase and help close the deficit in the balance of payments. In this case the elasticity of foreign exchange supply is greater than zero—foreign exchange receipts respond positively to a higher domestic price of foreign money.

3. When the elasticity of export demand is zero, then a 10 percent devaluation causes no increase in the quantity of exports and foreign exchange receipts fall by 10 percent. When the elasticity lies between zero and one, then the percentage increase in the quantity of exports is less than the percentage devaluation. In both instances devaluation causes a fall in the receipts of foreign exchange that worsens the deficit. Thus, the elasticity of foreign exchange supply is less than zero, or negative—on a graph the supply schedule slopes *downward* from left to right, unlike the normal supply schedule.

---

[4] For a definition of price elasticities, see footnote 15 in Chapter 15.

In summary, when the elasticity of export demand is greater than one (elastic), then devaluation causes an increase in the receipts of foreign exchange and helps close the deficit. When, on the other hand, the elasticity of export demand is less than one, or zero (inelastic), then devaluation lowers foreign exchange receipts and, insofar as the supply of foreign exchange is concerned, worsens the deficit. The elasticities of foreign exchange supply that we have discussed are shown in Figure 16-3, where e_s is the appropriate elasticity.

Under what conditions is export demand likely to be elastic? We can make only a few pertinent comments relating to the composition of exports, the relative importance of a nation's exports in world trade, and the presence of trade restrictions.[5] Generally speaking, the demand for manufactured products (especially "luxury-type" products) is more elastic than the demand for agricultural and other primary products, which is often inelastic. Many primary products satisfy basic needs and their consumption is relatively insensitive to price changes. The same is true of intermediate goods that are purchased as raw materials, semimanufactures, and the like, when these

---

[5] See also Chapter 15.

Figure 16-3   Elasticities of Foreign Exchange Supply

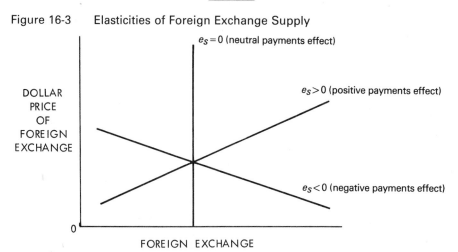

When the elasticity of *export demand* has a value of *one*, then the elasticity of *foreign exchange supply* is *zero*, as shown by the vertical supply schedule. When the elasticity of *export demand* is *more than one*, the elasticity of *foreign exchange supply* is *greater than zero*, as shown by the schedule sloping upward from left to right. When the elasticity of *export demand* lies *between zero and one*, then the elasticity of *foreign exchange supply* is *less than zero* (negative), as shown by the schedule sloping downward from left to right.

goods contribute only a small share to total costs of production. Such products face a derived demand that tends to be inelastic.

The demand facing a product with many substitutes is likely to be more elastic than a product with few or no substitutes. That is why a country whose exports are only a small fraction of world exports experiences a more elastic demand (other things equal) than a country like the United States, whose exports bulk large in world trade. There is a greater opportunity for substitution between a country's exports and the competitive exports of other countries when the country holds only a modest share of foreign markets.

One final point: Tariffs, quotas, cartels, and other restrictions that inhibit the free play of competition in world markets act to lower effective demand elasticities by limiting the role of price in buying decisions.

The Elasticity of Foreign Exchange Demand

The elasticity of the demand for foreign exchange depends mainly on the elasticity of the domestic demand for imports. When higher import prices in domestic currency cause a fall in the quantity of imports, then devaluation improves the balance of payments on the demand side. At the very worst, when the quantity of imports stays the same, devaluation has no effect on the balance of payments as far as foreign exchange demand is concerned.

When the *foreign exchange* price of imports does not change after devaluation (import *supply* is perfectly elastic), then the elasticity of import demand *fully* determines the demand elasticity of foreign exchange. We can distinguish two important cases.

1. When the import demand elasticity is *greater than zero*, then the quantity of imports decreases after devaluation and (given an unchanged foreign exchange price of imports) the quantity of foreign exchange demanded therefore also decreases. The higher the import elasticity, the greater the decline in the amount of foreign exchange in demand. In this case devaluation improves the balance of payments on the demand side.
2. When the elasticity of import demand is *zero*, then the quantity of imports does not change after devaluation and the *foreign exchange* value of imports is constant. In this case the demand for foreign exchange is perfectly inelastic (zero), and devaluation neither helps nor worsens the balance of payments on the demand side.

Figure 16-4 illustrates these two cases.

The elasticity of import demand will tend to be high when the composition of imports is heavily weighted with luxury-type consumer goods (such as automobiles and household equipment) and expensive capital goods (such as heavy machinery and transport equipment). Conversely, elasticity will tend to be low when most imports are raw materials, foodstuffs, and semimanufactures. Another factor is the degree of substitutability between

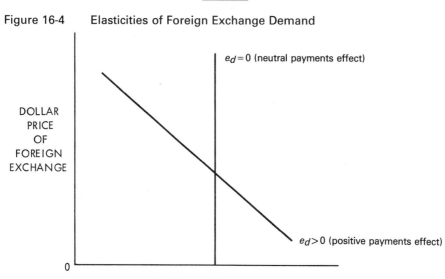

Figure 16-4   Elasticities of Foreign Exchange Demand

$e_d = 0$ (neutral payments effect)

DOLLAR
PRICE
OF
FOREIGN
EXCHANGE

$e_d > 0$ (positive payments effect)

0

FOREIGN EXCHANGE

When the elasticity of *import demand* is *greater than zero* (disregarding sign), then the elasticity of *foreign exchange demand* is also *greater than zero*, as shown by the demand schedule sloping downward from left to right. When the elasticity of *import demand* is *zero*, then the elasticity of *foreign exchange demand* is also *zero*, as shown by the vertical demand schedule.

import goods and domestic goods. When domestic substitutes are widely available at reasonable prices, then higher domestic prices for imports after depreciation will cause a switch to domestic sources of supply, thereby increasing the elasticity of import demand.

Elasticities of Export and Import Supply

In our analysis of the demand elasticities of export and imports, we assumed that export and import *supply* elasticities were infinite or perfectly elastic. Thus, the domestic price of exports and the foreign exchange price of imports did not respond to depreciation. This is an unrealistic assumption, and we must now take into account less-than-perfect elasticities of export and import supply.

The significance of supply elasticities may be understood if we make another unrealistic assumption, namely, perfectly inelastic (zero) export and import supplies. In that event devaluation has *no effect* on the balance of payments *regardless* of the demand elasticities. An export supply of zero elasticity means that the quantity of exports cannot be increased. Hence, a devaluation of 10 percent is promptly offset by a 10 percent *increase* in the domestic export price as foreign buyers bid for the same quantity of export goods. Thus, the *foreign exchange* price of exports remains the same, and there is no change in foreign exchange receipts. Similarly, an import supply of zero elasticity means that a 10 percent devaluation is promptly matched by a 10 percent cut in the foreign exchange price of imports as foreign suppliers strive to maintain sales in the devaluing country. Thus, the domestic price of imports stays the same after devaluation, and there is no effect on foreign exchange expenditures.

It would be tedious to recount the many combinations of demand and supply elasticities and their effects on the balance of payments. Suffice it to say that when demand elasticities are high, the effects of devaluation are most beneficial if supply elasticities are also high. Then lower foreign exchange prices can expand exports and higher domestic import prices can contract imports. On the other hand, when demand elasticities are low, devaluation is most beneficial (or least harmful) if supply elasticities are low, for then foreign exchange export prices fall less and domestic import prices rise less than otherwise.

When Is Exchange Depreciation Successful?

If the foreign exchange market is in stable equilibrium, then devaluation lessens or eliminates a deficit in the balance of payments, as shown in Figures 16-1 and 16-2. But if the foreign exchange market is in *unstable* equilibrium, then devaluation hurts rather than helps the balance of payments in deficit. Figure 16-5 shows that unstable equilibrium occurs when the supply curve has a negative slope and cuts the demand schedule from *below*.[6]

At the exchange rate 0–R, foreign exchange demanded exceeds foreign exchange supplied by F–H. In the attempt to wipe out this deficit, the exchange rate is devalued to 0–R'. But this only makes matters worse as the deficit increases in size to E–G.

What, then, is the requirement for stable equilibrium in terms of export and import elasticities? Devaluation *always* helps to lessen a deficit in the balance of payments if the sum of the export and import demand elasticities is greater than one, that is, $e_x + e_m > 1$. This is known as the Marshall-Lerner condition, and we may demonstrate its validity by citing two extreme examples. (The Marshall-Lerner condition assumes perfect elasticities of export and import *supply*.) Suppose the elasticity of export demand is zero and there is a 10 percent devaluation. Then foreign exchange receipts drop 10 percent; but if import demand elasticity is greater than one, foreign exchange expenditures decrease by more than 10 percent. Thus, the deficit becomes less. Again, suppose the elasticity of import demand is zero. Then foreign exchange expenditures do not change after depreciation; but if export

---

[6] In that event the sum of the supply and demand elasticities is negative. See Figures 16-3 and 16-4.

Figure 16-5   Unstable Equilibrium in the Foreign Exchange Market

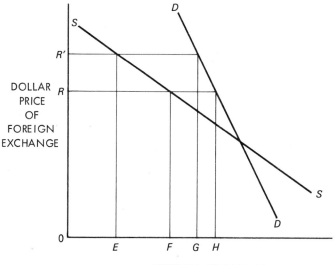

FOREIGN EXCHANGE

The schedule of foreign exchange supply (*S–S*) has a negative slope and cuts the schedule of foreign exchange demand (*D–D*) from below. Hence, the sum of the supply and demand elasticities is negative, putting the market in *unstable* disequilibrium. A devaluation from 0–*R* to 0–*R'* *widens* the balance of payments deficit from *F–H* to *E–G* instead of helping to close it. *Stable* disequilibrium requires that the sum of the *export* and *import* demand elasticities be greater than one (Marshall-Lerner condition). In that event, devaluation reduces a payments deficit and revaluation reduces a payments surplus.

demand elasticity is greater than one, a 10 percent devaluation leads to a greater than 10 percent increase in the quantity of exports and consequently an increase in foreign exchange receipts. Once again, the balance of payments improves.

When we introduce supply elasticities, we discover that the Marshall-Lerner condition is sufficient but not necessary. Even if the sum of demand elasticities is somewhat below one, the balance of payments can improve, provided that the supply elasticities are small enough.

What is the probability that the demand elasticities of exports and imports of a country will add to a sum greater than one? Today most economists believe the probability is high.[7] As far as elasticities are concerned,

---

[7] The IMF World Trade Model, covering a period through 1977, indicates a range of −0.5 to −1.0 for total imports and 0.5 to 1.5 for total exports. See Michael C. Deppler and Duncan Ripley, "The World Trade Model: Merchandise Trade Flows," *IMF Staff Papers*, March 1978, pp. 147–206.

therefore, a country can be reasonably confident that devaluation will improve its balance of payments. But elasticities are not the whole story. Devaluation also induces income and general price effects in the devaluing country that may nullify or compromise its effectiveness in remedying a payments deficit.

The Effect of Devaluation on the Terms of Trade

The effects of devaluation on the commodity terms of trade are uncertain.[8] It may seem obvious that devaluation *worsens* the terms of trade of the devaluing country: The foreign exchange price of its exports drops while the foreign exchange price of its imports usually stays the same. But this price behavior is by no means certain. We can see why if we understand that an exchange devaluation of, say, 10 percent is equivalent to a *duty* of 10 percent on all imports and a *subsidy* of 10 percent on all exports. An import tariff tends to *improve* the terms of trade by lowering the foreign exchange price of imports, but an export subsidy tends to *worsen* the terms of trade by lowering the foreign exchange price of exports. The net effect of *both* duty and subsidy on the terms of trade depends on the interaction of the supply and demand elasticities of both imports and exports.

The general rule states that a devaluation worsens the terms of trade if the product of the two supply elasticities is *greater* than the product of the two demand elasticities, or $(e_{sx})(e_{sm}) > (e_{dx})(e_{dm})$. Otherwise the terms of trade remain unchanged (the two products are equal) or improve (the product of the two supply elasticities is *less* than the product of the two demand elasticities).

ABSORPTION APPROACH TO EXCHANGE RATE ADJUSTMENT

In Chapter 15 we stated that adjustment to a current-account deficit under full-employment conditions calls for a reduction in *real* domestic expenditure regardless of whether adjustment occurs in a fixed-rate or a variable-rate system. Recall equation (18) in Chapter 15:

$$(1)\ B_c = Y - A.$$

When B_c is in deficit (negative), then A exceeds Y. Adjustment to a deficit demands, therefore, either (1) an increase in real Y, or (2) a decrease in real A. Since physical output cannot be expanded in the short run with full

---

[8] For a definition of the commodity terms of trade, see Chapter 21.

employment, adjustment to a deficit in such a situation requires a reduction in the real absorption of goods and services (an *increase* in real saving) to allow for higher exports and lower imports.

As we have seen in Chapter 15, income adjustment to a deficit on current account involves a decline in the level of aggregate demand. Thus, income adjustment via the foreign trade multiplier and monetary effects or via restrictive monetary and fiscal policies (the domestic multiplier) is *expenditure reducing*. In contrast, exchange depreciation is *expenditure switching*: It shifts domestic expenditures away from tradables by raising their prices in domestic currency relative to the price of nontradables.[9]

Expenditure Switching and Real Output

Where does the real output come from to support this expenditure switch? With full employment it can come only from a reduction in domestic absorption (A) that releases resources for the production of exportables and importables. Recall the statement for domestic absorption in terms of tradables and nontradables:

$$(2)\ A\ =\ S_n\ +\ D_x\ +\ D_m.^{10}$$

Hence, lower absorption requires a decrease in the domestic *supply* of non-tradables accompanied by a decrease in the domestic *demand* for tradables. Putting the matter somewhat differently, devaluation with full employment can be successful only if it is accompanied by an increase in domestic saving that matches the improvement in the balance of payments.[11] Can devaluation be expected to bring about the requisite increase in saving? The general answer is negative, because depreciation exerts no direct influence on saving.

In failing to increase saving and thereby decrease domestic absorption, devaluation with full employment will cause an inflationary rise in the price level that will partly or fully offset its initial effects on exports and imports. When devaluation raises exports and lowers imports, it injects income into the domestic economy and starts a cumulative expansion of money income. This higher money income stimulates higher expenditures on domestic goods whose supply cannot be expanded under full employment. The consequence, therefore, is inflation. If this general price rise is of the same order as the devaluation (say 10 percent), then the initial effects of devaluation are completely vitiated and the payments deficit remains the same. Devaluation may also stimulate a general price rise on the cost side. Higher domestic

---

[9] The role of relative price changes in effecting switches in real expenditure was explored in Chapter 15.

[10] See footnote 13 in Chapter 15.

[11] Recall that $X - M = S - I_d$. Assuming that I_d is autonomous, then a change in $X - M$ requires an equal change in S in the same direction, or $d(X - M) = dS$.

prices paid for imports of raw materials, capital equipment, and the like, may impose an upward pressure on domestic costs of production and the price level. The higher prices of imported consumer goods may encourage labor unions to ask for higher wages—and in countries where the wages of most workers are linked to a consumer price index, higher wages inevitably result when there is a substantial dependence upon such imports. It should be noted, however, that cost-push inflation would not occur in the absence of new money created by the government to finance it.

Under full-employment conditions, therefore, the income and price effects of devaluation limit its effectiveness, and in some instances they may nullify it entirely. Exchange rate adjustment provides an initial impulse for a switch in a country's resources from domestic to external use, but it does not guarantee that such a switch will actually take place. Hence, expenditure-switching policies must be supported by expenditure-reducing policies. Unless the domestic government contracts real absorption through monetary, fiscal, and (possibly) wage-price policies, depreciation can only lead to inflation and a perpetuation of the balance of payments deficit.

Because of its price and income effects, devaluation is likely to be more effective in removing a payments deficit when the domestic economy has substantial unemployment and excess capacity. Then the rise in money income and expenditure provoked by the depreciation will cause an expansion of real gross national product (Y). As noted earlier, governments tried to utilize the "employment effect" of depreciation by overdepreciating their currencies in the 1930s. In this situation it may be possible to have one's cake and eat it too, that is, to achieve an improvement in the balance of payments and an increase in real domestic expenditure at the same time. But this does not necessarily happen, because some of the increase in real expenditure induces higher imports via the marginal propensity to import. Even under conditions of widespread unemployment and excess capacity, therefore, the effectiveness of devaluation may be constrained by its income effects, although these are unlikely to fully offset its elasticity effects.

In sum, devaluation under full-employment conditions can effect adjustment in the balance of payments only when it is accompanied by expenditure-reducing policies that contract real domestic absorption. In the absence of such policies, devaluation will simply cause inflation that will nullify its initial balance of payments effects. Successful devaluation demands, therefore, more than a manipulation of the exchange rate; it must be part of a broader policy of international adjustment.[12]

---

[12] We are speaking here of devaluation to overcome an actual deficit in the balance of payments, which implies an adjustable-peg or managed-float system. In a flexible-rate system such a deficit would not appear because of continuous equilibrating adjustments in the exchange rate. Hence, there would be no income and price-level effects. The latter result from the elimination of a deficit caused by compensatory financing and a prior stabilization of the exchange rate.

The J-Curve

So far, in discussing the elasticity and absorption approaches to exchange rate adjustment, we have ignored the *time* it takes for full adjustment to occur. Changes in exchange rates do not effect an instantaneous adjustment of a current account deficit or surplus. The required change in domestic absorption can take up to two years, even when expenditure switching is supported by expenditure-reducing policies. Consequently, the initial impact of a *depreciation* (appreciation) is to *worsen* (improve) the current account. For some time after depreciation (devaluation), foreign exchange expenditures on imports fall only a little, while foreign exchange receipts may actually decline as the same export volume is sold at lower foreign currency prices. Eventually import and export volumes adjust to the new exchange rate, with a corresponding improvement in the current account. The time path of adjustment, therefore, is described by a *J-curve*, as depicted in Figure 16-6.

Figure 16-6   J-Curve: Delayed Effects of a Devaluation on Current Account

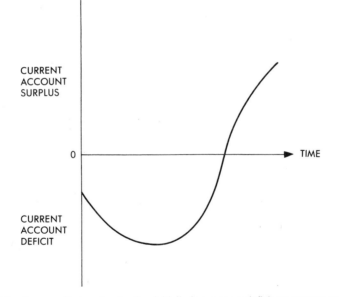

Because of the J-curve effect, a devaluation initially increases a deficit on current account rather than decreasing it. This happens because the *quantities* of exports and imports take time to respond to the new exchange rate. Hence, foreign exchange receipts decline and foreign exchange expenditures decline only a little. Eventually, when export and import volumes adjust progressively to the new exchange rate, the J-curve rises and devaluation improves the balance on current account.

The delayed effects of a change in the exchange rate are traceable to two sources. First, a change in the exchange rate is transformed into changes in the *domestic currency* prices of imports and in the *foreign currency* prices of exports (known as the "pass-through effect") only after some time. When a currency appreciates, for example, importers are commonly slow to lower their domestic currency prices, preferring instead to exploit higher gross margins. And when a currency depreciates, exporters may try to maintain their foreign currency prices by raising their domestic currency prices.[13] Second, even when a change in the exchange rate is passed through to importables and exportables, domestic and foreign buyers may be slow to respond to the new prices. That is to say, short-run price elasticities can be much smaller than long-term elasticities. Clearly, governments need to take the J-curve into account in their exchange rate policies.[14]

MONETARY APPROACH TO EXCHANGE RATE ADJUSTMENT

The elasticities approach to exchange rate adjustments is a *partial-equilibrium* analysis that deals only with the export and import sectors while ignoring the macroeconomic effects of a change in the exchange rate on the general price level and on real income. As pointed out earlier, the elasticities approach needs to be supplemented (or validated) by the absorption approach, which offers a *general-equilibrium* analysis that covers macroeconomic effects. Both of these approaches focus on current-account or "real" adjustment, with little attention to the remainder of the balance of payments, which is thought to passively accommodate the current account. In contrast, the monetary approach is a general-equilibrium analysis that explains exchange rate adjustment in terms of its effect on the money market, which in turn brings about equilibrating changes in both the current and capital accounts of the balance of payments.

In the following sections we look first at the monetary explanation of adjustment through an occasional devaluation or revaluation in an adjustable-peg or managed-float system. Then, as promised in Chapter 12, we take up the monetary explanation of exchange rate determination, particularly in a flexible-rate system.

---

[13] Kreinin estimated the pass-through effect of a dollar devaluation for U.S. imports to be between 30 and 55 percent within a year and for U.S. exports as nearly complete in the same period. See Mordecai E. Kreinin, "The Effect of Exchange Rate Changes on the Prices and Volume of Foreign Trade," *International Monetary Fund Staff Papers*, July 1977, pp. 317–18.

[14] For an examination of the J-curve effect on the adjustment path of the U.S. trade deficit after depreciation of the dollar in early 1985, see "Exchange Rates, Adjustment, and the J-Curve," *Federal Reserve Bulletin*, October 1988, pp. 633–644. The article concludes that the J-curve effect postponed improvement in the nominal trade balance but did not explain the *persistence* of the U.S. deficit. U.S. balance of payments policy in the 1980s is taken up in Chapter 19.

Adjustment Through Devaluation[15]

Let us assume that at a given exchange rate a country is running a deficit in its balance of payments as measured by a net balance on official reserves account. As we know, to monetarists this means that there is an excess supply of money ($M^s > M^d$) and the money market is in disequilibrium. Now suppose the government devalues its currency. Clearly, devaluation can eliminate the balance of payments deficit only if it can eliminate the excess supply of money. How is this possible?

We can explain the monetary version of the effects of devaluation in two steps. First, devaluation *raises* the domestic currency prices of tradables and also of nontradables, although to a lesser extent. This price inflation increases the demand for nominal money balances.[16] Second, the resulting higher demand for money causes an inflow of money from abroad as individuals and firms seek to restore their *real* money balances by cutting expenditures on imports of goods and services, by liquidating foreign financial assets (securities), or by borrowing from foreign lenders. These actions eliminate the balance of payments deficit or, if the devaluation is large enough, create a surplus.

The improvement in the balance of payments resulting from a devaluation continues only until *stock* equilibrium is restored in the money market, that is, until $M^d = M^s$. To monetarists, therefore, the effect of devaluation is *temporary*; over the long run it only raises the price level without affecting real economic variables. For that reason, monetarists argue that devaluation (or revaluation) is unnecessary in an adjustable-peg system; instead, authorities should reduce the domestic-credit element of the monetary base (D) or, in dynamic terms, restrain its growth rate below that of its trading partners.

To monetarists, the temporary effect of devaluation does *not* depend on changes in the country's terms of trade or on the demand and supply elasticities of tradables. The only requirement for adjustment is that the decrease in real money stocks causes a decrease in real absorption out of a given real income.

The monetarists use the same mechanism to explain adjustment to a balance of payments surplus through revaluation. A payments surplus means an excess demand for money ($M^d > M^s$) in the surplus country. By *lowering* the general price level, revaluation decreases the demand for money. Individuals and firms cut their money balances by buying more from abroad or investing and lending abroad. Once again, the effect is temporary, ceasing when equilibrium is restored in the money market.

---

[15] This and the following subsections draw on the presentation in Mordechai E. Kreinin and Lawrence H. Officer, *The Monetary Approach to the Balance of Payments: A Survey,* Princeton Studies in International Finance, no. 43 (Princeton, N.J.: Princeton University Press, 1978), Chapters 4 and 5.

[16] See equation (35) in Chapter 15.

The monetary approach to devaluation and revaluation can be reconciled with the absorption approach by recognizing that when absorption exceeds income (a deficit on current account), then the supply of domestic money stock exceeds its desired level, and conversely. Both the absorption and monetary approaches agree that exchange rate adjustment depends critically on the absence of new domestic money creation that would offset its effect on real money balances.

The assertion by monetarists that a change in the exchange rate will have *no* effect on real variables over the long run follows from their assumption of the *law of one price* in global markets for goods and services and for money and other financial assets. If, indeed, national markets were fully integrated with global markets through perfect international arbitrage, then the prices of importables and exportables would always remain in line with world prices. For instance, after a 10 percent devaluation, the domestic currency prices of exports and import-competing goods would also rise 10 percent, thereby foreclosing any switching through price effects. Insofar as the law of one price does not hold (and the empirical evidence says it does not, particularly in markets for differentiated goods and services), then a change in the exchange rate can have long-run switching effects on trade flows and other real economic variables.[17] And in that case, the elasticities approach can be useful in tracing and forecasting the magnitude of the switching effects. We shall have more to say about the law of one price in the next section.

Determination of Exchange Rates in a Freely Fluctuating Rate System

Monetarist and nonmonetarist economists agree that flexible exchange rates keep the balance of payments in continuing equilibrium. However, the monetarists do not believe that fluctuating rates are necessary to maintain long-run payments equilibrium, because they regard payments imbalances as self-correcting in a fixed-rate system. As we learned in Chapter 15, the money supply in a fixed-rate system adjusts gradually through changes in international reserves until equilibrium is restored in the money market.[18] In a freely fluctuating rate system, however, equilibrium is continuously maintained in the money market through domestic price changes that affect

---

[17] Himarios examined the relationship between nominal and real devaluation for fifteen countries covering a variety of exchange-rate systems over the period 1953–1973 and the same relationship for a second sample of fifteen countries over the period 1975–1984. He concluded that over a relevant policy horizon (three years) a *nominal* devaluation changes relative prices (becoming thereby a *real* devaluation) and affects the trade balance "positively and significantly." In over 80 percent of the cases, devaluation caused a long-run net improvement in the trade balance. See Daniel Himarios, "Do Devaluations Improve the Trade Balance? The Evidence Revisited," *Economic Inquiry*, January 1989, pp. 143–68.

[18] See p. 400.

the real value of money stocks. But how are exchange rates determined in such a system?

Monetarists answer that question in the first instance by saying that exchange rates, as the relative prices of national monies, are determined by the demand and supply of stocks of the several national monies.[19] Real factors, such as relative changes in national productivity, influence the exchange rate, but they work through monetary channels. A simple model can depict the fundamental reasoning of the monetary approach to exchange rate determination.

Monetarists begin with the proposition that the exchange rate, defined as the domestic currency price of a unit of foreign currency, is the ratio between domestic and foreign price levels:

$$(3) \ r = P/P^*,$$

where r is the exchange rate, P is the domestic price level, and P^* is the foreign price level. This equation is a statement of the purchasing-power parity doctrine that was described in Chapter 13. But monetarists do not assert, as does the doctrine, that relative price levels determine the exchange rate. Instead, equation (3) is simply a statement of the *law of one price* in a global market: Perfect commodity arbitrage makes the price levels of all countries equal when the levels are expressed in a common currency.

The domestic price level must also satisfy the conditions of equilibrium in the money market:

$$(4) \ M^{dr} = M^s/P,$$

where M^{dr} is the demand for *real* money stocks and M^s is the nominal money stock. Solving equation (4) for P, we get

$$(5) \ P = M^s/M^{dr}.$$

Substituting this expression for P and a similar one for the foreign price level in equation (3), we obtain.

$$(6) \ r = \frac{M^s/M^{dr}}{M^{s*}/M^{dr*}},$$

where M^{s*} is the foreign money stock and M^{dr*} is the foreign demand for real money balances. This equation states that the exchange rate equals the money supply/real money demand ratio in the domestic country divided by the foreign money supply/real money demand ratio.

---

[19] The balance of payments approach to exchange rate determination, which was presented in Chapter 12, views exchange rates as the relative prices of *national outputs*. The equilibrium rate is determined by *flows* of funds, not stock adjustments.

The demand for real money balances is dependent on real income and the nominal interest rate, or

$$(7) \ M^{dr} = f(y, i).$$

Substituting this expression for real money demand in equation (6) we get

$$(8) \ r = [M^s/M^{s*}] \ {}^s \ [f(y^*)/f(y)] \ [f(i^*)/f(i)],$$

where the asterisks indicate the foreign real income and nominal interest rate. Hence, the exchange rate equals the ratio of the foreign and domestic money stocks *times* the ratio of the foreign and domestic real income functions *times* the ratio of the foreign and domestic nominal interest rate functions.

The nominal rate of interest is composed of a *real* rate, which monetarists assume is the same in all countries (perfect international mobility of funds), and an *inflation premium*, which is the expected rate of increase in the domestic price level.

$$(9) \ i = i^r + E(p),$$

where i^r is the real rate of interest and $E(p)$ is the expected rate of inflation. And

$$(10) \ i^r = i^{r*},$$

where i^{r*} is the foreign real rate of interest.

Substituting the expression of i in equation (9) and a similar expression for the foreign interest rate (i^*) in equation (8), we arrive at:

$$(11) \ r = [M^s/M^{s*}][f(y^*)/f(y)] \ \{f[i^r + E(p)^*]/f[i^r + E(p)]\}$$

This equation shows the basic relationships of the monetary approach to the determination of exchange rates. Exogenous shifts in the domestic money stock or real income *relative* to the foreign money stock or real income and shifts in expected rate of domestic inflation *relative* to the expected rate of foreign inflation cause changes in the exchange rate.

In the short run, price expectations are the dominant influence on exchange rates because expectations are much more volatile than money stocks and real income. But fueling these expectations are divergent money/real income ratios among countries caused by divergent national monetary policies. Hence, a necessary condition for exchange rate stability is consistency among national monetary policies. Equation (11) also indicates that the most effective way to stop a depreciation in the exchange rate is a *permanent* reduction in the rate of growth of M^s announced by the monetary authorities in advance. Such an announcement (when it is believed by participants in the money market) will immediately lower the inflation premium on the interest rate and thereby cause an appreciation in the exchange rate.

Overshooting Exchange Rates

The monetary approach assumes *instantaneous* adjustment in international payments through movements in the exchange rate. As we observed in Chapter 15, adjustment can indeed occur rapidly through short-term capital flows as holders of financial assets (securities) respond to international shifts in interest rates, risks, and expectations. But adjustment in the goods market is another matter: Equilibrating changes in the volume and composition of expenditures on tradables and nontradables occur comparatively slowly. It is this lagged response that gives rise to the J-curve effect.

The lagged equilibrating response of the goods market (current account) in a flexible-rate system places the burden of *initial* adjustment entirely on the capital account. Hence, the initial change in the exchange rate (whether depreciation or appreciation) is greater than will be necessary to restore equilibrium when eventually the current account takes up some or all of the adjustment burden. This phenomenon is called "overshooting."

Let us trace the adjustment path in a flexible-rate system according to the monetary approach. We start with an increase in the domestic money stock that causes lower domestic interest rates and raises expectations of an eventual depreciation of the domestic currency. The resulting outflow of short-term capital from the domestic country due to interest-rate differentials, the portfolio effect, and the expectations effect (as described in Chapter 15) caused an *immediate* depreciation of the domestic currency. Subsequently, however, the domestic currency will *appreciate* throughout the rest of the adjustment that progressively occurs in the current account. This appreciation, however, will be less than the initial depreciation. In sum, the depreciation needed to clear the financial-asset market in the short run is greater than the depreciation needed to clear *both* the financial-asset and goods markets in the longer run. Overshooting intensifies the volatility of exchange rates in a floating-rate system.[20]

GENERAL EQUILIBRIUM IN AN OPEN ECONOMY WITH FLEXIBLE EXCHANGE RATES

As was true of a fixed-rate regime, equilibrium in the balance of payments (foreign exchange market) requires simultaneous equilibrium in a country's

---

[20] See Chapter 19.

goods and money markets. General equilibrium is depicted graphically in
Figure 15-9 in Chapter 15. It occurs at the point of intersection of the IS,
LM, and BOP schedules.

In a flexible-rate system, the exchange rate varies continually to keep
the balance of payments in equilibrium. *General* equilibrium is achieved by
shifts in the IS and BOP schedules induced by exchange rate movements
until the two schedules intersect on the LM schedule, which remains unaffected by such movements.

Figure 16-7 shows the markets for goods and money in equilibrium at
point E, with an interest rate i and national income Y. However, the balance
of payments is in *deficit* disequilibrium at E, given the initial exchange rate
S. (Remember: All points *below* the BOP schedule indicate a deficit (BOP
< 0).) This disequilibrium cannot endure. Because the amount of foreign
exchange demanded exceeds the amount supplied at E, the domestic currency depreciates from S to S'. This depreciation causes a decline in imports
and a rise in exports (an increase in X–M), which raises national income
via the foreign trade multiplier. Consequently, the IS schedule shifts to the
right from IS to IS'. Aggregate demand and supply are now equated at a

Figure 16-7   Adjustment to General Equilibrium Starting from a Balance of Payments Deficit in a Flexible-Rate System

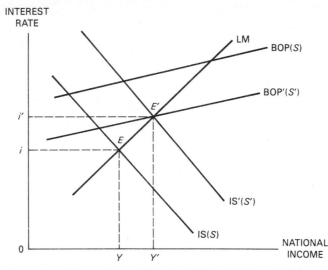

The goods and money markets are in equilibrium at E ($IS = LM$), but the balance of payments is
in deficit at E (BOP < 0), given the original exchange rate S. General equilibrium is restored at E'
after a depreciation from S to S' causes the IS schedule to shift to IS' and the BOP schedule to
shift to BOP'. At E' BOP $= 0$.

higher income level for any given interest rate. At the same time, the BOP schedule shifts downward: Equilibrium now occurs at a combination of lower interest rates and higher income levels than it did at the initial exchange rate S. General equilibrium is established at E', with national income at Y', the interest rate at i', and the exchange rate at S'.

SUMMARY

1. There are many possible kinds of variable-rate systems, ranging from a flexible-rate system to an adjustable-peg system. In a flexible-rate system movements in the exchange rate achieve a continuing short-run equilibrium in the balance of payments. In the adjustable-peg system exchange rates are occasionally varied by government action from one fixed level to another, and the choice of a new equilibrium rate is difficult.

2. The basic argument for flexible exchange rates is that they are the most effective means of market adjustment to balance of payments disequilibrium in the kind of world in which we live. It is alleged by proponents of flexible rates that long-run adjustment in a fixed-rate system is likely to be vitiated by domestic government policies of high employment and stability. The theoretical argument for an adjustable-peg system is less strong, because exchange rate adjustment is apt to come too late and be too big.

3. Economists have developed three different approaches to exchange-rate adjustment: the elasticities, absorption, and monetary approaches.

4. According to the elasticities approach, the effects of depreciation on the balance of payments depend on the elasticities of demand and supply of both exports and imports. Depreciation *always* improves the balance of payments when the sum of export and import demand elasticities is greater than one (Marshall-Lerner condition). Even if this sum is below one, depreciation improves the balance of payments, provided supply elasticities are small enough.

5. The effect of depreciation on the commodity terms of trade is uncertain. It depends on the size of the product of the two supply elasticities of exports and imports as compared with the product of their demand elasticities.

6. The absorption approach demonstrates that regardless of elasticities, depreciation with full employment can be successful only when it is accompanied by expenditure-reducing policies that contract real domestic absorption.

7. The J-curve illustrates that the initial short-run impact of depreciation is to worsen—not improve—the current account of the balance of payments.

8. The monetary approach explains the effects of depreciation on the balance of payments through its alteration of real money balances.
9. According to the monetary approach, exchange rates are determined by shifts in the domestic money stock or real income relative to the foreign money stock or real income and by shifts in the expected rate of domestic inflation relative to the expected rate of foreign inflation.
10. The lagged equilibrating response of the current account in a flexible-rate system places the burden of *initial* adjustment entirely on the capital account. Hence, the initial change in the exchange rate is greater than is needed for long-run equilibrium. This phenomenon is called " overshooting."
11. As was true of a fixed-rate regime, equilibrium in the balance of payments (foreign exchange market) requires simultaneous equilibrium in a country's goods and money markets.

QUESTIONS AND APPLICATIONS

1. (a) How does adjustment occur in a flexible-rate system?
   (b) How does it occur in an adjustable-peg system?
2. What is the basic argument for flexible exchange rates? Why have governments traditionally opposed flexible exchange rates?
3. (a) Assuming infinite supply elasticities, construct a graph to show the effects of depreciation when the elasticity of export demand is zero and the elasticity of import demand is zero. Does depreciation improve the balance of payments?
   (b) Using graphs, show how the effectiveness of exchange depreciation is determined by the elasticities of the supply and demand of foreign exchange.
   (c) What is the Marshall-Lerner condition?
4. "The effect of depreciation on the commodity terms of trade is uncertain." Explain.
5. (a) Using the absorption approach, explain why devaluation to eliminate a current-account deficit will be unsuccessful unless it is accompanied by higher domestic saving that matches any improvement in the balance of payments.
   (b) What steps can a government take to increase saving and thereby make devaluation effective?
6. Explain the reasons for a J-curve in exchange rate adjustment.
7. What is the monetary explanation of an exchange devaluation? An exchange revaluation?
8. (a) What is the law of one price?
   (b) Explain how the law of one price underlies the monetarist asser-

tion that a change in the exchange rate will have *no* long-term effects on the international trade balance.

9. Using equation (11), show the effect on the exchange rate of (a) an increase in the domestic money stock, (b) an increase in foreign real income, and (c) a fall in the expected domestic rate of inflation.

10. Explain the phenomenon of " overshooting."

11. **(a)** Using IS, LM, and BOP schedules, indicate a situation in which the goods and money markets of a country are in equilibrium but its balance of payments is in *surplus*.

    (b) Illustrate graphically how general equilibrium is restored after an *appreciation* of the country's exchange rate.

SELECTED READINGS

Alexander, Sidney S. "Effects of a Devaluation on a Trade Balance," *International Monetary Fund Staff Papers* 2 (April 1952): 263–78. Reprinted in *Readings in International Economics,* edited by Richard E. Caves and Harry G. Johnson. Homewood, Ill.: Richard D. Irwin, 1968.

Broughton, James M. *The Monetary Approach to Exchange Rates: What Now Remains?* Essays in International Finance, no. 171. Princeton, N.J.: Princeton University Press, October 1988.

Corden, W. M. *Inflation, Exchange Rates and the World Economy.* Chicago: The University of Chicago Press, 1981. Chapters 1, 2, and 3.

Friedman, Milton. "The Case for Flexible Exchange Rates." In *Essays in Positive Economics,* pp. 157–87. Chicago: University of Chicago Press, 1953.

Genberg, Hans, and Alexander K. Swoboda. "Policy and Current Account Determination under Floating Exchange Rates." *International Monetary Fund Staff Papers* 36 (March 1989): 1–30.

Isard, Peter. "Lessons from Empirical Models of Exchange Rates." *International Monetary Fund Staff Papers* 34 (March 1987): 1–28.

Johnson, Harry G. *Money, Balance of Payments Theory, and the International Monetary Problem.* Essays in International Finance, no. 124. Princeton, N.J.: Princeton University Press, 1977.

Kreinen, Mordechai, and Lawrence H. Officer. *The Monetary Approach to the Balance of Payments: A Survey.* Princeton Studies in International Finance, no. 43. Princeton, N.J.: Princeton University Press, 1978.

Krueger, Anne O. *Exchange-Rate Determination.* Cambridge: Cambridge University Press, 1983.

McKinnon, Ronald I. *Money in International Exchange.* New York: Oxford University Press, 1979. Chapter 6.

17

Nonmarket Suppression of External Payments Disequilibrium: Exchange Control

In Chapter 7 we examined tariff and nontariff restrictions on trade. A government may employ any of these restrictions to suppress a deficit in the balance of payments and foreign exchange market by lowering imports and thus the demand for foreign exchange. A government may also use export subsidies to stimulate export sales and thereby increase the supply of foreign exchange.[1] However, the most direct and comprehensive policy instrument to suppress a payments deficit is *exchange control*. In effect, exchange control replaces the free operation of the market with official decisions that determine the uses and availabilities of foreign exchange for all or specific transactions. When exchange control covers all transactions, then the government becomes a pure monopsonist and monopolist of foreign exchange.

THE ORIGINS OF EXCHANGE CONTROL

Exchange control was initially adopted by many governments during World War I, when it became necessary to conserve scarce supplies of gold and foreign exchange for the financing of imports vital to the national economy. Following the war, however, exchange control was abandoned everywhere, and by the second half of the 1920s most nations had returned to the gold standard and the full convertibility that characterized the prewar system of international payments. At that time it was widely believed that only the exigencies of war justified the use of exchange control, and few observers

---

[1] The variety of measures taken by the U.S. government in the 1960s to suppress a balance of payments deficit are described in Chapter 18.

expected to witness its revival in a period of peace. Yet, within a few years several governments had resurrected exchange control in the face of an event that was almost as convulsive as war in the suddenness of its impact on the international payments system—the international financial crisis of 1931.

The first peacetime use of exchange control by industrial countries arose as a response to the crisis of 1931, which unloosed a panicky run on the gold and foreign exchange reserves of one country after another.[2] The crisis began inconspicuously when the Credit-Anstalt bank in Vienna was declared insolvent in the summer of 1931. This caused a loss of confidence in the ability of Austria to honor its international short-term obligations, and there was an immediate large-scale withdrawal of funds from that country. Upon the failure of a large German bank in early July, the run by foreign creditors spread to Germany and to many Eastern European countries that had borrowed heavily on short term during the 1920s. Fearful of an exhaustion of its reserves, the German government stopped the flight of capital funds by introducing exchange control in August. By the end of the year, most countries in eastern Europe, as well as Denmark and Iceland, had also applied exchange control to halt an outflow of capital. Foreign-owned balances in the exchange control countries were now "frozen" and could no longer be freely transferred into gold or convertible foreign exchange. Similarly, residents of the exchange control countries were no longer able to send capital abroad.

The institution of exchange control in Germany next started a run on the British pound sterling. The large short-term loans that the United Kingdom had made to Germany were now immobilized by exchange control, and this created a doubt as to the capacity of the United Kingdom to liquidate its own heavy short-term international indebtedness. The panic rapidly depleted British reserves, but instead of following the example of Germany, the United Kingdom went off the gold standard in September 1931 and allowed the pound sterling to depreciate. In June of the following year, the British government established the Exchange Equalization Fund to stabilize the pound at a level below its former gold parity. A number of other countries allowed their currencies to depreciate along with the pound sterling and in this way gave birth to the Sterling Area.

By 1935 the international financial crisis and the global depression had split the international payments system into five groups.[3]

1. The *Sterling Area,* comprising principally the British Commonwealth and Scandinavian countries.

---

[2] In 1929 and 1930 a number of raw material exporting nations imposed exchange control to meet current account deficits brought on by the onset of depression in the industrial countries.

[3] League of Nations, *International Currency Experience* (Geneva: League of Nations, 1944), p. 198.

2. The *Dollar Area,* comprising the United States and most of the countries of Central America and northern South America.
3. The *Gold Bloc* countries of Western Europe.
4. The *Yen Area,* comprising Japan and Japan's possessions.
5. The *Exchange Control Area* of central and southeastern Europe, dominated by Germany.

Some countries, such as Canada, Argentina, Brazil, and Chile, did not fall completely into any one currency area. The Canadian dollar was depreciated about 10 percent against the dollar but remained convertible. The other three countries also depreciated but adopted exchange control that rendered their currencies inconvertible.

Exchange control was practiced by Germany, the Eastern European countries, and many countries in Latin America throughout the 1930s, long after the international financial crisis of 1931 had become history. Many new uses were found for exchange control, and this served to perpetuate its existence. The currencies of the Dollar Area, the Sterling Area, the Yen Area, and the principal countries of Western Europe (excluding Germany and Italy) remained fully convertible, however, up to the outbreak of World War II. During the war, all countries exercised tight control over their economies, and exchange control was only one of several instruments employed for that purpose.

After World War II most countries of the noncommunist world continued to restrict both current and capital transactions by means of exchange control.[4] In 1958 only eleven countries—all located in the Western Hemisphere—had *fully* convertible currencies that any holder could transfer freely into other currencies. All other currencies were inconvertible to one degree or another. This widespread use of exchange control had profound effects upon international trade and payments. It sharply limited the scope of multilateral trade and divided the free world into distinct currency areas. To the individual trader, exchange control meant that it was no longer possible to buy in the low-price market and sell in the high-price market without permission of the authorities. At times this permission was denied outright, and it was almost always limited in some way.

A massive liberalization of exchange restrictions started at the close of 1958, when ten countries in Western Europe established nonresident convertibility of their currencies on current account. In the early 1960s other industrial countries (including Japan) eliminated exchange restrictions on merchandise trade and, in most instances, on other current transactions as well. The industrial countries also greatly moderated their restrictions on capital transactions and some removed them entirely. Exchange control, therefore, is no longer a significant policy instrument for the countries of the industrial West.

---

[4] Since all international transactions of communist countries are channelled through state agencies, exchange control is an integral element of communist trading systems.

The less-developed countries have not matched the liberalization of the developed countries. The majority still retain exchange restrictions on trade and other transactions. For the developing countries, then, exchange control continues to be a major tool of foreign economic policy.

THE OBJECTIVES OF EXCHANGE CONTROL

Although the suppression of balance of payments disequilibrium has been the dominant objective of exchange control, it may also serve other important national objectives, such as the facilitation of national planning, the protection of domestic industries, and the creation of government revenue.

The Suppression of Balance of Payments Disequilibrium

When a nation is unwilling or unable to adjust to a persistent deficit in its balance of payments by deflating the domestic economy, by depreciating its rate of exchange, or by any other domestic measure of a fiscal or monetary nature, it must suppress the deficit by imposing direct controls over its international transactions. As noted above, the most important direct control utilized by contemporary governments is exchange control which regulates the acquisition and disposition of foreign exchange. Other forms of direct control—import quotas and import licenses—usually supplement exchange control, although at times they may be used as substitutes.

Exchange control was first used in peacetime mainly for suppression of the unique sort of disequilibrium that is provoked by a flight of capital. When exchange control is used solely for this purpose, there is no reason to restrict imports of merchandise and services, because the trouble is not in the current account. Moreover, exchange control need only be temporary, for once the panic has subsided, it may be lifted and most of the capital will return of its own accord. This last statement presupposes, however, a widespread belief that exchange control will not be reimposed. If there is doubt on this score, the cessation of exchange control will itself renew the capital flight. In this way, exchange control may perpetuate the loss of confidence and the speculative attitudes that engendered the original flight of capital. Fearing this consequence, governments tend to maintain exchange control long after the danger of capital flight is past.

There is another reason why exchange control that is imposed to restrain a capital flight may continue as a permanent feature of a nation's foreign economic policy. By maintaining an overvalued exchange rate, exchange control may itself create a current-account deficit in the balance of payments and induce further disequilibrium in the balance of payments. This is why many nations, once they have adopted exchange control, dare not abandon it.

The Facilitation of National Planning

Governments may use exchange control as a policy instrument (along with others) to attain certain national economic goals, such as full employment and economic development. In the communist countries, the economy is directed toward specific goals by a comprehensive set of controls that determine the allocation of all productive factors as well as the allocation of the national product. Since private enterprise is mainly forbidden, communist governments carry on most production and thereby execute the national plans they have drawn up. All international transactions are conducted by state trading agencies that behave in accordance with the dictates of the current national plans.

National planning in the market economies differs significantly from planning in the communist economies. In market economies, production rests largely in the hands of private entrepreneurs, and the price system is the main instrument in deciding the allocation of production and consumption. Consequently, noncommunist governments depend principally (although not exclusively) on fiscal and monetary policies instead of direct controls to implement their national economic programs. But since these programs are conceived in national terms, they sometimes demand an insulation of the national economy from the world economy. To achieve this insulation, governments may impose exchange and trade controls that are supplemented, at times, by state trading in specific commodities.

Since World War II the governments of less-developed countries in Latin America, Asia, and Africa have made economic development their preeminent policy goal. The policies associated with that goal have tended to create inflationary pressures that have, in turn, induced deficits in the balance of payments. Lacking adequate reserves, many countries have been forced to make immediate adjustments to these external deficits. Because of the objectives of national planning, however, the choice of methods of adjustment has been narrowly circumscribed. Deflation has been avoided because it would slow down the rate of economic growth. Similarly, exchange depreciation has promised little help because any subsequent domestic inflation would offset its effects on international payments. Rather than moderate the goals of national planning, governments have used exchange control and other direct measures to insulate the domestic economy from international repercussions. Apart from its insulation effect, the governments of less-developed countries have utilized exchange control to penalize imports of "nonessential goods" and favor imports of "essential goods" in accordance with criteria laid down by national development plans.

The Protection of Domestic Industries

By restricting imports, exchange control inevitably protects domestic producers against foreign competition. Therefore, exchange control will be supported by protectionist groups, which will seek to enhance its protective features. When exchange control is not consciously oriented toward protection but is set up simply to suppress an external deficit, it will not discriminate against those imports that have close domestic substitutes. All imports will be viewed indiscriminately as a drain on foreign exchange and they will be restricted only to stop that drain. When, however, exchange control also has a protectionist purpose, it will curtail imports of competitive products more stringently than imports of products not produced at home or in sufficient quantities. Once exchange control is established, it usually evolves in the direction of greater protection as a result of the lobbying activities of vested interests. This is also true of the import quotas and licenses that ordinarily accompany exchange control.

The Creation of Government Revenue

Exchange control is used in some countries to collect revenue for the government. In most instances this occurs where the exchange control authority sets the price at which it will buy foreign exchange below the price at which it will sell foreign exchange. For example, if the authority forces exporters to surrender dollar exchange at a rate of 10 pesos to the dollar and then sells dollar exchange to importers at a rate of 15 pesos to the dollar, it pockets 5 pesos for each dollar that it buys and sells.

Exchange control is used as a source of revenue mainly by developing countries. The reliance of nonindustrial countries on exchange control to provide government revenue is largely due to the difficulty of collecting income and other direct taxes. Many of these countries do not have the personnel and skills required to administer direct taxes, and often it is politically impossible to impose such taxes on wealthy individuals. By way of contrast, an exchange control system offers a ready-made apparatus for the collection of revenue with only slight additional administrative expense. Moreover, the tight regulations of exchange control make it more difficult to avoid the tax, whether in the form of a penalty exchange rate or an exchange tax.[5]

SINGLE-RATE SYSTEMS OF EXCHANGE CONTROL

No two nations have identical systems of exchange control. Some systems are lenient and have almost fully convertible currencies, whereas others carefully police all uses of foreign exchange and may strongly discriminate against certain currencies. Many other variations in systems of exchange control are attributable to differences in objectives, differences in administrative competence, and differences in economic conditions. It is possible,

---

[5] An exchange tax is a charge levied on transactions in foreign exchange.

however, to classify exchange control systems into two broad categories depending upon whether they employ one or several exchange rates.

Single-rate systems are administered by an exchange control authority that is the sole buyer and seller of foreign exchange. All foreign exchange transactions are carried on at one official rate of exchange. Exporters and others who receive foreign exchange from foreign residents are compelled to surrender it to the control authority at the official rate. Importers and others who must make payments to foreign residents must obtain permission to buy foreign exchange from the control authority at the official rate. The control authority also regulates the use of domestic currency (bank accounts) owned by foreign residents. Commercial banks are usually authorized to act as buying and selling agents of the exchange control authority. The key to the system of control is the requirement that all foreign exchange transactions involving domestic or foreign residents must pass through authorized banking channels.

The Surrender of Foreign Exchange Receipts

To regulate the expenditure of foreign exchange, the exchange control authority must make certain that all foreign exchange received by the nation's residents is actually surrendered to it. Otherwise foreign exchange that is not captured by the authorities may be used for illegal purposes, such as exporting capital, and thus it is not available to finance imports that the authorities consider desirable. Hence, surrender requirements must apply to all credit transactions in the balance of payments.

The surrender of foreign exchange to the control authority is usually accomplished in one of two ways. Under one method, all exports may be licensed by a trade control authority, and before the merchandise is allowed to pass through customs, the export license must be validated by an authorized bank. To obtain license validation, the exporter is required to inform the bank of the destination of the export shipment as well as the amount of the payment and the currency in which it is to be made. The exporter also agrees to surrender to the bank all receipts of foreign exchange. When the exporter arranges for payment by drawing a bill of exchange against the foreign importer or against a bank, the bill must be either discounted with the authorized bank or sent through that bank for collection. Thus, the authorized bank is certain to acquire the foreign exchange when payment is made on the bill.

In the second method, the surrender of foreign exchange receipts is insured by requiring the exporter to secure a sworn declaration from an authorized bank before the exports are allowed to pass customs. In obtaining the declaration, the exporter must inform the bank of the destination of the exports and the amount and kind of payment to be received for them. The exporter also agrees to surrender to the bank all receipts of foreign exchange within a stipulated period.

These two methods of effecting the surrender of foreign exchange receipts apply to merchandise exports only. It is more difficult for the control authority to capture foreign exchange receipts arising out of exports of services, gifts, and capital movements. Close watch must be kept over all foreign-owned bank balances in the exchange control country, foreign securities owned by domestic residents must be registered with the control authority and sometimes held by an authorized bank, and the international mails must be screened for domestic and foreign bank notes.

Failure to surrender foreign exchange in accordance with the regulations of the control authority is a criminal act. The guilty party may be punished by the imposition of a fine or, in the case of an exporter, denied permission to export in the future. Violations of the exchange control laws of Nazi Germany carried the death penalty. Nevertheless, evasions of exchange control are widespread, and the surrender procedures are never 100 percent effective.

The Allocation of Foreign Exchange Receipts

The exchange control authority is faced with several problems in the allocation of foreign exchange. First, it must decide how much foreign exchange to allot to the main categories of debit transactions of the balance of payments—merchandise imports, transportation services provided by foreigners, the servicing of foreign debts, travel expenditures of domestic residents, capital investment, and so on.

After reaching a decision on the overall amount of foreign exchange to be distributed to each of these categories, the control authority must next decide on the allocation of foreign exchange to the individual items within each category. It must also determine the applicants who will receive foreign exchange and the amounts they will be granted.

Finally, the exchange control authority must often decide upon the allocation of foreign exchange by countries or by currency areas, since it may have abundant supplies of some currencies and only scarce supplies of others. If all foreign currencies were convertible, this would not matter, but when several other countries also employ exchange control, it is no longer possible to settle a deficit through multilateral transfers.

Ordinarily the official rate of exchange *overvalues* the domestic currency. Regardless of the criteria used to allocate foreign exchange, therefore, it is not possible to satisfy the entire demand. The criteria of allocation will reflect the objectives of exchange control and current economic conditions. Imports that are considered vital to the nation's well-being will be afforded generous allotments of foreign exchange, while imports of "nonessential" items will receive only scanty allotments. Convertible currencies will be hoarded by the exchange control authority and released only for high-priority imports. On the other hand, inconvertible currencies may be sufficiently abundant to permit their use for low-priority imports.

The individual importer is particularly concerned with the method used to allocate foreign exchange to the applicants within each category. Among the several methods employed are the following:

1. individual allocation
2. exchange quotas
3. waiting list
4. prohibitions
5. tie-in import arrangement

The method of *individual allocation* involves the examination of each individual request for foreign exchange and, upon approval, the issuance of a license that permits the holder to buy a stipulated amount of foreign exchange from an authorized bank. The virtue of this technique is its flexibility. However, it encourages the bribery and corruption of officials, and it places in their hands the powers of life and death over the business enterprises engaged in importing. Efforts are often made to limit the arbitrary nature of individual allocation by requiring the authorities to use the past imports, capital, taxes paid, and so on, of the importing firm in deciding its exchange allotment. This procedure has the disadvantage of establishing fixed quotas for individual firms, and unless safeguards are established, it may create a special hardship for new or growing concerns.

Another method of allocation among applicants is the establishment for each category of imports of *exchange quotas* derived from estimates of the amount of foreign exchange that will be forthcoming over a specified period. Foreign exchange is then freely sold to all applicants on a first-come, first-serve basis until the respective quotas are exhausted. Although this technique limits the exercise of discretion on the part of officials, it suffers from inflexibility.

The *waiting-list* method resembles the quota method. The exchange control authority places each application on a waiting list and takes care of it when the foreign exchange becomes available. Hence, no application is rejected, but the importer may have only a vague idea as to when foreign exchange will be obtained. Unless the priority of exchange allocation is strictly decided by the date of application, the waiting-list technique becomes as arbitrary as the individual allocation of exchange.

Prohibitions are often used to rule out any foreign exchange for certain import items from specific countries or from all countries. Prohibitions are actually zero exchange quotas, and the same effect may be obtained by not issuing licenses when the method of individual allocation is used by the control authority.

Finally, mention should be made of the *tie-in import arrangement,* whereby foreign exchange is allocated for specified imports on the condition that the importer buy complementary or similar domestic products in a certain proportion. The object here is to stimulate particular kinds of domestic production rather than to protect the balance of payments. This method of exchange allocation is very similar to the mixing quotas discussed in Chapter 7.[6]

Import Quotas and Licenses

Single exchange-rate systems are usually strengthened by a system of *import quotas* or *import licenses*.[7] The most common procedure is to require that the importer first obtain an import license from the trade control authority. Import licenses will be issued in accordance with import quotas for specified imports or on an individual ad hoc basis in the absence of import quotas. Ordinarily the import license also serves as an exchange license permitting the importer to buy the foreign exchange necessary to finance the import shipment. In some countries however, an exchange license may be needed in addition to an import license; that is, the import license does not provide the importer with an automatic right to buy foreign exchange. The methods used to distribute import licenses among importers are similar to those used to allocate foreign exchange licenses.

As far as merchandise imports are concerned, import quotas or import licenses can do the same job as exchange control. In fact, they may do a better job. Import quotas and licenses allow only fixed quantities of merchandise to enter the country over a certain period, whereas exchange control simply limits the amounts of foreign exchange available for specified merchandise imports over a certain period. Under exchange control, therefore, variations in import prices or in the credit extended by foreign suppliers can lead to variations in the quantities of imports even though there is a fixed allotment of foreign exchange. This difficulty is avoided when exchange control is supplemented by import quotas and licenses. Of course, exchange control is more comprehensive than direct trade control, since it covers service and capital transactions in addition to merchandise transactions. The importance of merchandise, however, as compared to other items in the balance of payments makes a widespread application of import quotas and licenses a very close substitute for exchange control, with similar effects on international trade.

As has been noted, exchange control and quantitative import restrictions ordinarily are parts of the same overall system of direct control that is established by governments to suppress an external deficit. It follows, then, that international measures to remove or to reduce exchange control

---

[6] The tie-in import arrangement is also related to *countertrade arrangements* that allow imports into a country only if foreign suppliers also buy products from the importing country.

[7] The use of *export licenses* to compel surrender of foreign exchange receipts has already been mentioned. Export licenses may be used for several other purposes unrelated to exchange control, such as limiting exports of strategic military significance or conserving scarce commodities for use at home.

are likely to be ineffective unless steps are also taken to limit the use of import quotas and licenses.[8]

The Control of Nonresident Accounts

When a country employs exchange control to suppress a deficit in its balance of payments, it must regulate not only the foreign exchange transactions of its residents but also the use of domestic bank accounts owned by foreign residents. This is especially the case when the exchange control country is an international financial center like the United Kingdom, for then a large proportion of its international receipts and expenditures are made by debiting and crediting accounts maintained in its banking system by foreign residents.

At the end of 1958 the United Kingdom and several other European countries took a long step toward full convertibility by making freely transferable all nonresident accounts arising out of current transactions. Previously the British government did not allow foreign residents of nondollar countries to transfer their sterling balances to residents of dollar countries, although they were free to transfer such balances to residents of a nondollar country other than their own to finance transactions on current account. This procedure was necessary to insure that all British exports to dollar countries were paid for in dollars. Otherwise, say, a French resident might have used a sterling account to finance imports from the United States, and this sterling could then have been used by an American resident to finance imports from the United Kingdom, Thus, the United Kingdom would have lost the opportunity to earn the dollars the American importer would have had to pay if sterling had not been acquired from the French resident.

MULTIPLE-RATE SYSTEMS OF EXCHANGE CONTROL

In a single-rate system of exchange control, the exchange rate itself plays no role in the allocation of foreign exchange among transactions, applicants, currencies, and countries. Indeed, the overvaluation of the exchange rate intensifies the task of allocation by diminishing the amount of foreign exchange in supply and, at the same time, increasing the amount of foreign exchange in demand.

In multiple-rate systems of exchange control, however, two or more exchange rates are used to effect the allocation of foreign exchange, although

---

[8] The tariff is also an import restriction, but the uncertainty of its effects and the difficulties involved in changing it to meet new conditions make it a poor instrument of balance of payments adjustment.

they are usually used in conjunction with exchange licenses and direct trade controls. Because the task of allocation is at least partially carried out by differential exchange rates, multiple-rate systems rely far less upon administrative action than do single-rate systems. It is not surprising, therefore, that multiple-rate systems are associated with less-developed countries, which may also find them attractive as devices to raise revenue.

Multiple-rate systems exhibit a bewildering variety. At one extreme are the systems that depend upon two or more "free" markets to allocate foreign exchange, with few direct controls of any kind. At the other extreme are the systems that use two or more fixed official rates that are supplemented by exchange licenses, import quotas, and other quantitative controls characteristic of single-rate systems. Our description is confined to remarks about those features peculiar to multiple-rate systems: penalty and preferential rates, fluctuating "free" market rates, mixing rates, and exchange taxes and subsidies.

When multiple-rate systems use fixed official rates of exchange, the simplest form occurs when the exchange authority sells foreign exchange at a single rate that differs from the single rate at which it buys foreign exchange. When the selling rate is higher than the buying rate in domestic currency (the usual case), the difference accrues to the government as revenue.[9] More than two rates result when the exchange authorities buy exchange received for specific export goods at low *penalty* rates or at high *preferential* rates or sell exchange for "nonessential" imports at high penalty rates and for "essential" imports at low preferential rates. Ordinarily, penalty buying rates are applied only to exports that face an inelastic foreign demand that enables exporters to escape the incidence of the penalty rate by passing it on to foreign buyers. Sometimes mistakes are made, however, and then penalty rates depress the affected exports.

Many multiple-rate countries allow designated transactions in foreign exchange to be effected in a *free* market. In such a market, a floating rate of exchange adjusts the amount of foreign exchange in demand to the amount in supply. Since floating rates are ordinarily considerably higher than the official rate, they favor sellers of foreign exchange and hence encourage those transactions whose exchange receipts may be sold at floating rates. By the same token, buyers of foreign exchange at floating rates are penalized, and this tends to restrict transactions that must be financed in a floating-rate market. Floating-rate markets are used most frequently for invisible (service) and capital transactions and for high-priority exports and low-priority imports. At times, however, a country may use two or more floating-rate markets for most, if not all, foreign exchange transactions.

When a multiple-rate country wants to discriminate finely between

---

[9] The foreign exchange rate is defined here as the price in domestic currency of a single unit of a foreign currency. If the exchange authorities sell at an official rate of say, 5 pesos per U.S. dollar and buy at an official rate of say, 4 pesos per U.S. dollar, then they reap a gain of 1 peso for every U.S. dollar they sell.

different transactions by applying a large number of exchange rates, it may do so by *mixing* official rates with floating rates in varying proportions. Exporters are allowed to sell different percentages of their foreign exchange receipts on the "free" market, depending on their products. The higher the percentage, the greater the preferential treatment accorded to an exporter, because the free rate of exchange is ordinarily much higher (when expressed in domestic currency) than the official rate. Conversely, importers are penalized by making them buy a high percentage of their foreign exchange in the free market. The device of mixing rates enormously heightens the power of the control authority to discriminate between narrow classes of exports or imports—minute variations in effective exchange rates become possible. It should be noted, however, that mixing rates also demand closer administrative supervision of specific export or import items than do rates that apply to a broad class of items.

Countries may *tax* or *subsidize* certain transactions in foreign exchange for revenue or control purposes. The effect is to alter the buying rates of exchange for the transactions in question, thereby creating multiple rates. In 1987, for instance, Colombia imposed a 6.5 percent tax on exchange receipts from coffee exports while, at the same time, it gave tax credits on exchange receipts from several other export products.[10]

THE EFFECTS OF EXCHANGE CONTROL

We have investigated the origins, objectives, and nature of exchange control. What of its effects? The answer to this question is not simple. For one thing, the effects are manifold; for another, the effects vary greatly in intensity depending on the severity and comprehensiveness of exchange control. Here we can only briefly evaluate the principal effects of exchange control on international payments.

Inconvertibility and Bilateralism

By making a currency inconvertible, exchange control strikes at the heart of multilateral settlement, which permits a country to offset a deficit in one direction with a surplus in another direction. To illustrate, suppose that country A has traditionally run a deficit with country B that has been financed by a surplus with country C. But now country C imposes exchange control and no longer allows residents of country A to use its currency to buy the currency of country B. The effect is to force country A to balance its trade *bilaterally* with country B, either by cutting its imports from or

---

[10] For a detailed exposition of the Colombian system, see International Monetary Fund, *Annual Report on Exchange Arrangements and Exchange Restrictions* (Washington, DC: International Monetary Fund, 1988, pp. 154–59.

raising its exports to country B. Usually the first alternative is adopted, and, as a result, country B suffers a loss of exports to country A that may force it to restrict imports from a third country. Thus, exchange control, by disrupting the pattern of multilateral settlement, may compel other countries, one after another, to restrict imports and even to adopt exchange control in turn. A lower volume of trade is not the only consequence of this train of events. The *quality* of trade is also worsened, because it is no longer possible for the exporter to sell in the most profitable market or for the importer to buy in the least expensive market. The truth of this remark becomes clearer when we consider bilateral payments agreements.

Bilateral Payments Agreements

When several countries employ exchange control, there is usually an accumulation of bank balances owned by nonresidents that cannot be freely converted into other currencies. To liquidate these "blocked" balances and to avoid as much as possible the use of convertible currencies in the financing of trade, countries enter into bilateral payments agreements. In the 1950s the majority of trade between nondollar countries was financed in accordance with such agreements, which were often accompanied by trade agreements that specified the goods to be exchanged by the participating countries.

In the words of one authority, a bilateral payments agreement "provides a general method of financing current trade between two countries, giving rise to credits which are freely available for use by one country in making payments for goods and services imported from the other.[11] Bilateral payments agreements contain provisions relating to the unit or units of account that are to be used to finance the net balances of either country, the settlement of balances not covered by credits, the settlement of final balances at the conclusion of the agreement, the tenure of the agreement, and the transferability of balances. The credit and transferability provisions are of particular importance.

Most bilateral payments agreements establish reciprocal credits known as *swing credits*. These credits permit each country to have a deficit in its trade with the partner country up to a specified limit before settlement must be made in gold or dollars or in another agreed manner. At the conclusion of the agreement (which may run for several years), any outstanding balances must be settled in similar fashion. The presence of swing credits lessens the need of the partner countries to achieve an exact balance in their mutual trade, but it may expose the deficit country to a loss of gold or convertible currencies.

All bilateral payments agreements restrict in one way or another the transferability of domestic currency held by residents of the other partner

---

[11] Raymond F. Mikesell, *Foreign Exchange in the Postwar World* (New York: Twentieth Century Fund, 1954), p. 86.

country. This must be done if the agreement is to achieve its main function: the financing of trade with inconvertible currencies. The degree of transferability, however, may vary significantly in different agreements.

At one extreme are the restrictive *bilateral offset agreements* that allow no transferability to third currencies. Under this sort of agreement, usually found only between communist countries, any net balances are settled by an export of goods from the debtor country. Bilateral offset agreements, like barter, effectively prevent any multilateral settlement by destroying its very basis.

Exchange settlement agreements, as their name implies, allow for the settlement of final balances, and of balances beyond the swing credit, in gold, convertible currencies, or other agreed currencies. Although these agreements do not rigidly bilateralize trade, they do encourage bilateral settlement, since each partner country seeks to avoid having to pay gold or third currencies to the other.

The restoration of current-account convertibility by the important trading nations of Europe at the close of 1958 led to the dissolution of many payments agreements. Although sixty-nine agreements were in force at the end of 1987 between member countries of the International Monetary Fund, none involved a major trading country. Of some seventy-two agreements between member and nonmember countries, nearly all were with the communist countries. In conclusion, bilateral payments agreements are now extinct among major trading countries but are still common between the developing and communist countries.

The Redistribution of Money Incomes

The redistribution of money incomes that results from exchange control will vary depending upon the circumstances. Money income is diverted to the government by penalty selling rates of exchange, exchange taxes, exchange auctions, and the like. On the other hand, exporters and other sellers of foreign exchange may reap windfall profits when they are allowed to sell their exchange in floating-rate markets. In contrast, importers are apt to enjoy windfall profits in a single-rate system because the restriction of imports will push up their domestic prices. When exchange control protects domestic industry, its redistribution effects are similar to those of protective tariffs and quotas (see Chapter 7). In the last analysis, the consumer is likely to bear the incidence of exchange control in the form of higher prices for imports and their domestic substitutes.

The Evasion of Exchange Control

Exchange control encourages widespread evasion on the part of residents and nonresidents alike. Evasion of exchange regulations by residents is criminal, since it flouts domestic law. The exchange control country, however, has no jurisdiction over nonresidents who are located outside its boundaries and who may also evade its exchange regulations.

Bilateral payments agreements are often designed to lessen evasion of the exchange control of one partner country by residents of the other partner country, but the success of payments agreements in this respect depends upon the willingness and the ability of the government of the partner country to fulfill its obligations. The residents of free exchange countries, such as the United States, are able to evade the exchange regulations of other countries without violating domestic laws, since their governments are usually unwilling to enter into bilateral payments agreements with an evasion clause. Even if exchange control was fully effective in regulating all foreign exchange transactions within the exchange control country, it would not restrain much of the evasion practiced by nonresidents located abroad.

The number of evasion techniques is legion, including bribery and corruption of officials, false invoicing of exports and imports, and black market operations. False invoicing may involve the *underinvoicing* of exports so that part of the actual foreign exchange receipts is withheld from the control authority and placed by the importer or other agent in a foreign bank to the account of the exporter. The same thing may be accomplished through the *overinvoicing* of imports so that the importer obtains more foreign exchange than is needed to pay for the imports, the excess ending up in the importer's private bank account in a foreign country. Black market operations cover any illegal transactions in foreign exchange.

A SYNOPTIC VIEW OF CONTEMPORARY EXCHANGE CONTROL PRACTICES

Table 17-1 offers a synoptic view of the exchange control systems employed by members of the International Monetary Fund (IMF), which embraces almost all noncommunist countries. All the *highly industrialized developed* countries have now accepted Article VIII of the IMF agreement, which obligates them to refrain from restrictions on current payments.[12] However, two of the *less-advanced developed* countries, along with two-thirds of the developing countries, remain under Article XIV, which allows them to retain current account restrictions. At the end of 1987, three developed countries and seventy-five developing countries had such restrictions. However, no developed country had more than one rate of exchange for current transactions, while twenty-seven developing countries had multiple-rate systems. Restrictions on capital transactions are prevalent throughout the world: Only nine developed countries and twenty-one developing countries (mostly

---

[12] Article VIII and other features of the IMF Agreement are treated in Chapter 18.

TABLE 17-1   Summary Features of Exchange Control Systems of IMF
Countries at the End of 1987

	Developed Countries*	Developing Countries†	Communist Countries‡
Article VIII status	20	43	0
Article XIV status	2§	78	8
Restrictions on current transactions‖	3#	75	8
Restrictions on capital transactions**	13	100	8
Import rate(s) different from export rate(s)	0	27	7
Surrender of export proceeds required	10	103	8
Bilateral payments arrangements with IMF countries	1	33	7
Bilateral payments arrangements with non-IMF countries	1	20	8

* Twenty-two countries: United States, Canada, Western Europe, Japan, Australia, New Zealand, South Africa, and Finland.
† One hundred and twenty-one countries in Asia, Africa, and Latin America.
‡ Afghanistan, China, Hungary, Laos, Poland, Romania, Vietnam, and Yugoslavia.
§ Greece and Portugal.
‖ Other than restrictions for security reasons.
Greece, Iceland, and Portugal.
** Other than restrictions for security reasons. Resident-owned funds.

Source: Derived from International Monetary Fund, *Annual Report on Exchange Arrangements and Exchange Restrictions, 1988* (Washington, D.C.: International Monetary Fund, 1988), pp. 544–49.

oil exporters) did not have them. Also, only a small number of countries do not require their exporters to surrender foreign exchange receipts to the exchange authority (usually the central bank). It is evident that exchange controls of one sort or another remain very common in the world economy. Apart from their broad economic effects, such controls generate constraints and risks for international business enterprise, which must somehow learn to cope with them.

Is exchange control economically justified? The argument against exchange control is that its use raises obstacles to gainful international trade by restricting the convertibility of currencies, distorting price and cost relationships, discriminating between countries and currency areas, perpetuating balance of payments disequilibrium, and creating uncertainty and confusion. Hence, exchange control interferes with international specialization and trade in accordance with comparative advantage.

Despite this serious indictment, we have seen that exchange restrictions on current transactions have become a way of life for over half of the developing countries. The main explanation for the persistence of exchange control is that, although most nations pay lip service to the objective of free multilateral trade, they are unwilling to accept the monetary and fiscal disciplines necessary to sustain the convertibility of their currencies. Other objectives—full employment, economic development, national planning, and so on—are placed ahead of the attainment of international equilibrium. Exchange control then becomes a mechanism used to defend national policies against international repercussions, and under some circumstances exchange restrictions on current account may be justified as a second-best policy.

The achievement of a multilateral trading system does not require the abandonment of all forms of exchange control. Currencies used to finance current transactions in merchandise and services as well as in investment capital must be fully convertible. Exchange control, however, may be used to restrain an occasional capital flight without endangering multilateral trade. Another legitimate use of exchange control is its *temporary* employment to allow a nation enough time to make a fundamental adjustment to a persistent deficit in its balance of payments, assuming that its reserves are inadequate to perform the same task. Since the longer-term elasticities of the supply and demand of foreign exchange are ordinarily greater than their short-term elasticities, the temporary use of exchange control may also be justified as a policy instrument to ease adjustment after a devaluation. As we have observed, however, the *temporary* exchange control system commonly becomes a permanent system because of the vested interests that benefit from it.

SUMMARY

1. The direct interference of governments in the foreign exchange market is known as exchange control. Exchange control restricts the right of holders of a currency to exchange it for other currencies. It thereby renders a currency inconvertible.

2. Aside from its use during World War I, the first peacetime application of exchange control by industrial countries occurred in response to the capital flight unloosed by the international financial crisis of 1931. During the 1930s the exchange control area was centered in Germany and Eastern Europe, although several countries in Latin America also adopted exchange restrictions in the face of balance of payments difficulties.

3. After World War II most countries continued to restrict both current and capital transactions by means of exchange control. However, a massive liberalization by the industrial countries began at the close of 1958, when ten European countries established nonresident con-

vertibility of their currencies on current account. The majority of developing countries still retain exchange control as a major tool of foreign economic policy.

4. There are many objectives of exchange control. Foremost among them are the suppression of balance of payments disequilibrium, the facilitation of national planning, the protection of domestic industries, and the creation of government revenue. The versatility of ends that may be served by exchange control is an important factor behind its continued use in contemporary international trade.

5. A useful distinction may be made between single-rate systems of exchange control and multiple-rate systems. In single-rate systems, all foreign exchange transactions are carried on at one official rate of exchange. All foreign exchange receipts are surrendered to an exchange control authority that allocates foreign exchange expenditures by types of important transactions, by countries and currency areas, and by applicants. Single-rate systems make use of import licenses and quotas in allocating foreign exchange.

6. In a multiple-rate system of exchange control, two or more legal exchange rates apply to different foreign exchange transactions. Because at least part of the task of allocating foreign exchange to different uses is carried out by differential exchange rates, multiple-rate systems rely on administrative action far less than do single-rate systems. There is a bewildering variety of multiple-rate systems.

7. The most important effect of exchange control is its disruption of multilateral settlement and the forcing of international trade into bilateral channels. Exchange control thus limits the advantages to be gained from international specialization in a competitive world market. When several countries practice exchange control, blocked balances and the scarcity of convertible currencies raise formidable obstacles to trade. To liquidate blocked balances and to avoid the use of convertible currencies in the financing of mutual trade, exchange control countries negotiate bilateral payments agreements.

8. Exchange control also redistributes money incomes, since exporters, importers, or the government are able to enjoy monopoly profits depending upon the nature of the system.

9. Exchange control is evaded by both residents and nonresidents in many ways, including bribery and corruption of officials, false invoicing of exports and imports, and black market operations.

10. The main indictment of exchange control is its interference with international trade based on comparative advantage. The achievement of a multilateral trading system, however, is compatible with the use of exchange control to stop a capital flight and with its temporary use to provide time for fundamental adjustment to an external payments deficit.

QUESTIONS AND APPLICATIONS

1. What is exchange control?
2. (a) Trace the origins of exchange control in the 1930s.
   (b) What is the present situation in the world economy with regard to exchange control?
3. (a) What are the principal objectives of contemporary exchange control systems?
   (b) How does exchange control serve these objectives?
4. (a) Describe the single-rate system of exchange control.
   (b) What is the key to this system of control?
   (c) How may the control authority insure the surrender of foreign exchange?
   (d) What allocation problems does the control authority face?
   (e) What methods may be used to allocate foreign exchange to applicants?
5. What is the role of import quotas and licenses in single-rate systems of exchange control?
6. Why does exchange control involve the control of nonresident accounts?
7. (a) How does the multiple-rate system of exchange control differ from the single-rate system?
   (b) What features are peculiar to multiple-rate systems?
8. Distinguish between preferential and penalty buying and selling rates of exchange.
9. In the multiple-rate system, what is the function of floating market rates? Of mixing rates? Of exchange taxes?
10. Enumerate the principal effects of exchange control.
11. Describe the purpose and nature of bilateral payments agreements. Comment specifically on their credit and transferability provisions.
12. What is the "proper" use of exchange control?

SELECTED READINGS

Annual Report on Exchange Arrangements and Exchange Restrictions. Washington, D.C.: International Monetary Fund.

Bhagwati, Jagdish. *Anatomy and Consequences of Exchange Control Regimes.* Cambridge, Mass.: Ballinger, 1978

League of Nations. *International Currency Experience.* New York: Columbia University Press, 1944.

Lizondo, Jose S. "Unifying Multiple Exchange Rates." *Finance Development,* December 1985, pp. 23-24.

Nowak, Michael. "Black Markets in Foreign Exchange." *Finance Development,* March 1985, pp. 20-23.

Trued, M. N., and R. F. Mikesell. *Postwar Bilateral Payments Agreements.* Princeton Studies in International Finance, no. 4. Princeton, N.J.: Princeton University Press, 1955.

18

The Bretton Woods International Monetary System and Its Collapse (1945–1971)

For 25 years after World War II, the international monetary system, known as the Bretton Woods system, was based on stable and convertible exchange rates, with occasional devaluations of individual currencies to correct "fundamental" disequilibria in the balance of payments. This system had several strengths, but it also had flaws that were to prove fatal. Mounting pressures in the 1960s culminated in the collapse of the Bretton Woods system in 1971 and its unintended replacement with a regime of floating exchange rates. In this and the following chapter we examine the leading features of the Bretton Woods system, the reasons for its collapse, the nature and performance of the contemporary floating-rate system, and proposals for international monetary reform.

The Bretton Woods international monetary system was sustained by two institutions: the International Monetary Fund and the central reserve role of the U.S. dollar.

THE INTERNATIONAL MONETARY FUND (IMF)

While war still raged in Europe and Asia, representatives of the United States, Great Britain, and other Allied countries met at Bretton Woods, New Hampshire, in 1944 to reach final agreement on the postwar international monetary system. The delegates to the conference, who included the eminent British economist John Maynard Keynes, were mindful of the rise and fall of international monetary systems in the past and particularly of the monetary chaos that preceded the war. From 1870 to 1914, the international gold standard (centered in London) had reigned supreme, only to be abandoned at the outbreak of World War I.[1] Among the major countries, only the United States maintained the gold convertibility of its currency during that conflict. After a period of freely fluctuating exchange rates, the gold standard was painfully restored in the 1920s, but only in the modified form of a gold exchange standard whereby central banks held some or all of their reserves in sterling, dollars, or francs rather than in gold. Global depression, heightened by massive flows of speculative capital, forced the collapse of this system in the early 1930s; Great Britain halted the gold convertibility of the pound in September 1931, and the United States devalued the dollar by raising the price of gold from $20.67 to $35.00 an ounce in 1933. There followed a scramble by each country to protect its currency and trade vis-à-vis other countries. Competitive depreciations to promote exports and curb imports, inconvertible currencies, exchange control, currency blocs, and bilateral trade agreements became the order of the day.[2] Then came World War II.

The delegates at Bretton Woods were convinced that only an unprecedented degree of international monetary cooperation could hope to forestall a repetition of the 1930s. The outcome of their deliberations was the establishment of the International Monetary Fund, an international agency to administer a code of fair exchange practices and provide compensatory financial assistance to member countries in balance of payments trouble.[3]

The purposes of the IMF were clearly set forth in Article I of its Articles of Agreement:

1. To promote international monetary cooperation through a permanent institution which provides the machinery for consultation and collaboration on international monetary problems.
2. To facilitate the expansion and balanced growth of international trade, and to contribute thereby to the promotion and maintenance of high levels of employment and real income and to the development of the productive resources of all members as primary objectives of economic policy.
3. To promote exchange stability, to maintain orderly exchange arrangements among members, and to avoid competitive exchange depreciation.
4. To assist in the establishment of a multilateral system of payments in respect of current transactions between members and in the elimination of foreign exchange restrictions which hamper the growth of world trade.

---

[1] The mechanics of the international gold standard are discussed in Chapter 12.

[2] The collapse of the gold exchange standard in the 1930s is briefly treated at the beginning of Chapter 17.

[3] The Articles of Agreement of the Fund entered into force in December 1945. A second Bretton Woods agreement established the International Bank for Reconstruction and Development.

5. To give confidence to members by making the Fund's resources available to them under adequate safeguards, thus providing them with the opportunity to correct maladjustments in the balances of payments without resorting to measures destructive of national or international balances of payments of members

Code of Fair Exchange Practices

Upon entering the Fund, a country submitted a *par value* of its currency expressed in terms of gold or in terms of the U.S. dollar of the weight and fineness of gold in effect on July 1, 1944. All exchange transactions between member countries were to be effected at a rate that diverged not more than 1 percent from the par values of the respective currencies.

A member could change the par value of its currency only to correct a *fundamental* disequilibrium in its balance of payments and only after consultation with the Fund. If the Fund objected to the change but the member nevertheless went ahead with it, the Fund could declare that member ineligible to use its resources.[4] Although the Fund could object to a proposed change in the par value of a currency, it could not formally propose a change of its own accord. These provisions envisaged, therefore, a system of stable exchange rates with an occasional devaluation (depreciation) or revaluation (appreciation) to remove a persistent disequilibrium in the balance of payments.[5]

Article VIII of the agreement forbade members to restrict current (account) payments or to discriminate in their currency practices without the approval of the Fund. Members were also obligated to maintain the convertibility of foreign-held balances acquired or used in connection with current transactions. Thus, Article VIII clearly outlawed exchange control over international payments for merchandise and services. On the other hand, Article VI allowed members to control capital movements as long as current transactions remained unaffected.

There were two exceptions to the provisions of Article VIII. One exception occurred when the Fund declared a currency to be scarce because the demand for the currency threatened the Fund's ability to supply it. A scarce currency declaration authorized member countries to impose exchange control over all transactions in the scarce currency. The scarce currency provision explicitly recognized that free convertibility could not be sustained if most countries had persistent deficits with the same surplus country, for in that event multilateral settlement of the deficits was out of the question. This provision also applied pressure on the surplus country to take remedial measures to avoid discrimination against its trade.

---

[4] If the proposed change, together with all previous changes, whether increases or decreases, did not exceed 10 percent of the initial par value of the member's currency, the Fund would raise no objection.

[5] This is the adjustable-peg system described in the section "Variable Rates: Introduction" in Chapter 16.

The most important exception to the provisions of Article VIII, however, was found in the provisions of Article XIV. This article allowed a member country to retain exchange restrictions on current international transactions in effect when that country entered the Fund. Moreover, these restrictions could be adapted to changing circumstances to deal with balance of payments difficulties. The decision to abandon exchange restrictions permitted under Article XIV was left to the member country, but it was supposed to occur when such restrictions were no longer necessary to settle the balance of payments without undue dependence on the Fund's resources. Once a member abolished its exchange control over current payments and accepted the obligations of Article VIII, it could not reimpose similar exchange restrictions without the approval of the Fund.

Article XIV was conceived as a "transitional arrangement" that would not be necessary once the member countries had overcome the problems of readjustment that immediately followed World War II. Events proved otherwise, however, and it was not until 1961 that the major countries in Western Europe were able to accept the obligations of Article VIII. The last big trading country, Japan, came under Article VIII in 1964.[6] The remaining Article XIV countries were obliged to consult annually with the Fund on the continuance of exchange restrictions, but, as we noted earlier, the Fund had no power to decree their abolition. Nor did the Articles of Agreement specify the duration of the transition period.

Compensatory Financing by the Fund

In addition to administering a code of fair exchange practices, the Fund was also a source of compensatory financing for a member country experiencing a *temporary* disequilibrium in its balance of payments. The resources of the Fund came from the gold and currency subscriptions of its member countries.[7] Upon entering the Fund, each country was allotted a quota in accordance with its relative economic size. Twenty-five percent of a country's quota was paid to the Fund in gold and the remainder in the country's own currency.[8] Since quotas were calculated in the 1944 U.S. dollar, the dollar equivalents of nondollar currencies were determined by their respective par values. The Fund started operations in 1947 with aggregate quotas of $8 billion, but successive quota increases had raised the total to $28.5 billion by 1971. The largest quota was subscribed by the United States ($6.7 billion); the next largest by Great Britain ($2.8 billion).

The size of a country's quota was significant in two respects. First, it determined, approximately, the voting power of a member's executive di-

---

[6] By April, 1971 thirty-five countries had accepted Article VIII. The Fund never invoked the scarce-currency provision.

[7] In 1971, 117 countries of the noncommunist world were members of the Fund.

[8] When a country's gold reserves were low, it was permitted to join the Fund without full payment of its gold subscription, using its own currency as a substitute. Full payment was expected, however, when the country's gold reserves became adequate.

rector. Thus, the executive director of the United States had 21.9 percent of the voting power of the executive directors; the executive director of the United Kingdom had 9.2 percent. This gave these two countries a dominant voice in the operation of the Fund. Second, the size of a country's quota determined the overall amount that it could draw from the resources of the Fund.

A member country was entitled to buy from the Fund, with its own currency, the currency of another member subject to the following conditions:

1. The member desired to buy a currency to make currency payments consistent with the provisions of the Articles of Agreement.
2. The Fund had not given notice that its holdings of the desired currency were scarce.
3. The proposed purchase did not cause the Fund's holdings of the purchasing member's currency to increase by over 25 percent of its quota during the 12-month period ending on the date of such purchase nor to exceed 200 percent of its basic quota.
4. The Fund had not previously declared that the member desiring to purchase was ineligible to use the resources of the Fund.

In practice, the Fund freely allowed member countries to purchase other currencies up to the first 25 percent of their quotas (often called the *gold tranche*).[9] It also waived the twelve-month requirement in many instances. The Fund would not permit a country to draw beyond 25 percent of its quota, however, unless convinced that the country in question was following policies directed toward the eventual achievement of convertibility or the avoidance of exchange restrictions. Convertibility was a principal objective of the Fund, and it employed its resources accordingly.

The Fund also encouraged liberal exchange policies by negotiating *standby agreements* with interested member countries. Through these agreements, member countries received the Fund's guarantee that they would be allowed to draw on the Fund for the currency or currencies covered by the agreement within a specified period of time.

In addition to drawings under these general arrangements, a country could apply for a special drawing to obtain compensatory financing for a temporary decline in its export earnings. Intended to assist developing countries, such special drawings did not normally exceed 25 percent of a country's quota, but they could bring the Fund's holdings of a country's currency over the limit of twice its quota.

The resources of the Fund were intended to supplement the reserves of a country when it was faced with a temporary deficit in the balance of

---

[9] A country's *reserve position in the Fund* equalled its gold tranche *minus* any current utilization of its drawing rights *plus* the Fund's use of its currency to finance the drawings of other countries or to purchase gold. This reserve position was considered an unconditional asset that was part of a country's international reserves.

payments. Hence, the Fund provided only *short-term* financial assistance that was to be repaid by the borrowing country within the near future (3 to 5 years). The Fund was not a source of capital like the International Bank, and no member country could look to it for more than stopgap compensatory financing of an external deficit.

In 1962 the Fund's resources were supplemented by the *General Arrangements to Borrow,* which were negotiated by ten industrial countries. Under this agreement the Fund could borrow up to $5.9 billion from the "Group of Ten" to provide compensatory financial assistance to one or more of the participating countries.[10] In 1970, the Fund activated an entirely new facility to supply reserve assets to its members, known as *Special Drawing Rights (SDRs).* SDRs are treated later in the chapter.

Evaluation of the Fund

The IMF was originally intended to carry out its functions in a world economy enjoying a substantial degree of overall equilibrium and free of any persistent maladjustments, such as the dollar shortage or subsequent dollar glut. In such an economy, countries would adjust to temporary deficits in their balance of payments by resorting to their own reserves and, if necessary, to the resources of the Fund. Free convertibility would be maintained by all countries and exchange rates would be altered, after consultation with the Fund, only to correct a fundamental disequilibrium. In this way, the advantages of the gold standard—convertibility and fixed exchange rates—would be gained, while an occasional exchange devaluation would maintain equilibrium without the disadvantage of internal deflation. More specifically, the Fund was conceived as an antidote to the conditions of the 1930s. In those years convertibility was maintained between the dollar and the pound sterling (the key trading currencies), but its effects were compromised by disorderly exchange practices, including competitive depreciation and the spread of exchange control to Central and Eastern Europe and to Latin America.

In light of these observations, it is not surprising that the Fund could not fulfill its intended functions in the first decade of its existence. During those years nondollar countries showed persistent payments deficits and continued to restrict dollar payments. Moreover, unlike the 1930s, inflation rather than depression was the principal obstacle to external stability after World War II, and with few exceptions exchange rates were controlled to avert depreciation. During this period of restrictions and inconvertibility, the Fund was mostly a bystander and little use was made of its resources. This passive role ended abruptly with the Suez crisis in 1956–1957.

We can now see in retrospect that the Suez crisis coincided with the

---

[10] Participants in the General Arrangements to Borrow, known as the "Group of Ten," were Belgium, Canada, France, West Germany, Italy, Japan, the Netherlands, Sweden, the United Kingdom, and the United States. In 1964 Switzerland became an associate member.

end of the dollar shortage—in 1958 the U.S. balance of payments suffered the first of a continuing series of big deficits that replaced the dollar shortage with a dollar glut. When called upon at the end of 1956, the Fund quickly responded with compensatory financial assistance that was needed to overcome the trade disruptions and fears of the time. The resumption of convertibility by Western European countries at the end of 1958 carried with it the widespread abandonment of exchange controls on current transactions and later on capital transactions. With the accession of Japan to Article VIII in 1964, the Fund nearly achieved one of its basic purposes—the elimination of exchange controls for the bulk of world trade.

The return of convertibility, however, brought another problem in its wake—sudden, massive movements of speculative and flight capital among the financial centers of North America and Western Europe. As we shall see, this new source of instability, together with a progressive weakening of the dollar during the 1960s, ultimately forced a profound disruption of the Fund's par value system in 1971. We now turn to another aspect of the Bretton Woods monetary system as it evolved after World War II—the central reserve role of the U.S. dollar.

THE CENTRAL RESERVE ROLE OF THE U.S. DOLLAR

The Fund agreement laid the basis for the international monetary system after World War II. But the system evolved in a way that was not envisaged in that agreement. During the 1950s the United States emerged as the prime reserve country, with the dollar increasingly taking over the function of gold as an international reserve asset. No one planned this development; it arose as a response to the dominant postwar position of the United States in international trade and finance.[11] With well over half of all international money transactions being financed in terms of dollars, it became necessary for banks and business enterprises throughout the world to maintain dollar working balances.

In the early 1950s, as the European countries began to enjoy reserve surpluses, the most natural course of action for central banks was to convert those surpluses into dollar reserves rather than into gold. After all, interest could be earned on dollar assets and they could always be converted into gold at $35 per ounce if that ever became necessary.

The gold-exchange system that emerged in the 1950s is depicted in

---

[11] As one writer put it, the dollar and the pound sterling "became international currencies neither by Act of Congress (Parliament) nor by Act of God, but rather because they met various needs of foreign official institutions and foreign private parties more effectively than other financial assets could. " See Robert Z. Aliber, *The Future of the Dollar as an International Currency* (New York: Frederick A. Praeger,1966), p. 8.

Figure 18-1. All of the noncommunist countries maintained a stable relationship between their currencies and the dollar either directly or through the British pound. For members of the Fund this relationship was expressed

Figure 18-1   The Central Reserve Role of the U.S. Dollar in the Bretton Woods International Monetary System

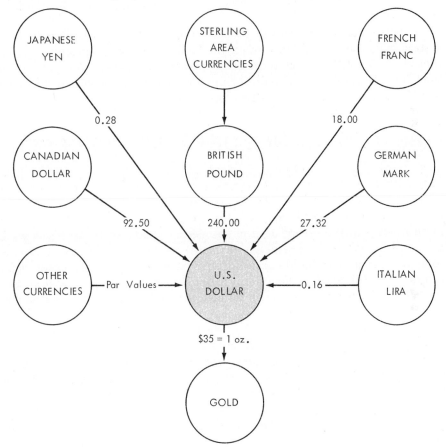

Note: Par values as of August 15, 1971, expressed as U.S. cents per currency unit.

In the Bretton Woods international monetary system, all IMF countries were obligated to maintain stable par values of their currencies expressed in terms of gold or in terms of the 1944 U.S. dollar. The U.S. dollar was the only currency convertible into gold (at a fixed price of $35 per ounce) for official monetary purposes. In practice, nondollar currencies were pegged to the dollar at rates of exchange that were altered only to adjust to a "fundamental disequilibrium" in a country's balance of payments. Hence, the designation of the Bretton Woods system as an "adjustable-peg" system.

in the par values of their currencies; for nonmembers (the most important being Switzerland) it was a result of an autonomous stabilization policy. The U.S. dollar stood at the center of this system, and it was the only currency directly convertible into gold for official monetary purposes. Before World War I the pound sterling performed a similar function, but the sterling area had shrunk to a small number of countries with mostly minor currencies. In this limited fashion, the United Kingdom also operated as a central reserve country. As the Bretton Woods system evolved, however, the reserves of most countries became a mixture of gold and dollars, with a growing dominance of the latter.[12]

The extraordinary role of the dollar in the international monetary system gave the U.S. balance of payments a significance far transcending that of other countries' balances of payments. And it was the inability of the United States to restore equilibrium after more than a decade of deficits that proved the undoing of the Bretton Woods system.

THE U.S. BALANCE OF PAYMENTS DEFICIT

In the 1960s the international monetary system was shaken by a series of crises in foreign exchange and gold markets. Although speculation against the dollar started as early as 1960, these crises became more frequent and more intense in the second half of the decade. Some of these crises were provoked by balance of payments disequilibria in nondollar currencies accompanied by massive shifts of speculative funds among the major financial centers. But the most pervasive source of instability was the weakness of the dollar, which, given its role as the central reserve currency, raised doubts about the viability of the entire system.

During the period 1958–1971, the United States experienced a persistent deficit in its balance of payments. At first, the tendency was to regard these annual deficits as temporary in nature and, not calling for any extraordinary measures by U.S. authorities. But by the fall of 1960 it had become obvious that the United States was facing a payments situation that was not self-corrective and showed signs of disconcerting permanency.

The complexity of the U.S. balance of payments, the mutual interdependence of its individual items, the many factors—economic and political—that have a causal bearing on international transactions, and, in some instances, the lack of sound quantitative data rendered impossible a precise determination of the cause or causes of the successive deficits. This is hardly surprising when we realize that a balance of payments is a summary of *all* the economic transactions between one country and the rest of the world over the year. It is also not surprising that economists disagreed—and some-

---

[12] See Table 18-6.

times sharply—as to the underlying cause or causes of the U.S. disequilibrium.

Analytical disagreements inevitably engendered policy disagreements. All sorts of remedial measures were urged upon the U.S. government by American and European economists. These included the "classical medicine" of internal deflation, dollar depreciation, gold appreciation, floating exchange rates, capital issues control, orthodox measures to increase world liquidity, and a basic reform of the international monetary system. These policy recommendations were often supported by cogent reasoning, but all of them were controversial in one way or another.

Table 18-1 shows the basic, net liquidity, and official reserves deficits of the U.S. balance of payments in 1970.[13] Table 18-2 indicates the net liquidity, official reserves, and basic deficits of the U.S. balance of payments during the period 1960–1971.

Financing the U.S. Deficits

During the years 1958–1971, the United States experienced a cumulative reserve deficit of $56 billion. The United States financed this deficit by drawing on its gold reserves and by incurring liquid liabilities to foreign central banks. Table 18-3 records the changes in U.S. reserve assets during those years.

As a central reserve country, the international reserves of the United States consisted mainly of gold. Gold reserves fell from $22.9 billion in 1957 to $10.2 billion at the end of 1971, or a total reduction of $12.7 billion. Exports of monetary gold, therefore, financed some 23 percent of the cumulative deficit. The other reserve assets provided only minimal compensatory financing for the period as a whole. The United States started using the currencies of other countries (mainly through bilateral swap agreements with foreign central banks) only in 1961, and SDRs were not activated until 1970.

The remaining cumulative deficit was financed primarily by an increase in liquid liabilities to official monetary institutions, as shown in Table 18-4. These liabilities rose from $7.9 billion in 1957 to $47.1 billion at the end of 1971, an increase of $39.2 billion.[14] This extraordinary rise in official liquid liabilities was possible only because of the central reserve role of the dollar. Dollars accumulated by foreign central banks were regarded as international reserve assets. A nonreserve country did not have this source of compensatory financing; it was compelled to rely on its own reserve assets

---

[13] The basic and official reserves transactions balances are described in Chapter 14. The *net liquidity balance* was intended to measure changes in the liquidity position of the United States by distinguishing *nonliquid* private short-term capital from *liquid* private short-term capital.

[14] Additional compensatory financing was supplied by an increase in nonliquid liabilities to foreign official agencies (item 14 in Table 18-1) and by liabilities to the IMF arising out of gold transactions.

TABLE 18-1   U.S. Balance of Payments in 1970 Showing the Basic, Net Liquidity, and Official Reserve Deficits (Billions of Dollars)

1.	Net balance on goods and services[1]	3.6
2.	Remittances, pensions, and other transfers	−1.4
3.	U.S. government grants[2]	−1.7
4.	Long-term U.S. government capital flows, net	−1.8
5.	Long-Term private capital flows, net	−1.5
6.	*Basic balance* (1 + 2 + 3 + 4 + 5)	−3.0
7.	Nonliquid short-term private capital flows, net[3]	−0.5
8.	Allocations of Special Drawing Rights (SDRs)	0.9
9.	Errors and omissions, net	−1.1
10.	*Net liquidity balance* (Basic balance + 7 + 8 + 9)	−3.8
11.	Liquid private capital flows: claims[4]	0.2
12.	Liquid private capital flows: liabilities[5]	−6.2
13.	*Official reserves transactions balance* (net liquidity balance + 11 + 12)	−9.8
14.	Nonliquid liabilities to foreign official agencies	−0.3
15.	Liquid liabilities to foreign official agencies	7.6
16.	U.S. official reserve assets	2.5
	(a) Gold	0.8
	(b) SDRs	−0.9
	(c) Convertible currencies	2.2
	(d) Gold tranche position in IMF	0.4

Note: Figures may not add because of rounding.

[1] Excludes military transfers under grants.

[2] Excludes military grants.

[3] Nonliquid short-term capital flows include changes in loans, collections, acceptance credits, and other credits to finance international trade.

[4] Changes in time and demand deposits and other negotiable instruments held abroad by U.S. residents.

[5] Changes in time and demand deposits and other negotiable instruments held in the United States by foreigners.

Source: Federal Reserve Bulletin (Washington D.C.: U.S. Government Printing Office, December 1971), Table 1, p. A74.

and limited external assistance from the Fund and other agencies. Although foreign central banks became increasingly reluctant to add to their dollar reserves in the 1960s, as a group they had no alternative. By 1963 U.S. gold reserves barely covered liabilities to foreign central banks, and by the end of 1970 coverage had fallen to 55 percent. Any concerted attempt by central banks to convert their dollar holdings into gold, therefore, would have forced the United States to abandon gold convertibility, which was the foundation of the Bretton Woods system. As it turned out, a massive flight from the dollar in 1971 (financed by a truly fantastic increase in official liabilities,

TABLE 18-2   Basic, Net Liquidity, and
Official Reserve Deficits in the U.S.
Balance of Payments, 1960–1971 (Billions of
Dollars)

Year	Net Liquidity Deficit	Official Reserves Deficit	Basic Deficit
1960	− 3.7	− 3.4	− 1.2
1961	− 2.3	− 1.3	0.0
1962	− 2.9	− 2.7	− 1.0
1963	− 2.7	− 1.9	− 1.3
1964	− 2.7	− 1.5	0.0
1965	− 2.5	− 1.3	− 1.8
1966	− 2.2	+ 0.2	− 1.7
1967	− 4.7	− 3.4	− 3.3
1968	− 1.6	+ 1.6	− 1.4
1969	− 6.1	+ 2.7	− 3.0
1970	− 3.9	− 9.8	− 3.1
1971	− 22.0	− 29.8	− 9.4

Source: U.S. Balance of Payments Trends (St. Louis: Federal Reserve Bank of St. Louis, April 1973), p. 3.

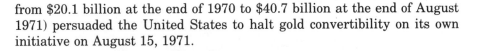

from $20.1 billion at the end of 1970 to $40.7 billion at the end of August 1971) persuaded the United States to halt gold convertibility on its own initiative on August 15, 1971.

Remedial Measures Taken by the U.S. Government before August 15, 1971

As we learned in earlier chapters, a country may adjust to a persistent deficit in its balance of payments in three broad ways: (1) through an internal deflation of prices and incomes relative to foreign prices and incomes; (2) through a devaluation of its exchange rate; or (3) through direct, nonmarket measures such as export promotion, exchange controls, and restrictions on trade and investment. In the 1960s the U.S. government chose the third way by adopting an extraordinary variety of measures to directly influence all of the major classes of transactions making up the balance of payments. They included measures to increase exports through promotional activities, measures to reduce U.S. government outlays abroad, measures to restrain private capital exports, and measures taken by the U.S. monetary author-

Table 18-3   Reserve Assets of the United States, 1957–1971
(Billions of Dollars)

End of Period	Total Reserve Assets	Convertible Currencies	Reserve Position in IMF	SDRs	Gold Stock	Gold Stock as Fraction of Official Liquid Liabilities
1957	24.8		2.0		22.9	2.90
1960	19.4		1.6		17.8	1.75
1963	16.8	0.2	1.0		15.6	1.08
1966	14.9	1.3	0.3		13.2	0.96
1967	14.8	2.3	0.4		12.1	0.78
1968	15.7	3.5	1.3		10.9	0.88
1969	17.0	2.8	2.3		11.9	0.99
1970	14.5	0.6	1.9	0.9	11.1	0.55
1971	12.2	0.2	0.6	1.1	10.2	0.22

Source: Federal Reserve Bulletin (Washington, D.C.: U.S. Government Printing Office, September 1969), Table 4, p. A75, and (January 1974), Table 4, p. A75. Liquid liabilities to official institutions are shown in Table 18-4.

TABLE 18-4   U.S. Liquid Liabilities to Foreign
Countries, 1957–1971
(Billions of Dollars)

End of Period	Official Institutions	Banks and Other Private Foreigners	Total Liabilities
1957	7.9	5.7	13.6
1960	10.2	7.6	17.8
1963	14.4	9.2	23.6
1966	13.7	14.2	27.9
1967	15.6	15.8	31.4
1968	12.4	19.4	31.8
1969	12.0	28.2	40.2
1970	20.1	21.8	41.9
1971	47.1	15.1	62.2

Source: Federal Reserve Bulletin (Washington, D.C.: U.S. Government Printing Office, December 1971), Table 6, p. A78, and (January 1974), Table 6, p. A75.

ities. Here we describe only capital restrictions and compensatory financing arrangements.

The first direct action to lessen the outflow of private capital was the imposition in mid-1963 of an *interest equalization tax* on the value of foreign securities bought by U.S. residents. This tax was effective in curbing the outflow of portfolio investment even though Canada, developing countries, and international financial agencies were granted exemptions. The tax forced foreign borrowers to raise funds locally or in European capital markets.

The curtailment of U.S. portfolio investment after mid-1963 was more than offset in 1964 by a big jump in U.S. bank loans to foreign borrowers and a further growth in U.S. direct investments. This precipitated a series of measures called the *voluntary restraint program*.

In a special balance of payments message to Congress in February 1965, President Johnson proposed a series of new steps to eliminate the payments deficit, including the application of the interest equalization tax to bank loans to foreigners of one year or more (except export credit), the voluntary cooperation of U.S. banks to limit their lending abroad, and the enlistment of U.S. business in a national campaign to limit direct investments abroad. Shortly thereafter, the Federal Reserve System and the Department of Commerce issued guidelines to commercial banks and business corporations, respectively, requesting them to achieve specified goals in restraining loans and investments abroad. Although the voluntary program was successful in limiting the outflow of direct investment capital, it was replaced in 1968 by *mandatory investment controls*.[15]

Although compensatory financing is not an adjustment to a persistent deficit, the U.S. monetary authorities sought to lessen the gold drain and forestall speculation by initiating measures that were described as the "first line of defense" for the dollar. Traditionally the United States had supported the dollar through a policy of passive stabilization. This policy shifted in May 1961, when the U.S. Treasury actively intervened in the foreign exchange market for the first time since the early 1930s. Using its Exchange Stabilization Fund, the Treasury's first intervention was limited to sales of forward West German deutsche marks to prevent excessive speculation in that currency, which could lead to a flight from the dollar. Later it extended its operations to other currencies in both spot and forward markets. Active stabilization of the dollar was massively reinforced in March 1982, when the Federal Reserve System entered the foreign exchange market on its own account (for the first time since the late 1920s) rather than simply acting as an agent of the Treasury. In the ensuing years the U.S. monetary authorities engaged in numerous transactions in all the leading currencies, mainly to prevent or moderate speculative capital movements in both the dollar and foreign currencies, especially the pound sterling.

---

[15] Restrictions on capital outflows were not lifted until 1974.

As part of its new intervention activity, the Federal Reserve System entered into a series of reciprocal currency arrangements (commonly called *swap agreements*) with the central banks of Western Europe, Canada, and Japan. Under these bilateral arrangements a foreign central bank provided standby credits to the Federal Reserve System in return for an equal amount of standby credits. At the end of 1964 the total amount of swap standby credits was over $2.3 billion; by 1971 it had climbed to $11.7 billion. The swap network benefited foreign countries, such as Italy and Great Britain, by supplementing their reserves with an assured access to dollars and, at the same time, afforded the United States a buffer to absorb sudden speculative drives on the dollar and thereby protected its gold reserves.

To reduce the "overhang" of U.S. liquid liabilities owing to foreign central banks, the U.S. Treasury issued a series of medium-term bonds payable in dollars or in specified foreign currencies for sale to foreign governments and central banks. In effect, these sales of medium-term bonds relieved pressure on U.S. gold reserves by giving foreign central banks an opportunity to acquire an earning asset payable in their own currencies.

None of the foregoing measures introduced by the U.S. monetary authorities reduced the U.S. basic deficit. But they lessened the gold drain and dampened speculative capital outflows by influencing sport and forward rates of exchange (especially forward rates), by interposing a buffer of foreign central bank credits, and by converting a part of U.S. liquid liabilities to a less liquid, more stable form.

Constraints Imposed on U.S. Payments Policy

In the 1960s, U.S. policymakers perceived many constraints that prevented them from making a fundamental adjustment to the balance of payments deficit. Conscious of U.S. leadership of the noncommunist world, they refused to cut back on military forces abroad or abandon foreign assistance to developing countries. Quite understandably, they also refused to deflate the economy to improve the balance of payments. In the first half of the 1960s, U.S. domestic policy was geared to expansion rather than contraction. Only in the late 1960s, when inflation got out of hand, did U.S. policymakers adopt anti-inflationary policies.

Why, then, did the United States not devalue the dollar in the 1960s? The answer to this question lies in the unique role of the dollar as a central reserve currency. This role conferred both benefits and costs on the United States. The clearest benefit was the willingness of foreign central banks to add dollars to their reserves, thus giving the United States a virtually unlimited and automatic access to compensatory finance and allowing it to postpone fundamental adjustment. The cost of this benefit was the commitment (as perceived by U.S. policymakers) to maintain a fixed link between the dollar and gold. Hence, the United States was not able to *initiate* a change in the external value of the dollar, which instead was dependent on the devaluations and revaluations of other currencies. It was also widely held that even if the United States did devalue the dollar by raising the price of gold, other countries would respond by devaluing their own currencies to the same extent and would thereby neutralize the effects of dollar devaluation on the balance of payments. There was also fear that a dollar devaluation would set off immense speculative activity endangering all countries. Only the monetary crisis of 1971 forced an abandonment of these perceptions and the undertaking of drastically new policies in August of that year.

MONETARY CRISES IN THE LATE 1960s

In the middle 1960s, the continuing weakness of sterling (the second central reserve currency) was a major cause of disturbances in foreign exchange markets. Starting in June 1967, tremendous speculative pressures built up against sterling, and in November it was officially devalued from $2.80 to $2.40. This action did not, however, restore stability in foreign exchange markets. Early in 1968, speculators turned to the London gold market in the expectation of a rise in the official price of gold. To maintain the London price at the official price of $35 an ounce, the United States and other members of the "gold pool" sold gold to the private market out of their own reserves.[16] During the first quarter of 1968, the United States lost $1.3 billion in gold, three-fourths of which went to support the London market.

This drain of official gold reserves to private speculators was stopped in March 1968, when the gold pool members agreed to abstain from any further sales to the London market and also not to buy private gold in the future. In this way there emerged the "two-tier" gold arrangement: an official price of $35 an ounce and a private price determined by private supply and demand. The decision to abandon all intervention in the London gold market served to freeze the amount of gold in official reserves—another step away from a gold-exchange standard and toward a dollar standard. Henceforth, central banks would engage in gold transactions only with other central banks.

Scarcely had the gold crisis abated when France was racked by widespread student and worker protests in May and June 1968. This political instability sparked a capital flight from the franc, especially into the West German deutsche mark. Although the French reserves fell drastically (France lost $2.8 billion in gold in 1968), the French government opted for

---

[16] The gold pool was devised in 1961 by the United States, the United Kingdom, Belgium, West Germany, Italy, the Netherlands, and Switzerland. The members of the pool agreed to share in the support of the London gold market.

exchange restrictions instead of devaluation. In 1969 there was a mounting expectation that the French deficit would force a devaluation of the franc while the West German trade surplus would force a revaluation of the deutsche mark. Stability was eventually restored by a franc devaluation of 11.1 percent in August and the declaration of a higher par value for the deutsche mark in October.

THE INTERNATIONAL MONETARY CRISIS OF 1971

Unlike the crises of the late 1960s, the crisis of 1971 was directly inspired by a loss of confidence in the dollar. In the third quarter of 1970, funds began to move at an enormous rate from the United States to financial centers in Europe and Japan. At first, these short-term capital flows were largely a response to interest-rate differentials, but in March 1971 (when interest-rate differentials had narrowed), expectations of changes in exchange rates began to feed a growing speculation against the dollar. The ensuing sequence of events is presented in Table 18-5.

The actions taken by the United States on August 15 marked the end of the Bretton Woods system. On that day (a Sunday), President Nixon suspended "temporarily" the gold convertibility of the dollar and imposed a "temporary" surcharge on dutiable imports into the United States. He

TABLE 18-5   Collapse of the Bretton Woods System: A Chronology of Events in 1971

January February	Large movement of interest-sensitive funds from the United States to Europe, pushing European currencies against dollar ceilings.
March April	Overt speculation appears in foreign exchange markets. A strong trade surplus and restrictive credit policy intensify buying pressure on the deutsche mark. U.S. official reserve deficit for first quarter reaches $5.5 billion.
May 3–4 May 5	Bundesbank forced to absorb a capital inflow of $1 billion. Bundesbank suspends support of the dollar after absorbing $1 billion in the first forty minutes of trading. Central banks of the Netherlands, Switzerland, Belgium, and Austria also terminate support of the dollar.
May 10	When foreign exchange markets reopen, the Swiss franc and Austrian schilling are revalued 7.07 percent and 5.05 percent, respectively, while the West German deutsche mark and Dutch guilder are allowed to float. Belgian market is split between official and financial markets.
June July	U.S. official reserves deficit soars to $11.3 billion for first half of year. U.S. trade deficit for second quarter is $1.0 billion. Outflow of speculative

TABLE 18-5   continued

	capital from United States continues. U.S. gold stock falls close to $10 billion.
August 1–14	U.S. Congressional subcommittee asserts the dollar is overvalued; calls for general realignment of exchange rates. Abrupt acceleration of capital flight from the dollar, which sells at its lowest level against the deutsche mark in twenty-two years.
August 15	President Nixon announces major new program: ninety-day freeze on wages and prices, new tax measures, 10 percent temporary surcharge on dutiable imports, and "temporary" suspension of the dollar's convertibility into gold.
August 16–20	West European governments keep their exchange markets closed. Fail to develop a coordinated response to U.S. measures.
August 23	European governments open foreign exchange markets on uncoordinated basis; each continues to adhere to pre-August 15 parity, but all except the French government cease to support the dollar. The French support commercial transactions market but not financial transactions market.
August 28	Japanese government suspends official intervention in the foreign exchange market. Yen immediately rises 4.7 percent.
September	Exchange rates of major trading currencies rise against the dollar, except commercial rate for French franc. But it is not a "pure" float: Many central banks continue to intervene on an ad hoc basis and some apply exchange restrictions.
September 15	Meeting of Finance Ministers of Group of Ten countries ends in total disagreement; U.S. demands—revaluation of other currencies, reduction in trade barriers, and more sharing of international defense burdens—shock foreign officials.
September 16	GATT urges the United States to end import surcharge.
October November	Pressure builds on the United States to end crisis; there is talk of retaliation in foreign countries. U.S. official reserves deficit reaches $12.1 billion for the first three quarters of year. Speculation intensifies.
December 1	U.S. Secretary of the Treasury surprises Group of Ten Finance Ministers at a meeting in Rome by suggesting a 10 percent dollar devaluation (rise in price of gold) as basis for negotiation.
December 14	At a meeting in the Azores, President Nixon and President Pompidou of France agree to work toward "prompt realignment of currencies through devaluation of the dollar and revaluation of some other currencies."
December 17–18	Group of Ten Finance Ministers meet at Smithsonian Institution in Washington, D.C. United States agrees to 8.57 percent devaluation of the dollar (rise in price of gold per ounce from $35 to $38) and end of surcharge in return for revaluation of other currencies. President Nixon hails outcome as "the most significant monetary agreement in the history of the world."

Chapter 18 – The Bretton Woods International Monetary System and Its Collapse

justified the suspension of convertibility as necessary to "defend the dollar against speculators" who "have been waging all out war on the American dollar." But the more important purpose was to compel foreign governments to raise the value of their currencies against the dollar. In effect, foreign governments were offered a simple choice: continue to maintain existing exchange rates by accumulating more dollars without gold convertibility *or* revalue exchange rates. The import surcharge was intended to place further pressure on them; it would not be taken off until foreign governments altered their "unfair" exchange rates.

The immediate response to the U.S. actions was a closing of foreign exchange markets in Europe and Japan. When they reopened, all of the major foreign currencies were left to float vis-à-vis the dollar, with the exception of the French franc. Hence, the system depicted in Figure 18-1 no longer existed; the Bretton Woods system had died and a new system was waiting to be born.

THE SMITHSONIAN AGREEMENT

The weeks following August 15 were rife with uncertainty, rumor, and tension. Taking a hard line, the U.S. government pressed the view that the dollar's troubles arose from the undervalued exchange rates, protectionist trade policies, and the inadequate defense-sharing expenditures of foreign governments. It demanded unilateral concessions in all three areas. Put on the defensive, the European and Japanese governments firmly resisted any change in the par values of their currencies, fearing the harmful consequences of revaluation on their exports and domestic economic situations. If the dollar is overvalued, they argued, then the United States should find a way to carry out a unilateral devaluation.

Meanwhile most of the leading currencies were floating at higher dollar values, but it was not a "clean" float, as central banks intervened in the market to prevent a full appreciation. France refused to float its currency for commercial transactions, although it permitted a floating rate for financial transactions. Foreign governments were reluctant to let their currencies float freely because they hoped to persuade the United States to devalue the dollar by raising the price of gold.

International monetary negotiations were undertaken within the framework of the Group of Ten. After several meetings, the United States agreed in mid-December to include a dollar devaluation in a general realignment of currencies. The details of this realignment were worked out by the Group of Ten on December 17 and 18 in a meeting at the Smithsonian Institution in Washington. The *Smithsonian Agreement* was then formalized by the IMF, which established a "temporary regime" allowing member countries to vary their exchange rates within margins of 2.25 percent on either side of the new "central rates" resulting from the currency realignment. In return for the revaluation of other currencies, the United States agreed to raise the price of gold from $35 an ounce to $38 an ounce (a dollar devaluation of 8.57 percent) and to immediately "suppress" its 10 percent import surcharge.

The Smithsonian Agreement gave the United States the currency realignment it had requested in return for a modest rise in the price of gold, a concession having no economic significance while the dollar remained inconvertible to gold. More importantly, it was an achievement of international monetary cooperation, a triumph of enlightened self-interest over economic nationalism. It reflected the universal acceptance of the need for agreed rules to govern exchange rates and exchange practices. Hence, the collapse of the Bretton Woods system on August 15 did not degenerate into chaos, as did the collapse of the international gold standard in the early 1930s. For all of its weaknesses, the Bretton Woods system had fostered intimate monetary cooperation on an unprecedented scale through the institutional machinery of the IMF and the Group of Ten. When the crunch came, this machinery proved equal to the challenge.

Although the Smithsonian Agreement prevented competitive exchange-rate behavior, it did not tackle the problems of durable international monetary reform. In retrospect, it was a futile attempt to perpetuate the adjustable-peg system, albeit with new currency alignments. With the second devaluation of the dollar in February 1973, the Smithsonian Agreement fell apart as other currencies were left to float against the dollar, thus marking the beginning of the contemporary international monetary system.

WEAKNESSES OF THE BRETTON WOODS SYSTEM

The poor performance of the Bretton Woods system in the 1960s is attributable mainly to three interrelated causes: (1) the problem of international liquidity formation centered on the dollar, (2) delays in balance of payments adjustment, and (3) disequilibrating short-term capital movements.

The Problem of International Liquidity Formation

International liquidity consists of (1) the world's supply of gold, foreign exchange, and other assets ("owned" reserves) that are freely usable to finance payments deficits and (2) available facilities for borrowing them ("borrowed" reserves). Over the longer run, the growth of international liquidity is dependent on the growth of international reserve assets or owned

TABLE 18-6   Growth and Composition of International Reserves of IMF
Countries, 1959–1971
(End of Period—Billions of Dollars)

Reserve Asset	1959	1965	1968	1969	1970	1971*	Increase (+) or Decrease (−) 1959–1971
Gold	37.9	41.9	38.9	39.1	37.2	36.2	+ 1.7
Foreign exchange	16.2	23.8	31.9	32.3	44.5	68.9	+52.7
U.S. dollar	10.1	15.8	17.5	10.0	23.9	45.7	+35.6
U.K. pound	7.0	7.1	9.7	8.9	6.6	7.1	+ 0.1
Difference	−0.9	0.9	4.7	7.4	14.0	16.2	+17.1
Reserve positions in Fund	3.2	5.4	6.5	6.7	7.7	6.3	+ 3.1
Special Drawing Rights (SDRs)	—	—	—	—	3.1	5.9	+ 5.9
Total reserves	57.4	71.0	77.3	78.2	92.5	117.3	+59.9

* End of September 1971.

Source: International Financial Statistics Washington, D.C.: International Monetary Fund, February 1970), pp. 13, 15, and (February 1972), pp. 18, 23.

General Note: Total may not add because of rounding. *Foreign exchange* mostly consists of U.S. liabilities to foreign official holders and, to a much lesser extent, U.K. liabilities to foreign official holders. From 1968, most of the *difference* is attributable to official holdings of Eurodollars, which do not appear as U.S. liabilities to official holders. *Reserve positions in the Fund* equal member countries' gold tranches plus the Fund's use of their currencies for drawings or gold purchases. *SDRs* are unconditional reserve assets created by the Fund.

reserves. Table 18-6 depicts the growth and composition of reserve assets between the end of 1959 and the end of September 1971.

The most striking feature of Table 18-6 is the prominence of the U.S. dollar. During this period, nearly all the growth in total reserves ($59.9 billion) came from an increase in the dollar holdings of foreign central banks—an increase of $35.6 billion in recorded U.S. liabilities and an increase of $17.1 billion in the "difference," which consists mostly of Eurodollar holdings.[17] The remaining growth ($7.2 billion) came from increases in reserve positions in the IMF and the creation of SDRs after 1969. Sterling reserves were stable over the period, while gold reserves actually decreased by $1.7 billion. As noted earlier, no gold was purchased by the major central banks from private sources after the agreement of March 1968.

---

[17] The Eurodollar market is discussed in "The Eurocurrency Market" in Chapter 19.

As the Bretton Woods system actually functioned, therefore, most of the growth in international reserves came from an increase in U.S. liabilities to foreign central banks. This growth was not planned; it was the result of U.S. balance of payments deficits. In particular, the growth had nothing in common with the required level of international liquidity. If the U.S. deficit were to turn into a surplus, then dollar reserves would fall regardless of the need for international liquidity. More fundamentally, the dollar could not supply new reserves on a sustainable basis over the long run because of an inherent *contradiction* of the gold-exchange standard. A sustained increase in the official liabilities of the central reserve country would eventually reduce the gold cover below 100 percent (as happened to the dollar in the mid-1960s) and a continuing increase would cause a progressive loss of confidence in the gold convertibility of the reserve currency. At some point, foreign central banks would force a breakdown of the system by demanding gold from the central reserve country or the central reserve country itself would declare its currency no longer convertible into gold. As we have seen, the latter happened on August 15, 1971, and its effect was to transform the international monetary system from a gold-dollar standard into a pure dollar standard, a most fragile arrangement because of the reluctance of foreign central banks to add more dollars to their reserves.

The liquidity problem of the Bretton Woods system, therefore, was twofold. In the short run, the amount of liquidity was dependent on erratic swings in the U.S. balance of payments, and in the long run, the dollar could not be counted on to supply new liquidity.

How much international liquidity is needed in a fixed-rate system? There is no simple answer to this question because it depends on the level of reserves each country *thinks* it should hold and the level it *actually* holds as a consequence of its policies. More generally, too much international liquidity is inflationary because countries are under little compulsion to make fundamental adjustments to deficits. Too little liquidity, on the other hand, forces countries to respond quickly to deficits by imposing restrictions, deflating their economies, or devaluing their exchange rates. If the supply of international liquidity does not keep pace with demand, then countries will seek to obtain reserves from each other, with the danger that they will slow down real economic growth to generate export surpluses or use restrictions to protect existing reserves.

In the 1960s there was widespread concern over the adequacy of international liquidity because of the expectation that the dollar would not continue to supply new reserves. Facilities for borrowed reserves were improved, notably by increasing the IMF quotas and strengthening the swap network among central banks. But borrowed reserves make no permanent contribution to the world's liquidity. Hence, attention was devoted to a scheme for the deliberate creation of a new reserve asset that came to be known as Special Drawing Rights (SDRs).

SDRs constitute international reserve assets that may be used in the settlement of balance of payments deficits by countries participating in the Special Drawing Account administered by the IMF. A decision to create SDRs requires the approval of a majority of the member countries holding 85 percent of the weighted voting power of the Fund. Once created, SDRs are distributed to participants in proportion to their Fund quotas. In 1969 it was agreed to allocate SDRs to the 104 participants in three annual stages: January 1, 1970 (SDR 3.4 billion); January 1, 1971 (SDR 2.95 billion); and January 1, 1972 (SDR 2.95 billion).[18]

Actually SDRs are merely bookkeeping entries punched out on a computer tape. What makes them a reserve asset is the commitment of the participating countries to accept SDRs in exchange for a convertible currency up to an amount equal to three times their own SDR allocations. Only one constraint is placed on a country's use of its SDRs for balance of payments settlements. It is expected to maintain over a five-year period average holdings of SDRs equal to 30 percent of its cumulative allocations. A country does not buy its SDRs, but all allocations of SDRs are subject to a market rate of interest, while member holdings of SDRs earn the same rate of interest.[19] Once placed on the books of the IMF, SDRs remain in existence as a permanent addition to the world's reserve assets.

Ironically, the first activation of SDRs coincided with a massive buildup of dollar reserves as short-term capital moved out of the United States in 1970 and 1971. As Table 18-6 indicates, total reserves rose from $78.2 billion to $117.3 billion between the end of 1969 and September 1971. Instead of a liquidity shortage, there was a liquidity surplus. Although the SDR facility did not solve the liquidity problem, it opened up the possibility of a gradual replacement of dollars with SDRs in international reserves. In that event, the dollar would eventually lose its role as a reserve currency, and reserve creation would no longer be dependent on U.S. deficits but rather on the collective judgment of the IMF member countries.[20]

Inadequate Adjustment Mechanism

In accordance with the Bretton Woods Agreement, countries were expected to maintain fixed exchange rates (within a band of 1 percent on either side of par values) and alter the par values of their currencies only to adjust to a fundamental disequilibrium in the balance of payments. In practice, the

---

[18] At the time one SDR unit was equal to one U.S. dollar. The SDR, now defined in terms of a bundle of currencies, was worth $1.37 in December 1988. As of April 1988, total SDR allocations were SDR 21.4 billion. The SDR has now become the official unit of account for the International Monetary Fund.

[19] Thus, a country that does not use its SDRs comes out even.

[20] The dollar would still remain the major *intervention* currency (the currency used by central banks to influence exchange rates) and the major *vehicle* currency (the currency used in the settlement of private international commercial and financial transactions).

U.S. dollar emerged as the central reserve currency with a fixed parity, while the other major currencies tended to maintain their parities even in the face of prolonged disequilibria. This almost rigid adherence to exchange parties encouraged speculation, provoked crises, and delayed adjustment.

Movements in the parities of the major currencies are depicted in Figure 18-2 for January 1947 to June 1970. Note the small number of parity adjustments. Furthermore, when parity changes were made, they were usu-

Figure 18-2   Movements in Parities of Currencies of Selected Industrial Countries, January 1947 to June 1970 (January 1947 = 100)

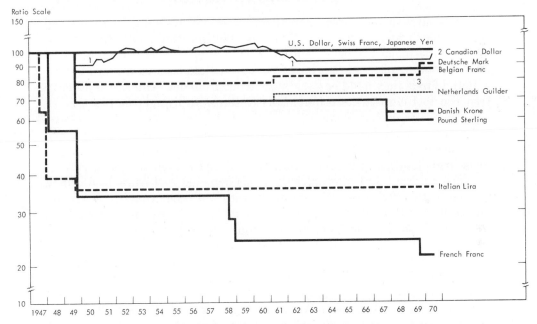

Source: The Role of Exchange Rates in the Adjustment of International Payments, A Report of the Executive Directors (Washington, D.C.: International Monetary Fund, 1970), p 9.
[1] The rates indicated are the par values agreed with the Fund except in the following cases: Swiss franc (nonmember currency); Japanese yen, to May 1953; Italian lira, to March 1960; French franc, January 1948 to December 1960; Canadian dollar, see footnote 2.
[2] Fluctuating rate, September 30, 1950 to May 1, 1962; and June 1, 1970–.
[3] Fluctuating rate, September 20 to October 24, 1969.

Over nearly a quarter century, most currencies *devalued* with respect to the dollar. Only the Japanese yen and the Swiss franc maintained a constant parity with the dollar. Upward movements of nondollar currency parities occurred only in crisis situations and then only in modest amounts for a few currencies. Because of this devaluation bias, the U.S. dollar had become overvalued by the 1960s—a failure of the international adjustment mechanism.

ally in a downward direction that devalued the currencies vis-à-vis the dollar. For the period as a whole, all currencies lost value vis-à-vis the dollar except the Swiss franc and Japanese yen, which maintained the same parity. As a consequence, the dollar became substantially revalued in terms of other major currencies, and even when it became apparent in the 1960s that the dollar had become overvalued, upward adjustments in parities occurred only rarely in crisis situations. Ultimately, the United States was compelled to take unilateral action to achieve a currency realignment.

Disequilibrating Short-term Capital Movements

A third source of weakness in the Bretton Woods system as it functioned in the 1960s was the enormous flow of disequilibrating short-term capital between the major financial centers. The emergence of a truly integrated international capital market based on Eurodollars created a growing pool of liquid funds that could be rapidly switched from one center to another in response to interest-rate differentials (interest arbitrage) or to expected adjustments in exchange rates.

The quick transfer of billions of dollars from one center to another had two broad consequences. First, it limited the freedom of national authorities to use monetary policy for domestic stabilization by intensifying the conflict between external and internal balance as depicted in Figure 15-5. When interest rates in one center rose above those in other centers, funds immediately left the country with the lower rates, and vice versa. More often than not, these shifts of funds were disequilibrating for the domestic economy or the balance of payments. In 1969 high interest rates in the United States attracted billions of dollars from European centers. Although this inflow improved the official reserves balance, it also partly nullified anti-inflationary policies of the U.S. government by swelling the money supply. In 1971 high interest rates in West Germany (induced by a restrictive monetary policy to impede inflation) drew in billions of dollars from abroad, thereby inducing further inflation and adding to a huge balance of payments surplus. Indeed, liquid funds became so sensitive to money market conditions in major-currency countries that some economists advocated using monetary policy primarily for balance of payments purposes and leaving domestic stabilization to fiscal policy.

A second consequence of the high international mobility of liquid capital was its disequilibrating impact on foreign exchange markets. In the 1960s speculation *against* currencies was demonstrably generated by delays in exchange rate adjustments. Deficit countries refused to devalue until it became obvious that they had to do so. Thus, speculators enjoyed a "no-lose" situation, since the *direction* of any adjustment was certain (if not the precise timing) and the adjustment most probably would be substantial.

Many industrial countries (including the United States) tried to influence or restrict short-term capital flows through a variety of special techniques: imposing selective taxation, limiting the foreign lending or borrowing of domestic commercial banks, prohibiting the payment of interest on foreign-held demand and time deposits, imposing reserve requirements on the foreign borrowings of domestic banks, intervening in forward markets, imposing selective exchange controls, and others. These techniques often proved effective in influencing changes in the foreign assets and liabilities of domestic commercial banks, but they had little or no effect on the short-term borrowing and lending by domestic nonbank business firms, to say nothing of leads and lags in international payments.

By and large, the industrial countries avoided comprehensive exchange controls over short-term capital movements even though they were permissible under the IMF Articles of Agreement. This reluctance stemmed from serious doubts about their feasibility and desirability. Short-term capital can move into and out of a country in so many ways that any attempt at full control requires a close regulation of all international transactions, current as well as capital. Hence, comprehensive exchange controls run the grave risk of "throwing the baby out with the bath water" by restricting legitimate international trade and investments and by curbing all short-term capital flows, not just speculative flows. The feasibility of unilateral controls is also limited; no single country can hope to control or even greatly influence the Eurodollar market because of its size and international scope. Most fundamentally, controls attack only the symptoms of disequilibrium rather than the causes.

SUMMARY

1. Agreement on the postwar international monetary system was reached at Bretton Woods, New Hampshire, in 1944. An international agency, the International Monetary Fund, was established to administer a code of fair exchange practices and provide compensatory financial assistance to member countries in balance of payments trouble.

2. In 1962, the Fund's resources were supplemented by the *General Arrangements to Borrow,* which enabled the Fund to borrow up to $5.9 billion from ten industrial countries (known as the "Group of Ten") to provide compensatory financial assistance to one or more of them. In 1970, the Fund activated an entirely new facility to supply to its members reserve assets, known as Special Drawing Rights (SDRs).

3. After World War II, the international monetary system evolved in a way that was not envisaged by the Bretton Woods agreement. In the 1950s, the United States emerged as the prime reserve country, with the dollar increasingly taking over the function of gold as an international reserve asset.

4. After 1958, the United States experienced a persistent deficit in its balance of payments. Three concepts of surplus and deficit were used by U.S. authorities in measuring disequilibrium in the balance of payments: the basic balance, the net liquidity balance, and the official reserves transactions balance.

5. During the years 1958–1971, the United States experienced a cumulative reserve deficit of $56 billion, which was financed by drawing down its gold reserves and by incurring liquid liabilities to foreign central banks.

6. In the 1960s, the United States undertook a variety of measures to remedy its balance of payments deficit. These included efforts to expand exports, to reduce U.S. government outlays abroad, to restrain U.S. private capital exports, to lessen the gold drain, and to discourage speculation. None of these measures involved a fundamental adjustment in the balance of payments. U.S. policymakers refused to cut back on military forces abroad, abandon foreign assistance to developing countries, deflate the economy, impose import restrictions, or devalue the dollar.

7. In the 1960s, the international monetary system was shaken by a series of crises in foreign exchange and gold markets. Although other currencies were involved in these crises (notably the British pound and French franc), the pervasive source of instability was the weakness of the dollar.

8. The international monetary crisis of 1971 was directly inspired by a loss of confidence in the dollar. Confronted with an enormous speculative run on the dollar, the United States suspended the gold convertibility of the dollar on August 15 and thereby forced the collapse of the Bretton Woods system. The United States also imposed domestic wage and price controls, as well as a 10 percent surcharge on all dutiable imports.

9. The immediate response to the U.S. actions was a closing of foreign exchange markets in Europe and Japan. When they reopened, all of the major foreign currencies (with the exception of the French franc) were left to float vis-à-vis the dollar. However, foreign governments were reluctant to let their currencies float freely to higher dollar values because they hoped to persuade the United States to devalue the dollar by raising the price of gold. Hence, central banks continued to intervene in foreign exchange markets and, in some instances, further appreciation vis-à-vis the dollar was prevented by exchange restrictions.

10. After weeks of uncertainty, the Group of Ten countries negotiated the Smithsonian Agreement on December 18, 1971. In return for the revaluation of the other currencies, the United States agreed to raise the price of gold from $35 an ounce to $38 an ounce. However, this agreement did not tackle the problems of fundamental international monetary reform.

11. The poor performance and eventual collapse of the Bretton Woods system is attributable to three interrelated causes: (1) the problem of international liquidity formation centered on the dollar, (2) delays in balance of payments adjustment and (3) disequilibrating short-term capital movements.

12. In response to widespread concern over the adequacy of international liquidity, agreement was reached in the late 1960s on facilities to create a new international reserve asset (SDRs). SDRs were first activated at the beginning of 1970

QUESTIONS AND APPLICATIONS

1. **(a)** What were the purposes of the International Monetary Fund?
   (b) What was the par value system of exchange rates?
   (c) What were the implications of the IMF rules on exchange rates?
2. Explain the compensatory financing system of the IMF.
3. "As the Bretton Woods system evolved, however, the reserves of most countries became a mixture of gold and dollars, with a growing dominance of the latter." Why did this development occur?
4. **(a)** Describe the remedial measures undertaken by the U.S. government before August 15, 1971, to overcome the deficit in the U.S. balance of payments.
   (b) Why did the United States not make a fundamental adjustment to its payments deficit in the 1960s by (1) deflating the domestic economy or (2) devaluing the dollar?
5. **(a)** Describe the actions of the United States on August 15, 1971.
   (b) Why did these actions bring about a collapse of the Bretton Woods system?
6. Be prepared to defend or criticize the U.S. decision to abandon the gold convertibility of the dollar on August 15, 1971.
7. **(a)** What was the Smithsonian Agreement?
   (b) Why was it only an "interim" agreement?
8. What was the problem of international liquidity formation? How was it related to the dollar? What is meant by the "inherent contradiction of the gold-exchange standard"?
9. What are SDRs? How are they created?
10. When are short-term capital movements "disequilibrating"?

SELECTED READINGS

See the list of readings given at the end of Chapter 19.

19

The Contemporary International Monetary System, the U.S. Balance of Payments, and Global Capital Markets

The second devaluation of the dollar in February 1973 brought in its wake floating exchange rates and a new international monetary system. Against the background of the Bretton Woods collapse, we describe in this chapter the principal features of the contemporary system and its performance, the emergence of global capital markets, and the persistent deficit in the U.S. balance of payments.

FOREIGN EXCHANGE ARRANGEMENTS

Figure 19-1 depicts the foreign exchange arrangements of countries in the contemporary international monetary system. The reader should compare Figure 19-1 with Figure 18-1, which depicts exchange practices under the Bretton Woods system. Under the Bretton Woods system, all foreign currencies were pegged to the dollar or to gold through the dollar. In sharp contrast, today the currencies of other industrial countries are floating with respect to the dollar, as shown by the dashed lines in Figure 19-1. Beyond that dominant feature, the contemporary international monetary system is a mixture of exchange rate arrangements. The Swiss franc, the Canadian dollar, the British pound, the Japanese yen, and the U.S. dollar are floating against all other currencies. Eight European currencies are aligned within margins of 2.25 percent, but they jointly float against the dollar and other currencies.[1] Fifty-three other currencies (forty-five developing and eight

---

[1] This is the European Monetary System, which is described in Chapter 10.

Figure 19-1   Exchange Rate Arrangements, March 31, 1989

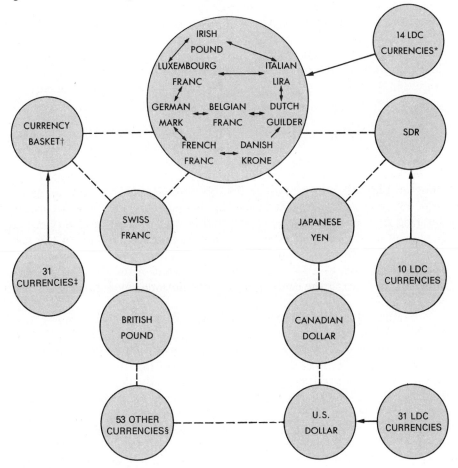

Legend: Floating rate ---; Pegged rate →.
* Pegged on the French franc.
† Other than SDR.
‡ 23 LDCs, 5 industrial countries, and 3 centrally planned economies.
§ 45 LDCs and 8 industrial countries. Exchange rates are floating independently or adjusted according to a set of indicators.

Source: International Monetary Fund, *IMF Survey,* May 1, 1989, p. 143.

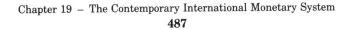

industrial countries) are either floating independently or are adjusted according to a set of indicators. The remaining currencies of developing countries (LDCs), however, are pegged either on a major currency or on a "basket" of currencies: 31 are pegged on the U.S. dollar, 31 are pegged on the French franc, 10 are pegged on the SDR basket, and 31 on non-SDR baskets.[2] In this respect, therefore, the contemporary system is a system of *currency areas*: the U.S. dollar area, the European Monetary System, the French franc area, and the SDR area. Exchange rates are stabilized within each area through occasional devaluations and revaluations but are allowed to float freely among the areas. The signal departure from the Bretton Woods system is the flotation of the U.S. dollar against other key currencies.

EXCHANGE RATE BEHAVIOR

As we know from our analysis of the determination of exchange rates in Chapter 12, exchange rates in a flexible-rate (or fluctuating-rate) system respond immediately to shifts in the supply and demand of foreign exchange deriving from changes in the export and import of goods and services and in the international purchases and sales of financial assets. In the short run, therefore, floating exchange rates are highly volatile, resembling the behavior of prices in a stock exchange. But what of the *long-run* behavior of exchange rates in the contemporary international monetary system over the 1980s?

Figure 19-2 depicts the nominal and real effective exchange rates of the U.S. dollar, the Japanese yen, and the West German mark—the dominant international currencies—over the period 1980–1989.[3] Our first observation is the *high volatility* of exchange rates for the period as a whole. In the first half of the 1980s, the nominal value of the dollar rose 60 percent. But then its value fell some 40 percent to reach in 1988 a value close to that of 1980. Hence, the value of the dollar took a roller coaster ride in the 1980s. The Japanese yen's nominal value rose and fell, and then starting in mid-1982 it rose steadily to reach in 1988 a level 95 percent above its 1980 level. The West German mark fell, rose, and fell, and then starting in 1985 it rose before flattening out in 1987, when it reached a level about 17 percent above its 1980 level.

---

[2] The SDR basket contains different percentages of five currencies: the U.S. dollar, British pound, West German mark, Japanese yen, and French franc. The currency mix of non-SDR baskets is particular to each country.

[3] *Nominal* exchange rates are actual rates of exchange; *real* exchange rates are nominal rates adjusted for relative changes in the purchasing power of the respective currencies. In this instance, the adjustment uses relative changes in unit labor costs. *Effective* rates are weighted rates that take into account the relative importance of a country's trading partners in direct bilateral relations with them. In this instance, the indices measure changes in the value of each of the three currencies against the currencies of seventeen other industrial countries.

Figure 19-2   Indices of Monthly Average Nominal and Real Effective Exchange Rates for the United States, Japan and West Germany, 1980–1989 (1980 = 100; Logarithmic Scales)

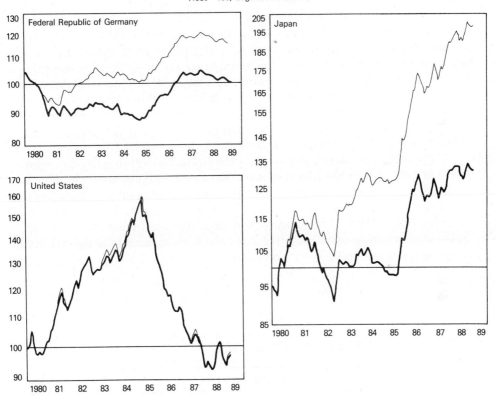

(1980 = 100; Logarithmic Scales)

Legend: ——— Real effective exchange rate ——— Nominal effective exchange rate
Note: The *real effective exchange rate* is the nominal rate adjusted for changes in purchasing power, using normalized unit labor costs in manufacturing and total trade weights based on 1980 trade data. The *nominal effective exchange rate* is the actual rate adjusted for the same weights as the real effective exchange rate indices.

Source: Based on *World Economic Outlook* (Washington, D.C.: International Monetary Fund), Chart 28, p. 91.

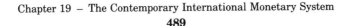

What caused these changes in nominal exchange rates? In the 1970s, the major influence on nominal rates was divergent rates of inflation. Because Japan and West Germany experienced notably lower rates of inflation than the United States, the yen and mark appreciated while the dollar depreciated over that decade. This behavior validated the purchasing-power parity doctrine, which states that changes in nominal exchange rates keep *real* exchange rates constant over the long run. But this explanation does not apply to the decade of the 1980s. For the three currencies to maintain purchasing-power parity during the 1980s, their *real* currency values would need to stay close to their 1980 index value of 100. As shown in Figure 19-2, however, the real values of all three currencies exhibit prolonged departures from the index value of 100. The behavior of the dollar's *real* exchange rate matches the dollar's nominal rate so closely that the two rates are almost described by the same curve. This means that the rate of inflation in the United States was about the same as the weighted aggregate rate of seventeen other industrial countries. In contrast to the dollar, the real values of the yen and mark diverge from the nominal values, but the former values also exhibit prolonged deviations from the index value of 100.

These changes in real exchange rates cannot be explained by divergent rates of inflation. Table 19-1 indicates that the average annual changes in unit labor costs (which reflect both changes in wages and productivity) of the United States were somewhat lower than in Japan and West Germany over the period 1981–1988. Clearly, the large changes in nominal exchange rates that actually occurred were *not* necessary to maintain the relative real values of the dollar, yen, and mark.

TABLE 19-1   Annual Percentage Changes in Unit Labor Costs for the United States, Japan, and West Germany, 1981–1988

Year	United States	Japan	West Germany
1981	7.2	5.1	5.2
1982	6.1	5.5	3.9
1983	−2.5	1.1	−0.5
1984	−2.0	−2.1	−0.3
1985	0.3	1.3	0.3
1986	0.5	2.2	4.0
1987	−1.2	−2.8	2.9
1988	0.3	−3.0	—
Average annual change	1.1	0.9	2.2

Source: World Economic Outlook (Washington, D.C.: International Monetary Fund, April 1989), Table A10, p. 135.

The prolonged changes in the real values of these three currencies have created huge imbalances in their current accounts by directly affecting international competitiveness (Table 19-2). Suffice it to say here that these net balances could be sustained only by equally huge international flows of capital.

What explains, then, the persistent changes in real exchange rates in the 1980s? What has prevented purchasing-power parity from eliminating these real changes? The basic answer to these questions is the markedly divergent macroeconomic policies of the United States and other industrial countries, which are discussed in the next section. These divergent policies brought about large international differentials in *real* interest rates, as indicated in Figure 19-3.

The relationships between interest rates and exchange rates is not a simple one. Both are influenced by changes in the supply and demand of money and other financial assets and by price expectations. Both, therefore, depend on national monetary and fiscal policies. Can interest-rate differentials, then, *cause* changes in exchange rates? The answer is *yes* when the differentials are real, but *no* when differentials are merely nominal. In the first instance, real differentials and exchange rates move in the same direction: A more positive (less negative) differential is accompanied by an appreciation in the currency, and conversely. In the second instance, nominal differentials and exchange rates move in opposite directions: A more positive (less negative) differential is accompanied by a depreciation in the currency, and conversely.

When interest-rate differentials among countries express *only* expected rates of inflation, they offer no inducement for persons and institutions to

TABLE 19-2   Net Balances on Current Account for the United States, Japan, and West Germany, 1981–1988

Year	United States	Japan	West Germany
1981	6.9	4.8	−3.6
1982	−8.7	6.9	5.1
1983	−46.3	20.8	5.3
1984	−107.1	35.0	9.9
1985	−115.1	49.2	16.6
1986	−138.8	85.8	39.3
1987	−154.0	87.0	45.0
1988	−135.3	79.5	48.5

Source: World Economic Outlook (Washington, D.C.: International Monetary Fund, April 1989), Table A30, p. 156.

Figure 19-3   Real Short-term Interest Rates of the United States and Other Countries in the Group of Seven, 1980–1989.

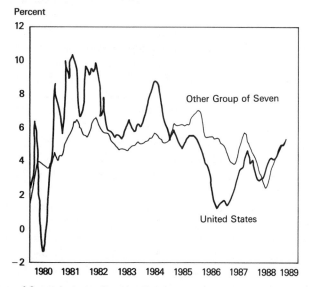

Note: The Group of Seven includes Canada, France, Italy, Japan, the United Kingdom, and West Germany. The seventh country is the United States. The interest rates are monthly rates on money market instruments of about ninety days maturity deflated by the private domestic demand deflator. The interest rate for the other countries in the Group of Seven is the weighted average of individual rates.

Source: World Economic Outlook (Washington, D.C.: International Monetary Fund, April 1989), Chart 32, p. 98.

switch money and other financial assets from one currency to another, that is, they do not induce an inflow of short-term capital into the high-interest-rate country. Nominal differentials, therefore, do not influence the exchange rate. However, when differentials arise from factors other than price expectations, they do offer an inducement to switch money and other financial assets to the high-interest-rate country, thereby causing an appreciation of that country's currency.

This happened to the dollar in the 1981–1985 period, when real short-term interest rates in the United States were significantly higher than real rates in other leading industrial countries. More generally, real-interest-rate differentials in the 1980s triggered vast movements of capital between the United States and the other industrial countries. These capital flows swamped the effect of trade flows on exchange rates.

THE PERSISTENT DEFICIT IN THE U.S. CURRENT ACCOUNT

We have seen that the *long-run* volatility of exchange rates in the 1980s has involved prolonged changes in their real values, owing to the persistent divergence between U.S. macroeconomic (fiscal and monetary) policies and those of other industrial countries, notably Japan and West Germany. This divergence was initiated in late 1979 when the Federal Reserve tightened monetary policy in an effort to lower a double-digit rate of inflation. But the divergence was tremendously magnified in 1981 when the new U.S. administration simultaneously started a long-term program of higher military expenditures, gave business firms more incentive to invest (through more generous depreciation allowances and investment tax credits), and gave consumers more disposable income to spend through cuts in personal taxes. Consequently, total domestic absorption rose at an average annual rate of 8.5 percent from 1981 through 1985 while gross national product rose at a lower annual rate of 7.9 percent. Total domestic absorption (national expenditure) rose from less than 99 percent of GNP in 1980 to 102 percent in 1985. This excess expenditure was possible only through a deficit on current account of the same amount. Recall equation (18) in Chapter 15: $B_c = Y - A$, where B_c is the net balance on current account, Y is the gross national product, and A is the domestic absorption of goods and services (consumption, domestic investment, and government expenditures). In short, the mix of new U.S. fiscal and monetary policies at the start of the 1980s caused excess domestic absorption and a corresponding current-account deficit.

But why did not the expansion of national spending induce a higher domestic output (Y) and thereby avoid a current-account deficit? The reason is the high real interest rates induced by both fiscal and monetary policies. The change in fiscal policy increased the demand for credit, leading to higher interest rates. (This effect was exacerbated by a decline in the already low personal savings rate.) At the same time, tight monetary policy sharply lowered inflation expectations, making *real* interest rates even higher. These rates made U.S. financial assets more attractive to foreign investors, who then shifted funds to the United States from other countries (portfolio effect). But to do so, they needed to buy dollars, which pushed up their external value. In turn, the dollar appreciation discouraged U.S. exports and encouraged U.S. imports. In sum, the dollar's appreciation *switched* U.S. national spending toward foreign goods and services (increasing U.S. imports) and, at the same time, *switched* foreign national spending away from U.S. goods and services (decreasing U.S. exports). This is shown in Figure 19-4. The rapid ascent of the dollar starting in 1980 brought about a rapid decline in the U.S. trade balance in 1982 after a lag of two years. The dollar reached its peak at the beginning of 1985 and then began a long descent to reach

Figure 19-4   U.S. Trade Balance and Trade-Weighted Value of the Dollar, 1978–1988

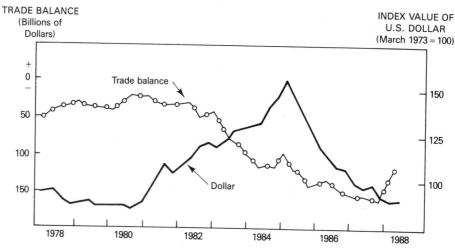

Note: The index value of the U.S. dollar is the weighted average of bilateral exchange rates between the United States and other Group of Ten countries (Canada, France, West Germany, Italy, Japan, the Netherlands, Sweden, Switzerland, and the United Kingdom).

Source: Based on Charts 1 and 2 in "Exchange Rates, Adjustment and the J-Curve," *Federal Reserve Bulletin,* October 1988, p. 633.

in 1988 a level close to its 1980 level. The trade balance has been slow to respond to this depreciation, although it showed some improvement in 1988.

These effects of U.S. macroeconomic policies in the first half of the 1980s were intensified by opposing macroeconomic policies in other industrial countries, namely, higher taxes and lower government spending, which induced lower real rates of interest.

The macroeconomic policies followed by the United States in the 1980s have had several unfortunate consequences. The 50 percent appreciation of the dollar in 1980–1985 (1) badly hurt U.S. export and import-competing industries, notably steel, automobiles, and nonelectrical machinery, and (2) magnified demands for U.S. import protection and generated trade disputes with Japan, the Economic Community, and other countries. The high U.S. real interest rates have (1) induced an enormous inflow of capital, making the United States the world's biggest debtor;[4] (2) slowed U.S. *domestic* in-

---

[4] Some of this capital inflow has taken the form of direct investment, including the acquisition of U.S. firms, office buildings, land and other real assets. See Chapter 23 for a discussion of foreign direct investment in the United States.

vestment; and (3) made it more difficult for Third World countries to manage their huge external dollar debts.[5]

The enormous current-account imbalances of the United States, Japan, and West Germany continue to haunt the world economy. To finance its current-account deficit, the United States would need to attract capital inflows amounting to $500 billion just to achieve a zero current-account balance by 1992. By then, its total international indebtedness would reach $1 *trillion*! Servicing this debt would require a trade surplus of some $70 billion a year.[6]

The rest of the world will not continue indefinitely to finance the U.S. current-account deficit.[7] At some point, foreign investors and central banks will refuse to transfer more capital to the United States. The nightmare scenario is an incident that provokes a massive capital flight from the dollar, pushing the dollar into a free fall and plunging the world into a financial crisis. To avert the possibility of this catastrophe, the United States needs to cut its domestic absorption by reversing its fiscal policy through some mix of lower government spending, higher taxes, and personal savings incentives. This contractionary fiscal policy would allow an easier monetary policy, reducing real interest rates. Unfortunately, this policy demands austerity and does not appeal to U.S. policymakers. Adjustment would be considerably eased by opposing changes in the macroeconomic policies of Japan and West Germany: tax cuts and higher real interest rates.

CENTRAL BANK INTERVENTION IN FOREIGN EXCHANGE MARKETS

Any inference from Figures 19-1 and 19-2 that the key currencies have been left to float freely against each other in response only to market forces would be erroneous. As a matter of fact, central banks have actively intervened in foreign exchange markets with compensatory financing intended to influence foreign exchange rates. Indeed, the amount of compensatory financing by central banks in the new system may well exceed the amount in the Bretton Woods system over a similar period of time. Intervention has been financed by central banks out of their international reserves, short-term borrowings from other central banks ("swap credits"), IMF credits, and borrowings from private banks. In light of this central bank activity, the contemporary system is correctly designated as a "managed float" rather than a "pure float."[8]

---

[5] See Chapter 21.

[6] Marina von Neumann Whitman, "United States and Japan Should Reorient Their Economies to Reduce Trade Imbalances," *IMF Survey*, November 14, 1988, p. 361.

[7] It may be argued that it is *unethical* for a rich country like the United States to borrow from the rest of the world; rather, it should be lending to the rest of the world.

[8] The terms "dirty float" and "clean float" are also used, respectively.

Arguments for Intervention

Why have national monetary authorities refused to allow exchange rates to respond freely to market forces? In theory, there would be no need for central bank intervention in a floating-rate market. Under conditions of perfect competition, exports and imports would respond immediately to changes in exchange rates so as to maintain current-account equilibrium in the balance of payments. In practice, however, the response of export and imports is not spontaneous but occurs only after a lag, which can take up to a year or more.[9] During the period of adjustment, therefore, surpluses and deficits appear in the balance of payments (as they do in a fixed-rate system) that need to be financed by the central monetary authorities. In the absence of such compensatory financing, it is argued, exchange rates during the adjustment period would fluctuate in response to speculation and other temporary factors in ways that could inhibit adjustment in exports and imports. Thus, there is ample justification for official compensatory action to "smooth" the short-run behavior of exchange rates as long as such action does not counteract fundamental economic forces and thereby delay real adjustment.

Another explanation of managed floating is the unwillingness of governments to let exchange rates float freely without limit when they perceive undesirable effects on employment, inflation, international competitiveness, and other matters of official policy concern. Hence, central banks may go beyond smoothing daily and weekly fluctuations in exchange rates to maintain them at levels that conform to their policy targets. In that event, a managed float takes on some of the characteristics of an adjustable-peg system by delaying fundamental adjustment and inviting speculation.

Economists generally advocate a standard of intervention that is called "leaning against the wind." Using this standard, a central bank opposes exchange rate movements but does not reinforce them: The bank sells foreign exchange when its currency is depreciating and buys foreign exchange when its currency is appreciating. Furthermore, a central bank does not try to maintain a target rate of exchange; it seeks to moderate the strength of the wind, not neutralize it. Again, a central bank intervenes "symmetrically" by leaning against both upward and downward movements of the exchange rate. In sum, intervention in accordance with this standard acts to smooth short-run fluctuations but does not attempt to influence the long-term trend of exchange rates that responds to changes in purchasing-power parities and real factors that affect international competitiveness.

Intervention in the 1980s

During the first half of the 1980s, U.S. officials saw no need to influence the dollar's value. Indeed, they treated the dollar's appreciation as a welcome

---

[9] As we have observed, when macroeconomic policies diverge radically among the leading industrial countries, current-account imbalances may persist for several years.

vote of confidence in the U.S. economy. But this laissez-faire policy was abandoned in September 1985, when the U.S. Treasury Secretary invited the finance ministers of Japan, West Germany, France, and the United Kingdom (these, plus the United States, are the G-5 countries) to a weekend meeting at the Plaza Hotel in New York. In the resulting *Plaza Agreement*, the ministers announced that the dollar was overvalued and that coordinated action was necessary to push down its value. However, no commitments were made to alter macroeconomic policies.

Table 19-3 describes four phases of the dollar's depreciation. In phase 1, the dollar's value reached a peak (in February 1985) and then started to fall. By the time of the Plaza Agreement, it had fallen by 9 percent. After central bank sales of dollars in February and March, intervention played little role in the subsequent decline. In phase 2, the dollar's decline picked up speed; by May 1986, its cumulative real depreciation reached 25 percent. To help push the dollar down, the U.S. monetary authorities bought $3.3 billion in foreign currencies. Initially, foreign central banks sold dollars, but by the end of this phase they had added $2 billion a month on the average to their international reserves. In phase 3, the earlier consensus that the dollar was overvalued dissipated. There was little U.S. intervention, but foreign central banks at times intervened heavily to support the dollar, increasing their reserves by $5.4 billion a month on the average. In this phase, the rate of depreciation slowed down; by February 1987, the cumulative real depreciation reached 34 percent.

In February 1987, the G-5 countries and Canada met in Paris and adopted the *Louvre Accord*. The central objective of the accord was to stabilize the dollar's value through equilibrating changes in macroeconomic policies and to prevent undue volatility in exchange rates through market intervention. In phase 4, the rate of dollar depreciation slowed considerably; the cumulative real depreciation reached 40 percent by February 1988. Large interventions were undertaken by the central banks in support of the dollar: Foreign central banks bought $7.1 billion on the average each month, and the U.S. monetary authorities sold $4.9 billion of foreign currencies in the April–June period and $5.0 billion in the August–January period.

How much central bank intervention influenced the behavior of the dollar over the 1985–1988 period is debatable. The purchase and sale of foreign exchange by central banks can add to or subtract from commercial bank reserves and, therefore, the money supply. But this monetary effect is nullified when changes in bank reserves resulting from intervention are "sterilized" by offsetting open market operations (the sale or purchase of securities by the central bank), a practice generally followed by the U.S. monetary authorities. Most economists agree that intervention can smooth short-run fluctuations in exchange rates but cannot stop a shift in rates to a new market equilibrium. Central bank reserves are simply too small compared with the funds available to private international investors. Intervention, therefore, is *not* a substitute for macroeconomic policy.

The depreciation of the dollar after February 1985 was market-driven.

TABLE 19-3   Four Phases in Depreciation of U.S. Dollar, February 1985 to February 1988

Phase		Average Monthly Nominal Depreciation* (Percent)	Cumulative Real Depreciation to Last Month of Period† (Percent)	Average Monthly Increase in Reserves of Group of Seven, excluding U.S.‡ (Billions of U.S. Dollars)	Intervention by U.S. Authorities
1. Pre-Plaza Agreement	February to September 1985	1.3	9	1.3	$565 million purchases of foreign currency, February–March.
2. Post-Plaza Agreement	September 1985 to May 1986	2.3	25	2.0	$3,301 million purchases of foreign currency, September–November.
3. Pre-Louvre Accord	May 1986 to February 1987	1.1	34	5.4	$50 million sales of foreign currency, January 1987.
4. Post-Louvre Accord	February 1987 to February 1988	0.8	40	7.1§	Purchases of foreign currency: $30 million in March, $631 million in August. Sales of foreign currency: $4,870 million, April–June; $5,040 million, August–January.

* In terms of nominal effective exchange rate of U.S. dollar (weights from the Fund's Multilateral Exchange Rate Model), monthly averages.
† Real effective exchange rate for U.S. dollar defined in terms of normalized unit labor costs.
‡ Foreign exchange reserves, aggregated over the six countries, end-monthly data.
§ Average for February 1987 to January 1988.

Source: World Economic Outlook (Washington, D.C.: International Monetary Fund, April 1988), Table 21, p. 55.

Although intervention affected the dollar's short-run behavior, it is almost certain that the 40 percent depreciation reached in February 1988 would have occurred without central bank intervention.

The Need for Policy Coordination

To repeat an earlier statement, the fundamental cause of the current-account imbalances and associated swings in the real values of the dollar, yen, and mark is the continuing divergence of the macroeconomic policies followed by the United States, Japan, and West Germany. So far, these three countries have failed to live up to their commitments in the Louvre Accord to achieve policy coordination. The chief culprit is the United States: Its seeming inability to eradicate the budget deficit (coupled with low private savings) insures a continuation of the international payments disequilibrium.

International policy coordination is based on formal agreements among countries to carry out specific policies in concert. Such coordination among the major industrial countries can greatly lower the adjustment costs of eliminating imbalances as compared with unilateral policy actions. With coordination, both deficit and surplus countries share the adjustment burden. This is not to gainsay the many pitfalls that can limit the effectiveness of policy coordination, including disagreements on how the world economy operates and should operate, imperfect information and forecasts, and the inability of governments to keep their promises because of national politics. Nor is international policy coordination a substitute for intelligent national policies.[10]

It is evident that further depreciation of the dollar alone cannot eliminate current-account imbalances. What is needed is international policy coordination that achieves a *decrease* in domestic absorption by the United States and, simultaneously, an *increase* in domestic absorption by Japan and West Germany.

THE CONTINUING ROLE OF THE INTERNATIONAL MONETARY FUND

The International Monetary Fund did not disappear with the demise of the Bretton Woods system. Indeed, it can be argued that the Fund's role in the contemporary international monetary system has become more important, not less so. The Fund has replaced its code of fair exchange practices with a program of surveillance over exchange rate policies and has greatly stepped up its financial assistance to member countries in balance of pay-

---

[10] Martin Feldstein, *Rethinking International Economic Coordination*, Oxford Economic Papers, 40, 1988, pp. 205–19.

ments difficulties. We offer here a brief review of the Fund's activities to bring up to date our earlier discussion of the Fund in Chapter 18.

Surveillance of Exchange Rate Policies

In 1978, the IMF adopted a new Article IV to replace the old article, which obligated member countries to maintain par values for their currencies. Under the new article, each member country is free to choose its own exchange arrangement, including the freedom to float. Member countries, however, undertake a general obligation to collaborate with the Fund and with other members to insure "orderly" exchange arrangements and to promote a *stable system* of exchange rates (but not a system of *stable exchange rates*). More specifically, members are "to avoid manipulating exchange rates or the international monetary system in order to prevent effective balance of payments adjustment or to gain an unfair competitive advantage over other members." The Fund is to exercise "firm surveillance" of the exchange rate policies of its members and is to adopt principles for their guidance.[11]

To undertake surveillance of exchange rate policies, the Fund has devised three principles for the guidance of member countries in their exchange rate policies:

(1) A member shall avoid manipulating exchange rates or the international monetary system in order to prevent effective balance of payments adjustment or to gain an unfair competitive advantage over other members.

(2) A member should intervene in the exchange market if necessary to counter disorderly conditions which may be characterized inter alia by disruptive short-term movements in the exchange value of its currency.

(3) Members should take into account in their intervention policies the interests of other members, including those of the countries in whose currencies they intervene.[12]

The Fund has also adopted principles and procedures for surveillance itself. The principles list "developments" that could trigger discussions between the Fund and a member country, including (1) protracted, large-scale intervention in one direction in the exchange market, (2) an unsustainable level of borrowing or lending for balance of payments purposes, (3) restrictions on current- and capital-account transactions, and (4) exchange rate behavior unrelated to underlying economic and financial conditions.

---

[11] Amendments to other articles in 1978 (1) reduce the role of gold by abolishing its official price and eliminating it as a unit of account in any par value system, and (2) obligate members to follow policies that will make the Special Drawing Right the "principal reserve asset" in the international monetary system. Collectively, the changes made in the Fund's Articles of Agreement in 1978 are known as the Second Amendment. The First Amendment in 1969 instituted the SDR.

[12] Executive Board Decision no. 5392–(77/63), adopted April 29, 1977.

In practice, surveillance occurs on both global and country levels. Global surveillance is intended to ascertain whether or not the balance of payments and exchange rate policies of member countries are mutually consistent. Country surveillance calls for identifying and encouraging the correction of inappropriate exchange rates and exchange rate policies of individual countries. Under Article IV, each country is required to notify the Fund promptly of any changes in its exchange arrangements and to hold annual consultations with the Fund.

In the 1980s, the behavior of exchange rates has highlighted the relation between exchange rates and demand management (monetary and fiscal policies) as well as the role of exchange rates in the adjustment process. A fundamental precept motivating the Fund's surveillance, therefore, is that stability in the exchange market should be accomplished through achievement of *domestic* economic stability. The Fund strives for greater coordination of domestic economic policies among its members and to that end it applies surveillance to countries in payments surplus as well as in payments deficit. But the Fund has no powers to *make* a member country adopt domestic policies that will support stability in the exchange market and international adjustment. As we know, widely divergent monetary and fiscal policies have induced highly volatile exchange rates in the contemporary system. The Fund sometimes can exert a strong influence on member countries that come to it for assistance, but its influence rests generally on the willingness of countries to live up to their responsibilities as members.

In recent years, the Fund has vigorously pushed for the use of indicators to promote policy coordination compatible with floating exchange rates. These indicators include GNP growth rates, inflation rates, interest rates, unemployment rates, fiscal deficit ratios, current-account and trade balances, monetary growth rates, reserves, and exchange rates.[13] The Fund now uses these indicators in its surveillance activities, with the addition of a commodity price indicator.[14]

Payments Adjustment Assistance

In the 1980s, the need of developing countries for assistance in financing balance of payments deficits has grown enormously under the impact of high oil prices, inflation, a general slowdown in the world economy, and the extraordinary growth of international debt in the Third World. The Fund has responded to this need by adding to its resources with quota increases supplemented by borrowed funds and by enlarging the access of member countries to those resources. Table 19-4 shows the outstanding Fund credit by facility and policy for the period 1982–1988.

---

[13] In 1986, the heads of the governments of the G-7 countries (G-5 plus Canada and Italy) in their *Tokyo Economic Declaration* asked their finance ministers to "review their individual economic objectives and forecasts collectively at least once a year" using these indicators.

[14] See *Annual Report 1988* (Washington, D.C.: International Monetary Fund).

TABLE 19-4 Outstanding Fund Credit by Facility and Policy, 1982–1988 (Billions of SDRs)

	1982	1983	1984	1985	1986	1987	1988
Regular facilities (tranches)	3.2	4.7	5.2	5.5	6.3	6.6	5.7
Compensatory financing facility	3.6	6.8	7.3	7.5	6.4	4.8	4.3
Buffer stock facility	—	0.3	0.4	0.2	—	—	—
Oil facility	0.6	—	—	—	—	—	—
Extended fund facility	2.1	3.3	5.6	6.5	6.5	6.2	5.8
Enlarged access policy/supplementary financing facility	5.3	8.3	13.3	15.2	15.3	14.0	12.0
Total	14.8	23.6	31.7	35.0	34.6	31.6	27.8

Source: Derived from *Annual Report 1988* (Washington, D.C.: International Monetary Fund), Table II.9, p. 95.

Until 1962, member countries obtained Fund credit only through the "purchase" of foreign currencies under quota arrangements, as described in the previous chapter. But subsequently, the Fund established facilities to finance specific needs of members, such as the oil facility set up in 1974 with borrowed funds to help oil-importing developing countries. Most recently, the Fund established in March 1986 a Structural Adjustment Facility and in August 1988, an Enhanced Structural Adjustment Facility. Table 19-5 explains the types of Fund assistance. The traditional source of Fund credit through tranches accounted for only one-fifth of total outstanding credit in 1988. A second departure from past practice is longer credit terms, ranging from five and a half to ten years in the case of the Enhanced Structural Adjustment Facility. Longer credit terms have moved the Fund toward the kind of development assistance provided by the World Bank, which is discussed in Chapter 21.

Periodic increases brought total quotas in the Fund to SDR 90 billion at the end of 1988. Also, starting in 1981, member-country access to Fund resources was enlarged by allowing a member to purchase currencies up to 150 percent of its quota in any single year and up to 450 percent over three years, with a cumulative limit of 600 percent, three times the old cumulative limit of 200 percent.

The first 25 percent of a member's quota (formerly subscribed in gold but now subscribed in SDRs or convertible currencies acceptable to the Fund)

TABLE 19-5   Types of Financial Assistance Provided by the International Monetary Fund

Tranche policies

First credit tranche

Member demonstrates reasonable efforts to overcome balance of payments difficulties in program. Performance criteria and purchase installments not used. Repurchases are made in 3¼–5 years.

Upper credit tranches

Member must have a substantial and viable program to overcome its balance of payments difficulties. Resources normally provided in the form of stand-by arrangements that include performance criteria and purchases in installments. Repurchases are made in 3¼–5 years.

Extended Fund facility

Medium-term program aims at overcoming structural balance of payments maladjustments. A program is generally for three years, although it may be lengthened to four years, where this would facilitate sustained policy implementation and achievement of balance of payments viability over the medium term. Program states policies and measures for first 12-month period in detail. Resources are provided in the form of extended arrangements that include performance criteria and drawings in installments; repurchases are made in 4½–10 years.

Enlarged access policy

Policy used to augment resources available under stand-by and extended arrangements, for programs that need large amounts of Fund support. Applicable policies on conditionality, phasing, and performance criteria are the same as under the credit tranches and the extended Fund facility. Repurchases are made in 3½–7 years, and charges are based on the Fund's borrowing costs.

Compensatory and contingency financing facility

The compensatory element provides resources to a member for an export shortfall and an excess in cereal import costs that are due to factors largely beyond the member's control. The contingency element extends assurance to help members with Fund-supported adjustment programs to maintain the momentum of adjustment efforts in the face of a broad range of unanticipated, adverse external shocks. Repurchases are made in 3¼–5 years.

Buffer stock financing facility

Resources help finance a member's contribution to an approved international buffer stock. Repurchases are made in 3¼–5 years.

Structural adjustment facility

Resources are provided on concessional terms to low-income member countries facing protracted balance of payments problems, in support of medium-term macroeconomic and structural adjustment programs. Member develops, and updates, with the assistance of the Fund and the World Bank, a medium-term policy framework for a three-year period, which is set out in a policy framework paper (PFP). Detailed annual programs are formulated prior to disbursement of annual loans, and include quarterly benchmarks to assess performance. Repayments ar made in 5½–10 years.

Enhanced structural adjustment facility

Objectives, eligibility, and basic program features of this facility parallel those of the SAF; differences relate to provisions for access, monitoring, and funding. A policy framework paper and detailed annual program are prepared each year. Arrangements include quarterly benchmarks, semiannual performance, and, in most cases, a midyear review. Adjustment measures are expected to be particularly strong, aiming to foster growth and to achieve a substantial strengthening of the balance of payments position. Loans are disbursed semiannually, and repayments are made in 5½–10 years.

Source: IMF Survey, Supplement on the Fund, September 1988, p. 2.

is known as the *reserve tranche*.[15] A member can obtain unconditionally from the Fund an amount of currency equal to its *reserve position*, which in turn equals its reserve tranche *plus* the Fund's use of its currency to finance the drawings of other countries *minus* any current utilization of its drawing rights. Because reserve tranches are considered the owned reserves of member countries rather than Fund credit, their use does not appear in Figure 19-4.

When a country obtains currencies in an amount beyond its reserve tranche, it uses its *credit tranche*. But this credit is conditional. To get it, a member must conclude an agreement with the Fund that commits that member to follow certain adjustment policies, including monetary and fiscal policies. The broad objective of Fund *conditionality* is the restoration and maintenance of equilibrium in the balance of payments in an environment of stable prices and sustainable rates of economic growth without resort to controls on trade or capital flows. In applying conditionality, the Fund sets quantifiable targets in its credit agreements for major adjustment variables, such as domestic credit growth and foreign borrowing. Conditional assistance is disbursed in installments and may be halted if the member fails to meet the agreed targets. Conditionality can give the Fund a strong leverage on member-country policies, but it is limited to countries that need to borrow from the Fund.

EMERGENCE OF A GLOBAL CAPITAL MARKET

A global capital market first emerged in the 1950s in the form of the *Eurocurrency* market. The movement to liberalize the *national* capital markets of the industrial countries started in the 1970s and gathered force in the 1980s. These developments stimulated a rapid growth of international capital movements, which have progressively integrated national capital markets and the Eurocurrency market to create a single global capital market with enormous financial resources. We offer here a brief description of the Eurocurrency market and then go on to identify the consequences of a global capital market for the operation of the international monetary system and national macroeconomic policies.

The Eurocurrency Market

The largest Eurocurrency market by far is in Eurodollars.[16] What are Eurodollars? Quite simply, *Eurodollars* are dollars that are deposited in foreign

---

[15] The reserve tranche was formerly called the gold tranche. See Chapter 18.

[16] Any currency can assume "Euro" form when it is held as commercial bank deposits outside the home country. Deutsche marks, yen, pounds sterling, and Swiss francs are the most common

commercial banks, including the foreign branches of U.S. banks (the greatest percentage of these dollars are in Europe). It is the foreign location of the banks that distinguishes Eurodollars from ordinary dollar deposits in U.S. banks. Eurodollars come into existence when someone transfers dollars from a U.S. bank to a foreign bank or when someone converts a foreign currency into dollars that are then deposited in a foreign bank. Actually the dollars underlying the Eurodollars resulting from such transfers never leave the U.S. banking system. A foreign bank accepting dollar deposits acquires a dollar balance in a U.S. bank, and when it lends Eurodollars, it draws down its U.S. dollar balance. Hence, transactions in the Eurodollar market involve shifts in the ownership of bank balances in the United States. We can demonstrate this fundamental fact with T accounts of participating banks.

Suppose a deposit holder (H) in a U.S. bank transfers $1 million to a Eurobank, for example, one located in London. Initially, let us assume also that the Eurobank maintains a demand account in the same U.S. bank. This transaction appears as follows in the U.S. bank's T account:

Assets		Liabilities	
		Demand deposit (H)	$-\$1$ million
		Demand deposit (Eurobank)	$+\$1$ million
Net change	$0	Net change	$0

Observe that the levels of the U.S. bank's assets and liabilities do not change: The ownership of a demand deposit has simply shifted from H to the Eurobank. The same transaction appears as follows in the Eurobank's T account:

Assets		Liabilities	
Dollar deposit (with U.S. bank)	$+\$1$ million	Time deposit (H)	$+\$1$ million
Net change	$+\$1$ million	Net change	$+\$1$ million

But now suppose that the Eurobank does *not* maintain a demand account with the U.S. bank (Bank I) but with another U.S. bank (Bank II). Then Bank I loses reserves to Bank II, as shown in its T account:

---

nondollar currencies used in this way. Hence, the Eurodollar market is correctly described as a "Eurocurrency" market. But even this designation is somewhat misleading, because some Eurocurrency deposits are held by banks located outside Europe, such as in Singapore. In brief, the Eurocurrency market has become a market for borrowing and lending the world's major convertible currencies.

Assets		Liabilities	
Reserves	− $1 million	Demand deposit (H)	− $1 million
Net change	− $1 million	Net change	− $1 million

The T account of Bank II shows the following changes:

Assets		Liabilities	
Reserves	+ $1 million	Demand deposit (Eurobank)	+ $1 million
Net change	+ $1 million	Net change	+ $1 million

Note that the level of assets and liabilities for the U.S. banking system as a whole remains the same: A deposit has merely moved from one U.S. bank to another. (Bank I, of course, is unhappy with the arrangement; it will seek to attract new deposits and hold on to existing deposits.)

The Eurobank may use the $1 million to convert into another currency for any purpose, lend dollars to nonbank borrowers, or, most likely, lend dollars to another Eurobank. Suppose the Eurobank (Eurobank I) decides to lend to a second Eurobank (Eurobank II) in the interbank market. The T account of Eurobank I shows the following changes:

Assets		Liabilities	
Demand deposit (with U.S. bank)	+ $1 million − $1 million	Time deposit (H)	+ $1 million
Interbank loan (to Eurobank II)	+ $1 million		
Net change	+ $1 million	Net change	+ $1 million

Eurobank II's T account looks like this:

Assets		Liabilities	
Demand deposit (with U.S. bank)	+ $1 million	Interbank loan (from Eurobank I)	+ $1 million
Net change	+ $1 million	Net change	+ $1 million

When one Eurobank lends dollars to another Eurobank, therefore, there is no effect on the level of assets and liabilities for the entire U.S. banking system: Ownership of a demand deposit simply shifts between the Eurobanks. As we have seen, one U.S. bank loses reserves to another when this deposit shift moves funds from the first U.S. bank to the second. In practice, Eurobank I will lend out somewhat less than $1 million, keeping the remainder as a transactions/precautionary reserve. But the reserve will be less than would be required by national monetary authorities for a deposit in domestic currency.

Some economists believe there is another source of Eurocurrencies, namely, their creation through a fractional-reserve system in much the same way as occurs in domestic banking systems. In that event, the total quantity of Eurodollars can exceed the underlying dollar balances. As a corollary, the Eurodollar market then not only facilitates the international transfer of liquid funds but also adds to their supply. The consensus today, however, is that the Eurocurrency market creates little, if any, additional liquidity. It is not an "engine of inflation."

Although centered in London, the Eurocurrency market is dominated by the European branches of the leading American banks. Banks seek out Eurocurrency deposits from individuals, banks, international traders, multinational corporations, and government agencies throughout the world by offering higher rates of interest than domestic banks. In turn, banks lend Eurocurrencies to the same groups at rates that are frequently lower than domestic rates. This is possible because the spread between borrowing and lending rates is smaller than in domestic markets as a consequence of the large size of most Eurocurrency transactions, intense competition, and the lower costs of smaller reserves against Eurocurrency deposits.

The development of the Eurodollar market was made possible by the establishment of free convertibility among the major currencies at the end of 1958 and by the broad acceptance of the dollar as an international transactions currency. But its explosive growth in the 1960s was mainly attributable to the U.S. balance of payments deficits and the policies adopted to correct them. On one hand, the persistent U.S. deficits continually added to the supply of dollars in foreign banks and, on the other hand, U.S. restrictions on capital exports (starting with the Interest Equalization Tax of 1963 and culminating with mandatory investment controls in 1968) stimulated the demand for Eurodollar funds by American companies operating abroad. The effect of these restrictions, therefore, was to move the international money market from New York, where it was subject to regulation, to Europe, where it was free of regulation.[17]

Although domestic financial markets have grown more rapidly than gross national products in the 1980s, the Eurocurrency market has grown even faster. Between 1975 and 1986, the *stock* of Eurocurrency bank loans

---

[17] Since Eurocurrency bank loans only supply short- and medium-term financing, the need of American companies to raise investment capital abroad to finance their foreign operations gave a strong boost to the Eurobond market. Eurobonds are long-term debt securities denominated in dollars or in other convertible currencies that are offered outside the country of the borrower. Dollar Eurobonds are sold only outside the United States, mainly in Europe. Hence, the Eurobond market is foreign both to borrowers and to most investors.

TABLE 19-6   Activities of the Eurocurrency Market, 1980–1986
(Billions of Dollars)

	1980	1981	1982	1983	1984	1985	1986
Bank loans[1]	81.0	144.4	96.0	73.5	108.5	110.3	82.8
Eurobonds	20.4	31.3	50.3	50.1	81.7	135.4	187.0
Equity-related bonds				8.0	10.9	11.5	22.3
Other facilities[2]					11.4	32.3	70.8
Total	101.4	175.7	146.3	131.6	212.5	289.5	362.9

[1] Credits extended by commercial banks to nonbanks wholly or in part out of Eurocurrency funds.
[2] Mainly commercial paper programs.

Source: International Capital Markets (Washington, D.C.: International Monetary Fund, January 1988), Table 41, p. 96.

grew at an average real rate of about 14 percent to reach $3.2 *trillion*.[18] At the same time, the stock of Eurobonds rose at an annual real rate of almost 21 percent to reach $618 billion. Table 19-6 indicates the activities of the Eurocurrency market over the period 1980–1986. Total financing provided by the market went from $101 billion in 1980 to nearly $363 billion in 1986. The Eurocurrency market has been very responsive to the needs of borrowers; it has moved beyond bank loans to short- and long-term securities.

Why has the Eurocurrency market grown so rapidly? Mainly because few countries regulate the foreign currency deposits of banks under their jurisdiction. Hence Eurobanks can compete strongly against domestic banks to attract foreign currency deposits.

Implications of a Global Capital Market

The progressive formation of a global capital market in the 1980s holds several consequences for the behavior of the international monetary system and the autonomy of national macroeconomic policies.

The most evident consequence of international financial integration is the enormity of short-term capital flows among the principal industrial countries. In the 1980s international flows of money overwhelmed international flows of goods and services in determining exchange rates. Because

---

[18] About two-thirds of the loans are *interbank* loans. Over one thousand banks of fifty different countries participate in the Eurocurrency market.

funds move quickly in response to actual and anticipated changes in interest and foreign exchange rates, international capital mobility has intensified the volatility of exchange rates.

Has the globalization of capital markets weakened the linkage between the instruments of U.S. monetary policy (discount rate and open market operations) and U.S. short-term interest rates? Economic theory supports the proposition that the integration of capital markets makes both the demand and supply of dollars more *interest-elastic*. Short-term securities issued by foreigners become closer substitutes of short-term dollar securities. Hence on the demand side, both U.S. and foreign investors become more sensitive to interest-rate differentials in arranging their portfolios. On the supply side, borrowers have the option of issuing short-term securities either in the U.S. or foreign capital markets.

Higher interest elasticity in the demand and supply of dollars implies that changes in U.S. bank reserves induced by actions of the Federal Reserve will have a smaller impact on U.S. short-term interest rates (and therefore less policy effectiveness) than formerly, when capital markets were more independent. Has this actually occurred? One study concludes that there is some evidence that the emergence of a global capital market has loosened the linkage between changes in bank reserves and short-term interest rates in the United States and has therefore "complicated" the use of monetary policy. Also, the greater influence of foreign economic factors in determining U.S. short-term rates has created more uncertainty about the impact of a change in U.S. monetary policy.[19] A widely accepted proposition is that international financial integration reduces interest-rate disparities among similar securities traded in different national capital markets. But we have seen that interest-rate differentials among industrial countries persisted throughout the 1980s. Is this proposition, then, false?

International financial integration means lower institutional barriers to the movement of funds in and out of national capital markets. Starting in the 1970s, such barriers have been dismantled in the industrial countries by deregulating national capital markets to make them more competitive and open to foreigners and by eliminating foreign exchange restrictions on the international flow of funds.[20] But this liberalization has not wiped out interest-rate differentials among those countries, because financial integration remains incomplete as long as each country has an independent monetary system with its own currency.

Because the global capital market remains *segmented* by different national currencies, shifts of funds from one national capital market to another assume an *exchange risk*. This risk prevents the equalization of interest

---

[19] Lawrence J. Radecki and Vincent Reinhart, "The Globalization of Financial Markets and the Effectiveness of Monetary Policy Instruments," *Quarterly Review* (Federal Reserve Bank of New York), Autumn 1988, pp. 18–27.

[20] Institutional barriers remain high in the developing countries.

rates. Interest parity theory states that equilibrium is achieved when an interest-rate differential is exactly offset by the cost of hedging.[21] And, as demonstrated in Chapter 13, speculation may prevent interest parity equilibrium. Even if institutional barriers become zero, therefore, interest rates will fail to equalize across countries because of the foreign exchange risk.

The significance of exchange risk is shown by the fact that short-term interest rates in the U.S. capital market track very closely with *Eurodollar* rates, as do the short-term rates in other major capital markets with their counterparts in the Eurocurrency market (yen rates with Euroyen rates, pound sterling rates with Eurosterling, and so on). In these cases, the near absence of institutional barriers between national markets and the Eurocurrency market and the absence of any exchange risk comes close to complete financial integration. The answer to our question, therefore, is that the elimination of institutional barriers reduces the divergence of interest rates among national capital markets for the same class of security. But as long as the global capital market falls short of complete integration with a single currency, it will fail to eliminate interest-rate differences across countries.[22] Summing up, the emergence of a global capital market has made exchange rates more volatile and more sensitive to national macroeconomic policies. High capital mobility has made national economies more interdependent and, for that reason, has weakened the autonomy of national policymakers in spite of the existence of floating exchange rates.

PERFORMANCE OF THE CONTEMPORARY SYSTEM

How has the contemporary system performed since it began in 1973? The answer to this question cannot be a simple "poorly" or "well," because it depends on assumptions about how an ideal floating-rate system *should* perform or how an alternative system *would* have performed in the 1970s, as well as the *actual* performance of the contemporary system. In short, the answer to this question is a value judgment. Our response to this question, therefore, is the modest one of making some relevant observations.

The actual performance of the contemporary system has fulfilled neither the dire prophecies of fixed-rate advocates nor the fond expectations of floating-rate advocates. On the one hand, floating rates have *not* inhibited international trade and investment or caused a disintegration of international capital markets. Traders, bankers, multinational enterprises, and others have learned to manage their affairs in a floating-rate environment.

---

[21] Recall equation (7) in Chapter 13: $i_{us} - i_{UK} = (F^* - S)/S$.
[22] See Bruce Kasman and Charles Pigott, "Interest Rate Divergences among the Major Industrial Countries," *Quarterly Review* (Federal Reserve Bank of New York), Autumn 1988, pp. 28–44.

On the other hand, floating rates have *not* brought about quick adjustments in trade flows through smooth changes in exchange rates. Instead, rates have been extremely volatile, while current-account adjustments in response to changes in relative prices and costs have occurred only slowly. Nor have floating rates enabled governments to pursue national policies without regard to their international consequences. Instead, governments have encountered difficulties with national policy autonomy because of the international integration of money and capital markets, notably the Eurocurrency market.

The high short-run volatility of exchange rates has intensified the debate on stable versus variable rates. Fixed-rate advocates argue that exchange rates in the contemporary system "overshoot" their proper equilibrium levels, causing excessive adjustments in national economies. But there is now substantial agreement among economists that short-run volatility in exchange rates is caused by volatile expectations about future rates and government policies that influence them. As "efficient" markets, foreign exchange markets respond to all available information, and they continuously receive new information that alters existing exchange rates. Moreover, although exchange rates have been more volatile than national price levels, they have been *less* volatile than the prices of other financial assets (stocks and bonds) and gold, which are also traded in organized markets.

The contemporary system has functioned through two turbulent decades marked by high but uneven rates of inflation, divergent national monetary and fiscal policies, two oil-pricing shocks, a slowdown in economic activity with rising unemployment, an international stock market crash, and several political crises, such as the Iranian seizure of American hostages and the Falkland islands conflict between Argentina and Great Britain. It is most doubtful that any fixed-rate system could have survived such turbulence without the imposition of stringent controls over international trade and capital movements by at least some of the major industrial countries. Highly volatile exchange rates have been a response to turbulence, not its cause.

The exchange rate is only one of several macroeconomic variables. In particular, exchange rates are strongly influenced by national monetary policies. Divergent monetary policies among countries, as we have seen, can create *real* interest-rate differentials (as well as nominal differentials) that instigate international flows of money and other financial assets. More profoundly, divergent monetary policies create different rates of inflation among countries and, therefore, shifting purchasing-power parities. Hence, exchange rate behavior should not be evaluated in isolation from other macroeconomic variables that were also highly volatile in the 1980s.

The experience of the past decade demonstrates that countries need to coordinate their macroeconomic policies in the contemporary system (even though they have somewhat more flexibility than in a fixed-rate system) if the countries want less volatile exchange rates. But coordinated policies will not insure stable foreign exchange markets: They are a necessary but not sufficient condition for stability. As long as the international environment remains turbulent, exchange rates will remain volatile. This is as it should be in a system in which exchange rates are the principal instrument of international adjustment. But coordinated national policies would certainly lessen exchange rate volatility.

The world economy in the 1980s experienced large swings in current-account balances and accompanying capital movements in an environment of uneven rates of inflation, general economic slowdown, and unemployment. With these conditions, a return to a fixed-rate system is most improbable. But if the leading industrial countries succeed in taming inflation and are willing to coordinate their domestic economic policies, then we can expect growing support for a fixed-rate system. The main threat today, however, is not a collapse of the international monetary system but rather protectionism. This new protectionism, which is spawned by divergent macroeconomic policies and structural maladjustments, will stifle international trade and investment in the 1990s if it is not successfully combatted.

SUMMARY

1. In sharp contrast to the Bretton Woods system, the currencies of other industrial countries are now floating with respect to the U.S. dollar.
2. Exchange rates have been highly volatile in the 1980s. Changes in real exchange rates among the dollar, yen, and mark cannot be explained by divergent rates of inflation. Rather, they are due to divergent macroeconomic policies that have brought about large international differentials in real interest rates.
3. In the first half of the 1980s, new fiscal and monetary policies increased total U.S. domestic absorption from 99 percent of GNP to 102 percent of GNP. This excess expenditure was possible only through a deficit on current account of the same amount.
4. The macroeconomic policies followed by the United States in the 1980s have had several unfortunate consequences. The 50 percent appreciation of the dollar in 1980–1985 hurt U.S. export and import-competing industries and magnified demands for import protection. High U.S. real interest rates induced an enormous inflow of capital (making the United States the world's biggest debtor), slowed U.S. domestic investment, and increased the burden of servicing the external debts of the Third World.
5. Central banks have continued to intervene in foreign exchange markets, and thus the contemporary system is best described as a *managed-*

float system. In general, intervention has followed the standard of "leaning against the wind."

6. Abandoning its laissez-faire attitude, the United States and other major industrial countries announced the Plaza Agreement in September 1985, which was intended to push down the value of the dollar. Actually, the dollar had started to fall in February of that year. The Louvre Accord of February 1987, agreed to by the G-5 countries and Canada, sought to stabilize the dollar's value through equilibrating changes in macroeconomic policies. But the Louvre Accord has so far failed to reduce significantly the divergence of macroeconomic policies, which is the fundamental cause of the huge current-account deficits of the United States with Japan and West Germany.

7. Further depreciation of the dollar alone cannot eliminate current-account imbalances. What is needed is international policy coordination that achieves a decrease in U.S. domestic absorption and an increase in the domestic absorption of Japan and West Germany.

8. The International Monetary Fund continues to play a role in the contemporary international monetary system. It undertakes surveillance of the exchange rate policies of member countries and extends far more adjustment assistance to developing countries than in the past. Conditionality gives the Fund strong leverage over the policies of the countries that use its credit.

9. A global capital market first emerged in the 1950s in the form of the Eurocurrency market. The liberalization of national capital markets started in the 1970s and gathered force in the 1980s. This movement has progressively integrated national capital markets and the Eurocurrency market to create a single global capital market. The resulting high international mobility of capital has made national economies more interdependent and, for that reason, has weakened the autonomy of national policymakers.

10. The contemporary international monetary system has functioned through two decades of economic and political turbulence. It is doubtful that a fixed-rate system could have survived such turbulence. As long as the major industrial countries remain unwilling or unable to coordinate macroeconomic policies, a return to a fixed-rate system is unlikely.

QUESTIONS AND APPLICATIONS

1. (a) Describe the structure of the contemporary international monetary system.
   (b) How does this system differ from the Bretton Woods system?
   (c) Some observers have described the contemporary system as a "nonsystem." Do you agree or disagree? Why?

2. Define *nominal effective exchange rate* and *real effective exchange rate*.
3. Why did the dollar, yen, and mark exhibit prolonged changes in *real exchange rates* in the 1980s?
4. What is the relationship between interest rates and exchange rates?
5. (a) Why did U.S. domestic absorption rise so strongly after 1980?
   (b) Explain how this rise in absorption was possible only through a deficit of the same amount in the U.S. current account.
   (c) Why did not the increase in U.S. absorption after 1980 induce higher output and thereby avoid a current-account deficit?
6. "The enormous current-account imbalances of the United States, Japan, and West Germany continue to haunt the world economy." Comment on this statement.
7. (a) Why have central banks intervened in foreign exchange markets in the contemporary system?
   (b) Distinguish a "managed float" from a "pure float."
   (c) Explain the intervention standard known as "leaning against the wind."
8. (a) What is the Plaza Agreement? The Louvre Accord?
   (b) What was the effect of central bank intervention during the period February 1985 to February 1988?
9. (a) What is international policy coordination?
   (b) Explain the reasoning behind this statement: "Further depreciation of the dollar alone cannot eliminate current-account imbalances. What is needed is international policy coordination."
10. Which principles guide the Fund's surveillance of exchange rate policies?
11. What is IMF "conditionality"? Can it be applied equally to deficit and surplus countries? Why or why not?
12. (a) What are Eurocurrencies?
    (b) How does the Eurocurrency market differ from national capital markets?
    (c) How does the Eurocurrency market facilitate the international transfer of funds?
13. Using T accounts, show what happens to bank assets and liabilities when (a) a deposit holder switches a dollar deposit from a Eurobank to a U.S. bank; (b) a multinational enterprise borrows from a U.S. bank and then deposits the dollars in a Eurobank.
14. (a) Why should a global capital market make the demand and supply of dollars more interest-elastic?
    (b) What are the implications for U.S. monetary policy of higher interest elasticity?
15. Why has not the emergence of a global capital market eliminated interest-rate disparities among the industrial countries?
16. Evaluate the prospects for a return to a fixed-rate international monetary system.

SELECTED READINGS

Cooper, Richard N. *Economic Policy in an Interdependent World.* Cambridge: M.I.T. Press, 1986.

De Vries, Margaret G. *The IMF in a Changing World, 1945–85.* Washington, D.C.: International Monetary Fund, 1986.

Dufey, Gunter, and Ian H. Giddy. *The International Money Market.* Englewood Cliffs, N.J.: Prentice-Hall, 1978.

Eichengreen, Barry, ed. *The Gold Standard in Theory and History.* New York: Methuen, 1985.

Federal Reserve Bank of New York. "Treasury and Federal Reserve Foreign Exchange Operations." *Quarterly Review.* Each issue.

Frankel, Jeffrey A. *Obstacles to International Macroeconomic Policy Coordination.* Princeton Studies in International Finance, no. 64. Princeton, N.J.: Princeton University Press, December 1988.

Funabashi, Yoichi. *Managing the Dollar: From the Plaza to the Louvre.* Washington, D.C.: Institute for International Economics, 1988.

Horne, Jocelyn, and Paul R. Masson. "Scope and Limits of International Economic Cooperation and Policy Coordination." *IMF Staff Papers,* June 1988, pp. 259–96.

International Monetary Fund. *Annual Report.* Washington, D.C.

———. *Articles of Agreement.* Washington, D.C.: International Monetary Fund. Latest edition.

———. *IMF Survey.* Biweekly.

———. *Economic Policy Coordination.* Washington, D.C.: International Monetary Fund, 1988.

———. *International Capital Markets.* Washington, D.C.: International Monetary Fund. No fixed issue date.

———. *International Financial Statistics.* Washington, D.C.: International Monetary Fund. Monthly.

———. *Strengthening the International Monetary System: Exchange Rates, Surveillance, and Objective Indicators.* Occasional Paper 50. Washington, D.C.: International Monetary Fund, February 1987.

———. *The Role of the SDR in the International Monetary System.* Occasional Paper 51. Washington, D.C.: International Monetary Fund, March 1987.

———. *World Economic Outlook.* Washington, D.C.: International Monetary Fund. No fixed issue date.

Kenen, Peter B. *Financing, Adjustment and the International Monetary Fund.* Washington, D.C.: Brookings Institution, 1986.

Solomon, Robert. *The International Monetary System, 1945–1976.* New York: Harper & Row, 1977.

Southard, Frank A., Jr. *The Evolution of the International Monetary Fund.* Essays in International Finance, no. 135. Princeton, N.J.: Princeton University Press, 1979.

PART THREE

INTERNATIONAL DEVELOPMENT

Over three-quarters of the world's people live in the developing countries of Asia, Africa, and Latin America at levels of income that remain far below those enjoyed by people in the rich, developed countries of North America, Western Europe, and Japan. Part Three examines the economic situation of the developing countries, the bearing of international trade on economic growth, the trade and other international economic policies followed by the developing countries in their effort to achieve economic development, and the problem of external debt.

20

The Developing Countries in the World Economy

One-third of the world's people live a daily round of grinding poverty. Occupying the vast stretches of Asia, Africa, and Latin America, these people inhabit more than one hundred countries that are committed to programs of economic development intended to break the vicious circle of poverty. Industrialization has become the supreme national goal of these developing countries; it dominates their economic policies and will probably continue to do so for generations to come. In particular, the drive for economic development shapes the attitudes, policies, and expectations of the developing countries in the areas of international trade, external assistance, and international investment.

In this and the following chapter we examine the role of international trade in economic development and the trade policies of the developing countries. We also look at the response that industrial countries are making to the needs and demands of the developing countries. But first we must comprehend the economic situation of the poor countries and the major obstacles to a betterment of their low standards of living, for it is this situation that generates the drive for development and the policies directed toward international trade and investment.

THE ECONOMIC SITUATION OF THE DEVELOPING COUNTRIES

Which are the developing countries? What are their major obstacles to further development? What is the record of three decades of development? These questions occupy our attention in the opening section.

Which Are the Developing Countries?

The most commonly used indicator to distinguish the developing from the industrial countries is gross national product (income) per capita.[1] Table 20-1 classifies countries according to this indicator.

Economic development and underdevelopment are complex phenomena with social, cultural, and political dimensions as well as an economic dimension. Hence, they cannot be fully measured by any single indicator. Nonetheless, most observers would agree that countries with per capita GNPs below $1,800 in 1986 are unquestionably nonindustrial countries. These poor countries, classified as low-income and lower-middle-income developing countries, account for 73 of the 120 countries listed in Table 20-1. At the same time, several countries in the upper-middle-income group, such as Brazil, Mexico, and Algeria, can hardly be described as modern industrial economies. This is also true of *high-income oil exporters*, whose per capita incomes have shot up since the quadrupling of oil prices at the beginning of 1974 but whose economies continue to bear the hallmarks of developing countries, which are discussed later in this chapter. Although the United Arab Emirates and Kuwait are in the highest per capita income category, they remain largely preindustrial societies badly in need of social and economic development.

It is impossible, therefore, to draw a line in Table 20-1 separating developing from developed countries. Per capita GNP is only a partial indicator of economic development. More fundamentally, the *developed* countries have not only surpassed the "threshold" level of annual per capita GNP (say $2,000) but have also demonstrated a capacity for sustained economic growth over a long period without concessional assistance (grants or low-interest, easy-payment loans) from external sources. However, the per capita GNP indicator offers certain advantages as a criterion of economic development: It distinguishes the least-developed from the most highly developed countries, it is quantitative, and it rests upon the empirical truth that a threshold level of per capita income is necessary, if not sufficient, for economic development.

The developing countries make up a highly heterogeneous group. In size of population they range from India, with almost 800 million inhabitants, to the many developing countries, such as Barbados, with less than 1 million inhabitants. Some are highly endowed with minerals or fertile agricultural lands; others consist mainly of arid desert or tropical rain forest. Some are much further advanced than others: Brazil possesses a major industrial center in its São Paulo region, Argentina has ten times the per

---

[1] Several terms are used to denote the developing countries: *poor, nonindustrial, underdeveloped, less-developed (LDC), South,* and *Third World.* These terms are used interchangeably in this and other chapters.

TABLE 20-1   Population and Per Capita GNP by Country Groups in 1986

Country Group[1]	Population (Millions)	Per Capita GNP[2] (Dollars)
Developing countries	3,761	610
Low-income countries[3]	2,493	270
Lower-middle-income countries[4]	691	750
Upper-middle-income countries[5]	577	1,890
High-income oil exporters[6]	19	6,740
Industrial countries[7]	742	12,960

[1] Only countries with a population of one million or more are included in this table. Also not included are the following nonreporting countries: Albania, Angola, Bulgaria, Cuba, Czechoslovakia, East Germany, North Korea, Mongolia, and the Soviet Union. Also not included is Taiwan, which ranks in the upper-middle-income group.

[2] To derive this data, the World Bank uses an exchange rate conversion method with the following steps: (1) GNP in local currency units is first expressed in weighted average prices of the base period 1984–1986; (2) this adjusted GNP is then converted to U.S. dollars at the GNP-weighted average exchange rate for the base period; (3) this adjusted dollar GNP is next converted into current dollars by adjusting for U.S. inflation with the implicit GNP deflator for 1984–1986; and (4) finally the current-dollar GNP is divided by the corresponding midyear population figure to get per capita GNP.

[3] Thirty-nine countries. Ranked in ascending order by per capita income: Ethiopia, Bhutan, Burkina Faso, Nepal, Bangladesh, Malawi, Zaire, Mali, Burma, Mozambique, Madagascar, Uganda, Burundi, Tanzania, Togo, Niger, Benin, Somalia, Central African Republic, India, Rwanda, China, Kenya, Zambia, Sierra Leone, Sudan, Haiti, Pakistan, Lesotho, Ghana, Sri Lanka, Mauritania, Senegal, Afghanistan, Chad, Guinea, Kampuchea, Laos, and Vietnam.

[4] Thirty-four countries. Ranked in ascending order by per capita income: Liberia, Yemen, Indonesia, Yemen Arab Republic, Philippines, Morocco, Bolivia, Zimbabwe, Nigeria, Dominican Republic, Papua New Guinea, Ivory Coast, Honduras, Egypt, Nicaragua, Thailand, El Salvador, Botswana, Jamaica, Cameroon, Guatemala, Congo, Paraguay, Peru, Turkey, Tunisia, Ecuador, Mauritius, Colombia, Chile, Costa Rica, Jordan, Syria, and Lebanon.

[5] Twenty-four countries. Ranked in ascending order by per capita income: Brazil, Malaysia, South Africa, Mexico, Uruguay, Hungary, Poland, Portugal, Yugoslavia, Panama, Argentina, South Korea, Algeria, Venezuela, Gabon, Greece, Oman, Trinidad and Tobago, Israel, Hong Kong, Singapore, Iran, Iraq, and Romania.

[6] Four countries. Ranked in ascending order by per capita income: Saudi Arabia, Kuwait, United Arab Emirates, and Libya.

[7] Nineteen countries. Ranked in ascending order by per capita income: Spain, Ireland, New Zealand, Italy, United Kingdom, Belgium, Austria, Netherlands, France, Australia, West Germany, Finland, Denmark, Japan, Sweden, Canada, Norway, United States, and Switzerland.

Source: Based on data in The World Bank, *World Development Report 1988* (New York: Oxford University Press, 1988), Table 1, pp. 222–23.

capita GNP of the least-developed countries, and the oil-exporting countries constitute a distinctive subset.

The developing countries also exhibit broad cultural, social, and political differences. Despite this diversity, they generally share common features: low levels of industrialization, low per capita incomes (except the oil-exporting countries), high illiteracy rates, a predominance of agriculture and other primary production, and a dependence on commodity exports. These common features set them off from the economically advanced countries located mainly in Western Europe and North America. Nonetheless, the developing countries can be adequately described today only in terms of three subgroups: (1) high-income oil exporters, (2) upper-middle-income economies, and (3) lower-middle-income and low-income economies. The upper-middle-income economies include the "newly industrializing economies" (notably, Brazil, Hong Kong, Mexico, Singapore, South Korea, and Taiwan), which have switched from commodity to manufactured exports and which possess high rates of industrial growth that are making their economies resemble more closely the industrial economies than those of other developing countries.

The inequality of per capita income among the world's nations is enormous. Figure 20-1 depicts this inequality with a Lorenz curve. If national

Figure 20-1   International Inequality of Income in 1986

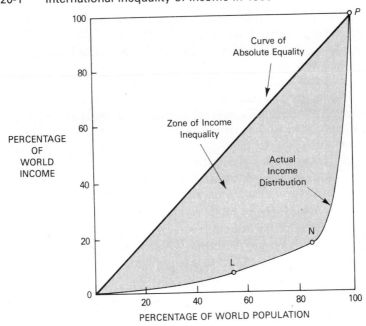

Source: The World Bank, *World Development Report 1988* (New York: Oxford University Press, 1988), Table A3, p. 188.

The international distribution of income is depicted by the 0–L–N–P curve. If per capital incomes among countries were absolutely equal, then income distribution would fall on the 0–P line: 20 percent of the world's population would earn 20 percent of the world's income, and so on. Hence, the gap between the 0–P line and the 0–L–N–P curve indicates income inequality.

per capita incomes were absolutely *equal*, the income distribution curve would be the diagonal line 0–*P*. For then 20 percent of the world population would earn 20 percent of the world income; 40 percent, 40 percent; and so on. (The curve of absolute *inequality* is the bottom and right sides of the figure.) The curve of *actual* income distribution determines the zone of income inequality, as shown in Figure 20-1. This zone is a large fraction of the entire space lying below the diagonal, indicating a high degree of income inequality. To demonstrate this inequality specifically, we have partitioned the income distribution curve into three income groups.

0–*L* represents the thirty-nine low-income developing countries that have 55.4 percent of the world's population but only 4.9 percent of its income (GNP). *L–N* denotes the fifty-eight middle-income developing countries, which have 26.9 percent of the world's population and 12.3 percent of its income. *N–P* represents the twenty-three high-income countries: four oil exporters, which enjoy 1.4 percent of the world's income but which have only 0.4 percent of its people, and nineteen industrial countries, whose 17.3 percent of the world's people receive 81.4 percent of the world's income.[2]

The poverty of the developing nations is not new; it has been a way of life for untold generations. What is new is the bitter awareness of poverty, the knowledge that it is not inevitable, and the determination to raise living standards one way or another. Many of the countries of Asia and Africa emerged from a colonial status to full political independence only after World War II. Independence has been accompanied by a virulent nationalism, high expectations, and, in some cases, antagonism toward the West.

What has been called "the revolution of rising expectations" is cause for both hope and fear. Of hope, for after centuries of stagnation the developing countries are now striving to create the conditions essential to economic and social progress. Of fear, for the frustration of their high expectations may turn these peoples toward violent revolution (as it has already done in some instances) and against the West.

Obstacles to Economic Development

The developing nations must overcome many obstacles to achieve a rate of investment that will provide a satisfactory rate of economic growth, especially in per capita terms. These obstacles are a complex set of internal and external factors. Although it is widely agreed that the basic restraints on growth derive from the very structure of the poor societies, external con-

---

[2] These nineteen industrial countries, plus Greece, Iceland, Portugal, Luxembourg, and Turkey, are the OECD countries. The OECD is the Organization for Economic Cooperation and Development. It has the following member countries: Australia, Austria, Belgium, Canada, Denmark, Finland, France, Germany, Greece, Iceland, Ireland, Italy, Japan, Luxembourg, the Netherlands, New Zealand, Norway, Portugal, Spain, Sweden, Switzerland, Turkey, the United Kingdom, and the United States. *OECD* is another designation for the developed or industrial countries. This group is also called the *West* or *North* . These terms are used interchangeably in this and other chapters.

ditions that hinder the exports of developing nations or limit the availability of financial assistance from abroad also can restrain growth.

To become mature economies, the developing nations must undertake a massive transformation of their societies, and this can be accomplished only by their own peoples and national leaders. To succeed, however, they need the capital goods and technology of the developed, industrial countries. This section looks at major obstacles to growth *within* the developing countries themselves; international trade and financial conditions that limit growth are taken up in the next chapter.

The situation of developing countries has been aptly described as interlocking sets of vicious circles that perpetuate economic stagnation and poverty. One of these vicious circles involves the savings-investment gap:

1. Productivity is low because investment is low.
2. Investment is low because saving is low.
3. Saving is low because income is low.
4. Income is low because productivity is low.

Thus, in a very real sense the poor nations are poor because they are poor.

Lack of Social Overhead Capital Social overhead capital supplies the services—power, transportation, storage, communications, education and so on—that are indispensable to modern industry and agriculture. The lack of this capital in the poor nations is a bottleneck to economic development. Inadequate transportation and communication facilities block the exploitation of attractive resources located in the interior regions of many countries in Latin America, Asia, and Africa. A country like India may lose up to one-third of its agricultural output because it lacks storage facilities to protect against spoilage, rodents, and other wastage. The absence of electrical power thwarts the establishment of the many industries dependent on it, as well as impeding community and urban development.

Educational facilities are a vital element of social overhead capital. The majority of the people in the least-developed nations are illiterate. Lacking the basic skills and training necessary for industrial production or modern agriculture, these people can make little contribution to economic development. The developing countries must stamp out illiteracy mainly by educating the new generation; unless this is done, there is little hope for the future.

Lack of Business Managers and Government Administrators The efforts of countless, mostly private, entrepreneurs gave Western Europe and North America the momentum to move into and beyond the takeoff stage of economic growth. Eagerly searching for new profit opportunities, these entrepreneurs combined factors of production in new ways and on a broader scale than ever before in history to produce new products for emerging markets. Later a large class of business managers arose to promote and administer the expanding private enterprise sectors of these economies.

Today professional preparation for careers in business is commonplace in the United States, Western Europe, and Japan.

In contrast, the developing nations generally lack a business class that is willing to invest in new industrial enterprises and has the know-how to manage them. Their business people are likely to be traders and merchants engaging in foreign trade, wholesaling, and retailing rather than in manufacturing. They tend to be speculative, looking for quick profits in real estate or monopoly market situations. Frequently the upper class in the poor societies disapprove of business, preferring to invest in land and rearing their children to be land-owning aristocrats, soldiers, lawyers, and diplomats instead of business executives. Partly owing to this class prejudice against business, foreigners dominate the commercial activity of many developing countries, such as the Chinese in Malaysia and European Jews in Latin America.

Lacking private entrepreneurs, the governments of the developing nations must take the lead in formulating and implementing national development plans. Here another problem arises: the shortage of trained government administrators. The result is often incompetence, worsened by endemic bribery and favoritism. Ineffective systems of taxation fail to mobilize financial resources for capital formation, investment is allocated in ways that do not promote economic growth, and public enterprises are operated at a loss, draining off scarce capital rather than creating it.

Cultural Blocks to Economic Growth   Old ways and new ways live side by side in the developing societies, and in many, the old ways remain dominant. Preindustrial attitudes toward work and belief in traditional ways are very hard to change. And yet they must be changed if the economy is ever to achieve takeoff: Workers must develop the motivation and discipline essential to industrial production, and peasants must become commercial farmers, open to technological innovations in agriculture.

Poor motivation, high turnover, absenteeism, and generally sloppy performance characterize the industrial workers of many developing nations. In the early stage of industrialization, an increase in wages may actually cause absenteeism because people work only to maintain a traditional standard of living, having no conception of a rising standard.[3] Peasants can offer stubborn resistance to changing their ways. Getting them to use commercial fertilizers, improved seed strains, crop rotation schemes, and so on, requires a time-consuming educational process that is likely to be only partially successful, as witnessed by the community development programs in India and Latin America.

Cultural blocks are often elusive and hard to identify. Once identified, they are hard to overcome. Nevertheless, they must be overcome, because

---

[3] This causes a "backward sloping supply schedule" for labor. This situation is not likely to last very long, particularly in urban areas where newly arrived workers are exposed to examples of higher standards of living.

prescientific, traditional attitudes and beliefs act to reinforce the vicious circles of poverty that plague the developing nations.

The Population Explosion It was not until 1800 that the world's population reached one billion. But today the world's population of five billion is growing at an annual rate of 1.8 percent. Most of this growth is occurring in the developing countries, where the annual growth rate is 2.1 percent. At that rate, the population of the developing countries will double in thirty-five years.

The issue here is not whether this vast number of people in the developing countries will be able to survive but rather how fast economic development would be able to proceed at a lower rate of population growth. It is clear that the population explosion is the single greatest obstacle to economic development. When population grows rapidly, the bulk of domestic investment is devoted to simply maintaining the current level of per capita income rather than increasing it. In other words, much of the increase in production of the poor countries is being consumed by the newly born.

Fundamentally, the population explosion is a consequence of the "public health" revolution in the poor countries. The introduction of modern medicine has cut death rates drastically (mainly in the early years of life) but has had little influence on birth rates, which often remain at the traditional high levels. Paradoxically, modern medicine, by saving lives, is making it more difficult to lift those lives out of poverty. Only recently have some governments of developing countries responded to this critical situation.

Three Decades of Development

Table 20-2 shows the rates of growth in population, GNP, and per capita GNP for the developing countries of the South and the industrial countries of the North over the period 1955–1984.

On the whole, the GNP of the developing countries grew more rapidly than the GNP of the industrial countries in all periods. But high growth rates in population constrained the growth of per capita GNP in the LDCs. It is noteworthy, however, that the LDCs as a group outpaced the industrial countries in the growth of per capita GNP in the 1970s (3.1 percent compared to 2.4 percent) despite high population growth. Not all LDCs, however, shared equally in this impressive performance. The low-income developing countries recorded economic growth rates significantly below those of the middle-income developing countries. But all in all, this performance of the developing countries compares very favorably with the historical growth rates of 2 to 3 percent experienced by the industrial countries over the last century.

The slowdown in the world economy and the eruption of an international debt crisis drastically lowered the growth rate of the middle-income developing countries in the 1980–1984 period. In contrast, the performance

TABLE 20-2   Growth of Population, GNP, and Per Capita GNP of the Developing and Industrial Countries, 1955–1984
(Average Annual Percentage Changes)

	1955–1970			1970–1980			1980–1984		
	Population	GNP	Per Capita GNP	Population	GNP	Per Capita GNP	Population[1]	GNP[2]	Per Capita GNP
Low-income developing countries	2.1	3.7	1.6	2.1	4.5	2.4	1.9	7.1	5.1
Middle-income developing countries	2.4	6.0	3.5	2.4	5.6	3.1	2.3	1.4	−1.4
All developing countries	2.2	5.4	3.1	2.2	5.3	3.1	2.0	3.0	0.7
All industrial countries	1.1	4.7	3.6	0.8	3.2	2.4	0.6	2.0	1.3

[1] 1980–1986.
[2] GDP.

Source: Derived from the World Bank, World Development Report 1982 (New York: Oxford University Press, 1982), Table 3.1, p. 21, and The World Bank, World Development Report 1988 (New York: Oxford University Press, 1988), Table A2, p. 187, and Table A4, p. 189.

of the low-income developing countries improved over the previous decade. The developing countries as a whole were able to improve per capita income in the 1980–1985 period only at the low annual rate of 0.7 percent. Although the growth rate of the industrial countries also experienced a sharp decline in 1980s, the low growth rate in population enabled them to achieve an annual growth in per capita income of 1.3 percent.

It is evident that three decades of development have brought substantial economic progress to the developing countries. This progress does not support those who believe that the LDCs are permanently sunk in hopeless poverty, and it offers encouragement to those who are committed to development. But the *absolute* levels of per capita income remain depressingly low for the least-developed countries. Even if the very high per capita growth rate achieved by the low-income developing countries were to continue, it would take fifteen years to double their average per capita income of $270.

CAPITAL FORMATION, ECONOMIC GROWTH, AND CONSTRAINTS ON DOMESTIC INVESTMENT

Capital formation—the creation of transportation, communications, and power facilities; the construction of factories; the acquisition of machines, tools, and other instruments of production—is an essential condition of economic growth. The harnessing of mechanical energies, the organization of mass production, the utilization of modern technology, the education and training of workers—all of these are dependent on the formation of capital. In the developed countries, capital resources per capita are high; in the developing countries, they are low.

Investment and National Output

To increase its stock of capital, a country must invest a part of its national product.[4] Investment reduces the resources available to satisfy immediate consumption, but it raises the level of consumption in the future by enhancing economic productivity. The relationship between new investment and a subsequent increase in real output depends on the marginal productivity of capital, which may be expressed as the *incremental capital-output ratio*, or k.

$$(1) \ k = I_t/\Delta V_{t+1}.$$

---

[4] More precisely, a country must invest an amount beyond that needed to maintain its existing capital stock (capital consumption is measured by depreciation) if it is to add to its capital stock. In the subsequent discussion we shall ignore the distinction between gross and net investment.

I_t is the investment in period t and ΔV_{t+1} is the resulting increment in real national output (gross domestic product) in the next period, which we shall take to be the following year. If, for example, $6 million of investment causes a $2 million increase in national output, then the capital-output ratio is 3.[5]

Given k, we can calculate the growth rate of a country's output once we know the annual rate of investment (r) expressed as a fraction (or percentage) of current national output.

$$(2)\ r = I_t/V_t.$$

Hence, the growth rate (g) of gross domestic product is r/k:

$$(3)\ g = r/k = (I_t/V_t)(\Delta V_{t+1}/I_t) = \Delta V_{t+1}/V_t.$$

To illustrate, if a country is investing 15 percent of its gross domestic product on an annual basis and its incremental capital-output ratio is 3, then its rate of growth is 15%/3, or 5%.

In measuring the progress of the developing countries, we are particularly interested in the *per capita* growth rate (w). If p is the annual rate of growth in population, then

$$(4)\ w = g - p = (r/k) - p.$$

(Strictly speaking, we should calculate w by dividing the index of gross domestic product by the population index, but when the population growth rate is less than 5 percent, which is empirically true, equation (4) will render a close approximation of the true value and is much more simple to compute.)

Returning to our previous example, if the annual rate of population growth is 2 percent, then the per capita growth rate in terms of equation (4) is

$$w = 15\%/3 - 2\% = 3\%.$$

Equation (4) tells us that a country can increase its rate of per capita growth by lowering its incremental capital-output ratio (k), by lowering its rate of population growth (p), or by raising its rate of investment (r). The incremental capital-output ratio is determined by many dynamic factors: As a country's capital stock increases relative to other productive agents, diminishing returns act to raise k, while a better allocation of investment, new technology, and improvements in human skills act to lower k by in-

---

[5] In both developed and developing countries, the incremental capital-output ratio generally falls between 2 and 5.

creasing the productivity of capital. Studies of long-term economic growth in the developed countries indicate that increases in productivity (decreases in k) account for a greater share of per capita income growth than the mere increase in capital utilized per worker at a constant level of technology.[6] It follows that the developing countries must continually work to lower k if they are to match the development experience of the advanced countries. As for population, we have already spoken about this growth constraint in the preceding section.

Given k and p, a country can increase its rate of growth by raising its rate of domestic investment (r). Negatively expressed, a country may fail to achieve a target rate of growth (say, 2 percent per capita per year) because r is too low. Suppose, for example, a country has an incremental capital-output ratio of 3, a rate of investment of 9 percent (rather than 15 percent as in our previous example), and an annual rate of population growth of 2 percent, then

$$w = 9\%/3 - 2\% = 1\%.$$

The relationship between domestic investment and economic growth has been emphasized by economists in growth models because it can be quantitatively defined, whereas the relationships between social and political factors and economic growth are both hard to quantify and fall outside the disciplinary boundaries of economics. Economists recognize, however, that investment is a *necessary* condition but not a *sufficient* condition for economic development. Investment must be accompanied by appropriate changes in attitudes, values, and institutions if an economy is to achieve a self-sustaining growth. Economic growth is only one element in the modernization of a traditional society. The foregoing remarks are not intended to dispute the importance of capital formation in the developing countries. Capital formation is the major instrument for the transformation of technical knowledge into technological innovation: Infrastructure investment in transportation and communication makes possible economies of scale, and social investment in education is necessary to improve human skills. It is correct, therefore, to view the rate of investment as a critical factor in economic development, although it is by no means the only critical factor. From this perspective, we now turn to a consideration of the constraints that may limit the growth of investment in the developing countries.

---

[6] For the 1929–1957 period in the United States, Denison attributes only 42 percent of the increase in output per worker to an increase in inputs (quality improvements in labor, more land, and more capital) and 58 percent to an increase in output per unit of input that mainly resulted from technological innovation and economies of scale. The increase in capital per worker (technology constant) explains only 9 percent of the growth rate. See Edward F. Denison, *The Sources of Economic Growth in the United States and the Alternatives before Us* (New York: Committee for Economic Development, 1962), Table 33, p. 270.

Constraints on Domestic Investment Faced by Developing Countries

The rate of domestic investment in a developing country may be constrained in three principal ways: (1) by the capacity of the country to absorb additional capital, (2) by the level of its domestic savings, or (3) by the availability of foreign exchange. With a given k, any one of these three constraints may impose a ceiling on the level of investment and, therefore, on the rate of growth in gross domestic product.

The *capital-absorption capacity* of a country depends on the availability of human factors (labor, managerial, and administrative) embodying skills that are necessary to transform investment funds (savings) into real investment. It also depends on the presence of an effective demand for the output resulting from investment. Suppose the target rate of growth is $\bar{g}$ and the rate of investment required to achieve this target rate is $\bar{r}$. Now let a be the country's current rate of capital-absorption capacity (expressed as a percentage of gross domestic product). Then if $\bar{r} > a$, absorptive capacity places a limitation on the rate of growth. Absorptive capacity is likely to be a critical constraint for an economy as a whole only when a country is in the early stages of growth.

In an open economy, gross *domestic* product assumes this form:

$$(5)\ GDP = C + I + G + (X - M).$$

This identity equation may be compared to that for gross *national* product, which is stated as equation (1) in Chapter 15. The only difference between the two is that exports (X) and imports (M) in the GDP identity are defined so as to exclude factor payments received from or paid to the rest of the world. Thus, GNP measures only the output resulting from factors of production owned by the country's residents, whereas GDP measures all output resulting from factors of production located on the country's territory regardless of their ownership.

Since gross domestic product equals gross domestic income (the sum of domestic consumption and domestic saving), it follows that domestic investment equals the sum of domestic saving and the import balance on current account that is financed by net borrowing from abroad:

$$(6)\ I = S + (M - X).[7]$$

In the absence of any net foreign borrowing $(M = X)$, then $I = S$, the rate of investment (r) equals the rate of domestic saving (s), and $r/k = s/k$. Now

---

[7] The derivation of this identity is the same as the derivation of equation (7) in Chapter 15.

assume that a country's target rate of growth is $\bar{g}$ and the required rate of investment is $\bar{r}$ while the rate of domestic savings is s. Then if $s < \bar{r}$, there is a *domestic savings gap* that will prevent the attainment of the target rate of growth: $g = s/k = r/k < \bar{r}/k = \bar{g}$.

When its savings gap is financed by net borrowing from abroad that permits an excess of imports over exports, then a country is able to achieve its target rate of growth: $\bar{I} = S + (M - X)$, where $\bar{I}$ is the required level of investment. If b is $(M - X)$ expressed as a percentage of gross domestic product (the rate of foreign borrowing), then $\bar{g} = s/k + b/k = \bar{r}/k$.

In the absence of capital-absorption and savings gaps, the growth rate of a developing country may still be constrained by a *foreign exchange (trade) gap*. That is to say, domestic savings are a necessary condition but may not be a sufficient condition for raising investment in a developing country to a desired level. The explanation of this situation rests on the import requirements of real capital formation coupled with the structural inability of a developing economy to transform savings into foreign exchange through an increase in exports or a decrease in imports. In order to invest, a developing country must acquire from abroad the capital equipment and other investment goods (such as structural steel) that it is unable to produce at home. If the output released by domestic savings can be allocated to exports or import substitution, then the foreign exchange necessary to purchase investment goods from abroad is forthcoming. In that event, there is no foreign exchange gap distinct from a savings gap, a situation that is true of the advanced, developed economies. But in developing countries, the capacity to reallocate resources is commonly limited by internal structural obstacles as well as external obstacles that curb export growth.

Because of the foreign content of capital formation, a developing country will require a certain level of imports $(\overline{M})$ to sustain a desired level of investment $(\bar{I})$. In the absence of external borrowing, a country can only obtain $\overline{M}$ through exports (X). If, therefore, $\overline{M} > X$, there is a trade or foreign exchange gap that blocks the attainment of I. The foreign exchange gap $(\overline{M} - X)$ will place a ceiling on actual investment. As was true of the savings gap, the foreign exchange gap may be closed by external assistance (B). When it is fully closed $(B = \overline{M} - X)$, then the foreign exchange gap no longer constrains the desired level of investment and growth.

Figure 20-2 offers a schematic representation of the three investment constraints. It is reasonable to hypothesize that in the early stages of economic development the critical constraint is absorptive capacity. At E, however, the critical constraint becomes the availability of foreign exchange. In late stages of development, an economy exhibits diversified production and has the capacity to adjust its exports and imports to the desired gap between investment and domestic saving. In Figure 20-2, this capacity is realized at L; after L, domestic saving becomes (and remains) the critical constraint on the rate of investment. The evidence suggests that the developing countries as a group are now in the middle stages of development

Figure 20-2   Capital-Absorption, Foreign Exchange, and Savings Constraints on the Rate of Investment

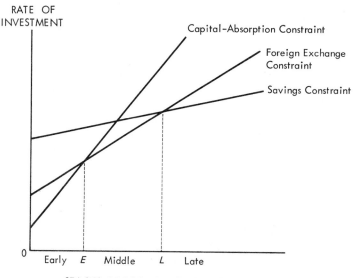

In the early stages of development, the critical constraint on investment is capital absorption. At *E*, however, foreign exchange becomes the critical constraint. In the late stage of development at *L*, savings becomes the critical constraint.

and hence the foreign exchange (trade) gap is the critical constraint for most of them.

Broadly speaking, two courses of action are open to the developing countries in the face of exchange gaps that will prevent the achievement of a target growth rate. The first course of action involves the use of policy instruments intended to reduce or eliminate the foreign exchange gap by expanding exports or contracting the level of required imports through import substitution. The second course of action is to obtain external financing of the foreign exchange gap from private and official sources.

THE DEMAND FOR A NEW INTERNATIONAL ECONOMIC ORDER

For a quarter century the developing countries have pressed collective demands on the developed countries for new policies and institutions that would orient the world economy toward economic development. These demands first came to a dramatic focus at the inaugural session of the United Nations Conference on Trade and Development (UNCTAD) held in Geneva in 1964. There the representatives of over seventy developing countries called upon both the West and East for action on a broad front as laid down in a report by Raul Prebisch, then Secretary-General of UNCTAD.[8] As a permanent agency of the United Nations, UNCTAD has continued to push vigorously for new policies in trade, aid, foreign investment, and technology.[9]

The general failure of the industrial countries to implement new policies and the remarkable demonstration of monopoly power by the OPEC cartel in late 1973 led to an intensification of demands that reached a formal culmination in the *Declaration and Action Programme on the Establishment of a New International Economic Order*, which was adopted by the General Assembly of the United Nations in May 1974.[10] In the declaration the members of the United Nations solemnly proclaimed their

> united determination to work urgently for THE ESTABLISHMENT OF A NEW INTERNATIONAL ECONOMIC ORDER based on equity, sovereign equality, interdependence, common interest and cooperation among all States, irrespective of their economic and social systems which shall correct inequalities and redress existing injustices, make it possible to eliminate the widening gap between the developed and the developing countries and ensure steadily accelerating economic and social development and peace and justice for present and future generations . . .

The declaration went on to state that

> the remaining vestiges of alien and colonial domination, foreign occupation, racial discrimination, *apartheid* and neo-colonialism in all its forms continue to be among the greatest obstacles to the full emancipation and progress of the developing countries and all the peoples involved.

Hence,

> it has proved impossible to achieve an even and balanced development of the international community under the existing international economic order. The gap between the developed and the developing countries continues to widen in a system which was established at a time when most of the developing countries did not even exist as independent States and which perpetuates inequality.

---

[8] *Towards a New Trade Policy for Development,* Report by the Secretary-General of the United Nations Conference on Trade and Development (New York: United Nations, 1964).

[9] The general purpose of UNCTAD is to promote the economic development of the Third World. Although the organization includes industrial and communist countries, it is dominated by the developing countries, because each country has an equal vote regardless of its size. UNCTAD can be regarded, therefore, as the OECD of the Third World. UNCTAD holds sessions about every four years.

[10] United Nations General Assembly Resolutions 3201 (S-VI) and 3202 (S-VI) (May 1, 1974). The declaration was adopted without a vote, but in debate several provisions were opposed by the United States and other industrial countries.

The declaration expressing the hope for a new international economic order (NIEO) was followed in December 1974 with the adoption of the *Charter of Economic Rights and Duties of States.*[11] The charter has several controversial provisions, including the right of a country to expropriate foreign property and determine any compensation to foreign owners and the right to associate in organizations of primary commodity producers (such as OPEC). The charter has as a fundamental purpose the establishment of the NIEO.

The Program of Action

The "Program of Action on the Establishment of a New International Economic Order," adopted by the United Nations General Assembly in 1974, identifies several efforts that should be taken to bring about "maximum economic cooperation and understanding among all States, particularly between developed and developing countries, based on the principles of dignity and sovereign equality." These efforts include actions to

(1) facilitate the functioning and further the aims of producers' associations;

(2) expedite the formulation of international commodity agreements to stabilize world markets for raw materials and primary commodities;

(3) improve access to markets in developed countries through the progressive removal of tariffs and nontariff barriers and the enlargement of the generalized systems of preferences;

(4) support initiatives in the regional, subregional, and interregional cooperation of developing countries, and thereby promote "collective self-reliance" among them;

(5) increase the flow of financial resources to the developing countries and mitigate the burden of external debt; and

(6) formulate and implement an international code of conduct for transnational corporations.

The first five actions (export cartels, international commodity agreements, access to industrial-country markets, regional integration, and external financial assistance) are treated in the next chapter. The regulation of transnational (multinational) corporations is left to Chapter 24.

Whither the NIEO?

The demands of the developing countries for a new international economic order proceed from a view of the international economy that differs radically from the liberal view of the developed countries. The *liberal view*, supported by economic doctrine centered on the theory of comparative advantage,

[11] United Nations General Assembly Resolution 3281 (XXIX), December 12, 1974. The resolution was adopted by a roll-call vote with 120 in favor, 6 opposed (including the United States), and 10 abstentions.

asserts that an open international economy of free trade will benefit all trading countries through the gains of international specialization. It follows that any government hindrances to the free international movement of goods and factors of production will make the international economy less productive than it otherwise would be. Similarly, any departures from perfect competition will generate market imperfections that distort the international allocation of resources. In particular, the liberal view contends that poor countries will benefit from the free flow of capital, technology, management, and other factors of production from the rich countries just as they will benefit from international specialization through trade. Among the major obstacles to economic development, therefore, are the highly protectionist policies of the poor countries and the massive intervention of their governments in the domestic economy.

The majority of Western economists hold to the liberal view, although few of them would accept it without qualification. Furthermore, the policies of the OECD countries and the principles underlying the GATT, the International Monetary Fund, the World Bank, and other international economic organizations all draw their inspiration from the liberal tradition, as does this book. It is the liberal conception of what the international economy is and should be that animates the response of the advanced countries to the demands for a new international economic order.

The developing countries demand a *managed* world economy directed toward economic development in place of the contemporary *market* world economy, which they believe helps the rich countries rather than the poor countries.

But demanding and getting are not synonymous. A series of North-South dialogues have produced little to please the LDCs. One may lament or celebrate the failure of the demands for a NIEO on ideological or political grounds, a matter that does not concern us here. What is of concern is that economic analysis raises serious doubts about the potential contribution of an NIEO to development in the LDCs. Almost certainly, therefore, a fully established NIEO would fail to live up to the economic promises of its declaration in 1974, however pleasing it would be to LDC governments for political reasons.

In any case, we are not likely to test that proposition, for a realization of an NIEO has been rendered most improbable by a slowdown of the world economy; severe macroeconomic imbalances among the United States, Japan, and West Germany; and intense global competition. In response to these changes, the industrial countries have turned inward, more resistant than ever to LDC demands. The decade of the 1980s, therefore, has probably marked the demise of the NIEO as an issue. But the passing of this issue does not eliminate the need for North-South cooperation in economic development. Indeed, relations between the rich and poor countries will remain one of the central issues of international economic policy into the next century.

SUMMARY

1. The drive for economic development shapes the attitudes, policies, and expectations of the developing countries in international trade, external assistance, and international investment.

2. The term *developing countries* generally denotes the noncommunist countries of Africa (except South Africa), the Middle East, Asia (except Japan), and Latin America.

3. The developing countries (LDCs) can be adequately described today only in terms of three subgroups: (1) high-income oil exporters, (2) upper-middle-income economies, and (3) lower-middle-income and low-income economies.

4. The developing countries must overcome many obstacles to achieve a satisfactory rate of economic growth, especially in per capita terms. The situation of the developing countries has been aptly described as interlocking sets of vicious circles that perpetuate economic stagnation and poverty. Major obstacles to economic development include lack of social overhead capital, lack of business managers and administrators, cultural blocks, and the population explosion.

5. The GNP of the developing countries as a group grew more rapidly than the GNP of the industrial countries over the past three decades. But per capita income remained at very low absolute levels for the low-income countries.

6. Capital formation is a necessary but not a sufficient condition for economic development. To increase its stock of capital, a country must invest part of its national product. The relationship between new investment and a subsequent increase in real output may be expressed as the *incremental capital-output ratio*, or k. Hence, the growth rate of gross domestic product is r/k, where r is the annual rate of new investment. The per capita growth rate, therefore, is $w = (r/k) - p$, where p is the annual rate of population growth.

7. The rate of domestic investment in a developing country may be constrained by the capacity of the country to absorb additional capital, by the level of its domestic savings, or by the availability of foreign exchange. In the absence of capital-absorption and savings gaps, the growth rate of a developing country may be limited by a *foreign exchange gap*. Broadly speaking, two courses of action are open to the developing countries in the face of exchange gaps that prevent the achievement of a target growth rate: (1) policies to expand exports or contract required imports, or (2) policies to obtain external financing from private and official sources.

8. For two decades the developing countries have pressed collective demands on the developed countries for new policies and institutions that would orient the world economy toward economic development.

9. In 1974 the General Assembly of the United Nations adopted the *Dec-

laration and Action Programme on the Establishment of a New International Economic Order, which was the formal culmination of the developing countries' demands.

10. The perception of the international economy held by the developing countries is shaped by a very different view from that of the West.

11. Economic analysis raises serious doubts about the potential contribution of an NIEO to development in the LDCs. The 1980s probably mark the demise of the NIEO as an issue.

QUESTIONS AND APPLICATIONS

1. "The situation of developing countries has been aptly described as interlocking sets of vicious circles." What is meant by this statement?

2. Why do many development experts consider the population explosion as the single greatest obstacle to economic development? Do you agree with them? Why or why not?

3. Suppose a country is investing 20 percent of its gross domestic product on an annual basis and its incremental capital-output ratio is 4. What, then, is the annual rate of growth of its gross domestic product? Suppose further that the annual growth rate of its population is 2.5 percent. What is the per capita annual growth rate of its gross domestic product?

4. Define the three constraints on the rate of domestic investment in a developing country. In the absence of a savings gap, how can a developing country have a foreign exchange gap?

5. What is meant by the phrase, "a new international economic order"?

6. Identify six efforts that should be taken according to the Program of Action on the Establishment of a New International Economic Order.

7. (a) What is the *liberal* view of the international economy?
   (b) How does this view differ from the view of the international economy underlying the NIEO?

SELECTED READINGS

See the list of readings given at the end of Chapter 21.

21

Trade Policies, External Assistance, and International Debt of Developing Countries

In Chapter 20, we observed that two broad courses of action are open to the developing countries in the face of exchange gaps preventing the attainment of target growth rates for their economies: (1) the use of policy instruments to encourage exports or discourage imports (import substitution), and (2) the use of external financing from private and official sources. These two courses of action are not exclusive, and most developing countries rely on both. The mix of trade and external financing varies across countries and across time, although a particular mix tends to dominate the policies of developing countries at a given period of time. In the 1970s, the developing countries generally relied on a mix of import-substitution trade policies and external financing. But in the 1980s, they shifted toward export-oriented policies as the availability of external financing diminished and import-substitution policies offered few, if any, opportunities to save foreign exchange.

This new direction of trade policies in the developing countries is the principal theme of this chapter. The chapter ends with an appraisal of the internation debt burden that now constrains the economic growth of many developing countries.

INTERNATIONAL TRADE AND ECONOMIC DEVELOPMENT

A foreign exchange or trade gap can constrain growth in a developing country, but can foreign trade also be an *autonomous* source of economic growth? The answer to this question is not a simple yes or no. Since international trade and economic growth are interdependent, trade may lead growth or growth may lead trade, depending on the circumstances.

In Chapter 3 we examined the effects of changes in factor endowments (which are associated mainly with economic growth) on international trade and showed that growth may be neutral, antitrade, or protrade.[1] We concluded that factor changes are a continuing phenomenon within countries, causing shifts in factor proportions and in comparative cost structures. We now reverse our analytical direction to look at the effects of changes in trade on economic growth and development.[2]

Conventional international trade theory (the Heckscher-Ohlin model) has ignored the growth effects of trade by assuming fixed supplies of homogeneous factors of production, the absence of technological innovation, and the sameness of production functions in different countries. By focusing on allocation effects, this theory demonstrates how international trade leads to a more efficient use of *existing* factors of production, thereby enabling countries to consume at a level beyond their production possibilities (transformation) curves. But it does not demonstrate whether or not international trade can shift the production possibilities curve outward as an independent agent of economic growth.

Although the H-O model is silent on the growth effects of trade, the classical and neoclassical stream of comparative advantage theory (to which the H-O model belongs) has argued that economic growth is stimulated by international specialization resulting from the free play of market forces. That is to say free trade not only utilizes existing factors of production more efficiently but also contributes to the quantity and quality of those factors. Rising exports lead to higher production in export industries, which in turn encourages higher investment to expand productive facilities and achieve economies of scale. Growing export industries open up new opportunities for employment and create new labor skills. This growth impulse spreads to the rest of the economy in a variety of ways: Other sectors are stimulated to provide inputs (raw materials, supplies, and capital equipment) to the export sector; the general economy is stimulated as the income effects of the dynamic export sector raise effective demand; and externalities (transportation, power, communication, and financial facilities created to support export industries), as well as labor and management skills, benefit the rest of the economy. Growing exports also finance growing imports, which stimulate growth by bringing in new products and technology and by compelling local import-competing industries to become more productive.

The majority of Western economists believe that international trade can be an "engine of growth" in the classical and neoclassical sense. To support this position, they can appeal to history, for the evidence is strong that in the nineteenth century exports led growth in Great Britain and several other now-advanced countries and have also done so since World War II in Western Europe and Japan.

---

[1] See Chapter 3.

[2] The effects of factor transfers (foreign investment and technology) on growth and development are treated in Chapter 24.

But if exports can be an "engine of growth," how do we explain the failure of the low-income developing countries to enter a self-sustaining growth process? Why has the growth effect of their exports been so weak? Our general answer is that underdeveloped economies lack the capacity to translate growth in their export sectors to other sectors. But this answer begs the question unless we draw a distinction between economic growth and economic development. *Economic growth* is an increase in an economy's output, but *economic development* includes not only growth but a political, social, and cultural transformation of society to overcome the obstacles we discussed earlier. It would seem that international trade can contribute a growth stimulus but that that stimulus is not powerful enough to transform preindustrial societies.

More specifically, a dynamic export sector will have only minimal growth effects when that sector has few *linkages* with the rest of the economy. The classical example is the "enclave" export economies of the mineral-exporting countries of Asia, Africa, and Latin America. Mineral exports were developed in these countries during the nineteenth century (for example, copper in Chile and tin in Malaysia) by foreign investors who provided the capital, technology, management, and markets for mineral exploration and production. The production process was capital-intensive, it employed few local workers, and most other inputs (machinery, tools, supplies, and even foodstuffs) were imported from abroad. Furthermore, the location of production was frequently geographically distant from centers of population in the host country. Apart from the few local inputs, much of the income generated in this sector was repatriated abroad by the foreign owners or accrued to a small upper class that spent it on imports of consumer goods unavailable at home. This absence of linkages between the export sector and other sectors created a *dual economy* consisting of a self-sufficient export sector using capital, advanced technology, and skilled labor and a primitive, self-sufficient domestic sector. Although the experience of the mineral-exporting developing countries is an extreme example of the failure of exports (or imports) to stimulate economic development, much the same can be said about the developing countries that relied on exports of agricultural products.

To conclude, international trade is *not sufficient* for economic development. Although it provides a growth stimulus, its effects may fail to spread beyond the export sector. What is necessary is the capacity of the economy to respond to that stimulus, a capacity that is dependent on the existence of political, social, and cultural conditions that are disposed toward growth. But if this capacity exists, then an economy can also respond to *domestic* growth stimuli.[3] Although its development effects may be limited, we should

---

[3] Thus, international trade may not even be necessary for economic development if a country has an extensive resource base and domestic markets large enough to support economies of scale in production. Few developing countries fit this description, but The People's Republic

keep in mind that international trade can lead to higher standards of living through the gains from trade even in the absence of any development effects. Thus, the argument against trade on development grounds is not an argument against trade on welfare grounds, although this distinction is commonly overlooked by the developing countries. Later in this chapter, we offer evidence to support the proposition that outward-oriented trade policies lead to more rapid economic growth than inward-oriented policies.

EXPORT PROBLEMS OF THE DEVELOPING COUNTRIES

The export growth of the developing countries has not kept pace with their rising import requirements for economic growth. In this section we examine problems that affect LDC exports.

Slow Growth of Commodity Exports

Over two-thirds of the exports of the low-income developing countries (excluding China and India) are agricultural raw materials and minerals that face a slow-growing demand in world markets. To make matters worse, the primary exports of the low-income developing nations have expanded more slowly than those of the developed nations: Technological innovations have greatly improved the productive capacities of primary industries (especially agriculture) in developed nations while the population explosion in developing nations has absorbed more of their primary output, leaving less for export. As a consequence, the industrial nations have increased their share of primary exports. Adding further to the troubles of the developing countries is the price instability of primary exports, accompanied at times by a longer-run deterioration in their prices relative to the prices of manufactures. Table 21-1 indicates that the volumes of the commodity exports of the developing countries grew much more slowly than the volume of their exports of manufactures over the years 1965–1984.

Why do commodity exports grow less rapidly than industrial exports? A full answer to this question would involve an examination of the specific supply and demand factors that influence the production and consumption of each of the many individual commodities. Such an examination is out of the question here. Instead we shall look at the main features of the demand for primary commodities in the industrial areas and their effects on the

---

of China, India, and Brazil may be examples. In the past, the Soviet Union and the United States may provide examples. Kravis, for instance, concludes that trade (and capital movements) were "handmaidens, not engines of growth" in the development of the United States in the nineteenth century. See Irving B. Kravis, "The Role of Exports in Nineteenth-Century United States Growth," *Economic Development and Cultural Change* 20 (April 1972): 387–405.

TABLE 21-1   Average Annual Percentage Growth of Export Volumes of the
Developing Countries by Product Category, 1965–1984

Product Category	1965–1973	1973–1980	1980–1984
Commodities			
Food	2.9	4.3	1.7
Nonfood	2.7	1.2	0.1
Metals and minerals	4.8	7.0	−0.2
Fuels	4.0	−0.8	1.8
Manufactures	11.6	13.8	9.5

Source: The World Bank, *World Development Report 1988* (New York: Oxford University Press, 1988), Table A8, p. 191.

primary exports of the developing areas. It is widely agreed that the slow, long-term growth of primary exports is traceable mainly to market conditions in the industrial areas rather than to supply conditions in the developing areas, although the latter should not be ignored.[4]

The *income elasticity of demand* for primary products tends to be low, taking on values below one.[5] This contrasts with the higher income elasticities for manufactured goods, which seldom fall below unity. To illustrate, a 4 percent increase in national income may cause only a 2 percent increase in the consumption of agricultural products (income elasticity equal to 0.5) but a 6 percent increase in the consumption of manufactured goods (income elasticity equal to 1.5). Thus, consumption of primary products in industrial areas does not keep pace with their general economic growth.

Low-income elasticities for foodstuffs reflect family spending patterns. As far back as 1857 Ernst Engel observed that a poor family spends a higher proportion of its income on food than a better-off family. Once a household has satisfied its needs for the basic necessities of food, shelter, and clothing, it spends additional income on durable consumer goods, personal services, travel, education, and the like.

The depressing effects of low-income elasticities on the consumption of primary commodities in the developed nations have been reinforced by a continuing stream of synthetic manufactured materials that replace natural

---

[4] Variations in supply conditions (such as crop yields) play a more important role in the short-run fluctuations of commodity exports.

[5] Income elasticity of demand measures the response in the amount demanded to a change in income, assuming the mathematical expression $(dQ/Q)/dY/Y)$. We can interpret this as the percentage change in amount demanded divided by the percentage change in income.

materials. Starting before World War I with rayon and manufactured nitrates, the development of synthetics has now reached flood proportions in the industrial nations. After World War II synthetic fibers, artificial rubber, and detergents strongly challenged cotton, wool, jute, abaca, oils, fats, natural rubber, and other commodities. Today, for example, the rubber used in the manufacture of passenger automobile tires in the United States is synthetic. To conclude, synthetics have cut deeply into the consumption of raw materials and are partly responsible for the relatively slow growth of commodity exports from the developing to the industrial countries. This is not to say that natural materials are doomed to be entirely replaced by synthetics. It does mean that they must compete in quality and price with manufactured substitutes.

All of the industrial countries have agricultural programs that protect their farmers from competition in the open market. Most frequently, this involves the maintenance of domestic agricultural prices at levels higher than those prevailing in world markets. To prevent foreign producers from capitalizing on this situation, imports are restricted by tariffs or quotas. The variable import levies of the European Community are an example of such restrictions. In addition to import restrictions that are by-products of agricultural support programs, European countries impose revenue duties or taxes on tropical agricultural products they do not produce at home.

To sum up, a variety of forces—low income elasticities, displacement by synthetics, import restrictions, and primary production in the industrial countries—have acted to curb the growth of primary exports from the developing countries.

In contrast to their primary-commodity exports, the manufactured exports of LDCs have increased sharply over the past quarter-century. But only a handful of developing countries (the newly industrializing countries) account for most of these exports. Clearly, the low-income developing countries need to diversify their exports away from commodities toward manufactures if they are to achieve the export growth needed to support economic development. The main problem facing LDC *manufactured* exports is not slow growth in world demand but rather the imposition of import restrictions by industrial countries to protect their traditional manufacturing industries. Protection is almost certain to intensify as the LDCs penetrate more deeply into the markets for manufactures of the industrial countries.

Short-Run Price Instability of Commodity Exports

In addition to slow growth, the commodity exports of developing countries are subject to frequent and sudden price changes that cause unpredictable short-run fluctuations in export earnings. This instability can be detrimental to economic growth when it disrupts development programs, because then the actual supply of foreign exchange falls short of the projected supply.

The price volatility of commodities in world trade results from low *price* elasticities of supply and demand. Cyclical and random shifts in demand in the industrial countries cause sharp price responses because the supply of commodities is relatively fixed in the short run. Prices also react violently to shifts in supply, such as crop-yield fluctuations, because the consumption of primary commodities in the industrial countries is relatively insensitive to price changes (price elasticity is below unity).

Deterioration in the Terms of Trade of Developing Countries

Some economists have postulated a persistent, long-run tendency for the terms of trade of the developing countries to deteriorate. Raul Prebisch explained this alleged tendency along the following lines.[6] Because of the slow growth in demand for primary commodities, only a declining proportion of the labor force in the developing countries can be absorbed in their production. Improvements in the productivity of primary activities cause an even further drop in that proportion. Thus, the labor force has to be shifted to industrial production, but this takes a very long time and meanwhile the surplus labor exerts a downward pressure on the real level of wages in the developing countries. Higher productivity in the primary export industries, therefore, is reflected in lower prices rather than in higher wages. Thus, the fruits of technical advance in the developing countries are passed on to the industrial countries. In the industrial countries, on the other hand, the relative shortage of labor and the strong labor unions keep wages rising in step with rising productivity, preventing any fall in prices. Hence, a persistent deterioration of the terms of trade of the developing countries is the result of fundamental structural differences between the industrial centers and the peripheral, developing countries.[7]

The Prebisch model is hardly proof of a built-in secular tendency for the terms of trade to turn against the developing countries. The historical record is ambiguous because of data inadequacies and the well-known difficulties of index number construction.[8] Worsening terms of trade have alternated with periods of improving terms of trade.[9]

---

[6] For a detailed presentation of his views, see Raul Prebisch, "Commercial Policy in the Underdeveloped Countries," *American Economic Review*, May 1959, pp. 251–73. Similar views are expressed by Gunnar Myrdal in *Rich Lands and Poor: The Road to World Prosperity* (New York: Harper & Row, 1957).

[7] Although different, the Prebisch model brings to mind the notion of "immiserizing growth" introduced in Chapter 3. Immiserizing growth is possible only when export demand is inelastic *and* protrade growth actually reduces domestic production of import-competing goods. These and other stringent assumptions make immiserizing growth a theoretical curiosity that is not likely to be matched by real experience in the developing countries. See Jagdish Bhagwati, "Immiserizing Growth: A Geometrical Note," *Review of Economic Studies,* June 1958, pp. 201–5.

[8] In practice, the net barter terms of trade is calculated as an index: $\Sigma P_{x1}/\Sigma P_{m1} \div \Sigma P_{x0}/\Sigma P_{m0}$, where ΣP_x and ΣP_m are weighted aggregates of export and import prices, respectively; 0 refers to the base period; and 1 refers to the year being compared with the base. The choice of the

Figure 21-1   Real Commodity Prices, 1970–1987

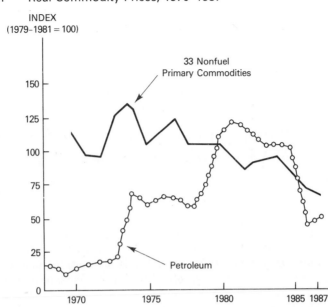

INDEX
(1979–1981 = 100)

33 Nonfuel
Primary Commodities

Petroleum

1970   1975   1980   1985 1987

Note: Real prices are annual average nominal prices in dollars, deflated by the annual change in the manufacturing unit value index (MUV), a measure of the price of industrial country exports to developing countries.

Source: The World Bank, *World Development Report 1988* (New York: Oxford University Press, 1988), Figure 1.6, p.25.

The evidence, as presented in Figure 21-1, indicates a sharp deterioration in the prices of commodities relative to the prices of manufactures between 1980 and 1987. Slower economic growth in the industrial countries depressed demand while technological innovation continued to cut demand for industrial raw materials. At the same time, the supply of commodities increased due to growing subsidies and trade protection in the industrial

base period is important, since a base period with highly favorable terms of trade is likely to show a subsequent deterioration and vice versa. In constructing index numbers, it is also difficult to allow for quality changes, which occur more frequently in industrial than in primary products. Another concept, known as the *income terms of trade,* multiplies the change in the net barter terms of trade by the accompanying change in the quantity of exports, thereby measuring the change in export *receipts* relative to import prices. Because it indicates a change in a country's capacity to import, the income terms of trade is a more appropriate concept for the developing countries, but it is seldom used by governments. Algebraically, the income terms of trade assumes this expression: $\Sigma P_x Q_x / \Sigma P_m$, where $\Sigma P_x Q_x$ is aggregate value of exports and ΣP_m is the weighted aggregate import price.

[9] For a recent study, see Enzo R. Grilli and Maw Cheng Yang, "Primary Commodity Prices, Manufactured Goods Prices, and the Terms of Trade of Developing Countries: What the Long Run Shows," *The World Bank Economic Review,* January 1988, pp. 1–48.

countries. For the 1970–1987 period as a whole, the real prices of nonfuel commodities and the real price of petroleum show very different patterns. In the 1970s, the real prices of nonfuel commodities were very unstable but they ended the decade at about the same level as they began it. In radical contrast, the real oil price rose eightfold in the 1970s as the oil cartel OPEC (Organization of Petroleum Exporting Countries) successfully exerted its monopoly power. But as that power waned in the 1980s, the real price of petroleum fell abruptly, causing serious adjustment problems for all oil exporters. (OPEC is discussed later in this chapter.)

TRADE POLICIES OF THE DEVELOPING COUNTRIES

The export problems of the developing countries are commonly aggravated by their own trade and general economic policies. The dominant goal of government policymakers in the developing countries is economic development, which is too often viewed as industrialization rather than self-sustaining economic growth. Since other goals are regarded as subordinate, the internal conflict of goals is resolved in favor of economic development except when events force policymakers to pay attention to matters such as inflation or the balance of payments. The policy tools chosen by many developing countries to advance their economic development have been economic controls, protection, and inflation; in so doing, they have rejected free markets, international specialization, and monetary stability. Unfortunately the neglect of internal and external balance and a disregard for the economics of comparative advantage have created problems that prevent the attainment of development targets. Two problems in particular deserve some comment: *inflation* and *import substitution*.

Inflation and Import Substitution

When developing countries seek to close savings gaps through budgetary deficits (rather than surpluses), the resulting creation of new money breeds inflation and balance of payments deficits. Reluctant to correct these deficits by cutting domestic spending (and thereby falling short of development targets) or by exchange devaluation (in the belief it would not work, would cause more inflation, or for political reasons), governments respond with import and exchange restrictions. As the inflation proceeds, therefore, exchange rates become increasingly overvalued, hindering exports and encouraging the circumvention of import controls. Eventually controls break down and devaluation takes place. But unless devaluation is accompanied by an austerity policy (higher taxes and cutbacks in government spending), the vicious circle starts up once again. To sum up, inflation, overvalued exchange rates, and exchange restrictions all too frequently limit the exports of developing countries.

During the 1930s, countries in Latin America progressively introduced regimes of high protection to restrict imports of consumer goods. Although initially provoked by the world depression, these protectionist policies were soon directed toward the promotion of internal industrialization. Isolated by import barriers, local enterprise was encouraged to manufacture consumer goods to replace imports. Because of a ready market and lack of foreign competition, import substitution proceeded quickly in shoes, clothing, household articles, and other nondurable consumer products. Furthermore, many European and U.S. companies were induced to set up plants in Latin American countries when their export markets were closed off by protection. During World War II, import substitution was intensified when many manufactured goods could not be imported from the industrial countries. After the war, import substitution was extended by some countries in Latin America (notably Mexico, Brazil, and Argentina) to cover durable consumer goods, such as automobiles and capital equipment. With political independence, many developing countries in Asia and Africa followed the lead of Latin America.

When an economy develops, import substitution occurs as a natural market phenomenon: Economic growth involves a continual domestic substitution of imports and their replacement by new import goods. But when import substitution is promoted through protectionist policies, then its national costs may exceed its national benefits. When protection is given to lines of production that do not have a potential comparative advantage, a country builds high-cost industries that are in fact a permanent drag on the economy. An indiscriminate policy of import substitution becomes, then, a policy of economic self-sufficiency and a perversion of the infant-industry argument.[10]

After sixty years of high protection, the Latin American countries have run out of easy opportunities for import substitution. Furthermore, the costs of import substitution are increasingly evident: diversified industrial plants that are entirely oriented toward the domestic market and whose level of cost, quality control, design engineering, and product innovation is noncompetitive in export markets. The absurdity of extreme import substitution in countries with small domestic markets that do not allow economies of scale is amply demonstrated by automobile production in several Latin American countries. In Colombia, Peru, and Chile the production costs of vehicles have run two to three times higher than the costs of similar vehicles in the international market. Apart from the social costs of inefficient resource allocation, it is even doubtful that local automobile production saved foreign exchange for these countries because they imported most of the materials and components.

---

[10] See Chapter 6 for an evaluation of the infant-industry argument.

More generally, import-substitution policies seldom decrease a country's dependence on imports; rather they shift the composition of imports from consumer goods to industrial inputs and capital equipment.

Summing up, indiscriminate import-substitution policies are self-defeating; they do not foster self-sustaining growth over the longer run, they are seldom net savers of foreign exchange, and they discourage exports of manufactured products. Fortunately policymakers in the developing countries are becoming more aware of the dangers of blanket import substitution.

Inward-oriented development policies involving inflation and import substitution have been rejected by some developing countries in favor of outward-oriented policies dependent on monetary stability and exports. These differences in policy orientation go a long way toward explaining the striking variations in the export performance of individual developing countries. These variations are found even among countries that face similar external market conditions.

Comparative Analysis of Outward- and Inward-Oriented Trade Strategies

Until recently, we have lacked empirical data on the relation between trade strategies and economic performance. But now this deficiency has been corrected by economists at the World Bank.[11] The World Bank study classifies forty-one developing countries according to the orientation of their trade strategies in two periods, 1963–1973 and 1973–1985. (These countries accounted for two-thirds of the total output of all developing countries in 1985.) Trade strategies are classified into four categories:

1. A *strongly outward-oriented* strategy does not use trade controls or uses only low-level ones. Also, the exchange rate does not discriminate between importables and exportables. Hence, production for the domestic market is not favored over production for export, and conversely.

2. A *moderately outward-oriented* strategy is biased toward production for domestic rather than export markets. But the average rate of effective protection is low, and the effective exchange rate is only slightly higher (the domestic price of a unit of foreign currency is lower) for imports than for exports.

3. A *moderately inward-oriented* strategy has an overall incentive structure that distinctly favors production for the domestic market. Effective protection is relatively high, the use of import controls and licensing is extensive, and the exchange rate is clearly overvalued.

4. A *strongly inward-oriented strategy* greatly favors production for the domestic market. The rate of effective protection is high, direct control and licensing disincentives to the traditional export sector

---

[11] See The World Bank, *World Development Report 1987* (New York: Oxford University Press, 1987), pp. 78–112.

are pervasive, positive incentives to nontraditional exportables are few or nonexistent, and the exchange rate is significantly overvalued.

The World Bank study demonstrates that trade strategies have a marked influence on industrial performance, manufactured exports, capital-output ratios, and gross domestic product.

Table 21-2 shows the average annual percentage growth of real manufacturing value added for the forty-one developing countries grouped by trade orientation (strategy). The table also lists the countries belonging to each group in the two periods. In the first period (1963–1973), the average growth of the strongly outward-oriented countries was 15.6 percent compared with only 5.3 percent average growth for the strongly inward-oriented countries. In the second period (1973–1985), growth rates were 10.0 and 3.1 percent, respectively.

Figure 21-2 is hardly surprising. Between 1965 and 1973, manufactured exports of the strongly and moderately outward-oriented countries grew by 14.8 and 16.1 percent, respectively. This compares with 10.3 and

TABLE 21-2   Average Annual Percentage Growth of Real Manufacturing Value Added for Forty-One Developing Countries by Trade Orientation, 1963–1973 and 1973–1985

	1963–1973	1973–1985
Outward-oriented	10.3	5.2
Strongly outward-oriented[1]	15.6	10.0
Moderately outward-oriented[2]	9.4	4.0
Inward-oriented	6.8	4.3
Moderately inward-oriented[3]	9.6	5.1
Strongly inward-oriented[4]	5.3	3.1

Note: Although Yugoslavia is listed as a moderatley inward-oriented country for both periods, the percentages in this table exclude it for lack of data.

[1] For 1963–1973 and 1973–1985: Hong Kong, South Korea, and Singapore.

[2] For 1963–1973: Brazil, Cameroon, Colombia, Costa Rica, Ivory Coast, Guatemala, Indonesia, Israel, Malaysia, and Thailand. For 1973–1985: Brazil, Chile, Israel, Malaysia, Thailand, Tunisia, Turkey, and Uruguay.

[3] For 1963–1973: Bolivia, El Salvador, Honduras, Kenya, Madagascar, Mexico, Nicaragua, Nigeria, Philippines, Senegal, Tunisia, and Yugoslavia. For 1973–1985: Cameroon, Colombia, Costa Rica, Ivory Coast, El Salvador, Guatemala, Honduras, Indonesia, Kenya, Mexico, Nicaragua, Pakistan, Philippines, Senegal, Sri Lanka, and Yugoslavia.

[4] For 1963–1973: Argentina, Bangladesh, Burundi, Chile, Dominican Republic, Ethiopia, Ghana, India, Pakistan, Peru, Sri Lanka, Sudan, Tanzania, Turkey, Uruguay, and Zambia. For 1973–1985: Argentina, Bangladesh, Bolivia, Burundi, Dominican Republic, Ethiopia, Ghana, India, Madagascar, Nigeria, Peru, Sudan, Tanzania, and Zambia.

Source: Based on The World Bank, *World Development Report 1987* (New York: Oxford University Press, 1987), Table 5.1, p. 87.

Figure 21-2 Average Annual Percentage Growth of Manufactured Exports of Forty-One Countries Grouped by Trade Orientation

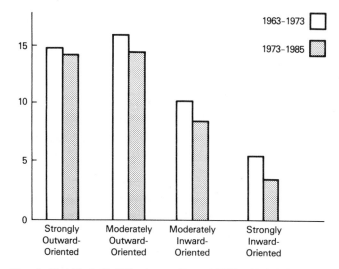

5.7 percent for the moderately and strongly inward-oriented countries, respectively. In the later period (1973–1985), growth rates were 14.2 and 14.5 percent compared with 8.5 and 3.7 percent.

Figure 21-3 indicates that the outward-oriented countries made more efficient use of their incremental capital resources than the inward-oriented countries. In both periods, the incremental capital-output ratio (the ratio of gross investment to the increase in GDP) was lower for the two outward-oriented groups than for the inward-oriented groups. In the first period, the ratio for the outward-oriented countries was 3.3 and for the inward-oriented countries, 5.2. Although the capital-output ratio deteriorated for all groups in the 1973–1985 period, it remained significantly lower for the inward-oriented groups.

Figure 21-4 shows a decline in the growth of real gross domestic product for both outward-oriented and inward-oriented countries. In the 1963–1973 period, the annual average growth for the strongly outward-oriented group was 9.5 percent, more than twice the 4.1 percent achieved by the strongly inward-oriented group. This gap widened in the 1973–1985 period (7.7 percent and 2.5, respectively).

It is evident that over the past quarter century the economic performance of developing countries following outward-oriented trade strategies

Figure 21-3   Average Annual Incremental Capital-Output Ratio of Forty-One Developing Countries Grouped by Trade Orientation

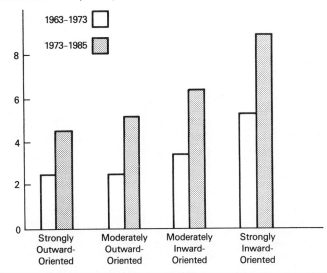

Source: Derived from The World Bank, *World Development Report 1987* (New York: Oxford University Press, 1987), Figure 5.2, p. 84.

has been superior to that of developing countries following inward-oriented strategies. This advantage of outward-oriented strategies is owing to the greater effectiveness of open markets over controlled markets in stimulating economic growth. The World Bank study demonstrates that open markets avoid the costs of protection, introduce international competition to domestic markets, and improve the efficiency of capital allocation.

The export problems of the developing countries are caused by both *external* market conditions (principally the slow growth and instability of commodity exports attributable to demand in the industrial countries) and *internal* conditions that are substantially influenced by the policies of developing countries. This conclusion points to another: Changes in the trade policies of the *industrial* countries are a desirable but not a necessary condition for an alleviation of the export problems of the developing countries. As is true of economic development in general, the major effort must come from the developing countries themselves.

OTHER POLICIES RELATING TO TRADE

In addition to their own trade policies, the developing countries have attempted to overcome foreign exchange gaps blocking economic growth by

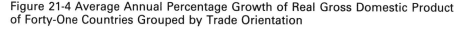

Figure 21-4 Average Annual Percentage Growth of Real Gross Domestic Product of Forty-One Countries Grouped by Trade Orientation

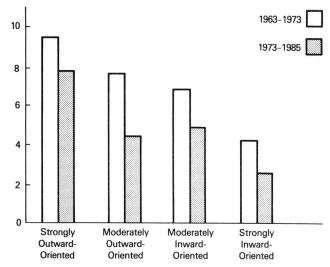

Source: Derived from the World Bank, *World Development Report 1987* (New York: Oxford University Press, 1987), Figure 5.2, p. 84.

resort to *multilateral* arrangements involving several countries. Some of these arrangements, notably international commodity agreements and export cartels, are intended to alleviate the problems of commodity exports. Other arrangements are aimed at opening up the markets of the industrial countries to the manufactures of developing countries. Much more comprehensive are regional integration schemes to promote economic growth through free trade among member countries.

International Commodity Agreements (ICAs)

International commodity agreements are arrangements between producing and consuming countries that seek to stabilize the prices of specific primary commodities (such as wheat, coffee, rubber, and tin) through measures that involve buffer stocks, export controls, and export-import commitments.

Analytically, we can distinguish two different functions of international commodity agreements: (1) moderating short-term price fluctuations caused by random disturbances in supply and demand, and (2) maintaining prices above their long-term equilibrium levels so as to transfer income from consumers to producers.

The contribution to economic development of agreements that only moderate short-term fluctuations in price is questionable. It can be shown

TABLE 21-3   Revenue Effects of Price Stabilization with Market Instability

	Shifts in Supply		Shifts in Demand	
	Increase	Decrease	Increase	Decrease
Free market	P ↓ Q ↑	P ↑ Q ↓	P ↑ Q ↑	P ↓ Q ↓
Stabilized price	P̄ Q ↑	P̄ Q ↓	P̄ Q	P̄ Q

that price stability *decreases* revenue stability when the cause of market instability is a shift in supply. Table 21-3 reveals why this is so.

In a free market, an increase in supply (a shift in the supply schedule to the right) leads to a decline in price (P) that is offset in some degree by an increase in the amount demanded (Q), and conversely with a decrease in supply. These offsetting changes in P and Q act to moderate the instability of revenues (PQ) received by producers. In contrast, price stabilization intensifies revenue instability when supply shifts occur, because the price (P̄) is held constant by the buffer stock agency through purchases of excess supply (when supply increases) or sales from the buffer stock (when supply decreases). Because producers can sell as much as they produce at P̄, their revenues (P̄Q) fluctuate directly with shifts in supply.

However, when market instability is caused by shifts in demand, then price stabilization also brings about revenue stabilization: P̄ and Q do not change and, therefore, P̄Q is constant. In contrast, in a free market shifts in demand cause P and Q to move in the same direction, with a corresponding instability in PQ.

What of the *amount* of revenue received by producers over time? Price stabilization *increases* total revenue over time when market instability is caused by supply shifts but *decreases* total revenue over time when market instability is caused by demand shifts.

In general, then, international commodity agreements are not effective policy instruments to stabilize commodity export revenues. Furthermore, they can damage rather than benefit the export earnings and welfare of developing countries.

This conclusion is supported by a study of the potential benefits to developing countries from the stabilization of the prices of 17 primary commodities based on actual price behavior over the period 1954–1973.[12] This study found that the *source* of price instability (whether demand or supply shifts) is a critical factor in determining the gain to producers and consumers

---

[12] Ezriel M. Brook and Enzo R. Grilli, "Commodity Price Stabilization and the Developing World," *Finance and Development*, March 1977, pp. 8–11.

Chapter 21 – Trade Policies, External Assistance, and International Debt

in terms of welfare (producers' and consumers' surplus) and income (total export earnings). If the price instability was caused by shifts in demand, then stabilization of the long-term price trend would *decrease* the gains of the commodity-exporting countries. Conversely, if the price instability was caused by shifts in supply, then exporting countries would gain from price stabilization. As shown in Table 21-4, the developing countries would benefit as *producers* from price stabilization in only five commodities—sugar, coffee, cocoa, cotton, and jute—while they would benefit as *consumers* from the price stabilization of wheat. In all other commodities (including all minerals), the developing countries would most probably suffer economic loss from price stabilization.

It follows from this analysis that international commodity agreements are not likely to help the developing countries unless they transfer resources to them via prices that are maintained above their long-run equilibrium levels. But such agreements are the most difficult to negotiate (because they

TABLE 21-4　Source of Price Fluctuations and Potential Benefits to Developing Countries from Price Stabilization

	Source of Export Price Fluctuations		Developing Countries' Exports Larger Than Imports	Developing Countries' Imports Larger Than Exports	Potential Benefit from Stabilizing Export Prices*
	Demand	Supply			
Wheat	X			X	+
Maize	X		X		−
Rice		X		X	−
Sugar		X	X		+
Coffee		X	X		+
Cocoa		X	X		+
Tea	X		X		−
Cotton		X	X		+
Jute		X	X		+
Wool	X		X		−
Sisal	X		X		−
Rubber	X		X		−
Copper	X		X		−
Lead	X		X		−
Zinc	X		X		−
Tin		X	X		−
Bauxite	X		X		−

Note: Benefit is marked by +; loss is marked by −.

Source: Ezriel M. Brook and Enzo R. Grilli, "Commodity Price Stabilization and the Developing World," *Finance and Development,* March 1977, p. 11.

oppose the interests of producers and consumers) and the most difficult to operate (because they oppose long-run market forces). For one thing, demand must be price inelastic; otherwise higher prices will cause a decline in export earnings. This rules out commodities that have partial substitutes (synthetic or natural) or are producible in the importing countries. In addition, the exporting countries forming an agreement must have a monopoly over supply and they must agree to restrict exports and eventually production. The higher the price, the more unstable the agreement: Exporting countries will have stronger incentives to export beyond their quotas and importing countries to look elsewhere for imports. All in all, the prospects of any substantial transfer of resources to the developing countries appear dim. Export diversification and external assistance offer far more promise as ways of relieving the foreign exchange gap.

The history of international commodity agreements is largely one of failure, and their outlook for the future is bleak. Some fifty ICAs, covering thirteen commodities, have been negotiated since 1931. But today only four (involving cocoa, coffee, rubber, and sugar) are active, and they play only a minor role in international commodity trade. A study of fifty-one agreements found that their median life was only 2.5 years.[13] The International Tin Agreement—long hailed as the most successful ICA—collapsed in 1985 as the buffer stock fund went bankrupt in a vain attempt to hold up the price of tin.[14] The Integrated Program for Commodities has been stalled since its proposal by UNCTAD in 1976.[15]

The failure of the Integrated Program for Commodities is hardly a matter of regret for its benefits for the LDCs are problematic, yet it carries economic costs (misallocation of resources) by freezing patterns of international specialization and thereby protecting inefficient producers. If the purpose of international commodity agreements is to stabilize LDC commodity export earnings, then *compensatory financing* is a superior policy instrument.

Basically, a compensatory scheme would sustain the import capacity of a developing country by matching any decline in its external purchasing power due to worsening terms of trade with an equal amount of external financial assistance. Several technical problems would have to be overcome to set up such an arrangement. First, it would have to be decided from which base year the terms of trade should be calculated. That is, to what degree (if any) should compensation be granted for a past deterioration in the terms

---

[13] Cited in Jere R. Behrman, *International Commodity Agreements: An Evaluation of the UNCTAD Integrated Commodity Program* (Washington, D.C. Overseas Development Council, 1977), p. 21

[14] See "Commodity Agreements and Commodity Markets: Lessons from Tin," *The Economic Journal*, March 1988, pp. 1–15.

[15] At the fourth UNCTAD meeting in Nairobi in 1976, it was resolved to negotiate eighteen international commodity agreements that would be financed by a *common fund* of $6 billion. Although the industrial countries accepted the idea of a common fund "in principle" (more for political than economic reasons), the Integrated Program for Commodities has not become operational due to lack of funding.

of trade? Once the scheme is in operation, should compensatory financing be based on yearly changes in the terms of trade or on some other time period? Suppose the terms of trade of a developing nation improved. Should the scheme compensate industrial countries whose terms of trade have deteriorated? How would the financing be shared by the industrial countries? These and similar questions suggest the difficulties in designing a workable mechanism that would be acceptable to the participating governments.[16]

If the purpose of international commodity agreements is to transfer resources from rich to poor countries, then official assistance programs can be far more effective, because they can be geared to the special development needs of individual LDCs. But the most promising remedy for LDC commodity export problems lies in diversification into other export commodities and into manufactures. The intense interest of the developing countries in international commodity agreements stems as much from the commodity concentration of their exports as from their overall dependence on commodities in general. Many developing countries earn most of their foreign exchange from exports of one or two commodities. Diversification into other export commodities facing different market conditions would reduce dependence on a single commodity. A more fundamental diversification calls for a shift toward manufactures.

Export Cartels

A *cartel* is an association of producers of a commodity that seeks to control the market through price-fixing, the allocation of market territories, supply restrictions, and other measures. A successful cartel, therefore, creates a monopoly or near monopoly that exploits the market by charging prices higher than it could obtain in a competitive market. A cartel becomes an international export cartel when it tries to dominate the world market by controlling the exports of member producers located in two or more countries. The remarkable success of the OPEC oil cartel in the 1970s stimulated efforts by the developing countries to establish export cartels in other primary products.

The OPEC Oil Cartel By the 1970s the industrial West had become highly dependent on a few developing countries to feed a growing appetite for oil. In 1972 the United States imported about one-third, Western Europe nearly all, and Japan all of their oil requirements. This high and rising dependence set the stage for the ascendancy of the OPEC oil cartel and the oil crisis of 1973–1974.

The Organization of Petroleum Exporting Countries was formed in

---

[16] Compensatory financing was started by the International Monetary Fund in 1963. The IMF Compensatory Financing Facility allows LDCs to obtain foreign exchange for up to 100 percent of their quotas to compensate for temporary shortfalls in export receipts from the medium-term values of their exports. Members using the facility are required to repay the facility when their exports recover. The European Community also has an export-earnings stabilization scheme (STABEX) for developing countries associated with the Community.

1961 by Iran, Iraq, Kuwait, Saudi Arabia, and Venezuela in response to a unilateral reduction in the posted price of crude oil in 1960 by the major multinational petroleum companies, a reduction that cut the oil revenues of these countries.[17] A surplus of oil in the 1960s weakened the bargaining power of the OPEC countries vis-à-vis the petroleum companies, which possessed the only worldwide marketing networks. Efforts by OPEC to control the supply of oil by allocating production among its member countries (prorationing) were frustrated by a reluctance to accept national export quotas.

In 1970, the multinational petroleum companies still maintained control over the price and volume of oil produced in the OPEC countries. Within a year, however, the balance of power shifted radically against the petroleum companies as the worldwide buyers' market turned into a sellers' market that promised to endure into the forseeable future. Holding 80 percent of the world's known oil reserves and providing 90 percent of the world's oil exports, OPEC quickly took advantage of this power shift in a series of historic confrontations with the petroleum companies that transformed the international petroleum industry. However, it was the first oil crisis (1973–1974) that demonstrated the awesome monopoly power of OPEC, probably as much to the surprise of OPEC as to the West.

An explosive combination of politics and economics in the fall of 1973 generated an embargo of oil exports to the United States and the Netherlands, a cutback in oil production, and a quadrupling of oil prices, forcing the world economy into an unprecedented energy crisis. The crisis was provoked by the Arab-Israeli war that started in October 1973. Deciding to use oil as a weapon, the Arab countries cut production by 25 percent and in December raised the price of oil to $11.65 per barrel.

The second oil crisis (1979–1980) was caused by the Iranian revolution, which shut off oil production in Iran, OPEC's second largest producer. OPEC quickly responded to the resulting oil shortage by doubling its price.

The first oil crisis raised the average *real* price of oil to almost five times the 1970 price ($19.90 per barrel compared with $4.10 per barrel). After 1974, a worldwide recession in 1975 and conservation efforts by the West brought about a gradual erosion in the real price of petroleum. This erosion was sharply reversed in 1979 when the second crisis began to take hold. By 1981, OPEC had succeeded in raising the real price of oil to more than eight times the 1970 level. OPEC's monopoly power appeared to be impregnable.

The two oil crises exerted profound effects on the world economy, causing structural, economic, and social changes of enduring significance. The sudden jump in the oil revenues of OPEC countries can be interpreted as an enormous tax on the oil-importing countries.

The OPEC price hike constrained economic growth in the non-oil coun-

---

[17] In 1989 OPEC had 13 members: Saudi Arabia, Kuwait, Iran, Iraq, Libya, United Arab Emirates (Abu Dhabi, Dubai, and five others), Nigeria, Venezuela, Indonesia, Algeria, Qatar, Ecuador, and Gabon.

tries in several ways. It caused a decline in real disposable income, which in turn induced cuts in real consumption and investment. On the cost side, high oil prices caused inflation and reduced permanently the energy intensity (and therefore productivity) of industry. Much of the slowdown in the world economy after 1974 can be attributed to the two oil crises.

After some lag, the oil-importing countries (particularly the industrial countries) began adjusting to the high price of petroleum through energy conservation measures, switches to non-oil energy sources, and higher production of oil outside the OPEC countries. Over the period 1973–1980, the ratio of total energy used per thousand dollars of gross domestic product in the West fell about two percent a year. By 1980, energy consumption was about 15 percent (equivalent to 10 million barrels of oil a day) lower than the level that would have occurred with no increase in the real price of energy.[18] Also, the share of petroleum in the total energy consumption of the industrial countries began to fall, a significant reversal of the situation before 1973.

The annual increase in energy use is a function of income growth and real price changes: $G = (a\,\Delta GDP) - (e\,\Delta P)$, where G is the annual growth in energy use, a is the income elasticity of energy, ΔGDP is the percentage change in GDP, e is the price elasticity of energy, and ΔP is the percentage change in the real price of energy. Although energy consumption is highly insensitive to real price changes in energy in the short run, it is far more responsive over the long run, when there is time to make adjustments in energy use. For the industrial countries, the long-run *price* elasticity of energy is estimated to be 0.4.[19] Hence, an increase of 10 percent in energy prices eventually causes a 4 percent decline in energy consumption. The long-run *income* elasticity of energy is estimated to be 1.0, that is, a 10 percent increase in GDP eventually causes a 10 percent increase in energy consumption.[20] The industrial countries adjusted to the high price of energy sustained by the OPEC cartel by lowering the income elasticity (a) and by raising the price elasticity of energy (e).

In the 1980s, adjustments in consumption by the industrial countries, a marked expansion of non-OPEC oil production, and a general slowdown in the world economy combined to erode OPEC's monopoly power. As shown in Figure 21-1, the price of oil fell precipitously in 1986, from $31 a barrel to $11 a barrel, a price somewhat lower in *real* terms than the price in 1972 before the first price hike. The immediate cause of this collapse was the abandonment of production controls by OPEC members. New controls have now been agreed to by the members. In mid-1989, the price of oil reached $20 a barrel, still far below the 1980 level. Negotiations among the OPEC countries on production controls are frequently bitter and filled with tension.

---

[18] The World Bank, *World Development Report 1981* (New York: Oxford University Press, 1981), p. 36.

[19] Ibid., p. 37.

[20] Ibid.

And the "free-rider" problem—the flouting of controls by some members—has weakened OPEC's authority.

Does OPEC remain an effective export cartel? Certainly it lost monopoly power in the 1980s. But the West is still highly dependent on OPEC oil. The long-run supply/demand equation, therefore, favors OPEC.[21] In the shorter run, however, OPEC's ability to raise oil prices depends on its ability to control output.

Prospects for Other Export Cartels OPEC's monopoly exploitation was warmly approved by some non-OPEC, low-income developing countries despite the fact that they were seriously hurt by high oil prices. It was viewed as a major step to rectify the imbalance of power and wealth between the rich and poor countries. OPEC's successful coup also inspired efforts to establish export cartels in other basic commodities produced by developing countries. At first glance, the prospects for other export cartels looked good. After all, a large proportion of the world's most important minerals (tin, chromium, bauxite, copper, manganese, and cobalt) that the North is deficient in are found in the South, to say nothing of tropical foodstuffs and raw materials.

This early enthusiasm for export cartels has now faded with the growing realization that few commodities lend themselves to cartelization. To qualify as a good candidate for cartelization, a commodity must possess certain features on both the demand and supply sides. First, its demand should be price inelastic in both the short and longer run. In other words, it should be a commodity that satisfies a vital need and has no close substitutes. Although not necessary, a stable and expanding demand is desirable since it makes it easier for the cartel to maintain a given price over a period of time and to avoid cutbacks in member country exports. Second, the cartel should control all or most of the export supply of the commodity, and it should be able to maintain control over the longer run. This means that export supply should be price inelastic: It cannot be increased by non-member countries very much or very soon. It is easier to hold the cartel together when export supply is also controlled by a small number of countries.

Of all the other minerals, bauxite probably comes closest (but not very close) to matching oil as a satisfactory candidate for cartelization. But if the short-run price elasticity of bauxite is low, the longer-run elasticity would appear to be high. In the short run, the aluminum companies are geared to specific types of bauxite, but in the longer run they can switch to other aluminum-bearing ones that are abundant in many countries, including the United States. In any event, a bauxite cartel was not able to prevent a decline in the price of bauxite in the 1980s.

No other primary products (agricultural or mineral) are satisfactory

---

[21] See Dermot Gately, "Lessons from the 1986 Oil Price Collapse," *Brookings Papers on Economic Activity* 2 (1986): 237–83.

candidates for export cartels formed by developing countries. The Intergovernmental Council of Copper Exporting Countries has not been able to prevent drastic declines in the price of copper: Its membership (Chile, Peru, Zambia, and Zaire) controls only about 30 percent of the world's copper production, and copper has several substitutes in different uses. Again, Zaire, Zambia, and Morocco account for most of the world's output of cobalt, but the demand for cobalt is price elastic, because nickel and tungsten are close substitutes. An attempt by Ecuador to form a banana cartel did not get off the ground. The fact of the matter is that oil is unique as a commodity for cartelization by the Third World. Either the developing countries do not control the supply of other minerals or their demand is price elastic. Also, the demand facing tropical foodstuffs is price elastic, especially in the long run.

To conclude, although developing countries may well try to form other export cartels in the future, the probability of success is very low. Both the fears of the industrial countries and the hopes of the developing countries regarding "commodity power" (which were so stimulated by the example of OPEC) find little support in the economics of supply and demand.

Preferential Treatment of Manufactures

The many difficulties encountered by primary exports (notably low income elasticities and synthetic substitutes) have convinced the developing nations that they must depend increasingly on industrial products to obtain a satisfactory, long-term growth in their exports. They are seeking a new pattern of international specialization whereby the industrial nations would export manufactures requiring advanced levels of technology while importing older and less complex manufactures from the developing nations. To help achieve this fundamental change, the LDCs in the first session of UNCTAD asked the industrial countries to give preferential treatment to LDC exports of manufactures.

Representatives of the developing countries asserted that the most-favored-nation policy is suitable between economies on the same level but not between rich and poor economies. They argued that preferential treatment for their industrial exports would be a logical extension of the infant-industry argument: If the infant industry needs protection in the domestic market, it needs even more protection in foreign markets in the form of preferences.

After several years of negotiations, eighteen developed countries agreed in 1970 to establish a generalized system of nonreciprocal and nondiscriminatory preferences on manufactured goods in favor of the developing countries. The United States did so in 1976. "Generalized" signifies that all the developed countries intend to participate, "nonreciprocal" means that the developed countries demand no concessions in return for preferential treatment, and "nondiscriminatory" means that all developing countries are to receive the same preferences. This agreement involves, therefore, a suspension with respect to the developing countries of the two traditional rules of international trade incorporated in GATT—most-favored-nation treatment and reciprocity.

Although the industrial countries generally agreed to offer duty-free entry to most of the products granted preferences, they excluded from any preferential treatment many products of greatest interest to the developing countries, notably textiles, clothing, and processed agricultural products. Furthermore, the preference offers are limited either by an escape clause (United States and several other countries) or by import ceilings (EC, Japan, and Austria).

We offer here some summary observations on these general preference systems (GSPs). First, preferences to the developing countries may be viewed as a "second-best" solution. The first-best solution is free trade in manufactured products among all countries, developed and developing alike. The economic analysis of preferences runs along the same lines as that for customs unions and free trade areas: trade diversion, trade creation, and dynamic effects.

Second, the preference systems offered by the industrial countries are weakened by the general exclusion of products such as textiles and processed foodstuffs, in which many developing countries have a comparative advantage. Third, preferences benefit mainly the most advanced developing countries with substantial manufacturing sectors. Fourth, developing countries cannot take advantage of whatever opportunities preferences offer their products unless they are willing to modify inward-oriented development policies that obstruct exports. Fifth, manufacturers in the LDCs must develop the capacity to compete in foreign markets not only in price but also in quality, promotion, channels of distribution, and the other areas of exporting marketing.

GSPs are transitional arrangements whose rationale is an extension of the infant-industry argument. Far more important than preferences to the future growth of LDC-manufactured exports is the general level of protection in the industrial countries. Thus the resurgence of protectionism in those countries is highly threatening to the trading interests of the Third World. By the same token, the developing countries have a compelling reason to work through GATT to eliminate nontariff trade barriers and to lower high effective tariffs on processed raw materials and resource-intensive manufactures. But to do so, the LDCs, particularly the middle-income countries, need to participate much more fully in GATT than in the past and to show a willingness to moderate their own restrictive import policies in return for more open markets in the West.

Regional Economic Integration

The great majority of the developing countries in Africa, Asia, and Latin America have small populations and national incomes. Consequently, their domestic markets are also small. Furthermore, autarkic economic development relying on import substitution is not possible: Small markets quickly limit growth, diversification, and economics of scale. In order to industrialize, therefore, small countries must find export outlets for their manufactures. It is not surprising, therefore, that developing countries seek to create institutional arrangements that will encourage mutual trade in manufactured goods. The most notable efforts in this regard are the regional schemes for economic integration that have been inspired by the outstanding success of the European Community. Table 21-5 identifies the principal integration efforts.

The most ambitious schemes for regional economic integration have been launched in Latin America. We offer here a brief description of them.

The Central American Common Market Five countries in Central America—Honduras, El Salvador, Nicaragua, Guatemala, and Costa Rica—established the Central American Common Market (CACM). The weight of the CACM in world trade is minimal; the member countries have a total population of 25 million, a per capita annual income of around $950, and a combined area about the size of France. Their economic problems are poverty, rapid population growth, overdependence on agriculture (over half of their exports consist of coffee, bananas, and cotton), and a dearth of development capital. The CACM is intended to accelerate economic development by widening market opportunities, increasing specialization, making possible economies of scale in industry, and attracting foreign capital.

The Treaty of Managua, which created the CACM in 1961, provided for the immediate removal of restrictions on one-half the products in mutual trade and the progressive elimination of remaining restrictions by 1966. The treaty also envisaged the promotion of regional industries, common finance and payments agencies, and other steps leading to eventual economic union with a common monetary system.

The CACM made very rapid progress in the early and middle 1960s. A customs union was virtually completed by 1966, along with freedom of capital movements. But then a series of political events disrupted the movement toward economic integration. Somehow, the CACM has survived these calamities, but it has never regained its earlier dynamism. It has failed to restore free trade or to have the member nations agree on a common external tariff. Widening political and economic differences among the member countries prevent any significant steps toward integration.

The Latin American Free Trade Association Started in 1960, the Latin American Free Trade Association (LAFTA) was the biggest integration scheme among developing countries until it was replaced in 1981 by the Latin American Integration Association (LAIA), which has the same member countries. These countries cover a territory twice the size of the United States and have a population exceeding 300 million. The average per capita GNP is higher than in other developing areas, but there are marked disparities among the members (per capita GNP ranges from a comparatively

TABLE 21-5 Principal Regional Integration Schemes among Developing Countries

Integration Scheme	Beginning Date	Country Membership	Planned Degree of Integration
Latin America			
Latin American Free Trade Association[1]	1960	Argentina, Bolivia, Brazil, Chile, Colombia, Ecuador, Mexico, Paraguay, Peru, Uruguay, Venezuela	Free Trade Area
Andean Common Market[2]	1969	Bolivia, Chile, Colombia, Ecuador, Peru, Venezuela	Common Market
Central American Common Market	1961	Costa Rica, El Salvador, Guatemala, Honduras, Nicaragua	Common Market
Caribbean Free Trade Association	1968	Antigua, Barbados, Guyana, Jamaica, Trinidad and Tobago, West Indies Associated States	Free Trade Area
Africa			
East African Economic Community[3]	1967	Kenya, Uganda, Tanzania (excl. Zanzibar)	Common Market
Asia			
Association of South-East Asian Nations	1975	Indonesia, Malaysia, Philippines, Singapore, Thailand	Free Trade Area

General Note: Free trade area and *common market* are defined in Table 10-1. A common market is associated with a *customs union* and also involves some harmonization of economic policies but falls short of an *economic union*.
[1] Replaced by the Latin American Integration Association in 1981.
[2] Chile withdrew in 1976.
[3] Broke up in 1977.

high figure in Venezuela to a low figure in Bolivia). Brazil, Argentina, and Mexico are much bigger than the other countries and are much more advanced in industrial development. Brazil alone has close to half the territory of LAFTA and over one-third of its population.

LAFTA commitments to negotiate duty reductions were far less rigorous than the automatic reductions in the EC and EFTA. In practice, moreover, trade liberalization was interpreted to mean that members were required to lower restrictions only on products they were already importing from each other in substantial volume, a major loophole because most of the foreign trade of the LAFTA countries was (and still is) with non-LAFTA countries. Another loophole was provided by escape clauses that allowed members to withdraw concessions. The LAFTA countries made full use of these loopholes, slowing trade liberalization to a crawl. Strong protectionist forces prevented countries from extending concessions on products that they produced at home.

In 1981, a stagnating LAFTA was superseded by the Latin American Integration Association. LAIA is far less ambitious than LAFTA. Its purpose is to create an area of economic preferences rather than a free trade area. LAIA's principal mechanism is "partial agreements" that may be negotiated among two or more member countries covering either individual industries or several economic sectors. Gone is LAFTA's national-list system of tariff concessions granted to all member countries. Partial agreements are viewed as the most realistic way to achieve some integration, but they will also engender further discrimination in tariff policies among member countries.

LAIA is a new phase of Latin American integration. But the obstacles that have stultified progress in LAFTA still remain: differences in levels of development and economic potential so great that some members gain far more from integration than others; deficiencies of transportation and communication that inhibit intraregional trade; divergent national economic, social, and development policies; heterogeneous production and cost structures that generate fierce opposition to trade liberalization; lack of market information, marketing channels, and financial facilities to support intra-LAFTA trade; uncertainty about the effects of trade liberalization; lack of a competitive spirit among local entrepreneurs; widely varying rates of inflation among member countries, coupled with unrealistic exchange rates; and others. But the key obstacle is economic nationalism: an emotional reluctance to accept any obligations that limit the nation's right to determine its own economic policies. As long as the spirit of economic nationalism flourishes in Latin America, any efforts toward economic integration (however grandiose in conception) will prove illusory as an effective instrument to promote economic development.

The Andean Common Market Fearful of becoming economic satellites of Brazil, Argentina, and Mexico, five small nations on the west coast of South America subscribed to the Andean Subregional Integration Agreement in Bogota in 1969. The overriding purpose of the agreement is the development of a modern industrial economy on a regional scale through the creation of a common market. Free trade within the subregion and a common external tariff is to be achieved by linear, automatic adjustments in duties along the lines followed by the European Community. However, the distinctive feature and central idea of the Andean Common Market (ANCOM) is the regional allocation of investment in those industries, such as steel, automobiles, and petrochemicals, that require a large market to attain economies of scale.

It is manifest that ANCOM contemplates a far higher degree of integration than LAFTA or even the CACM. Given their frequent changes in governments and economic philosophy, however, it is doubtful that the Andean countries can overcome the forces of economic nationalism that have so weakened other integration schemes. ANCOM suffered a major setback in 1976 when Chile withdrew its membership, objecting to the controls on foreign investment and high tariffs on imports.

Prospective Benefits of Regional Economic Integration In Chapter 10 we discussed both the *static* effects of economic integration (trade creation and trade diversion) and the *dynamic* effects (economies of scale, competition, enterprise size, product innovation, and new investment). The rationale for economic integration among the developing countries is based almost entirely on the dynamic effects; unlike economic integration among industrial countries, little attention is paid to trade effects. The immediate trade gains from economic integration among developing countries are small for several reasons. Their export sectors are oriented toward markets in North America, Europe, and Japan rather than toward neighboring countries. Also, a trading infrastructure in transportation, communications, finance, and marketing is notably lacking for intraregional trade. Finally, the factor endowments of developing countries belonging to a region tend to be similar, thus reducing the opportunities for short-term gains from trade.

The special case for economic integration among the developing countries, then, is that the creation of large regional markets will allow the establishment of regional firms that can benefit from the dynamic effects, especially from economies of scale. Conversely, the size of most developing economies is too small to provide a market outlet for the full-capacity production of the most efficient, lowest-cost plants in many industries.

To reap the dynamic benefits of economic integration, therefore, member countries must reach agreement on regional investment and compensation policies that will guide new investments in transportation, communications, industry, and agriculture. Agreement is necessary on the *location* of new industry (should a petrochemical plant be built in country A, B, or C?) and the necessary *regional allocation* of investment funds to that industry and location. It is abundantly clear that the member countries will not allow the marketplace to decide the location of regional industries. The less-developed countries fear the competitive strength of the more-developed countries; the poorest countries fear a widening of income gaps between them and other member countries. No country will enter (or remain in) a regional arrangement unless it expects to be better off as a member than as a nonmember. Hence, there must not only be a mechanism for the regional allocation of resources to new industries but also a compensatory mechanism (granting privileged treatment or otherwise transferring resources to member countries gaining the least) to assure a fair distribution of benefits.

At present no integration scheme has an effective regional investment policy, although there are provisions for one in CACM and in ANCOM. The obstacles to such a policy are many. In Latin America, where there are few "new" industries, vested interests and national pride greatly limit the scope of regional investment planning. Such a policy also requires a common policy toward foreign investors, something that is very difficult to achieve when countries compete for scarce investment capital in prestige industries. Another obstacle is the emphasis on reciprocity—the determination of each country not to give up more than it receives in return. But the gravest obstacle is economic nationalism, which favors national planning over regional planning, national industries over regional industries, and nationals over foreigners. In conclusion, developing countries will be able to obtain economies of scale and other dynamic benefits from regional integration schemes only when and if they design mechanisms to achieve a regional allocation of new investment and, at the same time, a "fair" share in the benefits of integration for all member countries.

EXTERNAL FINANCING OF THE DEVELOPING COUNTRIES

The second course of action open to developing countries for alleviating exchange gaps that constrain economic growth is to obtain external financing from private and official sources. But unlike foreign exchange *earned* through exports, foreign exchange *borrowed* through external financing requires that future interest and amortization payments be made to foreign lenders.[22] It follows that if the borrowing countries do not use external financing to increase investment in new productive capacity but instead use it to raise consumption, they will sooner or later become insolvent and unable to service their external debts. Indeed, this has happened to several middle-income developing countries in the 1980s.

The economic performance of the developing countries in the past three decades would not have been possible without a substantial flow of resources from the advanced, industrial countries. By providing compensatory fi-

---

[22] A developing country incurs no interest and amortization costs when external financing takes the form of grants. Also, when external financing takes the form of direct foreign investment, the host country incurs the cost of dividend payments (instead of interest) and capital repatriation (instead of principal). For a definition of direct foreign investment, see Chapter 23.

nancing of savings and foreign exchange gaps, external assistance has enabled developing countries to increase their rates of capital formation and economic growth. This assistance has paid for imports of equipment and other capital goods for investment in infrastructure, industry, and agriculture. Furthermore, technical assistance has directly enhanced productivity in the developing countries by transferring technology and human skills.

It would be erroneous to view external assistance as the only, or most crucial, factor in the economic performance of the developing countries. Although the correlation between growth and import capacity is high (a finding consistent with the operation of foreign exchange constraints), the correlation between the amounts of external assistance received by a country and its rate of economic growth is low. The explanation is the presence of many other factors that influence economic growth, notably export behavior and general domestic policies.

Net Flows of Capital to the Developing Countries

Table 21-6 shows the net flows of capital to developing countries in 1970, 1980, and 1987. After the oil crisis of 1973–1974, the sources of capital flows changed significantly in their relative importance. In 1970, official capital flows from OECD governments accounted for 51 percent of all capital flows and private capital flows accounted for 49 percent. But in 1980, the share of private capital flows reached 57 percent, mainly as a result of an enormous rise in private loans. For the most part, these loans were syndicated loans by commercial banks operating in the Eurocurrency market. To finance imports of higher-priced oil after 1973, the LDCs turned to multinational banks that borrowed funds from the OPEC countries. In this way the current-account surpluses of the OPEC countries were used to finance the current-account deficits of the LDCs. Most of these bank loans were made to the middle-income LDC's because low-income LDCs were considered unacceptable credit risks.

In the 1980s, new bank loans (portfolio investment) almost dried up as banks desperately tried to reduce their loan exposure in developing countries. Direct investment took up some of the slack, rising from $10.1 billion in 1980 to $20.1 billion in 1987. Also, official development assistance increased from $27.3 billion in 1980 to $41.5 billion in 1987. But these responses failed to maintain the real value of external assistance. In terms of 1986 prices and exchange rates, external assistance dropped from $86.2 billion in 1980 to $61.1 billion in 1987, a decline of almost 30 percent.

A few words are in order about the major categories of external assistance. *Official development assistance* involves the transfer of resources by the donor governments with the deliberate intent to promote economic development in the receiving countries. Only official development assistance, including grants and concessional (low-interest) loans for development made

TABLE 21-6   The Net Flow of Financial Resources from Industrial (OECD) Countries and Multilateral Agencies to Developing Countries, 1970, 1980, and 1987

	Billions of Dollars			Percent		
	1970	1980	1987	1970	1980	1987
Official development assistance	6.9	27.3	41.5	44	36	59
Bilateral grants	3.3	14.1	23.4	21	19	33
Bilateral concessional loans	2.4	4.0	6.6	15	5	9
Grants and loans from multilateral agencies[1]	1.2	9.2	11.6	8	12	17
Other official flows[2]	1.1	5.3	2.0	7	7	3
Private flows	7.0	40.4	23.1	44	54	33
Direct investment	3.7	10.1	20.1	23	13	29
Portfolio investment	1.2	18.8	1.5	7	25	2
Export credits	2.2	11.5	1.5	14	15	2
Grants by private voluntary agencies	0.9	2.4	3.3	5	3	5
Total net flows	15.9	75.4	70.0	100	100	100
Total net flows in 1986 prices and exchange rates	50.6	86.2	61.1			

[1] Mainly from the United Nations, European Community, International Development Association, and regional development banks.
[2] Mainly official export credits.
Source: Taken from "OECD Projects Recovery in Aid Flows Following 1 Percent Decline in 1987," *IMF Survey*, March 6, 1989, p. 69.

either bilaterally or through international agencies, fully deserves the designation "foreign aid." Other *official loans* consist mainly of official export credits, which, although they provide resources to the developing countries, are primarily intended to promote donor-country exports rather than economic development.

By their very nature, *private flows* cannot be directly manipulated by the governments of the industrial countries, although they are commonly subject to regulations of one kind or another. Private flows are the net consequence of decisions by an untold number of entrepreneurs, investors, bankers, and traders. The dominant motivation behind these decisions is the prospect of economic gain (profit, interest, or capital appreciation) for the decisionmakers or their organization. Nor do private flows involve grants or concessional loans. Properly speaking, therefore, private flows should not be considered "foreign aid," even though they may provide developing countries with resources that are not obtainable through official assistance, such as technology and industrial management. *Direct investment* occurs when business enterprises in the industrial countries acquire equity interests in affiliates in the developing countries.

How much official development assistance *should* the industrial countries provide to the developing countries? Economic analysis cannot answer this question, because it is essentially political in nature. However, the industrial countries have agreed to a target of 0.7 percent of their gross national products (at market prices). How close are they to this target? In 1988, only five of the OECD donor countries reached or exceeded the target: the Netherlands, France, and the three Scandinavian countries. Although the United States contributed more than one-fifth of the official development assistance in that year, the amount was only 0.2 percent of its GNP, ranking it last among the donor countries.

International Organizations Providing External Assistance

Although the bulk of official assistance to the developing countries has been supplied bilaterally by the industrial countries, substantial resources have also been channeled multilaterally through international organizations.

The most prominent international lending agencies make up the *World Bank Group*, which comprises the *International Bank for Reconstruction and Development* (IBRD or World Bank), the *International Development Association* (IDA), and the *International Finance Corporation* (IFC).[23] Each of these agencies has its own resources, lending terms, and policies.

The World Bank finances development projects on long term (ranging up to thirty-five years), for which it charges a market rate of interest. All of its loans must be guaranteed by governments in the borrowing countries and must be repaid in hard, convertible currencies. The World Bank obtains its loan funds from member-country subscriptions to its capital stock by selling its own bonds in international capital markets and by selling off its loan portfolios to private investors. Most World Bank loans are used to finance infrastructure investment in transportation, electric power, agriculture, water supply, and education.

The inability of many developing countries to qualify for World Bank loans and their high interest costs led to the formation of the IDA. The IDA extends credits to developing countries for up to fifty years. These credits are repayable in easy stages after a ten-year grace period and with no interest except a modest service charge. The IDA is frequently described as

---

[23] The IBRD came into being as a sister organization of the International Monetary Fund and began operations in 1946. The IFC was set up in 1956 and the IDA, in 1961; both are affiliates of the IBRD.

a "soft loan" agency while the World Bank is a "hard loan" agency. Unlike the World Bank, IDA does not have its own capital; it is dependent on a continuing replenishment of its funds by the member countries.

The IFC does not make loans to governments, as do the other agencies. Instead, it participates in industrial projects in conjunction with private investors, either as a lender or an investor in equity. The IFC has been able to function as a catalyst by bringing together private investors of the industrial and developing countries. The IFC obtains its investment funds from member country subscriptions to its capital stock, from its right to borrow from the World Bank up to four times its own unimpaired capital and surplus, and from the sale of its own investment portfolio to private investors (thereby "recycling" its investment funds).

The *United Nations Development Program* (UNDP) is the principal international agency in the field of technical assistance and preinvestment aid. It is intended to identify, investigate, and present to financial agencies those projects in developing countries that merit investment. Most of the UNDP assistance is actually carried out by specialized agencies and other bodies of the United Nations.

Several *development banks* have been established to provide multilateral assistance to developing countries in different regions of the world. The *Inter-American Development Bank* was started in 1960 by the United States and all the Latin American countries except Cuba. The bank has three categories of funds: ordinary capital used for loans at market rates ("hard-loan window"); special funds for loans on easy terms ("soft-currency window"); and a Social Program Trust Fund to finance low-income housing, education, and other social projects. The *African Development Bank* started operations in 1964 with a membership limited to independent African countries and an authorized capital of $250 million. The *Asian Development Bank* was established in 1966 with an authorized capital of $1.1 billion by nineteen Asian countries, eleven European countries, Canada, and the United States. The *European Community* provides assistance to developing countries through the European Development Fund and the European Investment Bank.

U.S. Foreign Aid Policy

Foreign aid has been a dominant element in American foreign economic policy since World War II. During the early postwar years U.S. government assistance was directed mainly toward the rehabilitation and recovery of Western Europe—the Marshall Plan era. At the start of the 1950s U.S. foreign aid became oriented toward rearmament of the free world, emphasizing military and defense support assistance. It was not until 1957 that U.S. foreign assistance turned toward the developing countries. In that year Congress approved the creation of the Development Loan Fund to finance projects in the developing countries. Formal recognition of this turn in U.S. foreign aid occurred in 1961, when a new agency—the Agency for International Development (AID)—was set up to administer economic and technical assistance programs. Today, U.S. bilateral development assistance relates mainly to food and nutrition, population and health, and education and human resources development.

In the conviction that the most dynamic economic progress in LDCs has been achieved by the "magic of the marketplace," the Reagan administration in 1981 launched a new foreign aid strategy that would strengthen the role of private enterprise in economic development. The principles underlying this strategy are as follows: (1) A growing U.S. economy can do more for LDCs than U.S. foreign aid; (2) the LDCs must put their own economies on a sound footing; (3) U.S. development assistance should continue to concentrate on the least-developed of the LDCs; (4) LDCs can best promote their development by attracting foreign investment, offering incentives to their farmers, and supporting the free flow of trade and capital; (5) more emphasis should be placed on U.S. bilateral aid and less on U.S. multilateral aid channeled through the World Bank and other international agencies; and (6) U.S. security aid to friendly LDCs threatened by hostile forces should take precedence over development aid.

The most ambitious effort to carry out the new U.S. aid strategy is the Caribbean Basin Initiative. Covering some twenty-five small LDCs in Central America, the Caribbean, and northern South America, the centerpiece of the initiative is the removal of U.S. import duties on the products of these countries for a period of twelve years, except for textiles and apparel and a limit on duty-free imports of sugar. Another feature is the extension of the 10 percent domestic investment tax credit to any new investments made by U.S. companies in the Caribbean Basin. A third feature is additional aid to Basin countries.

The new U.S. aid strategy is disappointing to the majority of LDCs that perceives the emphasis on the private sector as simply a way to reduce U.S. development assistance. This suspicion is fed by the secular decline in U.S. foreign assistance from 0.53 percent of U.S. GNP in 1960 to the current 0.20 percent. As noted above, this percentage is the lowest among the industrial countries.

EXTERNAL DEBT OF THE DEVELOPING COUNTRIES

The transfer of financial assistance from the industrial to the developing countries has gone through three phases since World War II. From 1945 to the late 1960s, the main forms of capital were official assistance, direct foreign investment, and trade finance. The current-account deficits of LDCs were mainly financed through international agencies and bilateral government arrangements.

In the second phase, the late 1960s to 1982, the world economy experienced two oil shocks, highly volatile exchange and interest rates, and wide swings in current-account balances. In this new environment, international banks shifted from trade finance to balance of payments finance. Bank loans to the developing countries accelerated and direct investment flows became less important. During this phase, official flows kept pace with private flows.

The third—and ongoing—phase began in August 1982, when Mexico, suffering from a sharp drop in its oil export revenues, announced a de facto moratorium on its amortization payments to foreign commercial banks. This action triggered a loss of confidence in the creditworthiness of LDCs in general. Banks immediately withdrew short-term credit lines and greatly restricted new medium- and long-term lending (see Portfolio Investments in Table 21-6). At the same time, budgetary pressures in several industrial countries constrained official development assistance. Also, OPEC's current-account surplus fell along with oil prices, thereby depriving the banks of new loanable funds. The third phase, then, witnessed a massive drop in external financing in response to an international debt crisis. But the origins of this crisis can be traced to the extraordinary rise in the external obligations of the developing countries in the second phase—a time of world inflation and negative real exchange rates. Because most private loans to the LDCs were in dollars with floating interest rates, both the risks of an appreciating dollar and higher interest rates were transferred to the borrowers.

The astounding rise in LDC external debt is indicated in Table 21-7. Between 1973 and 1988, total LDC debt rose more than tenfold! Debt owing private creditors (mostly banks) rose 8.5 times between 1973 and 1982, while debt owing official creditors rose 5 times. The biggest regional debtor, Latin America, accounted for over one-third of *all* LDC long-term debt. As the first ratio shows, external debt rose significantly faster than gross domestic product. The second ratio reveals that external debt became 1.5 times the value of LDC exports of goods and services in 1988.

This huge external debt has been incurred mostly by middle-income developing countries, particularly countries in Latin America. The ten largest debtors appear in Table 21-8. These countries alone are responsible for nearly two-fifths of the total LDC debt.

The key analytical issue is the capacity of LDC countries to make foreign exchange payments to service their external debts. The most commonly used measure of this capacity is the *debt service* ratio: scheduled interest and principal payments as a percentage of exports of goods and services. Between 1973 and 1982, this ratio jumped for developing countries as a whole from 14.0 percent to 18.9 percent. In 1988, it reached 19.3 percent. For the ten largest debtors, the ratios range from 20.0 percent (Malaysia) to 64.1 percent (Argentina). These ratios are extraordinarily high compared with past ratios, which were around 10 percent.

	1973	1982	1988
Total long-term debt	96.8	657.9	1045.1
Official creditors	48.3	244.8	481.3
Private creditors	48.5	413.1	569.8
Total long-term debt by region			
Latin America	36.6	267.7	381.3
Asia	27.0	140.8	256.5
Europe	11.6	91.5	137.1
Africa	13.1	98.9	172.1
Middle East	8.5	50.0	98.1
Ratio of external debt to GDP	16.6%	31.3%	36.2%
Ratio of external debt to exports of goods and services	88.7%	119.8%	147.6%
Debt service ratio*	14.0%	18.9%	19.3%

* Payments (interest and amortization) as a percentage of exports of goods and services.

Source: International Monetary Fund, *World Economic Outlook* (Washington, D.C.: International Monetary Fund,
1982), Tables 30-33, pp. 170–73; and International Monetary Fund, *World Economic Outlook* (Washington, D.C.:
International Monetary Fund, 1988), Tables A47, p. 175, and Tables A50–A51, pp. 180–82.

Despite widespread fears, the international debt crisis has not ended
in a worldwide financial collapse. The worst has been averted through a
rescheduling of debt payments by creditors, increased lending by international agencies, and adjustment efforts by debtor countries. But a huge "debt
overhang" (the contractual value of LDC external liabilities exceeds expected debt-servicing capacity) persists as an obstacle to economic growth
and a threat to the financial stability of the world economy. Table 20-2
reveals the drastic fall in the annual growth rate in the 1980s of the gross
national product of the middle-income countries.

Several measures need to be taken to deal with the international debt
problem. First, the prospects of a solution depend critically on whether
debtors will reform their own economic policies. The difficulties of many
countries stem from their failure to use external borrowing in the past for
investments that yielded returns higher than interest rates. Instead, borrowed funds were commonly used to finance balance of payments deficits
and offset capital flight caused by poor macroeconomic policies. The debtor
countries need to follow outward-oriented policies that will restore their
creditworthiness.

TABLE 21-8   Total External Long-term Debt and Debt Service Ratios of the
Ten Largest Debtors of the Developing Countries, 1970 and 1986

Country	Total Debt (Billions of Dollars)		Debt Service Ratio (Percent)	
	1970	1986	1970	1986
Brazil	5.1	97.2	12.5	41.8
Mexico	6.0	91.1	44.3	51.5
Argentina	5.2	43.0	51.7	64.1
Indonesia	2.9	35.7	13.9	33.1
Venezuela	1.0	32.4	4.2	37.4
Turkey	1.9	23.8	22.7	32.4
Egypt	1.7	23.7	38.0	23.8
Nigeria	0.6	21.9	7.1	23.4
Philippines	1.5	21.6	23.0	21.3
Malaysia	0.4	19.7	4.5	20.0
Total	24.4	410.1		

Source: Derived from the World Bank, *World Development Report 1988* (New York: Oxford University Press, 1988),
Table 18, pp. 256–57.

Second, there must be new capital flows from the industrial countries
to the LDCs to finance investment in productive capacity and thereby restore
higher growth rates. Because of interest and amortization payments, the
developing countries are now transferring net resources *to* the industrial
countries, amounting to $85 billion over the period 1982–1987. However,
the outlook for new private lending to the LDCs is poor due to the widespread
loss of confidence in their economic viability.

Third, the industrial countries need to follow higher-growth policies
and avoid protection that keeps out imports from the developing countries.

Fourth, there should be a return to lower *real* interest rates, which
would lower debt service ratios. (When the real interest rate exceeds the
rate of growth of exports, the debt service ratio tends to rise.) But lower
real interest rates depend on the ability of the United States to cut back on
its own international borrowing by improving its balance of payments.

Finally, there must be debt rescheduling and debt relief. *Debt rescheduling* does not reduce the present value of debt service; it merely defers
debt service. Rescheduling will work when a debtor faces only a liquidity
problem. *Debt relief*, in contrast, reduces the debt in whole or in part. Debt
relief is an appropriate action when a debtor faces an insolvency problem.

At the start of the international debt crisis, the problem was viewed
as mainly a lack of liquidity. Remedial action, therefore, focused on debt

rescheduling by private and official lenders. But toward the end of the 1980s, it became increasingly recognized that at least some countries faced insolvency—the inability to service external debt over the long term. Attention has thus turned to debt reduction. The most common debt reduction techniques are *debt buyback* (the debtor country buys the debt from a bank at a discount), *debt-for-debt swap* (a bank exchanges its loan for bonds issued by the debtor country at a discount or lower interest rate), and *debt-for-equity swap* (a bank exchanges its loan at a discount for local currency, which then finances an equity investment in the debtor country).

So far international commercial banks have been reluctant to engage in substantial debt reduction efforts. In 1989, the World Bank and the IMF approved a U.S. plan to reduce developing country debt by $70 billion within the next few years by persuading commercial banks to cut debts owing them. In return, the banks would receive either new bonds or equity shares in debtor country enterprises. To accelerate these debt swaps, the World Bank and the IMF would provide partial guarantees of interest payments and other support.[24]

SUMMARY

1. International trade is not sufficient for economic development. What is also necessary is the capacity of the economy to respond to an export stimulus, a capacity that is dependent on internal conditions disposed toward growth.

2. The key export problems of the low-income developing countries are traceable to the slow growth and instability of commodity exports on which they are so dependent for export earnings. There is no convincing evidence of a secular tendency for the terms of trade of the LDCs to deteriorate in trade with the industrial countries, but the terms of trade did worsen in the 1980s.

3. Over the past quarter century the economic performance of developing countries following outward-oriented trade strategies has been superior to that of developing countries following inward-oriented strategies.

4. International commodity agreements are arrangements between producing and consuming countries that seek to stabilize the prices of specific primary commodities through measures that involve buffer stocks, export controls, and import commitments or production controls. The prospects of any substantial transfer of resources to the developing countries through international commodity agreements appear dim.

---

[24] "World Bank and IMF Approve Plan to Cut Debt of Poorer Lands," *The New York Times,* April 5, 1989, p. 1.

5. A cartel is an association of producers of a commodity that seeks to control the market through price fixing, the allocation of market territories, supply restrictions, and other measures.

6. The OPEC oil cartel has raised oil prices with profound effects on the world economy. But in recent years, OPEC has lost much of its monopoly power as the West continues to decrease its use of energy in general and its use of OPEC oil in particular. Although non-oil-developing countries would like to establish export cartels, no other primary commodities (with the limited exception of bauxite) are satisfactory candidates.

7. Preferences for the developing countries may be viewed as a "second-best" solution. The best solution is free trade in manufactured products among all countries developed and developing alike.

8. Developing countries participate in several schemes for regional economic integration. The most ambitious schemes have been launched in Latin America: the Central American Common Market, the Latin American Free Trade Association, and the Andean Common Market. To reap the dynamic benefits of economic integration, the member countries must reach agreement on regional investment and compensation policies that will guide new investments in transportation, communications, industry, and agriculture.

9. The impressive economic performance of the developing countries in the past three decades would not have been possible without a substantial flow of resources from the advanced, industrial countries. But in the 1980s, the net flow of financial resources from the industrial countries to LDCs fell sharply in real terms, mainly in response to the international debt crisis.

10. Many international agencies provide assistance to the developing countries, including the World Bank Group, the United Nations Development Program, and regional development banks.

11. U.S. official development assistance has become a smaller and smaller percentage of total OECD assistance and of the U.S. GNP. The latest U.S. foreign aid strategy attempts to strengthen the role of private enterprise in economic development.

12. Between 1973 and 1988, the debt service ratio of the LDCs rose from 14.0 percent to 19.3 percent, extraordinarily high compared with ratios in the past.

13. Despite widespread fears, the international debt crisis has not ended in a worldwide financial collapse. But a huge debt overhang constrains economic growth in the LDCs.

QUESTIONS AND APPLICATIONS

1. Exports led the growth of several nonindustrial countries in the nineteenth century. Why, then, have exports failed to lead the growth of many developing countries in the twentieth century?

2. Why does the volume of commodity exports as a whole grow less rapidly than the volume of industrial exports in the world economy?

3. What factors cause the short-run price instability of commodity exports?

4. What are the commodity or net barter terms of trade? How does Prebisch explain the deterioration in terms of trade of the developing countries? Do you agree with his explanation? Why or why not?

5. "Indiscriminate import substitution policies are self-defeating." Discuss.

6. (a) Define strongly and moderately outward-oriented trade strategies and moderately and strongly inward-oriented trade strategies.

   (b) Compare the economic performance of countries following outward- and inward-oriented trade strategies over the period 1963–1985.

7. Describe the mechanisms for stabilizing prices under international commodity agreements. Are international commodity agreements likely to be effective instruments for transferring resources from the rich to the poor countries? Why or why not?

8. (a) What is an export cartel?
   (b) What are the requirements for an effective export cartel? Why?

9. "The OPEC oil cartel will break apart within the next decade." Do you agree with this statement? Why or why not?

10. Do non-oil export cartels formed by developing countries pose a major threat to the industrial West? Be prepared to defend your answer.

11. Discuss the pros and cons of preferential treatment of the manufactured exports of the developing countries.

12. Why is the rationale for economic integration among the developing countries based almost entirely on the dynamic effects?

13. (a) Why did the net flow of financial resources from the industrial to the developing countries decline in both nominal and real terms between 1980 and 1987?

    (b) Broadly speaking, what were the effects of this decline?

14. (a) What is the rationale behind the new direction in U.S. foreign aid strategy, which now emphasizes the role of private enterprise?

    (b) Why are so many LDCs dubious about this new direction?

15. (a) How can external debt become a "burden" to a developing country?

    (b) What economic factors would you investigate to estimate the debt service capacity of a given developing country?

16. (a) What is the international debt problem?
    (b) What measures need to be taken to deal with it? Why?

SELECTED READINGS

Bauer, P. T. *Reality and Rhetoric: Studies in the Economics of Development.* Cambridge: Harvard University Press, 1984.

Bhagwati, Jagdish N., ed. "A Symposium Issue on the Multilateral Trade Negotiations and Developing-Country Issues" (entire issue). *The World Bank Economic Review,* September 1987.

Bhagwati, Jagdish N., and John G. Ruggie, eds. *Power, Passions, and Purpose: Prospects for North-South Negotiations.* Cambridge: M.I.T. Press, 1984.

Cohen, Benjamin J. *Developing-Country Debt: A Middle Way,* Essays in International Finance, no. 173. Princeton, N.J.: Princeton University Press, May 1989.

Cohen, Daniel. "The Management of Developing Countries' Debt: Guidelines and Applications to Brazil." *The World Bank Economic Review,* January 1988, pp. 77–103.

Danielsen, Albert L. *The Evolution of OPEC.* New York: Harcourt Brace Jovanovich, 1982.

Dornbusch, Rudiger. *Dollars, Debts and Deficits.* Cambridge: M.I.T. Press, 1986. Part 2.

Edwards, Sebastian. *The Order of Liberalization of the External Sector in Developing Countries,* Essays in International Finance, no. 156. Princeton, N.J.: Princeton University Press, December 1984.

International Monetary Fund. *World Economic Outlook.* Washington, D.C.: International Monetary Fund. Annual.

International Monetary Fund and the World Bank. *Finance and Development.* Quarterly.

Kelley, Allen C. "Economic Consequences of Population Change in the Third World." *Journal of Economic Literature,* December 1988, pp. 1685–1728.

Krueger, Anne O. *Trade and Employment in Developing Countries: Synthesis and Conclusions.* Chicago: Chicago University Press, 1983.

Loehr, William, and John P. Powelson. *Threat to Development: Pitfalls of the NIEO.* Boulder, Colo.: Westview Press, 1983.

Organization for Economic Cooperation and Development. *Development Assistance.* Paris: Organization for Economic Cooperation and Development. Annual review.

Overseas Development Council. *The U.S. and World Development.* Washington, D.C.: Overseas Development Council. Annual.

Reynolds, Lloyd G. *Economic Growth in the Third World: An Introduction.* New Haven,Conn.: Yale University Press, 1986.

Rosenberg, Nathan, and L. E. Birdzell, Jr. *How the West Grew Rich.* New York: Basic Books, 1986.

The World Bank. *World Bank Atlas.* Washington, D.C.: The World Bank. Annual.

———. *World Development Report.* New York: Oxford University Press. Annual.

PART FOUR

INTERNATIONAL INVESTMENT/ MULTINATIONAL ENTERPRISE

In Parts One, Two, and Three, a macroscopic, national perspective was assumed in order to describe and analyze international economic relations. Although necessary, this perspective is no longer sufficient to explain the behavior of the world economy. Large multinational business enterprises now possess the financial and market power to make decisions that vitally affect the level, composition, and direction of international trade and investment. Multinational enterprises have become independent actors in the world economy, and there is no area of government policy that escapes their influence. The future evolution of the world economy will depend, therefore, not only on the behavior of national governments but also on the behavior of multinational enterprises as they strive to achieve their goals on a transnational scale. Part Four investigates the nature, scope, and economic role of multinational enterprises; the policies of the United States and other countries toward multinational enterprises; and the tensions that are generated by the complex relations between multinational enterprises and nation-states.

22
The Nature and Scope of Multinational Enterprise

In the 1960s, U.S. business firms went abroad on a massive scale unprecedented in the history of international enterprise. Today the production and sales of the foreign operations owned and managed by U.S. companies are more than three times the value of U.S. exports. The prevailing response of big American companies to market opportunities abroad is to establish producing affiliates in foreign countries. The dominant agency in the surge of U.S. business abroad is the multinational enterprise (MNE)—the large industrial or service corporation that possesses plants or other operations in many countries that produce for markets throughout the world. Many industrial firms in Western Europe and Japan have also become MNEs and they are emerging in newly industrializing countries, such as Mexico and South Korea, as well.

Because of their vast size, the worldwide operations of multinational companies are now a decisive force in shaping the patterns of trade, investment, and technology flows among nations. It has become impossible to understand the world economy without an appreciation of the many roles of multinational enterprises as producers, investors, traders, and innovators on a global scale. National governments must also reckon with this force because of its impact on domestic production, employment, trade, and the balance of payments. In so doing, they are commonly frustrated by the capability of multinational companies to far outrun national jurisdiction in taxation, antitrust, and other policy areas. Moreover, many governments view the multinational enterprise as a *political* threat, representing as it does an intrusion into the national domain by a company whose control is exercised by a headquarters located in another country. Even in the United States, the multinational enterprise has come under attack by labor and protectionist groups who charge it with exporting jobs and technology to the detriment of the U.S. economy.

The expansion of U.S. business into foreign production is not new. Today's multinational enterprises have roots that go deep into the American past. In the decades following the Civil War, the transformation of industrial corporations into national enterprises, together with notable improvements in transportation and communications, encouraged a number of American manufacturers with unique products to make investments in Canada and Europe. One of the pioneers, Singer, licensed a French company in 1855 to manufacture its new sewing machine (the first and last time Singer ever licensed a patent to an independent foreign concern), and in 1867 it established the first plant abroad, in Glasgow.[1] In 1879, Westinghouse started a shop in Paris to manufacture brakes; in 1882, Western Electric and International Bell Telephone Company jointly set up a manufacturing affiliate in Belgium; and by 1889, Eastman had incorporated a company in London to manufacture film for Kodak cameras imported from the United States.[2] In the 1870s and 1880s, then, many American companies with new products (screws, cash registers, elevators, steam pumps, locomotives, locks, and guns) were eagerly seeking export markets and, in some instances, entering into foreign production.[3]

It is noteworthy that this early movement of U.S. manufacturers abroad was based on new products, new methods of production, and new marketing methods that offered strong competitive advantages in foreign markets. From the very beginning, therefore, U.S. business investors appeared primarily as exporters of technology and management rather than exporters of capital. By the turn of the century, the presence of U.S. companies in Europe was sufficient enough to alarm some observers, who spoke of "the American invasion" in much the same terms as J. J. Servan-Schreiber did some seventy years later.[4]

Although its historical roots are deep, the multinational enterprise as we know it today is a recent phenomenon, emerging for the most part only since the mid-1950s. Before that time the inadequacies of the global infrastructure of communications and transportation, as well as the pervasive influence of restrictive government policies, rendered global business strategies nothing more than utopian dreams in the minds of a few entrepreneurs. The emergence of multinational enterprise systems directed and controlled by a single decision center had to await the dramatic postwar improvements in communications and transportation and the massive liberalization of international trade and payments that gathered steam in the late 1950s.

---

[1] See Mira Wilkins, *The Emergence of Multinational Enterprise* (Cambridge: Harvard University Press, 1970), pp. 38 ff. This book offers a detailed history of U.S. international business up to 1914.

[2] *Ibid.*, pp. 45, 51, and 59.

[3] *Ibid.*, p. 45.

[4] Three publications appeared in London in 1901–1902 entitled *The American Invasion*, *The American Invaders*, and *The Americanization of the World*. See Wilkins, *Multinational Enterprise*, p. 71. Also see J. J. Servan-Schreiber, *The American Challenge* (New York: Atheneum Publishers, 1968).

The many economic and political issues raised by the multinational enterprise are examined in later chapters. First, however, we need to learn something about the nature and scope of the multinational enterprise.

THE MULTINATIONAL ENTERPRISE AS AN INTERNATIONAL TRANSFER AGENT

We now examine the role of the multinational enterprise as an *international transfer agent* in the world economy. The multinational enterprise becomes an international transfer agent when it moves products and factor services (capital, technology, and management) among national economies. But let us turn first to the question of defining the multinational enterprise.

Some Definitions of the Multinational Enterprise

There is no single agreed-upon definition of the multinational (or transnational) enterprise. This is hardly surprising in view of the fact that "multinationality" has many dimensions and may be viewed from any of several different perspectives—economic, political, legal, managerial, and others.

Some observers regard *ownership* as the key criterion. In their view an enterprise becomes multinational only when the headquarters or parent company is effectively owned by nationals of at least two countries. Shell and Unilever, which are controlled by British and Dutch interests, are commonly cited as examples. By this ownership test, very few international companies may be called multinational. The dominant ownership interest in the overwhelming majority of big international companies is *uninational,* namely, American, British, French, or Japanese.[5] The ownership criterion has been rejected by most authorities.

A second definition of the MNE relies on the criterion of the *nationality mix* of headquarters management. An international company is seen as multinational only when the managers of the parent company are nationals of several different countries. Here again, very few international companies would qualify as multinational enterprises, because most have headquarters organizations that are entirely or mainly staffed with nationals of the home country. But uninational management may well prove to be a transitional phenomenon. Already it is commonplace for international companies to staff their foreign affiliates with local nationals all the way to the top levels, and some of these nationals are now being promoted to the parent headquarters.

---

[5] Of course, the shares of these companies may be held in comparatively small amounts by nationals of many countries. Indeed, several U.S. companies list their shares on stock exchanges in Europe and Japan. But the controlling ownership interest remains in the hands of nationals of the home country, where the parent company is located.

Multinational management, then, is more a consequence of the continuing evolution of the MNE than its distinguishing feature.

Most observers of large international companies have been concerned with their economic and business behavior. Accordingly, they have defined the MNE in terms of *organizational structure* or *business strategy*. Vernon sees the multinational enterprise as a "parent company that controls a large cluster of corporations of various nationalities."[6] Finding the essence of the multinational enterprise in its attempt "to treat the various national markets as though they were one," Behrman emphasizes the presence of a single management (strategy) center which guides the actions of foreign affiliates.[7] Perlmutter has distinguished three kinds of international companies by reference to the attitudes held by their top executives. *Ethnocentric* companies follow policies that are home country–oriented, *polycentric* companies follow policies that are host country–oriented, and *geocentric* companies follow policies that are world-oriented. To Perlmutter, a firm's multinationality may be judged by "the pervasiveness with which its executives think geocentrically."[8] More recently, the United Nations defined the essence of multinationalization (which it calls transnationalization) as "the internalization of international market transactions within an individual decision-making unit, the transnational corporation."[9]

The foregoing conceptions may be covered in a single definition of the multinational enterprise that contains both structural and strategic (attitudinal) elements. A multinational enterprise denotes a headquarters or parent company that

1. engages in foreign production and other activities through its own affiliates located in several different countries
2. exercises direct control over the policies of those affiliates
3. strives to design and implement business strategies in production, marketing, finance, and other functions that transcend national boundaries, becoming thereby progressively more geocentric in outlook

This definition is consistent with the approach taken in this and later chapters.

Unfortunately organizational structure and business strategy do not lend themselves to direct quantitative measurement. Thus, the definition of the MNE for statistical data–gathering purposes must rely on "proxy variables," such as the percentages of a company's assets, sales, earnings,

---

[6] Raymond Vernon, *Sovereignty at Bay* (New York: Basic Books, 1971), p. 4.

[7] Jack N. Behrman, *Some Patterns in the Rise of the Multinational Enterprise* (Chapel Hill: University of North Carolina, 1969), p. 63.

[8] Howard V. Perlmutter, "The Tortuous Evolution of the Multinational Corporation," *Columbia Journal of World Business*, January–February 1969, pp. 9–18.

[9] United Nations Center on Transnational Corporations, *Transnational Corporations in World Development* (New York: United Nations, 1988), p. 16.

employment, or production abroad. A company whose foreign sales are 25 percent or more of total sales is certainly heavily involved in international business on both operational and strategic levels, and in most instances it probably qualifies as a multinational enterprise. But there is no magic percentage at which a company is transformed into a multinational enterprise. The MNE is too complex a phenomenon to be captured by a single number. Any statistical definition of the MNE, however useful, is bound, therefore, to be arbitrary.

The Multinational Enterprise System

The multinational enterprise performs its role as an international transfer agent through institutional or organizational arrangements that collectively make up the *multinational enterprise system*. This system, as depicted in Figure 22-1, comprises the parent company and its foreign affiliates.

The parent company (denoted by the P circle) is the enterprise decision center that determines the goals and controls the operations of the entire system. The key decisions of the parent company relate to the establishment

Figure 22-1   The Multinational Enterprise System

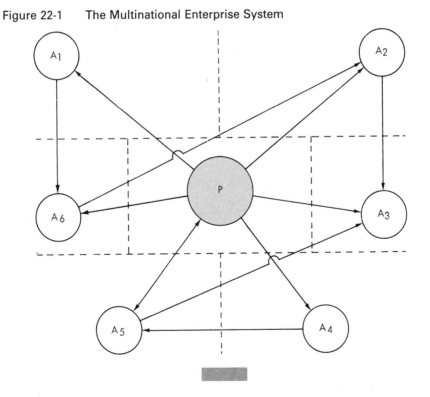

(or acquisition), country location, size, and "product mix" of its production affiliates; the direction, volume, and composition of transfers among the affiliates; and the national markets to be served by the affiliates. These strategy decisions generate a pattern of factor and product flows among the members of the system. The parent company and its affiliates (denoted by the A circles) are located in different countries, as indicated by the dashed lines. Most of the affiliates perform both production and marketing functions, but some perform only a marketing or financial function.

The affiliates are connected to the parent company and, in some instances, to other affiliates by a variety of cross-national flows of products, capital, technology, and management.[10] Flows of factor services, usually accompanied by product flows, generally move from the parent company to the affiliates. Any of these kinds of flows may also link pairs of affiliates. To illustrate, A_1 may transfer parts or components that it manufactures to A_6, which uses them to manufacture other products. A_4 may transfer certain finished products to A_5, which then resells them in the local market. Idle funds accumulating in A_2 may be transferred to A_3 to finance a capital expansion. A_5 may develop new technology that is transferred to A_3. A manager in A_6 may be transferred to a new position in A_2. Some products and factor services may also be transferred from an affiliate to the parent company, such as from A_5 to P.

One of the distinctive features of the multinational enterprise system is the rapid growth of interaffiliate transfers as managers in the parent company try to improve the performance of the entire system. Managers perceive a worldwide market for the company's products, and they work to build up interaffiliate transfers on regional or global levels to take advantage of similarities among national markets, economies of scale, and international specialization. Hence, the multinational enterprise system becomes progressively more integrated in production, marketing, finance, research and development, and management.

Several *external* constraints may limit the integration of a multinational enterprise system, and a parent company also encounters *internal* constraints, such as the domestic orientation of many managers. External constraints include all of the obstacles to international trade and payments that were examined in Parts One and Two. Most prominent are the restrictions imposed by governments on the flows of factor services, products, and current payments. When trade restrictions are severe, they inhibit interaffiliate product transfers. Furthermore, uncertainty about future government actions and unstable political conditions in some host countries may greatly enhance the risks of interdependence among affiliates. In Figure

---

[10] They are also connected by financial flows that represent the financing and payment of the real flows. These include product payments, capital funds, interest and dividend payments, royalties, and management fees. Our interest in this chapter is focused on the real flows of products and factor services rather than on the associated financial flows.

22-1, for instance, an interruption in the production or shipments of A_1 will halt the production of A_6 unless A_6 has access to another supplier. Or again, the host government may prevent A_5 from importing products from A_4 to fill out its product line.

As a result of external and internal constraints the parent company will seldom push the integration of its system to a logical extreme. Instead, integration is most likely to be partial, applying to some regions but not to the entire world or to some products but not to all products. In particular, many parent companies have been reluctant to integrate the operations of affiliates in the industrial countries with the operations of affiliates in the developing countries because of restrictions and political instability prevalent in developing countries.

To conclude, the multinational enterprise system functions as an international transfer agent for both products and factor services. Although the pattern of these transfers will depend on the parent company's strategy and various constraints, the parent company is the only source of certain factor services (notably, systemwide management) and is usually the principal source of capital and technology. However, as we have seen, the parent company may also initiate factor flows (as well as product flows) among the affiliates in different countries and from them back to itself. Hence, the multinational enterprise system recapitulates in microcosm the international economic system of trade and factor movements among national economies.[11] We now take a closer look at product and factor transfers within the multinational enterprise system.

Transfers of Product in the Multinational Enterprise System

As noted above, the multinational enterprise system generates many cross-national product transfers within the system itself.[12] These intra-enterprise product transfers are the direct consequence of the decisions made by the parent company managers relating to three strategy questions:

1. Where in the world are the markets for our final products?
2. Where should we locate our production facilities to supply those markets?
3. Where and from whom should we obtain the inputs (raw materials, parts, components, capital equipment) necessary to the manufacture of our final products?

---

[11] In different language, the MNE *internalizes* cross-national market transactions. The theory of internalization is treated in the next chapter.

[12] The system also generates cross-national sales to nonsystem customers and cross-national purchases from nonsystem suppliers. Both of these extra-enterprise transactions and the cross-national transfers within the system (intra-enterprise transfers) constitute the international trade created by the system.

For each country market of the multinational enterprise's final products, parent company managers must decide whether to produce within the market or export into it from a production base located in another country. For each production affiliate, parent company managers must decide whether to make or buy the necessary production inputs. If the decision is to make them, then the managers must decide whether to make them in the same country as the affiliate in question or to obtain them from an affiliate in another country. When the parent company is following a global strategy, these decisions will create some degree of system integration in marketing, production, or both.

Horizontal Integration   Figure 22-2 depicts a pattern of intra-enterprise product transfers resulting from a high degree of integration in the production of *final* products. Instead of having the parent company (P) and each foreign affiliate (the A's) produce full product lines, the parent company managers achieve a pattern of specialization among them, taking into account the scale of operations and the mix of factor services available at each of the country locations (including the home country); the logistical costs of storage, handling, and transportation; and the constraints imposed by import duties, quotas, and other trade restrictions. The transfer of final prod-

Figure 22-2   Product Transfers within the Multinational Enterprise System: Horizontal Integration

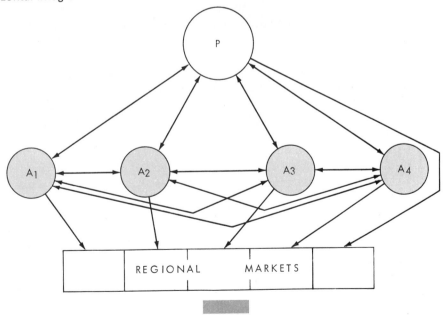

ucts among affiliates and between affiliates and the parent company enables the multinational enterprise system to offer full product lines in each country market at lower costs or higher quality levels than would be possible if those lines were entirely produced by each affiliate.

Furthermore, the parent company and each affiliate is assigned a *regional* market that it is best prepared to serve. For example, the French affiliate (A_1) serves all markets in the EC, the Mexican affiliate (A_2) serves all markets in Latin America, and so on. Hence, the parent company and the affiliates are exporting finished products to multicountry regional markets as well as participating in intra-enterprise trade. This multimarket approach can be the source of advantages separate from economies of specialization and scale derived from production. On the cost side, an international standardization of products in the multinational enterprise system makes possible the application of the same marketing policies to multicountry markets. For instance, the costs of designing an advertising program may now be spread over a hundred country markets. On the demand side, product standardization (involving the same product lines, trademarks, brand names, and packaging offered by all members of the system) helps to create a global product image that can stimulate demand throughout the world. In this way, the multinational enterprise can take advantage of communication links among consumers and industrial buyers in different countries.

Vertical Integration   Vertical integration in production also creates product transfers within the multinational enterprise system. Vertical integration occurs when a producer decides to produce at least some of the intermediate inputs required to make the final products. At the extreme, vertical integration can extend backward into raw material extraction, but for most producers (except for heavy industries, such as steel and other metals, chemicals, and oil refining), it is likely to go no further than the production of certain components and parts that are assembled into final products. Vertical integration becomes international in scope when a multinational enterprise system produces raw materials, components, or other inputs in one or more of its member companies (including the parent company) for use in production by member companies in other countries.

Figure 22-3 depicts one pattern of intra-enterprise product transfers that results from vertical integration in production. The parent company (P) transfers intermediate products to affiliates A_2, A_3, and A_4 for use in their production. At the same time, A_1 manufactures a component that is transferred to A_4, while A_2 and A_3 also manufacture inputs for A_4. Subsequently A_4 uses all these inputs to produce the final product, which is then sold to worldwide markets.

Vertical integration enables the multinational enterprise system to reap the advantages of international specialization and economies of scale, as was also true of horizontal integration. The classic example of vertical integration on a global scale is provided by the major petroleum companies,

Figure 22-3   Product Transfers within the Multinational Enterprise System: Vertical Integration

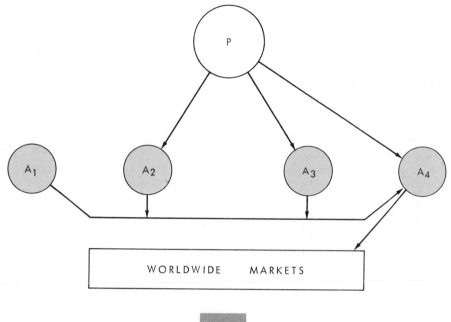

whose affiliates (located in developing countries) ship crude oil to refinery affiliates (mostly located in industrial countries), which in turn ship refined products to marketing affiliates for sale throughout the world.[13]

Transfers of Capital in the Multinational Enterprise System

The MNE is the dominant vehicle for direct foreign investment. For the most part, decisions to invest directly abroad are made by managers in multinational parent companies. Unlike portfolio investment, which is a pure transfer of capital, direct foreign investment is the transfer of a bundle of factor services that represent in their totality an extension of a business enterprise across national boundaries. In a behavioral sense, therefore, di-

---

[13] In the 1970s, governments in developing countries expropriated the crude-oil operations of the international petroleum companies. Instead of owning their own crude-oil affiliates, the international companies now obtain oil from developing countries under contractual arrangements. Nonetheless, the international petroleum companies retain much of their vertical integration. Expropriation is examined in Chapter 24.

rect foreign investment encompasses everything that MNEs do when they establish and manage their affiliates in different countries.[14]

We have observed that the direct investment activities of MNEs initiate a complex set of product and factor flows within a multinational system, which is an ongoing enterprise with expectations of continuing indefinitely into the future. It follows that no single act of direct investment and, even more so, no single product or factor flow can be fully understood without relating it to the entire system of which it is a part. In particular, any assessment of the economic effects of the MNE should consider the performance of the total system. As long as we avoid mistaking the part for the whole, however, fruitful economic analysis can proceed by investigating the constituent transfer functions of the multinational enterprise system.

The international transfer of *real* capital (plant, equipment, and inventories) commonly (but not always) occurs first as a *financial* transfer of capital funds.[15] In examining the flow of capital in the multinational enterprise system, therefore, we must consider the financial strategy of the parent company. Nonetheless, we should keep in mind that only when capital funds are converted into real capital do they contribute to production in the system.

Upon deciding to undertake new investment abroad, the parent company must then decide on the sources for financing the necessary capital expenditures. For a multinational enterprise pursuing a global strategy, the appropriate question is, Where in the world should we obtain financing for our affiliate in country Y? The answer to this question (and others like it) will determine the pattern of capital flows within the enterprise system and between the enterprise system and outside financial sources located in different countries.

Sources of Capital Financing   In deciding on the sources of financing for investment abroad, two questions are prominent in the deliberations of managers in most parent companies: (1) Should funds be obtained at home (the country of the parent) or abroad? (2) Should funds be obtained from sources *within* the system (parent company and affiliates) or from sources *outside* the system (investment banks, security markets, and other financial institutions)? Thus, the enterprise has four basic sourcing options, as depicted in Figure 22-4.

A choice of either option 1 or 2 results in the transfer of capital from the home country to a host country. The transfer may initially take the form of funds (financial transfer) or the form of capital equipment and inventory (real transfer).[16] Again, the transfer may represent an equity con-

---

[14] For a narrow definition of direct foreign investment as an international capital flow, see Chapter 23.

[15] For a discussion of capital as a factor of production, see Chapter 3.

Figure 22-4   Basic Capital-Sourcing Options for the Multinational Enterprise

	INTERNAL SOURCES	EXTERNAL SOURCES
HOME COUNTRY	1	2
FOREIGN COUNTRIES	3	4

tribution, a formal loan, or an informal advance. Under option 1, financing comes from the retained earnings of the parent company. Under option 2, the parent company obtains financing from financial institutions in the home country.

Under options 3 and 4, no net transfer of capital occurs between the home and foreign countries, because the funds are both raised abroad and invested abroad. Alternative 3 is available to the parent company only when it has affiliates with retained earnings.[17] When capital expansion in a given affiliate is financed by the affiliate's own earnings, no international transfer of capital takes place.[18] When, however, a given affiliate obtains capital funds (or real capital) from another affiliate located in a different country, there does occur an international transfer of capital. If, for example, the parent company directs a transfer of capital from its affiliate in Cologne to its affiliate in Paris, then capital moves from West Germany to France.

Under option 4, the affiliate may obtain capital from local financial institutions with or without the guarantee of the parent company. Or the parent company may raise capital funds under its own name from external sources in the host country of the affiliate. In both instances, the resulting capital flow is domestic, not international.[19] When, however, the parent

---

[16] Intangibles, such as patent rights, management services, and goodwill may also be capitalized. This practice is more common when the affiliate is a joint venture than when it is wholly owned by the parent company.

[17] The entire cash flow of affiliates (earnings plus depreciation allowances) may be used for capital financing, but we are concerned here only with a *net* expansion of capital.

[18] Since the retained earnings *could* be repatriated to the parent company, one can argue that the use of retained earnings should be considered a capital flow from the parent to the affiliate. However, in their financial decisions most multinational enterprises draw a distinction between repatriated earnings and earnings retained abroad.

[19] However, the sale of securities abroad by the U.S. parent company is entered in the U.S. balance of payments as a long-term capital inflow, but when the funds are spent on investment abroad an offsetting entry of a long-term capital outflow (direct investment) is also recorded. Hence, the transaction is merely a bookkeeping entry with no net effect on the balance of payments.

company (or more rarely, an affiliate) obtains external capital funds from a third country or from an international market (Eurocurrencies or Eurobonds), then capital flows to the host country from one or more third countries.[20]

The final choice of a capital-sourcing option depends on the strategy preferences of the parent company and on a variety of constraints. As to the choice between home country versus foreign country sources, apparently the majority of U.S. parent companies strongly favor the use of capital funds generated abroad by their affiliates, including their retained earnings and local loans obtained without the parent's guarantee. Although new affiliates depend much more on parent company funds, established affiliates are almost always compelled to obtain much of their financing from local sources. However, in those enterprises whose operations involve a large volume of exports shipped to affiliates from the United States, the parent companies frequently extend long-term inventory loans on open account.

The most recent benchmark census of U.S. direct foreign investment reveals that at the end of 1982 the aggregate investment of U.S. parent companies in their foreign affiliates was 15.4 percent of the total assets of those affiliates.[21]

Constraints on Capital-Sourcing Policies Numerous factors both at home and abroad act to constrain the capital-sourcing choices of parent companies. Here we mention only the more prominent ones without going into detail.

Exchange restrictions in the home country may limit the capital a parent company can invest abroad, as did controls in the United States in the late 1960s. Generally controls in the home country compel a parent company to rely more on foreign-source capital than it would otherwise care to do. Exchange restrictions in a *host* country may cause a parent company to rely more on local financing of an affiliate's capital needs because of a reluctance to transfer funds into an inconvertible currency. High rates of *inflation,* high *exchange risks,* or high *political risks* (such as a threat of expropriation) also favor local financing, other things being equal. All too often, however, a parent company encounters these conditions in developing countries that cannot provide local financing to meet all of the affiliate's capital requirements. In that event, the parent company has no choice but to transfer capital into the host country unless it is willing to limit the growth (and perhaps endanger the survival) of its affiliate.[22]

---

[20] Eurocurrencies and Eurobonds are described in Chapter 19.

[21] See U.S. Department of Commerce, Bureau of Economic Analysis, *U.S. Direct Investment Abroad: 1982 Benchmark Survey Data* (Washington, D.C.: U.S. Government Printing Office, December 1985), Table 2, p. 6, Table I.A.5, p. 36, and Table I.S.2, p. 50. U.S. parent companies numbered 2,245 and had 18,339 foreign affiliates, whose total assets were $1,348 billion. Parent company investment was $207 billion.

Some countries also limit the foreign-owned affiliate in its *access to local capital sources*. Somewhat paradoxically, the same countries may also limit the parent company's *ownership interests* in the local affiliate to a given percentage (commonly 49 percent). This ownership constraint can raise a serious financing problem for the joint-venture affiliate, because the parent company may be unwilling to lend to the affiliate as opposed to making an equity investment.

Taxation in home and host countries may also influence the source of capital financing in a multinational enterprise system as well as the kind of financing used (equity versus loan). To illustrate, the United States does not ordinarily tax foreign earnings until they are repatriated to the parent company, but it may tax capital transfers among foreign affiliates by regarding them as "constructive" loans or investments of the parent company. This tax policy encourages the retention of earnings in the affiliate and thereby encourages local financing. Probably the most important single effect of taxation in host countries on capital-sourcing decisions lies in the differential impact of the diverse tax systems on affiliate earnings and therefore the amounts available for new investment, either in the host country or elsewhere.

Varying *costs of capital* in different countries will also influence the choice of *external* capital sources. As the multinational enterprise becomes more global in its operations, it establishes intimate links with financial institutions in many countries and with international financial centers. Thus, it is in a position to raise capital in low-cost locations for transfer to high-cost locations. Regarding *internal* capital sources, the logical cost to the enterprise is the highest marginal opportunity cost of capital funds anywhere in the entire multinational enterprise system. Nonetheless, parent companies commonly make a decision to invest in a particular country without comparing investment opportunities in other countries (including the home country). Most parent companies do, however, have a desired rate of return on capital, which in effect is their internal cost of capital.

In closing, it should be evident that a U.S. parent company may undertake direct investment abroad without using its own capital resources or even without any transfer of capital from the home country to the host country. An inescapable conclusion is that *international capital transfers are not a necessary element of direct foreign investment.* Rather, the necessary element is an international transfer of management control.

Although not strictly necessary, direct foreign investment almost always involves at least *some* capital transfer from a parent company to its affiliate, especially when the affiliate is new. And, as we have observed,

---

[22] Hedging in forward exchange, swap arrangements, and investment guarantees provided by the home government may be used by the parent company to offset some of the risks. For a treatment of the U.S. investment insurance program, see Chapter 24.

capital-sourcing decisions in the multinational enterprise system may generate many capital transfers between second and third countries.

Transfers of Technology in the Multinational Enterprise System

The multinational enterprise functions as an *international innovation system* that goes far beyond the traditional mode of international technological diffusion through imitation.[23] Indeed, the comparative advantage of the MNE in world markets centers on its mastery of the innovation process far more than its mere size or financial strength. Multinational enterprises are research-intensive, and their remarkable growth proceeds from their capacity to create and market new products on a global scale.

Technology needs to be distinguished from *technological innovation*. Technology, as such, is a body of knowledge that is applicable to the production of goods and the creation of new goods. Technology, therefore, consists of ideas about products and how to make them rather than the products themselves or production facilities.[24] Today—with only modest exceptions—the source of new technology is scientific research and invention in industrial, government, and university laboratories.

Technological innovation, on the other hand, is the entire process whereby research and invention are converted into technology that is then applied to the production of "new" products or improvements in the production of "older" products. Innovation involves many activities performed by different groups of people: technical research, development (the conversion of research into industrial technology through process and product designs, engineering specifications, "scaling-up," and so on), production startup (all activities necessary to begin actual production), marketing startup (all activities necessary to launch a marketing program), and market research (the identification and measurement of market opportunities for new products). Taken together, these activities and their linkages comprise the innovation system. Because of its complexity, the process of innovation is subject to numerous failures. Many research discoveries are not developed into technology, available technology may not be used to transform production functions or create new products, and new products may not succeed in the marketplace for one or more reasons.

---

[23] For earlier discussions of technology in the context of international trade theory, see Chapter 5.

[24] Like all words that refer to a wide variety of phenomena, *technology* has no standard definition. In particular, the distinction between technology as knowledge and its embodiment in capital equipment, industrial processes, and products is commonly obscured by writers. The derivation of the word indicates that its essential meaning is that of a kind of knowledge.

International Transfer of Technological Innovation   Technological innovation may spread from one country to another either (1) through the transfer of technical knowledge (via licensing, trade, technical publications, official technical assistance programs, and other forms of communication) that is then "imitated" in new production functions and new goods by local business enterprises, or (2) through the transfer of innovation by multinational enterprises that establish operations in the recipient country via direct investment.

The first mode of innovation diffusion is critically dependent on the willingness and capacity of nationals to utilize the imported technology. Nations differ widely in this regard. Japanese entrepreneurs are able to turn imported technology quickly into new products that may even be exported to the country that was the source of the technology. A well-known example was their use of transistor technology to create the transistor radio, which found its biggest market in the United States, the source of the original technology.[25] The United States itself has used European technology to produce new products in advance of the originators. Evidence indicates that imitation works less quickly in Europe than in Japan or the United States. In the developing countries, however, imitation works slowly or not at all, because they lack the industrial and entrepreneurial skills that are necessary for innovation. As the pace of innovation quickens, lags in innovation (to say nothing of complete failure) place a nation at an increasing disadvantage in international competition. The consequences of the failure of a country's nationals to imitate foreign technology (or generate their own) may be alleviated, however, by the transfer of innovation within the multinational enterprise system.

A unique contribution of the multinational enterprise is the *internationalization of the entire innovation process*. The MNE undertakes technical research, development, production startup, marketing startup, and market research on a global scale. In this way the MNE overcomes the entrepreneurial gaps that constrain the spread of innovation through imitation alone.[26]

Multinational manufacturers set up production abroad to gain new markets or to hold on to markets that were first developed through direct exports. International investment strategy, then, is firmly market-oriented; the dominant consideration is the foreign market potential of products in which the company believes it has an advantage. If the investment region is highly developed, such as Western Europe or North America, most opportunities for multinational enterprises are found in new products that have not been imitated by local producers. This is why research-intensive

---

[25] A more recent example is the VCR.

[26] In contrast to entrepreneurial gaps among countries, the international mobility of technical knowledge is usually quite high.

industries are responsible for most of the U.S. direct investment in Western Europe.

When a multinational enterprise establishes operations in a new country, it does not simply duplicate its operations as they exist in the home or third countries. Adaptations to local conditions are usually necessary in production, in marketing, or in the product itself. As a company becomes more international, all the elements of its innovation system are affected by its foreign operations. When a company views itself as a single global entity, a multinational innovation system emerges that ties together research centers, production, and markets located throughout the world. Flows of information relating to market research, technical research, production programs, and marketing programs connect the parent company with its affiliates and connect the affiliates with each other to form one system guided by a dominant management center. In this way, each affiliate has access to both the inputs (scientific discoveries, manufacturing engineering specifications, and so on) and the outputs (new products) of the entire multinational enterprise system.

Not all multinational enterprises have fully internationalized their innovation systems. Many American multinationals still try out new products in the United States before producing them abroad and they concentrate R & D in U.S. laboratories. But as multinational enterprises become more and more global, the innovation function is expanded, since managers perceive the advantages of tapping research brains in several countries and quickly introducing new products in many national markets. We can reasonably expect, therefore, more dispersal of corporate R & D facilities; in effect, laboratories will be taken to the research workers rather than the other way around.[27] Some multinational enterprises economize on research expense by using the small and medium-sized production facilities of their affiliates for trial runs of new products.

The Transfer of Innovation to Developing Countries   Attracted by big, dynamic markets, U.S. industry has moved mainly into Western Europe and other economically advanced areas. Nonetheless, it would be erroneous to infer that the multinational enterprise has contributed little to technological innovation in the developing countries.

As indicated earlier, the capacity of local enterprise in developing countries to imitate imported technology is generally very limited and in some instances virtually nonexistent. Thus, the transfer of technology to these countries is a necessary but insufficient condition for innovation. Unfortunately the direct transfer of innovation by multinational enterprise is also subject to many constraints in the developing countries. Aside from restric-

---

[27] The principal arguments for the centralization of R & D in the home country are the ease of coordination and the avoidance of duplication. In view of the remarkable improvements taking place in long-distance communication, these arguments are not convincing when set against the advantages of decentralization.

tive government policies, which are taken up in Chapter 24, two factors especially inhibit innovation transfer: (1) small, stagnant, domestic markets, and (2) the absence of an industrial infrastructure consisting of people with technical and management skills, supporting industries, transportation, power, communications, and other services. Apart from the obvious limitations on sales potentials, small markets often require major and costly adaptations in product line and design, manufacturing, and marketing. The absence of an industrial infrastructure makes it very difficult to staff new affiliates with nationals at the technical and management levels. Furthermore, the scarcity of local suppliers of components and other production inputs forces the affiliate either to make many of its required inputs, to buy them from abroad (when permitted by the host government), or to develop local sources of supply through technical and financial assistance.

To begin production in a developing country, therefore, multinational enterprises are usually compelled to staff the new affiliate with expatriate technical and management personnel drawn from the parent company or affiliates in other countries. This arrangement is not only costly but may run counter to the nationalistic policies of the host government. Hence, multinationals strive to "nationalize" the affiliate staff as quickly as possible through training programs at the worker, technical, and management levels. The magnitude of this effort is seldom appreciated by host governments or critics of multinational enterprise.

To sum up, the multinational enterprise takes advantage of international technology and entrepreneurial gaps in producing and marketing new products on a global scale. Although international production is the principal vehicle used by the MNE to transfer technology to host countries, it is by no means the only vehicle. The establishment of local R & D facilities, the training and education of local nationals, the use of local subcontractors and suppliers, and the introduction of advanced management practices also serve to spread technology. Furthermore, the intra-enterprise product transfers (trade) of multinational enterprises and their licensing and cross-licensing arrangements with independent foreign companies transfer technology among countries. Multinational enterprises may also indirectly stimulate innovation in host countries by creating new primary markets (for example, the market for integrated circuits in Europe), by encouraging local companies to emulate them (positive demonstration effect), and by forcing local companies to innovate to withstand competition. The pace of innovation in Western Europe during the 1960s would have been much slower in computers, specialized plastics, electronic test and measuring instruments, numerically controlled machine tools, and many other new products if American companies had not invested there. Because Western Europe has an advanced industrial society, local companies would have eventually imitated these products on their own, but more slowly than the imitation that actually took place because of the direct innovation of U.S. companies in Europe. In the 1980s, European and Japanese multinationals have stepped up the pace of innovation in the United States by introducing new products, such as the VCR.

Transfers of Entrepreneurial Skills in the Multinational Enterprise System

The international transfer of entrepreneurial skills is the distinctive (and unique) function of the multinational enterprise system.[28] Entrepreneurial managers centered in the parent company take the initiative in combining natural resources (land), capital, labor, and technology in different countries to produce goods and services for sale in local and external markets. Ordinarily much of the capital and all of the technology are brought into a host country by the multinational enterprise, but it is the transfer of entrepreneurial skills that truly distinguishes the MNE from other modes of capital or technology transfer, such as portfolio investment or licensing. In brief, the multinational enterprise, as its name implies, transfers *enterprise* from one country to another.

We have already anticipated the transfer of entrepreneurial skills in our discussion of technology transfer because of our emphasis on technological *innovation*. We noted that the transfer of technical knowledge (technology per se) is a communicative process and that the transfer of technological innovation by the MNE requires not only the transfer of technical knowledge but also the transfer of management skills to overcome entrepreneurial gaps.

The international transfer of entrepreneurial skills by the multinational enterprise is not limited to technological innovation; it serves to mobilize all the factors of production for new tasks in new markets. The key decisions that result from the exercise of entrepreneurial skills by the parent company include answers to the strategic questions presented earlier: Where in the world are the best markets? Where in the world should we manufacture our products to supply these markets? Where in the world should we undertake R & D to create new products for future markets? Where in the world should we obtain financing for our capital investments? Where in the world should we recruit the technical and managerial staff for our parent company and affiliates? In short, entrepreneurial decisions determine the structure and evolution of the entire multinational enterprise system.

Two aspects of entrepreneurial management in the multinational enterprise deserve additional comment: (1) the perception of economic opportunity, and (2) the deliberate assumption of risk.

The Perception of Economic Opportunity Strongly oriented toward corporate growth through innovation, the managers of multinational en-

---

[28] We distinguish entrepreneurial skills, which innovate, from administrative skills, which direct and otherwise support the routine activities of a program or organizational unit.

terprises continually search for new economic opportunities. Their "opportunity horizons" are far broader than the horizons of domestic managers; they extend into many countries and world regions. What is a dazzling opportunity to a multinational manager may not even be noticed by a domestic manager in the same industry. In general, the managers of a multinational enterprise perceive far more opportunities than managers of uninational enterprises, if only because so many of their opportunities are generated by differences among national economies. For example, a given product is seldom in the same phase of its life cycle in all countries. A product that is experiencing market saturation in the United States may be in a growth stage in, say, Western Europe and not even on the market in some developing countries. Again, local competition may be very strong in one country but moderate in another. Aside from market differences, multinational managers can take advantage of international cost differences, they can alter the patterns of specialization and exchange among affiliate companies, and, in the longer run, they can shift the country locations of production, R & D, and other activities.

The perception of economic opportunity depends not only on the horizons of managers but also on their access to information about markets, competitors, new technology, government policies, and general economic and political conditions. Hence, multinational enterprises organize "strategic intelligence" systems to gather information from sources both inside and outside the enterprise. The intelligence systems of some firms (for example, the large petroleum companies) are superior to those of most national governments. Continuous scanning of the international horizon for new opportunities is a vital entrepreneurial activity of the MNE.

The Deliberate Assumption of Risk The perception of economic opportunity alone does not make an entrepreneur. The individual must also act to exploit the opportunity in an appropriate way. In so doing, the risks that accompany innovation must also be assumed. Multinational enterprises have demonstrated both a willingness and a capacity to assume risks in countries throughout the world.[29]

Although multinational managers ordinarily perceive far more opportunities than uninational managers, the risks involved tend to be greater. These risks may be broadly classified as *economic* and *political*. Economic risks proceed from uncertainty about demand, competition, costs, and other market conditions. They are the same in kind, if not in degree, for the multinational enterprise as for the domestic enterprise. The same, however, cannot be said of political risks. For the multinational enterprise, political risks emanate from uncertainty about political events of many kinds, such as war, revolution, coup d'etat, expropriation, taxation, devaluation or revaluation, exchange controls, and import restrictions. These events are po-

---

[29] In Chapter 4 we treated the subject of ignorance, uncertainty, and risk in international trade. What we said then is also pertinent to investment and the multinational enterprise.

litical (as opposed to economic), because they result from government actions or bear on the political authority of a nation, although they may be influenced (or even caused) by economic conditions. In addition to the economic risks of innovation, therefore, multinational enterprises must deliberately assume extraordinary political risks in performing their entrepreneurial role in the world economy.[30] The capacity of multinational enterprises to bear such risks is enormously enhanced by their great size and financial strength, their dispersal of operations in many countries, and the sophistication of their management.

THE CONTRIBUTION OF THE MULTINATIONAL ENTERPRISE TO THE WORLD ECONOMY

Does the multinational enterprise make a positive contribution to the world economy? From the perspective of liberal economic theory, the answer is certainly yes. It is instructive to repeat some statements about international trade and factor movements that were made in Chapter 5.

Both trade and factor movements bring about a superior allocation of resources among nations. Trade enables a country to take advantage of international specialization in production by exporting products with low opportunity costs and importing products with high opportunity costs. International factor movements achieve a better allocation of productive agents by transferring relatively abundant factors (such as technology and entrepreneurial skills) in one country to a second country where they are relatively scarce and where they may be combined with relatively abundant factors (such as natural resources and labor) in the production of goods and services. Under conditions of perfect competition, the flow of factors would continue until their marginal productivities (and prices) were the same everywhere. Then the international allocation of factors would be optimal, because any further factor movement would lower production and consumer satisfactions for the world as a whole. Although such an optimal allocation can hardly be achieved in the world as we know it, it follows that the greater the mobility of factors among countries, the better their international allocation and the higher the efficiency of the world economy.

In light of these theoretical considerations, it is evident that the multinational enterprise system is making a major contribution to the allocative efficiency of the world economy in carrying out its role as an international transfer agent. The contribution of the MNE has been compared with the earlier role of the national corporation in building a single national economy by moving capital, technology, and entrepreneurial skills from regions of

---

[30] Some political risks assumed by the multinational enterprise are treated in Chapter 24.

factor abundance to regions of factor scarcity. In the same way that the activities of national corporations helped to integrate regional economies into national economies, so the activities of multinational enterprises are helping to integrate national economies into a world economy.[31]

But the MNE's contribution to the static, allocative efficiency of the world economy is far less important than its contribution to the rate of innovation within that economy. The multinational enterprise is first and foremost an innovator. Through international production and trade, the MNE quickly spreads new ideas, new products, new production functions, new methods of management and organization, and other innovations on a global scale. *International innovation* defines the special contribution of the multinational enterprise; no other institution or group of institutions can match this contribution. And so, the multinational enterprise has become the preeminent agent of change in the world economy.

The positive contribution of the MNE to the world economy does not necessarily imply a positive economic contribution to each and every country, although the presumption is strong that all countries can share in the benefits of a more efficient and more dynamic world economy. The economic benefits and costs of direct foreign investment for both home and host countries are explored in Chapter 24. That chapter also takes up the controversial question of the *political* costs of the multinational enterprise, which may be perceived by some host countries as outweighing any net economic benefits.

SOME EMPIRICAL DATA ON MULTINATIONAL FIRMS

Table 22-1 ranks the world's fifty largest manufacturing companies by their worldwide sales in 1985 and also indicates the percentage of each company's worldwide sales made by its foreign affiliates. This percentage underestimates the *international involvement* of these companies because it excludes any home-country exports. Exports are particularly high for Japanese and West German companies. For instance, in 1985 Toyota Motor exported $12.2 billion of motor vehicles; Matsushita, $5.3 billion of electrical equipment; Volkswagen, $8.2 billion of motor vehicles, and Hoechst, $5.0 billion of chemicals. The sales of foreign affiliates, therefore, are of products manu-

---

[31] Some economists challenge the conclusion that multinational enterprises improve the allocative efficiency of the world economy on grounds that they are oligopolistic rather than purely competitive firms. Although the possible anticompetitive effects of the multinational enterprise should not be ignored, this position surely overstates the case. The national corporations that integrated regional economies into national economies were also, in essence, oligopolists. As we shall see in the next chapter, the MNE is mainly an institutional response to *exogenous* imperfections in the international markets for products (both intermediate and final) and technology.

TABLE 22-1 International Production of the World's Fifty Largest Manufacturing
Companies, 1985 (Billions of Dollars)

Rank	Firm	Home Country	Sector	Total Worldwide Sales[1] (A)	Sales of Foreign Affiliates[2] (B)	B/A (Percent)
1.	General Motors	USA	Motor vehicles	96.4	16.2	16.8
2.	Ford Motor	USA	Motor vehicles	52.8	16.0	30.3
3.	IBM	USA	Electrical equipment	50.1	21.5	43.0
4.	E.I. du Pont	USA	Chemicals	29.5	10.4	35.8
5.	General Electric	USA	Electrical equipment	29.3	3.1	10.6
6.	Toyota Motor	JPN	Motor vehicles	28.4	1.4	5.0
7.	ENI	ITA	Chemicals	24.5	—	—
8.	Unilever	NETH-UK	Food, drink	24.2	—	—
9.	Chrysler	USA	Motor vehicles	21.3	2.5	11.7
10.	Matsushita	JPN	Electrical equipment	21.2	1.5	7.0
11.	Hitachi	JPN	Electrical equipment	21.0	2.5	12.1
12.	Siemens	FRG	Electrical equipment	18.6	4.6	24.5
13.	USX	USA	Metals	18.4	1.1	5.8
14.	Philips	NETH	Electrical equipment	18.1	16.9	93.6
15.	Volkswagen	FRG	Motor vehicles	17.8	4.2	23.4
16.	Daimler-Benz	FRG	Motor vehicles	17.8	4.1	23.0
17.	Nestle	SWI	Food, drink	17.2	16.9	98.1
18.	B.A.T.	UK	Food, drink, tobacco	16.5	14.3	86.8
19.	Philip Morris	USA	Food, drink, tobacco	16.0	4.5	28.0
20.	Bayer	FRG	Chemicals	15.6	7.9	50.6
21.	Nissan	JPN	Motor vehicles	15.2	—	—
22.	BASF	FRG	Chemicals	15.1	4.3	28.4
23.	United Technologies	USA	Aerospace	15.0	3.0	20.0
24.	Hoechst	FRG	Chemicals	14.5	5.9	40.6
25.	Mitsubishi	JPN	Industrial equipment	14.5	0.3	1.8
26.	Fiat	ITA	Motor vehicles	14.2	3.9	27.2
27.	Toshiba	JPN	Electrical equipment	14.0	0.9	6.1
28.	Imperial Chemical	UK	Chemicals	13.9	—	—
29.	Boeing	USA	Aerospace	13.6	—	—
30.	Renault	FRA	Motor vehicles	13.6	4.8	35.1
31.	Proctor & Gamble	USA	Chemicals	13.6	3.4	25.1
32.	Beatrice	USA	Food, drink	12.6	2.8	21.9

TABLE 22-1   Continued

Rank	Firm	Home Country	Sector	Total Worldwide Sales[1] (A)	Sales of Foreign Affiliates[2] (B)	B/A (Percent)
33. RJR Nabisco		USA	Food, drink, tobacco	12.4	2.7	21.4
34. Honda		JPN	Motor vehicles	12.2	1.6	13.2
35. Nippon Steel[3]		JPN	Metals	12.0	—	0.2
36. ITT		USA	Electrical equipment	11.9	6.4	54.0
37. Thyssen		FRG	Metals	11.8	4.5	38.5
38. Dow		USA	Chemicals	11.5	6.3	54.8
39. McDonnell Douglas		USA	Aerospace	11.5	2.7	23.2
40. Rockwell		USA	Aerospace	11.3	0.9	8.4
41. Peugot-Citroen		FRA	Motor vehicles	11.2	4.8	42.6
42. Westinghouse		USA	Electrical equipment	10.7	0.9	8.4
43. Eastman Kodak		USA	Photographic equipment	10.6	3.2	30.5
44. Volvo		SWE	Motor vehicles	10.0	5.0	49.6
45. NEC		JPN	Electrical equipment	9.8	0.6	6.0
46. Goodyear		USA	Rubber	9.6	3.1	32.8
47. Lockheed		USA	Aerospace	9.5	0.2	2.2
48. Allied Signal		USA	Chemicals	9.1	2.0	22.5
49. General Foods		USA	Food, drink	9.0	1.7	19.3
50. Union Carbide		USA	Chemicals	9.0	2.6	29.2

[1] Consolidated sales for the enterprise and its subsidiaries.
[2] Consolidated sales of subsidiaries and affiliates outside the home country.
[3] The sales of Nippon Steel's foreign affiliates totalled less than $100 million.
Key: FRA—France, FRG—Federal Republic of Germany, ITA—Italy, JPN—Japan, NETH—Netherlands, SWE—Sweden, SWI—Switzerland, UK—United Kingdom, and USA—United States.

Source: Derived from United Nations Center on Transnational Corporations, *Transnational Corporations in World Development* (New York: United Nations, 1988), Annex Table B1, pp. 533 ff.

factured *outside* the home country, and they measure the *international production* of their parent companies, which is a distinctive feature of the multinational enterprise. Japanese and West German companies are now rapidly expanding their international production, following in the footsteps of companies headquartered in the United States, the United Kingdom, the Netherlands, and Switzerland. Not all of the top fifty manufacturing companies are multinational in an organizational or strategic sense, but all of them face competition from both domestic and foreign rivals.

Chapter 22 – The Nature and Scope of Multinational Enterprise

Dutch and Swiss firms show the highest levels of international sales (production) through foreign affiliates (Nestle [98.1 percent] and Philips [93.6 percent]), which reflects the small size of their home-country markets. Nearly half (twenty-four) of the top fifty firms are headquartered in the United States, followed by Japan (nine) and West Germany (six).

Table 22-2 ranks the world's ten largest petroleum companies. Two observations are pertinent. First, most of the petroleum companies depend heavily on the sales (production) of foreign affiliates. With the exception of Pemex, exports of petroleum products from the home countries are comparatively small. Nippon Oil and Pemex are not true multinationals: Nippon Oil's operations are mostly confined to purchasing oil outside Japan for sale inside Japan, and Pemex's operations are mostly limited to the production and sale of oil in Mexico and the export of oil from Mexico. Second, the United States is the dominant home country (six companies), followed by the United Kingdom (two companies).

In the 1980s, many firms in *service* industries—banking, investment services, insurance, retailing, accounting, advertising, market research, law, construction, publishing, air transportation, hotel services, and others—established foreign affiliates (as sole ventures, joint ventures, or fran-

TABLE 22-2   International Production of the World's Ten Largest Petroleum Companies in 1985 (Billions of Dollars)

Rank	Firm	Home Country	Total Worldwide Sales (A)	Sales of Foreign Affiliates (B)	B/A (Percent)
1.	Exxon	USA	86.7	59.0	68.1
2.	Royal Dutch Shell	NETH-UK	81.8	—	58.0[1]
3.	Mobil	USA	56.0	32.0	57.2
4.	British Petroleum	UK	53.1	29.2	55.4
5.	Texaco	USA	46.3	21.9	47.2
6.	Chevron	USA	43.8	13.6	31.0
7.	Nippon Oil	JPN	27.9	0.1	0.3
8.	Amoco	USA	26.9	6.0	22.2
9.	Atlantic Richfield	USA	21.7	2.1	9.8
10.	Pemex	MEX	20.4	—	—

[1] Percent for 1978.

Source: Derived from United Nations Center on Transnational Corporations, *Transnational Corporations in World Development* (New York: United Nations, 1988), Annex Table B1, pp. 533 ff.

TABLE 22-3   International Involvement of the World's Ten Largest Fast-Food and Restaurant Chains in 1986

Rank	Firm	Home Country	Total Worldwide Sales (Billions of Dollars)	Total Number of Units (A)	Number of Units Abroad (B)	B/A (Percent)
1.	McDonald's	USA	12.4	9,410	2,138	22.7
2.	Burger King	USA	4.5	5,024	451	8.9
3.	Kentucky Fried Chicken	USA	3.5	6,575	1,855	28.2
4.	Wendy's	USA	2.7	3,727	231	6.2
5.	Pizza Hut	USA	2.6	5,650	633	11.2
6.	Hardee's	USA	2.5	2,711	37	1.4
7.	Dairy Queen	USA	1.6	4,933	580	11.8
8.	Domino's Pizza	USA	1.5	3,608	100	2.8
9.	Taco Bell	USA	1.1	2,470	37	1.5
10.	Denny's	USA	1.1	1,176	56	4.8

Source: Derived from United Nations Center on Transnational Corporations, *Transnational Corporations in World Development* (New York: United Nations, 1988), Annex Table B17, p. 585.

chises) to penetrate world markets. Table 22-3 indicates the international involvement of the world's ten largest fast-food and restaurant chains. U.S. firms are the innovators in this business: *All* of the ten largest chains are headquartered in the United States.

SUMMARY

1. In the 1960s, U.S. business firms went abroad on a massive scale unprecedented in the history of international enterprise. Many industrial and service companies in Western Europe and Japan have also become multinational enterprises. Because of their vast size, the worldwide operations of multinational companies are now a decisive force in shaping the patterns of trade, investment, and technology flows among nations.

2. There is no single agreed-upon definition of the multinational enterprise. For our purposes, a multinational enterprise denotes a parent company that takes part in foreign production through its own affili-

ates, exercises direct control over the policies of its affiliates, and seeks to follow a worldwide strategy.

3. The manifold activities of the multinational enterprise may be usefully conceptualized as the performance of international transfer functions. The multinational enterprise becomes an international transfer agent when it moves products and factor services (capital, technology, and management) among national economies.

4. The multinational enterprise performs its role as an international transfer agent through institutional or organizational arrangements that collectively make up the multinational enterprise system. This system comprises the parent company, its foreign affiliates, and the relationships among them. The strategy decisions of the parent company generate a pattern of factor and product flows among the members of the system.

5. Intra-enterprise product transfers are the direct consequence of the strategy of the parent company. When the parent company is following a global strategy, its decisions will create some degree of horizontal and vertical integration.

6. Direct foreign investment is the transfer of a bundle of factor services that represent in their totality an extension of a business enterprise across national boundaries.

7. The international transfer of *real* capital by the MNE commonly (but not always) occurs first as a *financial* transfer of capital funds. The parent company must decide whether to obtain funds at home or abroad and whether to obtain funds from inside the enterprise or outside. The final choice of the capital-sourcing option depends on the strategy preferences of the parent company and on a variety of constraints: exchange restrictions, political risks, access to local capital sources, taxation, and capital costs. International capital transfers are not a necessary element of direct foreign investment, although they usually accompany it.

8. The multinational enterprise functions as an international innovation system that goes far beyond the traditional mode of international technological diffusion through local imitation. The MNE undertakes technical research, development, production startup, marketing startup, and market research on a global scale. It would appear that the multinational enterprise transfers more technology (and far more innovation) to the industry of developing countries than all the technical assistance and aid programs of governments and international agencies.

9. The international transfer of entrepreneurial skills is the distinctive (and unique) function of the multinational enterprise. Managers centered in the parent company take the initiative in combining natural resources (land), capital, labor, and technology in different countries to produce goods and services for sale in local and external markets.

10. The multinational enterprise makes a major contribution to the allo-

cative efficiency of the world economy, but its key contribution is innovation.

QUESTIONS AND APPLICATIONS

1. **(a)** Identify the three elements of the definition of multinational enterprise used in this text.
   (b) Why is an international holding company that owns foreign affiliates but does not exercise active control over affiliate policies excluded from the class of multinational enterprises according to our definition?
2. **(a)** What are the constituent elements of the multinational enterprise system?
   (b) "The strategy decisions of the parent company generate a pattern of factor and product flows among the members of the system." Explain.
3. Describe five external constraints that may limit the integration of a multinational enterprise system.
4. **(a)** What is international horizontal integration? International vertical integration?
   (b) Explain the possible advantages of each form of integration to the multinational enterprise. Are there any possible disadvantages?
5. Identify and discuss five constraints on the capital-sourcing policies of MNEs.
6. "International capital transfers are *not* a necessary element of direct foreign investment." Explain.
7. **(a)** Distinguish between technology and technological innovation.
   (b) How does technological innovation spread from one country to another?
8. "A unique contribution of the multinational enterprise is the internationalization of the entire innovation process." Explain.
9. **(a)** What are entrepreneurial skills?
   (b) Why are the political risks assumed by multinational enterprises described as "extraordinary" in the text?
10. Prepare a short report on a multinational enterprise of your choice, indicating its products, worldwide sales, international operations, and current situation.

SELECTED READINGS

Casson, Mark, and Associates. *Multinationals and World Trade*. London: Allen & Unwin, 1986.

Kindleberger, Charles P. *American Business Abroad.* New Haven, Conn.: Yale University Press, 1969. Lectures 1, 6.

Ohmae, Kenichi. *Triad Power: The Coming Shape of Global Competition.* New York: The Free Press, 1985.

Sauvant, Karl P. *International Transactions in Services.* Boulder, Colo.: Westview Press, 1986.

United Nations. *Multinational Corporations in World Development.* New York: 1973. Chapters 1, 2.

————. *Transnational Corporations in World Development: A Re-examination.* New York: United Nations, 1978. Chapters 1, 3.

————. *Transnational Corporations in World Development: Third Survey.* New York: United Nations, 1983. Chapters 1, 2.

————. *Transnational Corporations in World Development: Trends and Prospects.* New York: United Nations, 1988. Overview and Part 1.

23

Theories of Direct
Foreign Investment and the
Multinational Enterprise

This chapter examines theories advanced by economists to explain direct foreign investment and multinational enterprise (MNE). As a background for our discussion of these theories, we first offer a statistical overview of certain important features of direct foreign investment.

STATISTICAL OVERVIEW OF DIRECT FOREIGN INVESTMENT

There is a notable scarcity of statistical data on the multifaceted role of the multinational enterprise in the world economy. Conventional statistics are collected by governments and international organizations mainly to measure balance of payments transactions, that is, trade, service, capital, and monetary flows between the reporting country and the rest of the world. National income accounts do not distinguish foreign-owned production from locally owned production, and foreign trade statistics do not distinguish transactions between parent companies and their affiliates or between affiliates (intra-enterprise transactions) from transactions between independent exporters and importers. As a consequence, we lack reliable data on the location, size, and composition of the foreign production carried on by MNEs, as well as on the imports and exports associated with that production. On the financial side, we have only a sketchy knowledge of the aggregate current payments and receipts, sources and uses of capital financing, and size and distribution of earnings of multinational enterprises.

Because of poor statistics, both home and host governments can only guess how the decisions of MNEs affect production, employment, money supply, prices, exports, imports, the balance of payments, and other economic sectors. Thus, they are ill-prepared to devise rational policies toward multinational companies, running the risk that their actual policies will be either ineffective or counterproductive. Better statistics would remove much of the theoretical and policy-level confusion and debate about the economic role of MNEs, although they would hardly quiet debate about the MNEs political role. Given the economic importance of MNEs, we can expect national governments to improve their statistical coverage. In the end, however, the task will have to be taken on by an international agency, since no one government can hope to cover all the worldwide activities of multinational enterprises.[1]

Before looking at statistical data, it is desirable to define more precisely the meaning of *direct investment* and *book value*. The U.S. Department of Commerce defines *direct foreign investment* to include all foreign business organizations in which a U.S. person, organization, or affiliated group owns an interest of 10 percent or more.[2] The dollar values of direct foreign investments are the values carried on the books of the U.S. parent companies. The *book value* of an investment is its value at the time the investment was made; thus, it is a "historical" value that is not adjusted to changes in price levels. Since worldwide inflation has been common since the 1960s, the book values of direct investments made some years ago badly understate their current replacement values. The market value of U.S. direct investment abroad is almost certainly substantially higher than the reported book value.

Year-to-year increases in the book value of U.S. direct foreign investment are the net result of (1) the outflow of new capital from the United States, (2) new issues of securities sold abroad by U.S. companies to finance capital expenditures abroad (but not securities issued by their foreign affiliates or short-term borrowing abroad), (3) reinvested earnings of foreign affiliates, and (4) valuation of adjustments (which are mostly associated with liquidations of existing holdings).

Foreign affiliates of parent companies that are organized as foreign corporations are commonly called *subsidiaries*; foreign affiliates may also be organized as *branches* that parent companies use to conduct business in their own names and always have full ownership of. Unless there are special tax advantages for a branch, parent companies generally organize their affiliates as separate corporations. For this reason we shall at times use *subsidiary* as a substitute for *affiliate*.

---

[1] The Center on Transnational Corporations at the United Nations now compiles statistics on multinational corporations.

[2] U.S. Department of Commerce, *U.S. Direct Investment Abroad,* 1982 Benchmark Survey Data (Washington, DC: U.S. Government Printing Office, December 1985), p. 2. Other industrial countries use a similar definition. See Chapter 14 for an earlier definition of foreign direct investment as investment in enterprises located in one country but effectively controlled by residents of another country.

Direct Foreign Investment by the World's Principal Investing Countries

Table 23-1 shows the *stock* of direct foreign investment (DFI) by the major home countries and regions of multinational enterprises over the period 1960–1985.

In 1960, the DFI of all countries totaled $67.7 billion. The United States alone accounted for 47.1 percent of that amount and the other industrial countries accounted for most of the rest. In that year, the developing countries held only $700 million of DFI (1.0 percent of the world's total) and the centrally planned (communist) countries held none.

By 1985, the world's DFI had risen to $713.5 billion. The U.S. share had dropped to little more than one-third as multinational enterprises in other industrial countries, particularly those headquartered in Japan and West Germany, built up their foreign operations at a faster pace than U.S. multinational enterprises. The shares of the developing and communist countries remained small (2.7 percent and 0.1 percent, respectively), although they were higher than in 1960.

What of the future? It is probable that the U.S. share will continue to fall: *Outflows* of DFI from the United States are growing at a much slower pace than outflows from other industrial countries. The resulting drastic decline in the U.S. share of the world's average annual outflows of DFI is shown in Table 23-2. That share fell from 42.4 percent (for the period 1975–1980) to 19.0 percent (for the period 1981–1985). In sharp contrast, Japan's share rose from 5.5 percent to 11.0 percent and West Germany's share rose from 7.7 percent to 8.6 percent. This slow growth in U.S. DFI in 1981–1985 occurred at the same time as the appearance of large current-account deficits in the U.S. balance of payments. As noted in Chapter 19, the United States shifted from being the world's largest international investor to being the world's largest international debtor. This macroeconomic imbalance constrained outflows of DFI from the United States, which rose from $220.3 billion in 1980 to only $250.7 in 1985. But a more deep-seated structural reason was the appearance of new Japanese and West German multinationals at a pace that matched that of U.S. multinationals in the 1960s. The decline in the U.S. share of DFI reflects the structural shifts going on in the world economy as more and more countries catch up with the technology and other industrial resources of the United States.

U.S. Direct Investment Abroad

Where is U.S. direct foreign investment located? What is its distribution by industry? What is the distribution of sales by the majority-owned affiliates of U.S. multinational enterprises?

U.S. Direct Investment by Area Table 23-3 presents data on the area distribution of U.S. DFI for the period 1970–1986.

TABLE 23-1   Stock of Direct Foreign Investment by Major Home Country and Region, 1960, 1975, 1980, and 1985 (Billions of Dollars)

Country/Region	1960 Dollars	1960 %	1975 Dollars	1975 %	1980 Dollars	1980 %	1985 Dollars	1985 %
United States	31.9	47.1	124.2	44.0	220.3	40.0	250.7	35.1
United Kingdom	12.4	18.3	37.0	13.1	81.4	14.8	104.7	14.7
Japan	0.5	0.7	15.9	5.7	36.5	6.6	83.6	11.7
West Germany	0.8	1.2	18.4	6.5	43.1	7.8	60.0	8.4
Switzerland	2.3	3.4	22.4	8.0	38.5	7.0	45.3	6.4
Netherlands	7.0	10.3	19.9	7.1	41.9	7.7	43.8	6.1
All industrial countries	67.0	99.0	275.4	97.7	535.7	97.2	693.3	97.2
Developing countries	0.7	1.0	6.6	2.3	15.3	2.8	19.2	2.7
Centrally planned countries	—	—	—	—	—	—	1.0	0.1
All countries	67.7	100.0	282.0	100.0	551.0	100.0	713.5	100.0

Source: United Nations Center on Transnational Corporations, *Transnational Corporations in World Development: Trends and Prospects* (New York: United Nations, 1988), Table 1.2, p. 24.

TABLE 23-2   Annual Average Direct Foreign Investment Outflows by Home Country, 1975–1980 and 1981–1985 (Percentage)

Country or Type	1975–1980	1981–1985
United States	42.4	19.0
United Kingdom	17.4	20.8
Netherlands	9.4	8.8
West Germany	7.7	8.6
Japan	5.5	11.0
France	4.5	5.5
All industrial countries	98.8	98.0
Developing countries	1.2	1.8
World[1]	100.0	100.0
(Billions of Dollars)	40.3	45.3

[1] Excludes centrally planned countries of Europe.

Source: United Nations Center on Transnational Corporations, *Transnational Corporation in World Development, Trends and Prospects* (New York: 1988), Table V2, p. 77.

About three-fourths of U.S. DFI is located in other industrial countries, rising from a little more than two-thirds in 1970. It is noteworthy that direct investment in Japan is far lower than would be anticipated from the size of that country's gross national product. This "underinvestment" in Japan is a consequence of past restrictions on the entry of American companies coupled with cultural and institutional differences that make it difficult for Western firms to operate in Japan.

The primary location of U.S. DFI in the developing countries is Latin America. But that area has experienced a declining share, falling from 18.8 percent in 1970 to 13.3 percent in 1986. In contrast, the share of the newly industrializing countries of South and Southeast Asia has increased from 3.2 percent in 1970 to 5.8 percent in 1986. It is probable that this area will continue to increase its share in the 1990s at the expense of Latin America.

The inclination of U.S. multinational companies to invest in industrial countries is likely to continue in the 1990s in view of the limited market opportunities, slow economic growth, and high political risks in the majority of developing countries. In particular, we can anticipate a jump in U.S. DFI in Japan as that country takes further steps to open up its economy to foreign firms.

U.S. Direct Investment by Industrial Sector   As shown in Table 23-4, manufacturing accounted for the largest share of U.S. DFI in 1985. But manufacturing's share fell over the period while the share of services rose

TABLE 23-3   U.S. Direct Investment Abroad by Area, 1970, 1975, 1980, and 1986
(Billions of Dollars)

Area	1970		1975		1980		1985	
	Dollars	%	Dollars	%	Dollars	%	Dollars	%
Western Europe	24.5	31.4	49.5	39.9	96.1	43.6	122.9	44.5
Japan	1.5	1.9	3.3	2.7	6.2	2.8	11.3	4.1
Other industrial countries[1]	27.1	34.7	41.0	33.0	66.7	30.3	74.8	27.1
All industrial countries	53.1	68.0	93.9	75.6	169.0	76.7	209.1	75.7
Latin America	14.7	18.8	19.2	15.5	32.7	14.8	36.6	13.3
South and South-east Asia	2.5	3.2	5.7	4.6	8.5	3.9	16.0	5.8
Other developing countries[2]	7.9	10.1	5.4	4.3	10.0	4.5	14.2	15.1
All developing countries	25.0	32.0	30.3	24.4	51.3	23.3	67.0	24.3
World	78.1	100.0	123.2	100.0	220.3	100.0	276.1	100.0

[1] Australia, Canada, New Zealand, South Africa, and Bermuda.
[2] Africa, Western Asia, developing Oceania, and unspecified countries.

Source: United Nations Center on Transnational Corporations, *Transnational Corporations in World Development: Trends and Prospects* (New York: United Nations, 1988), Annex Table A.5., p. 520.

TABLE 23-4   Percentage Distribution of U.S. Direct Investment Abroad by Industry, 1975 and 1985

Industry	1975			1985		
	Developing Countries	Industrial Countries	World	Developing Countries	Industrial Countries	World
Extractive	20.0	26.4	26.4	27.6	19.9	23.1
Manufacturing	44.9	48.4	45.0	31.7	41.1	37.9
Services	24.5	22.2	24.3	34.5	34.4	33.7
Other[1]	10.5	3.0	4.3	4.5	6.4	5.2
All industries	100.0	100.0	100.0	100.0	100.0	100.0

[1] Agriculture, forestry, fishing, construction, transportation, communications, public utilities, and retail trade.

Source: United Nations Center on Transnational Corporations, *Transnational Corporations in World Development: Trends and Prospects* (New York: United Nations, 1988), Table V.4., p. 86.

from 24.5 percent to 33.7 percent. If this trend continues, services will become the dominant sector of U.S. DFI in the 1990s.

Sales by Majority-owned Affiliates of U.S. Companies   Table 23-5 indicates that the sales of majority-owned foreign nonbank affiliates of U.S. multinational companies reached $730.2 billion in 1982, about 3.5 times U.S. merchandise exports for that year. Around two-thirds of affiliate sales of all industries were local, that is, in the country of the affiliate's location. Around one-tenth of sales were to the United States and around one-fourth were to third countries.

The fraction of affiliate sales that went to the United States varies widely across industrial sectors, reflecting different purposes of DFI. Although companies enter into foreign production for specific reasons that relate to their own particular circumstances, we can distinguish three broad categories of foreign investors.

Manufacturing investors go abroad primarily to exploit foreign market opportunities. A much less common reason is to source intermediate products for use in the production of final products in the United States or third countries. Table 23-5 shows that about two-thirds of manufacturing affiliate sales were local in 1982. In contrast, less than 10 percent went to the United States ($26.2 billion out of $271.1 billion). Even this low percentage is deceptive, because almost four-fifths of these U.S. imports came from Canadian affiliates, largely in products covered by the U.S.-Canadian Automobile Agreement of 1965.[3] Excluding sales of Canadian affiliates, exports of foreign manufacturing affiliates to the United States in 1982 totaled only $5.4 billion, or 2.0 percent of their overall sales. Clearly, the main purpose of U.S. DFI in manufacturing is the penetration of foreign markets, not the supply of products for the home market.

Extractive investors in crude petroleum, mining, agriculture, and other primary industries go abroad to produce raw materials that are not available at home or are available only at a higher cost. Although the initial impulse of U.S. extractive investors is to obtain raw materials for use in the United States, many investors subsequently market raw materials to other countries, either to independent buyers or to their own manufacturing affiliates. It follows that extractive affiliates sell a higher fraction of their output to the United States and third countries than manufacturing affiliates. Table 23-5 indicates that local sales of mining affiliates were only 18.6 percent of their total sales, and local sales of affiliates in agriculture, forestry, and fishing were only 30.8 percent of total sales. The percentage of local sales of petroleum affiliates (64.2) is deceptive because it includes sales of both crude oil and manufactured refined products. When we consider sales of

---

[3] The agreement, which established free trade in new automobiles and parts between the United States and Canada, has greatly encouraged U.S. automobile companies to manufacture in Canada for sale in the United States. In effect, there is a single automotive industry in these two countries.

TABLE 23-5 Sales by Majority-owned Nonbank Affiliates of U.S. Companies in 1982 (Billions of Dollars)

Industrial Sector	Total Sales (A)	Local Sales (B)	(B) as % of (A)	Sales to United States	Sales to Third Countries	Intra-corporate Sales[1] (%)
All industries	730.2	478.0	65.5	76.8	175.5	21.9
Manufacturing	271.1	179.3	66.1	26.2	65.6	24.3
Extractive						
Petroleum	266.3	172.1	64.2	36.6	57.6	25.0
Crude oil & gas	45.1	17.4	38.6	18.1	9.6	48.1
Mining	4.3	0.8	18.6	1.2	2.3	13.6
Agriculture, forestry, fishing	1.3	0.4	30.8	0.5	0.4	64.4
Services						
Finance[2]	23.5	14.6	62.1	5.4	3.5	27.4
Wholesale trade	113.6	66.2	58.3	5.5	41.9	15.7
Services[3]	17.9	14.4	80.4	1.0	1.1	15.0
Other[4]	32.2	30.2	93.8	0.4	1.6	5.9

[1] Sales of foreign affiliates to parent company or to other foreign affiliates of the parent company.
[2] Finance (except banking), insurance, real estate, and holding companies.
[3] Hotels; business services; motion pictures; engineering, architectural, and surveying services; health services; and other services.
[4] Construction, transportation, communications, public utilities, and retail trade.

Source: U.S. Department of Commerce, *U.S. Direct Investment Abroad: 1982 Benchmark Survey Data* (Washington, D.C.: U.S. Government Printing Office, December 1985), Table III.E2, p. 226.

crude oil only, then local sales fall to 38.6 percent, sales to the United States become 40.1 percent, and sales to third countries, 21.2 percent.

Service investors make up a third category of direct foreign investors. These investors supply transportation, commerce, banking, insurance, business, hotel, and other services used by multinational companies and other customers. When their customers move abroad, service enterprises must follow them if they are to maintain business relations. A U.S. insurance company is poorly prepared to service a multinational client if it does not have branches or agencies in foreign countries. The wave of foreign investment by service companies in the 1960s, therefore, was a response to the appearance of multinational industrial enterprises that demanded services on a global scale. The reason service companies invest abroad is the reason manufacturers do, namely, to exploit foreign market opportunities, as indicated by the high level of local sales by service affiliates and the low level of their sales to the United States.

The last column in Table 23-5 reveals the percentage of affiliate sales that went to other members of the same multinational enterprise system, that is, to the parent company and other affiliates located in third countries. For all industries, this intracorporate trade is about two-fifths of affiliate sales, but it is almost half of crude oil sales, reflecting a high degree of global vertical integration in production.

REQUIREMENTS OF A THEORY OF DIRECT FOREIGN INVESTMENT

Direct foreign investment is the distinctive feature of multinational enterprise. Hence, a theory of direct foreign investment is also a theory of the multinational enterprise as an actor in the world economy.[4] As described in Chapter 22, direct foreign investment is not simply (or even primarily) an international transfer of capital but rather the *extension of an enterprise* from its home country into a foreign host country. The extension of enterprise involves flows of capital, technology, and entrepreneurial skills to the host economy, where they are combined with local factors in the production of goods for local or export markets. This transfer of a "bundle" of factor services remains under the control of the investing (parent) firm, as do the subsequent production and marketing activities of its subsidiary in the host country. Commonly, the transfer of factor services is accompanied by exports from the parent company of *intermediate* goods that are inputs in the subsidiary's production process or by exports of *final* goods channeled through the subsidiary's marketing facilities. In view of the nature of direct foreign

---

[4] As an *economic* theory, a theory of direct foreign investment would not, of course, seek to explain *all* facets of the multinational enterprise; it would ignore internal management processes as well as political and sociocultural factors.

investment, therefore, it is evident that a theory of direct foreign investment should be, first and foremost, a theory of international business enterprise.

What are the requirements, then, of a theory of direct foreign investment? Such a theory should answer three fundamental questions:

1. Why do firms go abroad as direct investors?
2. How can direct-investing firms compete successfully with local firms, given the inherent advantage of local firms operating in a familiar business environment?
3. Why do firms choose to enter foreign countries as producers rather than as exporters or licensors?

In answering these questions, a theory of direct foreign investment should also throw light on the following related questions:

4. Why is direct foreign investment dominated by large firms in oligopolistic markets?
5. Why does direct foreign investment occur in some industries and not in others?
6. Why does "reverse investment" occur at both country and industry levels (for example, when U.S. firms make direct investments in European countries and at the same time European firms make direct investments in the United States, usually in the same industries as well)?
7. Why are only a few countries the source of most direct foreign investment in the world?

Unlike trade theory, which stretches back at least to Adam Smith, direct foreign investment theory is a new domain for international economists. This is not surprising, because the contemporary scope of direct foreign investment and multinational enterprise is mainly owing to developments of the last quarter century. Although economists are now busily engaged in theory building, as yet no single dominant theory of direct foreign investment has emerged to match the Heckscher-Ohlin model of international trade.[5] Instead we have several theories, but we shall discover that, for the most part, they are complementary rather than rival explanations of direct foreign investment.

THE THEORY OF INTERNATIONAL PORTFOLIO INVESTMENT

Conventional economic theory has relied on a model of portfolio investment to explain the international movement of capital as a factor of production.

---

[5] However, as we saw in Chapter 3, the H–O model has come under attack from new theories of international trade, making its continued dominance highly questionable. Today both trade and investment theory are in intellectual ferment for much the same reason: The multinational enterprise (direct foreign investment) not only calls for explanation but it has also undermined the assumptions of conventional trade theory.

This theory postulates interest-rate differences among countries as the cause of international capital movements. Capital moves from country A to country B because the long-term interest rate (return on capital) is higher in country B than in country A, reflecting the comparative abundance of capital in the latter. Capital continues to move from country A to country B until interest rates are equal and the marginal product of capital in the two countries is the same.

This theory may be depicted in terms of the simple formula for capitalizing a stream of earnings, $C = Y/i$, where C is the value of a capital asset, Y is the stream of income produced by the asset, and i is the rate of interest.[6] Then capital moves from country A to country B when the value of an asset is higher in country A than in country B for the *same* income stream. Investors in country A will purchase the lower-priced asset in country B. This theory offers a good explanation of international movements of portfolio capital and short-term capital when account is taken of foreign exchange and other risks.[7]

But is a difference in i between two countries a good explanation of *direct* foreign investment? Do multinational enterprises establish foreign affiliates because they expect to earn higher rates of return on the same assets than at home? Or do they invest abroad because they expect to earn a higher income on the same assets than do local companies in the host country, the cost of capital (i) being the same for both?

Statistical data do not support the hypothesis that rates of return on direct foreign investment are higher than rates of return on home investment, particularly when the higher risks of foreign investment are taken into account. Sometimes they are, sometimes they are not. Nor can the country distribution of U.S. direct foreign investment be explained by yield differences between host countries and the United States.

The second hypothesis, that multinational enterprises expect to earn a higher income (Y) than local competitors, appears to be a better explanation. It is consistent with the observed fact that multinational enterprises must assume many costs of international business that are not assumed by local companies. They must overcome barriers imposed by distance, time, information gaps, nationality, culture, and other aspects of a foreign environment that are not experienced by uninational firms. These higher costs must be offset by higher incomes than are earned by local competitors. To earn a higher income, the multinational enterprise must possess advantages over local competitors that derive from its superior technology, its entrepreneurial and other management skills, and its worldwide organization.[8]

---

[6] The more elaborate formula discounts the stream of earnings for futurity to obtain its present value. The simple formula indicates that if an asset *permanently* generates an annual income of, say, $100, then it is worth $2,000 when capitalized at an interest rate of 5 percent.

[7] See the discussion of forward rates of exchange in Chapter 13.

[8] This is not to deny that large multinational enterprises may have better credit ratings than local companies, enabling them to raise capital funds more inexpensively. But local companies do not *necessarily* have lower credit ratings than multinational enterprises.

The hypothesis that direct foreign investment occurs because of differences in Y rather than differences in i is also consistent with the acquisition of local companies by multinational enterprises. Why should the MNE be willing to pay more for a company than local investors? The most plausible answer is that the MNE expects to earn higher profits (a higher Y) from the acquired company than do local investors. Furthermore, this hypothesis is consistent with the observed fact that European MNEs invest in the United States at the same time that American MNEs in the same industry are investing in Europe. Both sets of companies believe that they can compete effectively in each other's territory.

To conclude, the theory of international portfolio investment cannot adequately explain direct foreign investment. Indeed, by assuming perfect competition, this theory rules out *any* direct foreign investment. In perfectly competitive markets, local firms could buy the technology and other skills available to nonlocal firms. Hence, international firms possessing no advantages over local firms would have no incentive to produce abroad: They would incur costs of doing business abroad (not incurred by local firms) that would *not* be offset by higher sales revenues. In that kind of world, capital would move through international capital markets rather than through the mediation of the international firm, as occurs with direct foreign investment. It follows that an explanation of direct foreign investment must be found in departures from perfect competition (what the economist calls "market imperfections") that give the direct-investing firm one or more competitive advantages over local firms.

We now turn to three contemporary theories of direct foreign investment that agree on the importance of market imperfections but offer different approaches: the monopolistic advantage theory, the internalization theory, and the eclectic theory.

THE MONOPOLISTIC ADVANTAGE THEORY OF DIRECT FOREIGN INVESTMENT

The monopolistic advantage theory postulates that the investing firm possesses monopolistic advantages that enable it to operate subsidiaries abroad more profitably than local competing firms.[9] These advantages are specific to the firm rather than to its production locations. The advantages are owned by the firm and are not available to other firms on the open market. Hence, direct investment belongs more to the theory of industrial organization than to the theory of international capital movements. The monopolistic advan-

---

[9] The first systematic presentation of this theory was made by Hymer in his doctoral dissertation in 1960. (Stephen H. Hymer, *The International Operations of National Firms* [Cambridge: M.I.T. Press, 1976]). An early statement of the theory appeared in Charles P. Kindleberger, *American Business Abroad* (New Haven, Conn.: Yale University Press, 1969), Chapter 1.

tages of the investing firm fall into two broad categories: superior knowledge and economies of scale.

In presenting the monopolistic advantage theory of direct foreign investment, we shall distinguish between *horizontal foreign investment* and *vertical foreign investment*. Horizontal foreign investment occurs when the investing company enters foreign countries to produce the same product or products that are produced at home. It represents, therefore, a geographical diversification of the company's product line. In contrast, vertical investment occurs when the investing company enters foreign countries to produce *intermediate* goods that are intended for use as inputs in its domestic production process (backward vertical integration) or to produce or market its products at later stages closer to the final buyer (forward vertical integration). Backward vertical integration is particularly associated with extractive investment in petroleum and minerals, whereas most forward integration is associated with exporting, such as the establishment of an assembly plant or a sales branch. Product transfers within the multinational enterprise system based on horizontal and vertical investment are depicted in Figures 22-2 and 22-3.[10]

Two versions of the monopolistic advantage theory (superior knowledge and product life cycle) focus on horizontal investment, while a third version (oligopoly) focuses on vertical investment.

Superior Knowledge

Superior knowledge includes all *intangible* skills possessed by the firm that give it a competitive advantage wherever it undertakes operations: technology, management and organization skills, marketing skills, and the like. Monopolistic advantage derives from the firm's *control* over the use of its knowledge assets, which are transformed into differentiated products. All knowledge assets have the character of *public goods* in that the marginal cost of exploiting them through direct foreign investment is zero or very small relative to their returns. This is so because at any point in time the cost to the investing firm of acquiring its knowledge assets has already been incurred sometime in the past (sunk cost) and also because the supply of its knowledge assets is highly elastic (approaching infinity in some instances), since their use in one country does not preclude their use in another country.[11] Although the *marginal cost* of exploiting its knowledge assets in a foreign country is very low for the investing firm, local firms would need to invest the *full cost* to acquire similar assets.

---

[10] *Conglomerate foreign investment* is investment abroad to manufacture products *not* manufactured by the parent company. It is comparatively rare, occurring mainly as an unintended consequence of foreign acquisitions. For that reason, it will not be discussed here.

[11] Nor in a multiproduct firm does the use of knowledge assets for one product preclude their use for other products. Multinational enterprises engaged in horizontal foreign investment are overwhelmingly multiproduct firms.

The possession of superior knowledge allows the investing firm to create *differentiated products* with physical differences (deriving from technology skills) or with psychological differences (deriving from marketing skills) that distinguish them from competing products. In this way the firm gains a degree of control over product prices and sales that enables it to obtain an *economic rent* on its knowledge assets.[12] In brief, the investing firm with differentiated products controls knowledge that can be transferred to foreign markets at little or not cost.[13]

The monopolistic advantage theory indicates that horizontal direct foreign investment will be undertaken mainly by the more knowledge-intensive industries. This is confirmed by empirical data. Technology-intensive industries (such as petroleum refining, pharmaceuticals, industrial chemicals, farm machinery, office machinery, and transportation equipment) are the biggest source of U.S. direct investment abroad. But industries with high-level marketing skills, such as convenience foods and cosmetics, are also prominent direct investors abroad. The examples of Coca-Cola and Pepsi-Cola illustrate this point. On the other hand, the U.S. steel and textile industries, which are not knowledge-intensive, are notably absent from horizontal direct foreign investment despite the large size of many companies in those industries.

Product Life Cycle

Vernon's product life cycle model, which was described in Chapter 5, combines both trade and direct investment. Here we offer a few additional comments on this model, highlighting its investment features.[14]

By adding a *time* dimension to the theory of monopolistic advantage, the product life cycle model helps explain why U.S. manufacturers shift from exporting to direct foreign investment. The model asserts that U.S. manufacturers initially gain a monopolistic export advantage from product innovations developed for the U.S. market. In the *product introduction* stage (when production is not yet standardized and changes in design, production processes, and marketing require intimate contacts with research and development specialists, suppliers, and customers), production continues to be concentrated in the United States even though production costs in some foreign countries may be lower. However, when the product becomes standardized in its *product growth* phase, then the U.S. manufacturer has an incentive to invest abroad to exploit lower costs of manufacture and, more

---

[12] *Economic rent* is, for any factor, the return over and above its opportunity cost. Because the investing firm cannot control its knowledge assets indefinitely (since they will be eventually matched by competitors), their return is more precisely defined as a *quasi-rent* that will disappear over the long run.

[13] For an elaboration of this point from the perspective of industrial economics, see Richard E. Caves, "International Corporations: The Industrial Economics of Foreign Investment." *Economica,* February 1971, pp. 1–27.

[14] For Vernon's description of his model, see Raymond Vernon, *Sovereignty At Bay* (New York: Basic Books, 1971), pp. 64–112.

importantly, to prevent the loss of the export market to local producers. The U.S. manufacturer's first investment will be made in another industrial country where export sales are large enough to support economies of scale in local production. According to this model, then, U.S. horizontal foreign investment is essentially *defensive*—to hold on to markets built up through exports.

The monopolistic advantage of the U.S. manufacturer who first introduces a new product erodes over time. First, rival U.S. firms imitate (and sometimes improve on) the product; later, independent foreign firms imitate it. To sustain the viability of the foreign subsidiary, therefore, the U.S. manufacturer must delay product imitation with patent protection, product improvements, advertising, or new products. Since competition is mainly cost competition in the *product maturity* and *decline* phases, the U.S. manufacturer may also shift production from the country of the initial foreign investment to a lower-cost country, sustaining the old subsidiary with new products.

The product life cycle model was designed to explain U.S. exports and direct foreign investment in differentiated manufactured products. Thus, it cannot explain direct foreign investment by firms in other countries or the phenomenon of cross-investment. In the 1950s and early 1960s, the assumption that product innovations were first developed for the U.S. market and subsequently transferred to foreign markets via exports and direct foreign investment was justified by the overwhelming predominance of U.S. horizontal foreign investment. In the last decade, however, this assumption has been challenged by the rise of European and Japanese multinational corporations. It is now apparent that firms in other industrial countries are able to exploit monopolistic advantages through direct foreign investment in the United States and elsewhere.

The life cycle model is most relevant to manufacturers' *initial* entries into foreign markets as direct investors. However, by the same token, it loses relevance to multinational enterprises that have international production and marketing systems already in place. These global corporations are capable of developing new products abroad for subsequent sale in the United States, thereby standing the product life cycle model on its head. Or they can transfer new products from the United States directly to their existing foreign subsidiaries, thereby skipping the export stage. Although the United States remains the principal market and source of new products for U.S.-based multinational enterprises, their worldwide information and logistical systems (described in Chapter 22) create a pattern of investments and product transfers that bear little resemblance to the pattern postulated by the life cycle model. The inability of the model to explain the investment behavior of multinational corporations is recognized by Vernon.[15]

A final observation. In explaining why U.S. manufacturers invest

---

[15] Raymond Vernon, "The Product Cycle Hypothesis in a New International Environment," *Oxford Bulletin of Economics and Statistics* (November, 1979), pp. 255–67.

abroad, the product life cycle theory suggests an answer to the question raised previously: Why are only a few countries, notably the United States, the source of most direct foreign investment in the world? Although knowledge assets are firm-specific and, once created, may be easily transferred by a firm to other countries, a firm cannot create knowledge assets out of thin air. In the first instance, it depends on its home-country economy for the inputs necessary for their creation: scientists, engineers, managers, marketing specialists, and other human factors. A firm also needs a high-income, sophisticated domestic market for the early exploitation of its knowledge assets. As we discussed in Chapter 3, the availability of skill-intensive human factors is concentrated in a comparatively few countries, namely, the United States and other industrial countries. The same is true of high-income markets. It follows, therefore, that firms with knowledge assets are also concentrated in a small number of advanced countries and, as the monopolistic advantage theory demonstrates, these firms are the principal source of direct foreign investment.

Oligopoly

Direct foreign investors are, for the most part, big firms in oligopolistic industries characterized by only a few dominant members whose products may be differentiated or the same. Because the dominant members are so few (commonly eight or less), each of them is very sensitive to the competitive moves of the others. This *interdependence* among oligopolistic firms in the same industry is the essence of oligopoly; it is the source of distinctive oligopolistic behavior.

When an oligopolistic firm acts to obtain a competitive advantage by introducing a new product, entering a new market, or acquiring a new source of raw materials, then rival firms are forced to respond with counteractions. Not to do so would risk the loss of market position or growth to the advantage of the initiating firm. Indeed, the primary objective of oligopolistic firms appears to be *growth* (subject to a minimum profit constraint) rather than profit maximization. At the very least, each firm wants to grow as rapidly as rival firms; its *relative* rate of growth determines its relative size, which in turn determines its *relative* market power. For that reason, an oligopolistic firm is extremely sensitive to actions of rival firms that threaten its market share. A fall in market share is viewed with alarm even when the total market is expanding so rapidly that the firm's *absolute* profits and sales are rising. Equilibrium in an oligopolistic market exists, therefore, only when there is stability in the market shares of rival firms.[16]

---

[16] Competitive moves and countermoves frequently disrupt market equilibrium. To avoid price wars that hurt all members of the industry, oligopolistic firms try to maintain "market order" by implicit agreement to compete only in product differentiation, advertising, new market entry, and other forms of nonprice competition. Unless prevented by governments, oligopolists are inclined to replace implicit agreements with active collusion, including formal cartels.

Oligopolistic firms obtain monopoly profits (economic rent) because of entry barriers that keep new firms out of the industry. Common entry barriers are internal economies of scale that require large, lumpy investments of capital to be matched by newcomers; the control over scarce or low-cost raw material supplies through vertical integration; differentiated products; and knowledge assets, such as patents, trademarks, and brand names. In most manufacturing sectors, oligopolies are *heterogeneous* and produce differentiated products, and they derive monopoly profits partly from knowledge assets in the way described and partly from other entry barriers. However, oligopolies in basic manufacturing and natural resource industries (for example, steel, petroleum, and aluminum) are *homogeneous*, with member firms producing the same, nondifferentiated commodity. In the absence of superior knowledge, these industries must rely on other entry barriers to sustain monopoly profits, notably internal economies of scale and vertical integration.

What are the implications of oligopolistic behavior for direct foreign investment? We discuss them in terms of oligopolistic reaction, internal economies of scale, and vertical foreign investment.

Oligopolistic Reaction   Assume two firms, A and B, are members of an oligopolistic industry. Both firms are exporting their similar but differentiated products to country Y. Now suppose A establishes a manufacturing subsidiary in country Y. A's aggressive move is threatening to B for one or more reasons: (1) A's subsidiary in country Y could take market share away from B's exports because it can manufacture at a lower cost or mount a stronger marketing effort. If A has entered country Y on the condition that the host government impose import restrictions to create a protected market, then B is threatened with the loss of its entire export market. (2) If A's subsidiary in country Y is intended to be a key element in A's global enterprise system, either through integration in marketing or in production, then A could gain a worldwide competitive advantage over B. (3) Finally, and most threatening, A could obtain through its subsidiary in country Y (which may be an acquired local firm) new capabilities in technology, products, human skills, and knowledge that would enable A to upset the competitive equilibrium of the industry at home and abroad, leaving B and other rivals at a competitive disadvantage.

How should B counter A's investment in country Y? It could pursue any of several strategy options, but its most probable strategy would be to match A's investment in country Y with its own investment in that country. By keeping even with A, B can counter all the threats to its market position. This is a *risk-minimizing* strategy, akin to buying insurance, because the cost of B's investment is far more predictable than the consequences of *not* matching A's investment. B will, therefore, invest in country Y even if prospective returns are low, because in that event they are presumably also low for A.

The effect of this oligopolistic reaction is a "bunching" or entry concentration of foreign investments in a country by members of an oligopolistic industry. Sometimes called the "bandwagon effect," oligopolistic reaction appears to explain why many U.S. companies in the same industry have made investments in the same foreign country within a short space of time.

Knickerbocker made an empirical investigation of the effects of oligopolistic reaction on U.S. direct foreign investment in manufacturing.[17] Using a sample of 187 large U.S. corporations in twelve SIC two-digit industries and in twenty-three foreign countries, he found that almost half of the foreign manufacturing subsidiaries established by the sample corporations during the period 1948–1967 in any given industry and country were established in a three-year peak cluster and that three-fourths were established in a seven-year cluster. He also found that entry concentration was positively related to industry concentration but negatively related to product diversity. Wide-product-line firms were less likely to match a rival's foreign investment than narrow-product-line firms, because the former had a variety of ways to compete in foreign markets.[18]

In a related study, Flowers tested the hypothesis that the bunching of direct foreign investment entering the United States from Western Europe and Canada was tied to the degree of industrial concentration.[19] More concentrated industries in Western Europe and Canada were expected to show more active oligopolistic reaction in the time pattern of their U.S. investments. Statistical tests supported this hypothesis. The lumping of investment occurred within three years of the first investment, explaining about half of the European and Canadian subsidiaries established in the United States since World War II. Flowers also found that a cluster of reactive British investment in the United States tended to follow a preceding cluster of U.S. investment in the United Kingdom by a three-year lag. Thus, oligopolistic reaction offers some explanation of reverse or cross-investment.

To sum up, oligopolistic reaction appears to explain the bunching of foreign investments that causes a rapid proliferation of subsidiaries in a foreign country by members of an oligopolistic industry. However, since it deals only with *defensive* investment behavior, oligopolistic reaction does not explain why a firm makes the *first* investment in a foreign country.

Internal Economies of Scale in Production   Oligopoly is fostered by economies of scale that allow a few companies to supply an entire market. Can the economies of scale enjoyed by an oligopolistic firm become a source of monopolistic advantage over local firms and, therefore, an explanation of direct foreign investment? We have already noted that economies of scale are associated with the exploitation of knowledge assets specific to the firm

---

[17] Frederick T. Knickerbocker, *Oligopolistic Reaction and Multinational Enterprise* (Boston: Harvard University Graduate School of Business Administration, 1973).

[18] *Ibid.*, pp. 193–96.

[19] Edward B. Flowers, "Oligopolistic Reactions in European and Canadian Direct Investment in the United States," *Journal of International Business Studies,* Fall-Winter, 1976, pp. 43–55.

so that successive foreign investments are less costly than the initial one. But here we are speaking of economies of scale in physical production. Apart from knowledge assets, do internal economies of scale in production help explain direct foreign investment?[20]

In a two-country model, monopolistic advantages from scale economies in production are dependent on the investing firm's having a preferential access to capital in terms of both availability and cost. Although direct investors may indeed have greater access to capital than local firms in the developing countries (especially for large-scale, lumpy investments in natural resource industries), this is not generally true of local firms in foreign industrial countries. After all, large firms in Western Europe and Japan can obtain capital as easily as their counterparts in the United States. Such firms can match the economies of scale in production of a foreign firm that enters their home country. Thus, in a two-country model, internal economies in production do not offer a systemic explanation of direct foreign investment.

When we move from a two-country to a multicountry or world model, internal economies of scale assume a new importance. Through horizontal or vertical integration, the multinational enterprise can benefit from production economies that cannot be matched by local, nonmultinational firms. For example, suppose multinational enterprise A allocates the manufacture of a single product in its product line to its subsidiary in country Y for sale in multicountry markets. If the size of the domestic market in country Y is not sufficient to support optimal-size plants, then local firms will be operating suboptimal-size plants.[21] But A's subsidiary will have an optimal-size plant because it is geared to sales not only in country Y but also to sales in other markets through A's other subsidiaries. As a result, A's subsidiary will have lower unit costs of production than local firms, giving it a competitive advantage in the local market. More importantly, economies of scale through international specialization of production in many products and in many countries can give the multinational enterprise a competitive advantage in world markets (including the home country), apart from advantages in locating production in the least-cost countries. In effect, the multinational enterprise can escape the limits imposed on economies of scale by country market size more effectively through intra-enterprise product transfers than can the nonmultinational enterprise through exports to independent foreign buyers.

Vertical Foreign Investment   Vertical foreign investment is a prominent trait of homogeneous oligopolies in basic manufacturing and natural resources. U.S. companies in steel, aluminum, copper, and petroleum have all invested abroad to acquire sources of raw materials. Why this backward

---

[20] As we saw in Chapter 4, internal economies of scale in production can serve as a basis for international trade.

[21] This statement deserves some qualification. A local firm in a small domestic market might achieve optimal plant size through exports. But given the risks of exporting and the presence of import restrictions, most firms build plants scaled to the domestic market size.

integration into raw material sources? Why not obtain needed raw materials from independent foreign producers? The answers appear to be five: (1) sheer necessity, (2) the avoidance of oligopolistic uncertainty, (3) oligopolistic reaction, (4) the erection of entry barriers to new rivals, and (5) the technical advantages of vertical integration.

When prospective supplies of raw materials are running short and local foreign firms are not capable of discovering and exploiting new sources, an oligopolistic *industry* may be compelled to invest abroad. At the level of the oligopolistic firm, this motive may be accompanied by a desire to gain a competitive advantage over rival firms. Sheer necessity is at least a partial explanation of vertical foreign investments in the developing countries.

When the number of sources of a raw material is small and their exploitation requires large, capital-intensive investment (a common occurrence in minerals), then raw material producers are likely to be oligopolists. An oligopolist who depends on raw material as a critical input in production must, therefore, obtain it from another oligopolist. The first oligopolist can remove the bargaining disadvantages and uncertainties of this bilateral oligopoly most directly by vertical integration that affords control over the first oligopolist's *own* source of supply. Thus, the avoidance of oligopolistic uncertainty is a motive for vertical foreign investment.

As in the case of horizontal investment, oligopolistic reaction explains the proliferation of vertical foreign investments in the same country by members of an oligopolistic industry. Vertical foreign investments may also be intended to build barriers that prevent the entry of new firms into the industry. By denying to potential newcomers access to raw materials, the oligopolist is able to maintain market power. Finally, vertical foreign investment may also generate cost advantages through technical improvements in the coordination of the production and transfer of goods between different stages of production as compared to the coordination of independent producers through external markets. In effect, the oligopolist *internalizes* external economies of scale.[22]

Vertical foreign investment is not confined to raw material extraction. Manufacturing companies may invest abroad to source components for transfer to production units in the home or third countries. This kind of vertical investment is not related to oligopolistic behavior but is rather an effort to minimize production costs.

THE INTERNALIZATION THEORY OF DIRECT FOREIGN INVESTMENT

The monopolistic advantage theory asserts that direct foreign investment occurs because structural market imperfections enable individual firms to

---

[22] The technical advantages of backward integration may also extend to forward integration. Petroleum companies have not only invested abroad in crude oil extraction but in marketing outlets as well.

achieve monopoly power in foreign markets. The MNE is an institution embodying market imperfections and would not exist in a world of perfect competition. By definition, therefore, it is a monopolist.

The monopolistic advantage theory also throws light on the phenomenon of reverse investment. Because knowledge assets are firm-specific rather than country-specific, there is no contradiction in a U.S. company investing in, say, France while at the same time a French company invests in the United States. And because the two firms have differentiated products that appeal to different market segments, they may also belong to the same industry.

This theory also scores well in predicting the *industrial composition* of direct foreign investment. It answers the question, Which kinds of firms and industries are most likely to invest abroad? But the theory does not explain why some knowledge-intensive industries, notably aerospace, are large exporters but only small foreign investors. It would appear that the possession of knowledge and other firm-specific assets is a *necessary* but not a *sufficient* condition for direct foreign investment. A second condition is that a firm with a monopolistic advantage can obtain the highest economic rent for its proprietary assets only by investing abroad in production under its control. That is, the return from foreign investment must be higher than the returns from exporting or licensing.

The theory of internalization offers an explanation of why foreign investment may be a more effective way of exploiting foreign resources and markets than exporting or licensing. It is a theory, therefore, of the multinational enterprise, whose hallmark, as observed earlier, is international production.

The internalization theory postulates that (1) markets can fail to allocate factor services and goods efficiently due to natural and government-induced *externalities*, (2) markets and firms are alternative ways to organize the exchange of factor services and goods, (3) exchange is internalized within a firm when its costs are less than market exchange, and (4) the MNE is an institution that internalizes cross-national exchanges of factor services and goods through direct foreign investment (international production).

Markets become less-than-optimal allocators of resources when they fail to capture externalities in market prices. *Natural externalities* may be defined as ownership externalities, technical externalities, and public good externalities.[23] *Ownership externalities* occur when a seller is not able to charge users of a product. For instance, a knowledge innovator cannot charge users of that knowledge when the knowledge is disclosed without legal protection (patents and trademarks). *Technical externalities* occur whenever

---

[23] Jean-Francois Hennart, *A Theory of Multinational Enterprise* (Ann Arbor: University of Michigan Press, 1980), pp. 32–33. Another book on internalization is Alan M. Rugman, *Inside the Multinationals* (New York: Columbia University Press, 1981). The first book-length presentation of internalization theory is Peter Buckley and Mark Casson, *The Future of the Multinational Enterprise* (London: MacMillan, 1976).

a product experiences increasing returns to scale. *Public good externalities* occur in goods, such as knowledge, whose consumption by one individual does not lower the consumption by another individual. In addition to these natural externalities, government intervention in markets creates *artificial externalities* that cause a divergence between private and social costs and benefits: tariffs, subsidies and other incentives, taxes, price controls, exchange restrictions, investment performance requirements, and so on.[24]

Externalities may be regarded as the costs of organizing exchange— the costs of informing, monitoring, and rewarding buyers and sellers. Markets depend on prices to inform, monitor, and reward participants, and they become inefficient when externalities are not captured in prices. In contrast, firms organize exchange through central direction and control of their operations and employees: Arm's length market transactions give way to intrafirm transfers. In organizing exchange, firms incur the cost of systems to inform, monitor, and reward their employees. Internalization theory asserts that firms will replace external markets with internal flows of factor services and goods when the cost of doing so is less than the cost of organizing markets. Putting the matter somewhat differently, firms will internalize when they can capture more externalities through internal transfers than through sales and purchases in markets.

Market failure is most evident in the exchange of knowledge. When a firm creates new knowledge, that knowledge becomes a public good. But a public good cannot be priced by a market because its marginal cost is zero: New users of the good can be supplied at no additional cost. Furthermore, at a zero price, there would be no incentive for firms to create knowledge. This externality can be partly overcome by the assignment of property rights (patents and trademarks) to the innovating firm, enabling it to restrict the use of the knowledge. However, only some of a firm's knowledge can be legally protected; other knowledge must be protected through the firm's own efforts to prevent disclosure to outsiders. The most direct way to prevent disclosure and thereby earn monopoly rent is for the firm to internalize its knowledge. Instead of selling (licensing) its knowledge to outsiders, the firm applies that knowledge only to production under its control. Internalization theory explains *horizontal* foreign investment, therefore, as a response to market failure in knowledge. Internalization enables a firm to "appropriate" an economic rent for its knowledge that cannot be obtained in external markets.[25]

Internalization theory also explains *vertical* integration as a replacement of inefficient external markets. *Backward* integration occurs when (1) there are high costs in coordinating successive production stages by market

---

[24] See the discussion of the use of shadow prices to value the benefits and costs of direct foreign investment in Chapter 24.

[25] Stephen Magee, "Information and the MNC: An Appropriability Theory of Direct Foreign Investment," in *The New International Economic Order,* ed. Jagdish N. Bhagwati (Cambridge: M.I.T. Press, 1977), pp. 317–40.

prices when buyers and sellers are few in number, (2) exchange extends over a lengthy period of time, and (3) buyers and sellers experience a high degree of uncertainty. *Forward* integration becomes an efficient way of organizing exchange when there is a high degree of interdependence between the manufacturing firm and marketing channel agencies and it is costly to constrain that interdependence through market prices and market contracts.[26]

In sum, the theory of internalization posits that the multinational enterprise invests abroad in order to capture market externalities: economies of scale in production and marketing, the ownership and public-goods character of knowledge, and government-imposed market constraints. In so doing, the MNE accomplishes an international transfer of factor services and goods more efficiently than external markets. In other words, firm-specific knowledge and other assets lead to direct foreign investment whenever intrafirm transfers become less costly than external market transactions. From the perspective of internalization theory, the MNE is an institution designed to create and exploit internal markets.[27]

THE ECLECTIC THEORY OF DIRECT FOREIGN INVESTMENT

The theories of monopolistic advantage and internalization go a long way toward explaining direct foreign investment—but not all the way. In particular, these theories do not explain why the *pattern* of foreign involvement (the mix of export, licensing, and investment) by MNEs differs across countries. The only plausible explanation of different country patterns is the influence of *country-specific* factors on foreign investment as well as on other forms of international involvement.

The eclectic theory of direct foreign investment, associated with Dunning, helps explain cross-country differences in the pattern of international involvement by MNEs.[28] To Dunning, direct foreign investment implies that *location-specific* advantages favor a foreign host country but *ownership-specific* advantages favor the investing firm. International production, therefore, is attributable not only to the firm's monopolistic advantage and its ability to internalize that advantage but also to the presence of a foreign country in which production brings unique benefits to the firm. Because some market imperfections are related to country-specific endowments, the

---

[26] Hennart, *Theory of Multinational Enterprise*, Chapters 3 and 4.

[27] As revealed in Table 23-5, over two-fifths of the sales of U.S. majority-owned foreign affiliates in 1982 were intrafirm transfers. International transfers of knowledge and human skills (not shown in Table 23-5) are mostly intrafirm, that is, inside multinational enterprise systems. See also the presentation of a theory of intra-industry trade in Chapter 4.

[28] John Dunning, *International Production and the Multinational Enterprise* (London: George Allen Unwin, 1981), Chapter 2.

benefits of internalization for the MNE vary across countries.[29] The eclectic theory draws, therefore, on the theories of international trade (comparative advantage) and location and also on the theories of monopolistic advantage and internalization.

The principal contribution of the eclectic theory is an explanation of the distribution of international production by country. Both firm and country-specific endowments (natural resources, labor, energy, geographical location, markets, government policies, and so on) are necessary for foreign involvement. When it is most profitable for an MNE to internalize its monopolistic advantage in a foreign country, then the MNE favors investment in that country. Otherwise, it exploits the country market through export or licensing.

THE CHOICE AMONG EXPORT, LICENSING, AND DIRECT FOREIGN INVESTMENT

We can bring together the elements of the eclectic theory in a model that demonstrates how these elements influence a firm's choice of the entry mode best suited to a particular foreign country.[30] The variables are interpreted in present value terms because their values relate to a period of time that we take to be the same for the alternative entry modes.[31]

Assume that a knowledge-intensive firm F located in country A wants to service a market located in country B. *Total* production costs over a given period of time (including both fixed and variable costs) of F's product are P_a in country A and P_b in country B.

K represents the cost associated with a *disclosure* of the knowledge possessed by F when it grants a license to a firm in country B. Disclosure weakens F's monopoly advantage, lowering its economic rent in country B and possibly in third countries as well.

The *export marketing cost differential* is designated as M. It is the difference between export and domestic marketing costs and is positive because export marketing costs (communication, shipping, insurance, finance, and so on) are higher than domestic marketing costs.

Transfer costs, designated as T, are the extra costs of operating across

---

[29] Dunning also argues that the *industrial* composition of direct foreign investment is influenced by home country–specific factors. For example, internalization to secure foreign-based raw materials would be greater for MNEs whose home country has few raw materials than for MNEs whose home country is self-sufficient in them. See Dunning, *International Production and the Multinational Enterprise*, p. 33.

[30] The model draws on Alan M. Rugman, *Inside the Multinationals* (New York: Columbia University Press, 1981), pp. 54–60. For treatment of the choice of entry mode by international managers, see Franklin R. Root, *Entry Strategies for International Markets* (Lexington, Mass.: Lexington Books, 1987).

[31] We refrain from expressing the model's inequalities in present value terms to keep our presentation simple. For a mathematic expression of present value, see Chapter 24.

national boundaries as compared to operating at home. To operate in country B, firm F must direct, coordinate, and control a subsidiary located in a foreign political, economic, legal, social, and cultural environment. Just as M inhibits exports, so T inhibits direct investment. Since a high proportion of T is fixed, the initial foreign investment by F incurs the total transfer costs, but subsequent investments incur only small incremental expenditures.

We are now prepared to see how these five variables determine F's choice among export, licensing, and investment entry. To start, assume that $K = M = T = 0$. Under these conditions, exporting is the *only* way that F can service the market in country B. It will do so if production costs in country A are lower than production costs in country B. If, however, production costs are higher in country A, then F will remain a domestic firm. This is the world of the Heckscher-Ohlin model of international trade presented in Chapter 3. If M is positive while K and T stay at zero, F's exports will be somewhat restricted (assuming lower costs in country A), but exports will remain the only way F can enter country B's market. Zero knowledge disclosure cost (K) implies that F has no proprietary knowledge that gives it a monopolistic advantage in country B. Hence F can neither license nor invest in that country.

Now assume that K, M, and T are all positive. We have the following decision rules:

1. Export if $P_a + M < P_b + K$ (export is more profitable than licensing) *and* $P_a + M < P_b + T$ (export is more profitable than investment).
2. License if $P_b + K < P_a + M$ (licensing is more profitable than export) *and* $P_b + K < P_b + T$ (licensing is more profitable than investment).
3. Invest if $P_b + T < P_a + M$ (investment is more profitable than export) *and* $P_b + T < P_b + K$ (investment is more profitable than licensing).

Clearly, P_b is specific to country B, but M, T, and K are also influenced by country B. The value of M, for instance, is affected by transportation costs between A and B and by B's import duties. The value of T depends in part on F's knowledge and experience concerning country B and in part on B's investment climate. The value of K is influenced by the capability of local firms in B to exploit F's knowledge and by how segmented F's market is from the markets of third countries. It follows, therefore, that F's choice of entry mode for the same product may differ between country B and a third country as P, M, T, and K take on different values.

We can make certain plausible assumptions about the relationships between M, T, and K over time. At the start of F's involvement with country B, $M < T < K$, for F knows little about the country (which raises T) and it wants to protect its knowledge, which is at an early stage of the life cycle. Therefore, the probability is high that F will choose export as the most profitable initial entry mode. As time goes on, however, T falls relative to M because F learns more and more about country B through its export experience. At some point, then, F will invest in country B, particularly if production costs are lower in B. Over a longer period of time, K falls relative to T as F's product knowledge is imitated by other firms. Ultimately, therefore, F may license that knowledge (technology) to a local firm in country B.

This sequence—export, invest, license—is not certain. Government policies, in particular, may distort M, T, and K: Import restrictions increase M, a poor investment climate increases T, and those policies together increase the attractiveness of licensing.

The model is a neat depiction of the trade-offs between export, licensing, and horizontal investment. As do all theoretical models, however, it disregards variables that are deemed of lesser importance. Two missing variables deserve mention. First, by focusing only on costs, the model implicitly assumes that the revenues generated by the different entry modes are the same. But this assumption is unrealistic: Generally investment generates the highest revenue stream, exporting the next highest, and licensing the lowest. In any event, revenues need to be taken into account in deciding on the most profitable entry mode. Second, the model ignores *risk differentials* among the entry modes. Other things being equal, the higher risk of foreign investment as compared with exporting and licensing (both because a foreign subsidiary is exposed to more kinds of risk and because its risk exposure is greater) makes the trade-off favor them. This is particularly true for smaller firms that have only a limited capacity to bear risk, apart from the question of financing foreign investment. Thus, the greater risk also makes smaller firms less likely than large firms to invest abroad even when they possess knowledge assets.

TOWARD A SYNTHESIS OF INTERNATIONAL TRADE AND INVESTMENT THEORIES

In this closing section, we echo an earlier statement in Chapter 5 to the effect that the theory of international trade must become part of a broader theory of international enterprise. What is needed is a synthesis of international trade and investment theories to form a single theory of international economic involvement. Traditional theory has explained international trade in terms of a country's factor endowments relative to those of other countries. These endowments are *country-specific*. In contrast, the monopolistic advantage and internalization theories of direct foreign investment emphasize knowledge assets that are *firm-specific* and may be carried by the firm to any country. As the eclectic theory postulates, *where* production is located is influenced mainly by country-specific endowments but the international *control and ownership* of production is mainly owing to firm-specific endowments. A theory of international involvement, therefore, would center on the firm operating in imperfect factor and product markets within a world economy of dissimilar factor and market endowments at the country level. Given the recent developments in trade and investment theories, the outlook for a synthesis is favorable: Both sets of theories stress the importance of knowledge assets (technology and human skills) and both abandon the assumptions of perfect competition.

SUMMARY

1. In 1960, U.S.-based multinational companies were responsible for 47.1 percent of the world's direct foreign investment (DFI). But in 1985, the U.S. share was only 35.1 percent. This decline reflects structural shifts going on in the world economy as more and more countries catch up with the technology and other industrial resources of the United States.
2. About three-fourths of U.S. DFI was located in other industrial countries in 1986.
3. Manufacturing accounted for the largest share of U.S. DFI in 1985, but services may become the dominant sector in the 1990s.
4. In 1982, the sales of majority-owned nonbank affiliates of U.S. multinational enterprise reached $730.2 billion, about 3.5 times U.S. merchandise exports in that year. About two-thirds of these sales were local, one-tenth were to the United States, and one-fourth were to third countries. About two-fifths of the affiliates' sales were to the parent company or to other foreign affiliates of that country.
5. A theory of direct foreign investment should answer three fundamental questions: (1) Why do firms go abroad as direct investors? (2) How can direct-investing firms compete successfully with local firms given the inherent advantage of local firms operating in a familiar business environment? (3) Why do firms choose to enter foreign countries as producers rather than as exporters or licensors?
6. The theory of international portfolio investment cannot explain direct foreign investment. Indeed, by assuming perfect competition, this theory rules out *any* direct foreign investment.
7. The monopolistic advantage theory postulates that the investing firm possesses monopolistic advantages that enable it to operate subsidiaries abroad more profitably than local competing firms. These advantages fall into two broad categories: superior knowledge and economies of scale. Knowledge assets are specific to the firm, and the marginal cost to the firm of exploiting them in foreign investment is very low because they represent sunk costs. Superior knowledge allows the in-

vesting firm to create differentiated products with competitive advantages and thereby earn economic rent.

8. By adding a time dimension to the theory of monopolistic advantage, the product life cycle model helps explain why U.S. manufacturers shift from exporting to direct foreign investment. But the model cannot explain the investment behavior of full-blown multinational corporations.

9. The implications of oligopolistic behavior for direct foreign investment are discussed in terms of oligopolistic reaction, internal economies of scale, and vertical foreign investment.

10. The internalization theory of direct foreign investment postulates that multinational firms will internalize international market transactions when they can capture externalities through internal transfers. The MNE, therefore, is an institution designed to create and exploit internal markets.

11. The eclectic theory of direct foreign investment postulates that both firm- and country-specific factors are necessary to a firm's foreign involvement. When it is most profitable for an MNE to internalize its monopolistic advantage in a given foreign country, then it will invest in that country.

12. We can bring together the elements of the eclectic theory in a model that demonstrates how these elements allow a firm to choose the entry mode (export, licensing, or investment) best suited to a particular country.

13. A synthesis of international trade and investment theory is needed to form a single theory of international economic involvement.

QUESTIONS AND APPLICATIONS

1. Distinguish between *portfolio* and *direct* foreign investment.
2. (a) What is meant by the "book value"of direct foreign investment?
   (b) What are the sources of year-to-year changes in the book value of U.S. direct foreign investment?
3. (a) Why did the U.S. share of the world's DFI fall so drastically in the 1980–1985 period?
   (b) Do you anticipate the U.S. share will continue to fall in the 1990s? If not, why not? If so, why?
4. (a) How do you explain the *area* distribution of U.S. direct foreign investment?
   (b) How do you explain its distribution by economic sector?
5. (a) Distinguish three broad categories of direct foreign investors.
   (b) For each category, discuss the motivations of firms to invest abroad.
6. Why are more than half the sales of U.S. manufacturing affiliates

abroad local? Is this also true of the sales of U.S. extractive affiliates abroad? Why or why not?

7. (a) What is "superior knowledge"?
   (b) Why is superior knowledge specific to the firm?

8. (a) The marginal cost of exploiting knowledge assets in horizontal foreign investment is zero or very low. Why?
   (b) How can the investing firm obtain economic rent on its knowledge assets through horizontal foreign investment?

9. What are the limitations of the product life cycle theory in explaining direct foreign investment?

10. Explain the phenomenon of oligopolistic reaction and its effects on direct foreign investment.

11. Do internal economies of scale in production help to explain direct foreign investment? In what way?

12. How does oligopolistic behavior explain vertical foreign investment?

13. The possession of superior knowledge is a necessary but not a sufficient condition for horizontal foreign investment. Why?

14. (a) What are the postulates of the internalization theory?
    (b) What is the meaning of market failure?

15. What is the contribution of the eclectic theory of direct foreign investment?

16. How are M, T, and K likely to change over time? Why?

SELECTED READINGS

Buckley, Peter J. "The Limits of Explanation: Testing the Internalization Theory of the Multinational Enterprise." *Journal of International Business Studies*, Summer 1988, pp. 181–93.

Casson, Mark. *The Firm and the Market*. Cambridge: M.I.T. Press, 1987. Chapters 1, 2.

Caves, Richard E. *Multinational Enterprise and Economic Analysis*. Cambridge: Cambridge University Press, 1982.

Dunning, John H. *International Production and the Multinational Enterprise*. London: George Allen Unwin, 1981.

———. "The Eclectic Paradigm of International Production: A Restatement and Some Possible Extensions." *Journal of International Business Studies*, Spring 1988, pp. 1–31.

Hennart, Jean-Francois. A *Theory of Multinational Enterprise*. Ann Arbor: University of Michigan Press, 1982.

Hymer, Stephen H. *The International Operations of National Firms*. Cambridge: M.I.T. Press, 1976.

Kindleberger, Charles P., and David B. Andretsch, eds. *The Multinational Corporation in the 1980s*. Cambridge: M.I.T. Press, 1983.

Rugman, Alan M. *Inside the Multinationals*. New York: Columbia University Press, 1981.

24

Public Policy toward the
Multinational Enterprise

To effectively perform its role as an international transfer agent, the multinational enterprise must be able to move capital, technology, entrepreneurial skills, products, and funds freely throughout the world in response to market opportunity, costs, and competition. The contribution of the MNE to the efficiency and growth of the world economy is dependent, therefore, on the willingness of national governments to refrain from restricting its activities in ways that force it to suboptimize international production and trade for the world as a whole. But, as we have frequently observed, national governments are concerned only indirectly, if at all, with the maximization of the world's economic efficiency and growth. Rather, their concern is the protection and advancement of the national interest as they perceive it in any given situation. National governments, therefore, regard the multinational enterprise from the perspective of its political-economic benefits and costs to the nation—not to the world at large.

The activities of multinational enterprises bear directly on the balance of payments, production, trade, employment, growth, and international competitive position of both host and home economies. Furthermore, they raise fundamental political questions relating to external control over the domestic economy, extraterritoriality, and national sovereignty. Consequently, national governments seek to influence, regulate, and otherwise control the behavior of the multinational enterprise so as to promote their own perceived national interests, paying only scant attention to the effects of their policies on the world economy. Although the United States is the home country of about half the contemporary multinational corporations, the U.S. government is no exception to the preceding statement. In this chapter we look at U.S. policy toward the multinational enterprise, and then take up the policies of host countries and the overriding political question of national sovereignty and the multinational enterprise.

TRADITIONAL U.S. POLICY TOWARD THE MULTINATIONAL ENTERPRISE

What, then, is the policy of the U.S. government toward the MNE? As we shall discover, the answer to this question is not a simple one. Actually the United States does not have a policy toward the multinational enterprise. The rapid emergence of the multinational enterprise has caught the U.S. government unprepared to deal with it as a distinctive institution. Instead, the United States applies a variety of policies to different facets of the MNE, policies that were mostly formulated at a time when the multinational enterprise was not yet a policy issue, with the result that many of them are based on considerations unrelated to the multinational enterprise as a unique economic organization. Before we examine specific U.S. policies that affect the multinational enterprise, however, a brief review of traditional U.S. policy toward direct investment abroad by U.S. companies is in order.

The fundamental thrust of U.S. foreign economic policy since 1934 has been to extend the freedom of international trade and investment. Before World War II, U.S. foreign investment policy was a mixture of laissez-faire (letting U.S. companies invest abroad when and where they chose to do so) and strong diplomatic protection of U.S. companies in foreign countries. After World War II, U.S. policy shifted to active encouragement of direct foreign investment by American companies, at first as an instrument to help European reconstruction and somewhat later as a means (along with "transitional" foreign aid) to transfer resources to the developing countries. It was also recognized that U.S. foreign investment creates export markets for U.S. products, develops foreign sources of raw materials and fuels needed by U.S. industry, and affords profitable employment of U.S. capital. In the 1950s, the government also supported the foreign investment of U.S. companies as a way of alleviating the "dollar shortage" of foreign countries. Finally, direct foreign investment was viewed as a positive element in the struggle with the communist powers to keep the developing countries in the free world.

The onset of the persistent U.S. balance of payments deficit in 1958 weakened this supportive investment policy. Once promoted as a means of relieving the "dollar shortage," private foreign investment was accused in the 1960s of intensifying the "dollar glut." Capital outflows to Western Europe drew special criticism from government authorities, who asserted that Western Europe was no longer in need of U.S. foreign investment and, indeed, should step up its own foreign assistance and private investment in the developing countries. In 1962 the United States revised its tax code to strike down the use of "tax havens" by U.S. companies abroad and thereby accelerate the repatriation of their foreign earnings to the United States. And in 1965 the government initiated a "voluntary" restraint program (succeeded by a mandatory program in 1968) to curb the outflow of private direct investment to other industrial countries. At the same time, the United

States continued to actively support direct investment in the developing countries.

Steps taken to alleviate balance of payments deficits, therefore, split U.S. investment policy into two parts: active discouragement of private direct investment by U.S. companies in other industrial countries (when such investment involved the use of U.S. capital funds) and active encouragement of private direct investment in the developing countries. This switch in investment policy did not represent any disavowal of the traditional arguments favoring American investment anywhere in the world; rather, the switch was considered a temporary aberration that would be abandoned when the balance of payments recovered its strength.[1] Only in the late 1960s did labor and protectionist groups rise to challenge the traditional arguments by asserting that direct foreign investment by American companies had detrimental effects on the U.S. economy.

The traditional policy of the United States with respect to private foreign investment has involved treaties of friendship, commerce, and navigation with many countries; diplomatic assistance to American investors abroad; insistence on nondiscriminatory treatment of American investments; and, at times in the past, the military protection of American-owned property abroad, notably in Central American and Caribbean countries.

In recent years the U.S. government has negotiated investment treaties that deal more specifically with the conditions that affect investment abroad. These treaties have included provisions that protect the right of American investors to engage freely in business activities in a foreign country, including freedom from restrictions on the ownership or management of business enterprise. Other provisions may guarantee national or most-favored-nation treatment in taxation and other matters; reasonable requirements regarding the employment of local workers; the unrestricted remittance of earnings and repatriation of capital; and freedom from expropriation or prompt, adequate compensation in the event of expropriation.

In the 1980s, the United States reaffirmed its traditional policy, whose central feature is a belief that market forces should determine direct investment flows. But the dramatic rise in direct investment in the United States by foreign-based multinationals is now forcing a reconsideration of the traditional policy.

U.S. POLICY TOWARD DIRECT FOREIGN INVESTMENT IN THE UNITED STATES

Supporting the principle of national treatment at home as well as abroad, this country treats foreign investors the same as domestic investors. There

---

[1] Direct foreign investment controls were lifted in 1974.

are, however, some exceptions. Federal law does restrict foreign participation in U.S. companies associated with atomic energy, hydroelectric power, communications, air transport, coastal and inland water shipping, fishing, and the development of federally owned lands and mineral resources. Also, under regulations of the Department of Defense, foreigners are generally excluded from participation in, or access to, work covered by classified defense contracts. Furthermore, many states impose additional restrictions on foreign participation in banking, insurance, and land ownership, but these restrictions must be consistent with U.S. treaty obligations. Despite these exceptions, the entry of foreign companies into the United States is freer than entry into any other country in the world.

As the United States does not hinder the entry of foreign companies, neither does it encourage them with incentives. However, the individual states compete fiercely for the investment of foreign companies by offering inducements such as low-cost financing, the building of infrastructure facilities, and tax concessions. For example, to get Volkswagen's first manufacturing plant in the United States, Pennsylvania offered the West German company a $200 million package of loans, rail facilities, and highways. Most states also maintain offices abroad to attract foreign investors.

In the wake of the oil price hike, fears grew in the United States that the oil-rich Arab countries would initiate a massive takeover of American industry. In response to those fears (which have proved unwarranted), the U.S. government established a high-level interagency body to insure that foreign investments in the United States do not injure national interests, and a new office in the Department of Commerce was also created to monitor foreign investments.[2]

Figure 24-1 depicts direct foreign investment in the United States during the period 1970–1987. Its explosive growth in the 1980s is evident. In 1970, DFI in this country was only $13.3 billion and in 1980, only $68.4 billion. But then it took off, reaching $261.9 billion in 1987. Direct investment in the United States now exceeds U.S. direct investment abroad.

What explains this extraordinary growth? Undoubtedly, several factors—both macroeconomic and structural—are at work. The persistent U.S. deficit on current account provides foreign countries with an enormous dollar income to finance investments in this country. Also, the trade deficit fans the flames of import protection in the United States, which in turn induces foreign companies to circumvent actual and anticipated import barriers by establishing U.S. plants. Structural factors also promote direct investment in the United States: It is the world's largest single market, its economic growth was rapid in the 1980s, it has a high degree of political stability, and there is a comparatively low level of government interference in the

---

[2] The interagency advisory committee, the Committee on Foreign Investment in the United States, is charged with reviewing all major inward direct investments and has recently been given the authority to recommend exclusion of investments that would, in its judgment, hurt U.S. national interests.

Figure 24-1   Direct Foreign Investment in the U.S., 1970–1987

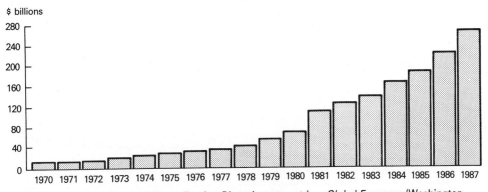

Source: U.S. Department of State, *Foreign Direct Investment in a Global Economy* (Washington, D.C.: U.S. Department of State, March 1989), p. 9.

economy. Another structural factor is the emergence of more Japanese and European multinationals with the financial and technological capability to compete directly in this country. To undertake global strategies, foreign multinationals *must* have a production and marketing presence in the United States.

Figure 24-2 shows direct foreign investment in the United States by major country. In 1987, the United Kingdom was still the leading source country ($74.9 billion), followed by the Netherlands. But the acceleration of Japan's investment, rising from a mere $200 *million* in 1970 to $33.4 *billion* in 1987, is almost certain to make Japan the most important source of direct investment for the United States in the 1990s.

Foreign multinational enterprises operating through their U.S. subsidiaries now account for a substantial share of the assets of U.S. manufacturing industries. As shown in Table 24-1, the share of U.S. affiliates of foreign multinationals almost doubled from 1971 to 1986, rising from 6.3 percent to 12.1 percent. In 1986, these affiliates held $240.5 billion of assets in the manufacturing industries of this country. For three industries, foreign ownership was more than one-fifth in 1986: chemicals and allied products; stone, clay, and glass products; and primary metal industries.

Since 1986, the penetration of U.S. manufacturing by foreign MNEs has continued apace. Four of the ten biggest U.S. chemical plants have foreign parents. Many household names, such as Firestone, General Tire, and Armstrong in the rubber industry, are owned by foreign companies (foreign-owned firms make 40 percent of the tires in the United States). There are now eight Japanese automobile assembly plants and more than 200 foreign suppliers (mostly Japanese) of automobile parts in the United

Figure 24-2   Foreign Direct Investment in the U.S. by Major Country, 1970–1987

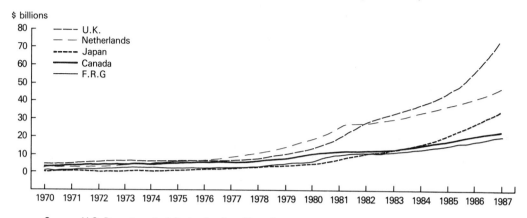

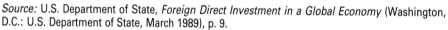

Source: U.S. Department of State, *Foreign Direct Investment in a Global Economy* (Washington, D.C.: U.S. Department of State, March 1989), p. 9.

States. In the 1980s, much of the expansion of direct investment occurred through the acquisition of U.S. companies by foreign multinationals. Table 24-2 lists the 12 largest foreign acquisitions during the period 1981–1988.

The unprecedented proliferation of foreign direct investments in the United States, often involving takeovers of well-known American companies, has aroused intense opposition by labor unions fearful of anti-union biases of foreign multinationals (particularly Japanese) and by U.S. firms fearful of new competition. These special interest groups are promoting legislation to curb new direct investments, particularly the acquisition of U.S. companies. In 1989, the Committee on Foreign Investment in the United States recommended for the first time that the president block a proposed acquisition—the acquisition of General Ceramics (a U.S. company engaged in a nuclear weapons program using critical technology) by Tokuyama Soda Company, a Japanese firm. Subsequently, Tokuyama withdrew its offer.

The massive flows of DFI into the United States are fundamentally an expression of the trend toward the globalization of the international economy that we have noted several times in this text. The policy issue for the 1990s is whether the United States fully participates in the emerging global economy or partly withdraws from it by restraining the entry of foreign multinationals as well as the entry of goods and services.

TABLE 24-1   Total Assets of U.S. Affiliates of Foreign-based Multinational Enterprises as a Percentage of Total Assets of All U.S. Businesses in Manufacturing, 1977 and 1986

Industry	1977	1986
Chemicals and allied products	15.4	32.5
Stone, clay, and glass products	7.3	22.8
Primary metal industries	6.2	20.5
Petroleum and coal products	12.0	14.9
Printing and publishing	4.5	11.8
Electric and electronic equipment	5.1	11.3
Food, tobacco, and kindred products	4.4	9.5
Paper and allied products	3.8	8.1
Fabricated metal products	2.8	7.6
Instruments and related products	3.3	6.4
Machinery, except electrical	3.7	5.5
Textile products	3.2	4.4
Rubber and plastics products	2.6	4.0
Transportation equipment	0.6	2.9
Other	2.1	5.6
All industries	*6.3*	*12.1*
Total affiliate assets in billions of dollars	*60.4*	*240.5*
Total assets of all U.S. businesses in billions of dollars	*963.0*	*1,994.1*

Source: "U.S. Affiliates of Foreign Companies: Operations in 1986," *Survey of Current Business,* May 1988, Table 4, p. 64.

U.S. PROMOTION OF DIRECT INVESTMENT IN DEVELOPING COUNTRIES

Since World War II, the United States has actively promoted private foreign investment in the developing countries, introducing investment insurance (guarantees) in 1948. Until 1971 most investment incentive measures were administered by the Agency for International Development (AID), but these functions were then transferred to a new institution, the Overseas Private Investment Corporation (OPIC), which was also given new authority and resources to promote investment.

OPIC offers the following programs and services to assist U.S. foreign investors in the developing countries:

TABLE 24-2 The Twelve Largest Acquisitions of U.S. Companies by Foreign-based Multinational Enterprises, 1981–1988

Foreign-based MNE	U.S. Company	Year	Value (Billions of Dollars)
British Petroleum (United Kingdom)	Standard Oil	1987	7.6
Campeau (Canada)	Federated Department Stores	1988	6.5
Grand Metropolitan (United Kingdom)	Pillsbury	1989	5.8
Royal Dutch Shell (Netherlands)	Shell Oil	1985	5.7
B.A.T. Industries (United Kingdom)	Farmers Group	1988	5.2
Campeau (Canada)	Allied Stores	1986	3.6
Unilever (Netherlands)	Chesebrough-Pond	1987	3.1
News Corporation (Australia)	Triangle Publications	1988	3.0
Nestle (Switzerland)	Carnation	1985	2.9
Elf Aquitaine (France)	Texasgulf	1981	2.7
Hoechst (West Germany)	Celanese	1987	2.7
Bridgestone (Japan)	Firestone	1988	2.7

Source: The New York Times, May 28, 1989, p. F9.

1. The *investment insurance program,* under which U.S. investors are provided coverage against the political risks of (a) expropriation and confiscation; (b) war, revolution, insurrection, and civil strife; and (c) inconvertibility of profits and capital.
2. The *investment guaranty program,* under which coverage against both political and commercial risks is provided for financial loans (mostly portfolio investments) by U.S. institutional investors, such as insurance companies.
3. The *direct investment fund program,* which provides dollar loans to help finance direct foreign investment projects.
4. The *investment survey program,* under which OPIC pays half the cost of an investment survey undertaken by a prospective U.S.

investor if subsequently the investor decides not to go ahead with the project.

5. *Services* that include the sponsorship of *investment missions* by American business people to foreign countries, the *planning and structuring* of investment projects, and *project brokering* to bring U.S. investors into contact with known opportunities abroad.

The incentive of most importance to multinational enterprises is the investment insurance program. Following are the eligibility requirements for such insurance:

1. The investor must be a U.S. citizen, a U.S. corporation at least 51 percent owned by U.S. interests, or a wholly owned affiliate (foreign or domestic) of such a corporation.
2. The investment must be a new project, including the expansion of an existing foreign operation.
3. The investment must be in a developing country that has signed an investment guarantee agreement with the U.S. government.
4. The application for risk coverage must be specifically approved by the foreign host government in writing.
5. OPIC must approve the investment as serving the host country's social and economic needs.[3]

Investment insurance is available to U.S. foreign investors up to a maximum of twenty years. The fee schedule for this insurance is expressed as a percentage of the risk coverage. In addition to current coverage, the investor may also obtain standby coverage, which allows the investor to increase coverage at a later time.

Has the investment insurance program stimulated U.S. direct investment in the developing countries? No conclusive answer is possible, but the following points are pertinent. First, like other incentives, investment insurance cannot turn an unprofitable investment into a profitable one. A multinational enterprise will not invest in a developing country simply because it can obtain insurance against political risks. If an investment project is judged to be unpromising on economic grounds, the enterprise will not go ahead with it even if investment insurance is available at no cost. Second, there may be situations where a multinational enterprise will not proceed with an economically attractive project in a developing country because political risks are deemed to be too high. Here the availability of insurance may tip the balance in favor of investment, although it is unlikely to do so if political risks are viewed as severe. After all, investment insurance covers only actual asset loss; it does not cover the investor's loss of pro-

---

[3] Investment Guarantee Agreements have been signed with over 90 developing countries, although some agreements do not cover all risk categories. The host government agrees to recognize the transfer of the rights and claims of the private investor to the U.S. government in the event of payment under the insurance contract, but the host government is not obligated to provide special treatment for the insured investment.

spective profits that made the investment desirable in the first place. In light of these considerations, investment insurance has probably encouraged some increase in U.S. direct investment in the developing countries. But investment insurance has not been able to alter the regional pattern of U.S. direct investment, which continues to favor the industrial areas.

U.S. TAX POLICY TOWARD THE MULTINATIONAL ENTERPRISE

Operating in many countries, multinational enterprises are subject to multiple tax jurisdictions. National tax systems are exceedingly complex, with many differences among them with respect to forms of taxation (for example, direct and indirect taxes), statutory rates, effective rates (what taxpayers actually pay), and the taxation of foreign-source income. Our interest in this section is the national taxation of foreign-source income and in particular the taxation of the income of multinational enterprises by the U.S. government.

Differences among national income tax systems influence several kinds of decisions made by the managers of multinational parent companies, notably the choice of country in which to locate operations, the legal form (branch or corporation) for the establishment of those operations, the method of financing operations (loan or equity, domestic or foreign), and the determination of the prices of products and other assets that are transferred among the many national units of the multinational enterprise system.[4] Because of its potency in influencing business decisions, both home and host governments frequently employ tax policy to promote or deter the investment and other activities of multinational enterprises.

Multiple Tax Jurisdictions

Multiple tax jurisdictions create two sets of problems: (1) "overlapping" jurisdictions, and (2) "underlapping" jurisdictions. When overlapping occurs, two or more governments claim tax jurisdiction over the same income of the same multinational enterprise. Hence, overlapping jurisdictions raise the problem of *double taxation*, a problem of immediate concern to enterprise managers. Conversely, underlapping occurs when some or all of the income of a multinational enterprise falls between tax jurisdictions and thereby escapes any taxation. The result is *tax avoidance*, which is a problem for governments. To understand how overlapping and underlapping can hap-

---

[4] Differences among national *indirect* tax systems also affect decisionmaking in the multinational enterprise because of their effects on production costs, prices, and the cost of transferring products among countries. See Chapter 10 for a discussion of the "tax frontier" in the European Community. The role of indirect taxes as nontariff trade barriers is treated in Chapter 7.

pen, we need to know something about the tax jurisdictions of national governments.

National governments may choose to exercise a *territorial tax jurisdiction*, a *national tax jurisdiction*, or both. Under a territorial tax jurisdiction, a government taxes only business income that is generated by operations located on the national territory. A government following this jurisdictional principle taxes both domestic and foreign-owned business operations taking place *within* its borders but exempts from taxation all foreign-source income that is earned by national companies *outside* its borders.

When a government exercises national tax jurisdiction, both the domestic *and* foreign-source incomes of national companies are liable for taxation by that government. Thus, the U.S. government (which follows the national principle, as do the majority of governments) taxes U.S. multinational enterprises on their worldwide incomes. If a government exercised *only* a national tax jurisdiction, it would exempt from taxation the income earned on its territory by nonnational companies owned by foreigners. But this does not happen because governments that claim a national tax jurisdiction also claim a territorial jurisdiction.

If all national governments were to adopt only a territorial tax jurisdiction, then the problem of double taxation would largely disappear for the multinational enterprise. Its affiliates would pay income taxes to their respective host governments, and dividends paid to the parent company by the affiliates would be exempt from taxation by the home government. Still remaining, however, would be the thorny problem of deciding where the income of a multinational enterprise was "rightfully" earned, a problem that is intensified by the ability of the enterprise to alter the national source of its income through adjustments in transfer prices. Given territorial tax jurisdiction only, a multinational enterprise could minimize its tax liabilities by arranging transfer prices so as to concentrate income in low-tax countries. Hence, governments would have to agree on the proper allocation among countries of the income of multinational enterprises to fully resolve the twin problems of double taxation and tax avoidance.

U.S. Taxation of Foreign-Source Income

In general, the U.S. government does not distinguish between income earned at home and income earned abroad. However, to minimize double taxation, the government does allow multinational enterprises headquartered in the United States to credit their U.S. income tax liabilities with income taxes paid to foreign governments.

Until the Revenue Act of 1962, the tax treatment of the foreign branches of U.S. multinational enterprises was basically different from the treatment of their subsidiaries that were incorporated in host countries. Considered a part of the U.S. parent company, the foreign branch was (and is) taxed by the U.S. government on its current income in the same way as domestic income, with credit granted for foreign taxes paid by the branch.

However, the foreign subsidiaries of U.S. multinational enterprises were viewed as legally distinct from the parent company, and as foreign corporations doing business on foreign soil, they were not subject to the tax jurisdiction of the U.S. government. Hence, the income of foreign subsidiaries was taxable by the U.S. government only when it was received by the U.S. parent company as dividends, royalties, management fees, or other forms of income. This tax treatment made possible the *deferral* of U.S. taxes on the foreign-source income earned by subsidiaries when that income was retained abroad rather than sent home to the parent company. To increase their tax deferrals, U.S. multinational enterprises frequently established nonoperating subsidiaries in "tax haven" countries, such as Panama and Switzerland, where taxes on foreign-source income were low or nonexistent. U.S. parent companies then channeled the earnings of their operating subsidiaries outside the United States to their tax-haven subsidiaries, where they became available for reinvestment in foreign countries throughout the world without payment of the U.S. corporate income tax.

In 1962 the Kennedy administration asked Congress to eliminate the tax deferral "privilege" for U.S.-owned subsidiaries located in industrial countries and also to eliminate all tax-haven subsidiaries regardless of their locations. Congress rejected the first request but agreed to the second request. The Revenue Act of 1962 struck hard at tax-haven subsidiaries by making their income subject to U.S. taxation when it was earned and regardless of whether or not it was repatriated to the United States. Specifically, when 30 percent or more of the income of a U.S.-controlled foreign subsidiary (more than 50 percent of the voting stock is held by the U.S. parent) takes the form of nonoperating, passive income (mainly dividends and royalties) received from other foreign subsidiaries controlled by the same U.S. parent, then that passive income is subject to immediate U.S. taxation with no deferral. If more than 70 percent of the income of a controlled foreign subsidiary is this sort of passive income, then *all* the income of the subsidiary is subject to immediate U.S. taxation. However, if less than 30 percent of a U.S.-controlled foreign subsidiary's income is nonoperating income received from subsidiaries of the same parent company, then the U.S. government taxes that subsidiary's income only when it is repatriated to the United States.[5]

To get its "fair share" of the income earned by U.S. multinational enterprises, the U.S. Treasury insists that a U.S. parent company use "arm's length" prices in all transactions with its foreign affiliates. Arm's length prices are the prices of the same or similar products and services that are paid or charged by the parent company in transactions with independent sellers and buyers. In the absence of such transactions (a common occurrence), arm's length prices are prices that represent full standard costs and

---

[5] This is the "30–70 rule." Nonrepatriated passive foreign-source income is known as "Subpart F income." In 1975, the U.S. Congress broadened the definition of Subpart F income to include income related to bribes and boycotts.

appropriate markups. Section 482 of the Internal Revenue Code gives the Treasury the authority to reallocate the income between a U.S. parent company and its foreign affiliates in accordance with the arm's length standards. The Treasury's interpretation of arm's length pricing has aroused much criticism from managers of multinational enterprises, who consider the Treasury's reallocations as frequently unrealistic and arbitrary. Nonetheless, the Treasury's authority to reallocate income is clearly necessary if U.S. parent companies are to be prevented from shifting income to foreign affiliates at the expense of U.S. tax revenue. It is rational for U.S. parent companies to establish transfer prices that will maximize the post-tax consolidated profits of the entire multinational enterprise system, and this behavior could very well involve shifting income from the United States (a high-tax country) to affiliates in low-tax countries either by charging low prices for the products and services it "sells" to its affiliates or by paying high prices for the products and services it "buys" from them.

Each national government insists that the units of a multinational enterprise operating on its territory make some taxable profits, although no other government has gone as far as the United States in reallocating profits. When the U.S. government reallocates the profits of a multinational enterprise in a way that is unacceptable to a foreign government, then the enterprise may experience double taxation. The U.S. government tries to overcome this problem by negotiating bilateral tax treaties with foreign governments whereby both signatories recognize the same allocation of income between related taxpayers. Bilateral tax treaties also contain provisions designed to eliminate other forms of double taxation and to prevent tax avoidance by nationals of the two countries.

OTHER U.S. POLICIES TOWARD THE MULTINATIONAL ENTERPRISE

This section offers a quick review of two other U.S. policies that bear on the multinational enterprise: antitrust policy and the Foreign Corrupt Practices Act.

Antitrust Policy

As business firms incorporated in the United States, the U.S. parent companies of multinational enterprises are clearly subject to antitrust laws of the United States.[6] But what may surprise many readers is the extent to

---

[6] The most important antitrust provisions are Sections 1 and 2 of the Sherman Act and Section 7 of the Clayton Act. Section 1 forbids contracts, combinations, or conspiracies "in restraint of trade or commerce among the several states, or with foreign nations." Section 2 makes illegal the monopolization of or attempt to monopolize "any part of the trade or commerce among the several states or with foreign nations." Section 7 prohibits a corporation from

which these laws also apply to their foreign affiliates, to their licensing arrangements with foreign companies, and to their acquisitions of foreign companies. Even foreign companies operating abroad come under the jurisdictional sweep of U.S. antitrust policy when their behavior has actual or potential anticompetitive effects in the United States.

The application of U.S. antitrust laws to business behavior outside the United States is sure to engender conflicts with the laws and policies of other countries. Indeed, the United States has been accused of "judicial imperialism" in seeking to apply its antitrust laws to the foreign operations of U.S. companies and even to the operations of foreign companies. The probability of conflicts is heightened by the wide diversity of national policies toward anticompetitive business behavior. Most developing countries have no antitrust laws, and the United States is sharply divergent from the other industrial countries in its antitrust philosophy and practice. EC policy, for instance, distinguishes between "good" and "bad" cartels and "good" and "bad" mergers.[7] Actually European governments strongly support mergers between national companies so that they may compete more effectively with the "American giants."

The mild enforcement of U.S. policy in the 1980s lessened antitrust conflicts with foreign governments. But as long as the United States claims extraterritorial jurisdiction for its antitrust laws, there remains the potential for future conflict.

Few subjects are as complex, contradictory, and uncertain as U.S. antitrust policy at home and abroad. It is a delight to lawyers, a challenge to economists, a brooding presence to business people, and a profound mystery to laymen. It raises many political, economic, and social questions that, for lack of space, cannot be treated here. In closing, therefore, we shall simply list the key issues that will continue to make U.S. antitrust policy a subject of controversy.

1. Does U.S. antitrust policy help or hurt the international economic position of the United States?[8] Does it promote or deter the attainment of other goals of U.S. foreign economic policy?
2. Does U.S. antitrust policy weaken the competitive strength of U.S. multinational enterprises vis-à-vis foreign companies that are sub-

---

acquiring another corporation "where in any line of commerce in any section of the country, the effect of such acquisition may be substantially to lessen competition, or tend to create a monopoly." In brief, Section 1 is an anticartel provision, Section 2 is an antimonopoly provision, and Section 7 is an antimerger provision.

[7] See Chapter 10, for EC rules governing competition.

[8] As far back as 1918, the U.S. Congress recognized that antitrust policy might hurt U.S. exports when it passed the Webb-Pomerene Act, which allows American companies to form export cartels. However, Webb-Pomerene Associations are prohibited from restraining trade within the United States or the trade of any U.S. competitor. In practice, these associations have not been important in U.S. exports, and they have been used mainly by primary producers, not manufacturers. The Export Trading Company Act of 1982 allows firms (including banks) to form export consortia, exempting them from current antitrust statutes. Comparatively few firms have taken advantage of this legislation.

ject to milder forms of antitrust regulation or to none at all? If so, is this result congruent with the national interest of the United States?

3. Should the United States seek to apply U.S. antitrust standards to the foreign operations of U.S. multinational enterprises? Or should the United States adopt a territorial jurisdiction, leaving the regulation of anticompetitive business behavior to each national government on its own territory?

4. Is the U.S. antitrust policy naive, given the oligopolistic character of U.S. and foreign multinational enterprises? To what extent is U.S. antitrust policy an ideological commitment rather than a realistic policy for the world economy of the 1990s and beyond?

5. Is U.S. antitrust policy alone sufficient to regulate the anticompetitive behavior of U.S. multinational enterprises? Can the United States achieve its antitrust goals by acting unilaterally?

6. What are the prospects for international antitrust regulation? How might it be achieved?

The Foreign Corrupt Practices Act

In the 1970s, some 500 U.S. corporations reported to the U.S. Securities and Exchange Commission (SEC) on "questionable payments" they had made to foreign government officials.[9] Total payments amounted to well over $1 billion. These revelations caused a furor in the United States and abroad: Some foreign governments were toppled, prominent persons were disgraced, several top U.S. executives lost their jobs, and in general there was acute embarrassment all around.

Why should U.S. corporations make questionable payments to foreign government officials and other influential people? Disclosures to the SEC reveal several motives: (1) to obtain or keep contracts for the sale of products and services; (2) to avoid taxes, tariffs, or exchange restrictions or resolve disputes over them; (3) to obtain preferential treatment from host governments; (4) to protect business assets from official interference or harassment; (5) to expedite the performance by government officials of duties to which a corporation is legally entitled; and (6) to influence the political process.[10] Evidently, the line between bribery *of* foreign officials and extortion *by* foreign officials cannot be neatly drawn in many cases of questionable payments.

As a result of the SEC investigations, the U.S. Congress passed the

---

[9] The SEC is charged with the administration of the federal securities laws, which require full and honest corporate financial records. Spurred by the Watergate Special Prosecution Force, which found eight corporations guilty of making illegal domestic political payments, the SEC in 1974 instituted injunctive actions against several corporations respecting questionable foreign payments and practices. Subsequently, the SEC encouraged voluntary corporate disclosures of such payments and practices. These disclosures were voluntary in name only: Refusal to disclose would bring SEC legal action.

[10] Thomas N. Gladwin and Ingo Walter, *Multinationals under Fire* (New York: John Wiley & Sons, 1980), p. 298.

Foreign Corrupt Practices Act (FCPA) in 1977. The act covers two areas of concern: accounting standards and payments to foreign officials. It requires companies to maintain accurate corporate books and records and to devise internal accounting controls to that end. Antibribery provisions contain criminal penalties for making payments to a foreign government official, a foreign political party, a party official, a political candidate, or to any person while "knowing or having reason to know" that the person will transfer any portion of the payment to any of the aforementioned recipients. Payments are unlawful under the FCPA when the purpose is to influence any act or decision of a foreign government or political party in order to obtain or retain business or direct it to another person. "Facilitating payments" that merely expedite matters by clerical or ministerial staff are exempted from prosecution.

The penalties are severe: up to $10,000 or five years' imprisonment, or both, for a convicted person and up to $1 million for a guilty company. The SEC enforces the accounting provisions and the Department of Justice enforces the antibribery provisions. The latter provisions apply without regard to whoever initiated the possibility of payment.

U.S. corporate spokesmen criticize the FCPA for its statutory ambiguities. What, for example, is the meaning of "reason to know" with respect to the actions of foreign agents and other third parties? What is the demarcation between illegal payments and legal (facilitating) payments? They also criticize the SEC and the Justice Department for not having adopted clear enforcement policies. They argue that the resulting uncertainty makes U.S. companies extremely cautious in their dealings with foreign officials and agents, causing a loss of business.[11]

No other country makes the bribery of foreign officials a *domestic* civil or criminal offense. The governments of other industrial countries either turn a blind eye to questionable foreign payments or actually encourage companies to make such payments if necessary to obtain foreign business. Because the peoples of all countries would benefit from an outlawing of improper payments to government officials, there is a strong argument for an international agreement to that purpose. But members of the United Nations have not been able to agree on an antibribery convention even though it would not be legally binding to the signatories. Despite the diplomatic efforts of the United States, the outlook for any binding agreement is bleak. For the foreseeable future, therefore, only U.S. MNEs will be subject to an antibribery law that covers their global operations.

---

[11] In general, research studies have *not* supported the allegation that the FCPA has caused U.S. companies to lose foreign business. A study by John Graham and Mark McKean, for instance, found that during the eight years after the act was passed, the U.S. share of imports of "corrupt countries" (where bribery is endemic) grew as fast as its share of imports of "noncorrupt countries." See "On the Take," *The Economist*, November 19, 1988, pp. 21–22.

Some Closing Observations on U.S. Policy toward the Multinational Enterprise

As observed earlier, the United States does not have a policy toward the multinational enterprise but instead pursues several policies that were formulated either at a time when the multinational enterprise was not a policy issue or for reasons unrelated to its unique characteristics. An examination of traditional policies toward direct foreign investment, the promotion of direct foreign investment in developing countries, tax policy, antitrust policy, and U.S. policy toward foreign investment in the United States substantiates that contention. Even the Foreign Corrupt Practices Act was the consequence of Watergate investigations of illegal corporate payments to a political campaign *inside* the United States.

Because of their importance to the American economy, new issues relating to U.S. and non-U.S. MNEs will continue to arise in the formulation of U.S. foreign economic policy. One example of an emerging issue is the performance requirements imposed on MNEs by host governments, such as local-content and export requirements. Host-government performance requirements (together with incentives offered to MNEs) distort international trade in ways that can be detrimental to U.S. economic interests. In effect, they are a form of protectionism.[12] The United States is now pressing GATT to address trade-distorting measures applied to foreign investment.

Contemporary U.S. policy toward the multinational enterprise calls to mind the fable of the blind man and the elephant. What is the multinational enterprise? Is it an international trader? An exporter of capital? An exporter of technology? An exporter of management? A possessor of considerable oligopolistic market power? A source of tax revenue? A major source of short-term capital movements? An institution subject to many national jurisdictions but not completely subject to any single jurisdiction? The answer, of course, is that the multinational enterprise is all of these things—and more.

U.S. policymakers need to transcend the traditional distinctions between trade, investment, and balance of payments policies if they are to develop a comprehensive policy toward the multinational enterprise. To design and implement such a policy, U.S. policymakers must obtain the answers to two fundamental questions: (1) What is the national interest of the United States in the multinational enterprise over the long run? (2) What comprehensive policy toward the multinational enterprise will enhance that interest?

The answer to the first question is dependent on the overall goals of U.S. foreign economic policy. The United States can choose to continue a liberal commercial policy or regress to the protectionist policy it espoused before 1934. In the final analysis, it is a choice between a world of economic interdependence and a world of autarkic economic blocs. The multinational

---

[12] See Chapter 8. Host-government policies are treated later in this chapter.

enterprise can promote the national interest of the United States only if that interest is defined in terms of an open, competitive world economy. A world of protectionist blocs would doom the multinational enterprise to eventual extinction.

Given a clear perception of the national interest in the multinational enterprise, U.S. policymakers should design a policy that optimizes the value of that institution to the United States. To a very substantial degree, the instruments of contemporary U.S. foreign economic policy are multinational enterprise systems headquartered in the United States. The success or failure of U.S. policies relating to export promotion, assistance to developing countries, East-West trade, taxation of foreign-source income, and the maintenance of competitive markets depends critically on the behavior of multinational enterprise systems. U.S. policymakers must learn much more about that behavior and how it can be influenced to serve the national interest. The development of an effective policy, therefore, will require more cooperation than heretofore experienced between the U.S. government and the representatives of multinational enterprises as well as between different agencies of the U.S. government. But it will also require closer cooperation between the U.S. government and foreign governments, extending even to the harmonization of specific policy areas such as taxation and antitrust. No single government can reasonably expect to regulate the conduct of multinational enterprise systems that operate in multiple national jurisdictions. Attempts by the U.S. government to do so engender extraterritorial disputes with other national governments that embitter international relations.

U.S. policymakers need to comprehend the rapid evolution of the multinational enterprise. In the years ahead many more firms will evolve from U.S. companies that happen to have extensive foreign operations into multinational enterprises that happen to have their headquarters in the United States. The question of U.S. policy toward the multinational enterprise becomes, therefore, part of the larger question of public policy toward the multinational enterprise by the community of nations. In particular, the national interests of foreign countries that host the affiliates of U.S. parent companies should not be ignored in the formation of U.S. policy. We now consider the national interests of host countries in the multinational enterprise and, more broadly, the conflict between the multinational enterprise and national sovereignty.

THE ECONOMIC BENEFITS AND COSTS OF DIRECT FOREIGN INVESTMENT TO HOST COUNTRIES

The multinational enterprise is perceived by policymakers in host countries as both an economic institution that creates benefits for and costs to the local economy and as a quasi-political institution that threatens the power and even the sovereignty of the nation. A lengthy examination of the policy issues generated by this twin role of the multinational enterprise would carry us far beyond the scope of this book and into the realm of political science and international law. Our purpose here is the more modest one of identifying the principal issues and, when possible, offering conceptual approaches to their objective analysis. All of these issues relate in one way or another to the mutuality and conflict of interests between national governments and the multinational enterprise. The crucial question, then, is whether both parties will learn how to expand the mutuality and contract the conflict of their individual interests. The answer to this question will determine the evolution of the world economy.

We begin by exploring the economic and then the political benefits and costs of direct foreign investment to host countries. Next we look at the constraints and risks that confront the multinational enterprise in host countries. We conclude the chapter by evaluating the need for international regulation of the multinational enterprise.

Direct foreign investment has multiple effects on the economy of a host country in terms of production, employment, income, prices, exports, imports, the balance of payments, economic growth, and general welfare. Some of these effects confer benefits on the host country; some of them incur costs. Some effects occur almost immediately, and some may take a generation. In this section we offer a conceptual approach to the measurement of the net benefit/cost ratio of direct foreign investment that takes into account its many effects and their impact over time.

The fundamental effect of direct foreign investment (representing the sum total of the many individual effects) is its contribution to the national income (net national product) of the host country over time. Closely related to this national income effect but deserving special treatment is the effect of direct foreign investment on the balance of payments of the host country over time.

The National Income Effect

What is the contribution to a host country's net national product of, say, the manufacturing affiliate of a multinational enterprise? Clearly it is less than the value of the affiliate's output, because some of the inputs used to manufacture that output (raw materials, parts, supplies, and so on) were produced by other firms. Our first approximation of the affiliate's contribution, therefore, is to subtract from the value of its output the value of all inputs purchased from other firms (including, of course, the parent company). Algebraically, if O represents the output of the affiliate and I represents the inputs purchased from local and foreign firms, then

$$(1) \text{ Benefits} = O - I.$$

This is the conventional expression of the *net value added* by a firm to national product. When all outside inputs are subtracted from the firm's output, we are left with the contribution of the factors of production directly employed by the firm as measured by the sum total of its factors payments (wages, salaries, interest, rent, and profits). Thus:

$$(2) \text{ Benefits} = O - I = F + R,$$

where F represents the affiliate's total factor payments to labor, capital, and land, and R represents the return (profit) to entrepreneurial management.

Conventional net value added, however, is not an adequate measure of the contribution of a *new* foreign-owned affiliate to the national product of the host country. It does not take into account the *opportunity cost* of the local factors of production employed by the affiliate, namely, the national product that those factors would have produced if they were *not* employed by the affiliate. Only to the extent that these local factors are used more productively by the affiliate than they would have been in its absence does their employment by the affiliate make a net contribution to national product. When the affiliate uses workers or resources that would otherwise be idle, then the opportunity cost is zero. At the other extreme, if the affiliate takes workers or resources away from other equally productive firms, then the opportunity cost is equal to the payments for their services by the affiliate. Our second approximation of the benefits of the affiliate, therefore, is to deduct the opportunity cost of the *local* factors of production used by the affiliate. Thus,

$$(3) \text{ Benefits} = (F + R) - N,$$

where N represents the opportunity cost of local factors.

So far we have considered only the direct benefits of the affiliate. To be complete, we must also include the *indirect* benefits, the net sum of its external economies and external diseconomies.[13] The external economies of the affiliate act to raise the productivity of other firms in the host country and thereby increase the national product. To illustrate, the affiliate may enable its local customers to cut costs or enter into more productive lines of activity by selling them established products at lower prices, by assuring them a reliable and adequate supply of products, by selling them new products, by offering technical assistance, and so on. The affiliate may also benefit local suppliers by providing a demand that enables them to achieve economies of scale and by offering them technical assistance to meet the affiliate's requirements. Competitive pressures exerted by the affiliate may force local

---

[13] Externalities are the economic effects of a firm's activities that are not reflected in that firm's costs or revenues. Externalities may directly affect the production activities of other firms or consumer welfare (as in the case of pollution). Our present discussion focuses on production externalities. For a treatment of externalities in the context of market failure, see Chapter 23.

firms to become more efficient. Training programs of the affiliate to upgrade the skills of its workers benefit other firms when workers leave the affiliate to enter their employ. More generally, the example of a modern, progressive enterprise may stimulate innovation by local entrepreneurs (positive demonstration effect). Against these and other external economies must be set any external *diseconomies* that decrease the productivity of local firms, such as losses in efficiency because of higher demands placed on them by the affiliate, structural unemployment caused by the competition of the affiliate, and the discouragement of local entrepreneurs (negative demonstration effect). Our third approximation of the affiliate's contribution to the national product of the host country takes into account its net external economies. Thus,

$$(4) \text{ Benefits} = (F + R) - N + L,$$

where L represents *net* external economies (external economies *minus* external diseconomies).

Our final approximation of benefits explicitly recognizes that the affiliate pays taxes on its net income (R) to the host government. R, therefore, is the sum of the after-tax income of the affiliate (R^*) and the income taxes paid by the affiliate to the host government (T). Thus,

$$(5) \text{ Benefits} = (F + R^* + T) - N + L.$$

The *costs* of direct foreign investment to the host economy are the sum total of all payments to the *foreign* factors of production (including technology) used by the affiliate (profits or dividends, interest, royalties, management fees, and so on) that are transferred out of the country. Thus,

$$(6) \text{ Costs} = E,$$

where E represents payments to foreign factors of production.

The net benefit/cost ratio of direct foreign investment to the host economy, therefore, is

$$\frac{(F + R^* + T) - N + L}{E}.$$

If the ratio is greater than 1, then benefits exceed costs to the host economy, and vice versa. Is this ratio likely to be greater than 1 for direct foreign investment in general? Both theoretical and empirical considerations support the assertion that direct foreign investment is generally beneficial to host economies.

Theoretically, it has been shown that under competitive conditions the net addition to the output of the host economy from direct foreign investment must *always* exceed the return to the investor because of the diminishing marginal product of capital. An inflow of foreign investment lowers the marginal product of *all* capital in the host economy and therefore reduces the net income on all previous foreign investments. Even when one drops the assumption of a diminishing marginal product of capital, host-government taxation would appear sufficient in most instances to insure that the net earnings of foreign investors are less than their contribution to national product, aside from any net external economies.

Empirical verification of the economic benefit/cost ratio of direct foreign investment is difficult to attain. Statistics on the foreign operations of U.S. multinational enterprises offer some basis for estimating factor payments (F), after-tax profits (R^*), and local taxes (T), but none at all for estimating the opportunity cost of local factors (N) or net external economies (L), which would be difficult to quantify in any event. F, R^*, T, and external factor payments (E) for U.S. direct investment in the developing countries are shown in Table 24-3 for the year 1982.

TABLE 24-3   Economic Benefits and Costs of U.S. Direct Investment in the Developing Countries in 1982 (Millions of Dollars)

Benefits of Direct Investment	
Factor payments by U.S. majority-owned affiliates (F)	
Employee compensation (F_1)	17,448
Interest, royalty, and	
	2,788
service payments (F_2)	20,236
Taxes paid to host government (T)	22,696
Net after-tax income (R^*)	11,030
Total benefit to national product ($F + T + R^*$)	53,962
Costs of Direct Investment	
Payments to foreign factors: royalty and service fees (E_1)	3,600
Payments to foreign factors: net interest, dividends, and	
reinvested earnings (E_2)	6,222
Total cost to national product ($E_1 + E_2 = E$)	9,822
Benefit/cost ratio before allowance for opportunity cost and net external economies [($F + T + R^*$) / E]	5.5

Source: U.S. Department of Commerce, *U.S. Direct Investment Abroad: 1982 Benchmark Survey Data* (Washington, D.C.: U.S. Government Printing Office, December 1985), various tables.

Table 24-3 indicates that U.S. investment in the developing countries made a sizable net contribution to national product in 1982. However, by ignoring opportunity cost, this estimate implicitly assumes that the opportunity cost of the local factors used by U.S. affiliates was zero. Nonetheless, even if we were to assume that the opportunity costs of labor were equal to one half the compensation received from U.S. affiliates, the contribution would remain positive.

Most probably, opportunity costs are on the low side in developing countries because of high unemployment, the presence of large endowments of unexploited resources, the low level of worker skills, and the frequently unproductive use of local savings. Thus, U.S. affiliates have added to national products by increasing the demand for unemployed or underemployed factors and by improving the allocation of factors. Most observers also conclude that U.S. affiliates have created net external economies that encourage economic growth in developing countries. Certainly the statistical evidence places the burden of proof on those who allege that national product would have been larger in the absence of direct foreign investment.

Our general conclusion that direct foreign investment offers net benefits to host economies should not be taken to mean that *every* foreign-owned affiliate necessarily makes a net contribution. When, for example, a host government exempts an affiliate from taxation, it may be questioned whether the benefits outrun the costs. Also, the foregoing analysis assumes that factor and goods prices in the host economy reflect their true scarcities and that the exchange rate does not seriously depart from the equilibrium rate. If such is not the case, the social contribution of foreign investment may be less than its social costs, although the same is also true of domestic investment. Finally, the benefit/cost ratio may shift over time, a subject we shall explore in a later section.

The Balance of Payments Effect

Direct foreign investment has numerous individual effects on the balance of payments of a host country that change significantly over time. The initial transfer of capital to the host country to establish, say, a manufacturing affiliate contributes a once-for-all benefit to the balance of payments. Once the affiliate starts operations, it may provide continuing benefits to the balance of payments by using some or all of its output for export or for import substitution. On the other hand, the affiliate may import raw materials or other inputs to sustain its operations at a continuing cost to the balance of payments. Profit repatriation and payments to foreign factors of production by the affiliate also constitute continuing drains on the host country's foreign exchange. Again, higher local income generated by the affiliate may induce more host country imports via the marginal propensity to import. Finally, if the affiliate is liquidated, any capital repatriation is a once-for-all cost to the balance of payments.

We can represent these benefits and costs algebraically as follows:

(7) Balance of payments benefits $= K + X + S,$

where K is the initial inflow of investment capital; X, the exports of the affiliate; and S, the replacement of imports by the affiliate's output (import substitution).

(8) Balance of payments costs $= (R^{**} + F^*) + (M + M^*) + D,$

where R^{**} is repatriated earnings; F^*, payments to other foreign factors of production; M, imports by the affiliate; M^*, imports induced by higher local income via the marginal propensity to import; and D, any disinvestment (liquidation) of the affiliate. The net benefit/cost ratio of direct foreign investment for the balance of payments of the host economy, therefore, is

$$\frac{K + X + S}{(R^{**} + F^*) + (M + M^*) + D}.$$

Over the long run, the balance of payments effect of direct foreign investment cannot be distinguished from its national income effect. We can understand why this is so by returning to equation (17) in Chapter 15, namely, $X - M = GNP - (C + I_d + G)$. This equation indicates that direct foreign investment will *improve* the balance of payments when its national income effect (increase in GNP) is not offset by an equal or greater increase in domestic absorption $(C + I_d + G)$. The most probable outcome over the long run is for domestic absorption to match an increase in gross national product so that the balance of payments effect of direct foreign investment becomes neutral.

Over the shorter run, however, direct foreign investment may cause a balance of payments deficit because factors of production in the host country are not fully mobile. Hence, the economy may not be able to shift quickly out of the production of "home" goods into the production of export or import-substitution goods so as to achieve the net export balance necessary to finance any net foreign-exchange expenditures associated with an affiliate. This condition of lagged adjustment is particularly representative of developing countries that have a structural inability to transform savings into foreign exchange through an increase in exports or a decrease in imports. As a consequence, developing countries commonly experience a foreign exchange constraint on their economic growth that is distinguishable from a savings constraint.[14] Over the shorter run, therefore, a net increase in imports of goods and factor services that are directly or indirectly attributable to the operations of a foreign-owned affiliate may cause a persistent deficit

---

[14] For a discussion of these constraints, see Chapter 20.

(a decrease in $X - M$) because of structural rigidities in the host economy that prevent an adjustment to the balance of payments. In other words, over the shorter run an affiliate may bring about an increase in domestic absorption that exceeds its own contribution to the national product.

Faced with foreign exchange constraints and heavy debt service burdens, policymakers in host developing countries are highly sensitive to the balance of payments effect of direct foreign investment. They regard with favor those foreign investment projects that will quickly replace imports or create exports so as to provide the foreign exchange necessary to finance the external transfer of earnings and factor payments. Conversely, foreign investment projects that are not import-saving or export-creating are likely to be discouraged by policymakers even though the projects in question will contribute significantly to economic growth. Thus, the foreign investment policies of many developing countries seek to maximize short-run balance of payments gains at the cost of sacrificing long-run gains in national income and economic growth.

Ideally a host country should maintain balance of payments equilibrium by resort to monetary, fiscal, and exchange rate policies, together with measures to speed up the reallocation of resources. But the fact is that policymakers in the developing countries must deal with immediate, pressing demands for scarce foreign exchange. In that situation, the short-run balance of payments effect of direct foreign investment tends to overwhelm the long-run national income effect in the formulation of policy. It is all the more necessary, therefore, to stress that the fundamental contribution of direct foreign investment to the host economy lies in the growth of national product through a superior allocation of resources, new technology, and improvements in local factor skills.

Disagreement on the Present Value of Benefits and Costs

So far our conceptual approach to the measurement of the national income and balance of payments effects of direct foreign investment is a static analysis that implicitly assumes that there is time for all the benefits and costs to occur. Since benefits and costs follow different time paths, a more useful approach views benefits as a future stream of annual increments to national income and costs as a future stream of external income and factor payments. To obtain the *present values* of these streams, it is necessary to discount future benefits and costs at an appropriate rate. The present value of benefits (costs), therefore, is the sum of the discounted annual benefits (costs) in the future. We can restate equations (5) and (6) in present value form as follows:

(9) Net present value of benefits =

$$\sum_{t=1}^{t=n} \left(\frac{[F_t + R_t^* + T_t] - N_t + L_t}{[1 + d]^t} \right).$$

(10) Net present value of costs =

$$\sum_{t=1}^{t=n} \left(\frac{E_t}{[1 + d]^t} \right).$$

In these equations, t is the number of years and d is the rate of discount. The higher the value of d, the greater the weight given to benefits and costs in the near future, and vice versa.[15]

When direct investors implicitly or explicitly discount future benefits and costs at a rate that differs from the rate used by the host government, then the two parties will disagree on the present value of those benefits and costs to the host country. Since it is rational for the multinational enterprise to use the marginal opportunity cost of its capital (the next best alternative use for it elsewhere in the world) to discount its own future benefits and costs, it tends to apply the same rate to discount future benefits and costs to the host country. When the host government seeks to maximize the income effects of foreign investment, the proper discount rate is the marginal productivity of capital in the host economy, a rate that should agree rather closely with the discount rate of the multinational enterprise. In that event, the investor and the host government will reach an easy agreement on the present value of the benefits and costs of a prospective investment. When, however, the multinational enterprise considers *political* risks to be high in the host country, it may add a risk premium to its discount rate so that the combined rate of the multinational enterprise exceeds the host government's rate. Then the enterprise will place a higher value on short-run benefits and costs than the host government.

However, apart from situations of high political risk, it is more common for the host governments of developing countries to discount the future more heavily than the multinational enterprise. Pressed by the need for immediate action to relieve foreign exchange shortages, to slow down inflation, to raise tax revenues, and to curb unemployment, host government officials generally place a much higher value on the early benefits and costs of foreign investment than on its more distant benefits and costs. As we have already noted, this concern with the shorter run frequently makes the balance of payments effects of a prospective foreign investment more critical in the eyes of government officials than its longer run national income effects. The

---

[15] The net present value of balance of payments benefits is

$$\sum_{t=1}^{t=n} \left(\frac{K_t + X_t + S_t}{[1 + d]^t} \right)$$

and balance of payments costs,

$$\sum_{t=1}^{t=n} \left(\frac{[R_t^{**} + F_t^*] + [M_t + M_t^*] + D_t}{[1 + d]^t} \right).$$

ensuing disagreement between the multinational enterprise and the host government on the present value of a proposed investment is most prominent in negotiations on entry. Once the investment is approved by the host government and the affiliate starts production, then disagreement is more likely to proceed from shifting perceptions of benefits and costs in the *current* period rather than the present value of benefits and costs over the indefinite life of the investment.

Using Shadow Prices to Value Benefits and Costs

Before considering shifting perceptions of benefits and costs over time, we should mention certain adjustments that a host government may make in market prices in order to value the *social* benefits and costs of a proposed foreign investment project. So far our conceptual approach to the national income and balance of payments effects of a direct foreign investment has relied on market prices to value the outputs and inputs of the foreign-owned affiliate with a single exception: the use of opportunity costs to value local labor inputs instead of wage costs. But market prices, particularly in developing countries, may not accurately reflect the relative scarcity of inputs or the relative desirability of outputs because of distortions created by monopoly, import restrictions, overvalued exchange rates, and other market imperfections. Given distortions, market prices will not direct an allocation of national resources that will maximize net social benefits, the objective of the host government. In this second-best world, therefore, a host government may replace actual market prices with social accounting or *shadow prices* to analyze a foreign investment project. Shadow prices are intended to measure accurately the social opportunity costs of inputs and the social utility of outputs.

We do not intend here to explore the often subtle world of social cost/benefit accounting.[16] Instead, we simply indicate the shadow price adjustments that a host government might make in a foreign investor's income statement for a proposed project. These adjustments are shown in Table 24-4.

In preparing the project's income statement for a representative year, the foreign investor uses market prices. The investor's estimates indicate a profit of 2.5 million pesos. Unwilling to accept actual market prices as a valuation basis, the host government adjusts the items in the investor's statement with shadow prices. Shadow prices remove the price distortions caused by import protection (which pushes the local price of widgets above

---

[16] Readers interested in the application of social cost/benefit analysis to foreign investment projects may consult Anandarup Ray, *Cost-Benefit Analysis: Issues and Methodologies* (Baltimore: Johns Hopkins University Press, 1984). See also Louis T. Wells, Jr., "Social Cost/Benefit Analysis for MNCs," *Harvard Business Review*, March–April 1975, pp. 40ff; and "Evaluating the Costs and Benefits of Multinational Enterprises to Host Countries: A 'Tool-Kit' Approach," in *International Production and the Multinational Enterprise,* ed. John H. Dunning (London: George Allen & Unwin, 1981), pp. 357–84.

TABLE 24-4   Shadow Price Adjustments of the Foreign Investor's Income Statement (Millions of Pesos)

Item	Investor's Income Statement (Market Prices)	Shadow Price Adjustments	Host Country's Social Income Statement (Shadow Prices)
Sales of widgets	20.0	−9.0	11.0
Cost of goods sold	14.0	−5.0	9.0
Local labor	6.0	−6.0	0.0
Imported raw materials	6.0	+1.2	7.2
Local raw materials	2.0	−0.2	1.8
Overhead	2.0	+0.4	2.4
Interest	1.5	+0.3	1.8
Remitted abroad	1.0	+0.2	1.2
Paid locally	0.5	+0.1	0.6
Profit	2.5		− 2.2

their import value) and by an overvalued exchange rate (which lowers the local currency value of imports). Although the actual exchange rate is $1 = P1.0, the shadow exchange rate is taken to be $1 = P1.2.

First, the host government assesses the social value of widget sales at 11 million pesos because the same quantity of widgets could be imported for that amount at the shadow exchange rate. Second, it prices local labor at a zero shadow wage rate because if the workers were not employed on the foreign investor's project, they would be idle. Third, the pre-duty value of imported raw materials is calculated at the shadow exchange rate, and local raw materials are valued at their international market prices (removing the price effects of any import protection) converted into peso prices at the shadow exchange rate. Fourth, overhead is adjusted with the shadow exchange rate. Fifth, interest remitted abroad is revalued at the shadow exchange rate while interest paid locally on P3 million in local loans to the project is adjusted to the social opportunity cost of local capital, which is 20 percent. After these adjustments, the social profit of the project becomes negative, calling for rejection by the host government. Alternatively, the social benefit/cost ratio is 0.83.

This illustrative analysis of a proposed foreign investment project has omitted consideration of externalities. If the host government values the project's externalities at 2.2 million pesos or higher, the project will pass the social benefit/cost test. Although social benefit/cost analysis, with its externalities and shadow prices, appears odd to private foreign investors,

more and more host governments in the developing countries are using it
to screen foreign investment proposals.

Shifting Perceptions of Benefit/Cost Ratios over Time

As perceived by host country policymakers, the benefit/cost ratio of a foreign-owned affiliate is likely to shift over time and, more often than not, in a negative direction. In the early years of an affiliate's operations, perceived benefits usually substantially exceed perceived costs. On the benefit side, the multinational enterprise brings new capital, technology, and entrepreneurial management to the host economy, and external economies are high as the affiliate trains workers, establishes connections with local suppliers and customers, and begins to compete in local markets. At the same time, perceived costs are usually low in the early years as the affiliate makes only modest profits (or incurs losses) that are mostly reinvested to build up its competitive position. As time goes on, however, host government officials frequently perceive a decline in benefits and a rise in costs. The multinational enterprise may no longer be transferring new capital and technology to the affiliate and the affiliate may generate fewer external economies as its operations become routine. On the other hand, profit repatriation may become ever larger as the affiliate achieves market success and has only modest needs for new capital. At some point, host government officials may even come to believe that the affiliate's operations could be performed entirely by local managers and workers and that external income and factor payments constitute a continuing cost with no offsetting benefits. Alternatively, they may believe they can negotiate more satisfactory arrangements with another multinational enterprise.

While the host government's perception of the benefit/cost ratio of an affiliate is shifting downward, the parent company's perception may be shifting upward. Managers in the parent company are inclined to interpret the rising production, sales, and local tax payments of the affiliate as evidence of its growing contribution to the host economy. Furthermore, they view repatriated profits as a reward for entrepreneurial efforts that go back to the birth of the affiliate. In effect, the multinational enterprise tells the host government, "Look at all we have done for you since we came to your country!" And the host government replies, "Yes, we appreciate that, but what have you done for us lately?" Figure 24-3 depicts this widening divergence between the benefit/cost perceptions of host government officials and multinational enterprise managers.

Up to point A, the host government is satisfied with the benefit/cost ratio of the affiliate and it may even believe it has the better of the arrangement with the multinational enterprise. As the zone of disagreement widens beyond point A, however, the host government will undertake measures to reverse the deterioration in its perceived benefit/cost ratio by de-

Figure 24-3   Divergence of Perceived Economic Benefit/Cost Ratios of an Affiliate Between the Host Government and the Multinational Enterprise

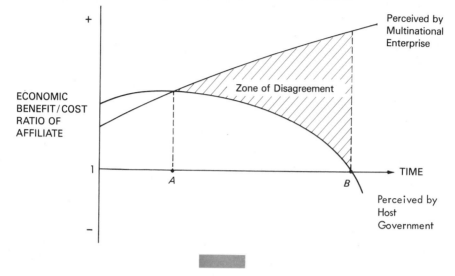

manding, for example, that the affiliate establish an R & D center, increase its exports, obtain more materials and components from local suppliers and less from abroad, promote nationals to top management positions, pay more taxes, and cease paying royalties to its parent company. If the host government's perception shifts beyond point B, where costs exceed benefits, then it may press the multinational enterprise to sell the affiliate to local investors. The ultimate action of the host government is a unilateral expropriation of the affiliate. Seldom, however, will the host government's perception of the *economic* benefit/cost ratio of an affiliate move beyond point B unless that perception is distorted by negative political factors that are unrelated to the economic performance of the affiliate.

These shifting perceptions of economic benefits and costs are closely associated with shifts in the relative power positions of the host country and the multinational enterprise. Before the initial investment is made, the host government is often in a weak bargaining position because the multinational enterprise usually has several options to invest in other countries. To obtain the investment, therefore, the host government may have to offer concessions, such as a tax exemption for the first five years of the affiliate's operations. Once the investment is made, however, the power balance tends to shift in favor of the host government. The multinational enterprise has now committed resources that may be lost if the affiliate does not maintain its viability. As the host country becomes less dependent on the affiliate for capital, technology, management, access to export markets, or external economies, it is in a better position to insist on new conditions to maintain (or increase) its share of economic benefits. As long as the multinational enterprise considers disinvestment more costly than accommodation to the host government's conditions, it will keep its affiliate in operation. On the other hand, it is in the economic interest of the host government to practice some restraint so as not to "kill the golden goose" by forcing the multinational enterprise to abandon local operations. The history of relations between the international petroleum companies and host developing countries is a classic example of the reversal of power positions over time.

The reversal of power positions need not be true of every direct investment; it may be slowed down or even halted when the multinational enterprise is able to keep the host country continually dependent on it for new technology, new products, or access to export markets. The power positions of IBM and other high-technology multinational enterprises have suffered little, if any, erosion in host countries for this reason.

The Coincidence and Conflict of Economic Interests

Our analysis of the benefits and costs of direct foreign investment points to a coincidence of economic interests between the multinational enterprise and the host country. As is true of other forms of economic specialization and exchange, direct foreign investment is a "positive sum game" that benefits both players. Within this fundamental harmony of interests, however, there is likely to be a continuing conflict of interests as both the multinational enterprise and the host country strive to maximize their respective shares of the net economic benefits of foreign investment.[17] This conflict may be exacerbated by different perceptions of the benefit/cost ratio of an affiliate held respectively by the parent company and the host government, perceptions that may change radically over time. The resolution of this continuing conflict depends essentially on the current power positions of the two parties. Ordinarily, both sides are constrained in their negotiations and bargaining by the recognition of their own interests regarding the activation and sustained performance of the affiliate in question. By pressing their own interests too hard, both risk the loss of actual or prospective economic gains. Hence, the conflict of economic interests between the foreign investor and the host government tends to be resolved to the satisfaction of both parties by a process of give and take that may be repeated many times over during the life of the affiliate.[18]

---

[17] The share of the *home* country is also at issue, particularly when a host country attempts to increase its benefit share by imposing performance requirements on the MNE investor.

[18] This statement assumes the absence of any serious *political* conflict between the multinational enterprise and the host government.

THE CHALLENGE OF THE MULTINATIONAL ENTERPRISE TO THE NATIONAL SOVEREIGNTY OF HOST COUNTRIES

Although there is a fundamental harmony of *economic* interests between host countries and the multinational enterprise, there is also a fundamental conflict of *political* interests that poses a challenge to the national sovereignty of host countries. Government officials, intellectuals, labor leaders, business people, and other groups in host countries regard the multinational enterprise as far more than a business institution that raises questions of only *economic* benefits and costs. From their perspective, the multinational enterprise contributes economic benefits but at the cost of imposing actual or potential constraints on the policy decisions of national authorities as well as threatening the "integrity" of the national community. They see the multinational enterprise as a political institution that can exercise decision-making power over key segments of the national economy from a headquarters located outside the national territory and beyond the jurisdictional reach of their government. They allege, therefore, that the multinational enterprise limits or thwarts the capacity of the host government to achieve economic, social, and other goals in pursuit of the national interest. Furthermore, representatives of host countries perceive the multinational enterprise as an actual or potential instrument for the extraterritorial application of the laws and policies of the parent company's home government. They view a multinational enterprise that is headquartered in the United States as an American enterprise that champions the interests of the United States and, in any event, is fully subject to the authority of the U.S. government. Finally, host country nationals see the multinational enterprise as an outsider, an intruder into the national community whose loyalty to the host country is questionable at best.

These perceptions of the political role of the multinational enterprise give rise to fears and allegations best described as *issues* that are subject to continuing disagreement, debate, and controversy within host countries (internal conflict of goals), between host countries and multinational enterprises, and between host and home countries. Moreover, these fears and allegations will remain issues in the future unless direct foreign investment and the multinational enterprise can be "depoliticized" by multilateral international agreements that spell out the rights and responsibilities of the multinational enterprise vis-à-vis national governments, together with limitations on the territorial jurisdiction of those governments. In this section we briefly treat the three major political issues of the multinational enterprise: the issue of national interest, the issue of extraterritoriality, and the issue of nationalism.

The Issue of National Interest

The issue of national interest arises on two levels: (1) the divergent policy goals of host governments and the multinational enterprise, and (2) the constraints placed on government policymaking by the independent power of the multinational enterprise to make decisions affecting the host country. It is alleged that the multinational enterprise ignores or opposes national policy goals and renders national policy instruments ineffective.[19]

Apart from the fact that a host government pursues social and national security goals that have no counterparts among the goals of the private multinational enterprise, goal conflicts between the two parties are almost certain to occur because of the profound difference in the perspectives of the respective decision-makers. The host government conceives its economic and other goals in *national* terms; it tries to maximize *national* values in its policies. In contrast, the multinational enterprise conceives its goals in *geocentric* terms; it tries to maximize *enterprise system* values on a global scale. Host government officials ask, "Is this policy good for our country?" Multinational enterprise managers ask, "Is this policy good for our worldwide company?" Clearly the answers to these two questions need not be the same.

The issue of national interest, however, is not simply a matter of a conflict of goals. Rather, the issue is the *power* of the multinational enterprise to act independently of national policies. Even if country and enterprise goals were always harmonious, no government would want to turn its power over to the multinational enterprise. On the other hand, if the multinational enterprise lacked power, then a host government could take measures to insure that the multinational enterprise always acted in the national interest. The power of the multinational enterprise comes from its possession of scarce capital, technology, and management and its capability to deploy these resources throughout the world. Thus, the multinational enterprise is able to award or deny economic benefits to host countries. This brings us to the second dimension of the national interest issue, namely, the constraints placed on national policymaking by the multinational enterprise, with a consequent loss of "national independence."

Many specific allegations have been made against the multinational enterprise with regard to its power to circumvent national policies. From the perspective of the host government, the multinational enterprise can manipulate intra-enterprise transfer prices to avoid local taxes, minimize import duties, circumvent exchange controls on capital outflows, and accomplish other purposes that are detrimental to the national interest. Other allegations relate to the investment and operating policies of the multinational enterprise. To illustrate, a multinational enterprise may decide that its global logistical system will benefit by shifting production from country A to country B or by lowering exports from country A in favor of more exports from country B. Or again, the multinational enterprise may decide

---

[19] For a discussion of national economic goals and policy instruments, see Chapter 1.

to undertake R & D only in the home country, a policy that makes the affiliates "branch plants" dependent on the parent's technology. Whether or not the multinational enterprise *actually* follows policies that are detrimental to the national interest is not the point; it is the capability of the multinational enterprise to do so that is at issue. No government, jealous sovereign that it is, cares to have a substantial or key element of the national economy controlled by decision centers located in another country.

The Issue of Extraterritoriality

Host countries may also perceive the multinational enterprise as a threat to national sovereignty because of its identification with the policies of the home government. Multinational enterprises headquartered in the United States are particularly suspect because of the extraterritorial claims of the powerful U.S. government. As we observed earlier, the U.S. government exercises jurisdiction not only over the U.S. parent company but over the entire multinational enterprise system as well. Moreover, the U.S. government has actually constrained the foreign operations of U.S. parent companies in order to carry out its policies regarding antitrust laws, East-West trade, and foreign investment.

Whereas the issue of national interest arises because the host country perceives the multinational enterprise as being too independent, the issue of extraterritoriality arises because the host country perceives the multinational enterprise as being too dependent on the home country.

In matters of jurisdictional dispute between two sovereign states, the multinational enterprise is caught in the middle. To avoid this unhappy situation, U.S. parent companies have undoubtedly prevented their foreign affiliates from taking actions that would get the parents in trouble with the U.S. government, whether the problem concerns export controls, antitrust policy, or foreign investment controls. To host governments, the subjection of U.S.-owned local companies to U.S. government policies constitutes a direct violation of their territorial sovereignty. For that reason, efforts by the United States or any other home country to use parent companies to extend their laws and policies beyond the national domain act to endanger the viability of the multinational enterprise.

Host countries may also be fearful that multinational enterprises will call upon their home governments to support them in disputes with host governments. Particularly sensitive to this possibility, Latin American countries uphold the Calvo Doctrine, which denies the foreign investor any right to obtain support from the home government in a dispute with the host government.

The Issue of Nationalism

In Chapter 1, we pointed out that nationalism injects an emotional energy into international relations, often inciting governments to behavior that undermines the achievement of their own political and economic goals. In no other realm of external economic relations is nationalism more prominent than in direct foreign investment and the multinational enterprise. Economic nationalists are apostles of the closed economy; they regard the multinational enterprise as an enemy that preaches the seditious doctrine of an interdependent world economy. To nationalists, it is essential that the government maintain absolute sovereignty over all business firms within the national domain. Hence, they reject the foreign ownership of local firms on the grounds that it serves as a channel for foreign influence on the economy, the society, and the national culture. The multinational enterprise is the unwelcome guest that establishes permanent residence in "our" country.

All countries experience nationalism to one degree or another. However, the most intense expression of economic nationalism today is found in the developing countries. Nationalists in these countries label direct foreign investment as "neocolonialism" or "economic imperialism," arguing that its purpose is to perpetuate economic and political dependence on the industrial countries. Governments in some developing countries consciously exploit nationalism to build loyalty to the state; political parties try to ride to power on the horse of antiforeign nationalism that pits "us" against "them." Frustrated by widening gaps between economic expectations and economic performance, governments are eager to use multinational enterprises as scapegoats for their own policy failures.

Nationalism in the developing countries has struck particularly hard at foreign investment in extractive industries. Natural resources are regarded as a national heritage that belongs to all the people. A common allegation against the foreign extractive investor is, "You take away our resources and leave us with an empty hole!" But the real grievance of nationalists is not the economic cost of direct foreign investment but rather the fact of foreign ownership, which sets the local affiliates of multinational enterprises outside the national society and national loyalties. Economic nationalists reject, therefore, the legitimacy of foreign ownership, regardless of the economic benefits it may bring to their country. Economic nationalism is by no means absent in the industrial countries, but it seldom dominates policies toward direct foreign investment.

Ambivalence and Tensions in Host Countries

The coexistence of economic benefits and political costs associated with direct foreign investment makes the attitudes and policies of host countries toward the multinational enterprise highly ambivalent and creates tensions that accompany any "love-hate" relationship. Unfortunately host countries are unable to resolve this ambivalence and relieve their tensions through an objective evaluation of economic benefits and political costs because there is no way to measure political costs and thereby establish trade-offs between the two. What, after all, is the political cost of foreign ownership? How much is a feeling of national pride that comes from the expropriation of a foreign-owned petroleum or copper company worth to a people? One might answer, it is worth as much as a people are willing to forgo in economic benefits. However, a people can know the economic consequences of these actions only if an objective appraisal of economic benefits and costs is made in advance by responsible authorities.

The most one can reasonably expect, then, is that increasingly host governments will evaluate the full economic benefits and costs of direct foreign investment in formulating their policies toward the multinational enterprise. This will minimize erratic shifts in policy that harm both foreign investors and host countries. But objective economic analysis will not remove ambivalence or cure tensions. These will persist as governments everywhere continue the struggle to maintain national sovereignty in a world economy that is reaching toward ever higher levels of global interdependence.

POLICIES AND ACTIONS OF HOST GOVERNMENTS TO MINIMIZE THE POLITICAL COSTS OF DIRECT FOREIGN INVESTMENT

The concerns in host countries over the political costs of direct foreign investment center on the actual or potential exercise of control over the national economy by foreign companies and by the home governments of those companies. The legal basis of control by a foreign parent company is its ownership of local affiliates. Hence, attempts to prevent, reduce, or eliminate *foreign ownership* constitute many policies and actions of host governments that are taken to minimize the political costs of direct foreign investment. Foreign investment regulations are also intended to maximize the host country's *economic benefits* within ownership constraints.

Restrictions on Foreign Ownership

All countries discriminate against the foreign ownership of local companies in at least some industries. In general, these restrictions are most severe in the developing countries, but they are by no means insignificant in the industrial countries.

Exclusion of Foreigners from Key Industries   Both industrial and developing countries exclude foreigners from direct investment in certain "key" industries that are regarded as essential to national security or as having a pervasive influence on the national economy and society. Key industries commonly include public utilities, airlines, shipping lines, communications media (television, radio, and publications), banks, and insurance companies. In developing countries, excluded industries may also encompass agriculture, forestry, fisheries, extraction (mining and petroleum), and basic industries (iron and steel, petrochemicals, and so on), which are sometimes reserved for state enterprise as well.

Requirements for Local Participation in Ownership In addition to excluding foriegn ownership from certain sectors of the economy, host governments may also require local ownership participation in some industries.

For many years, Mexico has pursued a policy of progressive "Mexicanization" of foreign-owned companies by converting them into joint ventures with local business interests. Another example is India. In 1977, the Indian government demanded that the Coca-Cola Company either transfer its know-how and a majority ownership share of its Indian subsidiary to Indian nationals or else cease to operate in India. Jealous of its trade secrets, Coca-Cola chose to withdraw. About the same time, IBM also pulled out of India, refusing to share its technology with a local partner.

In developing countries where there is no legal requirement for local ownership participation, the host government nonetheless may "persuade" foreign investors to enter into joint ventures with local entrepreneurs.

Prohibition of Acquisitions by Foreign Companies Even the governments of industrial countries that follow liberal policies toward new foreign investment may refuse to approve the acquisition (takeover) of a locally owned company by a foreign investor.

Expropriation

The expropriation of foreign-owned companies is the most dramatic action a host government can take to minimize the political costs of direct foreign investment. Broadly defined, *expropriation* includes any seizure of foreign-owned property by a host government. When foreign owners are not compensated for their seized properties, expropriation becomes *confiscation.* Most expropriation is also *nationalization*, which occurs when the host government assumes permanent ownership of the expropriated property. At a single stroke, then, expropriation deprives the foreign parent company of all ownership rights in its affiliate, including the right to control the affiliate's operations. The economic costs of expropriation to the host country may be extraordinarily severe. Apart from costs associated with the disruption of the affiliate's operations, expropriation commonly deters new foreign investment (which may be desired by the host government) and invites retaliation by the investor's home government.

Expropriation is a direct exercise of national sovereignty. Traditional international law has recognized the right of sovereign states to expropriate the property of foreigners, but it has also upheld an "international standard" that requires "prompt, adequate, and effective" compensation.[20] Since World

---

[20] "Adequate" compensation is payment of the full market value of the property. "Effective" compensation is payment in a convertible currency.

War I, this international standard has been repeatedly challenged by communist and developing countries. Because of the split between the West and the South (supported by the East), therefore, there is no generally accepted rule for compensation in cases of expropriation. Furthermore, the developing countries (where most expropriations occur) have been loath to enter into bilateral or multilateral treaties that commit them to "just compensation" in the event of expropriation.

INVESTMENT INCENTIVES AND PERFORMANCE REQUIREMENTS OF HOST COUNTRIES

We have now reviewed the policies and actions of host governments to minimize the political costs of foreign investment. For the most part, these are efforts to nationalize control by denying or limiting foreign ownership of domestic economic activities. However, as observed earlier, host governments also seek to maximize their share of the *economic* benefits of foreign investment. Somewhat paradoxically, they pursue this objective by offering incentives to attract foreign investors in the first instance, and then by imposing performance requirements on foreign investors.

Investment Incentives

Investment incentives are host-government policies or actions intended to increase the return to foreign investors above what it would be in the absence of such policies or actions. Table 24-5 shows the *percentage* of U.S. foreign affiliates that received incentives from host countries. The most common incentive for both industrial and developing countries was to offer tax concessions, but the industrial countries were more inclined to offer subsidies to foreign investors while the developing countries preferred to offer tariff concessions. Because of GATT obligations, the industrial countries have less freedom than the developing countries to alter their import duties.

The effectiveness of incentives in attracting foreign investment is questionable.[21] Because the vast majority of countries offers incentives, the incentives of one country are largely neutralized by the incentives of the others. Apart from matching the incentives of other countries, LDCs appear to use investment incentives to offset *dis*incentives, such as small markets, weak infrastructure, and disruptive host-government policies. But foreign investors enter a country only when they anticipate profitable operations, and incentives cannot create profitable operations, although they can make them more profitable.

---

[21] See Franklin R. Root and Ahmed A. Ahmed, "The Influence of Policy Instruments on Manufacturing Direct Foreign Investment in Developing Countries," *Journal of International Business Studies,* Winter 1978, pp. 81–94.

TABLE 24-5   Percentage of U.S. Nonbank Foreign Affiliates Receiving
Incentives from Host Governments, by Type and Country Area at Yearend 1982

Country Area	Tax Concessions	Tariff Concessions	Subsidies	Other Incentives	Number of Affiliates
Industrial countries	24.1	6.6	17.2	6.6	11,099
Developing countries	25.7	16.0	8.5	8.5	5,760
All countries	24.3	9.6	14.0	7.1	17,213

Source: U.S. Department of Commerce, *U.S. Direct Investment Abroad: 1982 Benchmark Survey Data* (Washington, D.C.: U.S. Government Printing Office, December 1985), Table II I.1, p. 135.

Not only are incentives generally ineffective in attracting foreign investment, they also are costly, reducing the net social benefits of foreign investment to the host country. The LDCs, therefore, have much to gain from regional or global agreements that would restrain the use of investment incentives. The prospects of such agreements, however, are very poor. In any event, LDC governments need to understand that policies aimed at improving the general investment climate can do much more to attract foreign investment than can incentives.

Investment Performance Requirements

Investment performance requirements include any host-government policies or actions that constrain the ownership or operations of a foreign-investment venture in the host country.

Table 24-6 indicates the percentage of U.S. foreign affiliates that were subjected to performance requirements by host governments. The most common LDC requirement was the use of local labor, followed by import limitation. The most common requirement in industrial countries was also local labor.

Performance requirements of special concern to home countries (as well as third countries) are export, import-limitation, and local-content requirements, for they distort the flows of trade and investment in ways that favor the host country to the detriment of other countries. Export requirements imposed on foreign affiliates not only increase a second country's imports but also may displace a third country's exports to the second country. This occurs without regard to the comparative advantage of the host country. Import-limitation and local-content requirements compel foreign affiliates to use local products regardless of their cost, and they are therefore forms

TABLE 24-6   Percentage of U.S. Nonbank Foreign Affiliates Subject to
Performance Requirements Imposed by Host Governments, by Type and
Country Area at Yearend 1982

Country Area	Export	Import Limitation	Local Content	Local Labor	Number of Affiliates
Industrial countries	1.1	0.5	0.6	3.9	11,099
Developing countries	2.6	3.3	2.1	15.0	5,760
All countries	1.6	1.4	1.1	7.6	17,213

Source: U.S. Department of Commerce, *U.S. Direct Investment Abroad: 1982 Benchmark Survey Data* (Washington, D.C.: U.S. Government Printing Office, December 1985), Table II.I3, p. 139.

of protection. Their trade-diversion effects have made performance requirements a growing issue between home- and host-country governments. The
United States is trying to get GATT to extend its mandate over trade-
distorting measures applied to foreign investment.

TOWARD AN ACCOMMODATION BETWEEN NATION-STATES AND THE MULTINATIONAL ENTERPRISE

Our analysis of the benefits and costs of direct foreign investment earlier
in this chapter demonstrated a coincidence of economic interests between
the multinational enterprise and host countries. Within this fundamental
harmony of interests, there is, of course, a continuing conflict of interests
as both the multinational enterprise and host countries strive to maximize
their shares of net economic benefits. But in the absence of political conflict,
this conflict over the division of gains can be resolved to the satisfaction of
both parties if they mutually recognize that their benefits are dependent on
the viability of the foreign investment in question. By pressing their own
interests too hard, both risk the loss of actual or prospective economic gains.
In principle, conflicts of economic interests are resolvable, because international economic transactions constitute a positive sum game in which
both participants can gain from its continuation and both can lose from its
cessation. The coincidence of economic interests rests on the contributions
that the multinational enterprise makes to the host economy as an inter-

national transfer agent of products, capital, technology, and entrepreneurial skills.

In spite of this fundamental harmony of economic interests, MNEs are opposed in many host countries on political grounds. This political conflict centers on control of their behavior within the host country. Host governments want control to maximize national sociopolitical values on a national scale; the multinational enterprise wants control to maximize enterprise economic values on a global scale. Unlike the conflict of economic interests, the political conflict is a power contest or zero sum game in which one party gains at the expense of the other.

Can governments slay the dragons of the multinational enterprise?[22] Certainly no government, acting individually, can do so, because it has jurisdiction over only one national element of the multinational enterprise system.[23] And it is difficult to imagine governments acting collectively to that end. But if many governments were to apply stiff performance requirements on the operations of MNEs within their territories, then they would seriously cripple the economic efficiency of multinational enterprise systems. Can MNEs slay the dragons of national sovereignty? Some scholars, viewing the nation-state as obsolescent, foresee political power passing to the multinational enterprise and other transnational functional institutions. But surely this is a fanciful notion in a world of intense nationalism. If, then, neither party is capable of destroying the other and achieving complete control over its own behavior, each can choose either to reach an accommodation with the other or else exacerbate the political conflict in pursuit of selfish interests.

Bilateral Accommodation at the National Level

At the bilateral national level, the range of accommodation between a national sovereignty and the multinational enterprise is defined by two extreme postures. For the national sovereignty, the extreme posture is the adoption of a policy of laissez-faire that allows the multinational enterprise to pursue freely its own interests regardless of the benefits and costs to that sovereignty. Laissez-faire policy, therefore, represents a full accommodation by the nation to the multinational enterprise. For the multinational enterprise, the extreme posture is the transfer of all ownership and managerial control of its local operations to the national sovereignty or its representatives while, at the same time, continuing to sustain those operations with

---

[22] Jack N. Behrman, "Can Governments Slay the Dragons of Multinational Enterprise?" *European Business,* Winter 1971, pp. 53–62.

[23] The U.S. government has the power to destroy *U.S.-based* multinational enterprises but not enterprises headquartered in other countries. In any event, U.S. policymakers do not perceive U.S. multinational enterprises as posing a threat to the national sovereignty of this country.

loan capital, technology, and management skills. By substituting contractual arrangements for ownership and control, the multinational enterprise becomes a service company that fully accommodates the political interests and nationalism of the host country.

Neither of these extreme postures is probable in the foreseeable future, although they may be assumed by individual nations and multinational enterprises in particular circumstances. The intellectual argument for a laissez-faire market economy has been decisively rejected by nations in the twentieth century for the doctrine of the welfare state, according to which the state should take on responsibilities for economic growth, employment, and social justice. Furthermore, even during the heyday of laissez-faire policies in the last quarter of the nineteenth century, economic nationalism never disappeared, since nations commonly used tariffs to discriminate against foreign business enterprise. Even on purely economic grounds, nations reject a laissez-faire policy that would allow concentrations of private economic power, institutionalized in MNEs and international cartels, to determine the world's pattern of industry and trade and the distribution of the world's income.

As we have discovered, the actual responses of national governments to the political costs of the multinational enterprise range from comparatively mild restrictions on foreign ownership to confiscatory expropriations. By impairing the capacity of MNEs to function as international transfer agents, these responses lower the contribution of MNEs to the world economy and, more often than not, to the host economy, regardless of their political justification. Given the national perspective and nationalistic attitudes of host governments, bilateral policies to minimize the political costs of MNEs are inevitably restrictive, since they are motivated by an intent to prevent, reduce, or eliminate foreign ownership and control. Bilateral accommodation by the nation-state, then, is a question of the degree of restriction on foreign ownership and control; the lower the degree of restriction, the higher the accommodation, but restriction is never entirely absent.

Will MNEs accommodate the political interests and nationalism of host countries by voluntarily abandoning ownership and control over their affiliates? In Chapter 22 we defined the multinational enterprise as a parent company that engages in foreign production through its own affiliates located in several different countries, exercises direct control over the policies of those affiliates, and strives to design and implement business strategies that transcend national boundaries. Hence, a general substitution of contractual service arrangements for the ownership and control of production affiliates would transform the multinational enterprise into an entirely different institution.

Some observers, sensitive to attitudes in many developing countries, believe that MNEs will evolve in that direction to eliminate political conflicts with host nations. But what is more probable is that they will enter into contractual arrangements (minority joint ventures, service contracts, coproduction schemes) as a *second-best* strategy only in those countries that prevent a *first-best* strategy of ownership and control.

We will witness, therefore, a proliferation of contractual arrangements as MNEs extend their activities into communist countries. However, in some of the more advanced LDCs (notably Hong Kong, Singapore, and Taiwan), policies toward MNEs are converging with those of the industrial countries as the economies of these developing countries come to resemble more and more those of the OECD countries. One noteworthy development in the advanced LDCs is the emergence of their own multinational enterprises; thus their views on MNEs are tempered by a growing home-country perspective on foreign investment.

In contrast to the East and much of the South, MNEs continue to have the freedom to pursue a first-best strategy in the West. The broad picture, then, is this: MNEs will follow a first-best strategy of ownership and control in the industrial countries and some advanced LDCs while adopting a second-best strategy of contractual arrangements in many developing countries and in the communist world. Unfortunately, this second-best strategy is second best not only for MNEs but also for the world economy. Lacking firm control, MNEs generally refrain from integrating country operations based on contractual arrangements with their global operations. The resulting fragmentation of operations (or lower degree of internalization) makes MNEs less efficient institutions, as suboptimization in individual host countries replaces optimization across national boundaries.

To conclude, bilateral accommodation offers no promise of any general resolution of the political conflict between the multinational enterprise and host nations. Moreover, when individual nations force an accommodation in ownership and control by the multinational enterprise, they limit its economic efficiency to the detriment of both the host and world economies. Is there, then, any way to broaden the range of accommodation so as to reduce the political costs of the multinational enterprise as perceived by host nations and, at the same time, preserve the economic efficiency of the multinational enterprise system?

Multilateral Accommodation at the International Level

The range of accommodation between the nation-state and the multinational enterprise would be enormously broadened by the multilateral agreements and institutions that conferred both rights and responsibilities on the multinational enterprise vis-à-vis national governments. Indeed, only through international agreements among governments can disputes between multinational enterprises and host countries be transformed from political issues into legal issues to be resolved by impartial international tribunals in accordance with agreed principles of equity.

Today the multinational enterprise has economic power without legitimacy, while many nations have legitimacy without economic power. The multinational enterprise has no transnational legal identity; it is an aggregation of *national* companies. It is dependent on a convention that obligates host governments to extend to foreign enterprise the national treatment they accord to domestic enterprise. Functioning as it does in a legal vacuum, the multinational enterprise has no legal rights or legitimacy as a multinational system and, accordingly, it has no legal responsibilities toward the world community. George Ball would fill that legal vacuum by an international treaty that would enable a parent company to be incorporated under an international companies law. This law would be administered by a supranational body composed of representatives from various countries that would exercise not only the ordinary domiciliary supervision but would also enforce antitrust laws and administer guarantees with regard to confiscatory expropriation.[24] Under this law, the parent company would trade its national legal identity for legal recognition in all countries. However, Ball's proposal—made over twenty years ago—has not struck a responsive chord among national governments.

The multinational enterprise also operates in a *policy* vacuum at the international level. To regulate international trade, governments have created GATT; to regulate international monetary relations, they have established the IMF. But where is the international machinery to regulate direct foreign investment and the multinational enterprise? So far only a few steps have been taken in that direction. In 1969, the International Center for the Settlement of Investment Disputes was set up under the auspices of the IBRD. Under the convention ratified by the participating governments, the private investor is granted the right for the first time to take direct international legal action against a national state. Once the private investor and the host country have consented to submit a dispute to the center, they come under the conciliation and arbitration provisions of the convention. In 1988, the Multilateral Investment Guarantee Agency (MIGA), a World Bank affiliate, came into existence. MIGA will complement the existing political risk insurance facilities of national governments (such as OPIC in the United States) and private insurers.

To fill the policy vacuum, a much broader approach has been suggested that would be directed toward the formation of a general agreement for the international corporation along the lines of GATT.[25] Apart from a single master agreement, specific international treaties for cooperation, coordination, and harmonization in taxation, antitrust laws, property rights, investment insurance, securities registration, patents, rights of establish-

---

[24] George W. Ball, "Cosmocorp: The Importance of Being Stateless," *The Columbia Journal of World Business,* November–December 1967, p. 29.
[25] Paul M. Goldberg and Charles P. Kindleberger, "Toward a GATT for Investment: A Proposal for Supervision of the International Corporation," *Law and Policy in International Business* 2 (1970): 295–325.

ments, repatriation of earnings and capital, and other policies would go a long way toward depoliticizing issues between the multinational enterprise and host countries. However, governments are not ready for such an institution, for nothing has been done to bring it into existence. A more likely development is the extension of GATT's jurisdiction to cover investment performance requirements.

The United Nations, the OECD, and other international organizations have worked on the formulation of codes of conduct for MNEs since the mid-1970s. But only the OECD countries have agreed on guidelines for MNEs.[26] The prospects remain bleak for a code of conduct that would be supported by both the industrial and developing countries. The issue dividing them is fundamental: The industrial countries want a code that places obligations on the host country as well as on the multinational enterprise, but the developing countries reject such a code as an infringement on their national sovereignty.

The international regulation of the multinational enterprise will not come quickly or all at once. But as governments come to recognize that uninational efforts to regulate MNEs are ineffective and carry a heavy national cost that is likely to prove unbearable in the long run, we can reasonably look forward to international agreements that will spell out the rights and responsibilities of MNEs in different areas of conduct. MNEs should welcome codes of conduct that spell out the rights and obligations of host countries as well as their own, for they can gain global legitimacy only through an international accommodation of their interests with national interests.

The 1970s were marked by confrontation between developing countries and the multinational enterprise on both bilateral and multilateral levels. But in the 1980s, the relationship between the two parties shifted from confrontation toward accommodation as LDCs liberalized their policies toward direct foreign investment. Expropriations have declined drastically, and there is much more acceptance by LDCs of international arbitration to settle investment disputes. Concern over the ownership issue has been displaced by concern over the performance criteria to be met by foreign investors. Fewer developing countries now see the MNE as a threat to their national sovereignty.

The liberalization of LDC policies toward the multinational enterprise is the resultant of many forces. Prominent among them is the international debt burden. By limiting resources available for domestic capital formation and by drying up imports of new loan capital from banks, the international debt problem has turned LDC governments toward the multinational enterprise as a source of capital and a means to achieve an expansion of industrial exports to earn badly needed foreign exchange. Another force is

---

[26] *International Investment and Multinational Enterprises* (Paris: The Organization for Economic Cooperation and Development, 1976).

the widening technology gap between the developing and industrial countries. Increasingly, LDCs perceive the MNE as a source of technological innovation that can overcome the weaknesses of their technological infrastructures.

Although LDC countries have liberalized their policies toward direct foreign investment and the multinational enterprise, they have not given up their belief that the MNE should be subject to some form of control. Their liberalization is a *pragmatic* accommodation to the MNE, not an ideological one. In the absence of international institutions to provide a legal or policy framework for regulating relations between MNEs and host countries, therefore, the accommodation of today can easily revert to the confrontation of the past.

SUMMARY

1. In the 1980s, the United States reaffirmed its traditional policy toward direct foreign investment and the multinational enterprise. The central feature of this policy is a belief that market forces should determine direct investment flows.

2. Direct foreign investment in the United States demonstrated extraordinary growth in the 1980s. Foreign MNEs now control a substantial share of the assets of U.S. manufacturing industries.

3. Since World War II, the United States has actively promoted private foreign investment in the developing countries through an investment insurance program that provides coverage against political risks. These and related programs are administered by the Overseas Private Investment Corporation (OPIC).

4. Operating in many countries, multinational enterprises are subject to multiple tax jurisdictions. This situation creates two sets of problems: double taxation and tax avoidance. Following the national rather than the territorial principle of tax jurisdiction, the United States taxes U.S. multinational enterprises on their worldwide income. To limit double taxation, the United States allows credits against foreign taxes; to limit tax avoidance, the United States insists that a U.S. parent company use "arm's length" prices in all transactions with its foreign affiliates.

5. The United States claims antitrust jurisdiction over the behavior of U.S. companies and their foreign affiliates regardless of where that behavior may take place. The rationale for this claim is that business behavior anywhere in the world may restrain U.S. exports or imports or have anticompetitive effects in the United States. As a result of seeking to apply the U.S. antitrust laws to the foreign operations of U.S. companies (and even to the operations of foreign companies), the United States has been accused of "judicial imperialism."

6. The Foreign Corrupt Practices Act (1977) prohibits payments by U.S. companies, directly or indirectly, to foreign government officials when the purpose is to influence official acts and decisions for business gain. The act is criticized for its ambiguity and its cost in lost U.S. sales abroad.

7. U.S. policymakers need to transcend the traditional distinctions between trade, investment, and balance of payments policies if they are to develop a comprehensive policy toward the multinational enterprise.

8. The multinational enterprise is perceived by policymakers in host countries as both an economic institution that creates benefits and costs to the local economy and a quasi-political institution that threatens the power and even the sovereignty of the nation.

9. The fundamental economic effect of direct foreign investment (representing the sum total of many individual effects) is its contribution to the national income (net national product) of the host country over time. Closely related to this national income effect, but deserving special treatment, is the effect of direct foreign investment on the balance of payments of the host country over time.

10. The net benefit/cost ratio of direct foreign investment for the national income of the host economy is

$$\frac{(F + R^* + T) - N + L}{E}.$$

There is both theoretical and empirical evidence that direct foreign investment generally offers net benefits to the host economy.

11. The net benefit/cost ratio of direct foreign investment for the balance of payments of the host economy is

$$\frac{K + X + S}{(R^{**} + F^*) + (M + M^*) + D}.$$

Ideally a host country should maintain balance of payments equilibrium by resorting to monetary, fiscal, and exchange rate policies, together with measures to speed up the reallocation of resources.

12. As is true of other forms of economic specialization and exchange, direct foreign investment is a "positive sum game" that benefits both players. Within its fundamental harmony of interests, however, there is likely to be a continuing conflict of interests as both the multinational enterprise and the host country strive to maximize their respective shares of the net economic benefits of foreign investment.

13. Although there is a fundamental harmony of *economic* interests between host countries and the multinational enterprise, there is also a fundamental conflict of *political* interests inasmuch as the MNE poses a challenge to the national sovereignty of host countries. This political conflict may be treated in terms of three major issues: national interest, extraterritoriality, and nationalism.

14. The coexistence of economic benefits and political costs associated with direct foreign investment makes the attitudes and policies of host countries toward the multinational enterprise highly ambivalent and creates tensions that accompany any "love-hate" relationship.

15. Many of the policies and actions of host governments intended to minimize the political costs of direct foreign investment are essentially attempts to prevent, reduce, or eliminate *foreign ownership*. Restrictions on foreign ownership include the exclusion of foreigners from key industries, requirements for local participation in ownership, and prohibitions against acquisitions by foreign companies.

16. Host countries commonly offer incentives to attract foreign investors and, at the same time, impose performance requirements on them. Bilateral accommodation offers no promise of any general resolution of the political conflict between the multinational enterprise and host nations. But the range of accommodation would be enormously broadened by multilateral agreements and institutions that conferred both rights and responsibilities on the multinational enterprise vis-à-vis national governments.

QUESTIONS AND APPLICATIONS

1. **(a)** Should the United States continue its laissez-faire policy toward investment in the United States by foreign MNEs? Why or why not?

   (b) Should the individual states offer incentives to encourage investment by foreign companies? Why or why not?

2. Has the U.S. investment insurance program stimulated U.S. direct investment in the developing countries? Be prepared to defend your answer.

3. **(a)** "Multiple tax jurisdictions create two sets of problems." What are they? How do they occur?

   (b) Describe the main features of U.S. tax policy toward foreign-source income.

   (c) How do the U.S. tax authorities seek to minimize both double taxation and tax avoidance?

4. **(a)** What is implied by the extraterritorial jurisdiction of U.S. antitrust policy?

   (b) Do the lenient antitrust policies of foreign governments place U.S. multinational enterprises at a disadvantage in competing against foreign multinational enterprises in world markets? Why or why not?

5. Be prepared to debate the following questions: (a) Is the Foreign Corrupt Practices Act good or bad for the United States? (b) Should it be revoked? (c) Should it be amended? If so, how?

6. Why is the conventional concept of *net value added* inadequate to measure the contribution of a *new* direct foreign investment to the national product (income) of a host country?

7. Does every foreign-owned affiliate necessarily make a net contribution to the economy of the host country? Be prepared to explain your answer.

8. "Over the long run, the balance of payments effect of direct foreign investment cannot be distinguished from its national income effect." Explain the reasoning behind this statement.

9. What is the coincidence and conflict of economic interests between host countries and the multinational enterprise (direct foreign investment)?

10. Explain the dynamics of shifting perceptions of economic benefit/cost ratios over time.

11. (a) Why do host countries offer incentives to foreign investors?
    (b) Why do host countries impose requirements on foreign investors?
    (c) Evaluate the effects of investment incentives and performance requirements on international trade.

12. "A second-best strategy of contractual arrangements (as substitutes for ownership and control) is second-best not only for the multinational enterprise but for the world economy as well." Explain the reasoning behind this statement. Do you agree with it? Why or why not?

13. Write a short essay entitled "Prospects for the International Regulation of the Multinational Enterprise."

SELECTED READINGS

Cohen, Robert, and Jeffry Frieden. "The Impact of Multinational Corporations on Developing Countries." In *The Challenge of the New International Economic Order,* edited by Edwin R. Reubens. Boulder, Colo.: Westview Press, 1981.

Frank, Isaiah. *Foreign Enterprise in Developing Countries.* Baltimore: Johns Hopkins University Press, 1980.

Gladwin, Thomas N., and Ingo Walter. *Multinationals under Fire.* New York: John Wiley & Sons, 1980. Chapters 9, 10.

International Center for the Settlement of Investment Disputes. *Annual Report.* Washington, D.C.: International Center for the Settlement of Investment Disputes, latest year.

Kumar, Krishna, and Maxwell G. McLeod, eds. *Multinationals from Developing Countries.* Lexington, Mass.: Lexington Books, 1981.

Lall, Sanjaya, and Paul Streeten. *Foreign Investment, Transnationals and Developing Countries.* Boulder, Colo.: Westview Press, 1977.

Organization for Economic Cooperation and Development. *International Investment and Multinational Enterprises.* Rev. ed. Paris: Organization for Economic Cooperation and Development, 1984.

_____. *National Treatment of Foreign-Controlled Enterprises*. Paris: Organization for Economic Cooperation and Development, 1985.

Overseas Private Investment Corporation. *Annual Report*. Washington, DC.: Overseas Private Investment Corporation. Annual.

_____. *Development Report*. Washington, DC: Overseas Private Investment Corporation. Annual.

United Nations Center on Transnational Corporations. *Transnational Corporations in World Development: Trends and Prospects*. New York: United Nations, 1988. Part 4.

Vernon, Raymond. *Storm over Multinationals*. Cambridge: Harvard University Press, 1977.

Glossary of Abbreviations and Acronyms

ACP – Africa, the Caribbean, and the Pacific region (Lome Convention).
ADB – Asian Development Bank.
AFDB – African Development Bank.
ASP – American selling price.

BTN – Brussels Tariff Nomenclature.

DAC – Development Assistance Committee (OECD).
DFI – Direct foreign investment.

EC – European Community.
EFTA – European Free Trade Association.
EMS – European Monetary System.

GATT – General Agreement on Tariffs and Trade.
GDP – Gross domestic product.
GNP – Gross national product.

H-O model – Heckscher-Ohlin theory of international trade.

IBRD – International Bank for Reconstruction and Development. Also known as the World Bank.
IDA – International Development Association.
IDB – Inter-American Development Bank.
IFC – International Finance Corporation.
IMF – International Monetary Fund.

LAFTA – Latin American Free Trade Association.

LAIA – Latin American Integration Association. LAIA is the successor of LAFTA.
LDC – Less-developed country. Also called developing, nonindustrial, or poor country. LDCs are designated collectively as the South.

MFN – Most-favored-nation principle.
MNE – Multinational enterprise. Also known as transnational enterprise or multinational company (corporation).

NIC – Newly industrializing (developing) country.
NIEO – New international economic order.
NTB – Nontariff trade barrier.

OECD – Organization for Economic Cooperation and Development. Also used to designate the industrial, advanced, or developed countries and, collectively, the West.
OPEC – Organization of Petroleum Exporting Countries.
OPIC – Overseas Private Investment Corporation.

RTA – Reciprocal Trade Agreements Act.

SDRs – Special Drawing Rights.

UNCTAD – United Nations Conference on Trade and Development.

Index

and factor movements as substitutes, 132–134; gains from, 12–14, 46–49; government regulation of, 10; and interregional trade, 14–15; methods of payment in, 281–285, 297; national interest in, 12–19
international trade and investment theories: complementarity of, 138–139; conventional. *See* Heckscher-Ohlin model; synthesis of, 635–636
International Trade Commission, 217, 220, 237
International Trade Organization, 194
international transaction, 349
interregional trade, 97; domestic specialization and, 14–15
interstate trade barriers, 15
intervention currency, 480
intervention price, in EC agricultural policy, 257
intrafirm trade, 110
intra-industry trade, 92, 110–115, 117; theory of, 114–115
inventions, 118
investment. *See also* international portfolio effect; direct, 26, 351–352, 354, 471, 569; domestic, in developing country, 530–532, 536; and market conditions, 269; and national income, 370–376; and national output, 527–529; in poor economies, 80–81; portfolio, 26, 352, 354, 471, 567, 619–621, 636; private, 226–230, 233, 568–569
investment incentives, 676–677
investment performance requirements, 677–678
investment policy, 26
Isaacs, Asher, 216
IS schedule, 402–403

Jacque, Laurent L., 333
J-curve, 426, 434
jurisdictional overlap, 9

Kasman, Bruce, 510
Kearl, J. R., 145
Keesing, Donald B., 89
Kenen, Peter B., 90
Kennedy Round, 198, 202, 219, 271, 272
key industries, exclusion of foreigners from, 674–675
Keynes, John Maynard, 448
Kindleberger, Charles P., 621
Knickerbocker, Frederick T., 627
knowledge, superior, 622–623
Kravis, Irving B., 89, 541
Kreinin, Mordecai E., 427, 428

labor: backward sloping supply schedule for, 524; free movement of, in EC, 259; heterogeneity and change in, 78–79; immobility of, 152; mobility of, 131–132; and technology, 119; varieties of, 69
laissez-faire, 20, 41, 679
land factors, 69, 77–78, 119
language, 8
Latin American Free Trade Association, 562–564
Latin American Integration Association, 562–564
Leamer, Edward E., 85
learning curve, 105
Leontief paradox, 84–88, 91
letter of credit, confirmed, irrevocable, 282–283
licensing, and choice of entry mode, 633–635
Linder model, 110–114, 116–117

linkages, between economic sectors, 540
liquidity effect, 395–396
List, Frederick, 156–157
Lloyd, P. J., 114
LM schedule, 402–403, 433
loans, 567–569
local-content laws, 189
location theory, 99
Lome Convention, 272
London, as international financial center, 298; before WWI, 294–295
London gold market, support of, 473
long-run average cost curve, 102–103
Louvre Accord, 497, 513
lower-middle-income economies, 521, 536
low-income economies, 527, 536
LRAC curve. *See* long-run average cost curve

MacBean, A. I., 270
macroeconomic policies, 491, 493–495, 497–499, 508–512
macroscopic perspective, 7
Magee, Stephen, 631
managed-float system, 410, 495–496, 512–513
managed world economy, 535
management, heterogeneity and change in, 79–80
managers: and economic development, 523–524; mobility of, 132
mandatory investment controls, 471
manufactures: comparative advantage in, 138; preferential treatment of, 560–561; trade in, 112–113, 114
manufacturing investors, 616
marginal propensity to consume, 375
marginal propensity to import, 375, 386–387
marginal propensity to save, 375, 386–387
marginal rate of substitution, 55–59, 65, 142
marginal rate of transformation, 51–65, 142
market extension, 269
market-oriented industry, 98
market requirements, in product life cycle, 128
market segments; effect on trade, 112; overlapping, 110–117
market world economy, 535
Marshall-Lerner condition, 421–422, 434
McKean, Mark, 654
Meade, J. E., 162
Mehta, Dileep, 123
mercantilism, 41
merchandise trade, 26; specialized intermediaries in, 17
metric system, U.S. policy on, 247
MFN policy. *See* most-favored-nation policy
microscopic perspective, 7
middle-income developing countries, 525
Mill, John Stuart, 392
minerals, production and trade, 100, 137, 540, 559
mini-steel mill, 104
mint parity, 309
monetary authorities, 310–312, 352
monetary base, 385
monetary crises, 473–476
monetary gold flow, 352
monetary policy, 8
monetary systems, national, 9–12
money, 385; demand for, 399; and protectionism, 147; supply, 399
money incomes, redistribution of, and exchange control, 451
money market, disequilibrium, 400–401

money stock, 385
Monnet, Jean, 265
monopoly, 100, 106–107, 116, 138, 161, 260
monopoly profits, 101–102, 116
monopsony, 160–161, 170
Morkre, Morris E., 241
most-favored-nation policy, 26, 184, 195, 197, 205, 216, 218, 220, 234
Multifiber Arrangement, 240
multilateral trade agreements, 199, 551–552; GATT, 193–212
multinational enterprises, 6, 7, 11, 37, 139; accommodation between nation-states and, 678–684; accounting standards for, 339; assumption of risk by, 599–600; capital financing, sources of, 590–592; capital-sourcing policies, constraints on, 592–594; contribution to world economy, 600–601, 606–607; definitions of, 7, 580, 582–584, 605–606; empirical data on, 601–605; foreign subsidiary's balance sheet, adjustment, 341; hedging by, 340, 344; history of, 580–581; horizontal integration, 587–588; host countries, ambivalence and tensions in, 673–674; international payments by, 281; as international transfer agents, 582–600, 606; intra-enterprise trade, 135–136, 586, 606; intra-industry trade, 115; market power of, 7; and national sovereignty, 669–674; oligopolistic power of, 135; political costs, 685–686; political-economic benefits, 639; scope of, 580, 605; and trade theory, 135–136; U.S. policy toward, 640–641; U.S. tax policy toward, 648–651; vertical integration, 588–589; in world economy, 609–610
multinational enterprise system, 584–586, 606
mutual recognition, 263

national defense, 18; and protectionism, 145
national economic policies, 8–9
national economies: interdependence of, 5, 38; structure of, and comparative advantage, 49
national income, 406; determination of, 370–375; and direct foreign investment, 657–661, 685
national interest, 671–672; and consumer welfare, 16, 37; and international economy, 1–39
nationalism, 3–5, 8, 18, 672–673
nationalization, 675
national planning, and exchange control, 441
national price levels, 333
national security: and protectionism, 155–156; and restriction of imports, 217
national sovereignty, 8, 36; and exchange rates, 10; and international payments, 10; principle of, 2
nations: cultural identity of, 8; domestic policies, 8–9; external political relations, 36–37; linguistic identity of, 8
nation-states, 36, 37; constituents of, 2; definition of, 3–4; international economic relations of, 5
natural resources, 77–78; immobility of, 131; scarcity of, 87–88; supply of, 69
negotiation groups, of GATT system, 207, 211
neofactor theory, 90–91
new international economic order, 532–537
newly industrializing countries, in world markets, 213